Stress and Coping in Autism

Stress and Coping in Autism

Edited by

M. Grace Baron

June Groden

Gerald Groden

Lewis P. Lipsitt

OXFORD
UNIVERSITY PRESS
2006

OXFORD
UNIVERSITY PRESS

Oxford University Press, Inc., publishes works that further
Oxford University's objective of excellence
in research, scholarship, and education.

Oxford   New York
Auckland   Cape Town   Dar es Salaam   Hong Kong   Karachi
Kuala Lumpur   Madrid   Melbourne   Mexico City   Nairobi
New Delhi   Shanghai   Taipei   Toronto

With offices in
Argentina   Austria   Brazil   Chile   Czech Republic   France   Greece
Guatemala   Hungary   Italy   Japan   Poland   Portugal   Singapore
South Korea   Switzerland   Thailand   Turkey   Ukraine   Vietnam

Copyright © 2006 by Oxford University Press, Inc.

Published by Oxford University Press, Inc.
198 Madison Avenue, New York, New York 10016

www.oup.com

Oxford is a registered trademark of Oxford University Press

Library of Congress Cataloging-in-Publication Data

Stress and coping in autism / edited by M. Grace Baron et al.
p. ; cm.
Includes bibliographic references and index.
Summary: "Looking at autism through the lens of stress and coping changes how one sees
and responds to the puzzle of autism. The diverse contributions in this edited volume enlarge
our knowledge of autism and offer strategies for ameliorating stress and for coping with the
challenging behavior associated with autism." –Provided by publisher.
ISBN-13 978-0-19-518226-2
ISBN 0-19-518226-X
1. Autism—Psychological aspects.   2. Stress (Psychology).   3. Adjustment (Psychology)
I. Baron, M. Grace.
[DNLM: 1. Autistic Disorder—psychology.   2. Stress, Psychological.   3. Adaptation, Psychological.
WM 203.5 S915 2006]
RC553.A88S85 2006
616.85'882—dc22   2005031838

9 8 7 6 5 4 3 2
Printed in the United States of America
on acid-free paper

Then I felt like some watcher of the skies

When a new planet swims into his ken.

—John Keats

We dedicate this book to all the children and adults with autism

and their families. Their courage and determination in

coping with the stresses of life give us a greater understanding

of human potential and of what is positive and possible.

Acknowledgments

We gratefully acknowledge the special contribution of Jean Murphy, director of Office Administration of the Groden Center, Inc., to the production of this volume. Her organizational expertise both structured and streamlined our work. We are grateful also to many Groden Center, Inc. staff for their expert secretarial and production support. We thank, finally, the many fellow teachers, researchers, and clinicians who have contributed to our thinking and our practice as expressed in this volume. As a group these Groden Center, Inc. colleagues buffered in various and essential ways the stress of creating an edited volume and brought satisfaction to our work.

Contents

Contributors

Tony Attwood, Ph.D.
The Asperger's Syndrome Clinic
Queensland, Australia

M. Grace Baron, Ph.D.
Wheaton College
Norton, Massachusetts
The Groden Center, Inc.
Providence, Rhode Island

Lawrence Bartak, M.A., Ph.D.
Monash University
Victoria, Australia

Verity Bottroff, Ph.D.
Flinders University
Stirling, South Australia

John Davis, M.M., B.A.
Brooklyn, New York

Anne M. Donnellan, Ph.D.
University of San Diego
San Diego, California

Jennifer M. Gillis, M.A.
Binghamton University
Binghamton, New York

Beth A. Glasberg, Ph.D.
Douglas Outreach
Rutgers University
Stony Brook, New York

Matthew Goodwin, M.A.
The Groden Center, Inc.
Providence, Rhode Island

Temple Grandin, Ph.D.
Colorado State University
Fort Collins, Colorado

Gerald Groden, Ph.D.
The Groden Center, Inc.
Providence, Rhode Island

June Groden, Ph.D.
The Groden Center, Inc.
Providence, Rhode Island

Sandra L. Harris, Ph.D.
Rutgers, The State University
of New Jersey
New Brunswick, New Jersey

Janice E. Janzen, M.S.
Eugene, Oregon

Martha R. Leary, M.A., CCC-SLP
Speech Language Pathologist
Halifax, Nova Scotia

Lewis P. Lipsitt, Ph.D.
Brown University
Providence, Rhode Island

Megan Martins, M.S.
Douglas Development
Disabilities Center
New Brunswick, New Jersey

Kathleen Morgan, Ph.D.
Wheaton College
Norton, Massachusetts

Clara Claiborne Park, M.A.
Williams College
Williamstown, Massachusetts

Jessica H. Park
Williamstown, Massachusetts

Jodi Patterson Robledo, Ph.D.
University of San Diego
San Diego, California

Raymond G. Romanczyk, Ph.D.
Institute for Child Development
Binghamton, New York

Luke Y. Tsai, M.D.
University of Michigan Medical School
Ann Arbor, Michigan

Diane Twachtman-Cullen, Ph.D.,
   CCC-SLP
Autism & Developmental Disabilities
Consultation Center, LLC
Higganum, Connecticut

Patricia Wisocki, Ph.D.
University of Massachusetts/Amherst
Wakefield, Rhode Island

Joanna Zeitz, Master of
   Disability Studies
Flinders University of South Australia
Blackwood, South Australia

Stress and Coping in Autism

Introduction

M. Grace Baron, Lewis P. Lipsitt,
June Groden, and Gerald Groden

A heightened urgency for a better understanding of the nature of autism sets the stage for this volume on stress and coping. While autism advocacy, research, and treatment efforts abound at the start of the twenty-first century, the underlying causes of autism, usually taken to mean the biological basis of this mysterious and frustrating developmental disorder, still elude us.

Beyond that, there seems to have been a remarkable increase in the incidence of autism. This not only increases the mystery among scientists and clinicians, but also severely taxes public as well as private resources that exist to accommodate the care, education, and treatment of such individuals. There are indications that the clinical definition of autistic developmental disorder has loosened in recent years, such that we now speak more broadly of an autism spectrum disorder (ASD) rather than simply autism. This expanded definition accommodates a greater variety of autistic disorders than was thought to exist earlier. This liberal definition, however, does not seem to account for all of the increase in the incidence of autism.

The mystery thus continues. We need to know more, and we need to look in places that, if not new, must be revisited and refreshed. To that end, this volume seeks to explore and understand a facet of ASD that has not yet been addressed with the vigor that, to us as clinicians and scientists, seems warranted.

Our aim in assembling here the best thinking, research, and observations of experts in the field of autism has been to explore the important role that we believe stress plays in the development and self-control of individuals with ASD.

This volume also highlights and celebrates the coping that is required of and possible for persons living with autism. A systematic examination of stress and coping in autism, we hope, will encourage and contribute not only to a science of preventing, curing, and treating autism, but also to the science of strength and resilience (Seligman & Csikszentmihalyi, 2000) aimed at creating the best possible lives for persons living with autism.

WHY IS STRESS IMPORTANT IN THE STUDY OF AUTISM?

The construct of stress has expanded our understanding of both typical and atypical human development in a revolutionary way. Research into a number of disorders that are often comorbid with a diagnosis of autism, such as anxiety, shyness, phobias, obsessive-compulsive disorder (OCD), and thought disorder, already include a systematic theoretical and applied analysis of the contribution of stress to the disorder. Autism, in its own right, might also benefit from such a focus for a number of reasons.

Anxiety, an indicator that someone is experiencing stress, was associated with autism as early as Kanner's (1943) first description of the syndrome. A few early clinical and research reports (e.g., Marks, 1987; Matson & Love, 1990) examined the correlation between fear and anxiety and autism. In 1994, Groden, Cautela, Prince, and Berryman presented the first systematic framework for using the concepts of stress and anxiety to describe and treat autism and proposed that those with autism may, in fact, have a special vulnerability to stress. We now have a better understanding that the clinical problems often associated with stress, such as anxiety, are more prevalent among people with pervasive developmental disabilities than in the general population.

Autism has long been seen as a problem of faulty or different arousal responses to environmental intrusions (Dawson & Lewy, 1989). This has given rise to continued speculation about the role of such patterns of arousal as diagnostic markers or even indicators of subtypes of autism. As early as 1979, Piggott's review of selected basic research in autism suggested that, "Children called autistic probably represent a complex of clinically similar manifestations in a variety of different physiological disturbance[s]. Objective markers are needed as to allow the demarcation of subgroups of autistic children for further study" (p. 199). More recently, Tordjman, Spitz, Corinne, Carlier, and Roubertoux (1998) offered a stress-based model of autism, integrating biological and behavioral profiles of individuals with ASD. They propose that stress and anxiety may be core problems of autism and that an analysis of differential responses to stress can lead to the identification of different subtypes. Similarly, Porges's *The Listening Project* (2002) documents hyperarousal and vagal disruptions in children with autism and offers a biologically based behavioral intervention designed to stimulate the social behavior of children with autism.

Some of the known biological or behavioral effects of stress (see McEwen, 2002; Sapolsky, 1998) can be seen in persons with autism. For example, there is recent evidence (Krause, He, Gershwin, & Shoenfeld, 2002) of suppressed immune system function in some persons with autism. Under- or oversensitivity to pain is a hallmark behavioral symptom for many with autism, and turbulent sensory and perceptual experiences are documented regularly in first-hand reports (e.g., Jones, Quigney, & Huws, 2003). Furthermore, from our clinical experience, some persons with autism when in a state of distress (e.g., in the presence of a feared stimulus, such as a dog) show a sharpening of cognitive-communicative and sensory skills, and may speak in full sentences when this is not the norm. Finally, so many of the behavioral disturbances of autism, especially the problems of self-injury and obsessive routines or stereotypes (as discussed in chapter 6 in this volume) bring a face validity to the assumption that stress may be a critical component of our understanding this disorder.

DOES STRESS CAUSE AUTISM?

We wish to dispel at the outset the notion that the point of this book is to say that stress causes autism. Rather, our emphasis is that stress is a contributor to the physiological, psychological, and overt behavioral manifestations, and not the cause, of autism. While a small set of empirical investigations (summarized in chapter 6 in this volume) have explored the impact of stress at various stages of development in autism, the focus of this volume is not primarily to determine the role of stress on the "pathology" of autism. We assume, as do other stress and coping researchers, that the contribution of stress to autism varies over time. There may or may not be a critical period, or critical periods, of influence. We simply do not know.

The current volume takes a more functional approach and asks, Do the constructs of stress and coping help us to understand better the characteristics of autism? Can these constructs also inform our assessment and our intervention in autism? Furthermore, we assume that having a child with autism or any other chronic condition can create an enduring stressor for families, caregivers, and teachers and that a focus on this reciprocal nature of stress can help us understand a family's dynamic and evolving adaptation.

INDIVIDUAL DIFFERENCES AND STRESS

Many observers, including parents of individuals with ASD, have noted that no two individuals with autism are alike. They grow, develop, and behave in unique ways, just as the population of youngsters and adults who are free of this disorder do. In particular, individuals with autism manifest anxiety and stress reactions.

But there are striking differences in the ways these reactions occur and in the intensity of the reactions. In turn, these stress reactions mediate other behaviors that are individualistic. It is our aim here to better understand the role that stress plays in the lives of individuals with autism.

Most of the literature concerning behavioral differences of individuals with autism has emphasized the cognitive problems associated with autism and the problems involved in facilitating learning in this population. The objectives of teachers, parents, and therapists are to enable better socialization, to improve communications skills (particularly those associated with speech and reading), and to integrate individuals in the ASD spectrum into a neurotypic age group of peers. The prevailing presumption is that if we can get their attention and instill lessons, they will be on the road to assimilation and a more normal track of development. Most of these approaches, we suspect, do not fully acknowledge the extremely important role that stress plays in mediating many of the inappropriate behaviors of individuals with autism and their delays in learning. Indeed, it is apparent from personal reports of individuals with autism that some kinds of attention to cognitive malfunctioning can instill fear and cause additional stress in the vulnerable individual with autism.

Many significant advances have been made in the past two decades in the understanding of stress in the development of individuals—those with disorders and those free of them. Yet, there has been only a smattering of attention paid, clinically and in the research literature, to the clear relevance of stress in understanding the problems of individuals with autism in the context of their families, their schools, and their own self-regulatory behavior. Too often the idiosyncratic features of the individual with autism are overtaken by the inevitable group labeling that goes with the disorder. As a result, the varying emotional thresholds and cognitive preparedness are ignored as the well-meaning therapist or teacher seeks to affect desired changes in behavior. In the Foreword to a very insightful and informative new volume by Bogdashina (2003), Wendy Lawson (2003) writes: "Many a time autistic individuals have been 'pushed' beyond their limits of sensory endurance. Often this is due to those relating to them not having understood how 'painful' it is to be overloaded by too much sound; visual stimulation; emotional or/and physical demand and environmental expectation" (p. 11). Further, Lawson challenges: "What if you couldn't separate an idiom from its literal translation? Might you feel terrified if someone said he had 'laughed his head off'? It demonstrates the extremes of emotion an autistic individual might travel through. Even today there is still literature that will tell you autistic individuals lack 'feeling'! This idea has been responsible for much of the abuse and misunderstanding that we have encountered as autistic people" (p. 12).

We seek in this volume to import reliable knowledge about stress from individuals with autism, from theories of stress reactions, and from the scientific literature contributing to our understanding of the role of stress in human development and behavior. Each chapter in this volume reflects the core concepts of stress theory as outlined by Hans Selye (1976) in his pioneering book, *The Stress of Life*. However, the volume also exemplifies the richness of theoretical and methodological pathways available for the study of stress and coping in human life.

The lead chapters in this volume, prepared largely by the editors, provide a scientific and clinical foundation for using the constructs of stress and coping in thinking about autism. The volume's other contributors are as diverse in their respective approaches to the understanding of autism as the individuals about whom they are speaking. Indeed, they are in some instances one and the same; some chapters are personal reports of individuals with autism who feel the effects of stress every day. These contributors give detailed first-person accounts, providing real-life meaning to and descriptions of a stressful life. Others, by weaving together empirical and theoretical observations related to stress, provide the framework for a creative new way to examine the underlying causes of the unique response patterns we have come to know as autism, and also the role of stress in the lives of persons with autism and its impact on their families. These authors offer educational and clinical strategies for stress-reduction, as well as masterful coping and self-control over life's inevitable stressors.

FOUNDATIONS FOR STRESS, COPING, AND AUTISM

The first two chapters in this volume provide a foundation for future theory, research, and practice in stress and coping in autism. The clinical utility of the stress construct in both assessment and treatment of autism is introduced in chapter 1. Groden's seminal work (see Groden et al., 1994) is expanded in this chapter and brings to this volume the Groden Center's 30-year history of rich and productive clinical work in autism. The authors review core assumptions about the role of stress in the lives of persons with autism and set the stage for the volume's other clinical contributions on how best to respond to stress with self-control and adaptive coping. Chapter 1 also introduces a number of clinical and educational strategies, including the use of the relaxation response, imagery-based rehearsal, and skills training to increase effective responding to stressors. The core theme of teaching persons with autism strategies for self-control over life's stressors is a theme that resonates in other chapters in this volume. In chapter 2, Baron, Lipsitt, and Goodwin provide an integrated biobehavioral view of stress, coping, and autism, and a research framework for applying the stress concept in understanding and treating autism. Their review of the history of the stress concept and summary of the empirical research to date on arousal, stress, and autism ends with the current research by the Groden Center clinical research team on stress and autism.

EXPERIENCE OF STRESS AND AUTISM

In chapters 3, 4, and 5, the authors exemplify the rich and often discordant sensory-perceptual worlds and the creative potential of autism, as well as the courage it takes to live a life with autism.

Temple Grandin's autobiographical books, *Emergence: Labeled Autistic* (1986) and *Thinking in Pictures and Other Reports From My Life with Autism* (1995), were among the first to tell us about the full experience of growing, learning, and living with autism. In chapter 3, she describes her life-long vulnerability to anxiety and stress, her adaptive responses to stressors, and the biobehavioral strategies she has found to "stop the constant stress."

For over 30 years, Clara Park has been a model and a champion of a family's adaptive coping to the challenges of autism (see Park, 1967). In chapter 4, she interviews her daughter, Jessy, to describe the "discouragements" (their word for stressors) of autism and their search, together, for the positive, normal life routines of work and play that can be, in their own words, "triumphs" over life's stressors. They show us that the best buffers to stress and the best learning for an individual with autism, family member, or caregiver is the adaptation and learning that is nurtured in the context of authentic relationship and lifelong support.

Chapter 5 provides a rich review of the life and circumstances of a musical savant born into slavery named Tom Wiggins, known to the American public as "Blind Tom." Davis, a pianist with intimate knowledge of Tom Wiggins' music, and psychologist M. Grace Baron give us a glimpse of Blind Tom's life-long stress and coping within the historical context of the mid-1800s. If social support is so essential to coping with life stress, this chapter provokes us to wonder what chance for adaptive coping might a black, blind, autistic, musical prodigy have in those times. Amazingly, neither the challenges of his condition nor the constraints of slavery prevented the blooming of Tom Wiggins' genius. This chapter also underscores the value and role of authentic relationships and rich life experience as buffers to stress.

EMERGING PATHWAYS FOR THE STUDY OF STRESS AND COPING IN AUTISM

Stress is based in, and affects, biology. In chapter 6, Morgan's in-depth review of the biobehavioral consequences of stress in a number of species provides a springboard for a provocative hypothesis that autism may, in fact, be a type of stress disorder. Morgan also suggests the neural and structural origins of maladaptive responses to stressors by persons with autism.

In chapter 7, Romanczyk and Gillis address the physiology of stress and options for its measurement. This chapter also offers a primer, or short course, for the researcher and clinician interested in integrating knowledge of stress into their work.

Two subsequent chapters offer reconceptualizations of the meaning and function of the characteristic behavioral responses of autism (e.g., lack of eye contact, disinterest in social interaction, repetitive behavior, insistence on sameness) as responses to environmental stressors. In chapter 8, Donnellan, Leary, and Robledo propose we view these characteristic behaviors as movement differences, rather than as useless, or even pathogenic, responses, and suggest that stress is both a trigger and an outcome of these behavioral differences. Similarly, Bartak, Bottroff, and Zeitz (chapter 9) offer a dynamic theory of autism that sees such behavior as secondary consequences of an individual's internal and external stressors or buffers to stress. Both these chapters conclude with application of these theories to clinical and educational practice over the lifespan of a person with autism.

STRATEGIES FOR COPING WITH STRESS

The next group of chapters provides families, teachers, and clinicians with a range of intervention and instructional strategies to reduce stress and to prevent or alleviate the anxiety, panic, fear, and other disruptive responses inherent in the condition of autism.

Three chapters address stressors in the home and other learning environments for persons with autism and for their families and teachers. In chapter 10, Glasberg, Martins, and Harris review the sources of stress in the lives of family members, consider ways that families cope more or less effectively with the stressors they encounter, and point out needs for future research on stress and coping for families.

In chapter 11, Twachtman-Cullen discusses the stressors of our complex world in general and of our teaching environments in particular. She presents the argument that decreased ability to communicate leads to stress, and stressors lead to decreased ability to communicate. This double bind requires thoughtful planning of our teaching environments and interaction strategies and a commitment to curriculum change and classroom-based, stress-reduction strategies.

Chapter 12 brings the wisdom and practicality of Janzen's years of teacher training and support (see Janzen, 1996) to the task of stress reduction. Parents, teachers, caregivers, job coaches, and other mentors can best maximize learning and independence by being aware of the fluctuations of stress in a learner's daily life. This chapter also encourages all teachers to become interpreters to help persons with autism navigate and cope through life's inevitable stressors.

This volume's next two chapters emphasize the strategies available to clinicians, counselors, family members, and other supporters for stress reduction in their work with persons with autism. In chapter 13, Attwood applies a cognitive-behavioral perspective to the treatment of persons with Asperger's syndrome. He highlights both the particular sensory and social challenges faced by this subgroup of persons with autism, as well as a number of creative individual and group strategies for clinical intervention.

In chapter 14, Wisocki addresses the erroneous belief that persons with developmental disabilities such as autism are incapable of comprehending the finality and the loss of death, and that they are unable to form the emotional bonds that underlie the experience of grief and loss. She presents the argument, instead, that the experiences of loss and death are significant disruptors for persons with autism. Wisocki guides clinicians and family members in supporting and preparing persons with autism to face life's final and ultimate stressor.

And finally, from a medical perspective, in chapter 15 Tsai offers treatment strategies and the psychopharmacologic alternatives for systematic assessment and treatment of the anxiety disorders that often accompany the experience of stress.

Persons with autism are rich in human experience, capacities and problems, and needs. Just like the rest of us, and maybe even more than the rest of us, they are challenged by life's stressors. We provide in this volume a source for future theoretical, educational, clinical, and research use of the stress construct in understanding and treating autism and other developmental disabilities. The stress construct will have heuristic value, we hope, for all in the field of autism. Beyond that, we venture to hope that our volume may contribute to the larger theoretical and applied effort to substantiate and validate the bio-psycho-social interplay of stress and coping in all of human life.

References

Bogdashina, O. (2003). Sensory perceptual issues in autism and Asperger syndrome: Different sensory experiences—different perceptual worlds. New York: Jessica Kingsley.

Dawson, G., & Lewy, A. (1989). Arousal, attention, and the socioemotional impairments of individuals with autism. In G. Dawson (Ed.), Autism: Nature, diagnosis, and treatment (pp. 49–74). New York: Guilford Press.

Grandin, T. (1995). Thinking in pictures and other reports from my life with autism. New York: Doubleday.

Grandin, T., & Scariano, M. (1986). Emergence: Labeled autistic. Novato, CA: Arena Press.

Groden, J., Cautela, J. R., Prince, S., & Berryman, J. (1994). The impact of stress and anxiety on individuals with autism and other developmental disabilities. In E. Schopler & G. B. Mesibov (Eds.), Behavioral issues in autism (pp. 177–194). New York: Plenum Press.

Janzen, J. (1996). Understanding the nature of autism. San Antonio, TX: Therapy Skill Builders.

Jones, R., Quigney, A., & Huws, J. (2003). First-hand accounts of sensory-perceptual experiences in autism: a qualitative analysis. *Journal of Intellectual and Developmental Disability, 28,* 112–121.

Kanner, L. (1943). Autistic disturbances of affective contact. *Nervous Child, 2,* 217–250.

Krause, I., He, M., Gershwin, E., & Shoenfeld, Y. (2002). Brief report: Immune factors in autism: A critical review. *Journal of Autism and Developmental Disorders, 32*(4), 335–337.

Lawson, W. (2003). Foreword. In O. Bogdashina, *Sensory perceptual issues in autism and Asperger syndrome* (pp. 11–12) New York: Jessica Kingsley.

Matson, J. L., & Love, S. R. (1990). A comparison of parent-reported fear for autistic and non-handicapped age-matched children and youth. *Australia & New Zealand Journal of Developmental Disabilities, 16,* 349–357.

Marks, I. M. (1987). *Fears, phobias, and rituals.* New York: Oxford University Press.

McEwen, B. (2002). *The end of stress as we know it.* Washington, DC: Dana Press.

Park, C. C. (1967). *The siege.* Boston: Little, Brown & Company.

Piggott, L. R. (1979). Overview of selected research in autism. *Journal of Autism and Developmental Disorders, 9*(2), 199–218.

Porges, S. (2002, November). *The listening project.* Paper presented to LADDERS conference, Danvers, MA.

Sapolsky, R. M. (1998). *Why zebras don't get ulcers.* New York: W. H. Freeman.

Seligman, M., & Csikszentmihalyi, M. (2000). Positive psychology: An introduction. *American Psychologist, 55*(1), 5–14.

Selye, H. (1976). *The stress of life.* New York: McGraw-Hill.

Tordjman, S., Spitz, E.,Corinne, A., Carlier, M., & Roubertoux, P. (1998). Biological and behavioral profiles of infantile autism: Interests of an integrated approach [in French]. *Psychologie Francaise, 43*(2), 185–195.

I

Foundations in Stress, Coping, and Autism

1 Assessment and Coping Strategies

June Groden, M. Grace Baron,
and Gerald Groden

Stress is assumed to have an important role in the development and expression of abnormal behavior in humans generally (Walker & Diforio, 1997), but there is a dearth of literature examining the role of stress in the lives of individuals with autism. Stress is in fact a problem, often overlooked but nonetheless important, in individuals with autism (Gillot, Furniss, & Walter, 2001; Kim, Szatmari, Bryson, Streiner, & Wilson, 2000; Muris, Steerneman, Merckelbach, Holdrinet, & Meesters, 1998; Stavrakaki, 1999), even though commonly observed characteristics of persons with autism suggest special vulnerability to stressors (Groden, Cautela, Prince, & Berryman, 1994). Stress can include environmental, or "exogenous," stimuli that disrupt behavior as well as characteristic, or "endogenous," response patterns of an individual or group. Stress and anxiety affect the cognitive, physiological, and overt behavioral responses of individuals with autism and pervasive developmental disorder (King, Hamilton & Ollendick, 1994).

This chapter addresses the characteristics of autism that make this population especially vulnerable to stress; assessment procedures to measure responses to stressors; and clinical, educational, and home/community-based strategies for stress reduction. Special emphasis is given to the role and value of self-control to reduce the stress in the lives of individuals with autism and to increase the use of proactive, adaptive, coping techniques.

Personal Reports

For many years, it was believed that persons with autism, characterized by social aloofness and separation from much of the everyday world, did not experience stress in the usual way. Individuals with autism who can report feelings verbally have told us differently. Fear, anxiety, worry, and even panic seem to contribute to the stress of living with autism. "No one really understands what the emotional suffering of a person with autism is like. It is the confusion that results from not being able to understand the world around me, which, I think, causes all fear. This fear then brings a need to withdraw" (Jolliffe, Landsdown, & Robinson, 1992, p. 12). Others report feeling "very nervous about everything, fear[ing] people and social activity greatly" (Volkmar & Cohen, 1985, p. 49), and that "the real world [was] terrifying. Stress showed in my speech, my actions, my relationship with others" (Grandin & Scariano, 1986, p. 79). Recent qualitative analyses of first-hand accounts of autism (Jones, Quigney, & Huws, 2003; O'Neill & Jones, 1997; chapter 8, this volume) document the turbulent sensory-perceptual experiences, interpersonal difficulties, and the disturbing awareness of being different that contribute to the stress of life with autism.

Characteristics of Autism Related to Stress

In addition to personal reports that attest to feelings of stress in persons with autism, individuals with autism may be especially vulnerable to stress in the domains described in the following sections. These domains include communication, socialization, sensory factors, physical factors, executive function and hardiness, and maladaptive behaviors.

Communication

Difficulty with verbal and nonverbal communication is a salient characteristic of autism. As such, a host of communication-related stressors are present for this population, including (1) expressing feelings; (2) processing verbal input that is spoken quickly; (3) deciphering language when many people are talking at once; (4) understanding words when they have no relevant concrete parallel; (5) attending to verbal input that is too complex or too long to discriminate what the message is; or (6) "getting stuck" on a certain sound or combination of sounds.

Even high-functioning people with autism or Asperger's syndrome who possess good verbal skills and who enjoy talking to others can feel frustrated by the requirements needed to hold a conversation, such as taking turns when speaking, beginning and ending appropriately, and maintaining a topic of interest to the listener. The inability to understand another person's perspective can limit conversational abilities. All of these situations and characteristics can lead to the experience of stress.

Socialization

The second area of development and behavior, socialization, is typically impaired by autism and promotes stress. Displaying an attachment to objects, repetitive isolated play and activity, lack of eye contact, and flat affect make it difficult for the child or adult with autism to form social relationships. Recent writings by adults with autism (e.g., Grandin & Scariano, 1986) have provided a clearer understanding of their difficulty with the social world, where cues are vague and ambiguous, expectations change rapidly, facial expressions and gestures add confusion, and clear rules for behaving are not available. Such conditions in the social world can be stressful for the person with autism and can result in avoidance behaviors that lead to solitary activity. The lack of social networks and the escape or avoidance of social situations can also reduce opportunities to practice social skills and to build social supports.

Sensory Factors

Significant impairment in auditory, visual, and tactile areas can lead to increased stress. For instance, hyperresponsivity to sounds is a commonly reported feature of autism. Clara Park (1982) describes such a response demonstrated by her daughter Jessy:

> We live in the midst of that hyperactivity to sound that so many observers have noted. Jessy has learned to control the intensity of her reactions to the clicks and buzzes and hums with which the twentieth century surrounds us. But she still notices them. "Guess what! The refrigerator turned on while the door opened! A loud click!" If Jessy is tuned to a sound it pierces through to her through conversation or distance. She hears the sound of the refrigerator—or its silence—two rooms away. Some sounds fill her with mysterious delight. Other sounds and phrases trigger an equally mysterious distress that seems, in its devastating suddenness, almost like an allergic reaction of the psyche. (p. 293)

Responses to visual stimuli such as light, color, shadow, or reflection may cause increased arousal of the nervous system in persons with autism. From their research on the cerebellum, Courchesne et al. (1994) postulated an impairment of individuals with autism to rapidly shift their focus of attention between visual and auditory stimuli. Atypical movement patterns (Hill & Leary, 1993) can be the result of sensory-based visual or tactile reactions to changes in floor surfaces or lighting. People with heightened sensory responses can often feel bombarded by the complexity of stimuli they encounter in everyday situations, such as different textures of clothing or food and certain types of touch.

Physical Factors

EEG abnormalities and seizure disorders are high in the population with autism. The incidence of seizures is markedly increased compared to typical and other psychiatric populations (Poustka, 1998). Konstantareas and Homatidis (1987) report greater incidence of ear infections in children with autism, and Mason-Brothers et al. (1993) report a significantly greater number of children with autism with recurrent otitis media, upper respiratory, and other infections. Otitis media has also been related to self-injurious behavior (O'Reilly, 1997). Pain and illness are stressors.

Executive Function and Hardiness

Executive function refers to goal-directed, future-oriented, cognitive abilities thought to be mediated by the frontal cortex (Duncan, 1986). They include planning, inhibition, flexibility, organization, and self-monitoring (Prior & Ozonoff, 1998). There is a body of literature suggesting that persons with autism have deficits in executive function (Prior & Hoffmann, 1990; Rumsey & Hamburger, 1988). These abilities are important as buffers to reduce stress. Hardiness (Huang, 1995) incorporates the ability to accept challenge and to have commitment, confidence, and self-control. Hardy persons are more likely to stay healthy and perceive life changes as positive and challenging through cognitive appraisal. Hardiness facilitates family adjustment and adaptation. Lacking these executive function skills and hardiness, persons with autism will experience more stress in their lives.

Maladaptive Behaviors

Behavioral characteristics of autism include repetitive motor behaviors, ritualistic patterns of carrying out certain activities, and an insistence on sameness, which results in the development of rigid routines. Interruption and prevention of rituals and routines presents a necessity to change that can occasion stress.

Other behaviors that are maladaptive include tantrums, aggression, and self-injurious behavior. It has been hypothesized that these behaviors are used by the population with autism and developmental disabilities as alternatives to more effective buffers. It is suggested that these behaviors may function as maladaptive coping strategies (Groden et al., 1994). When this occurs, the maladaptive behavior is reinforced, and the opportunity to learn and use adaptive coping strategies lessens. The flow chart in figure 1.1 illustrates the chain of events that can result from adaptive versus maladaptive coping strategies.

In the adaptive model, the individual experiencing stress implements one of the buffer strategies in his or her repertoire, leading to decreased stress and/or increased effective coping behavior. The individual is likely to be positively reinforced by the results of his or her behavior, leading to a further reduction in

Adaptive Model (Exhibited by persons with good coping strategies)	**Maladaptive Model** (Exhibited by persons with poor coping strategies, especially by individuals with developmental disabilities)
Stressors (promotion, death, separation, birth of a sibling, pain) ↓	Stressors (taking criticism, changes, inability to understand instruction, external control) ↓
Buffers (social networks, hardiness, internal locus of control) ↓	Inability to Use Buffers (lack of friends, communication deficits, lack of self-control) ↓
Adaptive Behaviors (assertiveness, socializing, exercise) ↓	Maladaptive Behaviors (aggression tantrum, self-injury, stereotypic behaviors) ↓
Reinforcement ↓	Punishment ↓
Stress Reduction	Increased Stress

Figure 1.1. Adaptive and maladaptive coping models in autism (from Groden, Cautela, Prince, & Berryman, 1994, with permission of Springer Science and Business Media).

stress. In contrast, the individual who exhibits the maladaptive model is disadvantaged in two ways: (1) he or she cannot access the range of buffers available to the general population, and (2) he or she may possess attributes of autism that cause more stress and anxiety. An inability to solve problems or to reduce stress can trigger maladaptive coping that may include crying, yelling, self-stimulatory behavior, or more severe behaviors, such as aggression and tantrums. These behaviors may also be functionally related to the stressor. For example, a child who is hungry, in pain, or just bored with the task at hand may lack the verbal skills to express such feelings, and might instead attempt to communicate through aggressive, self-injurious, or tantrum behavior. Such behaviors are frequently punished, which leads to an increase in stress and completes a loop of accumulating stress and anxiety.

It is important to consider both the stressors in a client's world and what might be done to diminish the impact of stress on the client. We turn now to how one might systematically assess stress in the lives of persons with autism.

MULTIMODAL ASSESSMENT OF STRESS

Assessments to evaluate stress in the typical population are often in the form of self-report interviews and paper-and-pencil tests, but these traditional assessments utilize verbal communication and have had limited use with individuals with autism (Bernston, Ronca, Tuber, Boysen & Leland, 1985). The multimodal approach to stress assessment described in this section offers the clinician and researcher a range of procedures, adaptable to persons with autism and developmental disabilities of all cognitive levels. This approach includes functional assessment, scales or schedules, informant interviews, and physiological measurement of stress responses.

Role of Functional Assessments in Identifying Stressors

Direct Observation

A functional assessment is a procedure developed by behavioral psychologists to identify events related to a challenging behavior and their role in its occurrence or maintenance. It typically involves the documentation of the behavior, its antecedents, and consequences over a number of occurrences.

It has become apparent that behavioral challenges of persons with autism are often precipitated by stressful events (Groden et al., 1994). These include specific, discrete stimuli and more general conditions or contexts that are referred to as setting events. Inasmuch as functional assessments are designed to identify stimuli that are antecedent to challenging behaviors, and since these stimuli are often stressors, it follows that functional assessments would be a helpful tool in identifying these stressors. For example, a functional assessment might reveal that a particular challenging behavior occurs most frequently when a student is required to perform multiplication tasks, a type of task that might be difficult (stressful) for the student.

Because stress can result in highly disruptive and dangerous behaviors, particularly among persons with autism spectrum disorders (ASD), it is important to have analysis methods or instruments that will facilitate thorough functional assessments and identify the details of behavioral incidents to identify stressors as quickly and accurately as possible.

Detailed Behavior Report

The Behavior Analysis Guide (BAG; Groden, Stevenson, & Groden, 1996) structures the functional assessment of behavior at the Groden Center. The BAG was developed to improve the quality of behavioral assessments and their resulting treatment plans by providing guidance in (1) observing and recording all potentially relevant information surrounding a behavioral incident; (2) organizing that information to make clear any recurring patterns; (3) understanding why events found to occur frequently in relation to the behavior might be functionally related to the behavior; and (4) developing analysis-based interventions. The Detailed Behavior Report (DBR) is used to record behavioral observations and is shown in figure 1.2 with sample information for an incident of aggressive behavior toward a staff member by John, a residential client.

Number ___1___   Detailed Behavior Report (DBR)

CLIENT John	STAFF Lisa
PROGRAM Adolescent 2	HOW RECORDED: Continuous/Sample___

Purpose: This form is used to record objective information regarding the target behavior, its antecedents and its consequences.

B E H A V I O R	Target Behavior (Describe in detail)	Aggression: hit Bob Roberts (staff) fairly strongly on the chest with both fists and was about to hit him again.
	Severity Rating	5(severe) ④ 3 2 1(mild) DURATION 1 - 3 seconds
	Precursors-body state,thoughts, emotions,verbals	Tense - stiffened body; tight lips
General	Schedule	DATE 3/14/92 DAY Saturday TIME 4:00 p.m.
	Location	Residence living room, in front of TV, on couch
	Activity	TYPE: Watching TV - favorite game show LENGTH ENGAGED: 30 min. MASTERED: Yes/No CHOICE: Yes/No MOVEMENT: High/Low RELEVANCY TO CLIENT: High/Low
ANTECEDENTS (Specific)	Personal/ Social/ Physical (Sequence of who was doing and/or saying what to whom)	STAFF INVOLVED: Lisa, Bob CLIENTS INVOLVED: Janet and Jim were in the room TONE OF INTERACTION: calm and matter-of-fact ENVIRONMENTAL CHARACTERISTICS: TV on at normal volume; Bob was sitting next to John on couch. When the TV program ended, I (Lisa) said to John, "You should vacuum the rug in your room now."
	Setting Events	Favorite staff member was on break
CONSEQUENCES	Program Consequences	Response prevention by staff until calm. John was required to vacuum rug after he had relaxed. He did not earn his reinforcer for the interval in which the aggression occurred.
	Non-program Consequences	Janet, another housemate, scolded John
	Perceived Function of Behavior	Expression of anger that he couldn't watch more TV and wanted to avoid vacuuming.

Figure 1.2. Detailed behavior report.

Using the DBR, all potentially relevant information about the occurrence of a challenging behavior is systematically collected, including antecedent and consequence details. Information is recorded in defined categories that include: (1) a description of the behavior, its severity and duration, and its precursors (client behaviors signaling the impending target behavior and often signaling stress); (2) general antecedents or conditions, such as date, day, time, activity, and location where the target behavior occurred; (3) specific antecedents, such as actions or cognitions of the individual, actions of others, and/or physical events, which often reveal the precise reasons for the behavior's occurrence; (4) setting events, which include those conditions, both immediate and distant in time, that influence whether the problem behavior will occur in the presence of a particular antecedent; (5) consequences, both planned and incidental; and (6) the perceived functions of the behavior, which are generally to obtain or avoid something or someone. Space is provided for recording sequences of events, if any, in the specific antecedent section.

When a sufficient number of DBRs are collected to sample events related to a challenging behavior, information from them are summarized onto the Detailed Behavior Report Summary (DBRS), another component of the BAG, to better reveal antecedent-behavior-consequence patterns (figure 1.3).

The recurring relationships (circled) that stand out in figure 1.3 are frequently observed precursors (e.g., licking lips, whining, tense lips) and more frequent occurrences of the behavior in the living room while engaged in leisure activities (e.g., drawing, watching TV, looking at magazine/pictures), or while reviewing his behavioral contract with his teacher. The specific antecedent categories (staff directed and staff informed) and the setting event (preferred staff absent) also are seen to be frequently associated with the target behavior, as are many of the consequences. Stimulus groups refers to antecedents, setting events, and consequences that are present in many of the incidents and whose joint presence might heighten the probability of a challenging incident over and above the presence of any one of them alone. In this case, a reasonable hypothesis for John's challenging behaviors is that he was upset by having to terminate his TV viewing to perform a task. The fact that his preferred staff was absent on each of the dates of his incidences might have provided an underlying level of stress that, given the above directions, the challenging behaviors were even more likely to occur. The consequences (i.e., response prevention and scolded by Janet) have been circled as each occurred with some frequency, and this might also have played a role in the maintenance of the challenging behavior.

Stress Survey Schedule

In addition to a functional analysis of behavior, more information can be obtained by personal interviews of teachers, parents, and caregivers, and by paper-and-pencil tests, such as survey scales. The Stress Survey Schedule for Persons with Autism and Other Developmental Disabilities (the Stress Survey Schedule; Groden et al. 2001) was developed as an instrument for measuring stress in the lives of persons with autism (figure 1.4). It can help identify which situations cause stress responses. The individual can then learn coping strategies to deal with this stress.

Using exploratory and confirmatory factor analysis, the Stress Survey Schedule identified eight components: changes, anticipation/uncertainty, social/environmental interactions, pleasant events, sensory stimuli, unpleasant events, food-related stress, and rituals. These stress dimensions are highly relevant to

Detailed Behavior Report Summary (DBRS)

CLIENT John	TARGET BEHAVIOR Aggression	# DBRs 12
PROGRAM Adolescent 2	PERIOD COVERED: from 3/14/92 to 3/28/92	

Purpose: This form is used to organize and summarize DBR information.
1. Number the DBRs in chronological order for the targeted behavior.
2. Write the specified behavior descriptor, antecedent, & consequence in the left columns under each category.
3. In the right columns, record the number of the DBR next to the corresponding behavior descriptor, antecedent, and consequence.

SEVERITY RATING		DURATION		PRECURSORS	
5(very hard)	2, 4, 9	< 1 min.	1,3,7,8,11	stiff body	1
4 (hard)	1,6,7,10	1-2 min.	2,5,6,10	tense lips	1,8,9,11
3 (medium)	8, 11	3-5 min.	4,9,12	licking lips	3,4,7
2 (light)	5, 12			whining	3,5,6,8,10
1 (not hard)	3			laughing	3,12

DAY OF WEEK		TIME	AM	PM	LOCATION	
Monday	9	9:00-9:59				
Tuesday	3, 4	10:00-10:59			living room	1,2,5,8,10
		11:00-11:59				
Wednesday	5, 7	12:00-12:59			hallway	3,6
		1:00-1:59				
Thursday	11	2:00-2:59			van	4
		3:00-3:59				
Friday	6, 12	4:00-4:59		1,7	dining room	7,12
		5:00-5:59		9,11		
Saturday	1, 10	6:00-6:59		10,12	bedroom	9,11
		7:00-7:59	5	2,6		
Sunday	2, 8	8:00-8:59	4	3,8		

ACTIVITY		STAFF		SPECIFIC ANTECEDENTS (from Worksheet)	
Leisure:		Lisa	1,3,6,9,11		
watching TV	1,2,5,8	Bob	1,4		
		Deb	2,4,5,8,12	Staff directed	1,2,4,7,8,10,11,12
drawing	7,10	Robin	3,10		
		Peter	7,8		
magazines	11,12	(Jeff)	(none)	Staff informed	3,6,9
Reviewing contract	3,6,9	CLIENTS		Client pushed	5
		Janet	1,3,5,7,8	John refused	8, 10
Waiting	4	Jim	1,7		
		Kristen	4,10		
		Tom	8		

SETTING EVENTS		CONSEQUENCES		FUNCTIONS OF BEHAVIOR	
Preferred staff absent	1-12	[Response prevention-P]	1-12	Cont. leisure & avoid task	1,2,7,8,10,11,12
		[Didn't earn reinforcer-P]	1-12	Obtain Rf	3,6,9
Leisure	1,2,5,7,8,10,11,12	[Had to complete task-P]	1,2,4,7,8,10,11,12	Express anger	5
Ill?	6	[Scolded by Janet -NP]	1,5,7	STIMULUS GROUPS	
Upset earlier	9			Staff direct, staff abs., leis. activ., no Rf, task compl., resp. prevention	

Figure 1.3. Detailed behavior report summary.

the problems of autism. In an analysis conducted at the Groden Center, 185 Stress Survey Schedules were completed for persons with autism. The items most frequently rated as moderate-to-severe or severe included (1) receiving a reprimand, (2) being told "no," (3) being in the vicinity of noise or disruption by others, (4) transitioning from a preferred to a nonpreferred activity, and (5) having to engage in a nonpreferred activity.

An individual stress profile can be obtained from the Stress Survey Schedule, which visually depicts the stress components that affect the individual's life. These data are especially helpful as a basis for developing programs to

THE STRESS SURVEY SCHEDULE FOR PERSONS WITH AUTISM
AND DEVELOPMENTAL DISABILITIES
The Groden Center, Inc.

Please rate the intensity of the stress reaction to the following events by filling in the appropriate circle:	None to mild	Mild to Moderate	Moderate	Moderate to severe	Severe
1. Receiving a present...	①	②	③	④	⑤
2. Having personal objects or materials out of order..............	①	②	③	④	⑤
3. Waiting to talk about desired topic...............................	①	②	③	④	⑤
4. Having a change in schedule or plans...........................	①	②	③	④	⑤
5. Being in the vicinity of noise or disruption by others..........	①	②	③	④	⑤
6. Waiting for preferred events......................................	①	②	③	④	⑤
7. Having a cold...	①	②	③	④	⑤
8. Being touched..	①	②	③	④	⑤
9. Having personal objects or materials missing..................	①	②	③	④	⑤
10. Having a change in task to a new task with new directions....	①	②	③	④	⑤
11. Going to the store..	①	②	③	④	⑤
12. Being prevented from completing a ritual.......................	①	②	③	④	⑤
13. Having a change in environment from comfortable to uncomfortable....................................	①	②	③	④	⑤
14. Being prevented from carrying out a ritual......................	①	②	③	④	⑤
15. Moving from one location to the next............................	①	②	③	④	⑤
16. Playing with others..	①	②	③	④	⑤
17. Having a change in environment from familiar to unfamiliar	①	②	③	④	⑤
18. Receiving activity reinforcement.................................	①	②	③	④	⑤
19. Having something marked as correct.............................	①	②	③	④	⑤
20. Being in the vicinity of bright lights.............................	①	②	③	④	⑤
21. Following a diet..	①	②	③	④	⑤
22. Having unstructured time..	①	②	③	④	⑤
23. Being allowed to attend a party or favored event..............	①	②	③	④	⑤

Figure 1.4. Sample page from the stress survey schedule.

teach coping skills. For example, if a person scores high on the "waiting in line" stressor, programs to reduce the stress might include cognitive strategies, such as saying to oneself, "I can handle this, it will be just a little while longer," using relaxation while standing in line, or keeping a favored activity, such as a hand-held electronic game or a book in their pocket, and then using it when they are waiting in line.

Physiological Assessment

To have an integrated clinical behavioral approach to research and therapy in stress with persons with autism, a thoughtful consideration of physiological responding is required. In this population, it is often impractical or impossible to obtain verbal reports about the personal experience of stress. A number of nonverbal physiological measures of the stress response, based on heart rate (HR), breathing rate, or hormonal differences, are available to the behavioral clinician. Preliminary investigations (Freeman, Horner & Reichle, 1999; Groden et al., 2005; Romanczyk & Matthews, 1998) have found that HR can be a robust measure of overall arousal in persons with autism. An HR measure can help clinicians learn about the subjective experience of arousal and stress in persons with autism. This is especially important when we consider the communication deficit of self-reporting for persons with autism. The development of a systematic protocol for the measurement of HR is currently being carried out at the Groden Center in Providence, Rhode Island. Because persons with autism are generally considered to be chronically in an overaroused (Rimland, 1964) or underaroused (Hutt, Hutt, Lee, & Ounsted, 1964) state, an HR measurement protocol can be particularly helpful in the assessment of stress.

The measurement of resting HR and changes in HR during a set of standardized activities provides an opportunity to integrate information on physiological arousal into a functional analysis of behavior and can guide prescriptive programming for persons with stress-related disorders. This observation protocol also provides a physiological and behavioral baseline for evaluating program interventions over time and, in a more general way, also contributes to the understanding of a client's clinical and behavioral functioning.

Heart Rate Assessment Protocol

At the Groden Center, a standardized assessment procedure has been developed. This procedure includes collecting HR measurements during 15 consecutive activities, each lasting 1–5 min. Baseline measures precede and alternate with a standard set of stimuli, including loud noise, uncertainty (a remotely controlled robot), unstructured time (sitting alone), edible reinforcement, a difficult task (folding towels), presence of an unfamiliar person, and physical exertion. Under special circumstance, other identified naturally occurring stressors can also be added. A videotape summary of the entire session allows for later analysis of observable behavior concomitant with the HR measures. Telemetric measurements can also provide information about arousal in natural settings.

Clinical Uses of HR Arousal Data

An examination of patterns of HR responding can contribute to behavioral and clinical assessment and treatment in a number of ways. In conjunction with other information about the client, such as medication history, HR data can help generate or validate hypotheses about the function of a particular problem behavior. Data on HR can also help identify clients who respond with heightened arousal to idiosyncratic stressors, respond to many stimuli with heightened arousal, are in a chronically aroused state, may have difficulty reducing the arousal response once aroused, or show no or little arousal response.

Heart rate measurements can also identify clients with lack of synchrony between observable behavior and HR response. Heart rate data expand a functional analysis of precursors to include the covert physiological responses that precede an overt problem behavior. The following case exemplifies the clinical use of HR data.

In a 15-year-old boy with a pervasive development disorder, not otherwise specified (PDD-NOS), two stimuli from the standard HR assessment procedure were also items identified by his mother and teachers on the Stress Survey Schedule as stressors. The two stimuli were "loud noise" and "difficult task." Heart rate data from the standard assessment showed increased arousal to loud noise and a difficult task, corroborating the caregiver reports. Interestingly, HR increases were not accompanied by concomitant motor movements; he appeared outwardly calm. Moreover, this young man's HR did not return to baseline, but remained at a high rate even after the stressor was removed. This finding coupled with his higher than average HR (92.74 beats/min vs. 80 beats/min on average) led to a hypothesis that this young man may be in a chronically aroused state. Once aroused, it appeared difficult for this young man to reduce arousal.

Heart rate assessment data also resulted in a clinical program that included continued practice and use of the relaxation response, both as a response to specific stressors and as a general contributor to well-being. The HR data showed that the presence of a familiar person served to reduce arousal. This led to a more systematic effort to introduce new situations only when a familiar person was with him, as well as imagery-based rehearsal strategies (detailed later in this chapter) to prepare for new stressors and social situations.

COPING WITH STRESS

Coping strategies play a critical role in an individual's physical and psychological well-being when he or she is faced with challenges, negative events, and stress (Westman, 2004). Lazarus (1993) defines coping as an individual's efforts to change thinking or overt behavior to manage stress. Historically, many programs that treat individuals with autism have neglected to include procedures to prevent or reduce responses to stressors, focusing instead on caregiver's efforts to change or control a problem behavior once it has already occurred. Literature on how to manage stress and activate "the resilience that is intrinsic" (McEwen, 2002, p. 135) recommends increasing social supports and exercise, providing outlets for frustration, and employing various ways to control and predict a stressor (Sapolsky, 1998).

In the field of autism, there has been energetic work in applying this clinical wisdom of stress reduction to the challenges experienced by families and caregivers of persons with autism. (In chapter 10, Glasberg, Martins, and Harris summarize this work.) However, relatively less literature is available addressing the coping needs of persons with autism. A recent review of the psychological literature (PsycInfo [electronic database]) revealed 121 citations related to coping and autism; the majority of the citations related to coping of family members. Only seventeen (14%) of these entries referred to either the challenges to persons with autism of coping with everyday life (e.g., Jones, Quigley, & Huws, 2003), or offered specific strategies for coping (e.g., Lord, 1996). This chapter focuses on the reduction of the impact of stress in the everyday lives, education and treatment of persons with autism.

No theory of the role of stress in autism is available, nor do we know the specific ways that stressors and overall stress levels influence behavior in autism. The remainder of this chapter highlights the role of attributional style, environmental arrangements, and individual skill level that we have found helpful in understanding the role of stress and coping in autism. It ends with a rationale and procedures for teaching self-control, one key coping skill often undervalued in the treatment of persons with autism.

Changing Attributions

Attribution is the explanation of causes of behavior that can affect an individual's coping style and programmatic decision making. Attribution can be viewed from the perspective of both the individual with autism and the caregivers. A clinician or teacher can help clients with autism to think positively about their ability to control stress and make adaptive responses to it.

There is a good deal of evidence in favor of the general proposition that an individual's attributional style influences how he or she responds to life events (Rutter, 1983). If a person feels that they can control their fate and have positive attributions, they are more likely to use self-control, self-reinforcement, positive imagery, positive assertions, and practices that will lead to a brighter future. If the individual can learn to recognize stressors and can make the attribution that something positive can be done, the chances are more likely that stress-reduction procedures will be used.

Caregivers' attributions can also affect treatment and educational decisions. If teachers, staff, or parents view maladaptive behaviors as the result of stress, they will more likely set up procedures that are positive and stress reducing. If, for example, they attribute maladaptive behaviors to "being bad," and view the person with autism as not having the ability to have control, there is a greater likelihood of setting up programs that use aversive procedures such as punishment, response costs, extinction, and so forth (figure 1.5).

Figure 1.5 shows how attribution influences perception, which then leads to program choices and design, and continues on to the implementation of therapeutic interventions stemming from the initial attribution. An example follows.

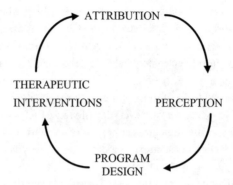

Figure 1.5. The role of attribution.

The teacher, John, notices that the student, Jamie, gets very upset, screams, and exhibits stereotypic behavior whenever there is a schedule change. John makes the attribution that a schedule change is a stressor for Jamie and notes his perception is that this perturbation is a difficult situation for his student. He designs a program that includes a request to do relaxation before he announces the change. He makes a change on a visual schedule so that Jamie both hears and sees the change, and the new program is pictured on the schedule board. He also reinforces Jamie for staying calm. In addition, the teacher might add some cognitive strategies that teach Jamie to say, "I can take this change. I will do something else I like." He implements these strategies whenever the classroom has a change in schedule.

In contrast, the teacher might not attribute the tantrum to a stressful situation and instead might perceive and interpret Jamie's usual outburst as a sign that Jamie is "a difficult student." He designs and implements a program to punish the behavior by using "x" on a contract, time-out, or exclusion. Similarly, a clinician or caregiver might see the tantrum as "just another characteristic of autism," a response that Jamie cannot control, or a behavior that is necessary to Jamie's self-expression. All these attributions may lead the teacher to feel hopeless or even to choose not to intervene. Programs are needed to teach individuals and caregivers the importance of their attributions.

As illustrated above, both the individual's and the caregiver's coping styles are based on attribution.

Environmental Strategies to Reduce Stress

Various arrangements of the physical and social environmental can also be useful in reducing an individual's exposure to stressful situations. Our growing awareness of the sensory-perceptual needs of persons with autism lead us to make accommodations for noise, crowding, lighting, and distracting movement in the physical surroundings. A daily schedule is an organizational tool that makes future events predictable and makes time concepts understandable. Daily schedules should allow time for both exercising and taking a break, and the physical location for these activities should be accessible.

Increasing a person's skills and abilities is another long-term adaptive method of reducing stress. For example, in a school setting, providing instruction in a way that matches the learning style of students with autism can help reduce their stress level. This would incorporate the use of visual supports and cues (Hodgdon, 1995), scheduling activities according to sensory and attentional needs (Janzen, 1996), breaking down learning tasks into manageable lessons, keeping directions simple, providing frequent experiences of success and positive reinforcement, implementing techniques to prepare for transitions, ensuring that opportunities for meaningful personal choices are available, and planning generalization strategies. Such instructional approaches make it more likely that the student will experience success. Repeated successes build confidence, self-esteem, and also increase the general level of reinforcement.

Selecting appropriate instructional objectives is as important as the method of instruction. Objectives must be functional, have long-term use to the learner, and increase independence. The area of social development, so stressful for individuals with autism, is one in which clear instructional objectives must be planned. From responding to greetings to more sophisticated skills such as being assertive and accepting constructive feedback, the acquisition of social skills reduces stress by increasing an individual's social competence. Building social interaction routines into daily activities provides the practice and positive reinforcement opportunities that can help a person function effectively in all social settings. In the areas of vocational and independent living goals, individuals' interests and abilities should be considered. Similarly, having some control over where one lives and what kind of work one does can help reduce the stressors related to those situations.

Importance of Self-Control in Managing Stress in Persons with Autism

One of the most effective ways to buffer the disruptive effects of a stressor is to achieve some degree of control over the stressor (Sapolsky, 1998). By using self-control, individuals can also be proactive in reducing stress by learning to act early, when first warning signs are evidenced (Hobfoil, 2001). By recognizing antecedents to stress and using self-control procedures, persons with autism can learn to deal effectively with a stressor. Unfortunately, one instructional objective often missing from programs for persons with autism is the skill of managing one's environment and one's own behavior—self-control. This may be the result of assumptions we make about what persons with autism cannot learn to do, instead of focusing on what these individuals can learn to do.

Assumptions about Self-Control and Autism

Teachers, clinicians, and parents who wish to help persons with autism learn self-control can, first, consider the assumptions we make about self-control and autism. It is not uncommon for professionals and parents alike to assume that persons with autism are limited or even unable to learn self-control, citing either their intellectual deficiencies (e.g., retardation) cognitive differences (e.g., lacking an ability to understand mental states of themselves or others), or the presumed neurological bases of some behaviors, such as self-injury or stereotypy. Such unexamined assumptions may in fact impose an unnecessary ceiling on growth, which leads to a barrier to self-management, and a requirement for life-long external controls imposed and managed by others.

Since 1976, the Groden Center programs have been focused on removing not only environmental, educational, and vocational barriers, but also the barriers that come from external control by others. We assume that people with autism, like all human beings, can learn self-control and reduce the impact of stress in their lives. One guideline for all clinicians, teachers, and caregivers should be, "If this person does not learn to make self-controlling responses, what external controls will have to be established and maintained during this child's life?" Guided by the thinking of early behavioral therapists (Cautela, 1973; Kanfer, 1977), we assume that self-control is not a higher personal quality that is possible for only some people of a certain cognitive range. As behavioral clinicians and teachers, we want to carry out each intervention with a person with autism with the explicit goal of teaching them to manage their own behavior, or in other words, to have self-control. We believe that self-control is a set of responses that any person can learn to make. Some describe self-control as a right of all humans. Because self-control is very satisfying for most humans, we assume that managing and controlling one's own environment and behavior can be also inherently rewarding for persons with autism. The techniques described in this chapter may increase perceived controllability over stressors.

Is self-control possible? The behavioral literature (e.g., Cautela, 1969; Rimm & Masters, 1974; Thorensen & Mahoney, 1974) describes self-control as procedures or strategies such as self-monitoring (as when a person records the number of laps jogged or the amount of piece work completed); self-instruction (as when an individual verbally directs his own behavior during assembly of an intricate machine or as one prepares to approach an anxiety-provoking situation); and self-reinforcement (as when one rewards oneself with leisure time after completing a difficult assignment). One can even broaden the definition of self-control to mean client involvement to the extent of helping to choose behaviors to be modified or intervention to be employed. To put it another way, we say that a child with autism has made a self-controlling response when he has learned to make a new, more appropriate response and when this new response is made in the apparent absence of external cues, prompts, or contingencies. We assume then that all individuals, typical or with special needs, have the right to as much freedom as possible from externally imposed and controlled contingencies over their behavior.

Learning and Using Self-Control

For persons with autism and other developmental disabilities, it is not enough to learn self-controlling responses to reduce stress. Learning to use self-controlling procedures in various life contexts is necessary for effective coping (Lazarus, 1993). A systematic program of stress reduction for persons with autism includes teaching and reinforcing the use of strategies for coping with stress in three general contexts: before, during, and after a stressful event occurs. Proactive strategies are taught for dealing with a stressor before it occurs. Reactive coping strategies are needed for times during which stress occurs and after the stress occurs. In the sections that follow, all the described interventions can be used as both proactive and reactive strategies.

A general program target of teaching self-controlling responses can also contribute productively to positive behavioral, educational, and clinical programs. For example, an alternative self-controlling response, such as taking a deep breath and doing the relaxation response, can be the targeted alternative in a Differential Reinforcement of Incompatible Behavior (DRI) program. The definition of DRI is the delivery of a reinforcer after a response that is incompatible or competes with a target response that is to be suppressed. The effect is to increase the frequency of the incompatible response (e.g., relaxation) and to decrease the frequency of the undesirable target response (e.g., aggression; Kazdin, 2001). Similarly, a communication program can teach self-controlling assertive and nonaggressive strategies if those are missing from a person's repertoire. Finally, a cognitively oriented clinician can teach a self-instructional strategy to reduce stress through the use of self-directive statements, such as, "If I take a deep breathe and relax, I'll be able to have self-control and get back to my work."

The following section details two procedures that enable persons with autism to make adaptive self-controlling responses to stressors. These include learning and using the relaxation response and using imagery-based rehearsal strategies to manage stress.

Relaxation

Cautela and Groden's (1978) publication, *Relaxation: A Comprehensive Manual for Adults, Children, and Children with Special Needs*, provides a guide to teachers, clinicians, and parents on how to adapt and teach Jacobson's (1938) progressive relaxation procedure to persons with autism. Systematic reinforcement, modeling, prompting, shaping, and fading procedures are used to teach the learner to discriminate and to label the feeling of muscles that are tight and muscles that are relaxed, to take deep inhaling and exhaling breaths, and to relax the entire body. Sometimes special equipment or toys are used to help teach the deep breathing response. Our experience with more than 30 years of teaching progressive relaxation to hundreds of children and adults with autism shows us that children and adults of all functioning levels can learn to relax muscle groups and take deep breaths. A number of reports demonstrate the effectiveness of relaxation training to treat behavioral disorders in clients with autism and other developmental disabilities (Calamari, Geist, & Shahbazian, 1987; Graziano & Kean, 1968; Harvey, Karan, Bhargava, & Morehouse, 1978; Lindsay, Baty, Michie, & Richardson, 1989; Lindsay, Fee, Michie, & Heap, 1994; McPhail & Chamove, 1989; Mullins & Christian, 2001; Steen & Zuriff, 1977; To & Chan, 2000).

The relaxation response, when learned, can function as an adaptive coping response that is incompatible with disruptive, stereotypic, or self-injurious behavior (Baron, Groden, & Cautela, 1988). After learning the relaxation response, the individual can be taught to identify situations in which stress occurs and then to use the relaxation response before, during, and after a stressful situation. Relaxation can also become part of a daily routine and will thereby help decrease general stress and anxiety by helping the individual identify both bodily signs of stress and the situations that elicit stress. One advantage of relaxation therapy is that it can be used in any setting—school, home, or workplace—whenever a stressful situation occurs. It is a positive, preventive strategy in which the learner actively reduces stress by engaging in a familiar routine that, through practice, has become inherently reinforcing. Research indicates that when the relaxation response is learned and practiced on a daily basis, it has a number of beneficial results throughout the day (Benson & Proctor, 1984).

Once the client has learned to make the relaxation response reliably, teachers and clinicians can incorporate programs to teach the relaxation response as a self-control procedure into individual educational or clinical plans using the following general program guidelines.

1. Determine the situations that produce stress and anxiety using the strategies and instruments described earlier in this chapter. Identify the antecedents that signal a stress response.
2. Practice the use of the relaxation response to the specific antecedents identified in the assessment as occurring before the stressful event. The antecedent is identified to the individual and the relaxation paired by either verbal, communication card, sign, or written word prompts.
3. Fade the use of prompts other than naming the antecedent and saying, "What do you do now?" to elicit the relaxation response.
4. Observe and reinforce the individual's efforts in real-life settings to identify a stressful situation and use the relaxation response to reduce the stress and make an adaptive response.

The following is an example of how this procedure is used with an individual. Barney was 24 years old and had a job at a local department store. He was sensitive to noise, and when he heard loud noises, he became upset and would scream, rock, and sometimes spit. His job was in jeopardy unless he could change this behavior. He had learned the relaxation procedure for adults and had practiced this on a daily basis. The following sequences were used for producing relaxation as a self-controlling response.

1. A behavioral observation was conducted at the job site, and it was noted that Barney had a continual problem when he heard the loud noise of the rolling carts that brought in new merchandise to the stockroom where he worked.
2. The job coach who worked beside Barney was taught to cue the relaxation response whenever she heard the sound of the rolling cart by saying, "Barney, the cart is coming. Take a deep breath and relax your whole body, stay relaxed, and keep on working." She then reinforced the relaxation response by checking his contract. She did this for about three weeks.
3. The job coach, upon hearing the sound of the rolling cart, said, "I hear the sound of the rolling cart. What do you do now?" Barney started to use relaxation and then continued working. He was reinforced for using the relaxation response.
4. After he had made this response for two weeks, the job coach withdrew the prompt, and Barney, upon hearing the sound of the rolling cart, began to self-cue the relaxation response. He was able to continue to use relaxation as a self-control procedure and keep his job.

In this case, it was crucial that the client learn a self-controlling response because the job coach would not always be available to monitor the procedure. In addition, once he learned to use relaxation, Barney was able to generalize the response to other stressful situations after they were identified. Disruptive behavior is incompatible with the relaxation response, and thus relaxation promotes adaptive behavior.

Picture Rehearsal

Picture rehearsal is a proactive instructional strategy, based on imagery techniques, using sequenced pictures and an accompanying script. The pictures and the script create a scene or story that describes when, where, and how to use a particular behavioral sequence and ends with reinforcement for successful performance (Groden, Cautela, LeVasseur, Groden, & Bausman, 1991; Groden & LeVasseur, 1995). The behavioral sequence depicted is typically a coping strategy, individually designed for use in a situation that has been identified as stressful for the learner. Picture rehearsal scenes are written within the positive reinforcement framework. Picture rehearsal scenes have three components: the antecedent (A), the behavior to increase (B), and the reinforcer or consequence (C). For each individual, this information is obtained from a number of sources, including a functional analysis of the target behavior, an ecological inventory, the Stress Survey Schedule, and reinforcement surveys. It is then put into the A—B—C format with pictures and a script for each component. Each scene is designed to match the individual's attention abilities, language level, sequencing abilities, picture preferences, and reinforcers. It depicts the desired sequence of adaptive behavior the individual can use in a stressful situation. Daily practice of the picture rehearsal scene increases the likelihood that the individual will be able to use it when the actual situation occurs. Picture rehearsal programs are a unique adaptation of imagery-based therapy. They combine a proven behavioral approach to learning with a visual support system that results in an effective, internally mediated self-control strategy.

Imagery-based picture rehearsal addresses the learning strengths of persons with autism by providing a visual system combined with structured interactive routines. Focusing on antecedent events and practicing coping strategies before stressful events occur places an emphasis on prevention. The scripts also include cognitive restructuring principles. This treatment technique identifies negative and/or unrealistic thoughts and attributions and attempts to modify them from negative self-references and attributions to positive ones (Corsini, 2002). An example of some modified, positive statements incorporated into the scripts might be, "I think to myself, I can do it," or, "I won't let this bother me."

The following example summarizes the procedure for creating and using a picture rehearsal scene in a classroom. More detailed information on how to construct scenes and use the picture rehearsal procedure can be found in *Coping with Stress Through Picture Rehearsal: A How-to Manual for Working with Individuals with Autism* (Groden, LeVasseur, Diller, & Cautela, 2002).

Assessing Stressors   Simon, a 10-year-old verbal boy with autism, is aggressive to his classroom aide and has tantrums that interfere with his learning and disrupt the class. Simon's parents and teachers completed the Stress Survey Schedule. Simon's responses were rated moderate-to-severe or severe on all of the items that were part of the component anticipation. Anticipation is defined as "a mental set or readiness to receive a stimulus that an individual either does or does not want to occur" (Groden et al. 2002). Results of DBR analysis indicated (see section on assessment in this chapter) that when Simon was waiting for an event to occur, he would talk loudly or have tantrums. Waiting in line for recess was particularly difficult.

Developing a Picture Rehearsal Scene   A picture rehearsal scene can be developed from the sample scenes in *Coping with Stress* (Groden et al., 2002, p. 275), which contains samples scenes for every item on the Stress Survey Schedule. Item #32, Waiting in Line, was identified as an appropriate scene for Simon (see figure 1.6).

Selecting Reinforcers   Each scene includes a reinforcing item chosen from the Reinforcement Survey Schedule (Groden et al., 2002). For Simon the reinforcing scene chosen was: "Now I imagine eating some ice cream."

Implementing the Picture Rehearsal Scenes   The scene is copied from the book and placed on index cards, and then Simon, his teacher, and staff schedule approximately 20 min at a specified time each day to work together. The staff first reads the scene to Simon, and then Simon repeats the scene pointing to each

Figure 1.6. Sample imagery scene: "waiting in line."

picture and answering questions pertaining to the scene. In this example, Simon is verbal and able to repeat the scenes and point. If Simon were nonverbal, he would point to the appropriate picture as the staff person repeated the scene. After about 100 sessions, Simon uses the scene before the identified stressor, which in this case, is recess.

Using the Picture Rehearsal Scene as a Proactive Coping Strategy in the Classroom   Simon continues to practice the scenes daily. However, before the identified event occurs, he reviews the scene with a prompt from a staff person. After two weeks of prompting from the staff person, he uses the scene independently by carrying small cards in his pocket and taking them out to review at the appropriate time. After a period of time, when he is able to memorize the scene and use it, he can identify the stressor and repeat the scene to himself.

As illustrated previously, an ongoing measurement of Simon's progress in coping with stressful situations was his increasingly independent use of the strategy outlined in the picture rehearsal scene and the resultant decrease in problem behavior.

FUTURE TRENDS

Although the concept of stress and procedures to reduce stress are widely used in the fields of sport psychology, behavioral medicine, and in the treatment of problem behaviors, such as depression, general anxiety disorders, and phobias, these procedures are rarely used in the population with autism. The principles of stress reduction have great application to persons with autism, and it would be a disservice if this arsenal of well-established, well-researched procedures were not used for their benefit.

Potential areas of future exploration include the following:

1. Using the concept of stress and procedures, such as relaxation, cognitive strategies, and imagery, and incorporating these methods into schools and programs working with children and adults with autism. This model is illustrated in the videos *Breaking the Barriers I* (Groden, Cautela, & Groden, 1989), *Breaking the Barriers II* (Groden et al., 1991), and *Breaking the Barriers III* (Groden, Spratt, & Fiske, 1998).

2. The addition of a stress assessment to diagnostic and assessment batteries. This assessment would examine stress levels for each individual and would be followed by individualized prescriptions of stress reducing and coping strategies. These would become part of an individual education and program plan, not only to reduce problem behavior, but also to increase well-being.

3. Research into the physiological factors associated with stress in the population with autism. The examination of biobehavioral responding (i.e., synchrony and dysynchrony between observable behavior and physiological measures) to stressors may contribute to classification and diagnosis and may help increase diagnostic clarity by identifying subgroups of individuals that show qualitatively different response patterns.

4. More research on specific stressors that affect children and adults with autism at different stages of development. For example, might there be hypersensitivity to some sensory stressors such as taste or texture of foods at different times in development? Or might we be able to anticipate and buffer the stressors associated with developmental milestones such as menstruation or preparing for graduation (Baron, 1990)?

PUTTING IT ALL TOGETHER: THE STRESS PREVENTION PYRAMID

Figure 1.7 illustrates the Stress Prevention Pyramid, which graphically depicts the main components of this chapter. A multimodal stress assessment is the foundation of the pyramid and includes observation (e.g., DBR), pencil-and-paper tests (e.g., the Stress Survey Schedule), and physiological measures (e.g.,

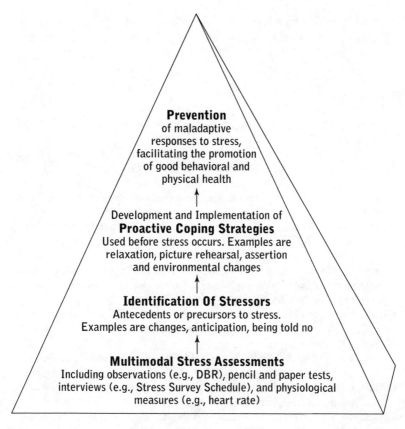

Figure 1.7. The stress prevention pyramid.

heart rate). This leads to the second level, identification of stressors, in which the information obtained from these assessments is analyzed, synthesized, and a list of separate and distinct stressors for each individual is produced. Therapists, teachers, caregivers, and multidisciplinary teams can then focus on antecedents or precursors to stress for each individual. The next tier designates the third step of the process, which is the development and implementation of proactive coping strategies. Coping strategies, such as relaxation, picture rehearsal, assertion, and environmental changes, are designed for each individual and each stressor. The children and adults with autism practice these strategies and then learn to use them proactively before the stress response occurs. These procedures, when used appropriately, enable self-control. The top of the pyramid, prevention, is the ultimate goal and the cumulative product of the proper implementation of the lower three tiers. Combining assessment, stressor identification, and implementing proactive coping strategies should lead to a decrease in maladaptive responses to stress and promote adaptive strategies that have a long-term positive effect on behavioral and physical health. The implementation of these strategies will also foster inclusion in social, school, and vocational settings and lead to an increased quality of life by providing more options for persons with autism.

References

Baron, G. (1990). Singular Voices. *Wheaton Quarterly*, Fall, 11–14. Norton, MA: Wheaton College.

Baron, G., Groden, J., & Cautela, J. R. (1988). Behavioral programming: Expanding our clinical repertoire. In G. Groden & G. Baron (Eds.), *Autism: Strategies for change* (pp. 49–73). Lake Worth, FL: Gardner Press.

Benson, H., & Proctor, W. (1984). *Beyond the relaxation response.* New York: Times Books.

Berntson, G. G., Ronca, A. E., Tuber, D. S., Boysen, S. T., & Leland, H. (1985). Cardiac reactivity and adaptive behavior. *American Journal of Mental Deficiency, 89,* 415–419.

Calamari, J., Geist, G., & Shahbazian, M. (1987). Evaluation of Multiple component relaxation training with developmentally disabled persons. *Research in Development Disabilities, 8,* 55–70.

Cautela, J. R. (1969). Behavior therapy and self-control: techniques and implications. In C. Franks (Ed.), *Behavior therapy: Appraisal and status* (pp. 323–340). New York: McGraw-Hill.

Cautela, J. R. (1973). Covert processes and behavior modification. *The Journal of Nervous and Mental Disease, 157,* 27–36.

Cautela, J. R., & Groden, J. (1978). *Relaxation: A comprehensive manual for adults, children, and children with special needs.* Champaign, IL: Research Press.

Courchesne, E., Townsend, J., Akshoomoff, N. A., Saitoh, O., Yeung-Courchesne, R., Lincoln, A. J., et al. (1994). Impairment in shifting attention in autistic and cerebella patients. *Behavioural Neuroscience, 108,* 848–865.

Corsini, R. (2002). *The dictionary of psychology.* New York: Brunner-Routledge.

Duncan, J. (1986). Disorganization of behavior after frontal lobe damage. *Cognitive Neuropsychology, 3,* 271–290.

Freeman, R., Horner, R., & Reichle, J. (1999). Relation between heart rate and problem behaviors. *American Journal on Mental Retardation, 104,* 330–345.

Gillot, A., Furniss, F., & Walter, A. (2001). Anxiety in high-functioning children with autism. *Autism, 5*(3), 277–286.

Grandin, T., & Scariano, M. (1986). *Emergence: Labeled autistic.* Novato, CA: Arena Press.

Graziano, A. M., & Kean, J. E. (1968). Programmed relaxation and reciprocal inhibition with psychotic children. *Behaviour Research and Therapy, 6*(4), 433–437.

Groden, G., Stevenson, S., & Groden, J. (1996). *Understanding challenging behavior: A step-by-step behavior analysis guide.* Providence, RI: Groden Center.

Groden, J., Cautela, J. R., & Groden, G. (1989). *Breaking the barriers I: The use of relaxation for people with special needs* [Video]. Champaign, IL: Research Press.

Groden, J., Cautela, J. R., LeVasseur, P., Groden, G., & Bausman, M. (1991). *Video guide: Breaking the barriers II: Imagery procedures for people with special needs.* Champaign, IL: Research Press.

Groden, J., Cautela, J. R., Prince, S., & Berryman, J. (1994). The impact of stress and anxiety on individuals with autism and developmental disabilities. In E. Schopler

& G. Mesibov (Eds.), *Behavioral issues in autism* (pp. 177–193). New York: Plenum Press.

Groden, J., Diller, A., Bausman, M., Velicer, W., Norman, G., & Cautela, J. (2001). The development of a stress survey schedule for persons with autism and other developmental disabilities. *Journal of Autism and Developmental Disorders, 17*(2), 207–217.

Groden, J., Goodwin, M. S., Baron, M. G., Groden, G., Velicer, W. F., Lipsitt, L. P., et al. (2005). *Assessing cardiovascular responses to stressors in individuals with autism and other developmental disabilities. Focus on Autism & Developmental Disabilities, 20*(4), 244–252.

Groden, J., & LeVasseur, P. (1995). Cognitive picture rehearsal: A system to teach self-control. In K. Quill (Ed.), *Teaching children with autism* (pp. 287–306). Albany, NY: Delmar.

Groden, J., LeVasseur, P., Diller, A., & Cautela, J. R. (2002). *Coping with stress through picture rehearsal: A how-to manual for working with individuals with autism and developmental disabilities.* Unpublished manuscript.

Groden, J., Spratt, R., & Fiske, P. (1998). *Breaking the barriers III: Intensive early intervention and beyond: A school-based inclusion program* [Video]. Champaign, IL: ResearchPress.

Harvey, J., Karan, O., Bhargava, G., & Morehouse, N. (1978). Relaxation training and cognitive behavioral procedures to reduce violent temper outbursts in a moderately retarded woman. *Journal of Behavior Therapy and Experimental Psychiatry, 9,* 347–351.

Hill, D., & Leary, M. (1993). *Movement disturbance: A clue to hidden competencies in persons diagnosed with autism and other developmental disabilities.* Madison, WI: DRI Press.

Hobfoil, S. E. (2001). The influence of culture, community, and all nested-self in the stress process: Advancing conservation of resources theory. *Applied Psychology: An International Journal, 50,* 337–421.

Hodgdon, L. (1995). Solving social-behavioral problems through the use of visually supported communication. In K. Quill (Ed.), *Teaching children with autism* (pp. 265–285). Albany, NY: Delmar.

Huang, C. (1995). Hardiness and stress: A critical review. *Maternal-Child Nursing Journal, 23,* 82–89.

Hutt, C., Hutt, S. J., Lee, D., & Ounsted, C. (1964). Arousal and childhood autism. *Nature, 204,* 909–909.

Jacobson, E. (1938). *Jacobson progressive relaxation.* Chicago: University of Chicago Press.

Janzen, J. (1996). *Understanding the nature of autism.* San Antonio, TX: Therapy Skill Builders.

Jolliffe, T., Landsdown, R., & Robinson, T. (1992). Autism: A personal account. *Communication, 3*(2b), 12–19.

Jones, R., Quigney, A., & Huws, J. (2003). First-hand accounts of sensory-perceptual experiences in autism: a qualitative analysis. *Journal of Intellectual and Developmental Disability, 28,* 112–21.

Kanfer, F. H. (1977). The many faces of self-control or behavior modification changes its focus. In R. B. Stuart (Ed.), *Behavioral self-management* (pp. 1–48). New York: Brunner/Mazel.

Kazdin, A. E. (2001). *Behavior modification in applied settings* (6th ed.). Belmont, CA: Wadsworth/Thomson.

Kim, J. A., Szatmari, P., Bryson, S. E., Streiner, D. L., & Wilson, F. J. (2000). The prevalence of anxiety and mood problems among children with autism and Asperger syndrome. *Autism, 4*(2), 117–132.

King, N. J., Hamilton, D. I., & Ollendick, T. H. (1994). *Children's phobias: A behavioral perspective*. New York: Wiley & Sons.

Konstantareas, M. M., & Homatidis, S. (1987). Ear infections in autistic and normal children. *Journal of Autism & Developmental Disorders, 17*(4), 585–594.

Lazarus, R. S. (1993). Coping theory and research: Past, present, and future. *Psychosomatic Medicine, 55*, 234–247.

Lindsay, W., Baty, R., Michie, A., & Richardson, I. (1989). A comparison of anxiety treatments with adults who have moderate and severe mental retardation. *Research in Developmental Disabilities, 10*, 129–140.

Lindsay, W., Fee, M., Michie, A., & Heap, I. (1994). The effects of cue control relaxation on adults with severe mental retardation. *Research in Developmental Disabilities, 15*, 425–437.

Lord, C. (1996). Treatment of a high functioning adolescent with autism: A cognitive-behavioral approach. In M.A., Reinecke, F.M., Dattilo, & A. Freeman, (Eds.), *Cognitive therapy with children and adolescents: A casebook for clinical practice* (pp. 394–404). New York: Guilford Press.

Mason-Brothers, A., Ritvo, E. R., Freeman, B. J., Jorde, L. B., et al. (1993). The UCLA-University of Utah epidemiologic survey of autism: Recurrent infections. *European Child & Adolescent Psychiatry, 2*, 79–90.

McEwen, B. (2002). *The end of stress as we know it.* Washington, DC: Dana Press.

McPhail, C., & Chamove, A. (1989). Relaxation reduces disruption in mentally handicapped adults. *Journal of Mental Deficiency Research, 33*, 399–406.

Mullins, J. L., & Christian, L. (2001). The effects of progressive relaxation training on the disruptive behavior of a boy with autism. *Research in Developmental Disabilities, 22*(6), 449–62.

Muris, P., Steerneman, P., Merckelbach, H., Holdrinet, I., & Meesters, C. (1998). Comorbid anxiety symptoms in children with pervasive developmental disorders. *Journal of Anxiety Disorders, 12*(4), 387–393.

O'Neill, M., & Jones, R. S. P. (1997). Sensory-perceptual abnormalities in autism: a case for more research? *Journal of Autism & Developmental Disorders, 27*, 283–293.

O'Reilly, M. (1997). Functional analysis of episodic self-injury correlated with recurrent otitis media. *Journal of Applied Behavior Analysis, 30*, 165–167.

Park, C. (1982). *The siege: The first eight years of an autistic child*. Boston: Little, Brown.

Poustka, F. (1998). Neurobiology of autism. In F. Volkmar (Ed.), *Autism and pervasive developmental disorders* (pp. 130–168). New York: Cambridge University Press.

Prior, M. R., & Hoffmann, W. (1990). Neuropsychological testing of autistic children through an exploration with frontal lobe tests. *Journal of Autism and Developmental Disorders, 20*, 581–590.

Prior, M. R., & Ozonoff, S. (1998). Psychological factors in autism. In F. Volkmar (Ed.), *Autism and pervasive developmental disorders* (pp. 64–108). New York: Cambridge University Press.

Rimland, B. (1964). *Infantile autism*. London: Methuen.

Rimm, D. C., & Masters, J. C. (1974). *Behavior therapy: Techniques and empirical findings*. New York: Academic Press.

Romanczyk, R., & Matthews, A. (1998). Physiological state as antecedent: Utilization in functional analysis. In J. Luiselli & M. Cameron (Eds.), *Antecedent control: Innovative approaches to behavioral support* (pp. 115–138). Baltimore, MD: Brookes.

Rumsey, J. M., & Hamburger, S. D. (1988). Neuropsychological findings in high-functioning autistic men with infantile autism, residual state. *Journal of Clinical and Experimental Neuropsychology, 10*, 201–221.

Rutter, M. (1983). Stress, coping, and development: Some issues and some questions. In N. Garmezy & M. Rutter (Eds.), *Stress, coping, and development in children.* New York: McGraw-Hill.

Sapolsky, R. M. (1998). *Why zebras don't get ulcers.* New York: W. H. Freeman.

Stavrakaki, C. (1999). Depression, anxiety and adjustment disorders in people with developmental disabilities. In N. Bouras (Ed.), *Psychiatric and behavioural disorders in development disabilities and mental retardation* (pp. 175–187). New York: Cambridge University Press.

Steen, P. L., & Zuriff, G. E. (1977). The use of relaxation in the treatment of self-injurious behavior. *Journal of Behavior Therapy and Experimental Psychiatry, 8*, 447–448.

Thorensen, C. E., & Mahoney, M. J. (1974). *Behavioral self-control.* New York: Holt, Rinehart & Winston.

To, M., & Chan, S. (2000). Evaluating the effectiveness of progressive muscle relaxation in reducing the aggressive behaviors of mentally handicapped patients. *Archives of Psychiatric Nursing, 14*, 39–46.

Volkmar, F. R., & Cohen, D. J. (1985). The experience of infantile autism: A first person account by Tony W. *Journal of Autism and Developmental Disabilities, 15*, 47–54.

Walker, E., & Diforio, D. (1997). Schizophrenia: A neural diathesis-stress model. *Psychological Review, 10*(4), 667–685.

Westman, M. (2004). Strategies for coping with business trips: A qualitative exploratory study. *International Journal of Stress Management, 11*(2), 167–176.

2 Scientific Foundations for Research and Practice

M. Grace Baron, Lewis P. Lipsitt,
and Matthew S. Goodwin

The concepts of stress and coping have been of enduring usefulness in the understanding of normal human behavior, and have contributed much to the behavioral and developmental sciences. Variations on the notion of human stress, most of them relating to the dynamic processes involved in the waxing and waning of the individual's comfort level, or "equilibrium," have been refined through discussion of coping mechanisms that optimize the comfort level or stability of the individual.

These ideas have also been useful in understanding deviations from normal mental functioning and the psychological processes through which adjustments are made to reduce tensions, conflicts, or anxiety. For example, the concept of defense mechanisms in Freudian theory originated as a way of explaining how individuals cope with stressful deviations from "normalcy." Surprisingly little attention, however, has been given to stress and its role in the development and behavior of individuals with autism spectrum disorders (ASD), despite the common understanding by those working with such individuals that much of their behavior seems intimately associated with stress; that is, it either stems from stress or produces stress in others. Difficulties with socialization, communication, and behavioral rigidity are hallmarks of ASD, and the display of problems in each of these aspects calls for a better understanding of them in terms of their developmental features and the stressful circumstances that may be implicated. The coping behaviors that accompany them are of no less importance.

We seek here to address scientific considerations in the understanding of stress and coping in individuals with ASD, hoping to shed light on, and perhaps guide our field toward, more relevant and heuristic approaches to future theory, research, and practice in the still young field of autism. To this end, and as a prelude to the remaining chapters of the volume, this chapter is dedicated to those individuals with ASD whose lives have touched ours. From them we have come to understand that while all individuals with ASD are unique, their similarities to one another and to nonautistic populations as well, provide us with confidence that the behavioral, developmental, and clinical sciences will together provide valuable advances in our comprehension of ASD.

A RATIONALE FOR THE BIOBEHAVIORAL STUDY OF STRESS AND COPING IN ASD

The search for an answer to the puzzle of autism can be aided by looking at the disorder in new ways. To date, biological studies have explored structural differences in neurochemistry (Anderson & Hoshino, 1997), brain systems (Minshew, Sweeney, & Bauman, 1997), and genetics (Courchesne, 1997; Rutter, Bailey, Siminoff, & Pickles, 1997; Volkmar, Klin, & Pauls, 1998). A broader and better understanding of ASD requires equal attention to the behavioral and physiological functioning of these individuals as they interact with the environment and their social milieu. Explorations of an individual's general adaptation response or adaptive stress response to life's inevitable perturbations, demands, and challenges may provide one way to study ASD as a dynamic connection not only between biological systems, but also across biological, psychological, and social systems. The constructs of stress and coping have contributed productively to a multisystem analysis of other conditions, such as anxiety, schizophrenia, panic disorder, phobias, post-traumatic stress disorder, and fragile X syndrome (Barlow, 2004). We expect it can do the same for ASD. Furthermore, the constructs of stress and coping appear to have special relevance to conditions like ASD, where individuals are prone to difficulties with modulating arousal. Patterns of over- and underarousal have long been noted in ASD and, as this chapter will discuss in more detail, new measurement systems have fueled an interest in the contribution of stress and coping to physiological and behavioral profiles.

The scientific reasoning for a systematic examination of stress and coping in ASD is also buttressed by the daily observations of clinicians and caregivers, elaborate first-person reports of the stress of life with ASD, and a growing appreciation of the impact of stress in modern life for all people. The personal worlds of sensation and perception, cognition, memory, learning, and the publicly observed behavior patterns of persons with ASD all promise to take on new meaning as we explore them through the lens of stress and coping. It is possible that a more rigorous examination of patterns of arousal and habituation in persons with ASD might point the way to functional rather than primarily descriptive diagnostic subcategories. Until then, more practical feasibility questions can guide research. For example, how can we best measure the effects of stress in persons with ASD? What are the effects of chronic and specific stressors in either motivating or interfering with adaptive behavior and the health and development of persons with ASD?

As clinical researchers, we also anticipate that the concepts of stress and coping will help us to better understand, educate, and treat persons with ASD. We anticipate that an individual's behavioral and physiological changes in response to stressors may prove to be a guiding and perhaps confirming measure of the short-range and long-range effectiveness of treatment procedures. Such data may also help us to predict treatment outcome and developmental pathways through life with ASD. It is also possible that, in the future, knowledge of an individual's pattern of response to chronic and/or phasic stress will routinely influence our choice of educational and treatment strategies.

We provide here some foundations for the systematic study of stress and coping in ASD. Following an introduction to the phenomenon of stress as it plays out in human nature and a proposal regarding its fit in ASD, the chapter reviews key concepts and terms related to the scientific study of stress, with special emphasis given to physiological investigations of stress and ASD. We then consider the concept of coping as it may apply in ASD, and suggest future directions for researchers and clinicians to enlarge our knowledge of stress and coping in ASD.

Stress and Human Nature

Textbooks on the psychology and physiology of stress generally treat it as a phenomenon inherent in natural development and, in humans, as a condition that can have deleterious as well as salubrious effects on an individual's well-being. A long line of historical writings exists in the fields of psychology and education on the role of stress in the functioning of ordinary individuals while growing up. The saliency of different kinds of stress at different developmental ages is often cited: the stress of an infant, for example, may relate especially to hunger and hurt; the toddler is stressed by his or her inability to reach a coveted object on a high table; the preschooler is stressed by the hoarding behavior of his playmate; the adolescent is stressed by the appearance of acne on his face; and the stresses of adults are too numerous to cite.

While individual differences are typically acknowledged in textbook treatments and manuals of psychopathological reactions, normative variations in typical responses and the diversity of reactions to normative experience are rarely emphasized. It is an unusual textbook that would say, for example, "Now here is what the extreme of this kind of stress reaction might look like," or, "The threshold for the occurrence of a stress reaction to some stimuli may, in some individuals such as those with ASD, seem quite bizarre to the uninformed onlooker."

To understand the role of stress in persons with ASD one must study those individuals not only as special cases, but also in the context of well-documented, "neurotypic" patterns of behavior found in normative populations and data sets. The rules governing the responses of individuals with ASD to either chronic or situational stress conditions are likely to bear similarities with those of neurotypic individuals, but application of those rules requires acknowledgment of the special conditions of personhood that inhere in being a person with ASD. A fitting analogy might be a glass of water and an ice cube: Both are the same substance, but their context and environmental conditions are different, and thus their respective states require that we address them differently.

The person diagnosed with ASD manifests, just like other humans, reflexes, learning capacities, motivations, social relationships, fascinations with the pleasures of sensation, and a propensity for avoiding annoying life conditions. In all of this, the individual with ASD is like other people. A short digression into the philosophy of science will help make this assertion clear.

Patterns of Human Behavior

Scientific statements of regularity, including regularities of behavior, are always based on replicable observations. Well-supported statements of fact are elevated to the status of "law," connoting that the statement is so well-supported by repetitive observation and testing that it can be regarded as highly reliable. Ohm's law, for example, is that kind of statement. According to Ohm's law, three conditions of an electrical circuit are all that are needed to describe the circuit: the amperage, I, the voltage, E, and the resistance, R. Physicists and electricians know the relationship as $E = I \times R$. Given any two of the measures, one can calculate the third by simple arithmetic. In a typical serial circuit, one can count on this relationship holding consistently. Individual differences in the construction of the wire and different methods of imposing resistances may exist, but one can always come back to the law to understand the "behavior" of the circuit. The law should always hold true.

While the constancies of electrical circuitry were found historically to be a reliable regularity of "nature," it was soon discovered that in some electrical circuits, this simple calculation ($E = I \times R$) did not work. Scientists found that there were not one, but two types of electrical circuits: one of them in series, the other in parallel. The arithmetic worked fine in series circuits, but not in parallel circuits. A further discovery was therefore required. For the law of the series circuits to be made whole, the resistances of the circuits in the atypical, parallel circuits needed to be understood differently, although still in terms of resistance. An adjustment needed to be made in the understanding of Ohm's law, which was valid and replicable for series circuits, but had to be amended for certain other "non-normative" circuits, like those in parallel. For these circuits, instead of the simple numerical value of the resistances being added together, one had to take the reciprocal of the resistances. Where the arithmetic understanding for the serial circuits was $R + R$, one needed to substitute $1/R + 1/R$ for the parallel circuits. Then the law worked!

As a result of the discovery of individual differences in electrical circuits, Ohm's law now has essentially two parts, one for series and one for parallel circuits. Both obey the common law, but the parallel circuits require a bit of adjustment—an adjustment principally in our way of seeing them, rather than in basic lawfulness. Philosophers of science call this kind of adjustment a composition law, which is an amendment of a prior understanding that must be made in order to retain an understanding of what is going on.

The moral of the story is that we don't discard a solidly supported manner of understanding something when a seemingly contradictory or unsupportive example is found. Rather, we seek ways of understanding the deviation in terms that have a track record of usefulness. This is the way it is, we believe, with individuals identified with an ASD. Like parallel circuits, persons with ASD are not beyond comprehension. They are humans who can be understood in very similar terms to those invoked for neurotypic individuals, but some adjustments in our understanding of the regularities must be made.

Theoretical Framework

In the remainder of this chapter, we seek to make the progression from basic scientific and clinical understandings of so-called normally functioning individuals under conditions of stress to comprehending individuals with ASD under their special burdens of stress.

On the one hand, we wish to understand stress and its varied effects on individuals with ASD in classical terms such as those of homeostasis, perturbations of equilibrium, and adaptation (Weiner, 1992). On the other hand, we have come to appreciate that adaptations on our own part are required to transport such concepts into the world of the individual with an ASD.

Subscribing here to a bipartite definition of stress, we focus both on stress reactions, which have to do with the manner or style of response that an individual manifests when confronted with an uncomfortably stimulating condition or extraordinarily surprising task, and on the pervasive condition of stressful anxiety that is not stimulus-specific (Miller, 1989). The former is largely a matter of external control and often measures can be taken to reduce the annoyance and help the individual return to a stable condition. The latter is an internal state that is more resistant to external controls. This pervasive stress results in lowered thresholds of response to upsetting stimulation and thus can be ameliorated, also through external, environmental manipulations.

In our task here, we find guidance in the classic work of Kanner (1944). He described the individual with ASD in terms that lend credulity to the importance of stress in the daily life of the individual. Kanner speaks of five characteristics of infantile autism: (1) the children's inability to relate themselves in the ordinary way to people and to situations, or to be encapsulated in an isolated world; (2) a failure to use language appropriately, some having no language, others having repetition patterns; (3) an anxiously obsessive behavior pattern designed to maintain sameness, limiting spontaneity, and leading to rage or panic when external conditions do not meet the individual's demands of the moment; (4) a fascination with objects rather than with people; and (5) good cognitive potentialities in some areas of functioning. These are generally agreed to be the distinguishing attributes separating individuals with ASD from those with mental retardation (Wolff, 1981).

Taken as a whole, these characteristics suggest quite clearly that life in its everyday features can be stressful for persons with ASD, and that such individuals will be more susceptible than the generality of individuals to stress reactions when unusual or unexpected conditions arise. We expect that, with qualifications of our understanding of neurotypic individuals, the rules of stressful conditions and reactions of the generality of human individuals will be relevant to understanding such reactions in persons with ASD.

We take the view, then, that ASD is a name for a set of attributes in individuals who share many similar characteristics to those regarded as neurotypic. They have a penchant for the pleasures of sensation, a strong inclination to avoid annoyances, and a proclivity for attachment to others. Moreover, holding to this view will help us understand better the impact that personal experiences and the social milieu have on individuals with ASD.

Yet, our insistence that such features of human development as the acquisition of attachment to others are obtained by persons with ASD in much the same way as neurotypic individuals may seem quite odd to those who perceive individuals with ASD as having attachment problems—devoid of real emotional interpersonal contact. We hope that chapters in this volume will help dispel this illusion.

Our knowledge about neurotypical individuals should have some bearing on how we perceive individuals with ASD and how we must come to understand them in their complexities. We presume that the knowledge psychologists, educators, and pediatricians have acquired in the last century—about human sensory development, learning processes, motivational attributes, emotions such as love and hate, and social development—will be relevant for an eventual better understanding of individuals with ASD.

It follows from this orientation that we must call upon the hypotheses and conclusions provided by past research in the general population, and we therefore refer particularly to the wisdom of stress theorists, such as Cannon (1928), Selye (1956), and McEwen and Lasley (2002), who use stress as an organizing construct for understanding one of the primary motivators of human behavior.

"Stress" originated from the Latin noun *strictus*, meaning tight or narrow, and the verb *stringere*, meaning to tighten. The term "stress" is used by engineers to refer to load (i.e., the force acting on an object) divided by the area over which it acts to result in strain, or the effects of the force on the object (e.g., weakening, change in shape). Medicine has borrowed this term from engineering to denote the state of health and stability when an individual is challenged or pressured.

The ability to maintain the constancy of the internal milieu despite changes in the surrounding environment was first described by Bernard (1879, as cited in Fox, 1996) as a characteristic feature of all living organisms. Cannon (1928, 1939) subsequently called this power to maintain consonance "homeostasis," the ability to remain the same or static. As a construct, homeostasis was introduced to describe and emphasize the dynamic process by which living systems maintain internal states within a functional range.

Selye (1956, p. 7) was the first to note that many medical conditions share common elements, even as they present with unique symptoms. Studying illnesses, he defined stress as the nonspecific, or "common," result of any demand on the body, whether the effect is mental or somatic. Stress, he further stated, can be dichotomized into distress (negative occurrences) and eustress (positive events).

Environmental conditions contributing to stress are typically referred to as stressors. The consequence of such stressors for individuals is called the stress response, comprising physiological, emotional, cognitive, and behavioral correlates. The stress response typically relates to three conditions connecting the stressor and the individual's response: (1) threat, the period before the stressful event occurs, (2) impact, the failure to thwart the stressor's occurrence, and (3) post-impact, when the individual may experience residual effects of the event. Many stressors do not impinge directly on the body, but rather are perceived, evaluated, and thwarted before they elicit a stress response. It is useful, also, to make a distinction between distal or contextual stress conditions and proximal stress stimuli, the latter being especially relevant for understanding immediate instigation of individual stress reactions.

INDIVIDUAL RESPONSES TO STRESS

Many parameters moderate the severity of psychological and physical responses to stress. These properties (Paterson & Neufeld, 1989; Turner, 1994) include:

- stressor's severity, or the amount of impact a stressor will have
- temporal factor, or the length of time before a stressor occurs
- event probability, or the likelihood of the stressor occurring

- novelty, or prior experience with the stressor
- duration, or how long the stressor will last
- ambiguity, relating to prediction of a stressor's severity, temporal factor, event probability, novelty, and duration
- controllability, or whether one's responses can affect the outcome.

Anticipation that an individual's given response to a stressor will be effective in reducing the perturbation is immensely important. This represents the ability to benefit from previous experience, the hope that one's own actions will be effective in coping, and the frustration that may ensue from anticipating failure. In the coping literature, coping responses are the means available to an individual for reducing activation in highly stimulating situations or increasing activation in understimulating situations. If an individual deems a stressful event uncontrollable, this may activate withdrawal responses and consequent physiological reactions supporting disengagement. Such an integrated specificity model of stress was proposed by Weiner (1992), who suggested that the resources available to the individual, including a personal history of learning to engage successfully to reduce the stress, can moderate the relationship between a stressor and physiological/cognitive outcomes.

BEHAVIORAL FACTORS IN STRESS

Whenever chronic or specific stressors affect an individual, these conditions are superimposed on a preexisting behavioral repertoire. When an individual encounters a threat, the prepotent reaction will be one either of flight or remaining at the site to defend against that threat (i.e., fight), and will depend in large part on the individual's prior experiences in similar situations. This learned behavior will be mobilized at the scene, and the response that is executed will depend on the hierarchy of available responses and their relative strengths (Spence, 1956).

Stress and other motivational factors impel an organism to do something. Extensive data exist to indicate that motivational conditions such as stress and anxiety have differential effects on the behavior of individuals, depending on the existing response hierarchy (Castaneda, 1956; Castaneda & Lipsitt, 1959; Castaneda & Palermo, 1955; Lipsitt & Spears, 1965). Thus, it may be presumed, although this has not yet been tested in individuals with ASD, that chronic or specific stressors may either facilitate or interfere with effective behavior.

PHYSIOLOGY OF STRESS

In the presence of a stressor, physiological systems necessary for mobilizing a response are activated, initiating widespread changes in the cardiovascular system, the immune system, the endocrine glands, and those brain regions that mediate emotion and memory. These physiological reactions mobilize the body to engage in defensive behaviors (i.e., "fight or flight") by increasing heart rate (HR) and blood pressure (BP), quickening respiration, oxygenating muscles, discharging adrenaline into the blood stream, and recruiting immune cells to rush to the site of an injury if one occurs. Once the stressor has passed, another set of physiological responses is activated, returning the body to a steady state by reducing HR and BP, slowing breathing, and facilitating digestion and absorption of nutrients. This process of maintaining equilibrium, also known as "homeostasis" or "allostasis," is critical to the well-being of individuals (McEwen & Lasley, 2002; Sterling & Eyer, 1988) and represents a useful mechanism for objectively assessing abilities for reactivity and adaptation (see chapters 6 and 7 in this volume.)

PHYSIOLOGY OF STRESS IN ASD

Researchers since the 1970s have used cardiovascular, electrodermal, and hormonal measures of the dynamic, self-regulatory autonomic nervous system (ANS) in individuals with ASD to investigate stress-related behaviors. One of the motivating factors for employing physiological indicators in persons with ASD, and our impetus for extended coverage of this research area, relates to the unreliable self-reports given by this population that prevent the use of traditional verbal assessments of stress (e.g., interviews, paper-and-pencil surveys; Hill, Berthoz, & Frith, 2004). Researchers have attempted to overcome this communication barrier and measure a variety of observable behaviors including engagement in stereotypical behavior, attention responses, habituation rates, and general arousal.

Stereotypical Behavior

Stereotyped behaviors, or "stereotypies," are generally defined as repetitive motor or vocal sequences that appear to the observer to be invariant in form and without any obvious eliciting stimulus or adaptive function (Baumeister & Forehand, 1973; Berkson & Davenport, 1962; Lewis & Baumeister, 1982; Ridley & Baker, 1982). Many different topographies of stereotypy have been identified (Lewis & Bodfish, 1998), the most prevalent among them being body-rocking, mouthing, and complex hand and finger movements (LaGrow & Repp, 1984).

Three studies have measured ANS responses while individuals with ASD engage in stereotypical behaviors (Lewis et al., 1989; Sroufe, Struecher, & Strutzer, 1973; Willemsen-Swinkels, Buitellar, Dekker, & van Engeland, 1998). Findings suggest there is a functional relationship between stereotypy and arousal in persons with ASD, such that changes in HR either precede or are a consequence of engaging in stereotypical motor movements. These results have been interpreted as evidence for engagement in stereotypical behavior in order to attain homeostasis.

Attention Responses

Typically, when an individual attends to a novel or intensive stimulus, but not a startle stimulus, HR slows and variability decreases (Andreassi, 1995). This receptivity to environmental input is a model of attention known as the orienting response (OR; Porges, 1976, 1984). Behaviorally, the OR is typified by shifting one's head toward the stimuli of interest and suppressing bodily movements. Physiological changes include an initial decrease in HR, increased electrodermal activity, pupillary dilation, and EEG desynchronization (Fox, 1996). In contrast to the OR, a defensive response (DR), or "rejection of environmental stimuli," occurs when stimuli of a high intensity elicit HR accelerations, increased BP, and orientation away from painful or noxious stimuli (Lacey, 1967). The DR is believed to be an adaptive strategy enabling an organism to avoid or escape the potential dangers of threatening stimuli (Stern, Ray, & Quigley, 2001).

Three studies have compared ANS correlates of attention in individuals with ASD to typically developing children in order to explore the relationship between sensory intake and autonomic arousal (Cohen & Johnson, 1977; Kootz & Cohen, 1981; Kootz, Marinelli, & Cohen, 1982). Results indicated that, as a group, individuals with ASD had high mean blood flow and low peripheral vascular resistance that failed to change with sensory intake, suggesting that these individuals are making defensive responses, thus limiting their sensory intake by rejecting environmental stimulation.

Habituation

Habituation is the reduction of an organism's response to repeated presentation of the same stimulus. Generally, the habituated organism does not resume its earlier reaction to a stimulus after a period without stimulation, or, if the normal reaction is resumed, it wanes on reexposure to the stimulus more quickly than before. In the latter case, repeated interruptions and resumption of the stimulus are followed by increasingly rapid decreases in response, and eventually the stimulus elicits no response (Fox, 1996).

Habituation studies indicate that individuals with ASD either fail to habituate to repeatedly presented stimuli (Barry & James, 1988) or produce slower habituation rates characterized by larger response amplitudes (Bernal & Miller, 1970; Stevens & Gruzelier, 1984; van Engeland, 1984) and longer response latencies (Stevens & Gruzelier, 1984). Taken together, these findings of atypical habituation suggest that individuals with ASD often experience continual arousal to repeated environmental stimuli.

General Arousal

Researchers have suggested that behavioral patterns of overarousal (Hutt, Hutt, Lee, Ounsted, 1964) and underarousal (DesLauriers & Carlson, 1969) seen in some individuals with ASD might be indicative of a primary defect in modulating arousal to novel social and sensory stimuli (Dawson, 1991; Dawson & Lewy, 1989; Kinsbourne, 1987; Ornitz, 1989; Ornitz & Ritvo, 1968). Poor arousal modulation may interfere with this population's ability to understand and engage with the environment (Lord & McGee, 2001; Prizant, Wetherby, Rubin & Laurent, 2003; Siegel, 2003), and contribute to the arousal differences seen between ASD and typically developing individuals. Although some studies find no arousal differences between these groups (Althaus, Mulder, Mulder, Aarnoudse, & Minderaa, 1999; Graveling & Brooke, 1978; Hutt, Forest, & Richer, 1975; MacCulloch & Williams, 1971; Stevens & Gruzelier, 1984; Toichi & Kamio, 2003; van Engeland, 1984), others have found greater sympathetic reactivity (e.g., increased HR, respiration, pupillary dilation) in persons with ASD (Angus, 1970; Cohen & Johnson, 1977; Kootz & Cohen, 1981; Kootz, Marinelli, & Cohen, 1982; Lake, Ziegler, & Murphy, 1977; Ming et al., 2005; Palkovitz & Wiesenfeld, 1980; Zahn, Rumsey, & van Kammen, 1987). Interestingly, only two studies have found lower than normal basal arousal levels in persons with ASD (DesLauriers & Carlson, 1969; Sigman, Dissanayake, Corona, & Espinosa, 2003).

CARDIOVASCULAR ASSESSMENT OF STRESS IN ASD

Research also suggests that combining physiological measures with behavioral measures can yield useful data with which to conceptualize and treat problematic behaviors in individuals with severe developmental disabilities (Boccia & Roberts, 2000; Freeman, Horner & Reichle, 1999; Romanczyk & Matthews, 1998). Encouraged by these reports and the use of stress and arousal as organizing constructs for understanding the behavior of individuals with ASD, investigators at the Groden Center have initiated a program of research to both assess the feasibility of telemetrically recording HR as a measure of sympathetic activity in individuals with ASD and to identify environmental conditions that can reliably elicit arousal responses in this population.

Groden et al. (2005) recorded HR in a laboratory setting with a *Polar V* telemetric HR monitor (Polar Electro, Inc.) in 10 individuals identified with ASD ranging in age from 13 to 37 years. Cardiovascular responses were recorded while the participants engaged in four potentially stressful situations adapted from The Stress Survey Schedule for Persons with Autism and Developmental Disabilities (Groden et al., 2001), including losing at a game, eating a preferred food, having a change in staff, and unstructured time. Sessions began with a baseline phase (sitting quietly) followed by exposure to the potentially stressful situations that alternated with rest phases (sitting quietly). Using time series analysis, the data for each participant was examined to see if mean HR responses were significantly different during each stressor phase compared with mean HR during baseline. Results of this study illustrated vulnerability to all four stressors in some of the participants.

Goodwin et al. (2004) repeated the experimental design and analysis plan from Groden et al. (2005) to provide a wider sample of potential stressors that can evoke significant arousal responses in individuals with ASD. Cardiovascular responses were recorded in five individuals with ASD (ranging from 12–20 years of age) to the presentation of three previously untested stressors from the Stress Survey Schedule, including exposure to a loud noise, engagement in a difficult task, and encountering an unpredictable stimulus, which in this case was attending to a remote control robot. This study also used a more sophisticated ambulatory apparatus (*LifeShirt,* Vivometrics, Inc.) for telemetrically recording cardiovascular reactivity. Results illustrated that participants tolerated the new ambulatory HR monitor and showed some significant arousal responses to all three added stressors.

Goodwin et al. (in press) compared the cardiac responses of five persons with ASD ranging in age from 8 to 18 years of age with five age- and sex-matched typically developing individuals. The participants engaged in six of the seven potentially stressful situations identified in Groden et al. (2005) and Goodwin et al. (2004). Findings revealed individual differences in stress responses within each group and, on average, lesser responsivity to the potential stressors in the individuals with ASD. However, the group with ASD elicited HR values of 20 beats per-minute (bpm) higher, on average, than the typically developing group during baseline and nearly every stress condition. The high basal HR in the group with ASD was interpreted as increased general arousal, and the reduced responsivity to the potential stressors was taken to be evidence for autonomic defensiveness (Lacey, 1967) or sensory rejection in an attempt to escape threatening stimuli.

These three studies have established experimental and statistical procedures for telemetrically assessing cardiovascular reactivity to environmental stressors in individuals with ASD. Participants were found to tolerate the telemetric devices, and the dependent variable HR proved to have measurement characteristics that suggest sensitivity to the stress-induced experimental conditions. Results showed variability in patterns of responses to environmental stressors that, despite the relatively small sample of individuals with ASD observed across these studies, suggest possible stress response patterns that can be tested in future studies. For instance, some participants with ASD showed high resting HR (e.g., 113 bpm) and no subsequent responsivity to stressors. Other participants with ASD showed more normative resting HR (e.g., 70 bpm) and cardiovascular increases to demands for socialization and behavioral flexibility. These preliminary findings suggest that including physiological measures in assessments of stress may enable differentiation of subtype responders within the diagnostic category of ASD.

Anecdotal observations of overt behavior in these studies also suggest that there may be dysynchrony between physiological and behavioral responding for some individuals with ASD. This is a potentially interesting development that deserves more systematic study, given that deficits in communication characteristic of persons with ASD require clinicians, educators, and caregivers to make inferences about internal states from overt behavioral responses. It may well be that some individuals with ASD look calm overtly, but are experiencing significant physiological arousal covertly.

Taken together, the experimental and measurement protocol developed in this program of research can yield potentially fruitful inquiry into both the types of stressors that can be arousing in persons with ASD and the nature of varying stress responses observed in this population. The protocol also provides a window for monitoring changes in one's stress response over time and, in turn, supports a more systematic examination of the construct of coping in persons with ASD.

Coping and ASD

Adaptation is inherent in human nature. In all people, a stressor activates a specific set of responses (i.e., physiological, cognitive, motor) that we call coping. People also protect themselves against anticipated stressors and, over time, develop predictable patterns of avoiding or responding to stressors that we call coping styles. Aldwin (2000) further distinguishes such coping styles from management skills that are routinized, everyday skills that forestall stress and assist coping with a particular situation. We assume that all of these facets of the term, "coping," can have fruitful application in the study of ASD. The research summarized so far has involved the study of individuals' responses to coping with particular stressors. We will now set the stage for the systematic investigation of coping in ASD, including both situationally specific management skills and more general coping styles of persons with ASD.

It is interesting that, until now, the concept of coping has been received scant attention in the rich and productive literature related to understanding, educating, and treating ASD, and we can speculate on why this is so. Perhaps this is the result of the necessary focus in our work as clinicians and teachers on ameliorating behavioral problems in and for those with ASD. Furthermore, our preferred, empirically supported, and often effective intervention strategies are built on protocols that use external strategies such as other person or environment-mediated strategies with relatively little focus on self-management or self-control responses made by persons with ASD. Too much of our understanding of the condition and life experience of those with ASD is focused on what is different and what may be missing or undeveloped in the psychological development of these individuals. We may assume implicitly that what we know about coping and human nature does not apply when a person has ASD. Let us, instead, return to the earlier lesson of Ohm's law and ask, What can we learn about the coping of our fellow humans with ASD by importing the knowledge we have about human coping and bringing that to bear on the special life conditions of those with ASD?

Research studies on coping tend to be either emotion-focused or problem-focused (Folkman & Lazarus, 1980). The former define and measure coping mostly in psychological terms such as subjective well-being, and the latter target more observable behavior, physiological measures, and health-related outcomes as indicators of effective coping. More recently (Lazarus, 2000; Aldwin, 2000), this dichotomous view has evolved to a more transactional approach that includes a systematic consideration of various contexts of stress—physiological, psychological, developmental, social, and cultural—and the dynamic interaction of the person with his or her environment. We now turn to the limited research literature on coping in ASD and then consider some implications of a transactional approach as applied to the study of coping in ASD.

LITERATURE ON COPING AND ASD

While the coping strategies over the life span of various human populations (e.g., the elderly, HIV-infected, trauma survivors) have been systematically investigated, there are few published reports and there has been little formal study of the coping strategies used by persons with ASD to manage the stressors of their lives. One might argue that some of the large volume of literature on how to ameliorate the behavioral problems of those with ASD would fit under the rubric of "teaching coping." However, in this chapter, we include only those published studies that have used the term "coping" explicitly.

Some of the studies take a problem-focused approach to teaching coping. Browning (1983) reports the use of a tape-recorded "memory pacer" worn by adolescents with autism to prompt coping with difficult social situations by making self-controlling responses. Nelson, Anderson, and Gonzales (1984) encourage the use of music to teach coping with change, to encourage participation using nonverbal means and as a pleasurable end in itself. Lord (1995) demonstrates the use of cognitive-behavioral strategies such as self-assessment of frustration level, labeling thoughts and feelings, self-instruction, and contingency contracting to help reduce problem behavior and facilitate coping with obsessive and aggressive urges. Similarly, a school-based anger-management program (Kellner & Tutin, 1995) teaches coping strategies for managing anger and reducing aggressive behavior using daily logs, contingency contracting, skill-building including the use of relaxation techniques, and thinking strategies, such as nor-malizing anger.

Some available reports have also focused on psychological or emotional as-pects of the coping response in those with ASD. Hendren, Taylor, Lemke, and Lemke's (1990) case study illustrates cognitive and relational strategies helpful in supporting a 12-year-old boy with autism as he coped with and prepared for his own death from cancer. Fegan and Rausch (1993) describe a number of strategies for coping with emerging sexuality for adolescents with autism. Bauminger (2004) provides a systematic sampling and description of both the expression and the understanding of jealousy in high-functioning children with autism. Results show that "high-functioning children with autism manifested jealousy in similar situations as did their typically-developing counterparts; yet, their understanding of the feeling was less coherent and associated cop-ing strategies less developed when compared with typical age mates" (p. 174). Finally, defense and successful coping strategies from childhood into adulthood with autism are illustrated in Ratey, Grandin and Miller's (1992) report of Tem-ple Grandin's experiences with hyperarousal (see chapter 4 in this volume for Grandin's personal reflections on coping with constant stress).

More comprehensive reviews (e.g., Jones, Quigley, & Huws, 2003; Patter-son, 2002; Strandt-Conroy, 1999; Young, 2000) of the first-hand experiences of ASD highlight a rich store of self-reported coping strategies that invite a more systematic qualitative and quantitative analysis. One conceptual framework for the application of the concepts of stress and coping in the life experience of those with ASD is provided by Groden, Cautela, Prince, and Berryman (1994). They assert that since commonly observed characteristics of persons with ASD suggest special vulnerability to stressors, we would do well to employ a variety of environmental and skill-building strategies to teach coping, and reduce stress and anxiety, in those with ASD. Chapter 1 in this volume expands this model to include cognitive (i.e., changing attributions) and psychosocial strategies, and highlights the value of teaching self-control as a general coping strategy.

On the whole, the available literature on ASD and coping includes promis-ing samples of both problem and emotion-based coping. How might the inter-ested researcher and clinician expand on this body of work and contribute to the systematic conceptualization, teaching, and research on coping in persons with ASD? Once more, we take our guide from the available literature on human coping.

APPLYING OUR UNDERSTANDING OF HUMAN COPING TO ASD

One cognitive shift in thinking about ASD may be vital to energizing future work in the area of coping in this population. We propose that coping occurs in those with ASD despite the absence of verifying self-report or the seeming maladaptive or unusual nature of behavioral adjustments to life stressors in ASD. This assumption sets the stage for seeing, expecting, and teaching a variety of better coping skills to those in our care. It also gives permission for and structure to our exploration and application of the rich available literature (e.g., Aldwin, 2000; Compas, Connor-Smith, Saltzman, Thomson, & Wadsworth, 2001; Lazarus, 2000; McEwen & Lasley, 2002; Sapolsky, 2002) on human coping to the world of ASD.

Modern-day conceptualizations of coping encourage a contextual view because people use different strategies in different situations and in different phases of a stress response. For example, we might use avoidant, or "disengagement coping" (e.g., leaving the room) in one circumstance and approach, or "engagement coping" (e.g., assertive behavior) in another. We should assume the same findings will hold when we study coping in persons with ASD. Similarly, individual variation in coping responses and styles should be expected even within the diagnostic categories of ASD shaped both by physiological susceptibility and personal learning history with stress. Implicit here is the call for a multidimensional and perhaps hierarchical model of coping in ASD. Factor analyses in child and adolescent research offer a variety of robust and theoretically meaningful coping dimensions (see Compas, Conner-Smith, Saltzman, Thomson, & Wadsworth, 2001) that may assist our analysis of coping by persons with ASD.

The coping literature tends to emphasize a person's control over the environment and his or her emotions. Aldwin (2000) argues that while instrumental responding may often be the best approach, less active responses (e.g., ignoring minor stress events, waiting for events and crises to pass) might expand the varieties of coping responses. Such strategies might be especially relevant in high arousal situations, or for persons with perceptual organization and/or motor planning and execution difficulties. Of particular interest here is the use of the relaxation response (Benson, 1975) that can be seen as both an active, instrumental response to reduce physiological arousal, and a more general means for providing a period of time and physiological state from which better instrumental choices might be made.

Researchers studying coping concur on the need to study coping on a variety of levels and over time. Compas et al. (2001) call for connecting coping to measures of psychological adjustment and biological patterns of stress reactivity and recovery. We hope that the biobehavioral research addressed in this volume can help extend this goal into ASD. We also encourage the continued development of qualitative and quantitative surveys, interviews, and observation tools that can provide standardized measures of stress that might be employed over the lifetime of persons with ASD. Similarly, there is a call for a systematic and serious consideration of the impact of both the physical environment (i.e., built-in, inescapable stressors) and the social and cultural milieu (what we have previously called the distal stimuli for stress reactions) in the development and expression of coping skills and styles. While doing so, we can emphasize the interactive, transactional nature of coping, reminding us to ask questions, even in the world of ASD, about the goodness of fit of a person with ASD and the reciprocal effect with his or her environment of caregivers and teachers. Finally, coping theorists remind us to tie coping not only to illness and disorders, but also to health and other positive effects for individuals. Those with ASD may, in fact, prosper from early and effective life challenges that teach coping in pivotal times and settings, enhance mastery and satisfaction, and provide a coping repertoire or even a coping style that would be useful in future stressful situations.

FUTURE DIRECTIONS FOR RESEARCH IN STRESS, COPING, AND ASD

General Research Guidelines for the Study of Stress and Coping in ASD

Careful, Thoughtful Protocols

The systematic study of stress and coping in ASD should include attention to the learning history, interaction, and reactivity of measurement in persons with sensory differences. Inclusion of procedures to help participants acclimate to the measurement process is particularly helpful. In physiological studies, this might include a set of pre-observation activities, such as familiarizing the participant with the evaluator, providing a measurement rationale appropriate to the participant's cognitive level, and introducing the participant to the observation setting and measurement apparatus using modeling, desensitization, and direct instruction as needed.

Multiple Measurements

Combining qualitative and quantitative methods of measurement, repeating assessments, and making observations in a variety of settings can enhance the study of stress and coping in ASD. Concomitant use of direct observation, survey instruments, and physiological measures enable a rich, multilevel description of an individual's stress responses. Repeated observation of an individual's stress reactivity allows an analysis of change or development over time. Conducting assessments across various settings leads to an appreciation of the differential impact that environmental conditions can have on an individual's reaction to a stressor.

Combined Single-Subject and Group Methodologies

A given stress condition may affect one individual and not another, or one individual markedly and another very little. Given these individual differences in stress responses, the heterogeneous nature of ASD, and the unlikely event that researchers know a priori which potential subgroups are likely to respond in idiosyncratic ways, inductive assessment strategies that employ mixed single-subject and group designs represent a useful methodology for studying stress responses in persons with ASD. In this framework, assessments could begin with an idiographic approach (Molenaar, 2004) that focuses on the behavioral variation over time within a single individual. After studying processes at the individual level, inductive approaches and systematic replication (Barlow & Hersen, 1984) can be undertaken to determine if there are similarities or differences in the processes between individuals. Such an approach has the potential to identify subgroup responders that can be tested prospectively in larger studies.

Lazarus (2000) argues for such combined within-persons, or "ipsitive," and across-persons, "normative," short-term and long-term research to study stress and coping in any clinical area. This combined approach may be especially important when using physiological measures, since early research (Lazarus, Speisman & Mordkoff, 1963) found almost no correlation between HR and skin conductance under conditions with stress and without stress using an across-persons method, but a nearly .50 correlation when a within-subjects method was used.

Standard Independent and Dependent Variables

Ideally, variables should be replicable, applicable to basic and applied researchers, and facilitate combined single-subject and group designs. Independent variables might include a wide sample of potential stressors commonly seen in individuals with ASD, including demands for socialization, communication, and behavioral flexibility. Dependent variables in physiological research might include noninvasive, tolerable measures of the sympathetic nervous system including, but not limited to, HR, blood pressure, and respiration rate. Recent research also suggests that cellular (e.g., oxidative stress; Ross, 2000), neuroanatomical (e.g., amygdala; Bachevaliera & Loveland, 2006), and hormonal (e.g., cortisol; Corbett et al., 2006) measures provide useful assessments of stress in ASD. Standards of reporting data obtained using these dependent measures would also be helpful. For instance, using HR as an example, it would be particularly informative to know the following data for an individual: (1) the average resting HR, (2) the average HR during a stressful event, (3) the average HR before, during, and after a targeted problem behavior, (4) the difference between resting HR and aroused HR, and (5) the time it takes for an aroused HR to return to its resting level. Similarly, we propose a standard protocol for comparing physiological responding with concomitant motor responses and, when possible, self-report and the use of systematic and subjective rating of stress. Finally, while self-reports are valuable when they can be obtained, we encourage the development of structured interviews and systematic reports from multiple informants.

New Conceptualizations of Stress and Coping

Future theories can approach the systematic study of the adaptation by individuals with ASD to stressful life events in a number of ways that have been useful when studying stress and coping in more typical populations (Wills & Cleary, 2000).

One can suggest types and dimensions of stressors relevant to a condition such as ASD, as well as strategies for coping with these stressors over time. June Groden's work on the Stress Survey Schedule (Groden et al. 2001) is an example of such an approach that promises to help identify stressors especially relevant to persons with ASD. Future research might help clarify the particular stressors and related coping strategies associated with key environmental changes (e.g., mainstreaming, teacher change, residential relocation) or developmental milestones (e.g., graduation, onset of puberty, death of a parent) for those with ASD.

Some theories emphasize the role of buffering or resilience variables such as temperament, social support, social skills, and so forth, while others focus on a family or caregiver's adaptation to a chronic stress condition. Alternatively, one can frame the role and value of teaching self-control over the stressors of life with autism (as is done in chapter 1, in this volume). Another buffering framework might be a more systematic effort to import, and adapt if necessary, the stress-reduction techniques that are effective with other populations. For example, authentic relationships and good social support, as well as predictability and personal control over stressors, are acknowledged as key buffers to stress (see McEwen & Lasley, 2002; Sapolsky, 1998). Similarly, Folkman & Moskovits (2000) suggest that positive affect (i.e., feeling happiness, relief, hope, pride) may facilitate one's coping with severe and prolonged stress and, in turn, one's resilience and the quality of one's general pattern of adaptation. This general approach, rooted in the growing movement of "positive psychology" (see Snyder & Lopez, 2002), may help expand the behavioral and clinical targets of our interventions beyond the familiar reduction of problem behavior. There would be value in a systematic examination of such constructs in the lives of those with ASD.

One might also emphasize the role of stress in the early development and expression of a particular problem or how it affects the health and behavior of an individual with ASD. The National Scientific Council on the Developing Child (2005), a multidisciplinary group of early childhood researchers, recently reviewed the effects of early and excessive stress with this conclusion:

> Stressful events can be harmful, tolerable, or beneficial, depending on how much of a bodily stress response they provoke and how long the response lasts. These, in turn, depend on whether the stressful experience is controllable, how often and for how long the body's stress system has been activated in the past, and whether the affected child has safe and dependable relationships to turn to for support. Thus, the extent to which stressful events have lasting adverse

effects is determined more by the individual's response to the stress, based in part on past experiences and the availability of a supportive adult, than by the nature of the stressor itself. This matters because a child's ability to cope with stress in the early years has consequences for physical and mental health throughout life. (p. 1)

Similarly, the biobehavioral research highlighted in this chapter and the contributions in this volume as a whole may have particular relevance in helping us to consider the lifelong impact that both temporary and chronic stress may have on the biological, cognitive, and behavioral responses characteristic of this population and to understand the various patterns of responding that are characteristic of the spectrum of ASD. Each of these approaches may be helpful to a future, concerted examination of the role of stress and coping in ASD. Each finds some form of expression in this volume.

Summary

We have argued in this chapter that the science of stress and coping can expand our knowledge of the human condition called ASD. Documenting the role of stress in a population that cannot reliably communicate the subjective experience of stress may contribute to a fuller understanding, more precise diagnosis, and more effective treatment of ASD. In turn, a systematic study of stress and coping in ASD may also contribute an innovative and reliable protocol to the larger clinical effort to substantiate and validate the biobehavioral effects of stress on children and adults.

Future research may help us see not only the differences, but also the similarities in the stress response of those of us with and without ASD. We expect the same patterns of individual differences in response to stress in persons with ASD as we find in the larger human population. A systematic focus on the coping strategies of those with ASD can reinforce, we hope, a view of those with ASD as fellow travelers on life's ever-challenging roads. Finally, implicit in this chapter is the assumption that stress is inevitable in all our lives, including those with ASD, and that seeking the "good life" does not mean eliminating all stress, but rather coping effectively with stress.

References

Aldwin, C. M. (2000). *Stress, coping, and development: An integrative perspective.* New York: Guilford Press.

Althaus, M., Mulder, L. J. M., Mulder, G., Aarnoudse, C. C., & Mineraa, R. B. (1999). Cardiac adaptivity to attention-demanding tasks in children with a pervasive developmental disorder not otherwise specified (PDD-NOS). *Biological Psychiatry, 46,* 799–809.

Anderson, G. M., & Hoshino, Y. (1997). Neurochemical studies of autism. In D. J. Cohen, & F. R. Volkmar (Eds.), *Handbook of autism and pervasive developmental disorders* (2nd ed., pp. 325–343). New York: Wiley & Sons.

Andreassi, J. L. (1995). Heart activity and behavior: Developmental factors, motor and mental activities, perception, attention, and orienting responses. *Psychophysiology: Human behavior and physiological response* (3rd ed., pp. 218–239). Mahwah, NJ: Erlbaum.

Angus, Z. (1970). Autonomic and cognitive functions in childhood psychosis. *Bulletin of British Psychology Society, 23*, 228–229.

Bachevaliera, J. & Loveland, K. A. (2006). The orbitofrontal-amygdala circuit and self-regulation of social-emotional behavior in autism. *Neuroscience and Biobehavioral Reviews, 30*, 91–117.

Barlow, D. H. (2004). *Anxiety and its disorders: The nature and treatment of anxiety and panic* (2nd ed.). New York: Guilford Press.

Barlow, D. H., & Hersen, M., (1984). *Single case experimental designs: Strategies for studying behavior change* (2nd ed.). New York: Pergamon Press.

Baumeister, A. A., & Forehand, R. (1973). Stereotyped acts. In N. R. Ellis (Ed.), *International review of research in mental retardation* (Vol. 6, pp. 55–96). New York: Academic Press.

Bauminger, N. (2004). The expression and understanding of jealousy in children with autism. *Development & Psychopathology, 16*, 157–177.

Benson, H. (1975). *The relaxation response.* New York: Avon Books.

Berkson, G., & Davenport, R. K., Jr. (1962). Stereotyped movements of mental defectives. 1. Initial survey. *American Journal of Mental Deficiency, 66*, 849–852.

Bernal, M. E., & Miller, W. H. (1970). Electrodermal and cardiac responses of schizophrenic children to sensory stimuli. *Psychophysiology, 7*(2) 155–168.

Boccia, M., & Roberts, J. (2000). Computer-assisted integration of physiological and behavioral measures. In T. Thompson, D. Felce, & F. Symons (Eds.), *Behavioral observation: Technology and applications in developmental disabilities* (pp. 83–97). Baltimore, MD: Paul H. Brookes.

Browning, E. R. (1983). A memory pacer for improving stimulus generalization. *Journal of Autism & Developmental Disorders, 13*, 427–432.

Cannon, W. B. (1928). The mechanism of emotional disturbance of bodily functions. *New England Journal of Medicine, 198*, 877–884.

Cannon, W. B. (1939). *The wisdom of the body.* New York: Norton.

Castaneda, A. (1956). Effects of stress on complex learning and performance. *Journal of Experimental Psychology, 52*, 9–12.

Castaneda, A., & Lipsitt, L. P. (1959). Relation of stress and differential position habits to performance in motor learning. *Journal of Experimental Psychology, 57*, 25–30.

Castaneda, A., & Palermo, D. S. (1955). Psychomotor performance as a function of amount of training and stress. *Journal of Experimental Psychology, 50*, 175–179.

Cohen, D. J., & Johnson, W. T. (1977). Cardiovascular correlates of attention in autistic children: Response times to proximal and distal stimulation. *Archives of General Psychiatry, 34*, 561–567.

Compas, B. E., Connor-Smith, J. K., Saltzman, H., Thomson, A. H., & Wadsworth, M. E. (2001). Coping with stress during childhood and adolescence: Problems, progress and potential in theory and research. *Psychological Bulletin, 127*, 87–127.

Corbett, B.A., Mendoza, S., Abdullah, M., Wegelin, J. A. & Levine, S. (2006).

Corisol circadian rhythms and response to stress in children with autism. *Psychoneuroendocrinology, 31*, 59–68.

Courchesne, E. (1997, July). *Discovering the biological basis of autism.* Paper presented at the Autism Society of America National Conference, Orlando, FL.

Dawson, G. (1991). A psychobiological perspective on the early socio-emotional development of children with autism. In D. Cicchetti & S. L. Toth (Eds.), *Rochester Symposium on Developmental Psychopathology: Vol. 3. Models and integrations* (pp. 207–234). Rochester, NY: University of Rochester Press.

Dawson, G., & Lewy, A. (1989). Arousal, attention, and the socioemotional impairments of individuals with autism. In G. Dawson (Ed.), *Autism: Nature, diagnosis, and treatment* (pp. 49–74). New York: Guilford Press.

DesLauriers, A. M., & Carlson, C. F. (1969). *Your child is asleep: Early infantile autism.* Homewood, IL: Dorsey Press.

Fegan, L., & Rausch, A. (1993). Sexuality and people with intellectual disability (2nd ed.). Baltimore, MD: Paul H. Brookes.

Folkman, S., & Lazarus, R. S. (1980). An analysis of coping in a middle-aged community sample. *Journal of Health and Social Behavior, 21*, 219–239.

Folkman, S. K., & Moskowitz, J. T. (2000). Positive affect and the other side of coping. *American Psychologist, 55*, 647–654.

Fox, S. (1996). *Human physiology* (pp. 5–9). Boston: Wm. C. Brown.

Freeman, R., Horner, R., & Reichle, J. (1999). Relation between heart rate and problem behaviors. *American Journal on Mental Retardation, 104*, 330–345.

Goodwin, M. S., Groden, J., Baron, G., Groden, G., Velicer, W. F., Lipsitt, L. P., Hofmann, S., & Hoppner, B. B. (2004, May). *Cardiovascular responses to stressors in individuals with autism.* Poster session presented at the annual meeting of the American Psychological Society, Chicago, IL.

Goodwin, M. S., Groden, J., Velicer, W.F., Lipsitt, L.P., Baron, G., Hofmann, S.H., & Groden, G. (in press). Cardiovascular arousal in autism. *Focus on Autism and Developmental Disabilities.*

Graveling, R. A., & Brooke, J. D. (1978). Hormonal and cardiac response of autistic children to changes in the environmental stimulation. *Journal of Autism and Childhood Schizophrenia, 8*, 441–455.

Groden, J., Cautela, J., Prince, S., & Berryman, J. (1994). The impact of stress and anxiety on individuals with autism and developmental disabilities. In E. Schopler, & G. Mesibov (Eds.), *Behavioral Issues in Autism* (pp. 178–190). New York: Plenum Press.

Groden, J., Diller, A., Bausman, M., Velicer, W., Norman, G., & Cautela, J. (2001). The development of a stress survey schedule for persons with autism and other developmental disabilities. *Journal of Autism, & Developmental Disorders, 31*, 207–217.

Groden, J., Goodwin, M. S., Baron, G., Groden, G., Velicer, W. F., Lipsitt, L. P., Hofmann, S. H., & Plummer, B. (2005). Assessing cardiovascular responses to stressors in individuals with autism and other developmental disabilities. *Focus on Autism and Other Developmental Disabilities, 20*(4), 244–250.

Hendren, R. L., Taylor, W. S., Lemke, B. J., & Lemke, P. A. (1990). An autistic boy copes with a terminal illness. *Journal of the American Academy of Child & Adolescent Psychiatry, 29*, 901–904.

Hill, E., Berthoz, S., & Frith, U. (2004). Brief report: Cognitive processing of our emotions in individuals with autism spectrum disorders and in their relatives. *Journal of Autism and Developmental Disorders, 34*, 229–235.

Hutt, C., Forrest, S., & Richer, J. (1975). Cardiac arrhythmia and behaviour in autistic children. *Acta Psychiatrica Scandinavica, 51*, 361–372.

Hutt, S. J., Hutt, C., Lee, D., & Ounsted, C. (1964). Arousal and childhood autism, *Nature, 204*, 908–909.

James, A. L., & Barry, R. J. (1980). A review of psychophysiology of early onset psychosis. *Schizophrenia Bulletin, 6*, 506–525.

Jones, R. S. P., Quigney, C., & Huws, J. C. (2003). First-hand accounts of sensory perceptual experiences in autism: A qualitative analysis. *Journal of Intellectual & Developmental Disability, 28*, 112–121.

Kanner, L. (1944). Early infantile autism. *Journal of Pediatrics, 25*, 211–217.

Kellner, M. H., & Tutin, J. (1995). A school-based anger management program for developmentally and emotionally disabled high school students. *Adolescence, 30*, 813–825.

Kinsbourne, M. (1987). Cerebral brainstem relations in infantile autism. In E. Schopler & G. B. Mesibov (Eds.), *Neurobiological issues in autism* (pp. 107–125). New York: Plenum Press.

Kootz, J. P., & Cohen, D. J. (1981). Modulation of sensory intake in autistic children: Cardiovascular and behavioral indices. *Journal of the American Academy of Child Psychiatry, 20*, 692–701.

Kootz, J. P., Marinelli, B., & Cohen, D. J. (1982). Sensory receptor sensitivity in autistic children: Response times to proximal and distal stimulation. *Archives of General Psychiatry, 38*, 271–273.

Lacey, J. I. (1967). Somatic response patterning and stress: Some revisions of activation theory. In M. H. Appley & R. Trumball (Eds.), *Psychological Stress: Issues in research*. New York: Appleton-Century-Crofts.

LaGrow, S. J., & Repp, A. C. (1984). Stereotypic responding: A review of intervention research. *American Journal of Mental Deficiency, 88*, 595–609.

Lake, C.R., Ziegler, M. G., & Murphy, D. L. (1977). Increased norepinephrine levels and decreased dopamine-β-hydroxylase activity in primary autism. *Archives of General Psychiatry, 34*, 553–556.

Lazarus, R. S. (2000). Toward better research on stress and coping. *American Psychologist, 55*, 665–673.

Lazarus, R. S., Speisman, J. C., & Mordkoff, A. M. (1963). The relationships between autonomic indicators of psychological stress: Heart rate and skin conductance. *Psychosomatic Medicine, 25*, 19–21.

Lewis, M. H., & Baumeister, A. A. (1982). Stereotyped mannerisms in mentally retarded persons: Animal models and theoretical analyses. In N. R. Ellis (Ed.), *International review of research in mental retardation* (Vol. 11, pp. 123–161). New York: AcademicPress.

Lewis, M. H., & Bodfish, J. W. (1998). Repetitive behavior disorders in autism. *Mental Retardation and Developmental Disabilities Research Reviews, 4*, 80–89.

Lewis, M., MacLean, W. E., Bryson-Brockmann, W., Arendt, R., Beck, B., Fidler, P. S., & Baumeister, A. A. (1989). Time-series analysis of stereotyped movements: Relationship of body-rocking to cardiac activity. *American Journal of Mental Deficiency, 89*, 287–294.

Lipsitt, L. P., & Spears, W. C. (1965). Effects of anxiety and stress on children's paired-associate learning. *Psychonomic Science, 3*, 553–554.

Lord, C. (1995). Treatment of a high-functioning adolescent with autism: A cognitive-behavioral approach. In M. A. Reinekke, F. M. Dattilio, & A. Freeman (Eds.), *Cognitive theropy with children and adolescents* (pp. 394–404). New York: Guilford Press.

Lord, C., & McGee, J. P. (2001). *Educating children with autism*. Committee on Educational Interventions for Children with Autism, Division of Behavioral and Social Sciences and Education, National Research Council, Washington, DC: National Academy Press.

MacCulloch, M. J., & Williams, C. (1971). On the nature of infantile autism. *Acta Psychiactrica Scandinavica*, *47*, 295–314.

McEwen, B., & Lasley, E. (2002). *The end of stress as we know it*. Washington, DC: Joseph Henry Press.

Miller, T. W. (1989). *Stressful life events*. Madison, CT: International Universities Press.

Ming, X., Julu, P. O., Brimacombe, M., Connor, S., & Daniels, M. L. (2005). Reduced cardiac parasympathetic activity in children with autism. *Brain & Development*, *27*, 509–516.

Minshew, N. J., Sweeney, J. A., & Bauman, M. L. (1997). Neurological aspects of autism. In D. J. Cohen, & F. R. Volkmar (Eds.), *Handbook of autism and pervasive developmental disorders* (2nd ed., pp. 344–369). New York: Wiley & Sons.

Molenaar, P. C. M. (2004). A manifesto on psychology as idiographic science: Bringing the person back into scientific psychology, this time forever. *Measurement: Interdisciplinary Research and Perspectives, 2*, 201–218.

National Scientific Council on the Developing Child (2005). Excessive stress disrupts the architecture of the growing brain (Working paper no. 3). Available: http://www.developingchild.net/reports.shtml [accessed February 7, 2006].

Nelson, D. L., Anderson, V. G., & Gonzales, A. D. (1984). Music activities as therapy for children with autism and other pervasive developmental disorders. *Journal of Music Therapy, 21*, 100–116.

Ornitz, E. M. (1989). Autism at the interface between sensory and information processing. In G. Dawson (Ed.), *Autism: nature, diagnosis, and treatment* (pp. 174–297). New York: GuilfordPress.

Ornitz, E., M., & Ritvo, E. R. (1968). Perceptual inconstancy in early infantile autism. *Archives of General Psychiatry*, *18*, 76–98.

Palkovitz, R. J., & Wiesenfeld, A. R. (1980). Differential autonomic responses of autistic and normal children. *Journal of Autism and Developmental Disorders*, *10*, 347–360.

Paterson, R. J., & Neufeld, R. W. J. (1989). The stress response and parameters of stressful situations. In R. Neufeld (Ed.), *Advances in the investigation of psychological stress* (pp. 7–42). Oxford: Wiley & Sons.

Patterson, J. (2002). *Social behavior of individuals with autism found in first-hand accounts*. Unpublished master's thesis, University of San Diego, San Diego, CA.

Porges, S. (1976). Peripheral and neurochemical parallels of psychopathology: A psychophysiological model relating autonomic imbalance to hyperactivity, psychopathology and autism. In H.W. Reese (Ed.), *Advances in child development and behavior* (Vol. 11, pp. 35–65). New York: Academic Press.

Porges, S. (1984). Physiologic correlates of attention: A core process underlying learning disorders. *Pediatric Clinics of North America, 31*, 371–385.

Prizant, B. M., Wetherby A. M., Rubin, E., & Laurent, A. C. (2003). The SCERTS model: A transactional, family-centered approach to enhancing communication and socioemotional abilities of children with autism spectrum disorder. *Infants and Young Children, 16*, 296–316.

Ratey, J. J., Grandin, T., & Miller, A. (1992). Defense behavior and coping in an autistic savant: The story of Temple Grandin, PhD. *Psychiatry: Interpersonal & Biological Processes, 55*, 382–391.

Ridley, R. M., & Baker, H. F. (1982). Stereotypy in monkeys and humans. *Psychological Medicine, 12*, 61–72.

Romanczyk, R., & Matthews, A. (1998). Physiological state as antecedent: Utilization in functional analysis. In J. Luiselli & M. Cameron (Eds.), *Antecedent control: Innovative approaches to behavioral support* (pp. 115–138). Baltimore, MD: Paul H. Brookes.

Ross, M. A. (2000). Could oxidative stress be a factor in neurodevelopmental disorders? *Prostaglandins, Leukotrienes, and Essential Fatty Acids, 63*, 61–63.

Rutter, M., Bailey, A., Simonoff, E., & Pickles, A. (1997). Genetic influences and autism. In D. J. Cohen, & F. R. Volkmar (Eds.), *Handbook of autism and pervasive developmental disorders* (2nd ed., pp. 370–387). New York: Wiley & Sons.

Sapolsky, R. (2002). *Why zebras don't get ulcers*. New York: Freeman.

Selye, H. (1956). *The stress of life*. New York: McGraw-Hill.

Selye, H. (1982). Foreword. In R. W. J. Neufeld (Ed.), *Psychological stress and psychopathology* (pp. v—vii). New York: McGraw-Hill.

Sigman, M., Dissanayake, C., Corona, R., & Espinosa, M. (2003). Social and cardiac responses of young children with autism. *Autism, 7*, 205–216.

Snyder, C. R., & Lopez, S. J. (2002). *Handbook of positive psychology*. New York: Oxford University Press.

Spence, K. W. (1956). *Behavior theory and conditioning*. New Haven, CT: Yale University Press.

Sroufe, L. A., Struecher, H. U., & Strutzer, W. (1973). The functional significance of autistic behaviors for the psychotic child. *Journal of Abnormal Child Psychology, 1*, 225–240.

Sterling, P., & Eyer, J. (1988). Allostasis: A new paradigm to explain arousal pathology. In S. Fisher & J. Reason (Eds.), *Handbook of life stress, cognition and health* (pp. 629–649). New York: Wiley & Sons.

Stern, R. M., Ray, W. J., & Quigley, K. S. (2001). Some basic principles of psychophysiology. In *Psychophysiological recording* (2nd ed., pp. 52–78). Oxford: Oxford University Press.

Stevens, S., & Gruzelier, J. (1984). Electrodermal activity to auditory stimuli in autistic, retarded, and normal children. *Journal of Autism and Developmental Disorders, 14*, 245–260.

Strandt-Conroy, K. (1999). *Exploring movement differences in autism through firsthand accounts*. Unpublished dissertation. University of Wisconsin-Madison, Madison.

Toichi, M., & Kamio, Y. (2003). Paradoxical autonomic response to mental tasks in autism. *Journal of Autism and Developmental Disorders, 33*, 417–426.

Turner, J. R. (1994). *Cardiovascular reactivity and stress: Patterns of physiological response*. New York: Plenum Press.

van Engeland, H. (1984). The electrodermal orienting response to auditive stimuli in autistic children, normal children, mentally retarded children, and child psychiatric patients. *Journal of Autism and Developmental Disorders, 14*, 261–278.

Volkmar, F., Klin, A., & Pauls, D. (1998). Nosological and genetic aspects of Asperger syndrome. *Journal of Autism, & Developmental Disorders, 28*, 457–463.

Weiner, H. (1992). *Perturbing the organism*. Chicago: University of Chicago Press.

Willemsen-Swinkels, S., Buitellar, J., Dekker, M., & van Engeland, H. (1998). Subtyping stereotypic behavior in children: The association between stereotypic behavior, mood, and heart rate. *Journal of Autism and Developmental Disorders, 28*, 547–557.

Wills, T. A., & Cleary, S. D. (2000). Testing theoretical models and frameworks in child health research. In D. Drotar (Ed.), *Handbook of research in pediatric and clinical child psychology: Practical strategies and methods* (pp. 21–50). New York: Kluwer Academic/Plenum.

Wolff, S. (1981). *Children under stress*. New York: Penguin.

Young, S. (2000). *Tears fall you can't see: Autism, personhood, and expression of self*. Unpublished doctoral dissertation, University of Wisconsin, Madison.

Zahn, T. P., Rumsey, J. M., & van Kammen, D. P. (1987). Autonomic nervous system activity in autistic, schizophrenic, and normal men: Effects of stimulus significance. *Journal of Abnormal Psychology, 2*, 135–144.

II

The Experience of Stress in Autism

3 Stopping the Constant Stress
A Personal Account

Temple Grandin

Puberty arrived when I was 14 years old, and nerve attacks accompanied it. I started living in a constant state of stage fright, the way you feel before your first big job interview or public speaking engagement. But in my case, the anxiety seized me for no good reason. Many people with autism find that the symptoms worsen at puberty. When my anxiety went away, it was replaced with bouts of colitis or terrible headaches. My nervous system was constantly under stress. I was like a frightened animal, and every little thing triggered a fear reaction.

For the next 20 years, I tried to find psychological reasons for the panic attacks. I now realize that because of the autism, my nervous system was in a state of hypervigilance. Any minor disturbance could cause an intense reaction. I was like a high-strung cow or horse that goes into instant antipredator mode when it is surprised by an unexpected disturbance. As I got older, my anxiety attacks got worse, and even minor stresses triggered colitis or panic. By the time I was 30, these attacks were destroying me and causing serious stress-related health problems. The intensification of my symptoms over time was similar to the well-documented worsening of symptoms that occurs in people with manic depression and that is common in other people with autism.

In my younger years, anxiety fueled my fixations and acted as a motivator. I probably never would have started my business or developed my interest in animal welfare if I had not been driven by the heightened arousal of my nervous system. At some point I realized that there were two ways to fight the nerves— either by fighting fire with fire or by retreating and becoming a house-bound agoraphobic who was afraid to go to the shopping center. In high school and college, I treated panic attacks as a kind of omen signifying that it was now time to reach the next door and take the next step in my life. I thought that if I faced my fears, the panic attacks would go away. Milder anxiety attacks propelled me to write pages and pages in my diary, though the more severe ones paralyzed me and made me not want to leave the house for fear of having an attack in public.

In my late 20s, these severe attacks became more and more frequent. The jet engine was blowing up, exploding instead of propelling me. My visual mind was going into overdrive since I was desperate to find a psychological explanation for the worsening attacks. I even started classifying different anxiety symptoms as having special meanings. I thought that diffuse anxiety was more psychologically regressive than anxiety-induced colitis because when I was sick from colitis, I did not feel nervous and fearful. While I was having bouts of colitis that lasted for months, I lost my fear of seeking out new things. The hyperaroused state of my nervous system seemed to manifest itself in different ways. The most severe anxiety left me house bound, whereas during colitis attacks I became fearless and would go out to conquer the world, following my internal map of visual symbols.

The more nervous I became, the more I would fixate, until the jet engine of anxiety started tearing me up. Visual symbols were not working, so I turned to medical science. I went to every doctor in town, but they found no physical cause for the headaches that accompanied my anxiety. I even went for a brain scan, but it did not provide an explanation either. Medical science was failing me, and I just took each day at a time and tried to get through it. My career was going reasonably well. I had just been elected as the first woman board member of the American Society of Agricultural Consultants. But I could barely function. I remember one horrible day when I came home sweating and in a total state of fear for absolutely no reason. I sat on the couch with my heart pounding and thought, "Will the nerves ever go away?" Then someone suggested that I try having a quiet period every afternoon. So, from four o-clock to five o'clock every afternoon, I watched *Star Trek*. This routine did help to calm my anxiety.

When I turned 34 years old, I needed an operation to remove a skin cancer from my eyelid. Inflammation from the procedure triggered the most terrifying and explosive attacks I had ever experienced. I woke up in the middle of the night with my heart pounding. My fixation had suddenly switched from cattle and finding the meaning of my life to a fear of going blind. For the next week I woke up every night at 3:00 a.m. and had nightmares about not being able to see. Headaches, colitis, and plain old anxiety were now replaced with an overwhelming fear of blindness. To a visual thinker, blindness is a fate worse than death. I knew I had to do something drastic to prevent a full-scale nervous breakdown. It was then that I turned to biochemistry to help me with the anxiety disorder I had lived with my whole adult life.

Before the eye operation, I was able to keep my panic attacks under control with vigorous exercise and the use of my squeeze machine. With this device I would apply pressure to my body. I invented the squeeze machine when I was

18 years old. After visiting my aunt's ranch in Arizona, I got the idea of building such a device, patterned after the cattle squeeze chute I first saw there. When I watched cattle being put in the squeeze chute for their vaccinations, I noticed that some of them relaxed when they were pressed between the side panels. I guess I had made my first connection between those cows and myself, because a few days later, after I had a big panic attack, I just got inside the squeeze chute at the ranch. Since puberty, I had experienced constant fear and anxiety coupled with severe panic attacks, which occurred at intervals of anywhere from a few weeks to several months. My life was based on avoiding situations that might trigger an attack.

I asked Aunt Ann to press the squeeze sides against me and to close the head restraint bars around my neck. I hoped it would calm my anxiety. At first there were a few moments of sheer panic as I stiffened up and tried to pull away from the pressure, but I couldn't get away because my head was locked in. Five seconds later, I felt a wave of relaxation and about 30 minutes later, I asked Aunt Ann to release me. For about an hour afterward I felt very calm and serene. My constant anxiety had diminished. This was the first time I ever felt really comfortable in my own skin. Ann went along with my odd request to get in the cattle chute. She recognized that my mind worked in visual symbols, and she figured that the squeeze chute was an important part of my journey in the visual symbol world. I don't think she realized at the time that it was the pressure from the chute that relaxed me.

I copied the design and built the first human squeeze machine out of plywood panels when I returned to school. Entering the machine on hands and knees, I applied pressure to both sides of my body. The headmaster of my school and the school psychologist thought my machine was very weird and wanted to take it away. Professionals in those days had no understanding of autistic sensory problems; they still believed that autism was caused by psychological factors. They wanted to get rid of my machine and alerted my mother, who became very concerned. Like the professionals, she had no idea that my attraction to pressure was biological.

Over the years, I improved the design of my machine. The most advanced version has two soft foam-padded panels that apply pressure along each side of my body and a padded opening that closed around my neck. I control the amount of pressure by pushing an air valve lever that pulls the two panels tight against my body. I can precisely control how much pressure my body receives. Slowly increasing and decreasing the pressure is the most relaxing. Using the squeeze machine on a daily basis calms my anxiety and helps me to unwind.

When I was young I wanted very intense pressure, almost to the point of pain. This machine provided great relief. The earliest version of the squeeze machine, with its hard wood sides, applied greater amounts of pressure than later versions with soft padded sides. As I learned to tolerate the pressure, I modified the machine to make it softer and gentler.

Because many people were trying to convince me to give up the machine, I had many ambivalent feelings about using it. I was torn between two opposing forces: I wanted to please my mother and the school authorities by giving the machine up, but my body craved its calming effect. To make matters worse, I had no idea at that time that my sensory experiences were different from those of other people. Since then, I've learned that other people with autism also crave pressure and have devised methods to apply it to their bodies. Tom McKean (1994) wrote in his book, *Soon Will Come the Light*, that he feels a low-intensity pain throughout his body, which is relieved by pressure.

DISCOVERING BIOCHEMISTRY

Six months before my eye surgery I read an article titled "The Promise of Biological Psychiatry" in the February 1981 issue of *Psychology Today*. The authors described the use of antidepressant drugs to control anxiety. Using the library skills that my teacher had taught me, I found an important journal article by Sheehan, Ballenger and Jacobsen (1980) at Harvard Medical School, with the impressive title, "Treatment of Endogenous Anxiety with Phobic, Hysterical and Hypochondriacal Symptoms," published in the *Archives of General Psychiatry*. This paper described research with the drug imipramine (brand name Tofranil) and phenelzine (brand name Nardil) for controlling anxiety. When I read the list of symptoms, I knew I had found the Holy Grail. More than 90% of Dr. Sheehan's patients had symptoms of "spells of terror or panic," were "suddenly scared for no reason," or had "nervousness or shaking inside." Seventy percent had pounding hearts or a lump in the throat. There was a long list of 27 symptoms, and I had many of them.

Even though I suspected that the medications described in the article were the answers to my problems, I put off getting them. I did not like the idea of taking medication. But the attacks following my eye surgery finally did me in. I took the paper out of my files and read it over and over. Like me, the patients in the study had failed to respond positively to tranquilizers such as Valium and Librium. I marked my symptoms on the symptom list, and I talked my doctor into giving me a 50-mg dose of Tofranil per day. The effects were quick and dramatic. Within two days, I felt better.

I had a great survival instinct; otherwise I would not have made it. The instinct to survive, along with my interest in science, helped me find treatments such as the antidepressant and the squeeze machine. My technical education also helped me. To get my degrees in psychology and animal science, I had taken veterinary and physiology courses. Reading complex medical articles was like reading a novel, and my training in library research taught me that the library was the place to look for answers.

My body was no longer in a state of hyperarousal after I took Tofranil. Before taking the drug, I had been in a constant state of physiological alertness, as if ready to flee from nonexistent predators. Many nonautistic people who are depressed and anxious also have a nervous system that is biologically prepared for flight. Small stresses of daily life that are insignificant to most people trigger anxiety attacks. Research is showing that antidepressant drugs such as Tofranil are helpful because they mimic adaptation to stress. After I had been on Tofranil for three years, I switched to desipramine (Norpramin), a chemical cousin of Tofranil, which was slightly more effective and had fewer side effects.

Taking these drugs caused me to look at myself in a whole new light. I stopped writing in my diary, and I found that my business started going much better because I was no longer in a driven frenzy. I stopped creating an elaborate visual symbolic world, because I no longer needed it to explain my constant anxiety. When I go back and read my diary, I miss the passion, but I never want to go back to those days. In the days before I took medication, anxiety drove my fixations. Interestingly, fixations I had before taking the medications have made a deep imprint on my emotions. Projects I created before taking these drugs still arouse more passion than those I started afterward do.

The nerve attacks returned after I had been on Tofranil for three months, but they were less severe than before. I figured out that my nerve attacks came in cycles, so I resisted the urge to increase the dose of Tofranil. I also knew from past experience that the attacks would eventually subside and that they tended to get worse in the spring and fall. The first relapse occurred during a new equipment startup at a meat plant. Stress can trigger a relapse. I just toughed out the nerve attack, and it finally went away. It took willpower to stay on the same dose when the relapses came, but the 50-mg dose I take has been working all these years. I have taken antidepressants for 13 years, and now I'm a true believer in biochemical intervention.

Taking the medication is like adjusting the idle screw on an old-fashioned engine. Before I took Tofranil, my "engine" was racing all the time, doing so many revolutions per minute that it was tearing itself up. Now my nervous system is running at 55 mph instead of 200 mph, as it used to. I still have cycles of nervousness, but they seem to go between 55 and 90 mph instead of between 150 and 200 mph. Before I took the medication, using the squeeze machine and intensive exercise calmed down my anxiety, but as I got older my nervous system became more difficult to tune. Eventually, using the squeeze machine to calm my nerves was like attempting to stop a blast furnace by spitting on it. At that point, medication saved me.

When I think back to the nerve attacks in the days before I took medication, I realize that I often had periods of several months when my anxiety was quite low, and then suddenly a panic attack would flip a metabolic switch, and my nerves would go from a tolerable 75 mph to a horrible 200 mph. It would then take several months for them to subside to 75 mph. It was like switching the speed on an industrial strength fan by pushing a button. My nervous system instantly jumped from a brisk breeze to a roaring hurricane. Today, it never gets beyond the brisk breeze level.

Panic attacks and anxiety occur in both people with autism and normal people. About half of high-functioning autistic adults have severe anxiety and panic. Lindsey Perkins, an autistic mathematician, states that when he tries to communicate with people, he begins to gag and feel panicky. Jack Gorman and his associates at Columbia University describe a process called kindling, which may explain such sudden increases in anxiety. In kindling, repeated stimulation of neurons in the limbic system of the brain, which contains the emotion centers, affects the neurons and makes them more sensitive. It's like starting a fire in kindling wood under the big logs in the fireplace. Small kindling fires often fail to ignite the logs, but then suddenly the logs catch on fire. When kindling occurred in my nervous system, I was on hair trigger. Any little stress caused a massive fear reaction (Gorman, Kent, Sullivan, & Coplan, 2000).

Even though I felt relief immediately after I started the drug, my behavior changed slowly. There were obvious improvements that everybody noticed immediately, but over the years there have been more subtle gains. For instance, many people who have attended my lectures for some time have noticed that they keep getting smoother and better. An old friend, whom I hadn't seen in seven years, since before I started taking medication, informed me that I now walked with my back straight rather than hunched up. I had stopped walking with a limp and seemed like a completely different person to her. I knew that I had sometimes hunched, but I never realized that I used to sound like I was always trying to catch my breath or that I was constantly swallowing. My eye contact had also improved, and I no longer had a shifty eye. People report that they now have a more personal feeling when they talk to me.

I had another rude encounter with the effects of biochemistry after I had a hysterectomy in the summer of 1992. An ovary was removed, which greatly reduced the estrogen levels in my body. Without estrogen, I felt irritable and my joints ached. I was horrified to discover that the soothing, comforting effect of the squeeze machine had disappeared; the machine no longer had any effect. My feelings of empathy and gentleness were gone, and I was turning into a cranky computer. I started taking low doses of estrogen supplements. This worked very well for about a year, and then the nerve and colitis attacks returned as they had been in the days before I started taking medication. I had not had a colitis attack for more than 10 years. The panic was like the hypervigilance I had felt before. A dog barking in the middle of the night caused my heart to race.

Remembering my pre-Tofranil days, I realized that I was almost never nervous when estrogen levels were at the lowest point, during menstruation, and I figured out that I had been taking too high a dose of estrogen. When I stopped taking the estrogen pills, the anxiety attacks went away. Now I fine-tune my estrogen intake like a diabetic adjusting insulin. I take just enough so I can have gentle feelings of empathy, but not enough to drive my nervous system into hypersensitivity and anxiety attacks. I think the reason my panic attacks started at puberty was that estrogen sensitized my nervous system. I also speculate that some of the unexplained cycles of nerves were caused by natural fluctuations in estrogen. Now that I am closely regulating my estrogen levels, the nervous cycles are gone.

Manipulating my biochemistry has not made me a completely different person, but it has been somewhat unsettling to my idea of who and what I am to be able to adjust my emotions as if I was tuning up a car. However, I'm deeply grateful that there is an available solution and that I discovered better living through chemistry before my overactive nervous system destroyed me. Most of my problems were not caused by external stresses such as a final exam or getting fired from a job. I am one of those people born with a nervous system that operates in a perpetual state of fear and anxiety. Most people do not get into this state unless they go through extremely severe trauma, such as child abuse, an airplane crash, or wartime stress. I used to think it was normal to feel nervous all the time, and it was a revelation to find out that most people do not have constant anxiety attacks.

Newer Medications

When I was looking for medications in 1981, newer medications such as Prozac were not available. Both practical experience and numerous scientific studies show that the serotonin reuptake inhibitors (SSRI) are effective for people with autism. I was lucky that Tofranil worked for me, but a wider range of people will benefit from medications such as Prozac, Zoloft, Paxil, and Luvox. Two friends of mine were totally stressed out from panic attacks and anxiety. They have found that Prozac has really improved their lives. SSRIs are especially helpful in high-functioning autism.

One must be careful about the dosage of an SSRI. Small doses will work and too much will cause insomnia, agitation, and aggression. Some people with autism need only one quarter of the normal starting dose listed in the *Physicians' Desk Reference* (2000) , but doctors sometimes make the mistake of prescribing too high a dose. I have heard many parents tell about terrible experiences with too much of an SSRI; if the person with autism starts to have insomnia or feels agitated, the dose must be reduced.

Hormone Effects

After I had a hysterectomy at the age of 46, I learned that the anxiety and panic attack cycles were due to hormones. I have been able to further control my anxiety by carefully regulating my intake of estrogen supplements and progesterone supplements. If I take estrogen alone I get nervous, but if I take estrogen and progesterone together, I remain calm. Today I still take Norpramin (desipramine), which works slightly better than Tofranil. Since I am stable on this old-fashioned medication, I was afraid to change it. I have found that my anxiety levels stay lowest if I take a very low dose of estrogen and progesterone for three weeks and then take a hormone holiday for one week. If I totally stop taking hormones, I get anxious. I have never stopped taking the Norpramin.

AUTISTIC EMOTIONS

Some people believe that people with autism do not have emotions. I definitely do have them, but they are more like the emotions of a child than of an adult. My childhood temper tantrums were not really expressions of emotion so much as circuit overloads. When I calmed down, the emotion was all over. When I get angry, it is like an afternoon thunderstorm; the anger is intense, but once I get over it, the emotion quickly dissipates. I become very angry when I see people abusing cattle, but if they change their behavior and stop abusing the animals, the emotion quickly passes.

Both as a child and as an adult, I have felt a happy glee. The happiness I feel when a client likes one of my projects is the same kind of glee I felt when I jumped off the diving board. When one of my scientific papers is accepted for publication, I feel the same happiness I experienced one summer when I ran home to show my mother the message I had found in a wine bottle on the beach. I feel a deep satisfaction when I make use of my intellect to design a challenging project. It is the kind of satisfied feeling one gets after finishing a difficult crossword puzzle or playing a challenging game of chess or bridge; it's not an emotional experience so much as an intellectual satisfaction.

At puberty, fear became my main emotion because of the hormone changes associated with adolescence. My life revolved around trying to avoid a fear-inducing panic attack. Teasing from other kids was very painful, and I responded with anger. I eventually learned to control my temper, but the teasing persisted, and I would sometimes cry. Just the threat of teasing made me fearful; I was afraid to walk across the parking lot because I was afraid somebody would call me a name. Any change in my school schedule caused intense anxiety and fear of a panic attack. I worked overtime on my door symbols because I believed that I could make the fear go away if I could figure out the secrets of my psyche.

The writings of Tom McKean (1994) and Therese Joliffe (1992) indicate that fear is also a dominant emotion in their autism. Therese stated that trying to keep everything the same helped her avoid some of the terrible fear. It is common for people with autism to report that they live in a world of daydreaming and fear. In my case the terrible fear did not begin until puberty, but for some autistic people it starts in early childhood. Sean Barron reported that he felt pure terror during the first five or six years of his life. The highly structured environment of the classroom reduced some of his fear, but he was often afraid and anxious in the hallways.

The intense fear and anxiety I used to experience has been almost eliminated by the antidepressant medication I've been taking for the last 23 years. The elimination of most of my fears and panic attacks has also attenuated many of my emotions. The strongest feeling I have today is one of intense calm and serenity as I handle cattle and feel them relax under my care. The feeling of peacefulness and bliss does not dissipate quickly like my other emotions. It is like floating on clouds. I get a similar but milder feeling from the squeeze machine. I get great satisfaction out of doing clever things with my mind, but I don't know what it is like to feel rapturous joy. I know I am missing something when other people swoon over a beautiful sunset. Intellectually I know it is beautiful, but I don't feel it. The closest thing I have to joy is the excited pleasure I feel when I have solved a design problem. When I get this feeling, I just want to kick up my heels. I'm like a calf gamboling about on a spring day.

My emotions are simpler than those of most people; I don't know what complex emotion in a human relationship is. I only understand simple emotions, such as fear, anger, happiness, and sadness. I cry during sad movies, and sometimes I cry when I see something that really moves me. But complex emotional relationships are beyond my comprehension. I don't understand how a person can love someone one minute and then want to kill him in a jealous rage the next. I don't understand being happy and sad at the same time. Donna Williams (1980) succinctly summarized autistic emotions in *Nobody Nowhere*: "I believe that autism results when some sort of mechanism that controls emotions does not function properly, leaving an otherwise relatively normal body and mind unable to express themselves with the depth that they would otherwise be capable of" (p. 203). As far as I can figure out, complex emotion occurs when a person feels two opposite emotions at once. American author Mark Twain (1977) wrote that "the secret source of humor is not joy but sorrow" (p. 119), and Virginia Woolf (1997) wrote, "The beauty of the world has two edges, one of laughter, one of anguish, cutting the heart asunder" (p. 21). I can understand these ideas, but I don't experience emotion this way.

I am like the lady referred to as S. M. in a recent paper by Antonio Damasio (1994) in *Nature*. She has a damaged amygdala. This part of the brain is immature in autism. S. M. has difficulty judging the intentions of others, and she makes poor social judgments. She is unable to recognize subtle changes in facial expression, which is common in people with autism. In developing many varied, complex ways to operate the squeeze machine on myself, I kept discovering that slight changes in the way I manipulated the control lever affected how it felt. When I slowly increased the pressure, I made very small variations in the rate and timing of the increase. It was like a language of pressure, and I kept finding new variations with slightly different sensations. For me, this was the tactile equivalent of a complex emotion and this has helped me to understand complexity of feelings.

I have learned how to understand simple emotional relationships that occur with clients. These relationships are usually straightforward; however, emotional nuances are still incomprehensible to me, and I value concrete evidence of accomplishment and appreciation. It pleases me to look at my collection of hats that clients have given me, because they are physical evidence that the clients liked my work. I am motivated by tangible accomplishment, and I want to make a positive contribution to society.

I still have difficulty understanding and having a relationship with people whose primary motivation in life is governed by complex emotions, as my actions are guided by intellect. This has caused friction between me and some family members when I have failed to read subtle emotional cues. I did not know that people could read emotion in another person's eyes. I only learned about this five years ago when I read about it in Simon Baron-Cohen's book, titled *Mind Blindness* (1995).

CONCLUSIONS

Today, the combination of the Norpramin and the two hormones taken in a three-week-on and one-week-off cycle is controlling the stress. Sometimes I fine-tune myself by changing the hormone schedule slightly. I have also found that doing 15 minutes of jogging in place is really helpful. This is an easy exercise that I can do when I travel. Vigorous aerobic exercise is very important.

I am always learning and improving. A person with autism never really grows up. Every day I learn more about how to get along with other people. My job and career make life worth living. Intellectual complexity has replaced emotional complexity in my life. I think it is very important for people with autism and Asperger's syndrome to have intellectually satisfying work. Young people with autism and Asperger'syndrome must be encouraged and mentored to develop their special talents into employable skills. I worked hard to make myself an expert in a specialized field. Developing expertise at a specialized skill or field will help to make up for social deficits. People respect and value talent. I am concerned that teachers and parents may get so concerned about social skills that the intellectual life of a young person with autism may be neglected. Neglecting intellectual development would be a great tragedy. I would have a very empty life if I did not have satisfying work, which has given my life meaning.

Acknowledgment

Parts of this chapter have been published in *Thinking in Pictures*, T. Grandin, 1996 (NewYork: Vintage Press; copyright 1995 Temple Grandin).

References

Baron-Cohen, S. (1995). *Mind blindness: An essay on autism and theory of mind.* Cambridge, MA: MIT Press.

Damasio, A. (1994). Impaired recognition of emotion in facial expressions following bilateral damage to the human amygdala. *Nature, 372,* 669–672.

Gorman, J. M., Kent, J. M., Sullivan, G. M., & Coplan, J. D. (2000). Neuroanatomical hypothesis of panic disorder, revised. *American Journal of Psychiatry, 157,* 493–505.

Joliffe, T., Lakesdown, R., & Robinson, C. (1992). Autism, a personal account. *Communication, 26*(3), 12–19.

McKean, T. A. (1994). *Soon will come the light.* Arlington, TX: Future Education.

Physicians' Desk Reference (54th ed., 2000). Montvale, NJ: Medical Economics.

Sheehan, D.V., Ballenger, J., & Jacobsen, G. (1980). Treatment of endogenous anxiety, with phobic, hysterical, and hypochondriacal symptoms. *Archives of General Psychiatry. 37*(1), 51–59.

Twain, M. (1997[1929]). *Following the equator, a journey around the world.* Hartford, CT: The American Publishing Company.

Woolf, V. (1997[1929]). *A room of one's own.* London: Grafton.

Williams, D. (1992). *Nobody nowhere.* New York: Times Books.

4 *Living with Autism*
A Collaboration

Clara Claiborne Park with Jessica Park

The somewhat unorthodox form of this chapter reflects the reality of family life with autism; it is, and must be, a collaboration. Our collaboration has lasted 45 years, from the time our daughter Jessy was 22 months old. It was then that we began to recognize the symptoms of what would soon be diagnosed as a classic case of Kanner's (1943) autism. We also began to realize that it would be up to us, her mother, her father, and her three older siblings, to help her grow. I need not describe here Jessy's slow progress out of childhood; that has been done at length elsewhere (C. C. Park, 1967, 1977, 1982, 1983, 1986, 1993, 2001a, 2001b; D. Park, 1974; Park & Youderian, 1974). What appears here is a reconstruction of an interview with Jessy at a 2001 symposium on autism at the Groden Center in Providence, Rhode Island, including selections from Jessy's own writings. Our chapter is a true collaboration; my questions both invite her responses and facilitate those she would not spontaneously offer. Inevitably they reflect my own perspective, as her responses reflect her own. Yet, because I know how easy it is to put words in her mouth—autistic speech, after all, commonly begins as echolalia—I take particular care not to do so.

The interview form is necessary because Jessy is not able to present an account that would be fully intelligible to someone who did not know her well. Only someone who has lived with her daily can ask the questions that will unlock her experience. Yet, Jessy is very much aware of that experience and is delighted to share it with an audience. But since her progress toward communicative speech has been slow and partial, her responses must be and are accompanied by some explanation [in brackets], and preceded by some account of the framework of her life today.

BACKGROUND

Jessy lives, as she has always done, at home with her mother and father. Since leaving school she has worked as a clerk in the Williams College mailroom. This year she attended the special appreciation luncheon for 25-year employees. She is an efficient worker: rapid, exact, and absolutely punctual. She saves all her money, balances her checkbook, and completes her own income tax forms. At home, she is in charge of the laundry, the vacuuming, and many other household tasks, and shares in the cooking. Her leisure time is increasingly occupied by her remarkable painting, which is readily sold and adds substantially to her income.

Jessy was not accorded a full school day until she was 13 years old; only then (a year before Public Law 91–142) did Massachusetts guarantee education for all children with special needs. Once at Mt. Greylock Regional High School, she remained until age 22, in a combination of a special class and what would now be called inclusion. At age 13, her remarkable mathematical skills were already in place; she had learned them at home with a rapidity and ease, which was all the more striking when compared with her slow and difficult learning of language. As the result of intensive teaching in high school, she learned to speak more intelligibly and to read and write at something like a fourth-grade level, skills without which she could not hold her present job. She also benefited from nine years of an excellent high-school art program.

Jessy was 20 years old when she wrote her first journal entries, not spontaneously, but as part of a home program to reinforce what she had learned at school. She has continued to write from time to time, willingly if not enthusiastically, enough to maintain her hard-won skills and even extend them. It is something more than a joke when I say that Jessy is the lowest-functioning high-functioning person with autism I have ever seen. Most high-functioning autistic people can and do speak for themselves, as is evident from Temple Grandin's contribution to this volume. Jessy can speak for herself, too, and only those who knew her in the long, silent years can realize what a miracle that is, for until she was five she had spoken only an occasional word, and she was eight before she could be understood beyond her family circle. Though Jessy's hesitations, mispronunciations, and fractured syntax improve, they do not disappear. She still needs me to encourage, prompt, and explain. For fuller intelligibility, I have added [also in brackets] comments I would not speak in her presence, even though I know she would be unlikely to understand them, or be embarrassed if she did. When we began our interview I couldn't know what she'd end up telling the audience. But I did know that whatever she said, it would be in its own way informative; Jessy would not only tell but also show what it's like to be a person with autism.

STRESSORS, DISCOURAGEMENTS, AND TRIUMPHS

Nearly 20 years ago, Jessy made a five-page list of things that regularly distress her. She headed it "discouragements." (We did not know the word "stressor" then.) Jessy liked making the list; she loves talking about her stressors—afterwards. It would not occur to her to list her triumphs. If she did, five pages would not be enough. Her presence at a symposium is a triumph, her enthusiastic participation even more so. Her painting is a triumph. Her job is a triumph, though she does not know it; many high-functioning autistic people do not manage to be employed at all. Her taxes are a particular triumph; Jessy has already returned to society far more than the cost of her special education. So why not begin there?

We would expect tax time to be stressful for Jessy. We would be wrong. One of the advantages of hearing directly from people with autism, as we increasingly do, is that we learn not to measure autistic experience by our own. For Jessy, taxes are definitely a positive experience.

Clara: Well, Jessy, tell about how you pay your taxes. Do you pay taxes?
Jessy: *Yeah!*
Clara: And what are you going to be doing in the next couple of weeks?
Jessy: I . . . will . . . pay . . . the . . . *income taxes* . . . at the beginning of April.
Clara: And who will make out the forms?
Jessy: (Smiling) Me!
Clara: And do you like to do that?
Jessy: Yeah! I'm doing it alone. Daddy used to help me.

[Daddy definitely did not like it as much as Jessy does. But Jessy likes to do things according to rule, and the forms are according to rule. She didn't like taxes 27 years ago, when she first began to pay them; she liked to see the numbers in her checkbook go up, not down. But she likes them now, the way she likes balancing her checkbook.]

Jessy: First I went to the post office and can . . . got . . . I got . . . Massachusetts state tax folders . . . books [she gropes for the right words] and the whole books [*sic*] of federal taxes, IRS, and then I stopped at the college library after work and I got the whole form . . . the whole work- sheet . . . ten . . . *two* copies of each of 1040 schedule A and B . . .

[Jessy talks about this enthusiastically now that it's done. But each stage provided its own stressors, as when the requisite forms were not available at the post office. That she was able to negotiate the process successfully, and independently, was one of the small triumphs which, along with stressors, make up her day.]

Jessy: . . . and schedule D, and . . . and . . . and . . .
Clara: And what did you do then?

Jessy: And put them in the folders and . . . then . . . and then I went to the public library and two copies each of schedule C and s-s-s-schedule SE (big smile) and even form 8606, and . . .

Clara: [since this shows no sign of stopping] *OK.*

Jessy: And *that* is for IRA (big smile).

Clara: And you know, I don't think we have time to tell them *all* about it—

Jessy: And . . . uh . . . and then I realize I need two sheets of EIC because I *think* I earned more *money* . . . not enough *money* . . . like those *limination* (limitation) of no child is getting higher.

Clara: OK.

Jessy would willingly talk forever about her tax preparation, or if it weren't quite forever, it would soon feel like it. Autistic people tend to get fixated on certain subjects and pursue them without regard to relevance or audience interest. "Drop it like a hot potato," we say now. Jessy thinks that's funny, and she'll cheerfully stop. But she won't stop on her own.

Today, however, she is glad to shift to another kind of triumph, as we show slides of some of her recent paintings, the paintings that make necessary the schedule SE for self-employment.

Jessy: And this is the silo from the Smith Caretaker Farm on Hancock Road. [Here's a small illustration of the effects of an impaired "theory of mind." Jessy's unerring memory can supply every fact about the painting, yet she omits the one the audience needs—the location of the farm in Williamstown, Massachusetts.]

Clara   (To the audience): And if any of you saw "Rage for Order," the autism section of the Oliver Sacks documentary *The Mind Traveler*, you saw Jessy at this farm, and the silo in the painting. You also saw her under stress when she was asked the kind of question she really doesn't like, which is the question that begins with "what."

Jessy: (Eagerly) Or *who*, or *where*, or *when*, or *why* . . . even *which*.

Jessy loves to recall these stressful episodes—after they're over. As Temple Grandin says of her childhood tantrums, "When I calmed down, the emotion was all over" (1995, p. 89). However intense the feeling, it can, she notes, be stored in memory and accessed much later without emotion (Grandin, 1995/2006). Thus Jessy revisits the painful scene with enthusiasm and even elaborates it with "where," "when," "why," and even "which," though I've never known them to cause problems. It's "what" and "who" that are the real culprits, number 7 on her list of discouragements. Jessy, who loves to classify, wrote it down in her own neat script, in the outline form she learned in school: "Questions that bother me. They are hard to answer and I sometimes say 'I don't know.' "

What-questions. What? What are you making? What are you doing?
Who-questions. Who is somebody? I try to prevent them by identify [*sic*] people's names [before she is asked].

Questions of happiness. Why are you smiling? I don't like them because they are too good to answer.

Stressors in autism are highly idiosyncratic. For most autistic people, such questions would be no more stressful than for you and me. For Jessy, however, they elicit the most intense emotions she ever feels, and her overreactions may be extreme. The usual one, a loud, sudden, hostile, "Why do you ask me that?!" is frightening enough for the innocent questioner, who was only trying to start a conversation. If things go badly, as they may if there have been other stressors that day, the scene becomes terrifying, as Jessy cries and shrieks out bizarre and piercing verbalizations that are audible through several closed doors. "Wee-alo, wee-alo" she screams, "La la," her face distorted, her heart pounding, every muscle in her body tense, her mouth open so wide we see her flattened tongue.

There are 22 different types of stressors on the discouragement list, which is far from complete. Among the most common is when things are out of place or missing. Recently, Jessy threw a sharp knife because she found it in the dishwasher where it wasn't supposed to be. She didn't hit anybody; she never does. But the friend who put the knife in the dishwasher didn't know that.

It is these overreactions to stress, rather than her remaining cognitive and communicative deficits, that are now the greatest difficulty for her and for those who live with her and work with her. Why do they elicit such intense emotion? We don't know.

[Jessy gets paid for her paintings, but painting isn't her real job. It occupies her spare time, but her job structures her life. Though it provides daily stressors, it brings her in contact with the outside world. Her job is her real triumph.]

Clara: Jessy, how much do you make now per hour in the mailroom?
Jessy: I think $10.18.

[In 25 years, Jessy has worked her way up from minimum wage. She's saved more money than any of her siblings—it's easy, since there's little besides chocolate that she wants to buy. But Jessy did go to the mall this morning.]

Clara: What did you buy, Jessy?
Jessy [with characteristic exactitude]: I bought Clarin's skin cleanser for all skin types, which is just gentle, and it's hard to make a choice between gentle, very gentle, and ultra-gentle which is a creamy kind, and hardly any fragrance. And the ultra-gentle is a big jar, and . . . and . . . much bigger, and it's lighter because it's creamy and the very gentle is heavy, it's thicker because it came from a tube and smells different, smells good so I chose the gentle kind.
Clara: OK.
Jessy: And I bought Godiva chocolates and Lindt chocolates at the mall. And . . . and . . . at the art shop I bought tantanium [sic].
Clara: Or was it cadmium?
Jessy: Nope. *Titanium* white, dioxide purple, and pern-a-ment [sic] lilac.

Clara: She's referring to the tubes of acrylics she buys for her multi-colored artwork. In her mind are the paintings she made for her first New York show. [Some of these are reproduced in *Exiting Nirvana*, which chronicles her growth into middle age and devotes a chapter to her painting.] That's another triumph.

Jessy: I never heard of triumphs. Is it another word for stressors?

Clara: No. Triumph is a word for something that's absolutely the best.

Jessy: Yes.

Clara: So now you have a new word. It's when you have done something *really good*. Have you heard of achievement?

Jessy: Yes.

Clara: It's a really big achievement. OK?

Jessy: *Yes!*

Clara: But along with the triumphs there are discouragements.

Jessy: And *excitements*? [This is another category from her journals.]

Clara (reading from Jessy's journal for July 1, 1978): "Many things seem to be discouraging me. I was sad about my impoliteness which is thank you."

[Jessy has illustrated the entry with a drawing of herself, captioned "thank you, I whispered." There is no stressor greater than being reminded to say, "Thank you."]

Clara: Can you tell about how you don't like to say "thank you"?

Jessy: I think it maybe it hurt my mouth when I say it. (Laughing) But I *exaggerated*.

Clara: I think so too. And it's too complicated to tell them about the hangman you see in people's eyes when you hear a politeness.

Jessy: Yes. A long time ago.

[The hangman, a word Jessy got from a song she sang at camp, used to hang from a clothesline, or even a cross. When he heard a "thank you" or "you're welcome," he jumped up and down.]

Clara: It was a long time ago—more than 25 years. But habits formed a long time ago remain. (Reading from Jessy's journal for 12/3/77): "I was discouraged about people sneezing."

[Autistic people may be hypersensitive to certain sounds, a sneeze, for instance.]

Clara: Or last night in the hotel, Jessy noted sounds I couldn't hear.

Jessy: From the other room. And also the groaning faucet.

Clara: But there can be more to it than sound. A sneeze is unexpected, and an unexpected sound is bad enough, but the sneeze is worse, because it suggests the possibility of a cold. (To Jessy) You know we try to hide our colds so you won't make a big fuss about it.

Jessy: Yeah.

Clara: But you're much better about that now. There used to be *lots* of discouragements. (Reading entry for December 3, 1978) "*Water* seems to be discouraging me."

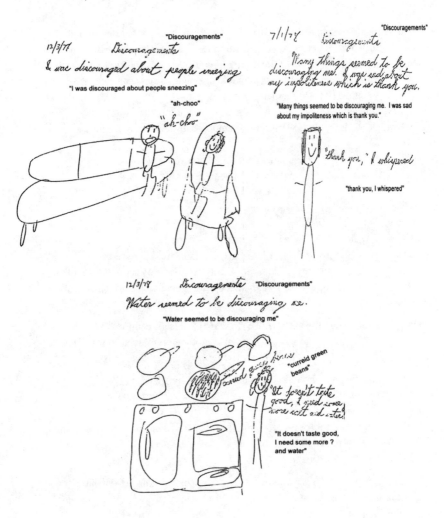

Figure 4.1. Jessy's stressors or "discouragements" as noted and illustrated in her journal.

[This was a major stressor. Jessy screamed for hours because she saw the word on a manhole cover.]

Jessy: But not any more. It outworked! I outworked! [Jessy formed this word on the model of "outgrown."]

Clara: Do you remember what you finally told me, why it was so bad?

Jessy: Because of a combination of fluffy in the middle, like one tall letter, and got to be at least two small letters on each side, but even, and a liquid, and part of the *car*!

Clara: Those three things Jessy called the "forbidden combination." That's a good example of an idiosyncratic stressor, also a good example of an autistic explanation—the only explanation you get.

Jessy: Yes, but I found with . . . the longest word, with fluffy in the middle, with five small letters on each side, *remembrance*!

[Thus, with the years, a major stressor becomes a triumph.]

Jessy (turning to her list): Oops, here's a long list of discouragements.

Clara: Too long to go through, much as Jessy would like to. But the list is indicative of the kinds of things that may bother an autistic person—interruptions, for example, as well as things out of place or missing.

Jessy: When our car is gone?

Clara: What do you think when things are missing?

Jessy: Because I want the car to go somewhere.

Clara: That's a *good* reason. But how about when a knife is missing, or the cat is missing. You don't even *like* the cat.

Jessy: Well—I don't like to have a pet in the house.

Clara: But nobody makes more of a federal case if the cat is missing, even for a short time.

Jessy: I used to say "lost, lost, oh lost."

Clara: The whole point is that everything should be in its place, the whole world as it should be, fully under control. But as stressors change and diminish, Jessy goes over her list and notes her progress, things she no longer has so much trouble with.

Jessy: Like those astro-things are outgrow?

Clara: Right—worrying about "astro-things"—stars, not seeing them, seeing them unexpectedly. And putting mail in student boxes.

Jessy: Putting a mail in the wrong box, wrong names in the right box, and repeating after somebody . . . somebody already filled them.

[Jessy hesitates because she has noticed an error in her entry, made fifteen years before; she corrects "fill" to "filled," and notes that this was "outworked by summer 1986."]

Clara: This is the kind of thing that creates difficulties in her job. Jessy is very fast and very efficient, but she doesn't like to make even the slightest mistake.

Jessy: Like [putting a mailing] a tenth of the way in? [Here as elsewhere, Jessy does not distinguish the significant from the trivial.]

Clara: She doesn't like others to make mistakes, either. (To Jessy) Are you always tactful when you point these things out?

Jessy: Yes.

Clara: I hope so.

There has since been slow but steady social progress; she'll go to the 25-year appreciation luncheon alone and behave beautifully. Despite all the discouragements and overreactions, she has managed to do the job, with all the interruptions and changes found in any office work. She has worked hard on this. Changes are very hard for autistic people; it's particularly hard to switch from one task to another. Discouragement number 20 is one example among many: "I hate being late. If the U.S. mail is late I'm afraid they will never come."

Eight years after Jessy made her list I discovered it again, tucked away among the cookbooks. Jessy, of course, was delighted to revisit it. Her comments astonished us: "This is what my life like." Do you remember saying that, Jessy, I asked her. It was such a mark of cognitive progress, of generalization. And she went on: "Like anything can be worn away and replaced by new things—bad things or good things. Like good things [happy obsessions] and bad things both worn away—some of them—and even replace new good things and discouragements."

Clara: Do the discouragements ever come back, Jessy?
Jessy: Nah.
Clara: Oh, Jessy, you told me they did.
Jessy: *Yeah.*
Clara (Reading again): "Not same discouragements much"—
Jessy: (Chiming in) Different.

[Discouragements and happy obsessions get "worn away" and new ones come, or we develop new ways of dealing with them.]

It was a great, great day when June and the Groden Center came into our lives, and especially when June asked Jessy to record the things that stressed her. Jessy loved doing this—after the fact. She wrote down the stressors, then what she did about it—the Groden desensitization routines, the "imagery scenes" in which the stressful stimulus is imagined, met with actual relaxation (STOP, R E L A X), and followed by self-congratulation for good behavior and an imagined reward. Each scene is written down on a series of cards, to be rehearsed twice a day. She brought them all with her and wanted very much to tell about them. There are many, many scenes now, and Jessy continually adds new ones.

Clara: Jessy, what scenes did you choose to practice today?
Jessy: Like obsessing?
Clara: Tell about obsessing.
Jessy: Means going on and on and on.
Clara: What's the first card?
Jessy: I find myself obsessing . . .
Clara: That's number one.
Jessy: And *stop*, and *relax*, drop it like a hot potato, and then thinking of rewards, like *banks*.
Clara: Tell about the reward today.
Jessy (instantly): Thinking about heating lamp on without a bathroom blower in place. Like in missing because it's *broken*. But next spring will soon install.
Clara: When June first showed Jessy how to make the imagery scenes—first the stressor, then that she doesn't like it, then relax, then feeling good

about how she handled it, then REWARD—June thought of lemonade or Godiva or—

Jessy (breaking in): chocolate chip *cookie*!

Clara: But that didn't cut it with Jessy. Rewards, like stressors, are idiosyncratic. Even Godiva is just chocolate, especially when you can buy your own. A reward has to be special, and it has to *fit*, to be a reward for the particular autistic person. Jessy, can you tell some rewards?

Jessy: (Sighs) It's hard to think.

Clara: Banks: And route 7 north of Manchester?

Jessy: Manchester *Center*.

Clara: Jessy isn't particularly interested in actually experiencing these rewards, she just likes to think about them. Right now she likes to think about casinos.

Jessy: Yes. I thought about the Foxwood Casino and the Las Vegas Casino.

Clara: But when I offered to take her to Las Vegas—she has the money—Jessy, do you want to go to Las Vegas?

Jessy: Nah, it's too far away.

[Perhaps what this tells us is that things are always more delightful in imagination than in reality, and Jessy knows that. Back to the journal and a typical stressor.]

Clara: Can you read your entry for 1/11/94?

Jessy: (Reading [see fig. 4.2]), "I cried and snapped about being asked to repeat myself. I wanted to have a perfect three weeks in my vacation but *I blew it*."

[In her journal, Jessy describes that she blew it when she had trouble pronouncing "Sri Lanka," where her father had told her he saw the green flash (one of her rewards), and he responded with, "What?" Being asked a *what* question stressed her; then Jessie describes how she coped with this stressor.]

Jessy: He said a *what* question. I took my mind off about almost perfect three weeks by reading books I made a long time ago.

[Jessy had a fit. She snapped, then cried and cried because she broke her perfect record. See figure 4.2, noting the contrast between this childlike drawing and the sophisticated draftsmanship of her painting in figure 4.3.]

Clara: This ties in so well with the Grodens' research about assessing stress in autism. It's so clearly a physiological thing, when Jessy snaps and cries, shrieks—Jessy, what is your heart like then?

Jessy: *Pounded, pounding.*

Clara: And when Jessy says it's pounding, it's pounding. When she sets herself a goal like that and blows it, it's so much worse. A minor stressor wouldn't get the full reaction. The imagery scenes and the relaxation techniques are an invaluable tool in controlling stress, but they are not a magic cure. In autism, there is no magic cure. The scenes mitigate, they help bring things under control—Jessy's control.

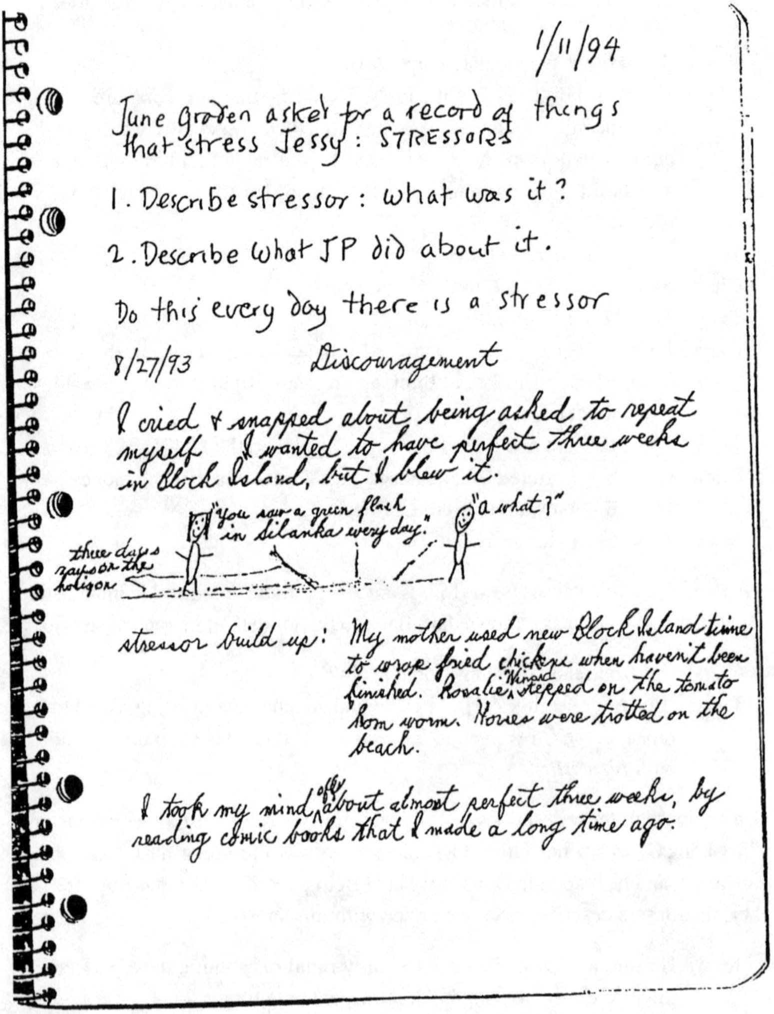

Figure 4.2. Jessy reviews and records her experience with a stressor or discouragement, the buildup to the stressor, and how she coped with the stressor.

At work, especially, the STOP, R E L A X helps control behavior that would certainly jeopardize her job. Yet the uncontrolled behavior may still erupt once she gets home, complete with "wee-alos" and "la-las," though the stressor may be hours in the past. I can help her, if I can get her to lie down with me and we do the relaxation process together. Sometimes, however, she resists and goes to her room to quiet down by herself, a process that now takes minutes instead of hours. Jessy has come a long way.

Figure 4.3. The Flatiron Building #3 with Jellyfish Sprite and Venus by Jessy Park (November 27, 2004).

CONCLUDING STORY

Years ago, this interview would have been impossible. Once Jessy couldn't talk at all, and it was many years after she spoke her first words that she was able to answer questions. To illustrate, let me conclude with a story from the past, when at 13 years of age Jessy was being examined by a school psychiatrist, an M.D., in preparation for her newly mandated full day of education. I don't think Jessy remembers this. It was back in the days when it was still hard for her to talk.

The protocol then was that the child was to be seen alone, without a parent. Never mind that this child's speech was both rare and fragmentary, that only those who knew her could get her to talk, let alone understand what she might say. I offered to help; of course I was refused. I don't know what went on behind the closed door, but I can guess—nothing. After 20 minutes the psychiatrist emerged, to tell me that Jessy had progressed from autism to (yes, he actually said this) childhood schizophrenia. I was savvy enough to pay no attention to this bizarre diagnosis—savvy enough, too, not to argue with the ignorance then widespread, even in the psychiatric profession. I did say that she was very good at mathematics and that we hoped that would be included in her education plan. He didn't think so. "If she learns to handle her periods," he told me, "she'll be doing well."

Jessy did learn how to handle her periods, which incidentally turned out not to be at all stressful, and much, much more. She's come a long way. And we, psychiatrists, psychologists, social workers, language therapists, teachers, and the families they now welcome and listen to have come a long way too, learning from each other and from the growing number of autistic people who can, with a little help from their friends, now speak for themselves.

Acknowledgment

We extend our thanks to Wendy Severinghaus, a long-time friend, whose knowledgeable and sensitive transcription made this chapter possible.

Jessy will be glad to send a copy of selections from her journal, at a cost of $5.00 to cover copying and mailing. Please send requests to Ms. Jessica Park, 29 Hoxsey Street, Williamstown, MA 01267.

References

Grandin, T. (1995). *Thinking in pictures and other reports of my life with autism.* New York: Doubleday.

Grandin, T. (1995/2006). *Thinking in pictures, expanded edition: My life with autism.* New York: Random House.

Kanner, L. (1943). Autistic disturbances of affective contact. *Nervous Child 2*, 217–250.

Park, C. C. (1967). *The siege.* Boston: Little Brown.

Park, C. C. (1977). Elly and the right to education. In R. E. Moneypenny & R. Johnston, (Eds.). *Contemporary issues in special education* (pp. 34–37). New York: McGraw-Hill.

Park, C. C. (1982). *The siege: The first eight years of an autistic child.* Boston: Little Brown.

Park, C. C. (1983). Growing out of autism. In E. Schopler & G. Mesibov (Eds.), *Autism in adolescents and adults* (pp. 279–295). New York: Plenum Press.

Park, C. C. (1986). Social growth in autism: A parent's perspective. In E. Schopler & G. Mesibov (Eds.). *Social behavior in autism* (pp. 81–99). New York: Plenum Press.

Park, C. C. (1993). *The siege.* Boston: Little Brown.

Park, C. C. (2001a). *The siege: A family's journey into autism.* Boston: Little, Brown.

Park, C. C. (2001b). *Exiting nirvana: A daughter's life with autism.* Boston: Little, Brown.

Park, D. (1974). Operant conditioning of a speaking autistic child. *Journal of Autism and Childhood Schizophrenia, 4*(2), 189–191.

Park, D., & Youderian, P. (1974). Light and number: Ordering principles in the world of an autistic child. *Journal of Autism and Childhood Schizophrenia, 4*(4), 313–323.

5 Blind Tom

A Celebrated Slave Pianist Coping with the Stress of Autism

John Davis and M. Grace Baron

Hindsight often provides an opportunity to look at a human being's coping and resilience in a comprehensive way, considering not only individual factors but also the social and cultural circumstances that may have contributed over time to that individual's unique story. For Thomas Wiggins, a slave who, as "Blind Tom," became one of nineteenth-century America's most famous pianist/composers, neither the challenges of a complex set of disabilities nor severe social constraints prevented the blooming of his talent.

That Wiggins' musical ability was able to develop despite severe mental impediments was apparent to virtually anyone who came into contact with him. Edward Seguin, an expatriate French physician living in the United States, was the first to attempt a scientific diagnosis of the pianist's unusual behavioral tendencies. In his seminal 1866 work, *Idiocy and Its Treatment by the Physiological Method*, Seguin concluded that Blind Tom was "another example of isolation of the mind (superficial idiocy), produced by the privation of a whole series of means of communication with the external world. For, though he is rather microcephalous, few of his symptoms point towards idiocy of centripetal origin" (p. 404).

More than a century passed before the use of the word "idiot" by Seguin and others in connection with Blind Tom was clarified. In *An Anthropologist on Mars*, Oliver Sacks surmised that "Although Tom was usually called an idiot or imbecile, such posturing and stereotypies are more characteristic of autism." But "autism," Sacks went on, "was not a term, or even a concept" in the 1860s (Sacks, 1995, p. 190). Not until the 1940s would Leo Kanner in Baltimore and Hans Asperger in Vienna simultaneously and independently coin the word "autism."

If Sacks is correct, Blind Tom was among the first documented autistic savants. The pianist has been a poster child for this elusive mental disorder ever since Seguin's diagnosis, a dubious distinction that, along with institutionalized racism, contributed greatly to the unfair dismissal of his musical accomplishments. Fortunately, today's more-evolved racial attitudes and recent renewed attention on Wiggins have called many of the inherited musical and extramusical assumptions about the prodigy into question. Concurrent with this reassessment, reported cases of autism have significantly increased, which in turn has led to more intensive study of the disorder, as well as its connection to savant syndrome, that "uncommon but spectacular condition in which people with various developmental disabilities, including autism, possess astonishing islands of ability and brilliance that stand in jarring juxtaposition to their overall mental handicap" (Treffert & Wallace, 2002, p. 78).

Early (Rimland & Hill, 1984) and more recent (Heaton & Wallace, 2004) reviews document that savant talent is most associated with autism. Though the rate of their co-occurrence is not known, experts agree that there is a high frequency of autism within savant syndrome. Heaton and Wallace (2004) even propose that autism's cognitive and behavioral traits are crucial underpinnings for savant skill development. Although estimates of correlation of savantism and autism vary, Treffert and Wallace report that more than 50% of known savants have autistic characteristics. One survey (Young, 1995) of savants documented characteristics of autism in all 51 of the participants, although some had never received a formal diagnosis. Nor is it unusual to find case reports (Miller, 1989, 1998) of complex patterns of disability (including intellectual, social, language, and motor impairments as well as blindness) in savant syndrome.

Congenital blindness also has a pattern of connection to autism. Keeler (1958) first described five preschool children born congenitally blind who "presented the most strikingly similar picture to infantile autism" (p. 64). More comprehensive studies of autism and congenital blindness confirm that "in some congenitally blind children, the syndrome of autism may arise though often without the full degree and/or quality of socioemotional impairment that are characteristic of sighted children with autism" (Hobson, Lee, & Brown, 1999, p. 55; see also Hobson & Bishop, 2003).

Although not all musical savants are blind, the triad of blindness, mental defect, and musical genius, according to Darold Treffert (1989), "occurs with startling regularity in the century-old literature; witness the stories of Blind Tom" (pp. 19–20). In this chapter we recount the stories of Thomas Wiggins to learn the sensory, social, and intellectual features of his particular way of being in the world and to set the stage for a fuller examination of his life stressors and his method for coping. Rather than formulate a definitive diagnosis of Wiggins' condition, our purpose here is to investigate possible correlations between the pianist's behavior as discussed in the historical record and what is known about savant syndrome in relation to current diagnostic criteria for autism spectrum disorder and pervasive developmental disorder. In doing so, we hope to encourage a fuller appreciation of Wiggins' artistry, his place in American musical history, and a richer telling of his life story of accomplishment, human resilience, and personal tragedy, as well as to provide a framework and invitation for continued and multilayered analysis of the role of stress and coping in the life of those with savant capabilities and developmental disabilities such as autism.

THE PHENOMENON OF "BLIND TOM"

Apparently, Wiggins, born in Georgia in 1849, delivered on the claims made in a broadside (see figure 5.1) publicizing his concert in Buffalo, New York, on January 19, 1866. "We yesterday were so fortunate as to attend a seance given by Blind Tom," wrote one reviewer in the same year in the *Albany Argus* (as cited in *Marvelous Musical Prodigy* [MMP], 1867) and continued,

> As an exhibition of incomprehensible genius, excelling in its simplest mani-
> festations the triumphs of severe art, we never saw the performances of this
> prodigy equaled. A wild, uncouth figure, angular at all points which should be
> curved, and curved at all points that should present acute lines—loose jointed,
> close-wooled, thick-lipped, sprawl-footed, with forehead almost covered with
> kinky locks, eyeballs prominent and distended, and an idiotic, staring ex-
> pression of countenance—in short, a regular specimen of the African in his
> unadulterated and barbarous condition, before he has been elevated by the
> influence of social surroundings or Caucasian infusion. (p. 23)

This demeaning rave went on to report on the various signature stunts advertised in the poster that Wiggins would pull off that January evening in the New
York state capital. When a member of the audience struck "a dozen or twenty
notes of the most difficult and intricate combinations, rapidly as possible" on
the stage piano, Blind Tom is described as awaking "from the ashes of idiocy"
(MMP, 1867, p. 23)

"'What notes are those, Tom?' asks the agent," the Argus critic passed on to
his readers, "and with voluble rapidity, the transformed idiot repeats them, each
by name, without a single error" (MMP, p. 24).

In a particularly discordant demonstration for which he was already famous,
Wiggins then played *Yankee Doodle* in B flat with his right hand and a C major
version of *Fisher's Hornpipe* with his left, all the while singing *Tramp, Tramp*
in yet a third key, "apparently without any effort whatever" (MMP, p. 24).

"Meanwhile, the review continued, "Tom grows most strangely antic," when
asked to mimic on the spot an original composition improvised by a local music
professor. As the volunteer played, the prodigy "claws the air with his hands,
whistles through his teeth, capers about and see-saws up and down," throwing
"himself into grotesque shapes, like an automaton at a fantocini show," only to
then sit down to recreate "note by note, perfectly" what he had just heard, and
"accompany that with variations" (MMP, p. 24).

Figure 5.1.
Advertisement for
Blind Tom concert,
January 19, 1866,
Buffalo, New York.

" 'Most marvelous,' you say, 'but can he express as well as he perceives?' " the Argus critic asked, curious about Blind Tom's way with more serious fare. " 'We will have this sonata, Tom,' " responded the musical director, offering Beethoven's *Pathetique* as exhibit A.

"Instantly the wonderful process of interpretation begins. This blind boy, who never saw a note of music in his life, plays you the entire work, while musical critics follow him with eyes and ears, and he makes no mistake—not one false register, or slur, or discord, or omission. . . . Were you to close your eyes during Tom's rendering of *Home, Sweet Home* by Thalberg," the *Argus* critic gushed on, "you could not tell but Thalberg himself was at the instrument, so perfect and so exquisite is the conception and the touch." As for Tom's interpretations of Chopin, Gottschalk, and Vieuxtemps, "you turn away convinced—surfeited with marvels, satisfied that you have witnessed one of the most incomprehensible facts of the time" (MMP, p. 24–25). Attempting to account for all he had just seen, the reviewer mused:

> Some curious metaphysical questions grow out of these remarkable demon-strations. What is this boy? A negro—belonging to an unintellectual race; him-self an idiot. But what is intellect and what is idiocy? Can he be an idiot with whom those achievements are most ordinary which in others are pronounced the grandest evidences of masterly genius? And what is it to be "developed?" Where is the narrow dividing line that separates the philosopher from the fool? Here is a monstrosity—a gorgon with angel's wings; a sunflower with the blush of a mignonette and the fragrance of a mountain rose. There is no law by which to measure and determine such exhibitions as this. . . . We only state what we saw in all its astonishing features, and leave our readers to determine for themselves whether . . . the soul of some unfortunate defunct musician, misbehaving on earth, has been banished into the awkward and angular body of Blind Tom. (MMP, 1867, p. 25)

While shocking today, such poetic, racially charged tributes to Blind Tom were not at all unusual during his lifetime. In fact, they were the norm and were embraced by Wiggins' former owner, longstanding guardian, and career archi-tect, General James Neil Bethune, a prominent Georgia anti-abolitionist news-paper publisher characterized in *The New York Times* as "the first editor in the South to openly advocate secession" ("Owner of 'Blind Tom' Ill," 1895). (For a sampling of Bethune's editorials in *The Corner Stone*, see Bethune, 1853–1861.) Almost from the start, Bethune's campaign to publicize Tom had been calculated to fan the fire of prevailing racial attitudes and the public's seemingly endless fascination with the freak show during a period when American society was just beginning to come to grips with slavery. Instead of a showcase for the truly artistic aspects of the prodigy's talent, a concert by "Blind Tom" (the stage name assigned to Wiggins by 1864 to elicit audience sympathy) soon became a forum for a litany of flamboyant, pianistic and extramusical stunts performed by an individual who, it was advertised, had no musical training and was mentally defective. Wiggins became renowned for his enormous repertoire, in-concert

"demonstrations," feats of the ear and memory, performances of complex classical compositions with his back to the piano, the elocution of well-known political speeches of the era in their original cadence and intonation, and convincing
recitations of texts in foreign languages he could not even speak, all accompanied by bestial grunts and the most horrible facial and bodily contortions. These
histrionics, instead of marginalizing his act, fueled a 50-year career that would
not end until 1904, just four years before his death in Hoboken, New Jersey
at age 59. By then, Wiggins had become the first American of African lineage
invited to play for the President at the White House, had performed throughout the United States as well as France and Great Britain, and, during the most
lucrative periods, had earned Bethune close to $100,000 a year, an astounding
annual sum equivalent today to $1.5 million dollars. In short, Blind Tom had
become a phenomenon, the first black superstar performer in America.

WIGGINS' TALENT AND ARTISTRY

With Wiggins' enormous success came praise from trustworthy sources. The
pianist's 1866 European tour brought confirmation of his ability from two musicians with unassailable credentials. "In justice to Blind Tom, I have much
pleasure in stating that I think him marvelously gifted by nature," wrote Ignaz
Moscheles, the illustrious Czech pianist, friend to Beethoven, and teacher of
Mendelssohn and Thalberg, after hearing Wiggins perform in England. "Tom's
technical acquirements are very remarkable," Moscheles concluded, "and his
entertainment full of interest for the musician and amateur" (quoted in MMP, p.
11). During the same European tour, Charles Hallé, the highly respected Ger-
man pianist and conductor and the first person to perform all 32 Beethoven piano
sonatas, echoed Moscheles' assessment. "I have this day, for the first time, heard
Blind Tom play on the pianoforte," he wrote, "and I was very much astonished
and pleased by his performance. . . . Altogether Blind Tom seems to be a most
singular and inexplicable phenomenon" (quoted in MMP, p. 10).

Albeit short of declaring Wiggins a profound interpreter of the European
masters, these glowing testimonials by two of the nineteenth century's greatest
pianists lie in stark contrast to a more negative assessment by another celebrated
keyboard virtuoso of the era, Louis Moreau Gottschalk of New Orleans. In his
Notes of a Pianist, Gottschalk (1881) questioned the public's ability to judge "an
art whose subtlety must necessarily escape the layman." With Tom, "we have to
deal with music [and] it is impossible for those competent in the art to permit the
continuance of the celebrity of Blind Tom, whose title to posterity as a musician
is, I fear, as authentic as that of the old Negress of Barnum is said to have been
[George] Washington's nurse" (pp. 166–167).

And who could blame Gottschalk for this dismissal? After all, he was the
New World's first internationally renowned concert pianist and one of the few

people in culturally bereft, mid-nineteenth century America whose opinion on musical matters can be trusted today. Furthermore, not even Wiggins could deny that his lofty reputation was based largely on a dubious talent for performing musical and nonmusical tricks in carnival-style concerts. Yet, there is no evidence in the literature that Gottschalk ever heard Blind Tom play, and, at least in terms of popularity, the slave pianist was the Louisiana virtuoso's only legitimate rival in the United States, a factor that subconsciously may have tainted his thinking.

More indisputable, however, is the compositional refinement of the approximately 20 published solo piano works attributed to Wiggins and what their inherent instrumental and artistic demands indicate about his level of musical accomplishment. (For a compact disc recording of 14 of these works, see *John Davis Plays Blind Tom*; Davis, 1999). On the surface, even the best works appear to be merely garden-variety salon pieces inspired by nineteenth-century American and European vernacular music: gallops (*Cyclone Galop*, *Oliver Galop*, and *Vivo Galop*), a waltz (*Wellenklange*), a polka (*Virginia Polka*), marches (*Grand March Resurrection* and *March Timpani*), a theme and variations (Wiggins' *Improvisations* on the Civil War song, *When This Cruel War Is Over*), and a nocturne (*Rêve Charmant*). *Wellenklange, Rêve Charmant*, and the introduction to *March Timpani*, a metrically altered direct quote of the opening measures of Chopin's *Waltz in A-flat Major, Opus 34, No. 1*, pay homage to Chopin, as does the *Grand March Resurrection* to Brahms. Ironically, *Water in the Moonlight* is inspired by *The Last Hope*, a staple of Blind Tom's repertoire composed by none other than his chief detractor, Gottschalk.

Upon closer examination, these and several other works are strikingly prescient. The atmospheric tremolos and explosive Lisztian flourishes in *The Rainstorm*, are precocious when one considers that the work was composed by Wiggins when he was 5 years old. The right-hand, off-the-beat accents superimposed over the steady left-hand stride bass in *Cyclone Galop* anticipate the syncopation of ragtime and jazz by nearly two decades. And the sound effects (e.g., tone clusters used to simulate cannon shots and the vocal imitation of a train and its whistle by the performer) in *Battle of Manassas* would not be reintroduced by composers until the twentieth century. *Manassas* became Wiggins' signature composition and remains one of the great battle pieces of any period.

And Wiggins' works are well-crafted. Although for the most part structurally simple, his pieces are imbued with charming melodies supported, particularly in *Water in the Moonlight, Rêve Charmant,* and *The Sewing Song*, by sophisticated harmonies and textures. Transitions, intentionally abrupt in upbeat dance pieces and *Battle of Manassas*, are appropriately smoother in the more lyrical works. The many notations in the printed music indicating subtle variations in tempo, dynamic shading, and expressions set these scores apart from most other published popular works of the era, often "dumbed down" for the amateur pianist. Clearly, Wiggins' pieces were serious works to be played by accomplished amateurs and professionals.

Unfortunately, no recordings of Blind Tom are known to exist that could shed light on his keyboard prowess. Rather tantalizing is the piano roll of *Battle of Manassas* released by The Autopiano Company in New York in 1904, the same year that Blind Tom gave his last New York concert. But according to remarks made by the ragtime pianist and piano roll expert, Trebor Jay Tichenor (personal communication, August 2, 2003), this performance was not by Wiggins at all, but was instead the product of a machine used to cut all rolls (so-called arranged rolls) prior to 1912. As further support for his argument, Tichenor also mentioned the failure of the Autopiano roll to explicitly identify Blind Tom as the performer, the usual practice in marketing later "hand-played" rolls.

Nonetheless, the physical and expressive demands of his compositions (as well as of those mainstream works by Bach, Beethoven, Mendelssohn, Chopin, and Gottschalk that made up the lion's share of his repertoire) suggest that Wiggins must have been an accomplished pianist. In *Cyclone Galop* and *March Timpani*, for instance, the high-speed leaps occurring simultaneously in both hands throughout as well as the octaves cascading to the end of *Wellenklange, Battle of Manassas*, and *Cyclone Galop* would have required many hours of intense practice to master. Shaping the musical phrases, given these technical challenges, would have taken even longer. The more lyrical pieces pose other kinds of problems. Sustaining the melodic line of *Reve Charmant, Water in the Moonlight*, and *Sewing Song* is no easy task for any pianist, nor is projecting the tune of *Water in the Moonlight* in relief of the work's dense supporting texture.

That Wiggins actually composed the works attributed to him has never been questioned. According to Thomas L. Riis, director of the American Music Research Center at the University of Colorado, "Few who heard Tom ever sought to dispute his authorship," and "no ghost writers for his pieces have been alleged by credible sources" (Riis, 2000, p. 36). A distinction, in fact, was always made in the published sheet music between those works actually written by Wiggins and those composed by others expressly for Blind Tom to perform.

EARLY INDICATIONS OF MENTAL IMPAIRMENT

Seguin's description of Wiggins as a child "from birth nearly absolutely blind, not seeing enough to direct his walk" who "till 5 or 6 years old . . . could not speak, scarce walk, and gave no other sign of intelligence than this everlasting thirst for music" (Seguin, 1866, pp. 404–405) raises the possibility that Tom, besides being blind, was at a very early age psychologically impaired. Typical of the characterizations ascribed to him was the description of Tom in the biography accompanying his program booklet as "born blind, and, learning nothing from sight, manifested in his early infancy so entire a want of intellect as to induce the belief that he was idiotic as well as blind" (MMP, 1867, p. 4). This image, used at a time when the term "idiot" was employed descriptively and not pejoratively, is further reinforced by Tom's mother, Charity. She explained under oath in 1886 that her son "was born blind. He never had any white to his eyes. They were as black as my hand," and that "he did not have the knowledge of other children. He has not until this day" ("Blind Tom's Mother," 1886).

Obsession with Sound

Tom's "first manifestation of interest in anything was his fondness for sounds," the program booklet claimed in apparent agreement with Seguin; "Musical sounds exerted a controlling influence over him." The publicity pamphlet went on, "All sounds, from the soft breathings of the flute to the harsh grating of the cornsheller, appeared to afford him exquisite enjoyment" (MMP, 1867, p. 4).

So single-minded was Tom's obsession with sound that it often took precedence over the safety and feelings of those around him. According to the program booklet, "he resorted to all the means in his power to make a noise. He dragged the chairs over the floor, rattled the dishes, beat the tin pans, and unless closely watched, punched or bit the younger children to make them cry" (MMP, p. 5). In fact, "The crying of children gave Tom great delight," wrote General Bethune's grandson, Norborne T. N. Robinson, Jr., who spent summers with Tom in the 1870s and 1880s on the Virginia farm to which the Bethunes relocated in 1868. "On one occasion he choked a younger brother nearly to death to make him cry. On another, Tom put a coal of fire on his baby sister's head as she lay in the cradle, singeing her hair so badly that to her dying day she had a bare spot on the side of her head" (Robinson, 1967, p. 343). And although in those instances "he will express sympathy for the sufferer and prescribe remedies for his relief, he cannot restrain his expressions of pleasure" (MMP, p. 5).

However, Robinson questioned the nefariousness of Tom's motives. "Looking back on my personal experiences with him, I cannot agree that he was cruel," he wrote. "His torture was simply a means to an end. I believe that if he could have gotten his sister and brother to cry simply by asking them, he would have done so." Bethune's grandson went on to recount how, to tease Tom, one of his aunts would pretend occasionally that she was going to whip her nephew. When "little Norborne," as Robinson referred to himself, would "whimper and effect fright, Tom would hover about like a hen over a chick, protesting and begging that I not be whipped. Finally my aunt would relent and tell Tom that because he asked it she would let me off" (Robinson, p. 352).

Sometimes, Tom was unaware of the imminent danger posed by noises he followed. One instance of this, related by Robinson, involved contrasting sounds produced by water dripping through two tin drainpipes of different size on the side of the Bethune house. "During a heavy summer rain storm, Tom crawled over to the spouts to enjoy the music, oblivious to the rush of water. He was nearly drowned when his mother rescued and revived him" (Robinson, p. 343). But instead of being permanently traumatized by the experience, Tom would return again and again to the site of this event, as if drawn by some magnetic force. "From his early childhood to the time he left home, whenever it rained, whether by day or night . . . he would go into that passage and remain as long as the rain continued" (MMP, p. 7). Out of this ritual would emerge a positive development, the composition of one of Blind Tom's most remarkable pieces. "When he was less than 5 years of age, having been there during a severe thunderstorm, he went to the piano and played what is now known as his *Rainstorm*" (MMP, p. 7).

Tom's pursuit of sound, whether strident or mellifluous, whether risky to him or others, led to what the program booklet deemed "the first indication of capacity, his power of imitating them" (MMP, p. 4). Charity recounted that, "If he heard a chicken crow before he was a year old, he would make the same noise. If he heard a dog bark, he would bark. And if he heard a bird sing, he would try to sing. . . . He would try to follow any noise that pleased him . . . So we had to watch him" ("Blind Tom's Mother," 1886).

"It was when he got away once, that his music talent was found out," Charity related in an anecdote later corroborated by others. "He crawled into the parlor when all the Bethune family were at dinner and got at the piano. The white people heard the sounds and they went to see who made them. They found Tom playing . . . he was only 1 . . . it completely 'stonished us" ("Blind Tom's Mother," 1886). Imagine the shock when the toddler, probably closer to 3 at this defining moment, blind from birth, deemed mentally impaired, and thrown in as mere chattel in an auction lot that sent him and his family to the Bethunes in 1850, was now discovered playing one of the General's daughter's piano pieces in the parlor while his owner's family was seated around the dinner table.

Tom's extraordinary ability to hear, seek out, imitate, and elaborate on complex auditory patterns in the natural world is strikingly similar to more recent findings concerning modern-day musical savants, who often possess absolute pitch, exceptional musical memories, and strong and persistent preference for musical stimuli (Heaton, 2003; Heaton, Pring & Hermelin, 1999; Sloboda, Hermelin & O'Connor, 1985; Young & Nettelbeck, 1995). Unlike the often-documented aversions or limited responses to sound in those with classic autism, musical savants, whether autistic or not, regularly show enhanced sonic sensitivities and an ability for auditory pattern recognition that may provide a scaffold for growing intellectual capabilities and the development of artistic talent (Treffert & Wallace, 2002). Often accompanying this preference and heightened appreciation for sound, however, is a lesser ability to perceive relevant social stimuli. All this appears to have been the case with Thomas Wiggins.

Other Hypersensitivities

Mirroring Tom's obsession with sound was an enormous appetite for food. "Tom was always a good man around the dining board," Robinson (1967, p. 354) summed up. This conclusion was corroborated by Joseph Poznanski, a New York-based pianist who testified that Tom "was an inordinate eater, . . . deficient of all senses except that of music and that which brings the consciousness of dinner time" ("Blind Tom's Mother," 1886). Joseph Eubank, who traveled with Wiggins for 12 years beginning in 1863, said that Tom "could never tell when he was hungry nor how much food was sufficient for him" ("Blind Tom's Mother," 1886).

Wiggins' penchant for overeating, according to *The Chicago Defender* (Magill, 1922), was related to an "acute sense of smell and touch." Whenever confronted with food, J. Frank Davis remarked, Tom "smelled of everything on the tray. If there was anything there which he disliked he set up a shouting until it had been removed" (Davis, 1908, p. 9). In fact, upon being presented any series of items to be identified, "one after another, . . . he would touch the object, smell it, and then pronounce its name" (MMP, 1867, p. 4). He would even satisfy his curiosity about an unfamiliar piano "by running his fingers over and smelling the keys" (MMP, p. 6).

Despite almost total blindness, Tom could also become transfixed by light. The program booklet described him at 3 or 4 years of age as spending much of his time "with his face upturned to the sun, as if gazing intently upon it, occasionally passing his hand back and forth with a rapid motion before his eyes." Pretty soon, however, Tom began "thrusting his fingers into his eyes with a force which appeared to be almost sufficient to expel the eyeballs from their sockets . . . From this, he proceeded to digging into one of them with sticks, until the blood would run down. All this must have been pleasant to him, or he would not have done it" (MMP, pp. 7–8).

Learning Process at the Piano

Contrary to the portrayal in Blind Tom's publicity materials (see fig. 5.1) of the pianist as musically unschooled, Wiggins' systematic keyboard education began the moment his talent was discovered. Mary, the oldest Bethune daughter and the family's most accomplished pianist, gave Tom his first music lessons (Robinson, 1967, p. 344). Soon, however, the limits of her expertise were eclipsed, and more professionally recognized instructors were called in. At some point during the Civil War, the Atlanta-based William Pinkney Howard would take Tom on as a pupil and accompany him on tour ("Law Report," 1865). Joseph Poznanski would later testify that he gave Tom lessons over nine successive summers in the 1870s and, during that period, transcribed many of Wiggins' original pieces for publication (Southall, 1999, p. 9).

Tom apparently worked very hard in preparation for the hundreds of recitals he was forced to give each year (for a breakdown of Wiggins' concerts, see Southall, 1979, 1983, 1999). Eugenie Abbott, who briefly trained Tom, wrote in *The Etude* that Wiggins "had gained great dexterity in his long years of playing, usually playing eight hours a day" (Abbott, 1940, p. 517). Bethune's grandson recalled how, even during his summer vacations on the Virginia farm, Tom usually began each evening reading through several duets with Bethune's daughter, Fanny, before wandering back to the Steinway grand in his own room to "play for hours. I have a distinct recollection of going to sleep listening to him" (Robinson, 1967, p. 353).

Musical savants, we now know from modern case studies (Miller, 1999), typically show a nearly "inextinguishable appetite for musical interactions of all kinds" (p. 39), taking quite naturally to periods of extensive practice with or without a tutor. Their implicit (unschooled) knowledge of harmonic structure in music usually provides a welcome base for formal and explicit learning and practice (Heaton & Wallace, 2003). However, it is not unusual for periods of intense focus and practice to alternate with episodes of more disorganized behavior.

In an attempt to describe the boy's learning process, Poznanski explained how "he would play on a piano and Blind Tom would caper around the room meanwhile. When he was done, Tom would seat himself at another piano and reproduce the sounds he had heard. He never forgot a piece he had thus learned" ("Blind Tom's Mother," 1886). A similar dynamic between teacher and pupil was present during Abbott's session with the former slave. According to her, Tom was "almost wild with joy" as she played for him, an elation manifested "through extreme bodily activity. . . . During the entire lesson, he was quiet and gentle, although he expressed great intensity of feeling" (Abbott, 1940, p. 517).

Abbott went on to recount how she would play short bits, maybe just a few phrases, two or three times if necessary, during which "Tom stood tense, all his being focused on the music." After hearing as much as Wiggins thought he could retain, "he indicated by words and sounds that he desired to play." At the keyboard, Tom "instantly recognized any wrong note he played and would shake his head, uttering disapproving sounds, and motion for me to play again. When he felt satisfied, we would go on, doing another portion in the same way . . . When we had accomplished a certain amount, we would go back and piece the parts together." During what Abbott described as "four hours of almost absolute concentration," she did not "remember that he ever wavered from the subject in hand," a consistency of focus she deemed "almost impossible by a person having his full mental faculties." By the end of the lesson, Tom could play the entire piece with "fine instinctive feeling for the music," having "worked to get all the variations of shade and color just as I had played it" (Abbott, 1940, p. 517).

In this manner and owing to his prodigious memory, Wiggins' repertoire grew to a purported 7000 established works (Southern, 1983; Trotter, 1878), an astounding figure for any pianist, even one at the highest professional level. Mainstream classical works made up the bulk of Blind Tom's strictly "by request" programs selected by audience members from eight possible categories on a list in the program booklet distributed beforehand (MMP, 1867, back cover).

Among "Classical Selections," were the *Pathetique, Moonlight,* and "*Pastorale*" *Sonatas* of Beethoven, two fugues from the *Well-Tempered Clavier* by Bach, several Mendelssohn *Songs Without Words*, three waltzes by Chopin, and the famous funeral march from his *Sonata in B-Flat Minor*. Opera transcriptions by Verdi, Rossini, Bellini, Gounod, Meyerbeer, and Donizetti were listed under the heading, "Piano Forte Solos." Included in "Fantasias and Caprices" were two Gottschalk compositions, as well as works by Liszt and E.T.A. Hoffman. Tom's own *The Rainstorm* and *Battle of Manassas* were listed under "Descriptive Music."

Without a doubt, the most evolved manifestations of Tom's imitative impulse are among the 100-or-so solo pieces attributed to him, approximately 20 of which were published. The *Rainstorm, Cyclone Galop, Voice of the Waves, Water in the Moonlight*, and *Daylight* stem from Wiggins' purported obsession with various natural phenomena. Tom's onstage "imitations" (as they were listed in his concert programs), including his pianistic evocations of a music box, a Dutch woman and hand organ, a harp, Scotch bagpipes and a Scotch fiddler, a church organ, guitar, and banjo, as well as the drum in *March Timpani* and the fife and drum in *Battle of Manassas*, are compositional outgrowths of his urge to replicate the sounds of musical instruments. *Sewing Song,* Tom's imitation of a sewing machine, is but one example of his many attempts to approximate at the keyboard the rhythmic clattering of mechanical devices. All are a window into the pianist's unique and insular world.

Tom's flexibility, inventiveness, and productivity in the musical domain, in fact, appear to match those of cognitively unimpaired talented musicians. Such abilities provide evidence to contrast musical savants from those, sometimes called pseudo-savants, with much more limited musical "splinter skills" (Heaton, Pring, & Hermelin, 1999).

Language Skills

The same inclination to imitate musical sounds, according to some sources, lay behind Tom's apparent precocious way with words. Despite Charity's report in 1900 of her son's lifelong stutter ("Mother of 'Blind Tom,' " 1900), Tom is described in his program booklet as having "talked earlier than other children; and he talked no baby talk." The pamphlet goes on to say that, although "he uttered his words . . . clearly and distinctly," he attached "no meaning to them," but seemed "to consider them merely sounds, which he imitated, as he did all others that he heard." Any words directed at him, whether a question, a command, a request, or as matter of information, "he simply repeated in the tones in which they had been uttered; and would repeat not only them, but conversations he had heard sometimes for hours at a time." In fact, "long after he was in possession of a vocabulary, with which . . . he might have sustained a respectable conversation upon any ordinary topic, he never attempted to express by words an idea, a feeling, or a want. His wants he expressed by a whine, which those about him had to interpret as best they could" (MMP, 1867, p. 4).

Out of this urge to mimic arose another curious verbal trait: Wiggins' habit of referring to himself in the third person. According to the program booklet, the first manifestation of this tendency emerged in connection with the composition of *The Rainstorm*, which Tom was said to have attributed to "what the rain, the wind, and the thunder said to him" (MMP, p. 7). This detached mode of expression, confirmed by others (e.g., Seguin, 1866, p. 405), eventually became a featured element of Blind Tom's concert presentation. The evolution of this practice was laid out in the publisher's preface to *Battle of Manassas*:

> The director of Blind Tom's concerts was at first accustomed himself to an-
> nounce the pieces to be played; . . . Noticing however that Tom often repeated
> to himself what had been said, . . . it occurred to him that it would be inter-
> esting to the audience to have Tom announce himself, which is now done, and
> he speaks of "This boy Tom," "This singular being," etc. with as much gravity
> and earnestness as if he were speaking of another person. (Blind Tom, 1866,
> p. 2)

Wit and Imagination

While Wiggins' language often appeared rote and echoic in nature, his diction, as reported by Bethune's grandson, was punctuated by numerous witticisms per-haps indicative of a more highly developed intelligence. "Tom said many things and used many expressions that became family by-words," Robinson (1967, p. 351) recalled fondly in connection with a story about his mother's visit with Tom at a New York hotel.

> "How do you like New York?" Mother asked.
> "I don't like it a bit," was Tom's reply.
> "Why not, Tom?" Mother pressed him.
> "Too many fellow beings," was Tom's laconic answer.

"For years," Robinson related, "if one of the family attended a dull party or had been thrown among undesirable people, the comment 'Too many fellow beings' always explained everything to the other members" (Robinson, 1967, pp. 351–352).

Accompanying Tom's wit was an active imagination that extended beyond the world of sound. "Much of the time Tom lived in a dream world all his own," Robinson wrote, and "he would hold long, audible conversations . . . with nu-merous non-existent characters of his own invention." His favorite among them was apparently a Doctor Smokeson, a vocal coach who, according to Robinson, became "one of the links that bound Tom and me together." Bethune's grandson told how he began to take singing lessons "from none other than the renowned Dr. Smokeson," whose persona was assumed by Wiggins himself. According to Robinson (1967), the lessons were initiated in the following way:

Catching Tom and me somewhere around the place, assiduously engaged in doing nothing, one of the aunts would suggest that it was time for a singing lesson. Whereupon Tom would walk out of the back gate, and disappear out of sight behind the tool shed. Soon he would return, not as Tom, but as "Dr. Smokeson," the renowned vocal teacher. We would greet each other with formality and the lesson would begin and continue until one or the other of us had had enough. I always addressed Tom as "Dr. Smokeson." What he called me I don't recall. It was not "little Norborne" as usual, but something more dignified. The "lessons" of course, consisted of nothing but Tom's accompanying me as I sang, and telling me to sing more loudly or softly according to his whim . . . I still wear the distinction of having received vocal coaching from one of the world's great musical geniuses. (pp. 349–350)

His wit and imagination notwithstanding, Wiggins was found to have a facile mind as far back as 1865. After subjecting Tom's skull to a series of caliper measurements, a procedure now universally considered pseudo-scientific, and observing the pianist's general behavior, a panel of phrenologists concluded that "He is by no means idiotic in any organ or faculty." While "he is odd," the report went on, "he is quite as far from being an idiot as are other sensible persons who can not make music" (Wells, 1865, p. 188). In 1900, Charity also described her son as "smart—very smart" ("Mother of 'Blind Tom,'" 1900), a never-explained about-face from her earlier stance.

Wiggins' intelligence, according to Robinson, would invariably manifest itself when Tom was "caught out on a limb." At those points, he "always came up with a prompt alibi." Robinson related how once, when the Bethune clan was having supper, there was "a sudden commotion at the end of the hall where Tom was having his evening meal. A chair was overturned, a door banged and, from outside in the yard, came sounds of violent retching." When everyone at the table got up to see what had happened, they found Tom bent over in seeming agony.

"What's the matter, Thomas?" asked Grandpa.
"I must have swallowed a fly," was Tom's quick reply.
"Fly nothin'," said Maria the waitress, out of earshot of Tom, "It was five saucers of oatmeal and six saucers of raspberries."

Wiggins' ability to think on his feet became especially evident in performance. "Members of the audiences before which he appeared were always trying to stump Tom," Robinson recalled, and "finally one night, they thought they had Tom stopped." That evening, as usual, a local musician was invited to the stage to perform an original piece on the piano for Blind Tom to mimic. The volunteer began with several traditional opening bars. But then, to everyone's amazement, the man stretched his hands out to opposite ends of the piano to play tremolos, pausing for dramatic effect before bending his head over the keyboard and striking a middle note with his nose. When Wiggins took his place at the piano, Robinson wrote, "the audience held its breath." After easily reproducing the few introductory bars, Tom ran his hands out to the extremities of the keyboard, only to hesitate. Clearly confused, he then repeated what he had just played, only to stop again. The third time, however, proved the charm. "All of a sudden he played it all over rapidly, shot his head down and banged the middle note with his nose. The audience almost tore the roof off" (Robinson, 1967, pp. 347–348).

Anecdotes such as these, illustrating Wiggins' penchant for role playing, on-the-spot adaptive thinking, and, as we'll see later, composing lyrics, suggest the seed of Tom's verbal creativity may have been his musical talent. It is quite possible that Tom's musical ability and the ongoing systematic development of these talents may have provided a stepping-stone for learning in other social, emotional, linguistic and artistic domains and may have provided a cognitive and perceptual (and thereby hereditary) basis for the development of his imagination, creativity, and talent. Theoretical explanations of the genesis and development of savant talent (see Heaton & Wallace, 2004; Miller, 1999) often highlight the role of such heightened perceptual abilities. A true savant, however, shows the ability to use these native abilities to improvise and invent (Miller, 1999). Moreover, it seems that the deficits in the creative and affective realms that are assumed in the developmentally disabled, and especially in classic autism, are often not present in savants (Heaton & Wallace, 2004). For example, Hermelin & Pring's research (1999) documents the ability of high-functioning children with autism to match excerpts of orchestra pieces to visual images of emotions such as love, fear, and anger. In fact, Heaton, Pring, & Hermelin (1999) propose that it may well be such a fuller, affective appreciation of music that distinguishes the true musical savant.

Body Language

Unusual bodily movements were a constant accompaniment to Wiggins' in-concert demonstrations. When an audience member was summoned onstage to perform, Tom, according to Seguin (1866, p. 406), "shows his satisfaction by his countenance, a laughing, stooping, with various rubbings of the hand, alternating with an increase of the sideway swinging of his body, and some uncouth smiles." Seguin went on to describe the same mannerisms reported the year before by phrenologists (Wells, 1865):

> As soon as the new tune begins. . . . Tom takes some ludicrous posture, expressive of listening, but soon lowering his body and raising on one leg, so that both are perfectly horizontal, and supported upon the other leg, representing the letter T, he moves upon that improvised axis like the pirouette dancer, but indefinitely. These long gyrations are interrupted by other spells of motionless listening, with or without change of posture, or persevered in and ornamented with spasmodic movements of the hands; this is his studying posture. (Seguin, 1866, p. 406)

That these gymnastics were considered by many to be the product of stage training was brought up in Wiggins' program booklet. "So far from this being the case," the biography refuted, "it is but a slight outcropping of his usual exercises" (MMP, 1867, p. 8). In fact, "the gyrations he performed on the stage," Robinson explained, "were but a toned-down sample of what he would do in his hotel room, on tour, or in the yard" (Robinson, 1967, p. 349). According to Bethune's grandson, somersaults, handsprings, and cartwheels were a daily occurrence on the Virginia farm. But Tom "never engaged in the plays of children or manifested any interest in them," the program booklet made clear. "His amusements were all his own" (MMP, 1867, p. 8).

These exercises, the phrenologists reported, left the pianist, at age 16, standing 5 feet 7 inches in height, and weighing 150 pounds, "one of the most compactly built, vigorous, and healthy persons that we have ever met." After demonstrating his repertoire of exercises to the committee, Tom was described as having "so developed his physique, that it will be hard to find a person of his age with a finer frame. . . . His legs are splendidly developed, and as hard as those of any gymnast. He has broad, square shoulders, a full chest, and a well-knot frame throughout, and we judge him to be as sound and healthy—the vision alone excepted—as a human being can well be" (Wells, 1865, p. 188).

Wiggins, by his teenage years, had become "solid, agile, and unbelievably powerful" (Robinson, 1967, p. 348), a description borne out by the countless engraved and photographic images that grace broadsides, concert programs, sheet music, cabinet cards, *cartes de visites*, and newspaper and magazine articles, all documenting the celebrity's appearance from boyishly lean in his youth to "very fat" ("Blind Tom's Return," 1887) late in life. Seguin also found Tom to be "well built," and his head "harmonious in its small, oblong, side-flattened shape," and his fingers "remarkably thin considering the constant use he makes of them on his instrument" (Seguin, 1866, pp. 404–405), a characterization that dovetails with Abbott's statement that "He had delicately formed flexible hands, for which the piano keyboard held no difficulties" (Abbott, 1940, p. 517), and Robinson's that "Tom had a forearm and fist that would be respected by Jack Dempsey or Joe Louis, plus fingers soft and delicate as those of a baby girl" (Robinson, 1967, p. 347).

A Short Fuse

On occasion, however, the chiseled physique of Wiggins' young adulthood in combination with an apparent hot temper had combustible consequences. "He was a powerful fellow," Joseph Eubank testified in 1886. "Once he knocked out a Louisville music teacher whom he disliked, and also pummeled the witness for trying to protect the teacher." Eubank also recounted how, on another night in a St. Louis hotel, Tom played a horn "very much to the discomfort of other occupants of the house." When Eubank tried to stop him, according to his testimony, Wiggins literally hurled him out of the room ("Blind Tom's Mother," 1886).

Tom's wrath, it appears, was most often directed at those who traveled with him. "A periodical riot," Robinson explained, would occur every September when Mr. Warhurst, Tom's manager, would travel to Virginia to take the pianist to New York to prepare for the concert season. One year, apparently, "Tom made everybody's life miserable, including his own, by announcing in violent terms every few minutes that he would never leave the farm as long as he lived. 'Goddam Mr. Warhurst,' yelled Tom, 'Tell-him-to-go-to-hell-I-ain't-coming-up-there,' all in one breath." An appeal to Wiggins' vanity, however, got this "grade A, blown-in-the-bottle, undiluted ham," into the carriage, according to Bethune's grandson. On the drive to the railroad station, "Tom would be men-tally miles away from the farm, on tour, playing before enthusiastic audiences" (Robinson, 1967, pp. 355–356).

W. P. Howard testified that he, too, "heard Tom, in his idiotic moments, use angry expressions against various parties" ("Blind Tom's Mother," 1886). Once, "a battle royal" followed some criticism from professional pianists in New York about Tom's faulty fingering, Robinson recalled, to which Wiggins apparently vowed, "with the whole-souled and picturesque profanity of which he had be-come master," that he would not alter his fingering. "In the end he was won over, but it took much persuasion" (Robinson, 1967, p. 345).

The pianist's violent streak sometimes surfaced in concert. According to J. Frank Davis, Tom once objected to the onstage characterization of him as an imbecile by his manager at the time, Mr. Gibson, by "hurl[ing] a chair at Gibson's head. Mr. Gibson being wise," Davis went on, "slightly changed his phraseology . . . and ever thereafter said, in a complimentary tone, 'Tom, as you can plainly see, is not only a great pianist, but is distinctly *non compos mentis*.' " From then on, "Tom would grin vacuously" whenever this point in the show was reached. In fact, Davis pointed out, "This became one of the negro's points of pride. 'Tom is non compos mentis,' he would say, proudly, when introduced to a stranger. To the day of his death, he never learned the meaning of the Latin phrase" (Davis, 1908, p. 9).

Expectations are that Wiggins' anger would have reached its apex during the two celebrated writ of habeas corpus suits that would interrupt his life and career, first in 1865 and then again in 1886. But, Tom seemed utterly unfazed on the eve of the first guardianship trial that would ultimately allow him to remain in the care of the Bethunes. "Having but a dim vision of surrounding objects," the *Cincinnati Enquirer* wrote, the 16-year-old spent the few hours prior to the hearing in the sheriff's office, engaging in "continual grimaces, twistings and squintings in endeavoring to trace the outline of persons and things" and, "in excellent style," entertaining those present with a vocal rendition of the *Star Spangled Banner*. "He seems to deport himself without any regard to the com-pany present," the article concluded, "and when tired of sitting, jumps to his feet, and goes through a series of genuflections and gymnastic movements of the most grotesque and original description" ("Law Report," 1865).

However, Wiggins' reaction would prove much different to the verdict in the second trial 20 years later. Against the pianist's wishes, Judge Bond, a federal judge in Baltimore, permanently turned Wiggins' guardianship over to General Bethune's ex-daughter-in-law, Eliza Bethune, in an arrangement shortsightedly authorized by Tom's mother. Upon her son's delivery to the court for the final exchange, an ugly, heart-wrenching scene took place. As reported by *The Baltimore Sun*:

> Charity Wiggins, his mother, came on from New York to meet Tom. When she saw him she said: "Tom, ain't you going to speak to your mother?" but he turned his back on her. Tom said: "I don't want to go; I won't go," and was almost in tears. The marshal said, "Yes, but people sometimes have to go where they do not want to," and Tom replied, "But they can fight." Then the marshal said, "Come on," but instead of coming on, Tom crowded back into a corner, and appealed to Mr. Bethune not to let him go. At length, after much coaxing and a promise that he should be brought back, he consented to get into a carriage, and with the officers and his mother, he was driven to the 3:20 train and left for New York. . . . Many of those present were much affected by the scene. ("Virginia affairs," 1887)

Resentment and Depression

Wiggins' subsequent conduct hints at how damaging this forced separation from General Bethune may have been to his enthusiasm for performing, his relationship with his mother, and his overall psyche. While the contention that, as a silent protest, he spent the last 20 years of his life in a self-imposed retirement in New York and New Jersey appears exaggerated (Southall, 1999, p. 168), several absences from the stage during this post-trial period, long enough to spawn both rumors of his death and the careers of several Blind Tom impersonators on the burgeoning vaudeville circuit, could indicate the negative effect the 1887 verdict may have had on his sense of security and well-being.

Any loyalty Tom may have felt toward his mother before the verdict appears to have turned to resentment afterward. In 1900, back in Georgia after a strained nine years with her son and Eliza Bethune in New York, Charity accused Eliza and Eliza's lawyer and future husband, Albert J. Lerche, of pitting Tom against her: "One day he said: 'Mother, you must go.' I said: 'Thomas, what put that into your head.' He said: 'If you don't go, we will make you go.' He put his hands out like as if to shove me out. I said: 'Thomas, who has been telling you to do this?' He said the people had, and was afterwards ashamed for the way he had acted." A lingering regret and bitterness seem to color Charity's interpretation of what happened. "When I was in New York, I signed away my rights. They won't let Thomas come to see me, and I am not allowed to see him" ("The mother of 'Blind Tom'," 1900, p. 13).

The emotional toll that Wiggins' lifelong isolation from his own family and race may have taken on him was never fully acknowledged by those responsible. "From infancy," Bethune's grandson wrote, "he stood apart and his association with the members of our family from my grandparents down to the youngest of my mother's brothers and sisters was one of close family intimacy. . . . As to Tom's relationship to other Negroes, my memory is not clear" (Robinson, 1967, p. 354).

J. Frank Davis argued that at no point did Wiggins "ever know that he was a negro." In fact, "It was his custom, in his disconnected way, to speak disparagingly of the black race", a contention borne out by an interchange Davis observed at a Boston shoeshine stand. Davis reported that while Tom

> sat, muttering, in the chair, the bootblack—a Negro—was gleefully recounting to another bootblack his story of a quarrel.
>
> "En' he says t' me," he said "Go on, yo' niggah—"
>
> Instantly there was an interruption. Blind Tom leaned forward and said in his soft, hesitating, stammering voice, "Are you—are you a nigger?"
>
> The bootblack looked at the towering, jet-black blind man and grinned. "I 'xpect I am," he replied.
>
> Ponderously Tom climbed down from the chair, one shoe shiny, the other untouched. "Tom ain't goin' to have his shoes blacked by no nigger," he said, definitely. And although he did, it was at a different shop and he didn't know the bootblack's color. (Davis, 1908, p. 9)

That a sense of remoteness and despair may have crept into Wiggins' outlook is suggested by the lyrics to the following song drawn from his in-concert repertoire:

Blind Tom

> Oh, tell me the form of the soft summer air,
> That tosses so gently the curls of my hair;
> It breathes on my lips, it fans my warm cheek,
> Yet gives me no answer, though often I speak;
> I feel it play o'er me, refreshing and kind,
> Yet I cannot touch it—I'm blind, oh, I'm blind.
>
> And music, what is it, and where does it dwell?
> I sink and I rise with its cadence and swell,
> While it touches my heart with its deep thrilling strain,
> Till pleasure, till pleasure is turned into pain.
> What brightness of hue is with music combined?
> Will any one tell me?—I'm blind, oh, I'm blind.
>
> The perfume of flowers that are hovering nigh—
> And what are they—on what kind of wings do they fly?
> Are not they sweet angels, who come to delight
> A poor little boy who knows not of sight?
> The sun, moon, and stars, are to me undefined,
> Oh, tell me what light is—I'm blind, oh, I'm blind.

Falsely attributed to Wiggins in several secondary sources (e.g., Southall, 1979, pp. 72–73) and retitled as "Blind Tom" and reprinted without credit in the pianist's publicity pamphlet (*MMP*, 1867, p. 20), these are actually Hannah F.

Gould's words to the William R. Dempster song, "The Blind Boy" (Dempster, 1842), with a copyright seven years before Wiggins' birth. Nevertheless, these lyrics must have resonated deeply with the pianist. The many references to blindness likely mirrored not only Wiggins' own lifelong struggle with his physical condition, but also the same loneliness and overwhelming rootlessness he shared with his fellow slaves, expressed by them in countless narratives and blues songs.

Equally imbued with double meanings characteristic of the blues are the lyrics to another song, this one explicitly attributed to Blind Tom in the published score:

Wilt Thou Bring My Baby Home?

Wilt thou bring my baby home?
Now he is satisfied,
Yes, he will be brought to you,
And I will see him aft'r a while.

I thought I heard my mother singing
And sitting there on the steps,
I think I see her with her sister,
Awaiting for the hack to come.

Wilt though bring my baby home?
Now he is satisfied,
Yes, he will be brought to you,
And I will see him aft'r a while.

Now the roses are in bloom,
And in the garden safe,
You may bring the can along,
And there it will be safe.

Go and ask my mother if she's ready,
To go and take a walk with me,
Tell me what time will you all be back,
We will be back at six o'clock.

Wilt though bring my baby home?
Now he is satisfied,
Yes, he will be brought to you,
And I will see him aft'r a while.

On the surface, the mutual longing of mother and child evoked here could be viewed as an expression of Wiggins' pining for his own mother, with whom a closer relationship was always denied. On a more symbolic level, the text hints at a possible urge to be reunited with the African homeland of his ancestors.

Before any conclusions can be drawn from these stories of Blind Tom, they must be evaluated with a critical eye. Among these firsthand accounts, the biography of Wiggins in his program booklet is most immediately troubling. After all, it was written by the Wiggins' handlers in part to publicize the more sensational aspects of his onstage and offstage persona. Later corroboration of much of its contents, however, by Seguin, an assuredly impartial observer, by Tom's biological mother, Charity, who presumably would want to portray her son in the most positive light, by the phrenologists who examined him, and by the array of former managers, teachers, and journalists who observed Wiggins firsthand, offset many of his promoters' potential biases. Even the rose-tinted glasses through which Bethune's grandson viewed Tom do not totally obscure the essence of his observations.

SOURCES OF STRESS IN WIGGINS' LIFE

The stories of Blind Tom depict a highly talented musician coping not just with blindness and the social, economic, and emotional hurdles presented by slavery and its aftermath, but also with the complex set of developmental disabilities that may have made him especially vulnerable to stress (see chapter 1). The record is replete with examples of Wiggins' difficulty in managing not just social and sensory sources of stress typical of those with autism and related disabilities, but also those larger contextual stressors arising out of both a documented awareness of injustices done to him and his ultimate separation from well-established life routines and sources of support.

Tom's childhood fascination with sound often to the exclusion of everything else suggests the presence of an "encompassing preoccupation with one or more stereotyped and restricted patterns of interest that is abnormal either in intensity and focus" and an "apparently inflexible adherence to specific, nonfunctional routines or rituals," both of which represent "restricted repetitive and stereotyped patterns of behavior, interests, and activities"(American Psychiatric Association [APA], 2000, p. 75). This fixation, when it became so strong as to render Wiggins oblivious to the pain he was inducing in himself and other children, hints at a "qualitative impairment in social interaction," and, more specifically, "a failure to develop peer relationships appropriate to developmental level" and a "lack of social or emotional reciprocity" (APA, 2000, p. 75), as well as being an example of what Bernard Rimland cites as stimuli often being "apprehended, but not comprehended" (Rimland, 1964, p. 86). Such maladaptive tendencies undoubtedly impeded Wiggins from forming strong social bonds that likely would have alleviated stress (chapter 1, this volume).

Wiggins' other obsessions, stemming from an apparent hypersensitivity to light and smell, also led to turbulent sensory perceptual experiences that are reported to cause great discomfort in persons with autism (Jones, Quigney, & Huws, 2003) When, as a small child, Tom virtually gouged his eyeballs out of their sockets with a stick as he relentlessly peered up at the sun, the light may have so aroused his nervous system that the resultant pain and bleeding became of only marginal importance to him. And Tom's inordinately strong reaction to any pleasing odor he encountered may have produced a level of stress that could only be relieved by binge eating, an affliction that fits Rimland's observation that, among autistic children, "feeding problems are almost the rule. Some children have ravenous appetites; others eat very little. Almost all have odd eating habits and preferences, however" (Rimland, 1964, p. 8).

Reports of Tom's language skills conflict, but they correspond, nevertheless, to communication-related stressors cited in chapter 1 of this volume. If, in fact, Wiggins did not speak until he was 5 or 6 years old, as Seguin (1866) stated, this trait could constitute a "delay in, or total lack of, the development of spoken language" (APA, 2000, p. 75). If, however, as the program booklet declared, Tom began talking earlier than other children, but out of a purely imitative, noninteractive impulse, this practice, what Rimland (1964) calls speech of a "peculiar noncommunicative kind" (p. 14), would be characteristic of those "individuals with adequate speech" who have "marked impairment in the ability to initiate or sustain a conversation with others" (APA, 2000, p. 75). His inability to express "an idea, a feeling, or a want" (MMP, 1867, p. 4) could also be viewed as an impairment in executive function, "the goal-directed, future-oriented" buffer to stress that allows a person to accept challenges, seek commitments, and develop confidence and self-control (chapter 1, this volume).

Verbally advanced or not, Wiggins' tendency to speak of himself in the third person may be an example of "stereotyped and repetitive use of language or idiosyncratic language,"(APA, 2000, p. 75) and is consistent with the observation that, for autistic children, "The words *I* and *Yes* are strikingly and consistently absent, often until the 6th or 7th year" (Rimland, 1964, p. 14). This detached mode of expression may have masked an anxiety in Tom toward expressing feelings (see chapter 1, this volume), and functioned as a means for him to keep his "fellow human beings" at arm's length.

Tom's on- and offstage gymnastic routines also had a distancing effect. Part physical exercise, part innocent play, they may have been another manifestation of his "apparently inflexible adherence to specific, nonfunctional routines or rituals" and his "marked impairment in the use of multiple nonverbal behaviors such as eye-to-eye gaze, facial expression, body postures, and gestures to regulate social interaction" (APA, 2000, p. 75). According to Groden, Baron, & Groden (chapter 1), such repetitive isolated play and activity is a behavioral pattern that, once reinforced, lessens "the opportunity to learn and use adaptive coping strategies" (p. 6) and becomes a stressor that "reduces opportunities to practice social skills and build social supports" (p. 3).

Also isolating were Wiggins' occasional tantrums, some of them violent. The accounts of Tom pummeling a witness after first knocking out a music teacher, tossing one manager out of a St. Louis hotel room, and hurling a chair at another manager's head during a concert indicate that Tom lacked self-controlling, alternate strategies for reducing stress (chapter 1, this volume).

The ruckus described by Robinson that Wiggins caused each year upon having to leave the Bethune farm for his annual touring season is more difficult to interpret. Although Bethune's grandson cast the story in the most positive light, his explanation that it was difficult for Wiggins to make the transition from summer vacation on the Bethune farm to life on the road is plausible. The tantrum, in fact, may have been just as Robinson implied: merely Wiggins' response to stress elicited by an unanticipated change in routine and schedule.

A darker explanation may lie at the root of Wiggins' outbursts. The Bethune family's successful appeal to Tom's vanity clearly shows that he enjoyed playing concerts and relished the attention he knew would accompany them. But the particular tantrum Robinson described, one that was similar to others that occurred on the eve of every upcoming concert season, could have been a manifestation of Wiggins' unacknowledged, suppressed anger at the prospect of being forced to play hundreds of concerts virtually for free and for the exclusive benefit of someone else. Examined in this context, Wiggins' acting out, veiled and indicative of anxiety over verbal communication, seems appropriate.

Also understandable is Tom's ultimate rejection of his mother. The lyrics to *Wilt Thou Bring My Baby Home* suggest that, at least up to the song's 1881 copyright date, the pianist's isolation from his mother had left him lonely and pining for the love and security she could have provided. Tom likely accepted that Charity, as a slave, was powerless to stop General Bethune from appropriating him.

The 1887 verdict in the second guardianship trial turned Wiggins' earlier sadness and resignation into out-and-out resentment. That his own mother, albeit naively, could have conspired to take her son out of the Bethune household, to which he had now grown so accustomed, and place him in the conniving hands of General Bethune's former daughter-in-law, was more than he could tolerate. When Tom turned his back on Charity in the courtroom, this gesture represented not just the end of an unfulfilled, anxiety-provoking relationship, but another family casualty of slavery.

Slavery was also behind the racist comments Wiggins hurled at the bootblack. At the least, Tom may have been mimicking the kind of cavalier, anti-Negro utterances he probably heard spoken many times in and out of the Bethune household. Just as likely, he was expressing a deep-rooted self-hate that historically has filtered into the psyche of oppressed people in a segregated society. Either way, these epithets were the residue of Wiggins' lifelong isolation from his family and fellow African Americans. Race was a never-acknowledged issue that clearly caused Tom great distress.

BUFFERS TO WIGGINS' STRESS

Our modern-day understanding of savant syndrome (Treffert & Wallace, 2002) and a growing appreciation of the role of stress in a life with autism (Groden,

Cautela, Prince, & Berryman, 1994) invite us to consider Wiggins' life, at least in his early years, as one of extraordinary coping and adjustment, not only to the stress of a disability, but also to slavery. Even the most stressful life has potential buffers, those features of the physical or social environment that reduce the impact of stress and facilitate adaptive coping. What were the buffers that reduced the potential harm of Wiggins' severe disability, and what supports nourished his musical talent? We seek answers in both Wiggins' skills and characteristics and in the arrangements of his environment.

The Power of Talent

Treffert and Wallace's (2002) study of savants, musical and otherwise, documents that sustained and improved "talents often help savants to establish some kind of normal routine or way of life" (p. 82) and thereby expand functional skills. The accepted approach with modern-day savants, Treffert reports, is to simultaneously encourage growth in talent while improving social skills, better language, and greater independence. Furthermore, Groden et al. (1994) argue that when successful, persons with autism may also have greater confidence and satisfaction. Although Wiggins' routine, in retrospect, can be seen as ultimately restricted by slavery and omnipresent "handlers," the historical record documents the self-esteem he derived from the development of his talent and the sense of purpose engendered by his daily ritual of practicing and performing.

The Pleasure of Talent

Recent firsthand reports on the sensory perceptual experiences of autism (Jones et al., 2003) have shown that, once stressful discomforts (e.g., going into a new environment, meeting new people) are under control, individuals with autism who can communicate about their inner experience describe their personal rituals and focused activities as creating states of serenity and/or perfect stimulation. In addition to the great joy Wiggins took during his infancy in the sustained sensory experience with sounds (e.g., listening to sounds, repeating sounds and words), the same combination of serenity and perfect stimulation could be observed in Tom after he discovered the piano, particularly when he engaged in the ritual and focused activity of practicing the instrument for hours each day. Abbott (1940, p. 517) described the quiet and gentle demeanor Wiggins assumed upon taking his place at the keyboard versus his "extreme bodily activity" as she played. Paradoxically, the sensory turbulence arising initially out of Wiggins' childhood obsession with random sounds—whether the product of nature, some mechanical device, a musical instrument, an animal on the Bethune farm, or another human being, all of which the boy was prone to imitate verbally and musically—may have been relieved simply by basking in those same sounds.

Contextual Buffers to Stress

Various arrangements of the physical and social environment (see Groden et al., 1994) may have reduced Wiggins' exposure to stressful situations or enhanced his ability to control stressful situations when they did arise. On the Bethune farm, Tom had a predictable daily schedule that included playing music for many hours. From the moment his musical talent was discovered, he received regular instruction that matched his free-wheeling yet disciplined learning style alternating music and movement and systematic keyboard instruction with creative music making.

Wiggins' interpersonal skills were further developed in and out of the Bethune household. Besides nourishing his musical talent, Tom's instruction also provided him regular opportunity to build social routines and social competence that helped him function in the Bethune household and the world of performance. Though tragically isolated at a young age from his own family, Wiggins learned vicariously the social routines of the Bethune family and their children at play. On tour, the pianist had no choice but to interact with the culture at large. Like modern-day savants (Treffert & Wallace, 2002), Tom's learning and performance routines gave him the opportunity to participate more fully in the world, and perhaps even to develop socially and cognitively.

Of course, none of this would have been possible without the Bethunes. However exploitative their motives may have been, it is unlikely that Tom would have achieved such personal and career success without their sustained financial and managerial input. One great contradiction of Tom's life is that the very family that limited his freedom and exploited his talent may have also provided Tom with an environmental framework for reducing his exposure to stressful situations and developing and achieving personal and public success.

A Sense of Self

Another buffer to the stress of life with autism can be the specific sense of accomplishment that comes from a savant's acknowledged talent (Treffert & Wallace, 2002). The constant positive feedback of his guardians, teachers, the press, and the listening public gave Wiggins a sense of accomplishment and pride in performance that led to greater confidence, self-esteem, and satisfaction, all important buffers to stress (see chapter 1, this volume). Sadly, some of this encouragement also involved the manipulation of Tom's ego for self-serving ends. Robinson, for example, documents his successful appeal to Tom's vanity (and pride in performance) in persuading the pianist to leave the Bethune farm for the rigorous New York concert season, for which Wiggins was not being paid.

Tom also may have developed, as many modern-day savants do, other cognitive and social-emotional skills that reflected an expanded sense of self-competence and increased range of emotion. Over time, these buffers allowed

Wiggins' demonstrated impairments to give way to more advanced conversational skills, an agile mind under pressure, a capacity for empathy and imaginative play, and a highly evolved musicianship. Accounts show that, by midlife, he was able to keep his anger in check, carry on witty, if still somewhat detached, conversations with those he felt comfortable, handle with ease any in-concert challenge presented, and even establish a caring friendship with "Little Norbonne," with whom he often engaged in role-playing pastimes. The creative and emotional depths Wiggins ultimately was able to plumb are borne out by the refinement of his published piano compositions and the songs lyrics he wrote and performed.

Sadly, however, no concerted effort to develop self-control seems to have been made where Wiggins' unusual body language was concerned. When the phrenologists observed that "Tom exercises himself in a manner which would doubtless be more seemly if he had sight," the implication is that blindness, not mental deficiency, lays at the root of his "queer antics." Moreover, the committee observed that "his twistings and wry faces he has never been taught to suppress," and "born a slave on a Georgia plantation, and being partially blind, he of course was not trained in decorous ways" (Wells, 1865, p. 188).

The Bethunes, it seems, could have tried harder to break those habits in Wiggins that only further alienated him from those with whom he came into contact. But, given General Bethune's well-documented paternalistic, pro-slavery views (see Bethune, 1853–1861) and a nineteenth-century America mostly hostile to blacks and endlessly drawn to the freak show, there appears to have been very little incentive to do so. If anything, Tom's handlers saw his remarkable talent and physical bearing as a commodity to be embraced and exploited.

Had Wiggins been born just a generation or two later, his idiosyncratic movements may have been viewed quite differently by those around him and by society at large. The slave musician's "primitive" concert deportment, after all, bears a striking resemblance to that of a more modern-day sightless, black pianist from Georgia, Ray Charles, whose omnipresent grin and herky-jerky torso at the keyboard were considered the ultimate in hip. Perhaps, as suggested by Thomas L. Riis, Blind Tom's crude social bearing may have even been cultivated by Wiggins himself. At a time when black men were "being lynched and burned across America on the average of two or three a week," he wrote, "keeping up the mask of idiocy and living a reclusive life in New Jersey might be judged the actions of an entirely sane and even highly intelligent individual" (Riis, 2000, p. 36).

Whether or not Tom actively sought to uphold the role of primitive performer and public recluse as a buffer to institutionalized racism and personal rejection, the end of his life was surely a sad and lonely one. The marginalization of his career during his last 20 years has been attributed to several factors: the pianist silent protest of a situation he deemed unacceptable, the poor promotional skills of Wiggins' new guardians, and simply a lack of public interest. What is clearer, however, is that, after the second guardianship trial, Wiggins led a diminished life brought on by the loss of those environmental buffers (constraining and controlling as they were) that may have facilitated his earlier coping. No longer was he part of the Bethune home in which he was most comfortable. Instead, he was ordered to reside in New York and New Jersey with those toward whom he harbored a tremendous amount of ill will: his mother, Charity; Eliza Bethune; and her future husband, Albert J. Lerche. It appears that this radical shift in his physical and social environment left the pianist unable to summon the same pure pleasure, sense of purpose, and pride in performance he had experienced over the previous 37 years in the more stable and familiar Bethune household, the same household that was so instrumental in curtailing his freedom before and after the abolition of slavery.

While Wiggins' life should never be examined independently of the adverse social circumstances unto which he was born, his final years, less active professionally, lonely, resentful, and depressed, remind us that stress for an autistic savant must be managed in the context of fair, loving relationships and unwavering support. We encourage others to consider such contextual factors in the analysis and description of savant skills. For only through a fuller examination of both stressors and buffers over a life span will we reach the goal suggested by Henley (2003) of understanding the connection between the development of talent and the savant's quality of life.

Acknowledgment

Extracts from Norborne T. Robinson's article, "Blind Tom, Musical Prodigy," are printed with the permission of the Georgia Historical Society.

References

Abbott, E. (1940, August). The miraculous case of Blind Tom. *The Etude, LVIII*(8), 517.
American Psychiatric Association. (2000). *Diagnostic and statistical manual of mental disorders Text revision* (4th ed). Washington, DC: Author.
Bethune, J. N. (Ed.). (1853–1861). *The corner stone,* Georgia Newspaper Project, vol. 8, no. 45. Athens, GA:University of Georgia Library.
Blind Tom (1866). *Battle of manassas.* Chicago: Root & Cady.
Blind Tom's mother. (1886, November 27). *New York Times,* p. 8.
Blind Tom's return. (1887, August 18). *New York Times,* p. 8.
Davis, J. (1999). *John Davis plays Blind Tom.* Newport, RI: Newport Classic, Ltd.
Davis, J. F. (1908, September). Blind Tom. *Human Life,* pp. 9–10.
Dempster, W. R. (1842). *The Blind Boy.* Boston: Oliver Ditson.
Gottschalk, L. M. (1881). *Notes of a pianist.* Philadelphia: Theodore Presser.
Groden, J., Cautela, J. R., Prince, S., & Berryman, J. (1994). The ijmpact of stress and anxiety on individuals with autism and developmental disabilities. In E. Schopler

& G. Mesibov (Eds.), *Behavioral issues in autism* (pp. 177–193). New York: Plenum Press.

Heaton, P. (2003). Pitch memory, labeling and disembedding in autism. *Journal of Child Psychology and Psychiatry, 44*, 543–551.

Heaton, P., Happe, F., Williams, K., & Cummins, O. (2003). Do social and cognitive deficits curtail musical understanding? Evidence from autism and Down syndrome. Manuscript submitted for publication.

Heaton, P., Hermelin, B., & Pring, L. (1999). Can children with autism spectrum disorders perceive affect in music? An experimental investigation. *Psychological Medicine, 29*, 1405–1410.

Heaton, P., Pring, L. & Hermelin, B. (1999). A Pseudo-savant: A case of exceptional musical splinter skills. *Neurocase, 5*, 503–509.

Heaton, P., & Wallace, G. L. (2004). Annotation: The savant syndrome. *Journal of Child Psychology and Psychiatry, 45*(5), 899–911.

Henley, D. R. (2003). Book review of *Bright splinters of the mind: A personal story of research with autistic savants*, by Beate Hermelin. *Art Therapy, 20*(3), 178–180.

Hobson, R. P., & Bishop, M. (2003). The pathogenesis of autism: Insights from congenital blindness. *Philosophical Transcripts of The Royal Society of London, 358*, 335–344.

Hobson, R. P., Lee, A., & Brown, R. (1999). Autism and congenital blindness. *Journal of Autism and Developmental Disorders, 29*(1), 45–56.

Jones, R., Quigney, A., & Huws, J. (2003). First-hand accounts of sensory-perceptual experiences in autism: A qualitative analysis. *Journal of Intellectual and Developmental Disability, 28*, 112–121.

Keeler, W. R. (1958). Autistic patterns and defective communication in blind children with retrolental fibroplasia. In V. Lewis, & G. M. Collis (Eds.), *Blindness and psychological development in young children* (pp. 64–83). Leicester, UK: The British Psychological Society.

Law report, probate court: Habeas corpus for 'Blind Tom,' the celebrated musical prodigy. (1865, July 20). *Cincinnati Enquirer.*

Local news: The habeas corpus in the case of Blind Tom. (1865, July 22). *Cincinnati Enquirer.*

Magill, C. T. (1922, August 19). Blind Tom: Unsolved problem in musical history. *The Chicago Defender.*

The marvelous musical prodigy (MMP), Blind Tom, the negro boy pianist (1867). New York: French & Wheat.

Miller, L. (1989). *Musical savants: Exceptional skill in the mentally retarded.* Hillsdale, NJ: Erlbaum.

Miller, L.K. (1998). Defining the savant syndrome. *Journal of Developmental and Physical Disabilities, 10*(1), 73–85.

Miller, L. K. (1999). The savant syndrome: Intellectual impairment and exceptional skill. *Psychological Bulletin, 125*(1), 31–46.

The mother of 'Blind Tom'. (1900, October 22). *Columbus Enquirer-Sun, Special Edition*, p. 13.

The owner of 'Blind Tom' ill. (1895, January 21). *New York Times*, p. 9.

Riis, T. L. (2000, March 5). The legacy of a prodigy lost in mystery. *The New York Times*, vol. 149, no. 51, pp. 35–36.

Rimland, B. (1964). *Infantile autism.* New York: Meredith.

Rimland, B., & Hill, A. (1984). Idiot savants. In J. Wortes (Ed.), *Mental retardation and developmental disabilities* (pp. 155–169). New York: Plenum Press.

Robinson, N. T. N., Jr. (1967, September). Blind Tom, musical prodigy. *The Georgia Historical Quarterly,* vol. 51, no. 3, 336–358. Savannah, GA: Georgia Historical Society.

Sacks, O. (1995). *An anthropologist on Mars.* New York: Alfred A. Knopf.

Seguin, E. (1866). *Idiocy and its treatment by the physiological method.* New York: William Wood.

Sloboda, J., Hermelin, B., & O'Connor, N. (1985). An exceptional musical memory. *Music Perception.* 3, 155–170.

Southall, G. H. (1979). *Blind Tom: The post Civil-war enslavement of a black musical genius.* Minneapolis, MN: Challenge Productions.

Southall, G. H. (1983). *The continuing "enslavement" of Blind Tom, the black pianist-composer (1865–1887).* Minneapolis: Challenge Productions.

Southall, G. H. (1999). *Blind Tom, the black pianist-composer, continually enslaved.* Lanham, MD: Scarecrow.

Southern, E. (1983). *The music of black Americans: A history* (2nd ed.). New York: W. W. Norton.

Treffert, D. A. (1989). *Extraordinary people: Understanding "idiot savants."* New York: Harper & Row.

Treffert, D. A., & Wallace, G. (2002, June). Islands of genius. *Scientific American, 286*(6), 78.

Virginia affairs: Blind Tom in court. (1887, August 17). *Baltimore Sun.*

Wells, S. R. (Ed.). (1865, December). Blind Tom. *American Phrenological Journal and Life Illustrated, 43*(6), 188.

Wiggins, T. (1881). *Wilt thou bring my baby home?* John G. Bethune.

Young, R. (1995). *Savant syndrome: Processes underlying extraordinary abilities.* (Ph.D. ed.). South Australia: University of Adelaide.

Young, R. L., & Nettelbeck, T. (1995). The abilities of a musical savant and his family. *Journal of Autism and Developmental Disorders, 25,* 231–248.

III

Emerging Pathways for the Study
of Stress, Coping, and Autism

6 Is Autism a Stress Disorder?

What Studies of Nonautistic Populations Can Tell Us

Kathleen Morgan

Is autism a stress disorder? Certainly many persons with high-functioning autism (Grandin, 1996; Williams, 1995; see also chapter 3, this volume) describe their experiences of autism as including profound and debilitating anxiety—the same kind of anxiety that characterizes disorders resulting from extremely stressful life experiences. In his original description of the disorder, Kanner (1943) characterized autism as including extreme anxiety and fearfulness. More recent investigations have shown a high degree of comorbidity (> 84%) for autism and one or more of the anxiety disorders (Bradley, Summers, Wood, & Bryson, 2004; Gillott, Furniss, & Walter, 2001; Green, Gilchrist, Burton, & Cox, 2000; Lainhart, 1997; Muris, Steerneman, Merckelbach, Holdrinet, & Meesters, 1998; Prater & Zylstra, 2002). Anxiety and depression also appear more often than one would expect by chance in first-degree relatives of persons diagnosed with pervasive developmental disorders. For example, in one study in which the relatives of 30 patients with autism were compared with relatives of those without autism, anxiety disorders and obsessive-compulsive illness were closely associated with having individuals with autism in the family (Wilcox, Tsuang, Schnurr, & Baida-Fragoso, 2003). Parents of children with autism have been found to have significantly higher rates of anxiety disorders compared to parents of children without autism (Piven et al., 1991). In another study of 36 families with child with autism, 64% had a first-degree relative with major depressive disorder, and 39% had a first-degree relative diagnosed with social phobia (Smalley, McCracken, & Tanguay, 1995). Higher-than-expected frequencies of anxiety or depression in first-degree relatives of persons with autism have been found in other studies (e.g., Abramson et al., 1992; Bolton,

Pickles, Murphy, & Rutter, 1998; Murphy et al., 2000; Piven & Palmer, 1999). The occurrence of these disorders is not unequivocally a consequence of caring for a child with autism (Piven et al., 1991).

These data clearly suggest a link between anxiety and autism, and exploring that link is, in part, the purpose for this volume. Although anecdotal reports and case studies make it clear that not all autistics suffer from anxiety, the fact that a substantial proportion do cannot be ignored. Many of the behavioral symptoms of autism—social withdrawal, repetitive movement, ritualistic or compulsive behavior, and atypical attention and cognitive function—are also symptoms of persons experiencing anxiety. Furthermore, the overlap between autism and anxiety is more than symptomatic, for many of the physiological underpinnings of one are shared by the other.

For most of my professional life, I have studied the long-term physiological and behavioral consequences of stress and anxiety. My subjects have included chimpanzees (Morgan et al., 2002), other primates (Morgan, Line, & Markowitz, 1998), and bears housed in zoos; rhesus monkeys (Line & Morgan, 1991; Line, Morgan, & Markowitz, 1991), guinea pigs, and rats (Morgan, Thayer, & Frye, 1999) maintained in research institutions; and even preschool students and their parents in the local community. In all cases, I have seen similarities between my stressed and anxious subjects and what I read in the literature about persons diagnosed with disorders in the autism spectrum. Animals and humans under stress are socially withdrawn, easy to arouse, and difficult to soothe. They are often hypervigilant, unable to sleep well, or unable to pay attention. They may make poor decisions and show impairment in their working memory. They frequently engage in repetitive and sometimes self-injurious behavior.

The purpose of this chapter is to review the consequences of stress and anxiety for behavior and biology, and to relate those, when appropriate, to behavioral and/or physiological correlates of autism. This review is intended to raise questions about the striking degree of overlap between biological and behavioral features of autism and those of anxiety. I do not promise, however, to provide any answers. Rather, it is my hope to stimulate debate and investigation into the possibility of a shared etiology for both disorders. It is also my hope that by raising these issues, the reader will come to recognize the likelihood of stress and anxiety as either underlying or contributing causes of some of the more problematic symptoms of autism and thus be motivated to make efforts to alleviate that stress whenever possible.

The definition of the word "stress" is part of the problem in any formal discourse on the subject. The term is used so broadly that some (McEwen, 2000a) have argued it is essentially useless. We use the word as a noun to describe a syndrome that appears to result from behavioral and physiological arousal. But we also use it to describe the phenomena that bring about that arousal, as in, "There's too much stress in my life!" The word stress, then, is used to refer to both the cause and consequence of behavioral and physiological arousal—an etymological accident that at first glance appears paradoxical.

But perhaps this is not the case. As we shall see, the kind of physiological arousal that can result from stress can potentiate sensitivity to arousal in the future. In that sense, stress is indeed both cause and consequence. Asking which comes first—the stressor or the stress—is a bit like asking the same question about chickens and eggs. In thinking about stress and the pervasive developmental disorders, this paradox is critical to understand. Do the symptoms of these disorders, such as social withdrawal and repetitive motion, come about as a consequence of an individual's hypersensitivity to stress? Or, do the hypersensitivities that so often characterize autism result in chronic arousal and distress that further potentiates the precipitating hypersensitivity?

What Is Stress?

In 1967, Thomas Holmes and Richard Rahe set out to develop a scale to measure life events that therapists and others could use to evaluate the amount of recent stress in a client's life. To do so, they asked 394 people to rank items in a list of possible life events according to how stressful they considered each life event to be. From the responses obtained, Holmes and Rahe developed the Social Readjustment Rating Scale (see table 6.1). Perhaps not surprisingly, the loss of a loved one through death or divorce was among the life events rated most stressful, and these appear at the top of the Holmes and Rahe scale. Other similarly aversive stressors include personal illness or injury, being fired from one's job, serving time in jail, and substantial debt.

Most of us agree that life events such as these are aversive. However, these were not the only kinds of events ranked by Holmes and Rahe's subjects as stressful. Included in their list were events that we generally celebrate, such as weddings, promotions, or winning the lottery. Thus, life events typically regarded as "positive," as well as those more often regarded as unpleasant, are considered stressful.

Regardless of the differences in emotional state normally associated with each of the situations listed in table 6.1, what they all share in common is a deviation from what is normally experienced—a change from the status quo for which the stressed individual feels unprepared. Stress is experienced when intrinsic or extrinsic demands exceed an individual's resources for responding to those demands (Dantzer, 1991), regardless of the overall emotional tone of the demanding situation. Animals and people often work hard to reduce those demands, as do the organ systems that make up their bodies, by maintaining the status quo with regard to their life circumstances. The tendency of a system to maintain a relatively constant state is referred to as homeostasis, or "same

Table 6.1. The social readjustment rating scale

Life event	Relative arbitrary value (0–100 points)
Death of spouse	100
Divorce	73
Marital separation	65
Jail term	63
Death of a close family member	63
Personal injury of illness	53
Marriage	50
Fired at work	47
Marital reconciliation	45
Retirement	45
Change in health of family member	44
Pregnancy	40
Sex difficulties	39
Gain of a new family member	39
Business readjustments	39
Change in financial status	38
Death of a close friend	37
Change to different line of work	36
Change in number of arguments with spouse	35
Having a large mortgage or loan	31
Foreclosure of mortgage or loan	30
Change in responsibilities at work	29
Child leaving home	29
Trouble with in-laws	29
Outstanding personal achievements	28
Spouse begins or stops work	26
Begin or end school or college	26
Change in living conditions	25
Change in personal habits	24
Trouble with boss	23
Change in working hours or conditions	20
Change of residence	20
Change of school	20
Change in recreation	19
Change in religious activities	19
Change in social activities	18
Having a moderate mortgage or loan	17
Change in sleeping habits	16
Change in number of family get-togethers	15
Change in eating habits	15
Vacation	13
Holidays	13
Christmas	12
Minor violations of the law	11

Reprinted from Holmes & Rahe (1967), with permission from Elsevier.

state." Many authors consider a stressor as anything that challenges or disrupts homeostasis (e.g., Cullinan, Herman, Helmreich, & Watson, 1995; Michelson, Licinio, & Gold, 1995; Selye, 1976). The challenge can be a physical one, such as having to run a marathon or being suddenly plunged into ice-cold water, or it can be purely psychological in nature, such as being called into the boss's office first thing in the morning. In either case, the stressor triggers a cascade of physiological events to prepare the body for meeting the challenge to homeostasis—the "fight-or-flight" response (see fig. 6.1).

Figure 6.1 summarizes one model of this cascade. In, 1936, when Hans Selye first set out to describe this cascade of events, he believed that biological responses to stress were the same, regardless of the nature of the stressor. Today, we understand that there are substantial variations in the nature of the body response, depending on the nature of the stressor, the temperament of the person being stressed, and other environmental factors (Broom & Johnson, 1993; Levine, Coe, & Wiener, 1989; Mason, 1971; Mason et al., 1976; Pacak & Palkovits, 2001; Pacak et al., 1998). In general, however, we can still depend on the pattern of responses that Selye originally described to understand how stress impacts a body. To understand the effects that stress might have on persons with pervasive developmental disorders, one needs to understand this cascade of physiological events that generally occurs each time a given situation or stimulus is perceived as stressful. This chapter describes that cascade, and when possible relates its components to some of the behavioral and physiological phenomena that accompany autism.

In the stress cascade, the first step is perceiving an event or situation as stressful. Stress, like beauty, is very much in the eyes of the beholder. This aphorism may seem trite, but it is essential for understanding the impact of stress on persons with autism. The aphorism reminds us that what is stressful to one person may not be stressful to another. Indeed, a stimulus that is stressful to the same person at a given point in time may be stress relieving at another time. For example, imagine you are driving along a dark, lonely country road, far from any sign of civilization, when your car breaks down. As you sit in your uncooperative car by the side of the road, your heart is pounding at every odd sound or apparent movement in the woods around you. Suddenly, the flashing red and blue lights of a police car coming to your aid appear in your rear-view mirror.

Contrast the feeling you get from seeing those flashing lights in your rear view mirror under this circumstance with the feeling you get when you see those same lights behind you while you are speeding down the highway, late for an important appointment. In each case, the stimulus (i.e., flashing red and blue lights) is the same. But the response to that stimulus is different, depending on whether those lights are perceived as salvation from being stranded or impending punishment in the form of a ticket. What is stressful in any given circumstance depends very much on how the viewer of the situation sees things and on how prepared he or she is to deal with the new set of circumstances.

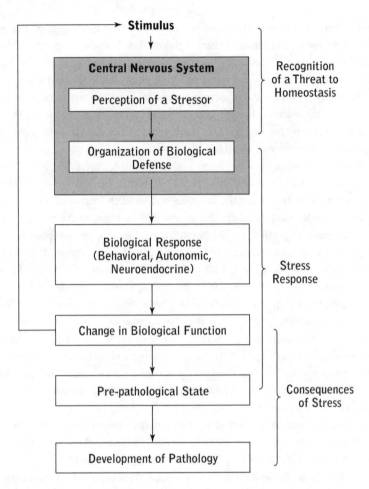

Figure 6.1. A model of response to stressful events (from Broom & Johnson, 1993).

To the degree that autism reduces the resources one has available to cope with challenges to homeostasis, the view of a given potential stressor is likely to be much different for autistic than for nonautistic persons. Imagine that you were suddenly whisked away by a party of aliens. They surround you, gesturing with their bodies and making sounds out of what appears to be a mouth. But you cannot understand any of their gestures or the sounds that they make. As you fail to respond to them, they grow more and more agitated, and the pitch and loudness of their sounds increases until it is quite painful. At the same time, they reach out to touch you. But their touch is accompanied by a feeling not unlike electric shock—it is simply that excruciating. Many persons with high-functioning autism have described experiences just like this arising from interactions with well-meaning family members and friends. One can only imagine how frightening it must be to understand the world so differently. Thus, it behooves us to remember how much stress is a matter of perception when discussing stress and autism.

Once a situation is perceived as stressful, the fight-or-flight response is engaged. To describe that set of body responses, let's consider a circumstance that most of us can agree is stressful. Imagine again that you are driving along an unfamiliar, winding road. As you come around a long turn, you see to your horror that among the vehicles in oncoming traffic is a truck that has pulled out into your lane, in an attempt to pass the car in front of it. The truck in your lane is only a few hundred yards away and coming toward you at high speed. You have little time to react. Just at the last moment, when it seems certain that a collision is inevitable, the car in front of the truck accelerates enough to let the truck back into the correct lane, and the two vehicles go thundering past you—a near miss.

The potential for physical harm that is inherent in an automobile accident typically challenges homeostasis for most people, and the feelings that result from the close brush with injury are typical of an exposure to stress. Your heart races, your palms feel sweaty, your stomach is full of "butterflies" and your breathing is rapid and irregular. You might cry out or tremble. You will probably have to pull over to the side of the road and stop the car for a few minutes until you get yourself under control again. While you sit there trying to calm down, you might bite your lip or wring your hands repetitively. It might be hard for you to stop thinking about the near accident that you just had, no matter how much you need to turn your attention back to the rest of your journey.

What causes these feelings and body responses? Upon determining a given stimulus to be a potential challenge to homeostasis, the body gears up to engage that threat in the only way, evolutionarily speaking, it knows how: it mobilizes the fight-or-flight response.

THE ROLE OF THE AMYGDALA IN THE FIGHT-OR-FLIGHT RESPONSE

Figure 6.2 shows some of the key brain structures involved in the fight-or-flight response, or "stress response." Among these are the hypothalamus, pituitary, amygdala, hippocampus, cingulated gyrus and prefrontal cortices, and hindbrain regions, such as the dorsal raphe nucleus and locus coeruleus (Carrasco & Van de Kar, 2003; Van de Kar & Blair, 1999). (A summary of the role of these structures and their associated neurotransmitters or hormones in the fight-or-flight is shown in table 6.2.)

When you round that turn and see the oncoming truck in your lane, incoming sensory information about the impending collision passes through neural relay stations to the amygdala (Pezzone, Lee, Hoffman, & Rabin, 1992), a part of the brain important for moderating fear and anxiety (Davis, 1992; Davis & Whalen, 2001; Kaline, Shelton, & Davidson, 2004) that also plays an active role in mod-

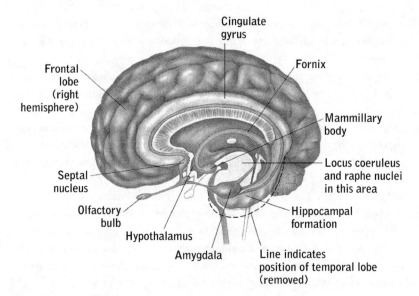

Figure 6.2. Key brain structures involved in the fight-or-flight response (Redrawn from Delcomyn, 1998, with permission of W.H. Freeman).

ulating the stress response (Bhatnagar & Dallman, 1998). For the image of that oncoming truck to stimulate the stress response, the brain needs to interpret it as a threat. The amygdala appears to be an important neural structure in facilitating this interpretation, as illustrated by the results of stimulating or damaging the amygdala.

Stimulating the amygdala in animals produces behavioral reactions associated with intense fear, and humans who have this area of the brain stimulated report intense anxiety and dread (Chapman et al., 1954; Kuhar, 1986). In contrast, lesions in this area of the brain appear to eliminate fear almost completely. For example, mice with lesions in the amygdala willingly approach cats (Carvey, 1998). Monkeys with bilateral lesions in the amygdala and surrounding temporal lobe, including the hippocampus, exhibit a syndrome characterized by excessive and unusual tameness, excessive orality, and hypersexuality (Kluver & Bucy, 1939).

In addition to its role in moderating fear, the amygdala appears to be important in determining the emotional tone of social interactions. Lesions restricted to the amygdala result in monkeys with profound deficits in social behavior. Not unlike persons with autism, these animals fail to initiate social contact and do not respond appropriately to social gestures from others (Kling & Brothers, 1992; Kling, Lancaster, & Bentone, 1970). Lesions to the medial temporal lobe (including the amygdala, parts of the hippocampus, and other limbic system structures) of monkeys cause them to initiate few social contacts and actively withdraw from approaches by other animals. These monkeys are also extremely

Table 6.2. A summary of the brain structures, hormones, and neurotransmitters that play a role in the stress response

Structure or substance	Function in the stress cascade
Amygdala	Part of the limbic system involved in the modulation of anger and fear; also sets the emotional tone for social interactions. Appears to be important in perception of a stimulus as a threat.
Adrenal cortex	Responds to stimulation by the pituitary hormone adrenocorticotropic hormone (ACTH) by releasing cortisol.
Adrenal medulla	Innervated by the hypothalamus via the sympathetic nervous system. Secretes norepinephrine (NE) and epinephrine.
Hippocampus	An area of the brain associated with spatial memory and emotion regulation. When stimulated by cortisol, it serves as one of the primary "brakes" on the stress response. Unfortunately, too much cortisol can kill cells in the hippocampus, effectively removing a major control on arousal and anxiety.
Hypothalamus	Controls pituitary glan. Communicates directly with the sympathetic nervous system via the neurotransmitter norepinephrin (NE) to sitmulate the adrenal medulla. Communicates with pituitary in the stress response via the hormone corticotropin releasing hormone (CRH).
Pituitary	The so-called "master gland." During stress, the pituitary releases adrenocorticotropic hormone (ACTH), prolactin, endorphins, enkephalins, and vasopressin.
Dorsal raphe nuclei	Involved in response inhibition during times of high arousal; uses the neurotransmitter serotonin (5-HT).
Locus coeruleus	Part of the reticular activating system that moderates overall arousal and attention; the brain's vigilance system. Uses the nerotransmitter norepinephrine (NE).
Endorphins	A substance that serves both as a neurotransmitter (when in the nervous system) and a hormone (in the bloodstream). Endorphins are the body's own natural painkillers. They are released by the pituitary in response to stress.
Vasopressin	Arginine vasopressin, also called "antidiuretic hormone," released by the pituitary primarily in response to stress. It helps to regulate body fluid by affecting vasoconstriction and renal function. It has also been implicated in the formation of normal social attachments in some species.
Cortisol	A hormone released by the adrenal cortex in response to its stimulation by ACTH. Mobilizes many of the body's resources in proparation for dealing with a threat (e.g., by keeping glucose circulating in the bloodstream for use by

(continued)

Table 6.2. (continued)

Structure or substance	Function in the stress cascade
Cortisol (continued)	active muscles). Also checks the stress response through its negative feedback effects on the hypothalamus, pituitary, and hippocampus. High levels of cortisol are classic indicators of an organism under stress.
Serotonin	A neurotransmitter that is broadly used in the nervous system. Abnormalities in serotonin function have been implicated in depression, anxiety, violent behavior, and autism.
Corticotropin releasing hormone	A short-lived hormone released by the hypothalamus in response to stress. Its function is to trigger the release of a number of stress-related hormones from the pituitary.
Norepinephrine (NE)	Another substance that serves both as a neurotransmitter (when in the nervous system) and a hormone (in the bloodstream). The adrenal medulla releases NE in response to stress, which results in increased heart rate, blood pressure, and respiration rate.

emotionally labile, throwing temper tantrums more readily than nonlesioned animals, and showing more self-directed stereotypies (Bachevalier, 1994, 1996). Similar emotionality, social withdrawal, easily triggered temper tantrums, and self-injurious repetitive behaviors are also characteristics of many persons with autism. Data from the animal literature suggest that having an intact and healthy amygdala appears to be necessary to react appropriately to other individuals or to dangerous and threatening situations. Could persons with autism have malfunctioning amygdalae?

Abnormalities in the amygdala have been found in some neuroanatomical studies of persons with autism (Aylward et al., 1999; Bauman & Kemper, 1994; Rapin & Katzman, 1998; Schumann et al., 2004; for a recent review, see Sweeten, Posey, Shekhar, & McDougle, 2002). Some of these abnormalities are similar to those produced by chronic stress, which has been found to alter the structure of the rodent amygdala and to increase behavioral indicators of anxiety in rats (Vyas, Mitra, & Chattarji, 2003). Sustained stress has also been found to enhance the amygdala's response to subsequent stress (Yaniv, Vouimba, Diamond, & Richter-Levin, 2003). These findings suggest that at least some kinds of amygdala damage can result in exaggerated fearfulness and anxiety, a condition which itself can sensitize the amygdala to future stress. Might some of the ease with which fear and startle can be triggered in some people with autism reflect an increased sensitivity to stress that is moderated, in part, by damage to the amygdala?

The degree to which amygdala abnormalities associated with autism reflect stress-related damage, as well as the impact of additional stress on persons with such damage, remain to be discovered. Once again, our "chicken or egg" question arises. From the standpoint of the practitioner dealing with a client, it may not matter which comes first. Whether amygdala abnormalities associated with autism result from the etiology of the disorder itself, or from subsequent stress derived from having the disorder, the net effect is the same. If the amygdala is abnormal in persons with autism, then that abnormality may contribute to their often exaggerated and abnormal fears and anxieties (Amaral, Bauman, & Schumann, 2003). Similarly, if a properly working amygdala is necessary for appropriate social engagement and appropriately modulated fear responses, and if stress interferes with the ability of the amygdala to work effectively, then it behooves practitioners dealing with clients with autism to evaluate the level of stress their clients might be experiencing and make significant efforts to reduce it.

LOCUS COERULEUS, RAPHE NUCLEI, NOREPINEPHRINE, AND SEROTONIN

Another set of neural players in the fight-or-flight response are the locus coeruleus and the raphe nuclei. The amygdala exchanges messages with both the raphe nuclei and the locus coeruleus (Carrasco & Van de Kar, 2003), regions of the brainstem that are part of the reticular activating system (RAS) and involved in attention and arousal. The locus coeruleus appears to be key in allowing us to rapidly switch our attention from generalities to the crisis immediately unfolding. In our near-accident scenario, it is critical for survival that you stop thinking about the itch on your arm, what you just had for dinner, or the appointments that you have slated for tomorrow. Instead, the situation calls for a single-minded focus on the life-threatening truck that is barreling toward you. The locus coeruleus acts as part of the brain's "vigilance" system. When stimulated by the amygdala or other incoming sensory stimuli that suggest a threat, it filters out distracting or irrelevant stimuli and allows selective orientation to the potential threat (Aston-Jones, Rajkowski, & Cohen, 1999, 2000). Focusing attention on a single fear-provoking stimulus is a hallmark of highly stressful situations, with increased arousal leading to a narrowing of attention (Easterbrook, 1959). For example, abused children have been shown to overly attend to facial expressions of anger, even when those expressions are inaccurate predictors of future events (Pollak & Tolley-Schell, 2003). Similarly, testimony regarding violent crimes is often compromised by the fear and arousal that cause witnesses to focus on weapons (Kramer, Buckout, & Eugenio, 1990; Steblay, 1992). Under stress, all attention is directed toward detecting and responding to the potential threat, to the detriment of other behavioral options.

The overfocus of attention that stress produces in fear-provoking situations is also seen in persons with autism (Casey, Gordon, Mannheim, & Rumsey, 1993; Courchesne et al., 1994; Rincover & Ducharme, 1987; Saulnier, 2003;

Wainwright-Sharp & Bryson, 1993). Even siblings of children with autism show deficits in attentional shift compared to siblings of children without autism (Hughes, Plumet, & Leboyer, 1999), suggesting a genetically mediated difference in these children regarding how attention is directed and modulated. This difference could lie in the performance of the locus coeruleus. Indeed, one of the earliest theories regarding the etiology of autism was that it derived from a dysfunction of the RAS, which includes the locus coeruleus (Rimland, 1964).

The chemical messenger that the locus coeruleus uses to direct attention is norepinephrine (formerly known as noradrenaline). The locus coeruleus is one of the brain's major suppliers of norepinephrine, particularly to areas of the decision-making forebrain (Foote, Bloom, & Aston-Jones, 1983; Sawchenko & Swanson, 1982; Ungerstedt, 1971). Norepinephrine is a chemical messenger that appears to act as a kind of general alarm signal (Carrasco & Van de Kar, 2003), and it plays an important role in the stress response. Stress such as that of the oncoming truck activates norepinephrine-containing neurons in the locus coeruleus (Abercrombie & Jacobs, 1987; Redmond, 1987), as do drugs that mimic the effects of stress (Redmond, Huang, Snyder, & Maas, 1976). Chronic stress has been shown to increase sensitivity of the locus coeruleus to additional stress (Jedema, Findlay, Sved, & Grace, 2001; Jedema & Grace, 2003). The sleep disturbances, hypervigilance, and increased sensitivity to startle that often result from chronic stress are thought to be a consequence of stress increasing the sensitivity of the locus coeruleus (Aston-Jones, Rajkowski, & Cohen, 1999). Could the sleep disturbances, hypervigilance, and hypersensitivity to sensory stimuli that accompany autism be the result of a sensitized locus coeruleus?

Several studies have suggested that noradrenergic neurotransmitter systems are indeed different in persons with autism than in persons without autism (Martineau et al., 1994; Taylor, 1993; Trottier, Srivastava, & Walker, 1999), and drug therapies that affect norepinephrine have been used successfully to treat some of the agitation, aggressivity, and impulsivity associated with autism (Craven-Thuss & Nicolson, 2003; Volkmar, 2001). If, as part of attention-moderating systems in general, the locus coeruleus of persons with autism is dysfunctional, then that dysfunction may render such persons unable to easily divert their attention from novel stimuli or other input that might be perceived as threatening. Hypervigilance itself is stressful, and stress sensitizes the locus coeruleus to incoming stimuli. Once again, regardless of which comes first—stress or biological phenomena that result in increased sensitivity to stress—the net result is the same: A person with selective attention for novel or potentially threatening stimuli whose very intensive attention to those stimuli exacerbates his or her attentional focus.

But the locus coeruleus is not alone in directing attention to threatening stimuli. The raphe nuclei also receive input about the oncoming truck from the amygdala. In comparison to the locus coeruleus, the raphe nuclei are a primary source for neurons using serotonin (5-hydroxytryptamine; 5-HT) as their chemical messenger, and neurons from these brain areas also project to many different parts of the forebrain (Azmitia & Segal, 1978; Stamford, Davidson, McLaughlin, & Hopwood, 2000). Serotonin is one of the most studied and least understood of the neurotransmitters. It appears as a chemical messenger early in neural development (Lauder, 1993), suggesting that it plays an important role in organizing the developing nervous system. (Whitaker-Azmitia, Druse, Walker, & Lauder, 1996). Indeed, treatments that reduce prenatal 5-HT levels in the developing nervous system delay neural growth in many brain regions (Lauder & Krebs, 1976) and alter the ability of receptors for 5-HT to bind to this chemical messenger (Whitaker-Azmitia, Lauder, Shemmer, & Azmitia, 1987). Stress or its consequences experienced by the developing fetus are among the treatments that can alter 5-HT levels in fetal brains (Peters, 1990), and thus prenatal stress may also alter normal development of the nervous system. This is another of the intersections between stress and autism, as disruption of neural development is one of the postulated causes of the autistic phenotype (Courchesne, 1997).

Like the locus coeruleus, the raphe nuclei containing 5-HT are also involved in attention and arousal, especially response inhibition during arousal. It is this part of the brain that focuses our attention and spurs us to immediate action.

However, the involvement of the raphe nuclei in attention and arousal is more complicated. The effects of the raphe nuclei on behavior depend on which nuclei are active. The dorsal raphe nuclei appear to play a role in sleep and wakefulness. Stimulating the dorsal raphe nuclei induces sleep in many animals, whereas lesions in this area result in chronic arousal and insomnia (Kelly, 1991). Disorders of sleep are common in persons suffering from anxiety disorders (Singareddy & Balon, 2002), as well as in persons with autism (Richdale, 1999). Might the sleep disturbances in both of these conditions result from disruptions in the dorsal raphe nuclei, exacerbated by stress?

Stimulation of the median raphe nuclei produces freezing behavior (Graeff & Silveira, 1978), which is common in animals that are extremely anxious or fearful. These mixed results complement similar findings on the effects of 5-HT on stress and anxiety, as we'll see in a moment. The raphe nuclei and their primary neurotransmitter, 5-HT, appear both to modulate the stress response and to be modulated by it (De Kloet, 1991; De Kloet, Korte, Rots, & Kruk, 1996; Maes, Meltzer, D'Hondt, Cosyns, & Blockx, 1995). For example, treatments that increase 5-HT under some conditions actually activate the stress response (Bagdy, Calogero, Murphy, & Szemeredi, 1989), while in other conditions such treatments suppress the response and reduce feelings of anxiety (Zangrossi et al., 2001). Current thinking is that altering 5-HT levels in the brain makes a person feel more or less stressed depending on the kind of neurotransmitter receptor that is affected by the alteration and how that receptor is affected.

The diversity of receptors for 5-HT makes a more detailed study of this topic problematic. At least seven different chemical families of 5-HT receptor have been identified (Hoyer, Hannon, & Martin, 2002; Hoyer et al., 1994), and drugs that stimulate different 5-HT receptors have different effects (Dinan, 1996). Drugs that stimulate $5\text{-HT}_{2A/2C}$ receptors, for example, increase the release of stress hormones (Levy, Baumann, & Van de Kar, 1994), as do drugs that block 5-HT_{1A} receptors (Serres et al., 2000; Van de Kar, 1997). Paradoxically, drug treatments that block 5-HT_{1A} receptors are commonly administered to persons with depression or anxiety disorders, where in some cases, but not all (e.g., Healy, 2003), they are associated with reductions in feelings of anxiety and despair (Nickel et al., 2003). Determining why drugs affecting 5-HT help some persons with debilitating anxiety and depression and hurt others has been keeping researchers very busy for the past several decades.

One recent development that may prove enlightening is the finding that some people with anxiety disorders have forms of the gene for 5-HT receptors that differ from those genes in nonanxious people. Variations in the form of the gene that codes for the serotonin transporter receptor in the 5-HT_{1A} family of 5-HT receptors have been associated with anxiety disorder in some individuals (Belliver, Roy, & Leboyer, 2002; Katsuragi et al., 1999; Osher, Hamer, & Benjamin, 2000). Polymorphisms, or different forms, of the 5-HT promoter gene have also been correlated with parent and teacher reports of shyness in grade-school children (Arbelle et al., 2003), suggesting a relationship between 5-HT and social behavior. Abnormalities in 5-HT systems have also recently been proposed as an underlying cause of the autistic phenotype (Chugani, 2002; Cook & Leventhal, 1996). Whole-blood serotonin levels are higher in persons with autism than in control populations (Anderson et al., 1987; Launay et al., 1988; Schain & Freedman, 1961) and in the near relatives of children with autism (Leboyer et al., 1999), suggesting abnormalities in 5-HT receptor binding in autism. In one study, higher 5-HT levels were correlated with higher levels of plasma norepinephrine, suggesting a chronic stress response in these persons (Cook et al., 1990).

Recently, genetic studies of populations with autism have revealed abnormalities in the genes that code for 5-HT receptors, particularly those involved in 5-HT reuptake (Anderson et al., 2002; Cook et al., 1997; Yirmiya et al., 2001). These data suggest some possible overlap in genetic markers for autism, anxiety, and depression. The evidence is not unequivocal, however (e.g., Persico et al., 2002), and this may be due to our as-yet limited understanding of the many functions of 5-HT in the nervous system. Although the mechanisms underlying the complexity of 5-HT's effects in autism or on stress are unclear, it is apparent that this chemical messenger plays a major role in influencing the overall tone of the stress response (Carrasco & Van de Kar, 2003; Fuller, 1992). If abnormalities in 5-HT contribute to heightened arousal and stress, then it is likely that persons with these abnormalities may be chronically anxious.

Hypothalamus and Limbic System

At the moment your brain determines an impending threat to life and limb, it sends some emotionally charged messages along with those sensory inputs to the amygdala. As already mentioned, the amygdala exchanges messages with the raphe nuclei, which uses 5-HT, and locus coeruleus, which uses norepinephrine. It also exchanges messages with the hypothalamus, an organ at the base of the brain that acts as the link between the nervous system and the endocrine system. The hypothalamus releases hormones and thus acts as part of the endocrine system, but it also uses neurotransmitters and communicates with other parts of the brain as part of the nervous system. In response to a perceived stressor, the hypothalamus responds both as part of the nervous system and endocrine system.

Both hormones and neurotransmitters are chemical messengers. The primary difference between them is the pathway they travel through the body. Hormones travel via the bloodstream, and neurotransmitters, as their name implies, travel via the nervous system. The same substance, therefore, can act as a hormone and as a neurotransmitter, depending on how it travels. (This is true for norepinephrine, for example.) Unlike hormones, neurotransmitters can communicate directly with their targets. Thus, the system that uses neurotransmitters as its chemical messengers is faster, and this is why the nervous system response of the hypothalamus is the fastest part of the stress response. Like the locus coeruleus, neural projections from the hypothalamus use the norepinephrine to send activational messages along sympathetic nervous system (SNS) fibers. The SNS is a part of the autonomic nervous system responsible for general arousal. It is the SNS that goes into high gear when you are watching horror movies or screaming in terror on the first drop of a roller coaster ride. The response of the SNS to stimulation from the hypothalamus is very rapid, and the degree of response is correlated with the degree of stress. The SNS innervates a number of different target organs, including many endocrine organs (see fig. 6.3), such as the sweat and salivary glands. The results of SNS communication with these organs is what gives you the sweaty palms and dry mouth you're experiencing after the near-accident described previously.

Another set of endocrine organs targeted by the SNS is the adrenals. It is the interior of an adrenal gland, the adrenal medulla, with which the SNS communicates directly. The stress-activated pathway from the SNS to the adrenal medulla is the sympathetic-adrenal-medullary pathway (SAM). When stimulated by the SNS in response to a stressor such as the oncoming truck in our example, the adrenal medulla secretes norepinephrine and epinephrine (also known as adrenaline) into the bloodstream. Note that in this case, norepinephrine is acting as a hormone rather than as a neurotransmitter. In general, norepinephrine and epinephrine have an excitatory effect on the body. They prepare the body for a physical engagement with the threat by increasing heart rate, increasing blood

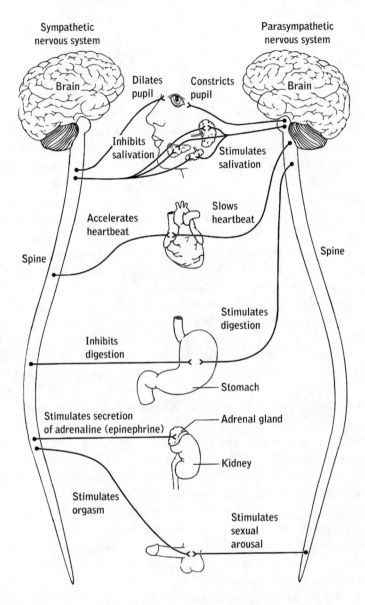

Figure 6.3. The sympathetic and parasympathetic divisions of the autonomic nervous system, and some of their effects (adapted from Sapolsky, 1998).

pressure, and delivering glucose to the brain and to skeletal muscles. It is the action of SAM in response to the near collision that is responsible for the rapid breathing, pounding heart, shakes, chills, and clammy skin that accompany a close call with danger.

Simultaneous with its actions in stimulating the SAM component of the stress response, the hypothalamus also acts as part of the endocrine system. Specifically, the hypothalamus releases a hormone called corticotropin-releasing hormone (CRH) into the short stretch of the circulatory system that connects it with the anterior pituitary. The anterior pituitary, when stimulated by CRH, releases prolactin, endorphins, and enkephalins, substances that blunt pain perception (Guillemin, Vargo, & Rossier, 1977), and vasopressin, a hormone involved in the maintenance of fluid levels in the body and also implicated in the formation of social attachments in some species (Carrasco & Van de Kar, 2003). In response to CRH, the anterior pituitary also secretes adrenocorticotropic hormone (ACTH), which triggers the activity of several others as part of the stress response.

Abnormalities in CRH and ACTH release are associated with the anxiety that accompanies major depression (Claes, 2004; Varghese & Brown, 2001; Young, Abelson, & Cameron, 2004) and with post-traumatic stress disorder (Goenjian et al., 2003; Rasmussen et al., 2001; Yehuda, Collier, Halligan, Meaney, & Bierer, 2004). Abnormalities in these hormones have also been found in victims of severe childhood abuse (Heim et al., 2002), who often suffer from excessive anxiety. Similarly, abnormalities in endorphin and vasopressin release have been found in persons with post-traumatic stress disorder (Baker et al., 1997; Newport et al., 2003). These findings suggest that severe or chronic stress leading to sustained anxiety has detrimental effects on the normal functioning of hypothalamic and pituitary responses to stress. Similar abnormalities in levels of beta-endorphin and ACTH have been found in some persons with autism (Curin et al., 2003; Gingell, Parmar, & SungumPaliwal, 1996; Tordjman et al., 1997). Might these abnormalities reflect a chronic state of stress in persons with autism?

Once released by the pituitary, ACTH travels through the bloodstream until it reaches the outer layer of the adrenal glands, the adrenal cortex. The pathway from the hypothalamus to the pituitary to the adrenal cortex is often referred to as the hypothalamic-pituitary-adrenal (HPA) component of the stress response. Upon stimulation by ACTH, the adrenal cortex releases a number of glucocorticoids (GC), substances so-called because of their role in glucose metabolism. Chief among these is cortisol. Elevation of cortisol in response to stress is so ubiquitous that an increase in cortisol levels is commonly used as an operational definition of stress. Cortisol increases in students taking exams (Ng, Koh, & Chia, 2003), in astronauts on long space missions (Stowe, Sams, & Pierson, 2003), in novice skydivers during their first jump (Chatterton, Vogelsong, Lu, & Hudgens, 1997), and in chimps (Muller & Wrangham, 2004) and baboons (Sapolsky, 1992) involved in social conflict. Cortisol is commonly elevated in persons with anxiety disorders and major depression (Sapolsky, 2000) and has also been found to be elevated in some children with autism (Richdale & Prior, 1992).

One role of cortisol is to assist with mobilizing the body's defenses for the potential threat. For example, cortisol helps keep glucose circulating in the bloodstream, so there is plenty of energy for muscles. Cortisol and other GCs help suppress functions such as growth and reproduction that are not needed while dealing with imminent threat. GCs also stimulate some aspects of the immune system while keeping others in check, thus helping protect the body from the effects of inflammation and aiding in the prevention of autoimmune disorders (Munck, Guyre, & Holbrook, 1984; Sapolsky, 2000).

However, another of cortisol's primary effects is to gradually stop the entire arousal episode. Thus, although cortisol is part of the emergency fight-or-flight response, helping to mobilize the body for dealing with a real or perceived challenge to homeostasis, it is also part of the process that ultimately returns the body to its resting, prearousal state (De Kloet, 1991). How does it do this?

One of the primary ways the body maintains homeostasis is through the use of negative feedback systems. A negative feedback system works like the thermostat system in a house. When you set the temperature on the thermostat, you are establishing the "set point" for thermal homeostasis in your house. As the temperature inside the house falls, circuits within the thermostat monitor the temperature change, and when it drops below your established limit, the heater comes on. Those same circuits in the house also monitor how high the temperature rises. Once ambient air temperatures are back to the thermostat setting, the system shuts itself off. In other words, the heating that was triggered initially by a fall in temperature is ultimately the very thing that shuts off the entire response.

The same thing happens in the body. A real or perceived threat to homeostasis—what we call a "stressor"—triggers a cascade of physiological events that results in increased levels of cortisol in the bloodstream. As the body's response to the stressor continues, plasma cortisol levels rise. Cells in the hypothalamus that monitor the bloodstream detect elevations of cortisol and other stress-related hormones, such as norepinephrine, and respond by decreasing secretion of CRH, and begin to put the brakes on the entire cascade. Similarly, cells in the pituitary respond to increased blood levels of cortisol by decreasing secretion of that cortisol-triggering substance, ACTH (De Kloet, 1995).

Finally, circulating cortisol affects another brain structure, the hippocampus, which responds by augmenting the braking effect that cortisol has on hypothalamic secretion of CRH. The hippocampus is a limbic system structure involved in spatial learning and memory. It receives input from several of the brain areas already mentioned, such as the raphe nuclei and the locus coeruleus. Similar to the amygdala, the hippocampus is also involved in emotion regulation. In the case of the extreme arousal we feel after the near-accident with the truck, the hippocampus is undoubtedly one of the most important "brakes" on that arousal (Feldman & Conforti, 1980; Herman, Cullinan, Morano, Akil, & Watson, 1995; Jacobson & Sapolsky, 1991; Sapolsky & Plotsky, 1990; Sapolsky, Krey, & McEwen, 1984a).

In small doses such as those released during exposure to acute stressors of moderate intensities, GCs such as cortisol are helpful. Glucocorticoids help the body replenish energy reserves after an immediate demanding situation, such as running away from a threat (McEwen & Wingfield, 2003). They also enhance memory formation, particularly for aversive events or stimuli that might signal danger in the future (Beylin & Shors, 2003; Sandi & Rose, 1994).

But under situations of severe acute stress or chronic stress, the story is different. Sustained exposure to cortisol has well-documented deleterious effects on the nervous system, which may result in altered behavioral and physiological responses to stress throughout one's lifetime. It really is true that stress is bad for you. For example, exposure to too much stress, and therefore too much cortisol, has been shown to inhibit metabolism in the brain (Horner, Packan, & Sapolsky, 1990; Kadekaro, Ito, & Gross, 1988) and to reduce the density of GC receptors in the hippocampus (Barbazanges, Piazza, LeMoal, & Maccari, 1996; Henry, Kabbaj, Simon, Le Moal, & Maccari, 1994; Sapolsky, Krey, & McEwen, 1984b; Sapolsky & McEwen, 1985; Tornello, Orti, DeNicola, Rainbow, & McEwen, 1982). Stress can also induce atrophy in the processes of hippocampal neurons, another way of applying the neural brake and making the fight-or-flight response less sensitive to incoming stimulation (Magarinos, McEwen, Flugge, & Fuchs, 1996; Magarinos, Verdugo, & McEwen, 1997; McEwen, 1994; Sapolsky, 1996; Vyas, Mitra, Rao, & Chattarji, 2002; Watanabe, Gould, & McEwen, 1992; Woolley, Gould, & McEwen, 1990). The hippocampus is among the few brain areas that continue to produce new neurons even in adulthood (Cameron & Gould, 1994; Gould, Beylin, Tanapat, Reeves, & Shors, 1999), a finding that has stimulated new research on the impact of aging on the brain. However, GCs have been found to inhibit the development of new neurons, or "neurogenesis," in the hippocampus (Duman, Malberg, & Nakagawa, 2001; Gould, Tanapat, McEwen, Flugge, & Fuchs, 1998), making damage to this area of the brain difficult, if not impossible, for the body to repair. Finally, in some circumstances, GCs have been found to cause outright cell death in the hippocampus (Arbel, Kadar, Silbermann, & Levey, 1994; Sapolsky, 1987, 1999; Sapolsky, Krey, & McEwen, 1985; Sapolsky, Uno, Rebert, & Finch, 1990; Uno, Tarara, Else, Suleman, & Sapolsky, 1989; Uno et al., 1990; Wolf, Convit, de Leon, Caraos, & Qadri, 2002). In short, cortisol in high or sustained doses is a neurotoxin. It can cause irreparable damage to the brain.

Remember that the hippocampus is one of the most important brakes on the fight-or-flight response, helping control the level of arousal and regulate emotions when we are under stress. It is also an important structure for memory and the formation of new learning. When prolonged or excessive exposure to cortisol damages this brain area, the result is the effective removal of one of the primary mechanisms for negative feedback on the stress cascade. What was once a nicely working negative feedback loop that allowed the body to return to homeostasis now becomes a feed-forward loop. The sustained increase in cortisol kills brain cells that ordinarily would help stop the secretion of cortisol. Less "brake" on the stress response system means more "fuel" to that system, so instead of a quick and effective return to baseline, the stress cascade continues unabated. The net result is an individual with a severely diminished ability to control his or her emotional lability. Such a person will be especially sensitive to stress—easily perturbed, unable to control arousal to challenging events or situations, and slow to calm down after becoming aroused. The individual is also likely to suffer from difficulties with concentration, learning, and memory (Bodnoff et al., 1995; Diamond, Fleshner, Ingersoll, & Rose, 1996; Kerr, Huggett, & Abraham, 1994; McEwen, 2000b; McEwen & Sapolsky, 1995). Indeed, disorders that are associated with hypersecretion of cortisol, such as Cushing's syndrome, post-traumatic stress disorder, Alzheimer's, and major depression, are also often characterized by increased irritability, anxiety, and memory deficits. Persons suffering from Cushing's syndrome, for example, frequently suffer from anxiety and depression (Loosen, Chamblis, Debold, Shelton, & Orth, 1992; Sonino & Fava, 2001), as one might expect if the body interprets high levels of GC as an indicator of a threat to homeostasis. Cushing's syndrome patients have reduced hippocampal volumes (Starkman, Gebarski, Berent, & Schteingart, 1992), as do animals exposed experimentally to high doses of GCs or to stress; so do some persons with autism (Aylward et al., 1999; Saitoh, Karns, & Courchesne, 2001). Cushing's syndrome patients show impaired performance in cognition and memory tasks (Forget, Lacroix, Somma, & Cohen, 2000; Mauri et al., 1993), which is positively correlated with levels of circulating cortisol (Starkman, Giordani, Berent, Schork, & Schteingart, 2001). Considering that exposure to high levels of GCs has been shown to damage the hippocampus, an area of the brain important not only in emotion regulation, but also in learning and memory, these effects of Cushing's syndrome are not surprising.

At least some neuroanatomical studies of persons with autism have found structural abnormalities in the hippocampus (Aylward et al., 1999; Bauman & Kemper, 1994; Raymond, Bauman, & Kemper, 1996; Saitoh et al., 2001; Sparks et al., 2002). Persons with autism show memory impairments (Bennetto, Pennington, & Rogers, 1996; Minshew & Goldstein, 2001; Russell, Jarrold, & Henry, 2002; Shalom, 2003), at least some of which are consistent with that seen in individuals with hippocampal abnormalities. The emotional dysregulation that characterizes those with hippocampal damage is one of the hallmarks of autism.

All these studies support the idea that stress and/or its concomitant physiological consequences can have profound and long-lasting deleterious effects on the brain and, consequently, on behavior, in ways that are strikingly similar to neuroanatomical and behavioral correlates of autism. Taken together, these studies show us that there are many ways to generate the kind of internal milieu that results in impairment of the nervous system's ability to self-regulate arousal. Among the consequences of that difficulty in emotion regulation are an increased sensitivity to disturbance, rapid and excessive arousal in response to such disturbance, a dramatically increased latency to soothe, and impaired memory and concentration. Behaviors such as these should be familiar to caretakers of children with pervasive developmental disorders, which beg the question, How many of the symptoms of autism are actually symptoms of stress? Alternatively, we might expect stress that results in chronic GC release to exacerbate characteristics of autism such as those previously described.

BEHAVIORAL RESPONSES TO STRESS AND ANXIETY

So far, this chapter has focused on neurological and physiological correlates of stress and anxiety and their similarities to biological correlates in autism. For the remainder of this chapter, I focus on two of the more common behavioral correlates of stress that are also observed in persons with autism, stereotypies, and self-injurious behavior (SIB).

Stereotypies are repetitive behaviors that are fixed in form and appear to serve no obvious function (Lawrence & Rushen, 1993; Mason, 1991; Mason & Turner, 1993). Such behaviors were among the first characteristics of autism to be described (Kanner, 1943) and are extremely common (Bodfish, Symons, Parker, & Lewis, 2000; Turner, 1999), so much so that they are among the defining characteristics of autism in the *Diagnostic and Statistical Manual of Mental Disorders*, fourth edition (American Psychiatric Association, 1994). Typical stereotypies in autism include repetitive manipulation of objects, hand-flapping, body-rocking, eye-poking, SIBs, and bizarre postures. The functions of stereotypies in persons with pervasive developmental disorders are much debated (e.g., Kennedy, Meyer, Knowles, & Shukla, 2000; Lewis & Bodfish, 1998), as are the functions of stereotypic behaviors in animals (see Lawrence & Rushen, 1993; Mason, 1991, for reviews). But a few studies suggest that stereotypies in persons with autism occur more frequently in situations that might be stressful (Hutt & Hutt, 1968, 1970; Militerni, Bravaccio, Falco, Fico, & Palermo, 2002), and are adaptations to assist the stereotyping individual in dealing with stress and arousal (Berkson, 2002).

Stereotypies also occur in populations without autism (Castellanos, Ritchie, Marsh, & Rapoport, 1996; Rafaeli-Mor, Foster, & Berkson, 1999; Soussignan & Koch, 1985; Tröster, 1994; Willemsen-Swinkels, Buitelaar, Dekker, & van Engeland, 1998), and in animals (Mason, 1991). They can be induced not only in humans and animals by drugs that stimulate arousal, such as amphetamines (e.g., Castner & Goldman-Rakic, 1999; Dickson, Lang, Hinton, & Kelley, 1994; Terlouw, de Rosa, Lawrence, Illius, & Ladewig, 1992), but also arise spontaneously in many captive animals. Among those who study animals, stereotypic or repetitive behavior is considered an indicator of stress (Broom & Johnson, 1993; Dawkins, 1990; Fraser & Broom, 1990; Lawrence & Rushen, 1993; Wiepkema, Broom, Duncan, & van Putten, 1983), as such behavior often occurs in environments that we might anthropomorphically consider boring or uncomfortable, and others in which the potential for anxiety is high (Hediger, 1964, 1992; Kiley-Worthington, 1977; Mason, 1991; Meyer-Holzapfel, 1968). In fact, stereotypic behavior is the most common problem that I am called upon to address in the work I have done consulting for zoos and animal laboratories (Morgan et al., 1998).

Debates about the function of repetitive behaviors in animals are just as intense as are debates about the functions of similar behaviors in humans. Some authors have proposed explicitly that stereotypies help animals cope with stress (Broom, 1991; Cooper & Nicol, 1991) or that such behaviors help animals to reduce arousal in the kind of aversive situations that often arise in captivity (Wood-Gush, Stolba, & Miller, 1983).

If such theories have any validity, then stereotypies should be associated with changes in physiology that reflect reduced arousal. Efforts to test this theory have had mixed results (Ladewig et al., 1993), and the available data are by no means unequivocal. However, a few investigations clearly support a coping hypothesis for the function of stereotypies. For example, heart rate (HR) is reduced during stereotypic leg-swinging in school children (Soussignan & Koch, 1985), during crib-biting in horses (Lebelt, Zanella, & Unshelm, 1998; Minero, Ödberg, Ferrante, & Canali, 1996), and during stereotypic behavior in pigs (Schouten & Wiegant, 1997). High-stereotyping sows also had lower mean HR after feeding (when stereotyping was most pronounced) compared to low stereotypers (Schouten & Wiepkema, 1991). It has also been found that HR decreases just before the onset of stereotypic behaviors in tethered pigs and increases once the animal switches back to nonstereotyped behavior (Wiegant et al., 1994). Considering that HR during stress is largely under the control of the SAM pathway, these results suggest that some stereotypies help reduce the SAM component of the stress response.

Stereotypies have also been found to lower HPA components of stress. In a study of stereotypy induced in rats by repeated administration of amphetamine, for example, performance of the stereotypies reduced plasma levels of corticosterone, usually elevated by amphetamine administration (Mittleman, Jones, & Robbins, 1991). Stereotyped shredding of cardboard and other materials by mice in a novel cage reduced the corticosterone response of these animals (Hennessy & Fox, 1987). Stereotypying chickens (Kostal, Savory, & Hughes, 1992), cattle (Redbo, 1998), pigs (Pol et al., 2002), and mink (Bildsoe, Heller, & Jeppesen, 1991) have lower baseline cortisol levels than do nonstereotyping conspecifics, suggesting that stereotypy helps animals cope better with the captive environment. Some research suggests that blocking the ability to perform a stereotyped behavior is stressful. For example, pigs were trained to chew on a chain in one study as a means of reducing frustration while waiting for a food reward in a delayed reward task. When the chain was removed so that the stereotypic chewing could not take place, plasma cortisol was elevated (Dantzer & Mormède, 1983). Similarly, blocking stereotyped jumping in captive voles increased their plasma corticosterone levels (Kennes & De Rycke, 1988). Blocking drug-induced stereotypies also increases HPA activity (Jones, Mittleman, & Robbins, 1989).

Some data from populations without autism suggest that stereotypies are a means of self-soothing in aversive situations. For example, a few studies show changes in plasma endorphin levels associated with stereotypies, suggesting that these behaviors are a kind of self-medication for distress. Plasma endorphin levels are higher in crib-biting horses (Lebelt, Zanella, & Unshelm, 1998; Mc-Greevy & Nicol, 1998). Administering an endorphin agonist such as morphine can induce stereotypic behavior (Pollock & Kornetsky, 1989), and blockade of endorphins with naloxone reduces stereotypic behavior in pigs (Cronin, Wiepkema, & van Ree, 1985), horses (Dodman, Shuster, Court, & Dixon, 1987), chickens (Savory, Seawright, & Watson, 1992), voles (Kennes, Ödberg, Bouquet, & De Rycke, 1988), and in some cases, persons with autism (Chabane, Leboyer, & Mouren-Simeoni, 2000).

The role of endorphins in stereotypic behavior is thought to change over time because the ability of naloxone to block such behaviors diminishes as the behaviors become more entrenched in the animal's repertoire (Cronin et al., 1985; Kennes et al., 1988). Cronin et al. and Kennes et al. suggest that although stereotypies may start out as stress-reducing habits that reward the body with endogenous opioids, over time these behaviors come under the control of a different neurological system, one more resistant to behavioral or pharmacological intervention.

Rather than helping cope with stress, it has also been proposed that stereotypies reflect stress in the form of conflict between competing motivations (Forrester, 1980; Ödberg, 1987; Wiepkema, 1985), such as the competing motivations of approach and avoidance. For example, chaffinches whose cage is placed near a stuffed owl show an increased amount of stereotypic preening, presumably reflecting the conflicting motivations of wanting to flee from the predator and wanting to approach and mob it (Rowell, 1961). Seemingly inappropriate behaviors that occur in such conflict situations are called "displacement" behaviors because it is assumed that they are performed instead of alternative but conflicting behavioral choices.

Displacement behaviors often resemble stereotypies in their form and apparent lack of function (Rushen, Lawrence, & Terlouw, 1993). Grooming and other self-directed behaviors are common displacement behaviors presumed to indicate that animals are stressed and anxious (Troisi et al., 1991), and reductions in self-directed behaviors are considered indicators of improved well-being (Clarke, Juno, & Maple, 1982; Lukas, Hoff, & Maple, 2003) because animals perform these behaviors at elevated rates when in stressful situations. For instance, rhesus monkey mothers show higher rates of self-grooming when their young infants move away from them, or when the mother—infant pair is approached by another monkey who routinely harasses the pair (Maestripieri, 1993). Similarly, baboon mothers show higher than normal rates of self-grooming after the birth of an infant, interpreted as an indicator of postpartum stress by researchers (Brent, Koban, & Raminez, 2002). Higher-ranking baboon males show higher rates of self-grooming, particularly in situations of high social tension (Easley, Coelho, & Taylor, 1987). The same is true for female baboons (Castles, Whitens, & Aureli, 1999). Both victims and initiators of aggression in groups of wild olive baboons (Castles & Whitens, 1998), barbary, and long-tailed macaques (Aureli, 1997) exhibit elevated rates of self-grooming after a fight. Rates of self-grooming also increase as the number of individuals in a captive group of chimps increases (Aureli & De Waal, 1997), suggesting increased social stress in crowded conditions. Even among nonautistic humans, social stressors increase rates of self-directed behaviors. For example, depressed and anxious outpatients who had difficulty describing their emotional states also showed higher frequencies of self-directed stereotypies (such as self-touching, scratching, and self-grooming) during interviews with helping professionals than did similar outpatients without such difficulties (Troisi et al., 2000).

Social stressors are not the only stimuli that can increase rates of self-grooming stereotypies. Cognitive challenge in the form of increasingly difficult discrimination tasks increases self-directed behaviors in chimpanzees (Leavens, Aureli, Hopkins, & Hyatt, 2001). Physical restraint stress induces body-shaking, a kind of self-grooming behavior, in dogs (Beerda, Schilder, van Hooff, deVries, & Mol, 1998), and disruption of feeding routines and schedules increases rates of self-directed behaviors in captive stump-tailed macaques (Waitt & Buchanan-Smith, 2001). Self-grooming stereotypies can also be reduced by anxiety-reducing drugs called anxiolytics (Moody, Merali, & Crawley, 1988; Schino, Perretta, Taglioni, Monaco, & Troisi, 1996; Schino, Troisi, Perretta, & Monaco, 1991), providing further evidence that repetitive self-directed behaviors are evidence of stress.

Another theory about the function of stereotypies in animals is that these behaviors help control arousal level under conditions such as captivity that often afford animals very little control (Fentress, 1976). In fact, "coping" in animals has been defined as the animal having some control over its own mental and physical stability (Fraser & Broom, 1990). Stereotypies may help animals exert control over otherwise uncontrollable situations by allowing them to influence their states of arousal. It is as though the animal were saying, "I can't control anything else about my life, but I can control *this*," the "this" being their own internal state of arousal. Animals subjected to a rate of stimulation lower than what is optimal for them, for example, may increase their arousal levels through the use of stereotypies. For example, pigs that perform stereotypies at relatively high rates also show more overall activity compared to pigs that show less repetitive behavior (Von Borell & Hurnik, 1991). Alternatively, individuals whose surroundings are stressfully unpredictable might increase predictability by engaging in repetitive behavior (Broom, 1981). Unpredictable situations, or those over which an individual has little control, are extremely stressful, as many studies have shown (e.g., Abbott, Schoen, & Badia, 1984; Davis & Levine, 1982). Rats that could not control or predict the onset of an electric shock had significantly more ulcers than did rats that could control the shock (Weiss, 1971). Commuters whose journey to work each day is unpredictable show higher levels of cortisol than do workers with more predictable trips (Evans, Wener, & Phillips, 2002), and tortured political activists who had expectations of arrest and torture because of their political activities showed less stress after their experiences than did torture survivors without prior expectations of such treatment (Basoglu et al., 1997). Children with autism often react badly to unpredictable situations (Ferrara & Hill, 1980; Hill & Frith, 2003). If persons with autism are more sensitive to stress, then perhaps their exaggerated distress when confronted with change is understandable.

In primates, deprivation of various kinds (e.g., social isolation, maternal deprivation) often results in profound stereotypies that include rocking, self-clasping, head-banging, self-biting, eye-poking, bizarre body and limb postures, and complex hand movements (Capitanio, 1986; Cross & Harlow, 1965; Erwin & Deni, 1979; Mason & Sponholz, 1963; Mitchell, 1970), similar stereotypies to those seen in persons with autism. Once established, deprivation-induced stereotypies in primates can be nearly impossible to interrupt (Ridley & Baker, 1982), just as has been found for other animals. Recall that early in the development of stereotypic behavior, opioid antagonists, such as naloxone, appear to be effective in reducing or eliminating the repetitive behavior. Over time, however, naloxone ceases to be effective, suggesting that the functional and biological bases of stereotypies change over the lifetime of the behavior. These findings may also help explain why opioid antagonists fail to interrupt stereotypic behavior in persons with autism more often than not.

STRESS AND SELF-INJURY

Some researchers have speculated that stereotypy can lead to self-injurious behavior (Chamove & Anderson, 1981; Kennedy, 2002; Oliver, 1995), and SIB itself is often stereotyped (Newell, Challis, Boros, & Bodfish, 2002). For example, captivity-induced excessive grooming, which is a kind of stereotypy, often leads to self-wounding through excessive licking, gnawing, scratching, and hair-pulling (Meyer-Holzapfel, 1968). Self-injurious behavior poses one of autism's most serious challenges (Woods, 1982). In one survey of self-injury among teenagers at schools for special-needs children, rates of SIB were significantly higher among teens with autism than they were among teens without autism (Kamio, 2002). Some studies estimate the prevalence of SIB in populations with autism to be as high as 40% (Bernstein, Hughes, Mitchell, & Thompson, 1987). In humans, SIB includes self-biting, eye-poking, head-banging, face-slapping, skin-picking, excessive scratching, self-cutting, and hair-pulling. The force used in these behaviors is near or at the low end of the level of force generated by boxing blows or karate kicks (Newell, Challis, Boros, & Bodfish, 2002). At times, the damage resulting from these self-inflicted injuries is severe enough to be life threatening (Schroeder et al., 2001).

Forms of SIB in animals include self-biting and hair-pulling in primates (Capitanio, 1986; Erwin & Deni, 1979; Reinhardt, Reinhardt, & Houser, 1986); feather-pulling in birds (Grindlinger, 1991; Jenkins, 2001; Samson, 1996); self-kicking in horses (Dodman, Normile, Shuster, & Rand, 1994); flank and other self-sucking in dogs (Hart & Hart, 1985; Houpt, 1991), goats (O'Brien, 1982), and cattle (Hafez & Lineweaver, 1968); and head-banging (Levison, 1970) and eye-poking in primates (Erwin & Deni, 1979). Many of these behaviors are similar or identical to SIB performed by persons with autism.

Self-biting is among the most serious abnormal behavior occurring in captive primates (Niemeyer, Gray, & Stephen, 1996; Reinhardt & Rossell, 2001), with serious self-wounding occurring in about 10% of all individually housed animals (Bayne, Haines, Dexter, Woodman, & Evans, 1995). In one study, self-biting was associated with the breaking of the skin to various degrees in 57% of all cases (Reinhardt, 1999), and the bites can be severe enough to break bones (Sackett, 1968). This kind of self-aggressive behavior occurs quite often among primates reared in isolation (Bellanca & Crockett, 2002; Capitanio, 1986; Kraemer & Clarke, 1990; Sackett, 1968), but it is certainly not restricted to individuals with impoverished early experiences (Novak, 2003).

Self-injurious behavior in captive primates is accompanied by behavioral signs of intense arousal, such as trembling and piloerection (Reinhardt, 1999, Tinklepaugh, 1928), and rapid increases in HR (Novak, 2003). Typically, the behavior occurs in emotionally arousing situations (Sackett, Novak, & Kroeker, 1999), such as having blood drawn (Lutz, Chase, & Novak, 2000), separation from cage mates (Chamove, Anderson, & Nash, 1984; Maple, Risse, & Mitchell, 1973; Redican, Gomber, & Mitchell, 1974), being threatened by a human caretaker (Allyn, Deyme, & Begue, 1976; Berkson, 1968; Cross & Harlow, 1965; Fittinghoff, Lindburg, Gomber, & Mitchell, 1974; Reinhardt, 1999), during and after social altercations (Anderson & Chamove, 1981; Arling & Harlow, 1967; Mason & Berkson, 1975; Zuckerman, 1932), when feeding or other caretaking schedules are changed (Levison, 1970; Waitt & Buchanan-Smith, 2001), during extinction trials in operant conditioning experiments (Gluck & Sackett, 1974), or when moved to a novel cage or room (Jorgensen, Kinsey, & Novak, 1998; Pond & Rush, 1983). Drugs that increase arousal, such as pemoline or caffeine, also increase self-aggression in laboratory rodents (Boyd, Dolman, Knight, & Sheppard, 1965; Genovese, Napoli, & Bolego-Zonta, 1969; Mueller & Nyhan, 1982; Turner, Panksepp, Bekkedal Borkowski, & Burgdorf, 1999).

Among the hypotheses to explain self-aggression is that it is a form of displaced aggression toward others (Chamove et al., 1984). In effect, it is as though the animal is thinking, "I really want to bite you, but I can't, and I am so upset I just have to bite something, so I'll bite myself." Some recent data, however, refute this idea. In several studies of rhesus monkeys showing high rates of SIB, increases in aggression toward other monkeys under a number of circumstances did not correlate with increases in SIB (Lutz, Marinus, Chase, Meyer, & Novak, 2003).

Another hypothesis is that SIB arises as a means for dealing with excessive anxiety or distress (Favazza, 1998; Reinhardt, 1999). Perhaps the pain resulting from the SIB distracts the individual performing the SIB from his or her troubles or redirects stress resulting from other internal or external events (Bennun, 1984; De Raedt, Schacht, Cosyns, & Ponjaert-Kristoffersen, 2002). This hypothesis is in keeping with the observed occurrence of self-aggression in animals under stressful situations. Similar data from human populations without autism also support this view. For example, SIB is not uncommon among incarcerated humans (Dear, Thomson, & Hills, 2000; Winchel & Stanley, 1991), where one can imagine that stress and anxiety are high. Indeed, prisoners who self-mutilate are also more irritable and report excessive levels of anxiety, depression, and despair (Bach y Rita & Veno, 1974; Yaroshevsky, 1975). Among some patients with retardation, SIB is associated with demands from teachers (Iwata et al., 1994), and similar demands as well as changes in routine evoke self-biting in boys with fragile X syndrome, a disorder that presents with symptoms similar to autism (Symons, Clark, Hatton, Skinner, & Bailey, 2003). Children with retardation who engage in hair-pulling (considered a mild form of SIB) typically do so under anxiety-provoking situations (Delgado & Mannino, 1969). In one study of 42 hospitalized self-injuring teenagers, the two most commonly given reasons for SIB were "to cope with feelings of depression" and "to release unbearable tension" (Nixon, Cloutier, & Aggarwal, 2002). These studies suggest that one of the functions of SIB is to help in coping with stress.

If SIB helps reduce arousal, then one might predict heightened arousal just before the onset of SIB and reductions in arousal levels after the occurrence of SIB. Some research using populations without autism supports these predictions. With regard to heightened levels of arousal in individuals showing SIB, for instance, a study of 72 clouded leopards across several zoos found a significant and positive correlation between GCs present in the feces and rates of SIB in these animals (Wielebnowski, Fletchall, Carlstead, Busso, & Brown, 2002). Male nail-biting college students have significantly higher galvanic skin conductance responses to moderate psychological stressors than do nonbiters (Morley, 2000). In one survey of college undergraduates with SIB, self-aggression was associated with a history of depression and anxiety (Rulf Fountain, 2001).

What about the ability of SIB to reduce arousal? Novak (2003) found that HR rapidly escalates just before the onset of self-biting in rhesus monkeys and plummets immediately after self-biting. In a study of human patients with a history of SIB, physiological measures of arousal (e.g., HR, respiration rate, skin conductance) decrease dramatically when these patients imagine themselves self-injuring (Brain, Haines, & Williams, 1998). College undergraduates who engage in hair-pulling report decreases in tension, boredom, anger, and sadness following a hair-pulling incident (Stanley, Borden, Mouton, & Breckenridge, 1995). Also, SIB appears to be associated with dysregulation of the HPA component of the stress response. Plasma cortisol levels tend to be lower in some persons with retardation who show SIB compared to similar persons without SIB (Verhoeven et al., 1999), and cortisol is also lower in monkeys showing high rates of SIB (Faucheux, Bouliere, & Lemaire, 1976; Novak, 2003; Tiefnebacher, Novak, Jorgensen, & Meyer, 2000); in fact, the higher the rates of SIB in these animals, the lower the plasma cortisol levels (Tiefenbacher et al., 2000).

Self-injurious behavior also appears to be associated with alterations in serotonergic systems (Kraemer & Clarke, 1990; New et al., 1997; Sivam, 1996). 5-Hydroxyindoleacetic acid (5-HIAA) is a major metabolite of serotonin (5-HT), and levels of 5-HIAA in cerebrospinal (CSF) fluid are reliable indicators of 5-HT concentrations in the brain (Stanley, Traskman-Bendz, & Dorovini-Zis, 1985). Low levels of 5-HIAA in CSF have been linked to SIB in depressed patients (Lopez-Ibor, Saiz-Ruiz, & Perez de los Cobos, 1985; Winchel & Stanley, 1991). Treating rhesus monkeys with high rates of SIB with tryptophan (a necessary precursor for 5-HT) reduced self-biting (Weld et al., 1998), and tryptophan also reduced self-biting in mice with amphetamine-induced SIB (Shishido, Watanabe, Kato, Horikoshi, & Niwa, 2000). Similarly, treatment with drugs that increase 5-HT levels in the brain by blocking its reuptake, such as serotonin-selective reuptake inhibitors (SSRIs), have been used effectively to reduce stereotypic behavior in vervet monkeys (Hugo et al., 2003) and to reduce hair-pulling in humans (Palmer, Yates, & Trotter, 1999). SSRIs have also been used with some success to treat SIB in children with autism (Kaufman, Vance, Pumariega, & Miller, 2001; McCracken et al., 2002; Posey, Geuenin, Kohn, Swiezy, & McDougle, 2001; Posey & McDougle, 2002; Zarcone et al., 2001). These data, along with other research reviewed previously regarding the relationships among stress, 5-HT, and autism, make a compelling case for increased sensitivity to stress as a characteristic of autism that explains one of its more distressing symptoms—self-injury.

The idea of SIB as a reducer of stress begs the question, How can subjecting one's body to so much pain possibly reduce stress? Think for a moment about how the body reacts to the mere threat of harm signaled by the sight of an oncoming truck in your lane of traffic. For most people, actual or imagined injury is anxiety provoking, not anxiety reducing. In my own observations of self-injuring primates at the California Primate Research Center, I could not imagine how monkeys that bit themselves so severely they required surgery could withstand their self-inflicted pain.

But animals and humans who engage in SIB probably do not react physiologically to stress or to painful stimuli the way "normal" animals and people do. In one study in which SIB patients with borderline personality disorder were asked to imagine themselves engaged in self-injury, pain perception was significantly reduced during the time the subjects imagined cutting or burning themselves (Bohus et al., 2000). Recall that SIB is reported by some self-injuring people to be a mechanism for reducing unbearable stress and anxiety (Nixon et al., 2002). Recall also that part of the physiological stress cascade is the release of endorphins and enkephalins (the body's natural painkillers) from the pituitary (Carrasco & Van de Kar, 2003). If SIB results, in part, as a reaction to chronic stress, then perhaps the increased threshold for pain that self-injuring individuals show is due to stress-induced increases in endorphin and enkephalin secretion.

Many studies clearly show that stress increases the threshold for pain (e.g., Amit & Galina, 1986). In fact, the phenomenon is so well-documented that it has its own name, "stress-induced analgesia" (SIA). Stress-induced analgesia explains why athletes wounded in competition or soldiers wounded on the battlefield so often report feeling no pain.

But you don't have to go into battle or run a marathon to experience SIA. Many other kinds of stress will have the same effect. Men in intensive and stressful military training, for example, have elevated pain thresholds (Yamaguchi, Toda, & Hayashi, 2003). Hypertension is thought to be in part a consequence of stress, and, indeed, people with high blood pressure also show greater pain tolerance (Ditto, France, & France, 1997; France, 1999; Guasti et al., 1999). In a study of 129 patients undergoing a surgical procedure at a hospital, elevations in HR during the procedure were significantly and negatively correlated with post-operative pain (Logan, Sheffield, Lutgendorf, & Lang, 2002). In other words, the more stressed people were by the impending surgery, the less post-operative pain they experienced. Similarly, the more stressed battered women in a shelter were and the higher their blood pressure, the more tolerant they were of pain (Nishith, Griffin, & Poth, 2002). Rats exposed to the stress of intensive gravity, such as the kind a fighter pilot or astronaut might experience, show reduced sensitivity to pain (Kumei et al., 2001), as do first-time parachute jumpers (Janssen & Arntz, 2001). Pinching slugs on the tail (Dalton & Widdowson, 1989), shocking a rat's paws or tail (Maier, Sherman, Lewis, Terman, & Liebeskin, 1983), and forcing rats to swim for long periods of time (Rizzi et al., 2001) result in a higher tolerance to pain. You might argue that in these latter cases, it is not stress, but pain itself that is altering pain sensitivity, just as hitting your thumb with a hammer makes a pinprick later in the day feel somehow less painful. But that does not appear to be the case. Take electric shock, for example, which has been found to increase pain tolerance in many animals, including humans (Willer & Ernst, 1986). When the shock is controlled by the individual receiving it, the shock can result in a small increase in pain tolerance. The same amount of shock, when uncontrollable and unpredictable, produces substantially more pain tolerance—evidence for the analgesic effect of stress in this situation, and not just pain itself (Maier, Drugan, & Grau, 1982).

How might excessive or chronic stress bring about an increased tolerance for pain? Again, part of the physiological consequences of stress is the release of the body's own natural painkillers, the opiatelike endorphins and enkephalins. One way that stress might raise pain thresholds is through elevating levels of these natural painkillers in the bloodstream, and some findings support this hypothesis. For example, plasma endorphin levels rise precipitously in first-time parachute jumpers just before their first jump, and those levels significantly predict pain thresholds after the jump. Furthermore, the pain-reducing effects of first-jump jitters can be blocked by drugs like naloxone that block the effect of endorphins (Janssen & Arntz, 2001). A stressful tail pinch resulting in increased pain tolerance in snails can also be blocked by naloxone (Dalton & Widdowson, 1989). Housing normally social mice by themselves results in increased pain tolerance in these animals (Puglisi-Allegra & Oliverio, 1983). Blocking the HPA component of the stress response with drugs that reduce cortisol levels prevents stress-induced reductions in pain sensitivity (Bogdanov & Yarushkina, 2000; Filaretov, Bogdanov, & Yarushkina, 1996).

Indeed, situations that we know are associated with increased sensitivity to stress also reduce sensitivity to pain. Prenatally stressed rats show exaggerated responses to stress, including increased activity of the HPA component of the stress response, and they also show greater pain tolerance that is diminished with naloxone (Kinsley, Mann, & Bridges, 1988; Takahashi, Kalin, Barksdale, Vanden Burgt, & Brownfield, 1988; Thayer, 1997). Combat veterans with posttraumatic stress disorder show increased pain tolerance when shown a videotape of dramatized combat (Pitman, van der Kolk, Orr, & Greenberg, 1990), which is also diminished by naloxone. Patients with major depression have higher pain thresholds (Adler & Gattaz, 1993; Dworkin, Clark, & Lipsitz, 1995; Lautenbacher, Spernal, Schreiber, & Krieg, 1999), as we would expect, knowing that major depression is associated with chronic increased HPA activity. So do elderly patients with Alzheimer's disease (Scherder et al., 2001), another disorder associated with sustained high levels of GCs and other stress hormones.

Conversely, people with conditions such as arthritis and fibromyalgia, in which levels of GCs are typically suppressed, are even more sensitive to pain (Chikanza, Petrou, Kingsley, Chrousos, & Panayi, 1992; Crofford et al., 1994; Lentjes, Griep, Boersma, Romijn, & De Kloet, 1997; Okifuji & Turk, 2002). Drugs that reduce anxiety in persons with depression or anxiety disorders also increase pain sensitivity in these patients (Kudoh, Katagai, & Takazawa, 2002; Willer & Ernst, 1986). These findings have led some researchers to speculate that SIB is a form of self-medication, in which the drugs of choice are those endogenous opiates, the endorphins (Thompson, Symons, Delaney, & England, 1995).

What does all this have to do with autism? Self-injury is common among persons with autism, and this chapter suggests that autism shares many behavioral and physiological characteristics with humans and animals under chronic stress. In keeping with this argument, some persons with autism also show increased tolerance for pain (Biersdorff, 1994; Cook et al., 1990). One of several hypotheses put forward to explain higher pain thresholds and rates of self-injury in persons with autism is that they have some kind of abnormality in their body's painkilling system (Schroder et al., 2001); perhaps, for example, the stress of perceiving the world so differently elevates endorphin levels in persons with autism.

A few studies provide support for this hypothesis. In one study of children with autism, plasma endorphin levels and severity of stereotypies were strongly correlated (Ernst et al., 1993). In other studies, drugs like naloxone that block endorphins were found to improve symptoms in persons with autism (Deutsch, 1986; Sandman, 1988; Walters, Barrett, Feinstein, Mercurio, & Hole, 1990). Higher levels of endorphins have been found in the blood (Tordjman et al., 1997) and cerebrospinal fluid of persons with autism (Gillberg, Terenius, & Lonnerholm, 1985). Adler and Gattaz (1993) suggest that increased pain tolerance in depressive patients may be a warning sign of impaired anxiety and coping in this population—in other words, a sign that depressed persons are stressed. France (1999) suggested that higher pain tolerance be used as a sign of possible hypertension. Could elevated pain thresholds in persons with autism be a warning sign of stress in this population?

SUMMARY

In this chapter I have reviewed some of the similarities in physiology and behavior between humans and animals suffering from stress and anxiety and related this to persons with autism. The purpose of this review was to explore the question, Is autism a stress disorder? Certainly what is known about the psychobiology of stress overlaps in interesting ways with what is known about the psychobiology of autism and suggests some provocative questions about those similarities. The literature we have reviewed makes it clear that excessive stress or anxiety can alter the brain in ways that promote hypervigilance and abnormal behavior, exaggerate fearfulness, disturb sleep, impair memory, and cause shifts in attention—all characteristics of autism. These behaviors, in return, can exacerbate feelings of anxiety, so that the entire cascade becomes one of constant emotional distress and arousal spiraling out of control. Thus, stress in a person who has difficulty moderating his or her emotional and behavioral responses to stimulation can produce a situation that, because of its potential for bringing about permanent physiological change, is self-perpetuating.

Such a situation may be part of the etiology for the autism phenotype—for surely a person with such a view of life would be prone to withdrawal from all kinds of provocative stimuli, including other people. It may also be a situation that derives from the autism phenotype, as being unable to understand others or tolerating sensory stimulation is always stressful to the person with autism. Recall that what is stressful is very much in the eye of the beholder. A person with autism who is unable to understand the social signals he or she receives from other people may find those people to be sources of stress and not the sources of comfort that they might be to persons without autism.

It is likely, therefore, that many persons with autism suffer from stress and anxiety, particularly in a world in which their realities and the realities of persons without autism do not share much in common. As we have reviewed, such stress and anxiety can only add to the physical and behavioral differences that keep these competing realities apart.

It behooves us, then, to increase our efforts to understand the overlap between autism and disorders deriving from stress, to assess the degree to which stress plays a role in the lives of persons with autism, and to reduce this stress as much as possible. As parents of persons with autism, as researchers interested in the etiology and treatment of the disorder, and as practitioners working with clients with autism, we will all benefit from the fruits of these labors.

References

Abbott, B. B., Schoen, L. S., & Badia, P. (1984). Predictable and unpredictable shock: Behavioral measures of aversion and physiological measures of stress. *Psychological Bulletin, 96,* 45–71.

Abercrombie, E. D., & Jacobs, B. L. (1987). Single-unit response of noradrenergicneurons in the locus coeruleus of freely moving cats: I. Acutely presented stressful and nonstressful stimuli. *Journal of Neuroscience, 7,* 2837–2843.

Abramson, R. K., Wright, H. H., Cuccara, H. L., Lawrence, L.G., Babb, S., Pencarinha, D.,et al. (1992). Biological liability in families with autism [Letter to the editor]. *Journal of the American Academy of Child and Adolescent Psychiatry, 31,* 370–371.

Adler, G., & Gattaz, W. F. (1993). Pain perception threshold in major depression. *Biological Psychiatry, 34,* 687–689.

Allyn, G., Deyme, A., & Begue, I. (1976). Self-fighting syndrome in macaques: Arepresentative case study. *Primates, 17,* 1–22.

Amaral, D. G., Bauman, M. D., & Schumann, C. M. (2003). The amygdala and autism: Implications from non-human primate studies. *Genes, Brain, and Behavior, 2,* 295–302.

American Psychiatric Association (1994). *Diagnostic and statistical manual of mental disorders* (4th ed.). Washington, DC: Author.

Amit, Z., & Galina, Z. (1986). Stress-induced analgesia: Adaptive pain suppression. *Physiological Reviews, 66,* 1091–1120.

Anderson, G. M., Freedman, D. X., Cohen, D. J., Volkmar, F. R., Hoder, E. L., McPhedran, P., et al. (1987). Whole blood serotonin in autistic and normal subjects. *Journal of Child Psychology and Psychiatry, 28,* 885–900.

Anderson, G. M., Gutknecht, L., Cohen, D. J., Brailly-Tabard, S., Cohen, J. H. M., Ferrari, P., et al. (2002). Serotonin transporter promoter variants in autism: Functional effects and relationship to platelet hyperserotonemia. *Molecular Psychiatry, 7,* 831–836.

Anderson, J. R., & Chamove, A. S. (1981). Self-aggressive behaviour in monkeys. *Current Psychological Reviews, 1,* 139–158.

Arbel, I., Kadar, T., Silbermann, M., & Levey, A. (1994). The effects of long-term corticosterone administration on hippocampal morphology and cognitive performance of middle-aged rats. *Brain Research, 657,* 227–235.

Arbelle, S., Benjamin, J., Golin, M. Kremer, I., Belmaker, R. H., & Epstein, R. P. (2003). Relation of shyness in grade school children to the genotype for the long form of the serotonin transporter promoter region polymorphism. *American Journal of Psychiatry, 160,* 671–676.

Arling, G. L., & Harlow, H. F. (1967). Effects of social deprivation on maternal behavior of rhesus monkeys. *Journal of Comparative and Physiological Psychology, 64,* 371–377

Aston-Jones, G., Rajkowski, J., & Cohen, J. (1999). Role of the locus coeruleus in attention and behavioral flexibility. *Biological Psychiatry, 46,* 1309–1320.

Aston-Jones, G., Rajkowski, J., & Cohen, J. (2000). Locus coeruleus and regulation of behavioral flexibility and attention. *Progress in Brain Research, 126,*165–182.

Aureli, F. (1997). Post-conflict anxiety in nonhuman primates: The mediating role of emotion in conflict resolution. *Aggressive Behavior, 23,* 315–328.

Aureli, F., & De Waal, F. (1997). Inhibition of social behavior in chimpanzees under high-density conditions. *American Journal of Primatology, 41,* 213–228.

Aylward, E. H., Minshew, N. J., Goldstein, G., Honeycutt, N. A., Augustine, A. M., Yates, K. O., et al. (1999). MRI volumes of amygdala and hippocampus in non-mentally retarded autistic adolescents and adults. *Neurology, 53,* 2145–2150.

Azmitia, E. C., & Segal, M. (1978). An autodiographic analysis of the differential ascending projections of the dorsal and median raphe nuclei in the rat. *Journal of Comparative Neurology, 179,* 641–688.

Bach y Rita, G., & Veno, A. (1974). Habitual violence: A profile of 62 men. *American Journal of Psychiatry, 131,* 1015–1017.

Bachevalier, J. (1994). Medial temporal lobe structures and autism: A review of clinical and experimental findings. *Neuropsychologia, 32,* 627–648.

Bachevalier, J. (1996). Medial temporal lobe and autism: A putative animal model in primates. *Journal of Autism and Developmental Disorders, 26,* 217–220.

Bagdy, G., Calogero, A. E., Murphy, D. L., & Szemeredi, K. (1989). Serotonin agonists cause parallel activation of the sympathoadrenomedullary system and the hypothalamo-pituitary-adrenocortical axis in conscious rats. *Endocrinology, 125,* 2664–2669.

Baker, D. G., West, S. A., Orth, D. N., Hill, K. K., Nicholson, W. E., Ekhator, N. N., et al. (1997). Cerebrospinal fluid and plasma beta-endorphin in combat veterans with post-traumatic stress disorder. *Psychoneuroendocrinology, 22*(7), 517–529.

Barbazanges, A., Piazza, P. V., LeMoal, M., & Maccari, S. (1996). Maternal glucocorticoid secretion mediates long-term effects of prenatal stress. *Journal of Neuroscience, 16,* 3943–3949.

Basoglu, M., Mineka, S., Paker, M., Aker, T., Livanou, M., & Gok, S. (1997). Psychological preparedness for trauma as a protective factor in survivors of torture. *Psychological Medicine, 27,* 1421–1433.

Bauman, M., & Kemper, T. (1994). *The neurobiology of autism.* Baltimore, MD: Johns Hopkins University Press.

Bayne, K., Haines, M., Dexter, S., Woodman, D., & Evans, C. (1995). Nonhuman primate wounding prevalence: A retrospective analysis. *Laboratory Animals, 24,* 40–44.

Beerda, B., Schilder, M. B. H., van Hooff, J. A. R. A. M., de Vries, H. W., & Mol, J. A. (1998). Behavioural, saliva cortisol and heart rate responses to different types of stimuli in dogs. *Applied Animal Behaviour Science, 58,* 365–381.

Bellanca, R. U., & Crockett, C. M. (2002). Factors predicting increased incidence of abnormal behavior in male pigtailed macaques. *American Journal of Primatology, 58,* 57–69.

Belliver, F., Roy, I., & Leboyer, M. (2002). Serotonin transporter gene polymorphisms and affective disorder-related phenotypes. *Current Opinion in Psychiatry, 15,* 49–58.

Bennetto, L., Pennington, B. F., & Rogers, S. J. (1996). Intact and impaired memory functions in autism. *Child Development, 67,* 1816–1835.

Bennun, I. (1984). Psychological models of self-mutilation. *Suicide and Life Threatening Behavior, 14,* 166–186.

Berkson, G. (1968). Development of abnormal stereotyped behaviors. *Developmental Psychology, 1,* 118–132.

Berkson, G. (2002). Feedback and control in the development of abnormal stereotyped behaviors. In R. L. Sprague & K. M. Newell (Eds.), *Stereotyped movements: Brain and behavior relationships* (pp. 3–15). Washington, DC: American Psychological Association.

Bernstein, G. A., Hughes, J., Mitchell, J. E., & Thompson, T. (1987). Effects of narcotic antagonists on self-injurious behavior: A single case study. *Journal of the American Academy of Child and Adolescent Psychiatry, 26,* 886–889.

Beylin, A.V., & Shors, T. J. (2003). Glucocorticoids are necessary for enhancing the acquisition of associative memories after acute stressful experiences. *Hormones and Behavior, 43,* 124–131.

Bhatnagar, S., & Dallman, M. (1998). Neuroanatomical basis for facilitation of hypothalamic-pituitary-adrenal responses to a novel stressor after chronic stress. *Neuroscience, 84,* 1025–1039.

Biersdorff, K. K. (1994). Incidence of significantly altered pain experience among individuals with developmental disabilities. *American Journal on Mental Retardation, 98,* 619–631.

Bildsoe, M., Heller, K. E., & Jeppesen, L. L. (1991). Effects of immobility stress and food restriction on stereotypies in low and high stereotyping female ranch mink. *Behavioural Processes, 25,* 179–189.

Bodfish, J. W., Symons, F. J., Parker, D. E., & Lewis, M. H. (2000). Varieties of repetitive behavior in autism: Comparisons to mental retardation. *Journal of Autism and Developmental Disorders, 30,* 237–243.

Bodnoff, S. R., Humphreys, A. G., Lehman, J. C., Diamond, D. M., Rose, G. M., & Meaney, M. J. (1995). Enduring effects of chronic corticosterone treatment on spatial learning, synaptic plasticity and hippocampal neuropathology in young and mid-aged rates. *Journal of Neuroscience, 15,* 61–69.

Bogdanov, A. I., & Yarushkina, N. N. (2000). The relationship between analgesia and corticosteroid levels in rats. *Neuroscience & Behavioral Physiology, 30,* 487–489.

Bohus, M., Limberger, M., Ebner, U., Glocker, F. X., Schwarz, B., Wernz, M., & Lieb, K. (2000). Pain perception during self-reported distress and calmness in patients with borderline personality disorder and self-mutilating behavior. *Psychiatry Research, 95,* 251–260.

Bolton, P. F., Pickles, A., Murphy, M., & Rutter, M. (1998). Autism, affective and other psychiatric disorders: Patterns of familial aggregation. *Psychological Medicine, 28,* 385–395.

Boyd, E. M., Dolman, M., Knight, L. M., & Sheppard, E. P. (1965). The chronic oral toxicity of caffeine. *Canadian Journal of Physiology and Pharmacology, 43*, 995–1007.

Bradley, E. A., Summers, J. A., Wood, H. L., & Bryson, S. E. (2004). Comparing rates of psychiatric and behavioral disorders in adolescents and young adults with severe intellectual disability with and without autism. *Journal of Autism and Developmental Disorders, 34*, 151–161.

Brain, K. L., Haines, J., & Williams, C. L. (1998). The psychophysiology of self mutilation: Evidence of tension reduction. *Archives of Suicide Research, 4*, 227–242.

Brent, L., Koban, T., & Raminez, S. (2002). Abnormal, abusive, and stress-related behaviors in baboon mothers. *Biological Psychiatry, 52*, 1047–1056.

Broom, D. M. (1981). *Biology of behaviour*. Cambridge, England: Cambridge University Press.

Broom, D. M. (1991). Animal welfare: Concepts and measurements. *Journal of Animal Science, 69*, 4167–4175.

Broom, D. M., & Johnson, K. G. (1993). *Stress and animal welfare*. London: Chapman & Hall.

Cameron, H. A., & Gould, E. (1994). Adult neurogenesis is regulated by adrenal steroids in the dentate gyrus. *Neuroscience, 61*, 203–209.

Capitanio, J. P. (1986). Behavioral pathology. In G. Mitchell & J. Erwin (Eds.), *Comparative primate biology*, vol. 2., Part A. *Behavior, conservation, and ecology* (pp. 411–454). New York: Alan R. Liss.

Carrasco, G. A., & Van de Kar, L. D. (2003). Neuroendocrine pharmachology of stress. *European Journal of Pharmacology, 463*, 235–272.

Carvey, P. M. (1998). *Drug action in the central nervous system*. New York: Oxford University Press.

Casey, B. J., Gordon, C. T., Mannheim, G. B., & Rumsey, J. M. (1993). Dysfunctional attention in autistic savants. *Journal of Clinical & Experimental Neuropsychology, 15*, 933–946.

Castellanos, F. X., Ritchie, G. F., Marsh, W. L., & Rapoport, J. L. (1996). DSM-IV stereotypic movement disorder: Persistence of stereotypies of infancy in intellectually normal adolescents and adults. *Journal of Clinical Psychiatry, 57*, 116–122.

Castles, D. L., & Whitens, A. (1998). Post-conflict behaviour of wild olive baboons: II. Stress and self-directed behaviour. *Ethology, 104*, 148–160.

Castles, D. L., Whitens, A., & Aureli, F. (1999). Social anxiety, relationships, and self-directed behaviour among wild female olive baboons. *Animal Behaviour, 58*, 1207–1215.

Castner, S. A., & Goldman-Rakic, P. S. (1999). Long-lasting psychotomimetic consequences of repeated low-dose amphetamine exposure in rhesus monkeys. *Neuropsychopharmacology, 20*, 10–28.

Chabane, N., Leboyer, M., & Mouren-Simeoni, M. C. (2000). Opiate antagonists in children and adolescents. *European Child and Adolescent Psychiatry, 9*(Suppl. 1), 44–50.

Chamove, A. S., & Anderson, J. R. (1981). Self-aggression, stereotypy, and self-injurious behavior in man and monkeys. *Current Psychological Reviews, 1*, 245–255.

Chamove, A. S., Anderson, J. R., & Nash, V. J. (1984). Social and environmental influences on self-aggression in monkeys. *Primates, 25*, 319–325.

Chapman, W. P., Schroeder, H. R., Guyer, G., Brazier, M. A. B., Fager, C., Poppen, J. L., et al. (1954). Physiological evidence concerning importance of the amygdaloid nuclear region in the integration of circulatory function and emotion in man. *Science, 120,* 949–951.

Chatterton, R. T., Vogelsong, K. M., Lu, Y. C., & Hudgens, G. A. (1997). Hormonal responses to psychological stress in men preparing for skydiving. *Journal of Clinical Endocrinology and Metabolism, 82,* 2503–2509.

Chikanza, I. C., Petrou, P., Kingsley, G., Chrousos, G., & Panayi, G. S. (1992). Defective hypothalamic responses to immune and inflammatory stimuli in patients with rheumatoid arthritis. *Arthritis and Rheumatism, 35,* 1281–1288.

Chugani, D. C. (2002). Role of altered brain serotonin mechanisms in autism. *Molecular Psychiatry, 7,* S16–S17.

Claes, S. J. (2004). CRH, stress, and major depression: a psychobiological interplay. *Vitamins and Hormones, 69,* 117–150.

Clarke, A. S., Juno, C. J., & Maple, T .L. (1982). Behavioral effects of a change in the physical environment: A pilot study of captive chimpanzees. *Zoo Biology, 1,* 371–380.

Cook, E. H., Jr., Courchesne, R., Lord, C., Cox, N. J., Yan, S., Lincoln, A., et al. (1997). Evidence of linkage between the serotonin transporter and autistic disorder. *Molecular Psychiatry, 2,* 247–250.

Cook, E. H., Jr., & Leventhal, B. L. (1996). The serotonin system in autism. *Current Opinion in Pediatrics, 8,* 348–354.

Cook, E. H., Jr., Leventhal, B. L., Heller, W., Metz, J., Wainwright, M., & Freedman, D. X. (1990). Autistic children and their first-degree relatives: Relationships between serotonin and norepinephrine levels and intelligence. *Journal of Neuropsychiatry & Clinical Neurosciences, 2,* 268–274.

Cooper, J. J., & Nicol, C. J. (1991). Stereotypic behaviour affects environmental preference in bank voles (*Clethrionomys glareolus*). *Animal Behaviour, 41,* 971–977.

Courchesne, E. (1997). Brainstem, cerebellar and limbic neuroanatomical abnormalities in autism. *Current Opinion in Neurobiology, 7,* 269–278.

Courchesne, E., Townsend, N. A., Akshoomoff, O. S., Yeung-Courchesne, R., Lincoln, A. J., James, H. E., et al. (1994). Impairment in shifting attention in autistic and cerebellar patients. *Behavioral Neuroscience, 108,* 848–865.

Craven-Thuss, B., & Nicolson, R. (2003) Amoxapine treatment of interfering behaviors in autistic disorder. *Journal of the American Academy of Child & Adolescent Psychiatry, 42,* 515–516.

Crofford, L. J., Pillemer, S. R., Kalogeras, K. T., Cash, J. M., Michelson, D., Kling, M. A., et al. (1994). Hypothalamic-pituitary-adrenal axis perturbations in patients with fibromyalgia. *Arthritis and Rheumatism, 37,* 1583–1592.

Cronin, G. M., Wiepkema, P. R., & van Ree, J. M. (1985). Endogenous opioids are involved in abnormal stereotyped behaviours of tethered sows. *Neuropeptides, 6,* 527–530.

Cross, H. A., & Harlow, H. F. (1965). Prolonged and progressive effects of partial isolation on the behaviour of macaque monkeys. *Journal of Experimental Research in Personality, 1,* 39–49.

Cullinan, W. E., Herman, J. P., Helmreich, D. L., & Watson, S. J., Jr. (1995). A neuroanatomy of stress. In M. J. Friedman, D. S. Charney, & A. Y. Deutch (Eds.). *Neurobiological and clinical consequences of stress:.From normal adaptation to PTSD* (pp. 3–26). Philadelphia: Lippincott-Raven.

Curin, J. M., Terzic, J., Petkovic, Z. B., Zekan, L., Terzic, I. M., & Susnjara, I. M. (2003). Lower cortisol and higher ACTH levels in individuals with autism. *Journal of Autism and Developmental Disorders, 33,* 443–448.

Dalton, L. M., & Widdowson, P. S. (1989). The involvement of opioid peptides in stress-induced analgesia in the slug *Arion ater. Peptides, 10,* 9–13.

Dantzer, R. (1991). Stress, stereotypies and welfare. *Behavioural Processes, 25,* 95–102.

Dantzer, R., & Mormède, P. (1983). De-arousal properties of stereotyped behaviour: Evidence from pituitary adrenal correlates in pigs. *Applied Animal Ethology, 10,* 233–244.

Davis, H., & Levine, S. (1982). Predictability, control, and the pituitary-adrenal response in rats. *Journal of Comparative Physiological Psychology, 96,* 393–404.

Davis, M. (1992). The role of the amygdala in fear and anxiety. *Annual Reviews in Neuroscience,15,* 353–375.

Davis, M., & Whalen, P. J. (2001). The amygdala: Vigilance and emotion. *Molecular Psychiatry, 6,* 13–34.

Dawkins, M. S. (1990). From an animal's point of view: Motivation, fitness, and animal welfare. *Brain and Behaviour Science, 13,* 1–61.

Dear, G. E., Thomson, D. M., & Hills, A. M. (2000). Self-harm in prison: Manipulators can also be suicide attempters. *Criminal Justice & Behavior, 27,* 160–175.

De Kloet, E. R. (1991). Brain corticosteroid receptor balance and homeostatic control. *Frontiers in Neuroendocrinology, 12,* 95–164.

De Kloet, E. R. (1995). Steroids, stability, and stress. *Frontiers in Neuroendocrinology, 16,* 416–425.

De Kloet, E. R., Korte, S. M., Rots, N.Y., & Kruk, M .R. (1996). Stress hormones, genotype, and brain organization: Implications for aggression. *Annals of the New York Academy of Sciences, 794,* 179–191.

Delgado, R. A., & Mannino, F. V. (1969). Some observations on trichotillomania in children. *Journal of the Amercan Academy of Child Psychiatry, 8,* 229–246.

De Raedt, R., Schacht, R., Cosyns, P., & Ponjaert-Kristoffersen, I. (2002). Pain-provoking behaviour as a driven reaction to psychological distress: The bio-psycho-social neurotic loop model. *New Ideas in Psychology, 20,* 59–87

Deutsch, S. I. (1986). Rationale for the administration of opiate antagonists in treating infantile autism. *American Journal of Mental Deficiency, 90,* 631–635.

Diamond, D. M., Fleshner, M., Ingersoll, N., & Rose, G. M. (1996). Psychological stress impairs spatial working memory: Relevance to electrophysiological studies of hippocampal function. *Behavioral Neuroscience, 110,* 661–672.

Dickson, P. R., Lang, C. G., Hinton, S. C., & Kelley, A. E. (1994). Oral stereotypy induced by amphetamine microinjection into striatum: An anatomical mapping study. *Neuroscience, 61,* 81–91.

Dinan, T. G. (1996). Serotonin and the regulation of hypothalamic-pituitary-adrenal axis function. *Life Sciences, 58,* 1683–1694.

Ditto, E., France, J., & France, C. R. (1997). Risk for hypertension and pain sensitivity in women. *International Journal of Behavioral Medicine, 4,* 117–130.

Dodman, N. H., Normile, J. A., Shuster, L., & Rand, W. (1994). Equine self-mutilation syndrome (57 cases). *Journal of the Veterinary Medical Association, 15,* 1219–1223.

Dodman, N. H., Shuster, L., Court, M. H., & Dixon, R. (1987). Investigation into the use of narcotic antagonists, in the treatment of a stereotypic behaviour pattern (crib-biting) in the horse. *American Journal of Veterinary Research, 48,* 311–319.

Duman, R. S., Malberg, J., & Nakagawa, S. (2001). Regulation of adult neurogenesis by psychotropic drugs and stress. *Journal of Pharmacology and Experimental Therapeutics, 299,* 401–407.

Dworkin, R. H., Clark, W. C., & Lipsitz, J. D. (1995). Pain responsivity in major depression and bipolar disorder. *Psychiatry Research, 56,* 173–81.

Easley, S. P., Coelho, A. M., & Taylor, L. L. (1987). Scratching, dominance, tension, and displacement in male baboons. *American Journal of Primatology, 13,* 397–411.

Easterbrook, J. A. (1959). The effect of emotion on cue utilization and the organization of behavior. *Psychological Review, 66,* 183–201.

Ernst, M., Devi, L., Silva, R. R., Gonzalez, N. M., Small, A. M., Malone, R. P., & Campbell, M. (1993). Plasma beta-endorphin levels, naltrexone, and haloperidol in autistic children. *Psychopharmacology Bulletin, 29,* 221–227.

Erwin, J., & Deni, R. (1979). Strangers in a strange land: Abnormal behaviors or abnormal environments? In J. Erwin, T. L. Maple, & G. Mitchell (Eds.), *Captivity and behavior: Primates in breeding colonies, laboratories, and zoos* (pp. 1–28). New York: Van Nostrand Reinhold.

Evans, G. W., Wener, R. E., & Phillips, D. (2002). The morning rush hour—Predictability and commuter stress. *Environment and Behavior, 34,* 521–530.

Faucheux, B., Bouliere, F., & Lemaire, C. (1976). Decreased reactivity in partially isolated, autoaggressive macaques. *Biology and Behavior, 1,* 329–338.

Favazza, A. R. (1998). The coming of age of self-mutilation. *Journal of Nervous and Mental Disease, 186,* 259–268.

Feldman, S., & Conforti, N. (1980). Participation of the dorsal hippocampus in glucocorticoid negative feedback effect on adrenocortical activity. *Neuroendocrinology, 30,* 52–55.

Fentress, J. C. (1976). Dynamic boundaries of patterned behaviour: Interaction and self organization. In P. P. G. Bateson & R. A. Hinde (Eds.), *Growing points in ethology* (pp. 135–169). Cambridge, England: Cambridge University Press.

Ferrara, C., & Hill, S. D. (1980). The responsiveness of autistic children to the predictability of social and nonsocial toys. *Journal of Autism and Developmental Disorders, 10,* 51–57.

Filaretov, A. A., Bogdanov, A. I., & Yarushkina, N. I. (1996). Stress-induced analgesia: The role of hormones produced by the hypophyseal-adrenocortical system. *Neuroscience & Behavioral Physiology, 26,* 572–578.

Fittinghoff, N. A., Lindburg, D. G., Gomber, J., & Mitchell, G. (1974). Consistency and variability in the behavior of mature, isolation-reared, male rhesus macaques. *Primates, 15,* 111–139.

Foote, S. L., Bloom, F. E., & Aston-Jones, G. (1983). Nucleus locus coeruleus: New evidence of anatomical and physiological specificity. *Physiology Review, 63,* 844–914.

Forget, H., Lacroix, A., Somma, M., & Cohen, H. (2000). Cognitive decline in patients with Cushing's syndrome. *Journal of the International Neuropsychology Society, 6,* 20–29.

Forrester, R. C. (1980). Stereotypies and the behavioural regulation of motivational state. *Applied Animal Ethology, 6,* 386–387.

France, C. R. (1999). Decreased pain perception and risk for hypertension: considering a common physiological mechanism. *Psychophysiology, 36,* 683–692.

Fraser, A. F., & Broom, D. M. (1990). *Farm animal behaviour and welfare.* London: Baillière Tindall.

Fuller, R. W. (1992). The involvement of serotonin in regulation of pituitary-adrenocortical function. *Frontiers in Neuroendocrinology, 13,* 250–270.

Genovese, E., Napoli, P. A., & Bolego-Zonta, N. (1969). Self-aggressiveness. *Life Science, 8,* 513–515.

Gillberg, C., Terenius, L., & Lonnerholm, G. (1985). Endorphin activity in childhood psychosis. Spinal fluid levels in 24 cases. *Archives of General Psychiatry, 42,* 780–783.

Gillott, A., Furniss, F., & Walter, A. (2001). Anxiety in high-functioning children with autism. *Autism, 5,* 277–286.

Gingell, K., Parmar, R., & SungumPaliwal, S. (1996). Autism and multiple pituitary deficiency. *Developmental Medicine and Child Neurology, 38,* 545–549.

Gluck, J., & Sackett, G. (1974). Frustration and self-aggression in social isolate rhesus monkeys. *Journal of Abnormal Psychology, 83,* 331–334.

Goenjian, A. K., Pynoos, R. S., Steinberg, A. M., Endres, D., Abraham, K., Geffner, M. E., & Fairbanks, L. A. (2003). Hypothalamic-pituitary-adrenal activity among Armenian adolescents with PTSD symptoms. *Journal of Traumatic Stress, 16,* 319–323.

Grandin, T. (1996). *Thinking in pictures and other reports from my life with autism.* New York: Vintage.

Green, J., Gilchrist, A., Burton, D., & Cox, A. (2000). Social and psychiatric functioning in adolescents with Asperger syndrome compared with conduct disorder. *Journal of Autism and Developmental Disorders, 30,* 279–293.

Grindlinger, H. (1991). Compulsive feather picking in birds. *Archives of General Psychiatry, 48,* 857.

Gould, E. Beylin, A., Tanapat, P., Reeves, A., & Shors, T. (1999). Learning enhances adult neurogenesis in the hippocampal formation. *Nature Neuroscience, 2,* 260–265.

Gould, E., Tanapat, P., McEwen, B. S., Flugge, G., & Fuchs, E. (1998). Proliferation of granule cell precursors in the dentate gyrus of adult monkeys is diminished by stress. *Proceedings of the National Academy of Sciences, 95,* 3168–3171.

Graeff, F. G., & Silveira, F. G. (1978). Behavioral inhibition induced by electrical stimulation of the median raphe nucleus of the rat. *Physiology and Behavior, 71,* 477–484.

Guasti, L., Gaudio, G., Zanotta, D., Grimoldi, P., Petrozzino, M. R., Tanzi, F., et al. (1999). Relationship between a genetic predisposition to hypertension, blood pressure levels and pain sensitivity. *Pain, 82,* 311–317.

Guillemin, R., Vargo, T., & Rossier, J. (1977). Beta-endorphin and adrenocorticotropin are secreted concomitantly by pituitary gland. *Science, 197,* 1367.

Hafez, E. S. E., & Lineweaver, J. A. (1968). Suckling behaviour in natural and artificially fed neonate calves. *Zeitschrift für Tierpsychologie, 25,* 187–198.

Hart, B. L., & Hart, L. A. (1985). *Canine and feline behavioral therapy.* Philadelphia: Lea and Febiger.

Healy, D. (2003). Lines of evidence on the risks of suicide with selective serotonin reuptake inhibitors. *Psychotherapy and Psychosomatics, 72,* 71–79.

Hediger, H. (1964). *Wild animals in captivity.* New York: Dover. Hediger, H. (1992). *The psychology and behavior of animals in zoos and circuses.* New York: Dover.

Heim, C. Newport, D. J., Wagner, D., Wilcox, M. M., Miller, A. H., & Nemeroff, C. B. (2002). The role of early adverse experience and adulthood stress in the prediction of neuroendocrine stress reactivity in women: A multiple regression approach. *Depression and Anxiety, 15,* 117–125.

Hennessy, R. B., & Fox, T. (1987). Nonedible material elicits chewing and reduces the plasma corticosterone response during novelty exposure in mice. *Behavioral Neuroscience, 101,* 237–245.

Henry, C., Kabbaj, M., Simon, H., Le Moal, M., & Maccari, S. (1994). Prenatal stress increases the hypothalamo-pituitary-adrenal axis response in young and adult rats. *Journal of Neuroendocrinology, 6,* 341–345.

Herman, J. P., Cullinan, W. E., Morano, M.I., Akil, H., & Watson, S. J. (1995). Contribution of the ventral subiculum to inhibitory regulation of the hypothalamo-pituitary-adrenocortical axis. *Journal of Neuroendocrinology, 7,* 475–482.

Hill, E. L., & Frith, U. (2003). Understanding autism: Insights from mind and brain. *Philosophical Transactions of the Royal Society of London Series B—Biological Sciences, 358,* 281–289.

Holmes., T. H., & Rahe, R. H. (1967). The social readjustment rating scale. *Journal of Psychosomatic Research, 11,* 213–218.

Horner, H. C., Packan, D. R., & Sapolsky, R.M. (1990). Glucocorticoids inhibit glucose transport in cultured hippocampal neurons and glia. *Neuroenendocrinology, 52,*57–64.

Houpt, K. A. (1991). Feeding and drinking behavior problems. *Veterinary Clinics of North America: Small Animal Practice, 21,* 281–298.

Hoyer, D., Clarke, D. E., Fozard, J. R., Hartig, P. R., Martin, G. R., Mylecharane, E. J., et al. (1994). VII. International Union of Pharmacology classification of receptors for 5-hydroxytryptamine (serotonin). *Pharmacology Reviews, 46,* 157–204.

Hoyer, D., Hannon, J. P., & Martin, G. R. (2002). Molecular, pharmacological, and functional diversity of 5-HT receptors. *Pharmacology, Biochemistry, and Behavior, 71,* 533–554.

Hughes, C., Plumet, M. H., & Leboyer, M. (1999). Towards a cognitive phenotype for autism: Increased prevalence of executive dysfunction and superior spatial span amongst siblings of children with autism. *Journal of Child Psychology and Psychiatry, 40,* 705–718.

Hugo, C., Seier, J., Mdhluli, C., Daniels, W., Harvey, B. H., De Toit, D., et al. (2003). Fluoxetine decreases stereotypic behavior in primates. *Progress in Neuro-Psychopharmacology and Biological Psychiatry, 27,* 639–643.

Hutt, C., & Hutt, S. J. (1970). Stereotypies and their relation to arousal: A study of autistic children. In S. J. Hutt & C. Hutt (Eds.). *Behaviour studies in psychiatry* (pp. 175–204). Oxford: Pergamon.

Hutt, S. J., & Hutt, C. (1968). Stereotypy, arousal, and autism. *Human Development, 11,* 277–286.

Iwata, B. A., Pace, G. M., Dorsey, M. F., Zarcone, J. R., Vollmer, T. R., Smith, R.G., et al. (1994). The functions of self-injurious behavior: An experimental/epidemiological analysis. *Journal of Applied Behavior Analysis, 27,* 215–240.

Jacobson, L., & Sapolsky, R. (1991). The role of the hippocampus in feedback regulation of the hypothalamic-pituitary-adrenocortical axis. *Endocrine Reviews, 12,* 118–134.

Janssen, S. A., & Arntz, A. (2001). Real-life stress and opioid-mediated analgesia in novice parachute jumpers. *Journal of Psychophysiology, 15,* 106–113.

Jedema, H. P., Finlay, J. M., Sved, A. F., & Grace, A. A. (2001). Chronic cold exposure potentiates CRH-evoked increases in electrophysiologic activity of locus coeruleus neurons. *Biological Psychiatry, 49,* 351–359.

Jedema, H. P., & Grace, A. A. (2003). Chronic exposure to cold stress alters lectro-physiological properties of locus coeruleus neurons recorded in vitro. *Neuropsychopharmacology, 28,* 63–72.

Jenkins, J. R. (2001). Feather picking and self-mutilation in psittacine birds. *Veterinary Clinics of North America: Exotic Animal Practice, 4,* 651–667.

Jones, G. H., Mittleman, G., & Robbins, T. W. (1989). Attenuation of amphetamine-stereotypy by mesostriatal dopamine depletion enhances plasma corticosterone: Implications for stereotypy as a coping response. *Behavioral Neural Biology, 51,* 80–91.

Jorgensen, M. J., Kinsey, J. H., & Novak, M. A. (1998). Risk factors for self-injurious behavior in captive rhesus monkeys (*Macaca mulatta*). *American Journal of Primatology, 45,* 187.

Kadekaro, M., Ito, M., & Gross, P. M. (1988). Local cerebral glucose utilization is increased in adrenalectomized rats. *Neuroendocrinology, 47,* 329–334.

Kalin, N. H., Shelton, S. E., & Davidson, R. J. (2004). The role of the central nucleus of the amygdala in mediating fear and anxiety in the primate. *Journal of Neuroscience, 16,* 5506–5515.

Kamio, Y. (2002). Self-injurious and aggressive behavior in adolescents with intellectual disabilities: A comparison of adolescents with and without autism. *Japanese Journal of Special Education, 39,* 143–154.

Kanner, L. (1943). Autistic disturbances of affective contact. *Nervous Child, 2,* 217–250.

Katsurgi, S., Kunugi, H., Sano, A., Tsutsumi, T., Isogawa, K., Nanko, S., & Akiyoshi, J. (1999). Association between serotonin transporter gene polymorphism and anxiety-related traits. *Biological Psychiatry, 45,* 368–370.

Kauffmann, C., Vance, H., Pumariega, A. J., & Miller, B. (2001). Fluvoxamine treatment of a child with severe PDD: A single case study. *Psychiatry-Interpersonal and Biological Processes, 64,* 268–277.

Kelly, D. D. (1991). Sleep and dreaming. In E. R. Kandel, J. H. Schwartz, & T. M. Jessell (Eds.). *Principles of neural science* (3rd ed., pp. 792–804). Norwalk, CT: Appleton & Lange.

Kennedy, C. H. (2002). Evolution of stereotypy into self-injury. In S. R. Schroeder, M. L. Oster Granite, & T. Thompson (Eds.), *Self-injurious behavior: Gene-brain-behavior relationships* (pp. 133–1143). Washington, DC: American Psychological Association.

Kennedy, C. H., Meyer, K. A., Knowles, T., & Shukla, S. (2000). Analyzing the multiple functions of stereotypical behavior for students with autism: Implications for assessment and treatment. *Journal of Applied Behavior Analysis, 33,* 559–571.

Kennes, D., & de Rycke, P. H. (1988). Influences of performance of stereotypies on plasma corticosterone and leucocyte levels in the bank vole (*Clethrionomys glareolus*). In J. Unshelm, G. van Putten, K. Zeeb K, & I. Ekesbo (Eds.), *Proceedings of the International Congress on Applied Ethology in Farm Animals* (pp. 238–240). Kuratorium for Technology and Building in the Agriculture, Darmstadt, Germany.

Kennes, D., Ödberg, F. O., Bouquet, Y., & De Rycke, P. H. (1988). Changes in naloxone and haloperidol effects during the development of captivity-induced jumping stereotypy in bank voles. *European Journal of Pharmacology, 153,* 19–24.

Kerr, D. S., Huggett, A. M., & Abraham, W. C. (1994). Modulation of hippocampal long-term potentiation and long-term depression by corticosteroid receptor activation. *Psychobiology, 22,* 123–33.

Kiley-Worthington, M. (1977). *Behavioural problems of farm animals*. London: Oriel.

Kinsley, C. H., Mann, P. E., & Bridges, R. S. (1988). Prenatal stress alters morphine- and stress induced analgesia in male and female rats. *Pharmacology, Biochemistry and Behavior, 30,* 123–128.

Kling, A., & Brothers, L. (1992). The amygdala and social behavior. In J. Aggleton (Ed.), *Neurobiological aspects of emotion, memory, and mental dysfunction* (pp. 353–377). New York: Wiley & Sons.

Kling, A., Lancaster, J., & Bentone, J. (1970). Amygdalectomy in the free ranging vervet. *Journal of Psychiatric Research, 7,* 191–199.

Kluver, H., & Bucy, P. C. (1939). Preliminary analysis of the functions of the temporal lobes in monkeys. *Archives of Neurology and Psychiatry, 42,* 979–1000.

Kostal, L., Savory, C. J., & Hughes, B. O. (1992). Diurnal and individual variation in behaviour of restricted-fed broiler breeders. *Applied Animal Behaviour Science, 32,* 361–374.

Kraemer, G. W., & Clarke, A. S. (1990). The behavioral neurobiology of self-injurious behavior in rhesus monkeys. *Progress in Neuro-Psychopharmacology and Biological Psychiatry* (Suppl. 14), 141–168.

Kramer, T. H., Buckout, R., & Eugenio, P. (1990). Weapon focus, arousal, and eyewitness memory: Attention must be paid. *Law and Human Behavior, 14,* 167–184.

Kudoh, A., Katagai, H., & Takazawa, T. (2002). Increased postoperative pain scores in chronic depression patients who take antidepressants. *Journal of Clinical Anesthesia, 14,* 421–425.

Kuhar, M. J. (1986). Neuroanatomical substrates of anxiety: A brief survey. *Trends in Neuroscience, 9,* 307–311.

Kumei, Y., Shimokawa, R., Kimoto, M., Kawauchi, Y., Shimokawa, H., Makita, K., et al. (2001). Gravity stress elevates the nociceptive threshold level with immunohistochemical changes in the rat brain. *Acta Astronautica, 49,* 381–390.

Ladewig, J., de Passillé, A. M., Rushen, J., Schouten, W., Terlouw, C., & von Borrell, E. (1993). Stress and the physiological correlates of stereotypic behaviour. In A. B. Lawrence & J. Rushen (Eds.). *Stereotypic animal behaviour: Fundamentals and applications to welfare* (pp. 97–118). Wallingford, England: CAB International.

Lainhart, J. E. (1997). Psychiatric problems in individuals with autism, their parents and siblings. *International Review of Psychiatry, 11,* 278–298.

Lauder, J. M. (1993). Neurotransmitters as growth regulatory signals: Role of receptors and second messengers. *Trends in Neuroscience, 16,* 233–240.

Lauder, J. M., & Krebs, H. (1976). Effects of p-chlorophenylalanine on time of neuronal origin during embryogenesis in the rat. *Brain Research, 107,* 638–644.

Launay, J. M., Ferrari, P., Haimart, M., Bursztejn, C., Tabuteau, F., Braconnier, A., et al. (1988). Serotonin metabolism and other biochemical parameters in infantile autism: A controlled study of 22 autistic children. *Neuropsychobiology, 20,* 1–11.

Lautenbacher, S., Spernal, J., Schreiber, W., & Krieg, J. C. (1999). Relationship between clinical pain complaints and pain sensitivity in patients with depression and panic disorder. *Psychosomatic Medicine, 61,* 822–827.

Lawrence, A. B., & Rushen, J. (Eds.). (1993). *Stereotypic Animal Behaviour: Fundamentals and Applications to Welfare*. Wallingford, England: CAB International.

Leavens, D. A., Aureli, F., Hopkins, W. D., & Hyatt, C. W. (2001). Effects of cognitive challenge on self-directed behaviors by chimpanzees (*Pan troglodytes*). *American Journal of Primatology, 55,* 1–14.

Lebelt, D., Zanella, A. J., & Unshelm, J. (1998). Physiological correlates associated with cribbing behaviour in horses: Changes in thermal threshold, heart rate, plasma, endorphin, and serotonin. *Equine Veterinary Journal Supplement, 27,* 21–27.

Leboyer, M., Philippe, A., Bouvard, M., Guilloud-Bataille, M., Bondoux, D., Tabuteau, F., et al. (1999). Whole blood serotonin and plasma endorphin in autistic probands and their first degree relatives. *Biological Psychiatry, 45,* 158–163.

Lentjes, E. G., Griep, E. N., Boersma, J.W., Romijn, F. P., De Kloet, E. R. (1997). Glucocorticoid receptors, fibromyalgia and low back pain. *Psychoneuroendocrinology, 22,* 603–614.

Levine, S., Coe, C., & Wiener, S. G. (1989). Psychoneuroendocrinology of stress: A psychobiological perspective. In F. R. Brush & S. Levine (Eds.), *Psychoneuroendocrinology* (pp. 341–377). San Diego, CA: Academic Press.

Levison, C. A. (1970). The development of head banging in a young rhesus monkey. *American Journal of Mental Deficiencies, 75,* 323–328.

Levy, A. D., Baumann, M. H., & Van de Kar, L. D. (1994). Monoaminergic regulation of neuroendocrine function and its modification by cocaine. *Frontiers in Neuroendocrinology, 15,* 1–72.

Lewis, M. H., & Bodfish, J. W. (1998). Repetitive behavior disorders in autism. *Mental Retardation and Developmental Disabilities Research Reviews, 4,* 80–89.

Line, S. W., & Morgan, K. N. (1991). The effects of two novel objects on the behavior of singly caged adult rhesus macaques. *Laboratory Animal Science, 41,* 365–366.

Line, S. W., Morgan K. N., & Markowitz, H. (1991). Simple toys do not alter behaviour of aged rhesus monkeys. *Zoo Biology, 10,* 473–484.

Line, S. W., Morgan K. N., Markowitz, H., & Strong, S. (1990). Increased cage size does not alter heart rate or behavior in female rhesus monkeys. *American Journal of Primatology, 20,* 107–113.

Logan, H. L., Sheffield, D., Lutgendorf, S., & Lang, E. (2002). Predictors of pain during invasive medical procedures. *Journal of Pain, 3,* 211–217.

Loosen, P. T., Chambliss, B., Debold, C. R., Shelton, R., & Orth, D. N. (1992). Psychiatric phenomenology in Cushing's disease. *Pharmacopsychiatry, 25,* 192–198.

Lopez-Ibor, J. J., Jr., Saiz-Ruiz, J., & Perez de los Cobos, J. C. (1985). Biological correlations of suicide and aggressivity in major depressions (with melancholia): 5-hydroxyindoleacetic acid and cortisol in cerebral spinal fluid, dexamethasone suppression test and therapeutic response to 5-hydroxytryptophan. *Neuropsychobiology, 14,* 67–74.

Lukas, K. E., Hoff, M. P., & Maple, T. L. (2003). Gorilla behavior in response to systematic alternation between zoo enclosures. *Applied Animal Behaviour Science, 81,* 367–386.

Lutz, C., Marinus, L., Chase, W., Meyer, J., & Novak, M. (2003). Self-injurious behavior in male rhesus macaques does not reflect externally directed aggression. *Physiology and Behavior, 78,* 33–39.

Lutz, C. K., Chase, W. K., & Novak, M. A. (2000). Abnormal behavior in singly-housed *Macaca mulatta*: Prevalence and potential risk factors. *American Journal of Primatology, 51,* 72.

Maes, M., Meltzer, H.Y., D'Hondt, P., Cosyns, P., & Blockx, P. (1995). Effects of serotonin precursors on the negative feedback effects of glucocorticoids on hypothalamic-pituitary adrenal axis function in depression. *Psychoneuroendocrinology, 20,* 149–167.

Maestripieri, D. (1993). Maternal anxiety in rhesus macaques (*Macca mulatta*). 1. Measurement of anxiety and identification of anxiety-eliciting situations. *Ethology, 95,* 19–31.

Magarinos, A. M., McEwen, B. S., Flugge, G., & Fuchs, E. (1996). Chronic psychosocial stress causes apical dendritic atropy of hippocampal CA3 pyramidal neurons in subordinate tree shrews. *Journal of Neuroscience, 16,* 3534–3540.

Magarinos, A. M., Verdugo, J. M. G, & McEwen, B. S. (1997). Chronic stress alters synaptic terminal structure in hippocampus. *Proceedings of the National Academy of Sciences of the United States of America, 94,* 14002–14008.

Maier, S. F., Drugan, R. C., & Grau, J. W. (1982). Controllability, coping behavior, and stress induced analgesia in the rat. *Pain, 12,* 47–56.

Maier, S. F., Sherman, J. E., Lewis, J. W., Terman, G. W., & Liebeskind, J. C. (1983). The opioid/nonopioid nature of stress-induced analgesia and learned helplessness. *Journal of Experimental Psychology: Animal Behavior Processes, 9,* 80–90.

Maple, T., Risse, G., & Mitchell, G. (1973). Separation of adult male from adult female rhesus monkeys (*Macaca mulatta*). *Journal of Behavioral Science, 1,* 321–336.

Martineau, J., Herault, J., Petit, E. Guerin, P. Hameury, L., Perrot, A., et al. (1994). Catecholaminergic metabolism and autism. *Developmental Medicine and Child Neurology, 36,* 688–697.

Mason, G. (1991). Stereotypies: A critical review. *Animal Behaviour, 41,* 1015–1037.

Mason, G. J., & Turner, M. A. (1993). Mechanisms involved in the development and control of stereotypies. In P. P. G. Bateson, P. H. Klopfer, & N. S. Thompson (Eds.), *Perspectives in ethology: Vol. 10. Behavior and evolution* (pp. 53–85). New York: Plenum Press.

Mason, J. W. (1971). A re-evaluation of the concept of "non-specificity" in stress theory. *Journal of Psychiatric Research, 8,* 323–333.

Mason, J. W., Maher, J. T., Hartley, L. H., Mongey, E. H., Perlow, M. J., & Jones, L. G. (1976). Selectivity of corticosteroid and catecholamine responses to various natural stimuli. In G. Serban (Ed.), *Psychopathology of human adaptation* (pp. 147–171). New York: Plenum Press.

Mason, W. A., & Berkson, G. (1975). Effects of maternal mobility on the development of rocking and other behaviors in rhesus monkeys: A study with artificial mothers. *Developmental Psychobiology, 8,* 197–211.

Mason, W. A., & Sponholz, R. R. (1963). Behaviour of rhesus monkeys raised in isolation. *Journal of Psychiatric Research, 1,* 299–306.

Mauri, M., Sinforiani, E., Bono, G., Vignati, F., Berselli, M. E., Attanasio, R., & Nappi, G. (1993). Memory impairment in Cushing's disease. *Acta Neurologica Scandinavica, 87,* 52–55.

McCracken, J. T., McGough, J., Shah, B, Cronin, P., Hong, D., Aman, M. G., et al. (2002). Risperidone in children with autism and serious behavioral problems. *New England Journal of Medicine, 347,* 314–321.

McEwen, B. S. (1994). Corticosteroids and hippocampal plasticity. *Annals of the New York Academy of Sciences, 746,* 134–142.

McEwen, B. S. (2000a). The neurobiology of stress: From serendipity to clinical relevance. *Brain Research, 886,* 172–189. McEwen, B. S. (2000b). Effects of adverse experiences for brain structure and function. *Biological Psychiatry, 48,* 721–731.

McEwen, B. S., & Sapolsky, R. (1995). Stress and cognitive function. *Current Opinion in Neurobiology, 5,* 205–216.

McEwen, B. S., & Wingfield, J. C. (2003). The concept of allostasis in biology and medicine. *Hormones and Behavior, 43,* 2–15.

McGreevy, P., & Nicol, C. (1998). Physiological and behavioral consequences associated with short-term prevention of crib-biting in horses. *Physiology and Behavior, 65,* 15–23.

Meyer-Holzapfel, M. (1968). Abnormal behavior in zoo animals. In M. W. Fox (Ed.), *Abnormal behavior in animals* (pp. 476–503). Philadelphia: W. B. Saunders.

Michelson, D., Licinio, J., & Gold, P. W. (1995). Mediation of the stress response by the hypothalamic-pituitary-adrenal axis. In M. J. Friedman, D. S. Charney, & A. Y. Deutch (Eds.), *Neurobiological and clinical consequences of stress: From normal adaptation to PTSD* (pp. 225–238). Philadelphia: Lippincott-Raven.

Militerni, R., Bravaccio, C., Falco, C., Fico, C., & Palermo, M. T. (2002). Repetive behaviors in autistic disorder. *European Child and Adolescent Psychiatry, 11,* 210–218.

Minero, M., Ödberg, F. O., Ferrante, V., & Canali, E. (1996). Preliminary results on the relationship between heart rate and cribbing in horses. *Proceedings of the International Workshop on Methods and Techniques in Behavioural Research,* Utrecht, The Netherlands, 70–71.

Minshew, N. J., & Goldstein, G. (2001). The pattern of intact and impaired memory functions in autism. *Journal of Child Psychology and Psychiatry, 42,* 1095–1101.

Mitchell, G. (1970). Abnormal behaviour in primates. In L. A. Rosenblum (Ed.), *Primate behaviour: Developments in field and laboratory research* (Vol. 1., pp., 195–249). New York: Academic Press.

Mittleman, G., Jones, G. H., & Robbins, T. W. (1991). Sensitization of amphetamine-stereotypy reduces plasma corticosterone: Implications for stereotypy as a coping response. *Behavioral & Neural Biology, 56,* 170–182.

Moody, T. W., Merali, Z., & Crawley, J. N. (1988). The effects of anxiolytics and other agents on rat grooming behavior. *Annals of the New York Academy of Science, 525,* 281–90.

Morgan, K. N., Line, S. W., & Markowitz, H. (1998). Zoos, enrichment, and the skeptical observer: The practical value of assessment. In D. J. Shepherdson, J. D. Mellen, & M. Hutchins (Eds.), *Second nature: Environmental enrichment for captive animals* (pp. 153–171). Washington, DC: Smithsonian Institution Press.

Morgan, K. N., Mondesir, F. L., Buell, K., Guy, P., Carmella, V., Hunt, C., & Pizarro, S. (2002, June). *Changes in chimp behavior, visitor behavior, and visitor attitude with a change in exhibit.* Poster presented at Animal Behavior Society, Bloomington, IN.

Morgan, K. N., Thayer, J. E., & Frye, C. A. (1999). Prenatal stress suppresses rat pup ultrasonic vocalization and myoclonic twitching in response to separation. *Developmental Psychobiology, 34,* 205–15.

Morley, D. S. (2000). Psychophysiological reactivity to stress in nail biters. *International Journal of Neuroscience, 103,* 139–154.

Mueller, K., & Nyhan, W. L. (1982). Pharmacologic control of pemoline induced self-injurious behaviour in rats. *Pharmacology, Biochemistry, and Behavior, 16,* 957–963.

Muller, M. N., & Wrangham, R. W. (2004). Dominance, cortisol, and stress in wild chimpanzees (*Pan troglodytes schweinfurthii*). *Behavioral Ecology and Sociobiology, 55,* 332–340.

Munck, A., Guyre, P. M., & Holbrook, N. J. (1984). Physiological functions of glucocorticoids in stress and their relation to pharmacological actions. *Endocrine Reviews, 5,* 25–44.

Muris, P., Steerneman, P., Merckelbach, H., Holdrinet, I., & Meesters, D. (1998). Comorbid anxiety symptoms in children with pervasive developmental disorders. *Journal of Anxiety Disorders, 12,* 387–393.

Murphy, M., Bolton, P. F., Pickles, A., Fombonne, E., Piven, J., & Rutter, M. (2000). Personality traits of the relatives of autistic probands. *Psychological Medicine, 30*(6), 1411–1424.

New, A. S., Trestman, R. L., Mitropoulou, V., Benishay, D. S., Coccaro, E., Silverman, J., & Siever, L. J. (1997). Serotonergic function and self-injurious behavior in personality disorder patients. *Psychiatry Research, 3,* 17–26.

Newell, K. M., Challis, J. H., Boros, R. L., & Bodfish, J. W. (2002). Further evidence on the dynamics of self-injurious behaviors: Impact forces and limb motions. *American Journal on Mental Retardation, 107,* 60–68.

Newport, D. J., Heim, C., Owens, M. J., Ritchie, J. C., Ramsey, C. H., Bonsall, R., et al. (2003). Cerebrospinal fluid corticotropin-releasing factor (CRF) and vasopressin concentrations predict pituitary response in the CRF stimulation test: A multiple regression analysis. *Neuropsychopharmacology, 28,* 569–576.

Ng, V., Koh, D., & Chia, S. E. (2003). Examination stress, salivary cortisol, and academic performance. *Psychological Reports, 93,* 1133–1134.

Nickel, T., Sonntag, A., Schill, J., Zobel, A. W., Ackl, N., Brunnauer, A., et al. (2003). Clinical and neurobiological effects of tianeptine and paroxetine in major depression. *Journal of Clinical Pharmacology, 23,* 155–168.

Niemeyer, C., Gray, E. G., & Stephen, T. (1996). Improving the psychological well-being of nonhuman primates by providing appropriate therapeutic devices [abstract no. 678]. In Proceedings of the *XVIth Congress of the International Primatological Society/XIXth Conference of the American Society of Primatologists,* Madison, WI.

Nishith, P., Griffin, M. G., & Poth, T. L. (2002). Stress-induced analgesia: Prediction of posttraumatic stress symptoms in battered versus nonbattered women. *Biological Psychiatry, 51,* 867–874.

Nixon, M. K., Cloutier, P. F., & Aggarwal, S. (2002). Affect regulation and addictive aspects of repetitive self-injury in hospitalized adolescents. *Journal of the American Academy of Child & Adolescent Psychiatry, 41,* 1333–1341.

Novak, M. A. (2003). Self-injurious behavior in rhesus monkeys: New insights into its etiology, physiology, and treatment. *American Journal of Primatology, 59,* 3–19.

O'Brien, P. H. (1982). Self-sucking behaviour by a feral goat. *Applied Animal Ethology, 8,* 189–190.

Ödberg, F. (1987). Behavioural responses to stress in farm animals. In P. R. Wiepkema & P. W. M. van Adrichem (Eds.), *The biology of stress in farm animals* (pp. 135–149). Dordrecht, The Netherlands: Martinus Nijhoff.

Okifuji, A., & Turk, D. C. (2002). Stress and psychophysiological dysregulation in patients with fibromyalgia syndrome. *Applied Psychophysiology and Biofeedback, 27,* 129–141.

Oliver, C. (1995). Annotation: Self-injurious behavior in children with learning disabilities: Recent advances in assessment and intervention. *Journal of Child Psychology and Psychiatry, 36,* 909–927.

Osher, Y., Hamer, D., & Benjamin, J. (2000). Association and linkage of anxiety-related traits with a functional polymorphism of the serotonin transporter gene regulatory region in Israeli sibling pairs. *Molecular Psychiatry, 5,* 216–219.

Pacak, K., & Palkovits, M. (2001). Stressor specificity of central neuroendocrine responses: Implications for stress-related disorders. *Endocrine Reviews, 22,* 502–548.

Pacak, K., Palkovits, M., Yadid, G., Kvetnansky, R., Kopin, I. J., & Goldstein, D. S (1998). Heterogeneous neurochemical responses to different stressors: A test of Selye's doctrine of nonspecificity. *American Journal of Physiology, 275,* 1247–1255.

Palmer, C. J., Yates, W. R., & Trotter, L. (1999). Childhood trichotillomania. Successful treatment with fluoxetine following an SSRI failure. *Psychosomatics, 40,* 526–528.

Persico, A. M., Pascucci, T., Puglisi-Allegra, S., Militerni, R., Bravaccio, C., Schneider, C., et al. (2002). Serotonin transporter gene promoter variants do not explain the hyperserotonemia in autistic children. *Molecular Psychiatry, 7,* 795–800.

Peters, D. A. (1990). Maternal stress increases fetal brain and neonatal cerebral cortex 5-hydroxytryptamine synthesis in rats: A possible mechanism by which stress influences brain development. *Pharmacology, Biochemistry & Behavior, 35,* 943–947.

Pezzone, M. A., Lee, W. S., Hoffman, G. E., & Rabin, B. S. (1992). Induction of c-fos immunoreactivity in the rat forebrain by conditioned and unconditioned aversive stimuli. *Brain Research, 597,* 41–50.

Pitman, R. K., van der Kolk, B. A., Orr, S., & Greenberg, M. S. (1990). Naloxone-reversible analgesic response to combat-related stimuli in posttraumatic stress disorder. A pilot study. *Archives of General Psychiatry, 47,* 541–544.

Piven, J., Landa, R., Gayle, J., Cloud, D., Chase, G., & Folstein, S. E. (1991). Psychiatric disorders in the parents of autistic individuals. *Journal of the American Academy of Child and Adolescent Psychiatry, 30,* 471–478.

Piven, J., & Palmer, P. (1999). Psychiatric disorder and the broad autism phenotype: Evidence from a family study of multiple-incidence autism families. *American Journal of Psychiatry, 156,* 557–563.

Pol, F., Courboulay, V., Cotte, J. P., Martrenchar, A., Hay, M., & Mormede, P. (2002). Urinary cortisol as an additional tool to assess the welfare of pregnant sows kept in two types of housing. *Veterinary Research, 33,* 13–22.

Pollak, S. D., & Tolley-Schell, S. A. (2003). Selective attention to facial emotion in physically abused children. *Journal of Abnormal Psychology, 112,* 323–338.

Pollock, J., & Kornetsky, C. (1989). Evidence for the role of dopamine D1 receptors in morphine induced stereotypic behavior. *Neuroscience Letters, 102,* 291–296.

Pond, C. L., & Rush, H. G. (1983). Self-aggression in macaques: Five case studies. *Primates, 24,* 127–134.

Posey, D. J., Geuenin, K. D., Kohn, A. E., Swiezy, N. B., & McDougle, C. J. (2001). A naturalistic open-label study of mirtazapine in autistic and other pervasive developmental disorders. *Journal of Child and Adolescent Psychopharmacology, 11,* 267–277.

Posey, D. J., & McDougle, C. J. (2002). Risperidone: A potential treatment for autism. *Current Opinion on Investigational Drugs, 3,* 1212–1216.

Prater, C. D., & Zylstra, R. G. (2002). Autism: A medical primer. *American F. mily Physician, 66,* 1667–1674.

Puglisi-Allegra, S., & Oliverio, A. (1983). Social isolation: Effects on pain thresholds and stress induced analgesia. *Pharmacology, Biochemistry & Behavior, 19,* 679–681.

Rafaeli-Mor, N., Foster, L., & Berkson, G. (1999). Self-reported body rocking and other habits in college students. *American Journal of Mental Retardation, 104,* 1–10.

Rapin, I., & Katzman, R. (1998). Neurobiology of autism. *Annals of Neurology, 43,* 7–14.

Rasmussen, A. M., Lipschitz, D. S., Wang, S., Hu, S., Vojvoda, D., Bremner, J. D., et al. (2001). Increaesed pituitary and adrenal reactivity in premenopausal women with posttraumatic stress disorder. *Biological Psychiatry, 15,* 965–977.

Raymond, G. V., Bauman, M. L., & Kemper, T. L. (1996). Hippocampus in autism: A Golgi analysis. *Acta Neuropathologica, 91,* 117–119.

Redbo, I. (1998). Relations between oral stereotypies, open-field behavior, and pituitary-adrenal system in growing dairy cattle. *Physiology and Behavior, 64,* 273–278.

Redican, W. K., Gomber, J., & Mitchell, G. (1974). Adult male parental behaviour in feral-and isolation-reared rhesus monkeys (*Macaca mulatta*). In J. H. Cullen (Ed.), *Experimental behaviour: A basis for the study of mental disturbance* (pp. 131–146). Dublin, Ireland: Irish University Press.

Redmond, D. E., Jr. (1987). Studies of the nucleus locus caeruleus in monkeys and hypotheses for neuropsychopharmacology. In H. Y. Meltzer (Ed.), *Psychopharmacology: The third generation of progress* (pp. 363–372). New York: Raven Press.

Redmond, D. E., Huang, Y. H., Snyder, D. R., & Maas, J. W. (1976). Behavioral effects of stimulation of the nucleus locus coeruleus in the stump-tailed monkey (*Macaca arctoides*). *Brain Research, 116,* 502–510.

Reinhardt, V. (1999). Pair-housing overcomes self-biting behavior in macaques. *Laboratory Primate Newsletter, 38,* 4.

Reinhardt, V., & Rossell, M. (2001). Self-biting in caged macaques: Cause, effect, and treatment. *Journal of Applied Animal Welfare Science, 4,* 285–294.

Reinhardt, V., Reinhardt, A., & Houser, D. (1986). Hair-pulling and eating in captive rhesus monkey troops. *Folia Primatol (Basel), 47*(2–3), 158–164.

Richdale, A. L. (1999). Sleep problems in autism: Prevalence, cause, and intervention. *Developmental Medicine & Child Neurology, 41,* 60–66.

Richdale, A. L., & Prior, M. R. (1992).Urinary cortisol circadian rhythm in a group of high functioning children with autism. *Journal of Autism & Developmental Disorders, 22,* 433–447.

Ridley, R. M., & Baker, H. F. (1982). Stereotypy in monkeys and humans. *Psychological Medicine, 12,* 61–72.

Rimland, B. (1964). *Infantile autism: The syndrome and its implications for a neural theory of behavior.* Englewood Cliffs, NJ: Prentice Hall.

Rincover, A., & Ducharme, J. M. (1987). Variables influencing stimulus overselectivity and "tunnel vision" in developmentally delayed children. *American Journal of Mental Deficiency, 91,* 422–430.

Rizzi, A., Marzola, G., Bigoni, R., Guerrini, R., Salvadori, S., Mogil, J. S., et al. (2001). Endogenous nociceptin signaling and stress-induced analgesia. *Neuroreport, 12,* 3009–3013.

Rowell, C. H. F. (1961). Displacement grooming in the chaffinch. *Animal Behaviour, 9,* 38–63.

Rulf Fountain, A. (2001). Self-injurious behavior in university undergraduate students (doctoral dissertation, University of Amherst). *Dissertation Abstracts International: Section B. The Sciences and Engineering, 62,* 596.

Rushen, J., Lawrence, A. B., & Terlouw, E. M. C. (1993). The motivational basis of stereotypies. In A. B. Lawrence & J. Rushen (Eds.), *Stereotypic animal behaviour: Fundamentals and applications to welfare* (pp. 41–64). Wallingford, England: CAB International.

Russell, J., Jarrold, C., & Henry, L. (2002). Working memory in children with autism and with moderate learning difficulties. *Journal of Child Psychology and Psychiatry, 37,* 673–686.

Sackett, G. P. (1968). Abnormal behavior in laboratory-reared rhesus monkeys. In M. W. Fox (Ed.), *Abnormal behavior in animals* (pp. 293–331). Philadelphia: W. B. Saunders.

Sackett, G. P., Novak, M. F. S. X., & Kroeker, R. (1999). Early experience effects on adaptive behavior: Theory revisited. *Mental Retardation & Developmental Disabilities Research Reviews, 5,* 30–40.

Saitoh, O., Karns, C. M., & Courchesne, E. (2001). Development of the hippocampal formation from 2 to 42 years: MRI evidence of smaller area dentata in autism. *Brain, 124,* 1317–1324.

Samson, J. (1996). Behavioral problems of farmed ostriches in Canada. *Canadian Veterinary Journal-Revue Veterinaire Canadienne 37*(7), 412–414.

Sandi, C., & Rose, S. P .R. (1994). Corticosterone enhances long-term retention in one-day old chicks trained in a weak passive avoidance learning paradigm. *Brain Research, 647,* 106–112.

Sandman, C. A. (1988). Beta-endorphin disregulation in autistic and self-injurious behavior: A neurodevelopmental hypothesis. *Synapse, 2,* 193–199.

Sapolsky, R. M. (1987). Glucocorticoids and hippocampal damage. *Trends in Neuroscience, 10,* 346–349.

Sapolsky, R. M. (1992). Cortisol concentrations and the social significance of rank instability among wild baboons. *Psychoneuroendocrinology, 17,* 701–709.

Sapolsky, R. M. (1996). Stress, glucocorticoids, and damage to the nervous system: The current state of confusion. *Stress, 1,* 1–11.

Sapolsky, R. M. (1999). Glucocorticoids, stress, and their adverse neurological effects: Relevance to aging. *Experimental Gerontology, 34,* 721–729.

Sapolsky, R. M. (2000). Glucocorticoids and hippocampal atrophy in neuropsychiatric disorders. *Archives of General Psychiatry, 57,* 925–935.

Sapolsky, R. M., Krey, L. C., & McEwen, B. S. (1984a). Glucocorticoid-sensitive hippocampal neurons are involved in terminating the adreno-cortical stress response. *Proceedings of the National Academy of Sciences, 81,* 6174–6177.

Sapolsky, R. M., Krey, L. C., & McEwen, B. S. (1984b). Stress down-regulates corticosterone receptors in a site-specific manner in the brain. *Endocrinology, 114,* 287–292.

Sapolsky, R. M., & McEwen, B. S. (1985). Down-regulation of neural corticosterone receptors by corticosterone and dexamethasone. *Brain Research, 339,* 161–165.

Sapolsky, R. M., & Plotsky, P. M. (1990). Hypercortisolism and its possible neural bases. *Biological Psychiatry, 27,* 937–952.

Sapolsky, R. M., Uno, H., Rebert, C. S., & Finch, C. E. (1990). Hippocampal damage asociated with prolonged glucocorticoid exposure in primates. *The Journal of Neuroscience, 10,* 2897–2902.

Saulnier, C. A., Jr. (2003). Sensory reactivity in children with and without autism (doctoral dissertation, University of Connecticut, 2003). *Dissertation Abstracts International: Section B. The Sciences & Engineering, 63(10-B),* 4923.

Savory, C. J., Seawright, E., & Watson, A. (1992). Stereotyped behaviour in broiler breeders in relation to husbandry and opioid receptor blockade. *Applied Animal Behaviour Science, 32,* 17–26.

Sawchenko, P. E., & Swanson, L. W. (1982). The organization of noradrenergic pathways from the brainstem to the paraventricular and supraoptic nuclei in the ra. *Brain Research Reviews, 4,* 275–325.

Schain, R. J., & Freedman, D. X. (1961). Studies on 5-hydroxyindole metabolism in autistic and other mentally retarded children. *Journal of Pediatrics, 58,* 315–320.

Scherder, E., Bouma, A., Slaets, J., Ooms, M., Ribbe, M., Blok, A., & Sergeant, J. (2001). Repeated pain assessment in Alzheimer's disease. *Dementia and Geriatric Cognitive Disorders, 12,* 400–407.

Schino, G., Perretta, G., Taglioni, A. M., Monaco, V., & Troisi, A. (1996). Primate displacement activities as an ethopharmacological model of anxiety. *Anxiety, 2,* 186–191.

Schino, G., Troisi, A., Perretta, G., & Monaco, V. (1991). Measuring anxiety in non-human primates: Effects of lorazepam on macaque scratching. *Pharmacology, Biochemistry, & Behavior, 38,* 889–891.

Schouten, W. G. P, & Wiegant, V. M. (1997). Individual responses to acute and chronic stress in pigs. *Acta Physiologica Scandinavica* (Suppl. 640), 88–91.

Schouten, W. G. P., & Wiepkema, P. R. (1991). Coping styles of tethered sows. *Behavioural Processes, 25,* 125–132.

Schroeder, S. R., Oster-Granite, M. L., Berkson, G., Bodfish, J. W., Breese, G. R., Cataldo, M. F., et al. (2001). Self-injurious behavior: Gene-brain-behavior relationships. *Mental Retardation and Developmental Disabilities Reviews, 7,* 3–12.

Schumann, C. M., Hamstra, J., Goodlin-Jones, B. L., Lotspeich, L. J., Kwon, H., Buonocore, M. H., et al. (2004). The amygdala is enlarged in children but not adolescents with autism: The hippocampus is enlarged at all ages. *Journal of Neuroscience, 24,* 6392–6401.

Selye, H. (1936). A syndrome produced by diverse nocuous agents. *Nature, 138,* 32.

Selye, H. (1976). *The stress of life.* New York: McGraw-Hill.

Serres, F., Li, Q., Garcia, R., Raap., D. K., Battaglia, G., Muma, N. A., & Van de Kar, L. D. (2000). Evidence that G_z proteins couple to hypothalamic $5-HT_{1A}$ receptors *in vivo. Journal of Neuroscience, 20,* 3095–3103.

Shalom, B. (2003). Memory in autism: Review and synthesis. *Cortex, 39,* 1129–1138.

Shishido, T., Watanabe, Y., Kato, K., Horikoshi, R, & Niwa, S. I. (2000). Effects of dopamine, NMDA, opiate, and serotonin-related agents on acute methamphetamine-induced self-injurious behavior in mice. *Pharmacology, Biochemistry, and Behavior, 66,* 579–583.

Singareddy, R. K., & Balon, R. (2002). Sleep in post-traumatic stress disorder. *Annals of Clinical Psychiatry, 14,* 183–190.

Sivam, S. P. (1996). Dopamine, serotonin, and tachykinin in self-injurious behavior. *Life Sciences, 58,* 2367–2375.

Smalley, S. L., McCracken, J., & Tanguay, P. (1995). Autism, affective disorders, and social phobia. *American Journal of Medical Genetics, 60,* 19–26.

Sonino, N., & Fava, G. A. (2001). Psychiatric disorders associated with Cushing's syndrome: Epidemiology, pathophysiology and treatment. *CNS Drugs, 15,* 361–373.

Soussignan, R., & Koch, P. (1985). Rhythmical stereotypies (leg swinging) associated with reductions in heart-rate in normal school children. *Biological Psychology, 21,* 161–167.

Sparks, B. F., Friedman, S .D., Shaw, D. W., Aylward, E. H., Echelard, D., Artru, A. A., et al. (2002). Brain structural abnormalities in young children with autism spectrum disorder. *Neurology, 59,* 184–192.

Stamford, J. A., Davidson, C., McLaughlin, D. P., & Hopwood, S. E. (2000). Control of dorsal raphe 5-HT function by multiple 5-HT1 autoreceptors: Parallel purposes or pointless plurality? *Trends in Neuroscience, 23,* 459–465.

Stanley, M., Traskman-Bendz, L., & Dorovini-Zis, K. (1985). Correlations between aminergic metabolites simultaneously obtained from samples of CSF and brain. *Life Sciences, 37,* 1279–1286.

Stanley, M. A., Borden, J. W., Mouton, S. G., & Breckenridge, J. K. (1995). Non-clinical hair-pulling: Affective correlates and comparison with clinical samples. *Behaviour Research & Therapy, 33,* 179–186.

Starkman, M., Gabarski, S., Berent, S., & Schteingart, D. (1992). Hippocampal formation volume, memory dysfunction, and cortisol levels in patients with Cushing's syndrome. *Biological Psychiatry, 32,* 756–765.

Starkman, M. N., Giordani, B., Berent, S., Schork, A., & Schteingart, D. E. (2001). Elevated cortisol levels in Cushing's disease are associated with cognitive decrements. *Psychosomatic Medicine, 63,* 985–993.

Steblay, N. M. (1992). A meta-analytic review of the weapon focus effect. *Law and Human Behavior, 16,* 413–424.

Stowe, R. P., Sams, C. F., & Pierson, D. L. (2003). Effects of mission duration on neuroimmune responses in astronauts. *Aviation, Space and Environmental Medicine, 74,* 1281–1284.

Sweeten, T. L., Posey, D. J., Shekhar, A., & McDougle, C. J. (2002). The amygdala and related structures in the pathophysiology of autism. *Pharmacology, Biochemistry, and Behavior, 71,* 449–455.

Symons, F. J., Clark, R. D., Hatton, D. D., Skinner, M., & Bailey, D. B., Jr. (2003). Self-injurious behavior in young boys with fragile X syndrome. *American Journal of Medical Genetics, 118A,* 115–121.

Takahashi, L. K., Kalin, N. H., Barksdale, C. M., Vanden Burgt, J. A., & Brownfield, S. (1988). Stressor controllability during pregnancy influences pituitary-adrenal hormone concentrations and analgesic responsiveness in offspring. *Physiology and Behavior, 42,* 323–329.

Taylor, E. (1993). Neurotransmitters, overactivity and other psychiatric disturbance. *Educational & Child Psychology, 10,* 46–55.

Terlouw, E. M. C., de Rosa, G., Lawrence, A .B., Illius, A. W., & Ladewig, J. (1992). Behavioral responses to amphetamine and apomorphine in pigs. *Pharmacology, Biochemistry, and Behavior, 43,* 329–340.

Thayer, J. E. (1997, May). *Prenatal stress affects opioid-mediated nociception.* Poster session presented at the American Psychological Society, Biology and Behavior Symposium, Washington, DC.

Thompson, T. Symons, F., Delaney, D., & England, C. (1995). Self-injurious behavior as endogenous neurochemical self-administration. *Mental Retardation & Developmental Disabilities Research Reviews, 1,* 137–148.

Tiefenbacher, S., Novak, M. A., Jorgensen, M. J., & Meyer, J. S. (2000). Physiological correlates of self-injurious behavior in captive, socially-reared rhesus monkeys. *Psychneuroendocrinology, 25,* 799–817.

Tinklepaugh, O. L. (1928). The self-mutilation of a male Macacus rhesus monkey. *Journal of Mammalogy, 9,* 293–300.

Tordjman, S., Anderson, G. M., McBride, P. A., Hertzig, M. E., Snow, M. E., Hall, L M., et al. (1997). Plasma beta-endorphin, adrenocorticotropic hormone, and cortisol in autism. *Journal of Child Psychology and Psychiatry and Allied Disciplines, 38,* 705–715.

Tornello, S., Orti, F., DeNicola, A. F., Rainbow, T. C., & McEwen, B. S. (1982). Regulation of glucocorticoid receptors in brain by corticosterone treatment of adrenalectomized rats. *Neuroendocrinology, 35,* 411–417.

Troisi, A., Belsanti, S., Bucci, A. R., Mosco, C., Sinti, F., & Verucci, M. (2000). Affect regulation in alexithymia: An ethological study of displacement behavior during psychiatric interviews. *Journal of Nervous and Mental Disease, 188,* 13–18.

Troisi, A., Schino, G., D'Antoni, M., Pandolfi, N., Aureli, F., & D'Amato, F. R. (1991). Scratching as a behavioral index of anxiety in macaque mothers. *Behavioral and Neural Biology, 56,* 307–313.

Tröster, H. (1994). Prevalence and functions of stereotyped behaviors in nonhandicapped children in residential care. *Journal of Abnormal Child Psychology, 22,* 79–97.

Trottier, G., Srivastava, L., & Walker, C. D. (1999). Etiology of infantile autism: A review of recent advances in genetic and neurobiological research. *Journal of Psychiatry and Neuroscience, 24,* 103–115.

Turner, C., Panksepp, J., Bekkedal, M., Borkowski, C., & Burgdorf, J. (1999). Paradoxical effects of serotonin and opioids in pemoline-induced self-injurious behavior. *Pharmacology, Biochemistry, and Behavior, 63,* 361–366.

Turner, M. (1999). Annotation: Repetitive behavior in autism: A review of psychological research. *Journal of Child Psychology and Psychiatry, 40,* 839–849.

Ungerstedt, U. (1971). Mapping of the central dopamine, noradrenaline, and 5-ydroxytryptamine pathways. *Acta Physiologica Scandinavica Supplement, 367,* 1–43.

Uno, H., Lohmiller, L., Thieme, C., Kemnitz, J. W., Engle, M. J., Roecker, E. B., & Farell, P. M. (1990). Brain damage induced by prenatal exposure to dexamethasone in fetal rhesus monkeys: I. Hippocampus. *Developmental Brain Research, 53,* 157–167.

Uno, H., Tarara, R., Else, J. G., Suleman, M. A., & Sapolsky, R. M. (1989). Hippocampal damage associated with prolonged and fatal stress in primates. *Journal of Neuroscience, 9,* 1705–1711.

Van de Kar, L. D. (1997). 5-HT receptors involved in the regulation of hormone secretion. In H. G. Baumgarten & M. Göthert (Eds.), *Handbook of experimental pharmacology: Serotonergic neurons and 5-HT receptors* (pp. 537–562). Berlin, Germany: Springer.

Van de Kar, L. D., & Blair, M .L. (1999). Forebrain pathways mediating stress-induced hormone secretion. *Frontiers in Neuroendocrinology, 20,* 1–48.

Varghese, F. P., & Brown, E. S. (2001). The hypothalamic-pituitary—adrenal axis in major depressive disorder: A brief primer for primary care physicians. *Primary Care Companion to the Journal of Clinical Psychiatry, 3,* 151–155.

Verhoeven, W. M. A., Tuinier, S., van den Berg, Y. W. M., Coppus, A. M. W., Fekkes, D., Pepplinkhuizen, L., & Thijssen, J. H. H. (1999). Stress and self-injurious behavior: hormonal and serotonergic parameters in mentally retarded patients. *Pharmacopsychiatry, 32,* 13–20.

Volkmar, F. R. (2001). Pharmachological interventions in autism: Theoretical and practical issues. *Journal of Clinical Child Psychology, 30,* 80–87.

Von Borell, E., & Hurnik, J. F. (1991). Stereotypic behavior, adrenocortical function, and open field behavior of individually confined gestating sows. *Physiology and Behavior, 49,* 709–713.

Vyas, A., Mitra, R., & Chattarji, S. (2003). Enhanced anxiety and hypertrophy in basolateral amygdala neurons following chronic stress in rats. *Annals of the New York Academy of Sciences, 985*, 554–555.

Vyas, A., Mitra, R., Rao, B. S. S., & Chattarji, S. (2002). Chronic stress induces contrasting patterns of dendritic remodeling in hippocampal and amygdaloid neurons. *Journal of Neuroscience, 22*, 6810–6818.

Wainwright-Sharp, J. A., & Bryson, S. E. (1993). Visual orienting deficits in high-functioning people with autism. *Journal of Autism & Developmental Disorders, 23*, 1–13.

Waitt, C., & Buchanan-Smith, H. M. (2001). What time is feeding? How delays and anticipation of feeding schedules affect stump-tailed macaque behavior. *Applied Animal Behaviour Science, 75*, 75–85.

Walters, A. S., Barrett, R. P., Feinstein, C., Mercurio, A., & Hole, W. T. (1990). A case report of naltrexone treatment of self-injury and social withdrawal in autism. *Journal of Autism and Developmental Disorders, 20*, 169–76.

Watanabe, Y., Gould, E., & McEwen, B. S. (1992). Stress induces atropy of apical dendrites of hippocampal CA3 pyramidal neurons. *Brain Research, 588*, 341–345.

Weiss, J. M. (1971). Effects of coping behaviour in different warning signal conditions on stress pathology in rats. *Journal of Comparative Physiological Psychology, 77*, 1–13.

Weld, K. P., Mench, J. A., Woodward, R. A., Bolesta, M. S., Suomi, S. J., & Higley, J. D. (1998). Effect of tryptophan treatment on self-biting and central nervous system serotonin metabolism in rhesus monkeys (*Macaca mulatta*). *Neuropsychopharmacology, 19*, 314–322.

Whitaker-Azmitia, P. M., Druse, M., Walker, P., & Lauder, J. M. (1996). Serotonin as a developmental signal. *Behavioural Brain Research, 73*, 19–29.

Whitaker-Azmitia, P. M., Lauder, J., Shemmer, A., & Azmitia, E. (1987). Postnatal changes in serotonin receptors following prenatal alteration in serotonin levels: Further evidence for functional fetal serotonin receptors. *Developmental Brain Research, 33*, 285–289.

Wiegant, V. M., Schouten, W. G. P., Helmond, F. A., Wiepkema, P. R., Loyens, L. W. S., & Janssens, C. J. J. G. (1994). Opioids and stereotypies in coping with chronic stress. *Regulatory Peptides, 53*, 237–238.

Wielebnowski, N. C., Fletchall, N., Carlstead, K., Busso, J. M., & Brown, J. L. (2002). Noninvasive assessment of adrenal activity associated with husbandry and behavioral factors in the North American clouded leopard population. *Zoo Biology, 21*, 77–98.

Wiepkema, P. R. (1985). Abnormal behaviours in farm animals: Ethological implications. *Netherlands Journal of Zoology, 35*, 279–299.

Wiepkema, P. R., Broom, D. M., Duncan, I. J. H., & van Putten, G. (1983). Abnormal behaviour in farm animals. *Report of the Commission of the European Community* (pp. 1–16). Luxembourg: European Community.

Wilcox, J., Tsuang, M. T., Schnurr, T., & Baida-Fragoso, N. (2003). Case-control family study of lesser variant traits in autism. *Neurobiology, 47*, 171–177.

Willemsen-Swinkels, S. H. N., Buitelaar, J. K., Dekker, M., & van Engeland, H. (1998). Subtyping stereotypic behavior in children: the association between stereotypic behavior, mood, and heart rate. *Journal of Autism and Developmental Disorders, 28*, 547–557.

Willer, J. C., & Ernst, M. (1986). Diazepam reduces stress-induced analgesia in humans. *Brain Research, 362,* 398–402.

Williams, D. (1995). *Somebody somewhere: Breaking free from the world of autism.* New York: Three Rivers Press.

Winchel, R. M., & Stanley, M. (1991). Self-injurious behavior: A review of the behavior and biology of self-mutilation. *American Journal of Psychiatry, 148,* 306–317.

Wolf, O. T., Convit, A., de Leon, M. J., Caraos, C., & Qadri, S. F. (2002). Basal hypothalamo pituitary-adrenal axis activity and corticotropin feedback in young and older men: Relationships to magnetic resonance imaging-derived hippocampus and cingulate gyrus volumes. *Neuroendocrinology, 75,* 241–249.

Wood-Gush, D. G. M., Stolba, A., & Miller, C. (1983). Exploration in farm animals and animal husbandry. In J. Archer & L. I. A. Birke (Eds.), *Exploration in animals and humans* (pp. 198–209). London: Van Nostrand Reinhold.

Woods, T. (1982). Reducing severe aggressive and self-injurious behavior: A nonintrusive, home based approach. *Behavioral Disorders, 7,* 180–188.

Woolley, C. S., Gould, E., & McEwen, B. S. (1990). Exposure to excess glucocorticoids alters dendritic morphology of adult hippocampal pyramidal neurons. *Brain Research, 531,* 225–231.

Yamaguchi, K., Toda, K., & Hayashi, Y. (2003). Effects of stressful training on human pain threshold. *Journal of the International Society for the Investigation of Stress, 19,* 9–15.

Yaniv, D., Vouimba, R., Diamond, D., & Richter-Levin, G. (2003). Effects of novel versus repeated mild stressful experiences on long-term potentiation induced simultaneously in the amygdala and hippocampus in freely behaving rats. *Annals of the New York Academy of Sciences, 985,* 556–557.

Yaroshevsky, F. (1975). Self-mutilation in Soviet prisons. *Canadian Psychiatric Association Journal, 20,* 443–446.

Yehuda, R., Golier, J. A., Halligan, S. L., Meaney, M., & Bierer, L. M. (2004). The ACTH response to dexamethasone in PTSD. *American Journal of Psychiatry, 161,* 1397–1403.

Yirmiya, N., Pilowsky, T., Nemanov, L., Arbelle, S., Feinsilver, T., Fried, I., & Ebstein, R. P. (2001). Analysis of three coding region polymorphisms in autism: Evidence for an association with the serotonin transporter. In E. Schopler, N. Yirmiya, C. Shulman, & L. M. Marcus (Eds.), *The research basis for autism intervention* (pp. 91–101). New York: Plenum Press.

Young, E. A., Abelson, J. L., & Cameron, O. G. (2004). Effect of comorbid anxiety disorders on the hypothalamic-pituitary-adrenal axis response to a social stressor in major depression. *Biological Psychiatry, 15,* 113–20.

Zangrossi, H. Jr, Viana, M. B., Zanoveli, J., Bueno, C., Nogueira, R. L., & Graeff, F. G. (2001). Serotonergic regulation of inhibitory avoidance and one-way escape in the rat elevated T maze. *Neuroscience & Biobehavioral Reviews, 25,* 637–645.

Zarcone, J. R., Hellings, J. A., Crandall, K, Reese, R. M., Marquis, J., Flemming, K., et al. (2001). Effects of risperidone on aberrant behavior of persons with developmental disabilities: I. A double-blind crossover study using multiple measures. *American Journal on Mental Retardation, 106,* 525–538.

Zuckerman, S. (1932). *The social life of monkeys and apes.* New York: Harcourt, Brace.

7   *Autism and the Physiology of Stress and Anxiety*

Raymond G. Romanczyk
and Jennifer M. Gillis

Over the past three decades, there has been a substantial evolution of behaviorally oriented treatments for autism. Initially, treatment focused on changing individual behavior through manipulation of consequent events. This progressed to a repertoire-focused perspective, in which treatment emphasized an attempt to develop the individual's range of skills and address complex behavior such as social skills, expressive language, and generalization of behavior. In the last 10 years, treatment has centered more on an antecedent events perspective (Luiselli & Cameron, 1998). This evolution has been a process of incorporation and emphasis rather than replacement. In parallel, much progress has been made in understanding the biology of autism. Interestingly, the overlapping points of these two important domains have not received much research or applied attention. In this chapter we discuss the important contribution of the constructs of stress and anxiety to assist in treatment formulation from a psychophysiological perspective.

Antecedent events are important in understanding and ameliorating clinically significant problem behavior, but the complexity of the analysis process and the diversity of the influences and patterns of antecedent—behavior relationships has been understated in the literature (Romanczyk, Lockshin, & O'Connor, 1992). Some of our most common language referents to important psychological and physiological processes (e.g., stress, anxiety), suffer from a lack of precise definitions and can actually impede provision of appropriate services by oversimplifying complex processes.

To use physiological variables in behavioral assessment and intervention, it is necessary to operationalize such processes. This is similar to what is done in defining complex behavior: We transform colloquial terms for behavior into operational definitions that permit reliable measurement. The same holds true for physiological variables. However, because most physiological events are not observable in the same way as behavior, we use transducers to monitor physiological processes and transform the signals from transducers into meaningful and reliable measures that can be quantified in a precise manner. Often, the term "biofeedback" is used to describe this process of recording "hidden" physiological processes and making them observable to an individual through an auditory or visual display. This process permits further measurement of interactions of environmental events with the individual's behavior as well as physiological status. This complex process of extracting meaningful information from physiological processes to be used in assessing and modifying behavior is often referred to as psychophysiological measurement.

We have a long-standing interest in psychophysiological monitoring (e.g., Romanczyk, Gordon, Crimmins, Wenzel, & Kistner, 1980) as a possible variable of importance in antecedent and functional analyses. From our earliest attempts, we observed a high degree of individual variability and found a lack of generally agreed upon appropriate measures of physiological status in the literature. This is, in part, because of the complex issues associated with constructs such as anxiety and stress. Use of the more correct term, "arousal," still leaves problems in measurement and interpretation.

While not minimizing these difficulties, our work in this area suggests that the use of psychophysiological measures can provide a useful context for the conceptual analysis of problem behavior. While our focus is on autism, the conceptual and methodological issues presented here have implications for other clinical populations as well.

ANXIETY

Anxiety is a concept conspicuously underrepresented in the literature concerning developmental disabilities in general, and it is especially underrepresented with regard to autism. This lack of coverage is independent of the orientation of the writer, whether he or she represents the psychodynamic, biological, behavioral, or any other school of thought. When referencing autism and anxiety, it is usually in the context of simply explaining the behavior of the individual rather than as part of a sound conceptual and clinical analysis geared for treatment, such as, "He gets anxious around the other children."

This lack of attention to such a basic phenomenon is puzzling, as the term anxiety pervades not only our common day-to-day conversations and writings in the popular press, but also is pervasive within the educational, psychological, medical, and other diverse disciplines. Perhaps it is still a vestige of the outdated view that developmental disorders were orthogonal to other disorders, as opposed to the more current conceptualization of comorbidity of disorders. The relatively recent acknowledgment of dual diagnosis has yet to make a substantial impact.

Although emphasis in many different public and professional contexts concerns anxiety reduction, this is too limited a perspective. As Barlow (1988) so accurately observes in his classic volume on anxiety, "Without anxiety, little would be accomplished. The performance of athletes, entertainers, executives, artisans, and students would suffer; creativity would diminish; crops might not be planted. And we would all achieve that idyllic state long sought after in our fast-paced society of whiling away our lives under a shade tree. This would be as deadly for the species as nuclear war" (p. 12). The same holds true for individuals with autism: It is anxiety modulation and coping that is of concern, not simply the elimination of anxiety.

Because of the pervasiveness of multiple contexts and meanings for anxiety, it is a word that must be used with caution in a clinical context as it carries an array of meanings and connotations. Clearly, anxiety is not a word that is easily defined. In fact, anxiety is best construed as a construct; that is, a description of a set of interrelated events rather than a "thing," in and of itself.

As many researchers and clinicians have done (Romanczyk & Gillis, 2005), one can conceptualize anxiety as a series of interrelated subcomponents that can include the following broad areas of human behavior:

- Cognition. What is the individual thinking and feeling? Such information is beyond the realm of current measurement technology. It is by definition a private event; therefore, we cannot have access to it.
- Self-report. The information the individual provides to describe the internal cognition and feeling. It is important to note that cognition and self-report are not equivalent. It should not be presumed that self-report is necessarily an accurate reflection of private events.
- Overt behavior. The individual's observable behavior patterns that are assumed to be reflective of anxiety. This could include observing someone perspiring where the ambient temperature would not normally elicit a response such as fidgeting, pacing, or avoiding eye contact.
- Performance. The quality, quantity, and rate of task oriented behavior. Simple examples include how well one does on tests, putting toys in a toy box, writing a letter, or reciting the alphabet. Judgment is not based on how the product is produced, but rather the quantity and quality of the product.
- Physiology. Measures of bodily processes that do not have an immediate or apparent visual component, including heart rate (HR), blood pressure, respiration, galvanic skin conductance response (SCR), and EEG. Because this type of information is often not easily available to the observer, greater reliance is placed on the other three observable categories—self-report, behavior, and performance.

One of the difficulties with the construct of anxiety is that these various subcomponents do not typically correlate well with one another for a given individual. This speaks to the complexity of our use of the term "anxiety," and how, in fact, it is a multifaceted event that is highly interactive not only with our current biological state, but also with our learning history, current emotional status, and the physical and social environment. Virtually everyone has experienced a sense of detached anxiety wherein, for some reason, it is not clearly obvious to the individual or others present that a state of anxiety or tension exists. A common example is when an individual is engaging in certain forms of public speaking where cognitively one is experiencing no discomfort and then "notices" a feeling of being physically anxious, such as through sweating or increased HR. For this individual, there is an experience of a detachment of these feelings of anxiety. Certainly the reverse is often true for children. They may engage in certain activities or participate in situations that are not anxiety-provoking for them, but the reaction of an adult can immediately generate such feelings in the child.

Anxiety at appropriate levels is important for adaptive functioning. There are many environmental hazards that must be avoided and these are often learned through the process of anxiety induction. The resultant anxiety response is learned through the association of certain stimuli with unpleasant consequences. Thus, for some individuals with autism, lack of anxiety is a significant clinical problem that can have serious negative consequences. However, excessive anxiety produces significant decrements in the person's ability to cope with various situations and can lead to maladaptive behavior. In this context, we must also differentiate state anxiety from trait anxiety. Trait anxiety is an enduring experience that can be chronic, as well as ranging in intensity. State anxiety reflects the changing, usually situation-specific, experience of anxiety. Virtually everyone experiences this form of anxiety at some time. State anxiety that is linked to common environmental events, such as social contact, can produce chronic anxiety reactions that appear to be trait anxiety due to the persistence and frequency of anxiety responses.

STRESS

Stress is not a simple, easily defined phenomenon. Rather, it is quite complex and composed of several factors. Most definitions of stress and stressors tend to be circular and do not provide useful information. When the term "stress" is used, it typically (and incorrectly) refers to either a stressor or stress response. A stressor is an individual response to an environmental event that produces, or results in, a stress response. The stress response is the individual's reaction to the real or imagined aversive situation. There is currently no universal scientific definition for stress. Although some researchers continue to develop theories of stress and refine their own definitions, other researchers disagree altogether on the definition and existence of stress. For example, Pollack (1988) suggests that stress may only be a "manufactured concept, which has by now become a 'social fact' " (p. 390).

There are several competing theories of stress:

- Life events approach (Paykel & Rao, 1984). According to the life events approach, an external (not internal or psychological) change occurs in an individual's social or personal environment. The perception of this change is stressful to the individual and adaptation is essential. The difficulty with this approach is determining whether stress is dependent on an objective number of life events or the appraisal of the specific life events.
- Daily hassles and uplifts approach (Kanner, Coyne, Schaefer, & Lazarus, 1981). Hassles are the daily interactions with the environment that may be defined or characterized as irritating, frustrating, or distressing demands. Uplifts are the positive daily interactions with the environment. According to this approach, the relationship between life events and health are mediated by daily hassles and uplifts. In general, it has been found that daily hassles are more related to health outcomes than how they mediate life events.
- Transactional approach (Lazarus & Folkman, 1984). According to this theory, stress is best described as a "rubric consisting of many variables and processes" (p. 12). There are many components in this rubric that influence the definition of a stressful event for a given individual. These components include causal antecedents (personal and environmental variables); mediating processes (appraisals and coping style); immediate effects (affect, physiological changes); and long-term effects (psychological well-being, health, and social functioning; Lazarus, DeLongis, Folkman, & Gruen, 1985).

Because stress is a poorly defined construct, it is important to look at the antecedents, processes, and consequences when considering an approach to understanding stress. According to Lazarus et al. (1985), a stressor is defined by the appraisal of an individual as to their vulnerability to an environmental event. Therefore, perception of a stressor will cause a physiological reaction within the individual, leading to symptomatic changes (e.g., dizziness, HR increasing), which are labeled as a stress response. Unfortunately, no single measure of stress response exists. As suggested by Lazarus and Folkman (1984), the measurement of stress should include the measurement of stressors or antecedents (i.e., environmental variables appraised by the individual as a stressor), intervening variables (i.e., coping styles), and strains or outcomes (i.e., anxiety). The manifestation of changes in the body's chemistry during a stress response is often measured by the individual's self-report of the physical symptoms related to the stress response or by physiological measures. Physiological measures of stress are preferable, especially measurement of physiological changes that are thought to be precursors to disease. The limitation or difficulty with physiological measures is that they may not positively correlate with self-report measures.

Stress Response

The physiological response associated with stress, or in response to a stressor, is commonly termed the "fight-or-flight" response. This physiological response prepares the body for the demanding efforts of either fighting or fleeing. The stress response will depend on the immediate physical and social context and on whether the situation is perceived as a stressor to the individual.

There is a common notion that there is "good stress" and "bad stress." What differentiates the two is what occurs after the stress is relieved. If a stunning piece of art is created, or a new swimming record is made, then we attribute these positive outcomes to good stress. On the other hand, bad stress leads to negative personal outcomes, such as health problems, increased anxiety, or panic attacks. An individual's cognitive appraisal of stress usually determines what type of stress they are experiencing, even though the physiological mechanisms remain very similar. The experience of stress may be episodic or chronic. The physiological changes within the body are quite different, depending on which type of stress someone is experiencing. If a stress experience is episodic, physiological changes return to normal. However, if a stress experience is chronic (the threat does not cease), the stress response is continuous, as are the physiological changes.

Basic Physiological Mechanisms of Stress

The physiology of stress is quite complex and involves several specific hormones controlled by the autonomic nervous system (ANS). There are two main branches of the ANS: the sympathetic and parasympathetic branches. The sympathetic branch is involved with the stress response. It activates the adrenal glands to secrete stress-related hormones—namely, epinephrine, norepinephrine, and cortisol. The parasympathetic branch does just the opposite; that is, it returns our body back to homeostasis by releasing acetylcholine and is involved in relaxation.

The sympathetic branch stimulates the release of epinephrine and norepinephrine. Epinephrine is a hormone involved in the body's metabolism of glucose. When released, epinephrine stimulates the release of stored nutrients in muscles to increase the body's energy for strenuous exercise, as in the fight-or-flight response. Norepinephrine is considered a neurotransmitter; it is secreted in the brain. It mediates both behavioral and physiological responses. The brain areas involved with the release of norepinephrine include the hypothalamus, frontal cortex, and the lateral basal forebrain. Both epinephrine and norepinephrine increase blood flow to the muscles as a result of increasing the heart's blood output.

Once a cognitive appraisal of a stressor occurs, the limbic system is activated, which in turn activates the hypothalamus. Once this occurs, the hypothalamus coordinates the appropriate motor responses required for the emotion associated with a particular stressor. There are two basic stress response systems, both controlled by the hypothalamus: the sympathetic adrenal medullary (SAM) response system and the hypothalamic-pituitary-adrenal (HPA) axis. Both SAM and HPA regulate the cardiovascular and immune systems. (For a detailed description of these two response systems, see Clow, 2001.)

In addition to the ANS, the endocrine system is also involved in the stress response. The endocrine system is composed of a network of glands and hormones located throughout the body, which regulate metabolic functions that require endurance rather than speed. The pituitary gland is stimulated by the hypothalamus to release vasopressin (responsible for constriction of blood vessels), adreno-corticotrophic hormone (ACTH), and thyrotropic hormone (TTH). The thyroid gland, which releases thyroxine, is also involved in the stress response. Thyroxine is associated with increased perspiration, HR, and exaggerated breathing. The release of thyroxine is also related to the effects of long-term stress.

The adrenal glands are the third set of glands of the endocrine system associated with the stress response. The adrenal glands, located above the kidneys, release both corticoids and noradrenalin. Cortisol is a type of glucocorticoid because it affects glucose metabolism and is also responsible for some of the detrimental effects on the immune system. Glucocorticoids break down protein and convert it to glucose, help make fats available for energy, increase blood flow, and stimulate behavioral responsiveness, presumably by affecting changes in the brain. The process begins with glucocorticoid secretion from the paraventricular nucleus (PVN) of the hypothalamus, whose axons terminate near the anterior pituitary gland. Neurons in PVN secrete a peptide, corticotropin-releasing factor (CRF), which stimulates the anterior pituitary gland to secrete ACTH. ACTH stimulates the adrenal cortex to produce glucocorticoids in response to CRF. These harmful effects of stress are produced by prolonged secretion of glucocorticoids. Although the short-term effects of glucocorticoids are essential, the long-term effects are harmful and often lead to a decreased immune system response, cardiovascular problems (e.g., increased blood pressure, strokes, heart attacks), an inhibition of growth, infertility, and diabetes, to name a few.

Measurement of Stress

For all types of measurement, it is important to consider individual differences that may influence stress. There is a wide array of individual variables, such as the use of different coping strategies when there is a stressor in the environment, the degree of social support such as family members, conflict at work and other areas of a person's life that may positively or negatively influence stress, as well as the individual's own perception of stress. In an attempt to address this complexity, often both quantitative and qualitative methodologies are used in stress research, samples of which are briefly described below (for an excellent review of different stress research methodologies, see Robson, 1993):

- Quantitative measures. The use of quantitative measures of stress is encouraged as much as possible since these types of measures tend to be more objective and can be used in complex statistical analysis. Types of quantitative methods include the use of surveys, epidemiological studies, experiments, and daily diary questionnaires and experience sampling (Jones & Kinman, 2001).
- Self-report measures. Many studies use self-report to measure stress. However, it is well-known that self-reports may include significant bias. One method used to address this problem is the use of an observer's report (e.g., another family member) that may be used as a reliability check of the self-report. In general, surveys are most typically used to collect data on stress, stressors and variables that interact with and affect stress.
- Questionnaires and diaries. Daily diary questionnaires and experience sampling are also used in stress research, however both have complex data interpretation limitations. A robust and complex quantitative method for the study of stress is the use of experiments.
- Qualitative methods. Qualitative methods are also used in the forms of literature reviews and meta-analyses (Jones & Kinman, 2001).

Epidemiological studies use a range of methodologies, but surveys are the most common method. These studies gather stress-related data over long periods of time or a large span of geographical areas in order to provide information about trends or relationships of stress and other variables. For example, individuals with a higher socioeconomic status and a higher level of job control tend to have less long-term stress.

Arousal

To understand the complex constructs of anxiety and stress, we must first address the basic process of arousal. The activation of the sympathetic branch of the ANS produces arousal responses. Arousal activation is observed by responses, such as increase in sweat gland activity, increased HR, increased blood pressure, dilation of the pupils, and other glandular responses. Such responses are often described as preparation by an individual for responding immediately to a stressful event (Andreassi, 1989). Similar to the general concept of anxiety, a variety of behavioral responses are related to varying levels of arousal, and a moderate amount of physiological arousal is required for optimal learning to occur. On the other hand, high arousal can lead to an extreme anxiety response resulting in the development of anxiety disorders, such as panic attacks. In contrast, certain forms of intense arousal can be perceived as very pleasurable, such as athletic competition. Therefore, understanding how physiological arousal is linked to different behaviors could prove to have clinical utility.

Arousal has been used to explain a number of aspects of autism, including self-injury, social avoidance, and escape behavior. Historically, research has indicated three possible arousal dysfunctions: underarousal (Rimland, 1964), overarousal (Hutt, Hutt, Lee, & Ousted, 1964), and poor modulation of arousal (Ornitz & Ritvo, 1968). However, there are few data on the physiological functioning of children with autism to support any of these theories. Research has indicated that physiological responsivity was diminished and correlated with behavioral unresponsiveness (Bernal & Miller, 1971). However, opposing findings have also been reported, with some studies showing elevated skin conductance levels (SCL). For example, Palkowitz and Wisenfeld (1980) found that a group of 10 individuals with autism displayed significantly higher resting SCL and more spontaneous skin conductance responses (SCR) than a group of 10 normally developing subjects of the same chronological age. Elevated HR was sometimes found in both children with and without autism (Cohen & Johnson, 1977; James & Barry, 1984). Other researchers have observed normal HR (Palkowitz & Wisenfeld, 1980) and SCL (van Engeland, Roelofs, Verbaten, & Slangen, 1991).

Data interpretation has been difficult because of inconsistency in diagnostic terminology and classification and not enough reporting of subject characteristics. Additionally, obtaining reliable physiological data from young children with severe disabilities can be complicated and time-consuming. Interpretation of results is also difficult, as children with autism may be reacting to the stress of being tested because this type of testing is typically invasive in the sense that transducers must be attached to the body and movement must be constrained. Within different studies, experimenters utilize different ways to reduce subject movement, fear responses, and escape responses. Various acclimatization procedures are likely used, but infrequently reported. Heterogeneity in age and functioning level of children with autism and medication effects may also play a role in the differences among studies. Therefore, multidisciplinary studies are needed to evaluate possible associations among behavioral, clinical, and psychophysiological data, and how they relate to sensory, perceptual, and cognitive processes (James & Barry, 1980).

Overall, a review of the literature indicates that no characteristic of the central nervous system (CNS) functioning can be definitively linked to autism (James & Barry, 1980). The one pattern that has emerged from the research is that children with autism display responses that are different from those of children without autism. However, the precise nature of the differences has yet to be discerned. Turpin (1989) suggests that researchers are moving away from general arousal theories to the examination of stimulus-response relationships to provide more specific explanations of behavior. At this time, it may be more useful to utilize physiological assessment on an individual basis to determine relationships among behavioral, environmental, and physiological events.

Population differences, while elusive, do merit continued research. As an example, Belser and Sudhalter (1995) investigated the issue of arousal modulation in males with fragile X syndrome. They note that their search of the literature over the last 10 years "failed to identify a single publication with both the words 'arousal' and 'fragile X syndrome' in its abstract" (p. 271). This is in contrast to speculation about the role of arousal (Braden, 1992; Romanczyk, 1992; Scharfenaker, Braden, & Hickman, 1991), again underscoring the interest in conceptualizations utilizing arousal/anxiety and also the great difficulty associated with doing well-controlled research in this area.

PSYCHOPHYSIOLOGY

Human psychophysiological measurement and interpretation is a complex process, both pragmatically and conceptually. Improvements in measurement procedures have occurred at a fast pace with concomitant cost reductions, and it is no longer prohibitive to use psychophysiological measurement on a routine basis.

Psychophysiological measurement is the detection of physiological events in relation to behavior (Surwillo, 1990). Physiological events may be considered antecedents, determinants, concomitants, or the result of behavior. Physiological phenomena and psychological events can occur together, but they are not necessarily correlated. However, in some cases, physiological responses may reliably precede certain behaviors. If behavior could then be predicted from physiological states, then problem behaviors could potentially be preempted through physiological monitoring in a feedback process (Romanczyk & Matthews, 1998). Psychophysiological assessment illuminates processes that cannot be observed directly but that may help us understand—and possibly predict—behavior. Physiological data have been explored primarily by conducting global evaluations of groups of individuals to learn what characteristics a given population may share. For example, some studies (reviewed in chapter 2 in this volume) have examined the physiological states of children with autism to determine whether consistent patterns are evident which could provide diagnostic or treatment information. Unfortunately, such studies have provided little consistency regarding physiological patterns of individuals with autism as a whole. In contrast, little research has been conducted examining the clinical utility of physiological assessment on an individual basis for individuals with autism.

Psychophysiological measurement and interpretation is a highly complex topic area, particularly with a developmentally disabled population. Nevertheless, an overly cautious atmosphere with respect to research and clinical utilization of physiological measurement seems to have resulted (Romanczyk, Lockshin, & O'Connor, 1992).

PHYSIOLOGICAL MEASUREMENT

The use of physiological measures can seem cumbersome and confusing when one considers the many decisions required and information needed to conduct a psychophysiological assessment. There are three commonly used techniques, however, that are comparatively easy to use and that are minimally invasive which we describe here (from Romanczyk & Matthews, 1998): HR, skin temperature, and electrodermal activity.

Heart Rate

The heart is a closed system that primarily oxygenates blood to be recirculated or pumped back throughout the body. Cardiac activity fluctuates and varies in response to multiple stimuli and can be utilized in the study of fear and anxiety. Heart rate is a very basic measure of cardiac functioning. It is the frequency of contractions for a given time period, and is initiated for each beat by spontaneous depolarization in the sinoatrial node per unit time. Increases in HR are related to activation of the sympathetic division of the ANS. Decreases in HR are also related to activation of the parasympathetic division, specifically from the vagus nerve (Siddle & Turpin, 1980).

The widespread usage of HR in psychophysiological research and treatment reflects the commonly held belief that cardiac activity parallels level of arousal. However, the relationship between HR and arousal is not a linear function (Siddle & Turpin, 1980). Malmo and Shagass (1949) found that individuals who had somatic complaints evidenced greater cardiac responsiveness to stress than those who did not have somatic complaints. Heart rate has also been found to decrease in response to simple stimuli and increase in response to threatening stimuli, including startling stimuli such as a gun shot, or stimuli that require some type of cognitive processing, such as mental arithmetic (Blair, Glover, Greenfield, & Roddie, 1959; Davis, Buchwald, & Frankmann, 1955; Sternbach, 1960, respectively). During exercise, HR increases due to increases in sympathetic activity and overall decreases in activity of the vagus nerve (Wolf, 1979). Cardiac activity can be conceptualized as paralleling the level of arousal. However, there is not a simple linear relationship between HR and arousal, so caution in interpretation is necessary. Heart rate can be influenced by many factors, including stress, emotion, and movement (Wolf, 1979) and the degree of individual variability.

To measure HR, a physical connection to the subject is required; many potential artifact problems can occur due to the mechanics of the connection. Typically, an active electrode is placed on a person's right wrist while a second electrode used as a ground is located on the left leg. It is important to obtain adequate contact with the skin and use of an electrode cream is recommended. Extreme care must be taken to prevent ground fault, which would allow a current to flow across the heart. Although electrodes placed at various sites permit very accurate measurement, for the purposes of measuring HR as opposed to performing cardiac diagnosis profiles, electrodes are placed on a highly localized site rather than on opposing limbs. Localization also helps with subject movement, as any movement of the electrode or the cable connecting the electrode to the instruments can cause artifact in the measurement.

It is also possible to measure HR by photoelectric plethysmography. Plethysmography is possible because, with every heartbeat, there is a change in blood flow to various parts of the body. This change in blood flow can be measured by the change in volume of a particular body part. A plethsmograph can monitor the change in optical density through the skin (Cromwell, Weibell, Pfeiffer, & Usselman, 1973). Photoelectric plethysmography measures the arrival time of the blood flow "pulse," which is used to calculate HR. A photoelectric plethysmograph is typically placed on the subject's fingertip or earlobe.

There are limitations in using the photoelectric plethysmograph. For example, movement of the finger can cause a shift of the photocell or the light source and thereby add artifact to the measurement (Cromwell et al., 1973). A second source of error results from the light source. Heat can be produced by the light source and produce an increase in circulation beneath the light, which will change the resistance of the photocell producing artifact (Cromwell et al., 1973). However, devices using light-emitting diode technology effectively eliminate this problem.

Skin Temperature

The measurement of skin temperature has frequently been used in biofeedback along with electromylogram readings (muscle tension). Measurement can be quick and simple through the use of temperature sensitive liquid crystals (TSLC), similar to the flexible bands placed on the forehead to measure children's temperature. However, few studies have been conducted to examine the utility of these low-cost devices, typically used in the context of stress reduction and personal biofeedback.

As part of a study conducted in our laboratory, skin temperature was used as an adjunct with galvanic skin conductance (GSC). The study involved five undergraduate students participating in a range of activities while GSC and skin temperatures were measured using TSLCs to determine differential responses across activities and measurement sites (right vs. left hand). Each subject participated in seven sessions. The activities included differential movement of the right and left hand, resting, blowing up a balloon, popping a balloon, relaxing, and emotional imagery. Wide individual variations were found for GSC across subjects and activities. However, there was virtually no variation of skin temperature across activities using the TSLCs, indicating differential sensitivity compared to GSC. Due to the limited research in this area and our results, the measurement of skin temperature using the TSLC method should be considered with caution if one is attempting to measure behavior-specific variation.

Electrodermal Activity

Skin conductance is perhaps the most frequently used measure of physiological arousal. Because arousal is highly correlated with sweat gland activity and skin conductance is directly related to sweat gland activity, this permits straightforward measurement. In the context of psychophysiology, sweat gland activity is often referred to as the galvanic skin reflex (GSR), electrodermal activity (EDA; Fowles, 1986), or as a function of measurement GSC procedures. Changes in EDA will occur with a wide variety of sensory and psychological stimuli. The momentary fluctuations of EDA that occur with stimulation have been termed "phasic responses," whereas relatively stable EDA is referred to as the "tonic level" (Venables & Christie, 1973; Venables & Martin, 1967).

Phasic and tonic responses are related to sympathetic nervous system activity. The secretory portion of the eccrine sweat gland has a profuse nerve supply via cholinergic fibers of the sympathetic nervous system (Andreassi, 1989). Sweat gland secretions are mediated by the sympathetic nervous system in response to acetylcholine (Venables & Christie, 1980). The secretions contain salt, which makes the skin electrically conductive.

There are several areas on the body that have sweat glands. The preferred sites for EDA measurement are the soles of the feet and the palms of the hands. Both sites have the highest density of sweat glands and do not contain hair follicles or sebaceous glands, which may affect the EDA measurement (Fowles, 1986). Although the center of the palm shows greater responsivity than the fingers, it is more susceptible to movement artifacts (Venables & Christie, 1980). These can be diminished by firmly fixing the electrodes on the fingers; however, placement on the finger decreases the potential total area with which the electrode can be in contact with the skin, as opposed to the broad areas of the palm or feet. This leads to fewer sweat glands in the current loop, thereby decreasing the absolute SCL (Venables & Christie, 1980). It is therefore important to standardize the placement and the size of the electrode to ensure equally sized areas are in contact with the electrode (Lykken & Venables, 1971) and to maximize the comparability of measurements across sessions.

Two forms of electrical activity of the skin are typically studied. These are endosomatic and the more commonly recorded exosomatic EDA. Exosomatic EDA is measured by passing an external electrical current through the skin to obtain SCL or skin resistance (SR) readings. These indicate the amount of electrical current that the skin will allow to pass. The type of method employed determines whether SCL or SCR is the outcome measure. With endosomatic EDA, skin potential is recorded by measuring voltage differences at two points on the skin (Venables & Christie, 1980). A committee report in 1981 recommended the use of SCL over skin potential (Fowles, Christie, Edelberg, Grings, Lykken, & Venables, 1981). The simple linear relationship between SCL and sweat gland secretion found by Darrow (1964) makes SCL conceptually appealing. Skin conductance is usually favored because the equipment and technique are easier. Most investigators prefer to use units of conductance over resistance values. One reason for this is that conductance values are more suitable for obtaining means and for use in other statistical manipulations. Additionally, conductance increases with higher levels of arousal or activity of the organism and decreases at low levels, a relationship that is more easily understood, as opposed to resistance measurement, which is inversely related to arousal.

Three analyses are often used in skin conductance interpretation. First, the SCL is the average level of conductance during a given period of time, which is also referred to as tonic level. Second, the SCR is the number of conductance changes that have a characteristic waveform "peak" characterized by specific onset and decay time and amplitude above a specified threshold during a given time period, also referred to as a phasic response. The third type of analysis measures the magnitude of the SCR, defined as a positive increase as indexed to the tonic level immediately preceding the SCR (Andreassi, 1989). Therefore, EDA is composed of slow tonic changes in baseline level and fast changes reflected in phasic response. Both are mediated by the sympathetic nervous system.

EDA is reactive to a variety of factors (e.g., room temperature, humidity, movement), so comparison across sessions can be difficult. Increases in room temperature or humidity can activate the thermal regulatory function of the skin. This would stimulate secretion of larger amounts of the sweat and subsequently produce higher SCL readings. Another potential problem is movement of the surface on which an electrode is attached, which changes the total area which is in contact with the electrode (Venables & Christie, 1980). This is more pronounced with dry electrodes than with electrodes used in combination with electrode gel.

The condition of the skin (e.g., dry skin, calluses, whether the hands were recently washed) can also affect EDA. For example, skin that is callused tends to be thick and dry, which leads to higher resistance readings and therefore lower skin conductance measures. Washing the hands with soap and water removes the salt from the skin, which causes a decrease in skin conductance readings (Venables & Martin, 1967). Skin-related problems can be alleviated by enforcing the standard procedure that all participants wash and dry their hands immediately before the electrodes are fixed to the surface (Venables & Christie, 1980).

Another common problem that may precipitate a change in EDA is if the individual becomes bored, curious, or displeased with wearing the monitoring device. Another important consideration is the prohibition of the use of the equipment and transducer by some individuals, especially those who are uncooperative or display high frequency and/or intensive disruptive behavior. Although there are always potential problems with the use of EDA (or any other measurement), standardization for the individual subject is the key to interpretation and generalization of data across sessions. That is, clinical use is concerned less with "absolute" measurement in order to compare to other individuals. Rather, emphasis is placed on within-subject changes, reproducible measurement procedures, and pattern of responses. It is important to emphasize that electrodermal activity should not be thought of as *the* measure of arousal, but rather simply as reflecting specific aspects of arousal (Stevens & Gruzelier, 1984).

Cortisol Levels

Cortisol is of particular interest as an index of stress and, moreover, negative emotion, as it is the result of stimulation of the HPA axis. Typically, measurement of cortisol or ACTH (the precursor to cortisol) is taken approximately 20 min after the presentation of a stressor in order to measure the highest level of cortisol levels (or HPA activity). There are two common ways of measuring cortisol.

The first procedure measures the cortisol levels in the blood. The procedure to extract blood can be a stressor itself and is difficult to perform, especially with persons with autism or individuals with a phobia of blood or needles/syringes. Another disadvantage of measuring cortisol levels this way is that cortisol is typically bound to a protein when in the blood. Only 10% of the cortisol in the blood is unbound, which is the cortisol of interest when measuring stress.

The second measurement procedure allows the researcher to collect only the free cortisol. This procedure uses the individual's saliva by placing a cotton ball underneath the individual's tongue for about 2 min. Conducting research with individuals with autism using these methods would be quite difficult because many individuals have a fearful response to needles/syringes and may not tolerate having a cotton ball in their mouth for 2 min. It is understandable that there is little research with individuals with autism in this area, given the nature of the current methodologies for measuring cortisol.

Clow (2001) guides the reader to Kuby (1997) for a more detailed exploration of the current topics regarding the measurement of the physiology of stress.

APPLICATION OF AROUSAL TO A MODEL

An illustration of concepts such as stress, anxiety, and arousal, as applied to a specific clinical problem, has been presented by Romanczyk, Kistner, and Plienis (1982) and Romanczyk (1986). Self-injurious behavior (SIB) is sometimes observed in individuals with autism and can be very difficult to treat. This is perhaps best illustrated in the case of individuals who have undergone a period of severe restraint as a protective mechanism for their SIB. Such individuals are often seen to behave in a frenzied fashion when restraints are removed. The individuals display severe distress and what may be termed panic. The operant/respondent model presented by Romanczyk et al. (1982) and Romanczyk (1986), hypothesizes that experience with restraint leads to a conditioning history wherein restraint is associated with the removal of demands and aversive environmental events, as well as the cessation of SIB. Since SIB produces pain, which in turn produces arousal, it is therefore the case, in a respondent fashion, that restraint is associated with the reduction of arousal, and thus becomes a powerful positive conditioned stimulus. Paradoxically, SIB in some individuals can be seen as its own eliciting event. For an individual with a history of restraint, seeking restraint is an effective method of arousal reduction. Once achieved, the negative reinforcement value of arousal reduction serves to increase the probability that this form of escape behavior will be used in the future. The behavior that results in restraint is SIB, which completes the vicious circle. Over time, the degree to which overt arousal can be observed may be significantly reduced. This observation is critical to maintaining the construct perspective; multiple measurement procedures are important. It should not be assumed, as discussed above, that various aspects of anxiety and arousal will co-occur consistently.

Krasner and Ullmann (1973) illustrate the importance of learning history, especially escape/avoidance learning, by stating, "A person may avoid situations without experiencing any physiological arousal; or, to put it differently, he may avoid situations in order not to be aroused. In college certain professors or courses are reputed to be tough and are accordingly avoided. A student may go to great lengths to avoid these ogres without ever having had any experience with the professors or the subject matter they teach" (p. 98).

This model attributes both respondent and operant properties to SIB. Initial occurrences of SIB are respondents and may be elicited thereafter. However, environmental events also act to shape and maintain responding through operant conditioning. Development of this model of SIB is further complicated by the possibility of predisposing physiological variables (e.g., dysfunction of sensory stimulation modulation, neurological and biochemical influences) that may increase the probability of SIB. Early experience with painful stimuli, such as otitis media or simple accidents, may also play an important role.

It is important to emphasize that the operant/respondent model is not an either/or model, with respect to its two learning process emphasis. The question is not which component is "true" for a given individual, but rather what is the relative contribution of each learning component to the SIB of a given individual. Further, and more explicitly, this model is not exclusive of biological influences.

CLINICAL UTILIZATION

It is often appealing to apply approaches that use new technology to pursue the physiological and neurological bases of behavior. However, the fields of behavior therapy and applied behavior analysis have strongly and continuously affirmed the great utility of viewing the environment and behavior as critical variables in their own right. Thus, there is a critical need to consider the conceptual validity as well as clinical utility (the prediction of behavior and the extension to the development of appropriate and effective treatment programs) to determine the relative contribution of adding psychophysiological measurement to behavioral assessment. There is growing evidence of conceptual validity, but little has changed with respect to clinical utility (Turpin & Clements, 1993). Better conceptual models are needed to drive psychophysiological research and methods of assessment. Also, clearly there is a need for continued efforts to address the problems of intrusiveness and application in naturalistic, in vivo environments, as most physiological studies take place within a carefully controlled research environment.

Psychophysiological assessment can provide objective information about arousal or emotional states. However, there is not always a good relationship between psychophysiological measures and behavior measures. These measures must be part of a multimodal assessment. It has been evident across research studies that there is a wide range of variability to physiological measures across and within individuals. Within a study of 14 children with autism conducted recently in our laboratory, each child had a different response to assessment conditions within and across days. Some children never showed a reactive physiological response regardless of situation ($n = 3$), other children were highly reactive with no apparent consistency across time and day ($n = 7$), while still other children had more consistent reactivity across time and/or day ($n = 4$). Therefore, comparisons across children, even within a given autistic population, may not be useful and physiological measurement in normative environments appears to serve best as a tool for individual assessment.

Physiological assessment, as part of the functional assessment process, may influence the creation of effective treatment programs that may include components not otherwise addressed (Freeman & Horner, 1996). The importance of investigating arousal is also inferred from the successful use of relaxation for challenging behaviors (e.g., Cautela & Baron, 1973; Cautela & Groden, 1978; Groden & Baron, 1991; Steen & Zuriff, 1977). Within a developmentally disabled population, these studies indirectly indicate that anxiety and arousal are possible antecedent factors to be considered within the development of interventions. Physiological measurement may be able to indicate the critical times when relaxation techniques should be utilized. Relaxation as treatment or a treatment component for SIB has been used for quite some time, but without the explicit conceptual underpinning. Thus, relaxation or counterconditioning procedures appear to be one reasonable approach to take with respect to intervention. Although a number of studies have used relaxation as a component for intervention, few published studies have included psychophysiological measurement in conjunction with their intervention programs to assess arousal directly (Romanczyk, Lockshin, & O'Connor, 1992). This is likely due to the continued complexity of using physiological equipment and methods in a clinical setting.

We use psychophysiological measurement selectively, and most typically during the "development" stage of constructing interventions. As an example, we have recently completed a long-term project concerning significant phobias in children with autism. Based on a multisite survey, we estimated that perhaps as many as one-third of children with autism have significant phobias, as defined by the *Diagnostic and Statistical Manual of Mental Disorders* (*DSM-IV-TR*; American Psychiatric Association, 2000), except for the criteria of "person recognizes that the fear is excessive or unreasonable" (p. 449), which is often not possible to assess for many individuals with autism. In response to this, we assessed specifically for phobias in our program's population, and according to parental report, a full one-third of the children in our program had significant phobia to medical examination. (There was a wide range of other phobias, but we will focus on the medical examination phobia here.)

An assessment procedure was developed that included GSC measurement. Using appropriate medical instruments and an examination room, with both nurse and clinical staff as therapists, we developed a treatment protocol. Most common feared instruments included the sphygmomanometer (40%), thermometer (36%), otoscope (36%), and tongue depressor (40%).

GSC was an important assessment and process-monitoring dimension, in addition to behavior observation, to assess anxiety. The majority of the children participating were nonverbal, and, as a result, many of the standard self-report procedures were not functional. Using GSC allowed us to assess our exposure hierarchy and to assess variation in responses across children. Our effort was to develop a standardized intervention procedure that did not require either highly trained or intensely supervised staff. We wanted to preserve the precision of a totally individualized intervention, with the benefits of a manual intervention that made it possible to serve many children.

Thus, GSC was used in the assessment and initial treatment development phase. It was also used to assess treatment process in conjunction with behavioral measures. We identified a subgroup of children who displayed physiological arousal that preceded their behavioral responses to the stimulus presentation. For other children, the two measures changed simultaneously. This underscores the utility of a multimethod approach: We were able to improve our accuracy and timing of identification of a response that in turn allowed for greater accuracy of implementation of treatment procedures. GSC was then phased out so as to make the service delivery system developed efficient and cost effective. The program was highly effective, with 16 of 18 children meeting criterion over a period of 1 to 9 months (mean of 4.5).

CONCLUSION

Choosing a psychophysiological measure may seem like a difficult task. Selection involves considering the rationale behind the decision to use a measure and the definition of the arousal construct. Theories of arousal are complex, with little research to directly assist the clinician in choosing a psychophysiological assessment measure. A reasonable choice should result from observations of behavior and the specific clinical problem that is to be addressed. It is also important to consider the context of the assessment and practical considerations, such as instrumentation, cost—benefit analysis, and time-course within a sound case conceptualization.

Issues of individual differences in activation and reactivity must also be considered. Comparisons should be made within individuals involving the examination of patterns of responses rather than absolute values. At this time, the process of psychophysiological assessment across standardized situations, as well as clinically significant situations, is not refined enough to make consistent and meaningful comparisons across individuals. Psychophysiological assessment may find its best clinical use in the assessment of individuals as part of a functional analysis to determine patterns of responses and their relationship to physiological and environmental events.

References

American Psychiatric Association (2000). *Diagnostic and statistical manual of mental disorders: Text revision* (4th ed.). Washington, DC: Author.

Andreassi, J. L. (1989). *Psychophysiology: Human behavior and physiological response.* Hillsdale, NJ: Erlbaum.

Barlow, D. H. (1988). *Anxiety and its disorders.* New York: Guilford Press.

Bernal, M. E., & Miller, W. H. (1971). Electrodermal and cardiac responses of schizophrenic children to sensory stimuli. *Psychophysiology, 7,* 155–168.

Belser, R., & Sudhalter, V. (1995). Arousal difficulties in males with fragile x syndrome: A preliminary report. *Developmental Brain Dysfunction, 8,* 270–279.

Blair, D. A., Glover, W. F., Greenfield, A. D. M., & Roddie, I. C. (1959). Excitation of cholinergic vasodilator nerves to human skeletal muscles during emotional stress. *Journal of Physiology, 148,* 633–647.

Braden, M. L. (1992). Behavioral assessments. In R. J. Hagermann & P. McKenzie (Eds.), *International Fragile X Conference Proceedings* (pp. 161–163). Denver, CO: Spectra.

Cautela, J. P., & Baron, M. G. (1973). Multifaceted behavior therapy of self-injurious behavior. *Journal of Behavior Therapy and Experimental Psychiatry, 4,* 125–131.

Cautela, J. P., & Groden J. (1978). *Relaxation: A comprehensive manual for adults, children, and children with special needs.* Champaign, IL: Research Press.

Clow, A. (2001). The physiology of stress. In F. Jones & J. Bright (Eds.), *Stress: Myth, theory, and research* (pp. 47–61). Essex, England: Pearson Education .

Cohen, D. J., & Johnson, W. T. (1977). Cardiovascular correlates of attention in normal and psychiatrically disturbed children: Blood pressure, peripheral blood flow, and peripheral vascular resistance. *Archives of General Psychiatry, 34*(5), 561–567.

Cromwell, L., Weikell, F. J., Pfeiffer, E. A., & Usselman, L. B. (1973). Biomedical instrumentation and measurements. Englewood Cliffs, NJ: Prentice-Hall.

Darrow, C. W. (1964). The rational for treating the change in galvanic skin response as a change in conductance. *Psychophysiology, 1,* 31–38.

Davis, R. C., Buchwarld, A. M., & Frankmann, R. W. (1955). Autonomic and muscular responses and their relationship to simple stimuli. *Psychological Monographs, 69,* 1–71.

Fowles, D. C. (1986). The accrine system and electrodermal activity. In M. G. H. Coles, E. Donchin, & S. W. de Porges (Eds.), *Psychophysiology systems, processes, and applications* (pp. 51–96). New York: Guilford Press.

Fowles, D. C., Christie, M. J., Edelberg, R., Grings, W. W., Lykken, D. T., & Venables, P. H. (1981). Publication recommendations for electrodermal measurements. *Psychophysiology, 18*, 232–239.

Freeman, R., & Horner, R. H. (1996). *The relationship between physiological arousal and problem behavior*. Paper presented at the 22nd annual meeting of the Association for Behavior Analysis, San Francisco, CA.

Groden, G., & Baron, M. G. (Eds.). (1991). *Autism: Strategies for change*. New York: GardnerPress.

Hutt, C., Hutt, S. J., Lee, D., & Ousted, C. (1964). Arousal and childhood autism. *Nature, 204*, 908–909.

James, A. L., & Barry, R. J. (1980). A review of psychophysiology in early onset psychosis. *Schizophrenia Bulletin, 6*, 506–525.

James, A. L., & Barry, R. J. (1984). Cardiovascular and electrodermal responses to simple stimuli in autistic, retarded, and normal children. *International Journal of Psychophysiology, 1*, 179–193.

Jones, F., & Kinman, G. (2001). Approaches to studying stress. In F. Jones & J. Bright (Eds.), *Stress: Myth, theory and research* (pp. 17–45). Essex, England: Pearson Education.

Kanner, A. D., Coyne, J. C., Schaefer, C., & Lazarus, R. S. (1981). Comparison of two modes of stress measurement: Daily hassles and uplifts versus major life events. *Journal of Behavioral Medicine, 4*, 1–39.

Krasner, L., & Ullmann, L. (1973). *Behavior influence and personality: The social matrix of human action*. New York: Holt, Rinehart, & Winston.

Kuby, J. (1997). Overview of the immune system. In D. Allen (Ed.), *Immunology* (pp. 3–24). New York: W. J. Freeman.

Lazarus, R. S., DeLongis, A., Folkman, S., & Gruen, R. (1985). Stress and adaptational outcomes: The problem of confounded measures. *American Psychologist, 40*, 770–779.

Lazarus, R. S., & Folkman, S. (1984). *Stress, appraisal and coping*. New York: Springer.

Luiselli, J. K., & Cameron, M. J. (Eds.). (1998). *Antecedent control: Innovative approaches to behavioral support*. Baltimore, MD: Paul H. Brookes.

Lykken, D. T., & Venables, P. H. (1971). Direct measurement of skin conductance: A proposal for standardization. *Psychophysiology, 8*, 656–672.

Malmo, R. B., & Shagass, C. (1949). Physiologic study of symptom mechanisms in psychiatric patients under stress. *Psychosomatic Medicine, 11*, 25–29.

Ornitz, E. M., & Ritvo, E. R. (1968). Perceptual inconstancy in early infantile autism. *Archives of General Psychiatry, 2*, 389–399.

Palkowitz, R. J., & Wisenfeld, A. R. (1980). Differential autonomic responses of autistic and normal children. *Journal of Autism and Developmental Disorders, 10*, 347–360.

Paykel, E. S., & Rao, B. M. (1984). Methodology in study of life events and cancer. In C. L. Cooper (Ed.), *Psychosocial stress and cancer*. Chichester, England: Wiley & Sons.

Pollock, K. (1988). On the nature of social stress: Production of a modern mythology. *Social Science and Medicine, 26*, 381–392.

Rimland, B. (1964). *Infantile autism*. New York: Appelton-Century-Crofts.

Robson, C. (1993). *Real world research, a resource for social scientists and practitioner-researchers*. Oxford: Blackwell.

Romanczyk, R. G. (1986). Self-injurious behavior: Conceptualization, assessment and treatment. In K. D. Gadow (Ed.), *Advances in learning and behavioral disabilities* (vol. 5, pp. 29–56). Greenwich, CT: JAI Press.

Romanczyk, R. G. (1992, June). *The role of arousal and anxiety in self-injurious behavior: Implications for treatment*. Paper presented at the third international Fragile X Conference, Snowmass, CO.

Romanczyk, R.G., & Gillis, J. M. (2005). Treatment approaches in autism: Evaluating options and making informed decisions. In D. B. Zaer (Ed.), *Autism specturm disorders: Identification, education and treatment* (3rd ed., pp. 515–535). Mahwah, NJ: Erlbaum.

Romanczyk, R. G., Gordon, W. C., Crimmins, D. B., Wenzel, Z. M. and Kistner, J. A. (1980). Childhood Psychosis and 24-hour rhythms: A behavioral and psychophysiological analysis. *Chronobiologica, 7*, 1–14.

Romanczyk, R. G., Kistner, J. A, & Plienis, A. (1982). Self-stimulatory and self-injurious behavior: Etiology and treatment. In J. Steffen & P. Karoly, (Eds.), *Advances in child behavioral analysis and therapy* (vol. 2., pp. 189–254). Lexington, MA: Lexington Books.

Romanczyk, R. G., Lockshin, S., & O'Connor, J. O. (1992). Psycho-physiology and issues of anxiety and arousal. In J. K. Luiselli, J. L. Matson, & N. N. Singh (Eds.), *Self-injurious behavior: Analysis, assessment and treatment* (pp. 93–121). New York: Springer-Verlag.

Romanczyk, R. G., & Matthews, A. L. (1998). Physiological state as antecedent: Utilization in functional analysis. In J. K. Luiselli & M. J. Cameron (Eds.), *Antecedent control: Innovative approaches to behavioral support* (pp. 115–138). Baltimore, MD: Paul H. Brookes.

Scharfenaker, S., Braden, M., & Hickman, L. (1991). An integrated approach to intervention. In R. J. Hagerman & A. C. Cronister-Silverman (Eds.), *Fragile X Syndrome: Diagnosis, treatment, and research* (pp. 327–372). Baltimore, MD: Johns Hopkins University Press.

Siddle, D. A., & Turpin, G. (1980). Measurement, quantification, and analysis of cardiac activity. In I. Martin, & P. H. Venables (Eds.), *Techniques in psychophysiology* (pp. 139–246). New York: Wiley & Sons.

Steen, P. L., & Zuriff, G. E. (1977). The use of relaxation in the treatment of self-behavior. *Journal of Behavior Therapy and Experimental Psychiatry, 8*, 447–448.

Sternbach, R. A. (1960). Correlates of differences in time to recover from startle. *Psychosomatic Medicine, 22*, 143–148.

Stevens, S., & Gruzeiler, J. (1984). Electrodermal activity to auditory stimuli in autistic, retarded, and normal children. *Journal of Autism and Developmental Disabilities, 14*, 245–260.

Surwillo, W. W. (1990). *Psychophysiology for clinical psychologists*. Norwood, New Jersey: Ablex.

Turpin, G. (Ed.) (1989). *Handbook of clinical psychophysiology*. New York: Wiley & Sons.

Turpin, G., & Clements, K. (1993). Electrodermal activity and psychopathology: The development of the palmar sweat index (PSI) as an applied measure for use in clinical settings. In J. Roy, W. Boucsein, D. C. Fowles, & J. H. Gruzelier (Eds.), *Progress in electrodermal research* (pp. 49–59). New York: Plenum Press.

van Engeland, H., Roelofs, J. W., Verbaten, M. N., & Slangen, J. L. (1991). Abnormal electrodermal reactivity to novel visual stimuli in autistic children. *Psychiatry Research, 38*, 27–38.

Venables, P. H., & Christie, M. J. (1973). Mechanisms, instrumentation, recording techniques and quantification of responses. In W. F. Prokasy & D. C. Raskin (Eds.), *Electrodermal activity in psychological research* (pp. 1–124). New York: Academic Press.

Venables, P. H., & Christie, M. J. (1980). Electrodermal activity. In I. Martin & P. H. Venables (Eds.), *Techniques in psychophysiology* (pp. 3–67). New York: Wiley & Sons.

Venables, P. H., & Martin, I. (1967). The relation of palmar sweat gland activity to level of skin potential and conductance. *Psychophysiology, 3*, 302–311.

Wolf, S. (1979). Anatomical and physiological basis for biofeedback. In J. V. Basmajian (Ed.), *Biofeedback-principles and practice for clinicians* (pp. 81–91). Baltimore, MD: Williams & Wilkins.

8 *I Can't Get Started*

Stress and the Role of Movement Differences in People with Autism

Anne M. Donnellan, Martha R. Leary,
and Jodi Patterson Robledo

> Someone who has much better inherent communication ability than I do but who has not even taken a close look at my perspective to notice the enormity of the chasm between us tells me that my failure to understand is because I lack empathy.
>
> —Jim, as quoted by L. Cesaroni and M. Garber

In the public perception, the word autism conjures up an image of a person rocking back and forth, hands flapping in front of eyes that seem to focus in an unknown space—a person remote from and disinterested in the social milieu (Cowley, 2000, 2003; Nash, 2002). For many years, professional descriptions, definitions, and common assumptions about people with autism have reinforced that image and named the unusual ways of moving and acting as "behaviors." Within the professional world that arranges and provides support for people with autism , the word "behavior" often became shorthand for bizarre, bad, repetitive, self-stimulatory, or useless ways of spending time. Much of the literature is concerned with manipulating, managing, or eliminating behaviors with little or no reference to how these might reflect the experience of the labeled individual. Moreover, the professional models for addressing autism are usually couched in social definitions (e.g., avoiding eye contact, disinterest in social interaction, no imaginative play) that reflect our experience as much as, or more than, that of the labeled person. Because of the communication difficulties pathognomonic to the disorder, these individuals often have difficulty explaining their behavior. Thus, we end up assuming our experience of them matches their own experience, an inadequate substitute for their perspective at best.

Despite this obvious breech, many professionals believe that we already understand what autism is, if not the exact cause of the disorder (Donnellan, 1999). In fact, the description of autism is too often a teleological exercise with the same symptoms used to both describe and explain it. When one asks why the person displays "autistic symptoms," one is told that he does it because he "has autism," or because he does not have a "theory of mind module," which is why he is autistic, and his autism is why he does what he does.

If parents and professionals are to begin to understand the phenomenon called autism, and through this understanding provide personalized support, it seems evident that the expressed experience of those who are categorized as autistic must be included (Lovett, 1996). Therefore, in this chapter, the words of those with autism will be used to explore the stress with which these individuals live. We will use the literature on "movement differences/disturbances" (Donnellan & Leary, 1995; Leary & Hill, 1996) to help guide that exploration and identify accommodations that might help to minimize stress.

Research that explores the relationships between autism and movement differences has been accumulating slowly since Kanner (1943, 1944) first described repetitive movements, insistence on sameness, differences in the use of facial expression, and limited use of gesture as characteristics of autism. Our reviews of the literature have uncovered historical references to movement differences for people with symptoms associated with autism (Earl, 1934; Kahlbaum, 1874/1973; Rutter, 1966; Rutter, Greenfield, & Lockyer, 1967), as well as more recent research (Donnellan & Leary, 1995; Leary & Hill, 1996). Young and Donnellan (1997) found that the movement differences most commonly cited in the literature include gross and fine motor difficulties (Gittelman & Birch, 1967); initiation failure or difficulties (Damasio & Maurer, 1978; Maurer & Damasio, 1982; Rutter et al., 1967; Schopler, Reichler, & Renner, 1986; Wetherby & Prutting, 1984); awkwardness and clumsiness in arms and legs; facial-grimacing or teeth-grinding (Bender, 1947; Kanner, 1943); and hyperkinesis or hypokinesis (Gittelman & Birch, 1967; Menolascino, 1965; Rutter, 1966; Rutter, et al 1967; Wortis, 1958). Although movement differences are frequently mentioned in the literature on autism, few papers exist that focus on the implications these symptoms might have for the people labeled with autism. Early works by Damasio and Maurer (1978) and Maurer and Damasio (1982) are particularly noteworthy exceptions.

Our work over the past 12 years has focused on understanding symptoms of movement differences in people labeled with autism and in people with other labels, such as Parkinson's disease, postencephalitic Parkinson's disease, Tourette's disorder, and catatonia (Donnellan & Leary, 1995; Leary & Hill, 1996; Leary, Hill, & Donnellan, 1999; Patterson 2002a, 2002b; Strandt-Conroy, 1999; Strandt-Conroy & Donnellan, in preparation). Our emphasis has been on understanding the symptoms commonly associated with movement differences, rather than on the syndromes, diagnostic categories, or etiologies. Our interest has centered on the possible effects that differences in movement may have on a person's ability to organize and regulate movement in order to communicate, relate to others, and participate in his or her family and community. Conversely, we have an interest in how moving differently affects the image a person projects to others, leading others to make assumptions about a person's interests, potential for forming relationships, intellectual functioning, and emotions.

Through most of this chapter, we use the term "movement difference," rather than "movement disorder" or "movement disturbance," to acknowledge that not all of the differences that people experience need be viewed as pathological. Rather, moving and behaving differently is merely part of their day-to-day experience. For example, the person who twirls in a small circle after standing or before sitting may be described as moving differently. The act of twirling does not impact negatively on life and, for most people, is not necessarily a problem. It may, in fact, be an accommodation or a way that a person may temporarily get around difficulties in making the transition from standing and sitting. It may thus be seen as no more odd than straightening one's tie before beginning a speech. When movement differences cause harm or truly disrupt a person's ability to participate, the term "disturbance" may be applied. Difficulties with self-injurious or aggressive behaviors or difficulties of overall activity, such as stupor or frenzy, would fall into the category of movement disturbance. The terms "disorder" and "disturbance" are commonly used in the literature for other diagnostic categories as well. For these reasons, we will generally use the term "movement difference" except where movement disturbance would obviously apply.

This chapter offers information on the symptoms of movement differences reported and observed for some people with autism. We will present the range and intensity of expression of symptoms with first-person accounts of how the symptoms have affected people's lives. We will consider stress both as a trigger for unusual, atypical, or uncontrolled movements, as well as an outcome for people who have significant differences in their ways of moving and behaving. Finally, we address some of the implications for supporting people challenged with these differences.

WHAT IS A MOVEMENT DIFFERENCE?

Leary, Hill, and Donnellan (1999) defined a movement difference as a difference, interference, or shift in the efficient, effective use of movement. It is a disruption in the organization and regulation of perception, action, posture, language, speech, thought, emotion, and/or memory. Typically, the word "movement" refers to observable actions, such as posture, muscle tone, head and eye movements, facial expression, vocalization, speech, whole body movements, reaching, gesturing, running, and walking. Our use of the word movement is consistent with research that considers internal mental processes of sensory perceptions (e.g., touch, taste, smell, vision, hearing, proprioception), language, thoughts, and emotions as aspects of human movement.

There is a unity of perception, action, emotion, and thought reflected in the writings of many authors interested in movement. The physicist, martial artist, and movement innovator Moshe Feldenkrais (1972) wrote: "Our self-image consists of four components that are involved in every action: movement, sensation, feeling and thought" (p. 10). In his fascinating book, *Awakenings*, Oliver Sacks (1990) wrote of the experiences of his patients with postencephalitic Parkinson's disease. The diagnosis for these patients was movement disorder. The variety of manifestations of symptoms encompassed many hidden aspects of human experience, including difficulty with perception of the passing of time, interest in normal activities, fatigue, memory, and recurring thoughts.

Esther Thelen (1995), a developmental psychologist, has researched and described movement in relation to child development. In her view, perceptions, movement, thoughts, and emotions can be linked by having coincidentally (and possibly routinely) co-occurred. Experience may selectively reinforce them as a bundle. They can be unbundled or softly assembled as required by the context. The individual is always operating within an environment or context and, as the context changes, systems scan, adjust, and shift as necessary to meet new demands. These contextual shifts play a vital role in movement. Context changes come together in such a way as to allow the movement to emerge; the movement and, indeed, the person are part of the context.

No one component is causal in determining the movement. As these are dynamic systems, all components and context determine the product (Thelen, 1995; Thelen & Smith, 1994). Thelen and Smith further explained, "even behaviors that look wired in or program-driven can be seen as dynamically emergent: behavior is assembled by the nature of the task, and opportunistically recruits the necessary and available organic components (which themselves have dynamic histories) and environmental support" (p. 73).

An example of this is seen in the dynamic nature of speech. Speech is not lost or gained; rather it emerges when all components and context, appropriately regulated and organized, allow its production. For many persons, autistic or not, stress makes speech difficult and even impossible at times. Paradoxically, for some people with movement differences, stress can help produce speech. The late Arthur Shawlow, Nobel laureate and father of an adult son with autism, reported that his son could say a complete, and original, context-appropriate sentence about once every 8–10 years. He asked an audience at the Autism Society of America conference how many parents had similar experiences and about 15 sets of parents raised their hands. They met briefly and compared notes. Most of the labeled children of these individuals were able to speak under extreme, often negative, circumstances. Some had only spoken once or twice in a lifetime (A. Shawlow, personal communication, July, 1996).

INTERPRETING SYMPTOMS OF MOVEMENT DIFFERENCES IN PEOPLE WITH AUTISM

Parents, teachers, and people who themselves experience these movement differences have consistently reported disturbances of sensation and movement asso-

Table 8.1. Symptoms of movement differences found in autism

Symptoms	Research
Apraxia/dyspraxia or difficulties in motor planning and sequencing of movements	Ayres (1979); Biklen (1990); Brasic, Barnett, Will, Nadrich, Sheitman et al. (2000); DeMyer, Alpern, Barton, DeMyer, Churchill, et al. (1972); Jones & Prior (1985)
Abnormalities of gait and posture	Bond (1986); Ornitz (1974); Vilensky, Damasio, & Maurer (1981)
Parkinsonian symptoms such as akinesia/dyskinesia or difficulties initiating or switching movements, freezing, or stopping movements	Damasio, & Maurer (1978); Maurer & Damasio (1982)
Tourette's disorder, including stereotyped movements, vocal, verbal and physical tics, and obsessive-compulsive traits	Comings & Comings (1991); Realmuto & Main (1982); Sverd (1991); Wing & Attwood (1987)
Catatonia or catatonic-like phenomena including mutism, echolalia, repetitive movements, automatic obedience, odd hand postures, interruption and freezing of movements, increased slowness affecting passivity, and apparent lack of motivation and frenzy, excitement, or agitation	Ahuja (2000); Chaplin (2000); Hare & Malone (2004); Kahlbaum (1973); Realmuto & August (1991); Wing & Attwood (1987); Wing & Shah (2000)

ciated with autism (e.g., Rubin et al., 2001). Researchers have studied autism in relation to a number of disturbances of sensation and movement. These findings are summarized in table 8.1.

Autism, apraxia, Parkinson's disease, Tourette's disorder, and catatonia comprise clusters of symptoms diagnosed through behavioral observation. The co-incidence of symptoms does not necessarily denote one particular etiology. However, examination of the similarities of symptoms among these various syndromes may assist us in understanding aspects of autism that present challenges to people in communicating, relating to others, and participating in typical activities. We are interested in understanding the possible neurological basis for many symptoms of autism that are currently considered to be "behaviors." In contrast, a social interpretation of these symptoms may leave people with the assumption that the symptoms with which people struggle are matters of choice, apathy, or learned behavior. For example, aggression during an episode of catatonic frenzy is viewed differently if the neurological aspects of the person's experience are considered. Would punishment be used to change the behavior of a person with a recognized neurological symptom? Would criticism and discouraging descriptions such as "laziness" be applied to a person in a catatonic stupor? Would a person with Parkinson's disease be scolded for reacting slowly when instructed to do something? Assumptions based on our social interpretations of symptoms may not always be helpful. We need a clearer understanding of people's experiences if we are to provide appropriate care and support that boosts self-confidence and is the product of collaboration rather than control.

Social interpretation of these symptoms is not unique to autism. Symptoms of sensory and movement differences in people labeled with developmental disorders may also be interpreted as a part of mental retardation or a learning difficulty without acknowledgment of the possible neurological basis for the symptoms. Rogers (1992) and his colleagues believe that unusual and abnormal movements of people labeled as mentally retarded or as having an intellectual handicap are often viewed as a side effect, a part of the retardation, or as a kind of self-stimulation. When people with movement disorders such as Parkinson's disease or Tourette's disorder show the same unusual movements, the behaviors are acknowledged for their neurological base and described in neurological terms; thus for one group, there is a social interpretation of behavior and for another group, there is a neurological description. Many of us have accepted without question the implicit message that unusual movements presented by people with autism are volitional and pleasurable. Table 8.2 illustrates the different labels given to behavior dependent on a person's diagnosis.

During the early 1990s, a small group of people, working both independently and as a team, were committed to increasing the understanding of symptoms in autism. One of the products of this synergy was an exploratory analysis using the symptoms of autism in a sample of published research accounts and the *Diagnostic and Statistical Manual of Mental Disorders*, third revised edition (*DSM-III-R*; American Psychiatric Association, 1987) to compare with symptoms of movement disturbance as categorized in the Modified Rogers Scale (Leary & Hill, 1996). Rogers (1992) and his colleagues have carefully examined movement differences as an integral part of some psychiatric and developmental disorders. They viewed the symptoms of catatonia, for example, as neurologically based movement disorders. The Modified Rogers Scale (Lund, Mortimer, Rogers, & McKenna, 1991) has been used to detail the motor disorders associated with catatonia, schizophrenia, and developmental disabilities.

The exploratory analysis presented by Leary and Hill (1996) helped us understand the wide range and complexity of symptoms of movement disturbance (see table 8.3). It was clear that at least some individuals labeled with autism have symptoms fitting most of the categories of the Modified Rogers Scale, suggesting the possibility that the core characteristics of autism may be based, in part, on the presence of neurological symptoms that affect sensation and movement. As documented in several disorders affecting sensation and movement, such as Parkinson's disease, catatonia, and Tourette's disorder, these symptoms frequently interfere with, and may even supplant, a person's intentional movement.

Table 8.2. Differences in labeling

People with movement disorders	People labeled with autism
Akinesia	Noncompliance
Festination	Behavior excess
Bradykinesia	Laziness
Bradyphrenia	Mental retardation
Tics	Aberrant behavior
Obsessions	Autistic behavior

Because people with autism have grown up with these differences, their behaviors have been affected by the experience of sensory and movement challenges. As practitioners, we had relied upon the possible communicative intentions of a person's behavior as guideposts for providing them with support. In considering the possibility that some behaviors may not be intentional, even though they might be "communicating" vital information about an individual, we were faced with a new challenge. Movement and sensory differences may affect a person's ability to perceive, act, and respond accurately—that is, in a way that reflects his/her intention. Thus, our understanding of people's behaviors needed fine-tuning. We now had to consider that our intuitive interpretations of behavior needed to include the possibility that the observed behavior was the result of difficulties organizing and regulating sensation and movement. In other words, "Behaviors may not be what they seem" (Leary & Hill, 1996, p. 44).

FIRST-HAND EXPERIENCES OF INDIVIDUALS WITH AUTISM

Within the last two decades, numerous individuals with autism have shared their unique experiences of living with autism resulting in a plethora of published first-hand accounts. Many professionals are seeking out and listening to these individuals to better understand this complex disorder (Cesaroni & Garber, 1991; Patterson, 2002a; Strandt-Conroy, 1999; Young, 2000). Individuals have been able to share their experiences through interviews, personal communication, and published accounts. These accounts come from individuals who can speak or type independently. In almost every first-hand account, individuals with autism report the experience of the stress of living in bodies that often do not work and move the way they want them to, resulting in extreme anxiety in their day-to-day lives.

A common theme that has emerged in the first-hand accounts fits in well with the dynamic systems model described earlier. That is, stress and difficulties with sensation and movement are described by labeled people as not necessarily having a cause and effect relationship. They suggest that the relationship would be better described as a causal loop, instead of a linear as "A causes B" or "B causes A." Instead, stress and difficulties with sensation and movement interact dynamically.

Table 8.3. Autism research and diagnostic criteria compared with features of movement disturbance

Features of movement disturbance[a]	Autism research	DSM III-R criteria for autism
Posture		
Simple abnormal posture	Flexion dystonia: Maurer & Damasio (1982); odd hand postures: Wing & Attwood (1987), Walker & Coleman (1976)	Failure to cuddle; odd hand postures
Complex abnormal posture	Posturing: Realmuto & August (1991); freezing: Wing & Attwood (1987)	Odd body postures
Persistence of imposed postures	Catalepsy: Realmuto & August (1991)	Catatonic posturing
Tone		
Abnormal tone	Abnormalities in muscle tone: Gillberg, Rosenhall, & Johansson (1983), Maurer & Damasio (1982)	Failure to cuddle
Gegenhalten (springy resistance to passive movement)		
Mitgehen (anglepoise lamp–raising of arm in response to light touch)		
Abnormal movements, face, and head		
Simple brief/dyskinesialike; repetitive, rhythmical ticlike	Myoclonic jerk of head: Walker, Coleman, Ornitz (1976); bruxism: Bebko & Lennox (1988), Ornitz & Ritvo (1976); mouthing: Walker & Coleman (1976)	
Simple sustained/grimacelike; spasmodic, not completely fixed	Disturbances in facial expression: Maurer & Damasio (1982); grimace or rigidity for no apparent reason: Schopler et al. (1986), Walker & Coleman (1976); decreased use of facial expression: Schopler et al. (1986)	Lack of facial responsiveness

212

Table 8.3. (continued)

Complex mannerism/stereotypyilike; turning away, side to side, searching movements.	Looks out of corners of eyes; avoids looking adult in the eye: Schopler et al. (1986); eye-gaze/ocular abnormalities: Churchill & Bryson (1972), Hutt & Ounsted (1966), Mirenda et al. (1983)	Facial expression and gesture is absent or minimal or socially inappropriate in form; lack of eye contact
Abnormal movements, trunk and limbs		
Simple brief/dyskinesialike; random/repetitive, rhythmical ticlike	Involuntary motor tics: Wing & Attwood (1987), Comings & Comings (1991), Realmuto & Main (1982); choreiform and athetoid movements: Maurer & Damasio (1982), Walker & Coleman (1976); dyskinesia: Maurer & Damasio (1982)	Arm flapping; abnormalities of motor behavior; gesture is absent or minimal or socially inappropriate in form
Simple sustained/ dystonialike; abnormal muscle stretch and flex	Flexion dystonia: Maurer & Damasio (1982)	
Complex mannerism/ stereotypyilike	Motor stereotypies: DeMyer et al. (1972), Hutt et al. (1965), Kern et al. (1984), Maurer, & Damasio (1982), Meiselas et al. (1989), Ornitz & Ritvo (1976), Ornitz (1974), Ornitz & Ritvo (1968), Ritvo et al. (1971), Sorosky et al. (1968), Walker & Coleman (1976)	Motor stereotypies include peculiar hand movements, rocking, spinning, dipping and swaying movements of the whole body
Abnormal ocular movements		
Increased blinking		
Decreased blinking		
Eye movements; to and fro, roving, conjugate		

Table 8.3. (continued)

Features of movement disturbance[a]	Autism research	DSM III-R criteria for autism
Purpose movement		
Abruptness/rapidity of spontaneous movements; suddenness quality		
Slowness/feebleness of spontaneous movements; weak, languid, labored	Bradykinesia: Maurer & Damasio (1982); dyspraxia: DeMyer (1975), DeMyer et al. (1972), DeMyer et al. (1981), Jones & Prior (1985)	
Exaggerated wuality to movements; nourishes/flurries of adventitious movements		
Iterations of spontaneous movements; gesture, mannerism repeated	Spatial/logic symmetrizing and ordering: Frith (1971), Kanner (1943), Prior & Hoffman (1990), Prior & Macmillan (1973); obsessive-compulsive behaviors: Baron-Cohen (1989), Frith (1971), Kanner (1943), Maurer & Damasio (1982); object exploration through proximal senses: Frith & Hermelin (1969), Goldfarb (1956), Masterton & Biederman (1983), Maurer & Damasio (1982), Ornitz (1974); Sorosky et al. (1968); self-injurious behavior: Favell et al. (1978), Gabony (1991), Gedye (1989), Guess & Carr (1991), Rolider & VanHouten (1985), Walker & Coleman (1976), Winchel & Stanley (1991); persistent strange or peculiar body movements despite attempts to discourage them: Schopler et al. (1986); perseveration: Chess (1972), Frith (1970, 1971), Hoffman & Prior (1982), Kanner (1943), Maurer & Damasio (1982)	Abnormalities of motor behavior; self-injurious behavior

Table 8.3. (continued)

Other: echopraxia/blocking/ambitendence; copying action/freezing/an opposing action interruption	Echopraxia: Carr (1979), Konstantareas (1985); hypermimesis: Bartak, Rutter, & Cox (1975), Curcio & Piserchia (1978), DeMyer (1975, 1976), Rutter (1974)	Repetitively mimics actions
Gait		
Exaggerated associated movements		
Reduced associated movement	Loss of associated movements: Bartak et al. (1975), DeMyer et al. (1972), Maurer & Damasio (1982), Vilensky et al. (1981)	
Slow/shuffling	Brandykinesia: Maurer, & Damasio (1982)	
Manneristic, bizarre	Gait disturbance: Bond (1986), Hutt et al. (1964), Maurer & Damasio (1982), Sorosky et al. (1968), Vilensky et al. (1981); toe walking: Schopler et al. (1986)	Walking tiptoe; jumping
Speech		
Aprosodic; abnormal rate, volume, intonation	Dysprosody: Baltaxe (1981), Ornitz & Ritvo (1968); poor speech volume modulation: Baltaxe (1981), Ornitz & Ritvo (1968); abnormal tone, rhythm, volume: Schopler et al. (1986)	Abnormal speech melody
Mutism	Mutism: Curcio (1978), Konstantareas (1985), LaVigna (1977), Maurer & Damasio (1982), Ornitz & Ritvo (1968), Ritvo et al. (1971); lack of communicative initiations: Curcio (1978), Loveland & Landry (1986), Maurer & Damasio (1982), Mundy et al. (1990), Ornitz & Ritvo (1968), Prizant & Wetherby (1985), Rapin (1987), Ritvo et al. (1971)	Language may be totally absent

Table 8.3. (continued)

Features of movement disturbance[a]	Autism research	DSM III-R criteria for autism
Indistinct/unintelligible speech; mumbling, poor articulation, nonsocial speech	Use of jargon: Schopler et al. (1986); vocal, verbal tics: Comings & Comings (1991), Realmuto & Main (1982), Wing & Attwood (1987)	
Other: echolalia/palilalia/ speech mannerisms	Echolalia: Baltaxe & Simmons (1977), Kanner (1943), Ornitz & Ritvo (1968), Paccio & Curcio (1982), Prizant & Duchan (1981), Prizant & Rydell (1984), Rapin (1987), Simon (1975); topic preseverations: Kanner (1943); unconventional expression of intent: Prizant & Wetherby (1985)	Delayed or immediate echolalia; verbal stereotypies including repetition of words, phrases
Overall behavior Marked overactivity	Catatonic excitement: Wing & Attwood (1987); extreme response to minor environmental changes: Campbell et al. (1972), Geller et al. (1981), Kanner (1943), Ornitz & Ritvo (1968), Prior & Macmillan (1973); hyperkinesis: Sorosky et al. (1968); explosive/violent movement episodes: Campbell et al. (1972)	Catatonic phenomena, particularly excitement or posturing; aggressive behavior
Marked underactivity	Hypomimesis: Bartak et al. (1975), Curcio (1978), Curcio & Piserchia (1978), Dawson & Adams (1984), DeMyer (1975), DeMyer et al. (1972, 1981), Schopler et al. (1968); almost never initiates: Schopler et al. (1986); almost never responds to the adult: Schopler et al. (1986); catatonic stupor: Realmuto & August (1991); decreased responsiveness: Lovaas et al. (1971), Ornitz & Ritvo (1968), Prizant & Wetherby (1985), Rapin (1987)	Indifference to affection or physical contact; no or impaired imitation

216

Table 8.3. (continued)

Excessive compliance/ automatic obedience	
Poor/feeble compliance	
Other: negativism	Command negativism/blocking/substitution: Clark & Rutter (1977), Morrison et al. (1971), Volkmar (1986), Volkmar et al. (1985), Wallace (1975)	Oppositional behavior; aversion to physical contact
Other: engages in rituals	Ritualistic behavior: Frith (1971), Kanner (1943), Maurer & Damasio (1982), Prior & Macmillan (1973)	Ritualistic, repetitive actions: following routines in a repetitive way

Reprinted with permission from Leary & Hill (1996).

[a] Movement features represent items adapted from the Modified Rogers Scale (Lund, Mortimer, Rogers, & McKenna, 1991).

Stress can play a significant role in a person's ability to organize and regulate actions and postures. It can also affect speech and language, as well as emotions, perceptions, and memories. Often stress can cause unusual sensations and movements to escalate (Brenner, Friedman, & Merrit, 1947). Some individuals report that they may feel physically unaware of their body and movements (e.g., Blackman, 1999; Hale & Hale, 1999; Williams, 1996a, 1996b, 2003). Williams (1996b), for example, reported how stress affected her movement, causing her to feel pushed beyond her limits. She described three involuntary situations that might occur during an episode of stress. She might become dissociated, thus causing her to lose all conscious connection with her movements. Or she might shut down completely, causing her movement to become involuntarily "frozen." She likened this to the feeling of "test anxiety." Finally, overload from stress might cause her painful sensory hypersensitivity. She also described the feeling of stress spiraling out of control, taking her to a point where she was completely unaware of her body in space.

Stress can be immense when sensations and movements are unreliable and unpredictable. Imagine having to cross the street. You know that you only have a certain amount of time to get to the other side. Knowing in the back of your mind that you might become stuck and unable to move when you are in the middle of the street would cause a great deal of anxiety and stress. If this stress causes you to avoid such situations, it will have a direct impact on your daily activities.

In the following section, first-hand accounts are used to explore the complexity of the dynamics of autism, stress, sensation, and movement differences.

Experiences of Stress and Anxiety

Donna Williams has written numerous insightful books describing her experience of autism. Recently, she published *Exposure Anxiety—The Invisible Cage* (2003). Similar to conditions such as agoraphobia and reward deficiency syndrome, Williams defined exposure anxiety as a "self-parenting survival mechanism, an intense often tic-like involuntary self-protection mechanism that jumps in to defend against sensed 'invasion' " (p. 10). Williams went on to describe it as "feeling your own existence too close up, too in your face" (pp. 10–11), like a "vulture" that was watching and waiting, affecting every moment, especially when the situation was stressful: "The more I wanted to say or show something, the more my own Exposure Anxiety was tuned in, hanging on my every expression. My body, my facial expression, my voice and my words were pulled about by some wild horse inside of me. I'd want to say I was sad, my face would be beaming. I'd want to sit calm and still and enjoy a sense of company, my body would be propelled into wild diversion responses demonstrating discomfort and hyperactivity. I'd try to tell someone I liked them and swear at them, try to show caring and be compelled to do something to repel them" (p. 103).

Struggling against the will of her body was something that Williams had to deal with on a daily basis. Williams also described the complex self-protective responses often necessary to cope. She raised interesting questions about how exposure anxiety affects movement and how these differences can appear so odd:

> Why can someone with Exposure Anxiety be expressively and naturally laughing out loud out in the back garden but somehow "stuck", compliant, or performing when in front of others? Why they can't get together to make breakfast once you are up, or run the bath, or get dressed, but seem to do a whole range of things which might prove they were capable of these? Why might someone with Exposure Anxiety be able to initiate communication with their own reflection and yet unable to respond as themselves when shown affection? Or be able to initiate an activity, but when you try to initiate exactly the same activity with them, appear uninterested, distracted or disowning? Why, although they have an ability, do they appear to freeze and become incapable in front of others or when asked to perform a task on command? (Williams, 2003, pp. 21–22)

Having all these questions and few answers lead to a number of emotions, including stress and anxiety. Many individuals with autism report that fear, anxiety, and stress are the dominant emotions of their every day life.

Challenges in Organizing and Regulating Actions

Sensory and movement differences can have a direct impact on the individual's action. This can involve difficulties initiating and executing movements. It can also affect difficulties with stopping, combining, and switching movements. Organizing and regulating sensory information and movement to perform tasks may be frustrating for people with these differences. Extreme emotions can cause the individual to become stuck, unable to stop a movement. Sean Barron (Barron & Barron, 1992) recalled, "All I wanted was to be like the other kids my age. It felt as if I was weird and strange on the outside, but inside I wasn't like that. The inside person wanted to get out and break free of all the behaviors that I was a slave to and couldn't stop" (p. 181). For many of these individuals, as for Sean, simple movements can lead to repetitions or perseveration, even if the individual wants to stop the movement.

Some individuals report that they get stuck and unable to initiate movement. Williams (1996b) described this experience as a "suffocating and frightening experience of helplessness" (p. 171). Williams (1996a) recalled, "I found myself physically stuck and physically disconnected. I struggled to 'remember' how to cross the room or open a drawer, but I was now trying to remember with my body and my body had little memory of moving as me. Inside of me I was thinking, Come on, leg, you know what to do. But it was like my body couldn't hear me, like I had no body-memory" (p. 99).

It is little wonder that the fear of being stuck like this in public would cause these individuals to live in a nearly constant state of stress and panic. When asked if he feels stress when he is stuck, Charles Martel Hale, Jr. (Hale & Hale, 1999) replied, "Yes. It feels like I am doing a marathon just to move" (p. 35).

Feeling disconnected from your body has been likened to being a puppet on strings with someone else in control. Williams (1996a) stated, "If not for a sense of humor I might have killed my body outright in retaliation" (p. 89). Often, Williams would want to go in one direction, but her body would take her in another. Her body seemed to be off on a track of its own. This complete lose of control of the body may cause frustration, anxiety, and stress within these individuals. Charles recalled that his movement disorder is most apparent when he is unable to respond to someone or something in an appropriate manner (Hale & Hale, 1999). Although his intelligence told him how to respond, his body would not always follow along: "For instance, when I should be smiling, sometimes I know that I am not smiling but may be even frowning. This causes me a great deal of pain and makes me look as though I am not comprehending when, in fact, I am crying to respond in an appropriate manner" (p. 32).

Sean Barron (Barron & Barron, 1992) recalled the intense frustration and stress when he was unable to perform fine motor tasks, such as buttoning or tying his shoes: "Many times I ripped the buttons off my shirts and broke my laces because I was so furious with the damn things when they refused to work" (p. 200). Temple Grandin recalled feelings of stress when being asked to perform two motor tasks at the same time: "Getting all the parts to work together is a monumental task" (Grandin & Scariano, 1986, p. 26). Transferring the knowledge of the movement to actual performance of the task left these individuals completely exhausted. Jim, a participant in a study by Cesaroni (1990), reported that combining and synchronizing movements was as difficult as trying to make your eyes blink at opposing times.

Individuals with autism say that knowing that others judge them by their actions causes them pain, stress, and frustration. Charles is constantly stressed by the fact that how he moves within his environment affects the way he is perceived: "I hope people will begin to understand that appearances do not always indicate how a person thinks and responses do not show our abilities. . . . I know that it is difficult for anyone to understand unless he has the problem himself. If people could give us a chance in life to prove ourselves, many people would be happier and feel a part of society and not just misfits" (Hale & Hale, 1999, pp. 32–33).

Experience of Perceptual Differences

Perception can also be greatly affected through this loop of stress and movement differences. Williams (1996a) recalled that escalators provoked dizziness and loss of awareness of where her body was in space. For Grandin (1995), various stimuli such as a telephone ringing or the arrival of the mail, could cause a full blown stress attack. Tito Rajarshi Mukhopadhyay (2000) found that open space was a stressor for him. Open space made him feel as though his body was being scattered. Tito's reaction to this stressor would be to tantrum. This fear of open spaces caused him stress for many years.

These individuals tell of experiencing differences in sensory integration where information from one sense may blend with another sense. For some individuals, labeled people as well as those who are not, this may be pleasant. For others it is a stressor. This blending of senses is known as synesthesia, which may result in hearing colors, seeing music, and tasting objects (Ramachandran & Hubbard, 2003). Jim, a participant in Cesaroni's study (1990), described his experience with synesthesia: "Sometimes the channels get confused, as when sounds come through as color. Sometimes I know that something is coming in somewhere, but I can't tell right away what sense it's coming through" (p. 74).

Other individuals describe an inability to process two or more sensations that are occurring at the same time. Rand (as cited in Strandt-Conroy, 1999) described this difficulty combining different kinds of sensory input as, "sometimes only one thing can go in at one time. So the sight could go in first, then fade out because the sound is coming in. When the sight fades only the sound is left, it is the only information the person is getting, which makes it sound louder because it is all he can focus on" (p. 79).

Some individuals with autism report that difficulty with organizing and regulating sensory information causes them to have unusual responses to sensations of hearing, vision, touch, taste, and smell. Judy Barron (Barron & Barron, 1992) described many of the sensory experiences that brought stress into her son Sean's life: "The one thing that did hurt him was having his scalp touched; when I washed his hair he squirmed and cried out, trying to push my hands away. Though I was as gentle as possible, it was obviously painful to him. It was even worse when I brushed his hair—he screamed 'OW!' over and over, wrenching away from me" (p. 34).

Sean noticed that these sensory experiences made him different from others, causing him anxiety every day (Barron & Barron, 1992). He described sitting in a bathtub as painful. He was extremely sensitive to the squishy feeling around him: "When they insisted I 'sit right,' it only compounded the problem. I had no choice—I had to sit in an unnatural way, so baths were a trying experience. Also it made me feel that there was something wrong with me because I had to sit that way" (p. 96). Even a bath, a very relaxing sensation to many people, caused Sean extreme discomfort and distress.

Temple Grandin (Grandin & Scariano, 1986) was very clear about the effect of sensory overreactions in her daily living: "The clamor of many voices, the different smells, perfume, cigars, damp wool caps and gloves—people moving about at different speeds, going in different directions, the constant noise and confusion, the constant touching, were overwhelming" (p. 21). Grandin also described how these overwhelming reactions would often cause her to act out: "I would invariably react by hitting another child or by picking up an ashtray or anything else that was handy and flinging it across the room" (p. 20).

From time to time, we all experience difficulties with a repetitive thought, but people with sensory and movement differences report unmanageable repetitive thoughts. Kathy, another participant in the Strandt-Conroy (1999) study described how intrusive thoughts could lead her to distraction and stress:

> I think in some situations it's just harder for me not to have intrusive thoughts. Some autistic people, they say, block things out or they shut things down or whatever. My mind doesn't think—I'm not able to stop an intrusive thought or block something out unless it's something really, really, really mild—but if it's severe, it all comes in and there's no way I can stop it. I'm not able to tune out anything. Intrusive thoughts would be nonsense syllables or something. I don't understand why this is—but if I was trying to study a foreign language or if I tried to study anything with odd-sounding words, I'd get nonsense syllables and stuff would pop in my mind and anxiety. It doesn't make a bit of sense. I don't know why it happens. (pp. 125–126)

Other individuals described their defenses against an environment that caused them so much stress. Lucy Blackman (1999) described how she had to accommodate to perceptual inconstancy: "On the good days, my world was one of time and 'feeling' and light and movement all in one, but fear or other unpleasant sensations fragmented my surround, so I relied on activities such as swaying, humming and running in circles, which defended me against uninterrupted exposure to my sound-environment" (pp. 34–35).

Blackman (1999) went on to describe the behaviors she used to accommodate her sensitivity to overwhelming auditory stimulation: "Because other people's sound processing was alien to me, I had no idea that sound should not be like a pressure-cooker lid. I put my hands to my ears for loud sudden noises, but the continuous clamor of everyday life was only relieved by movement. Even in the classroom there was visual stimulation and noise, which combined with my own breathing and a buzzing effect that I think was my own inner ear. I rocked, swayed and scampered, even though I knew how to sit in one place and that it was expected of me" (p. 51).

Donna Williams (1996b) told how constant adaptations and accommodations to unusual sensory experiences can be emotionally and mentally stressful, especially after years of these experiences: "After 10, 20, or 30 years, people with systems integration problems, due to whatever reason, have pretty much developed adaptations to their difficulties which might be mentally and emotionally difficult to change. Also, in correcting an underlying problem someone has taken many years adapting to, the impact of these changes upon one's identity and personality may sometimes be more than the mind or emotions can handle in too big a dose" (p. 67).

Challenges of Speaking

Sensory and movement differences can also have a profound effect on speech, language, and all aspects of communication. Within a conversation there is a labyrinth of complexity. For people with sensory and movement differences, even typical daily interactions can be extremely anxiety-provoking. Lindsay (one respondent quoted in Strandt-Conroy, 1999), expressed the intense stress caused by conversation:

> 1. Paying attention to the other person in the first place is difficult enough, and causes enough anxiety, add 2. The stress of me dealing with this onslaught of noise from this strange person . . . 3. The knowledge that they expect me to be able to understand what they are saying, and 4. The effort of trying to do this . . . 5. That they figure I'm supposed to have thoughts on this . . . whatever it is, and of course, they are (or were) supposed to give THEIR thoughts on the subject, I now have one more thing to add to my list of things I've got to do . . . figure out what their thoughts are on the subject, and then see if I can in any way make that acceptable to me in any way, even though I don't understand it (understanding is way too impossible and difficult a concept that I don't even bother with it . . .) and more often than not I cannot. And 6. I am now supposed to EXPRESS my opinions (or pseudo opinions), fluently, coherently, and rapidly!! 7. The fact that this is impossible, **PLUS** 8. The expectation/demand that all of this WILL be met, and anything else is unacceptable, and unacceptability is not allowed!!!!! And 9. The entire interaction (which is repeated endlessly throughout the entire encounter) is supposed to take place in a matter of a few seconds!!!!! (pp. 114–115)

Coordinating the sensations and movements involved in speech is a lot to handle in a matter of seconds. It is no wonder that many individuals appear to withdraw or limit their participation in situations that require these kinds of interactions. Yet, trying to avoid them would certainly have a negative impact on your social life and cause additional stress and anxiety.

Although stress typically increases difficulties with speech, these individuals can sometimes perform better under stress (Sacks, 1990). As noted earlier, many parents of individuals with autism report that during extremely stressful situations their children, whom they say never speak, are able to get words out very clearly, such as, "Fire, everyone get out of here," or "I'm very hungry." Temple Grandin (Grandin & Scariano, 1986) recalled a similar experience:

> It also was sort of a miracle that I had been able to get the word "ice" out clearly and succinctly. As an autistic child, difficulty in speaking was one of my greatest problems. Although I could understand everything people said, my responses were limited. I'd try, but most of the time no spoken words came. It was similar to stuttering: the words just wouldn't come out. Yet, there were times when I said words like "ice" quite clearly. This often occurred during a stressful period such as the car accident when stress overcame the barrier which usually prevented me from speaking. (p. 14)

On the other hand, many individuals report that they want to speak, but combining all the actions appropriately is often an impossible task. Lucy Blackman (1999) experienced this in many daily interactions: "My speech really just bulges out of my mouth like a balloon, and the real thoughts in my head just keep on a direct line. The direct line and the balloon are related, but they do not correspond, and the more the balloon bulges, the less sense it makes, until it bursts, leaving nearly all my thoughts scattered, and me wild with anger and shame" (p. 135).

Thomas McKean (1994) described his experience with speech: "There are, on occasion, still times when I want to talk, but I can't. I can try and try and try, but I can't talk. There is a fear holding me back. I do not know what it is I am afraid of, I only know that it is a feeling of fear unlike any other feeling of fear I have ever known. It is not that I do not want to talk, it is that I am unable to at that moment" (p. 39).

Donna Williams (1992) reported a similar experience of fear regarding communication: "The anxiety of my inner battle was becoming unbearable. I could say words but I wanted to communicate. I wanted to express something. I wanted to let something out. The anxiety would have been so easy to give in to; whereby I would again lose all awareness of self and my surroundings" (p. 19).

Williams (1992) described increased difficulties finding words and initiating speech as her emotional intensity increased: "At worst, the stress of direct, emotionally loaded communication either blocks the brain's ability to retrieve all or any of the words needed to speak a fluent sentence or won't allow the process of articulation to begin, leaving the words echoing within the speaker's head. The frustration of this can lead, as I described, to the deafening scream of frustration that may or may not get out of the speaker's mouth" (p. 208).

And, Lindsay, as reported in Strandt-Conroy (1999), stated how he accommodates himself to the stress of retrieving and initiating speech: "What I do is think in ideographs or thought-pictures and then translate them into speech as I go, which normally gives my speech a slight hesitancy, and the degree of this hesitancy is a very good stress-gauge. When I am under a good deal of stress my speech becomes markedly hesitant, but when I am comfortable in a situation then the hesitancy is something that only I can notice" (p. 116).

Routines, Rituals, and Perceptual Motor Habits

Perceptual motor habits are those skills that a person has acquired through extensive experience. Perceptual motor habits allow us the freedom to move, think, and talk without conscious attention to performing a skill. Sensory and movement differences can also have an effect on a person's ability to establish and sustain perceptual motor habits. For some people with sensory and movement differences, it is difficult to establish perceptual motor habits or, once established, the perceptual motor habit must be performed in the same way each time. A lack of flexibility in this skill base may mean that combining the skill with other events or in different settings forces the person to use conscious thought to perform the skill. People report that enormous effort is needed to think about moving in the most mundane ways. Geneva, a participant in a study by Strandt-Conroy (1999), pointed out how using conscious thought for movement and perception brought increased stress to her everyday life:

> People don't realize the major problem that nobody ever sees or realizes is how much conscious thinking we have to do just to function. Walking takes thinking. So if I am walking and you ask me a question I could trip or I could mess up the sentence and put the wrong word in. Or have to stop and say what did you say? I can walk with my girl friend down the street and carry on a conversation as long as she is right there but I have to look down at the sidewalk. I have to keep track of where the sidewalk is and where any obstacles are and all that stuff and sometimes if I have to keep walking and I feel like I am going to blow any second I make sure the path is clear ahead of me and close my eyes and continue walking. (p. 124)

Often people establish routines as an accommodation to difficulties with perceptual motor habits. When fewer aspects of a task vary, they report that less effort is needed to perform the task. Rand reported in Strandt-Conroy (1999) that routine and sameness assist him in finding meaning in his environment:

> Some people who are different like routines. They like to know what is going to happen next, and they like it to be the same thing that happened last time. When information, which is sights, sounds, tastes, smells, and touches, goes into their head, if it is information they're used to because they've had this information before, it can go into their head on the same pathways to the same places and get processed the same way as before. So if someone learns that a picture hanging on a wall usually hangs straight, if they see a picture hanging straight, that information is easy to process because it is the same as before. It goes along the same pathways to the same places, maybe those places are checkpoints that decide what the information means. Like it is flat, it is colorful, it is scenery, it is hanging straight on the wall. So it gets to the same result. It is a picture. But if a picture is hanging crookedly, it might start being processed along the same pathways to the same checkpoints, but then it might suddenly stop at some checkpoint because something is not the same as before so some checkpoint made a different decision about the information. Then the information might go off that pathway along different pathways, and whenever different pathways have to be used they could turn out to be bad ones, which means the information could just stop completely or get backed up or go off on wrong pathways. So it might never get to the same result, that it is a picture, or it might finally get there, except that it took longer and was a lot more work. (pp. 126–127)

EXPERIENCES WITH EMOTIONAL REGULATION AND EXPRESSION

Sensory and movement differences can also affect an individual's emotional expression. When a person uses his or her voice, gestures, and facial expressions in unusual ways, we may find it puzzling. When, in addition, we cannot see and hear the conventional expressions of emotion, we may assume the person does not feel emotion. Kathy, a participant in Strandt-Conroy (1999), reported feeling as though she was on an emotional roller coaster. Barbara, a participant in the same study, reported that there was never a time when she felt completely free of concern about emotions. Others report similar challenges in controlling emotions, expressing emotions, identifying emotions, and changing emotions. Barbara explained: "I think I've had times where I wasn't able to express how I was feeling and sometimes it was hard to experience my feelings directly. And one of the biggest problems was that I tried to express how I felt and people just didn't understand, my feelings were just so much different than another person that they just simply disregarded it" (Strandt-Conroy, 1999, p. 105).

Not having her feelings understood or recognized could trigger intense anxiety for Barbara. This kind of stress is reported by the participant in Jolliffe, Lansdown, and Robinson (1992) who stated, "It occurs at any time, but always when I know I have to go somewhere stressful. Sometimes the pain is so bad that my whole body becomes stiff and then I am unable to move" (p. 14).

There is also an assumption that people with autism do not want to interact with others. People's reactions to behaviors they do not understand can lead to isolation for many people with autism. Barbara described this in the Strandt-Conroy (1999) study as,

> I had no meaningful relationships with anybody. An autistic person has to jump through hoops in order to be accepted by others. I wasn't good enough for anybody. They didn't like my behavior and I couldn't make friends very good—there was nobody around I could be myself with because the only people were involved with me were those who were paid to make me behave. There was nobody I knew then that would let me be myself. There was nobody who would like me as I was. I felt unwanted. I would be told 'people won't accept you if you do this—people won't accept you if you do that.' There's no way I could've made myself quiet enough and calm enough and attractive enough to make people accept me. It just wasn't in there" (pp. 109–110).

Although many individuals report that they have challenges when it comes to emotions, it is not an absence of interest in emotional interaction. They continue to try to relate to others. Jim, in the Cesaroni (1990) study, shared his perspective regarding the common assumption that people with autism lack empathy: "Someone who has much better inherent communication ability than I do but who has not even taken a close look at my perspective to notice the enormity of chasm between us tells me that my failure to understand is because I lack empathy" (pp. 94–95).

Cesaroni (1990) pointed out that "Jim raised an interesting question which merits consideration: if a large amount of effort and energy is devoted in trying to understand others' perspectives, does Jim have less empathy than those people who not only do not understand him, but who do not even notice they do not understand him?" (p. 95).

Concluding Remarks on First-hand Accounts

The first-hand reports from people with autism provide us with powerful insights into how stress affects their symptoms and how the appearance of their symptoms is affected by stress. People need support that acknowledges their differences, accepts them the way they are, and provides them with the tools they need to learn and to cope with a world that may often be overwhelming. Donna Williams (2003) comments on treatment instruction and education that emphasizes "normality" while ignoring a person's true nature: "If you gain expression or skills that are not connected to self, they represent feels like a façade [*sic*], a cardboard reality, a parody. It can work for survival if you are really pushed, but it is not really the kind of stuff you can use as a basis for an enjoyable existence because it's disconnected from any internal emotional intrinsic reward. Such apparent 'success' may feel intensely alienating and isolating" (p. 290).

Understanding how sensory and movement differences affect everyday existence is an important step. Finding ways to assist a person to accommodate and to promote body movement control and awareness are also key. Throughout this discovery process, we need to rethink commonly held assumptions about these individuals in order to listen to them and provide them with the appropriate support, presuming competence and seeing them as complete human beings, not as individuals with something missing. The voice of the labeled individual must be included in our new understanding of autism and sensory and movement differences. On this basis, we can begin to address them as people who need unique accommodations and support.

Stress, sensation, and movement have a direct impact on daily living. Speaking, facial expression, action, and emotion are all organized and regulated by sensation and movement. A person's emotional state and the level of intensity of emotions, whether these are positive or negative in nature, may make the balance between inhibition and activation more difficult to achieve (Brenner et al. 1947; Leary & Hill, 1996; Maurer, 1992, 1993). For many, unusual sensations and movements are less pronounced and less problematic when a person is distracted (Brenner et al. 1947). Distraction may be an effective support strategy for some people and in some situations. The following section provides more accommodations for individuals experiencing sensory and movement differences.

ACCOMMODATIONS

We draw on the historic works of Aleksander Romanovich Luria, a Russian psychologist and neurologist, in using the term "accommodations" to describe those supports that temporarily assist a person with difficulties in sensation and movement control, in participation, and behavior regulation. Luria (1932/1976) details many accommodations devised by or for individual people in his book, *The Nature of Human Conflicts*. After years of research working directly with people challenged by differences in their abilities to organize and regulate sensation and movement, he wrote of the need for people to develop accommodations or substitutions for the usual methods of motivation that may not be available to people during an episode of movement disturbance. Years later, Oliver Sacks (1990) credited Luria for his understanding of the importance of accommodating rather than battling such problems by force of will. Sacks used a metaphor to describe the process of accommodating to the challenges of organizing and regulating sensation and movement: "Neither defiance nor denial is of the least use here: one takes arms by learning how to negotiate or navigate a sea of troubles, by becoming a mariner in the seas of one's self. 'Accommodation' is concerned with weathering the storm" (p. 265).

Accommodations are personalized strategies that assist in temporarily overcoming differences in learning style, sensory integration, and/or movement. We all use accommodations to temporarily compensate for difficulties we may have in starting, executing, and stopping movements. We may also need accommodations for combining and switching behavior, thoughts, perceptions, speech, language, memories and emotions. Some common accommodations include the use of gesture, touch, and rhythm. Also, behavior rituals, sequences, and changing the aspects of tasks have proven effective, as well as visualization, music, and other strategies. These accommodations will be different for each person and the person's need for accommodations may vary from day-to-day or hour-to-hour. Accommodations may be effective for a time and then lose their effectiveness for a person. It is always a good idea to have a "menu" of possible accommodations for a particular person, considering alternative accommodations when needed.

Accommodations cannot be explained in a developmental framework. That is, for most accommodations there are no prerequisite skills, no linear progressions. Although some factors may seem to play a more central role in assisting a person to accommodate, it is often an array of accommodations that allow skills to emerge. Given appropriate supports from past experience, other people, and the environment, a person may be able to demonstrate competencies that have not been evident before. Broderick and Kasa-Hendrickson (2001) provide a thoughtful qualitative analysis of one teen labeled with autism and his acquisition of reliable speech at age 13. The authors viewed this young man's progress as reflecting a dynamic systems model for development, as described by Thelen and Smith (1994), rather than the more traditional linear model for development. Broderick and Kasa-Hendrickson note that no single component of the array of supports for speaking appeared more important than another and his development did not follow the usual expected sequence of learning to "listen, speak, read, write" (p. 23). Instead, his emerging speech "was a complex, dynamic, and fluid expansion of [his] expressive communication system, a system in which he continues to integrate both speech and typing in complex and novel ways" (p. 22). They emphasized that the whole experience of communicating and receiving support to speak was greater than the sum of the individual supports provided.

Labeled people often devise their own accommodations, without the assistance of others. For example, people who have difficulty passing through a doorway or making other transitions, such as from wood flooring to carpet, report that taking a step backward during the transition may ease their ability to move and avoid their getting "stuck" in a doorway. Others may wave or flap to help propel themselves through. Some of the accommodations that people have devised for themselves may appear unusual or bizarre to others. Family and professionals may recommend that a person change a particular accommodation for a specific reason (e.g., because the accommodation causes damage to or hurts self or others or limits a person's access to many environments). It is, therefore, critical to recognize the possible function that an unusual behavior may serve and to provide alternative accommodations to fulfill that function.

Accommodations are strategies that people use to find the balance they need to regulate sensation and movement when the natural, unconscious mechanisms are not enough (Donnellan & Leary, 1995). Accommodations do not necessarily replace instructional strategies but may be used to personalize more conventional programs. The following accommodations have been developed by individuals who exhibit movement differences and by the professionals and family members who support them (Donnellan et al. 2003; Williams, 1992; 1994; 1996a; 1996b; 2003). The descriptions of accommodations we provide here are not exhaustive, as this is meant only to be a brief introduction. Nonetheless, because accommodations are so personalized, there is no limit to the style and number of accommodations that can be created. There are as many accommodations as there are people and situations to use them (Donnellan & Leary, 1995). Although these accommodations are in no way a cookbook or how-to guide, we hope they will spark interest and creativity when it comes to providing and creating accommodations.

Accommodations for Organizing and Regulating Actions

People often experience difficulties initiating, executing, stopping, combining, continuing, and switching actions and postures, including movements of the whole body, facial expression, gestures, and head movements. They and their families or caregivers often work out ways of supporting movement that is functional, timely, and done with less effort. These accommodating strategies can boost a person's confidence and may reduce stress that results from unreliable movement.

Use of Touch   Some individuals with autism have reported the use of touch as a very useful accommodation. For some, a gentle touch to their arm, shoulder, or back can help initiate an action. The film *Awakenings,* based on the book by Sacks (1990), illustrates how one patient is able to stand and move only when the nurse is touching his back. Touch is the preferred way to gain some people's attention, such as touching an arm or hand, and waiting for attention before speaking.

Use of Rhythm   Rhythm is a well-known facilitator for most people. In fact, many couples credit their ability to dance well together for the onset of their relationship. Using a rhythm, tempo, or any rhythmic sound can be especially helpful during transition times. Moving with another person in rhythm can be used to help initiate action for people with movement differences. Sacks (1990) reported that one of his patients was able to initiate action when he walked with her. She explained that she felt the power of his walking, which assisted her in her own movements. Some individuals report that performing a task to a certain tune or rhythm can often help as well. Music is often a preferred activity for people labeled with autism. Children who show little imitative ability or emotional expression can be seen to jump, dance, and smile with a favorite television character dancing to music. The use of music as an accommodation must be personalized. Sacks (1990) relates that one patient only moved to music that "moved" her. Some people hum or sing softly to themselves while working or playing. Rhythm can be found in many activities, including reading aloud from a storybook or reciting poetry. Some individuals comment that slight sounds in the environment, such as the sound of a clock ticking, can provide the necessary tempo. Ralph Maurer (1993), a psychiatrist specializing in understanding people labeled with autism, has noted that people who rock their bodies, walk with skating-type movements, or otherwise move rhythmically may be trying to compensate for difficulties in establishing a rhythm for movement. He recommended that supporters pay close attention to the rhythm that people use when rocking. Matching this rhythm may provide a way for a supporter to enhance a relationship with a person.

Use of Imagery   Many people in sports, business, and health have used imagery-based programs successfully. June Groden and her colleagues, in collaboration with Joseph Cautela, successfully adapted covert conditioning procedures for people with special needs that are based on visualization and imagery (Groden, Cautela, LeVasseur, Groden, & Bausman, 1991). Imagery and visualization may help some individuals to get started or stay with an activity, as well as to cope with possible disruptions in specific situations. Grandin (1995) reported how she easily thought in pictures; her thoughts were similar to that of a film. Actual visual representations, such as photographs or drawings, are often used to establish an image. For other people, imagining a detailed scene may be enough. Luria (1932/1976) reported that his patient, Ivan, had great difficulty getting out of his bed in the morning. Ivan used a combination of visual representation and imagery to accommodate to this difficulty. He painted a tree next to his bed so that he could arise in the morning by imagining himself climbing the tree.

In addition to imagery-based accommodations, many people use things that they are able to see or read to help accommodate. Some move well when they see sequences or steps that are written in words or represented in drawings. Others have told us that looking toward a destination or watching someone else move can provide the support they need. The placement of objects can be a useful accommodation, for example, providing the motivation to do a task when the tools are assembled and visible. Objects can be used to cue an established skill or perceptual-motor habit, such as seeing the dishtowel as a cue to dry and put away the dishes. Even a simple gesture or facial expression may provide the needed trigger for an individual. Remembering the last time the sequence was performed may help some individuals perform it again. Specifically going through the steps of the action in one's mind prior to an event may also be helpful.

Use of Words   There are many ways to use spoken or written words as accommodations. In this chapter, we cover a few verbal accommodations related to organizing and regulating actions and behavior that may be useful for some individuals.

The ritualized use of key words, or "catch phrases," may be a helpful accommodation for some people. People report that hearing the words said in a specific tone of voice or from a specific person may help them initiate an action or maintain self-control. Saying these words softly or silently to oneself or listening to a recording of a specific voice may be used as an accommodation. One person mentioned that carrying a short note in her pocket helped her to get through difficult times.

Use of Preparation   Preparation for change and transition may present a special challenge for people with unusual sensory and movement abilities. Transitions are often reported to be times of uncertainty; many people are aware that minor changes will stretch their flexibility and tap their energy. Some people report that they have a less stressful experience if a situation is explained from their own point of view in advance. Perhaps because some people need more than the usual amount of time for organizing and regulating their actions and emotions, they appreciate getting information on events well before the event is to occur.

Many people have experience with stories told to them during a quiet and calm time and which relate to future events. Carol Gray (1994, 2000) has assembled many good examples of social stories that provide guidelines for using stories more effectively. It is helpful to know details such as who, what, when, where, and how long. These stories may be in written form or spoken. When a story is repeated, some people appreciate the sameness and want to hear the same words, while others like the story to contain other words and new details. People frequently report that the best situation for listening to these kinds of details is one that does not require looking directly at the speaker or repeating the information provided. For some, tests of comprehension, such as answering questions about the information, are not helpful or necessary. Other people like the opportunity to repeat back the information in order to use it for themselves whenever needed. Preparation for change may reduce the stress of anticipation by supporting a person's confidence and assisting in planning.

Use of Prompts   The use of verbal prompts to support a person to initiate or complete a task may be an appropriate accommodation for some people, in some situations. Experience and reports from others, however, indicate that many people become unable to perform a task without those spoken prompts. When a person is learning a task that should be done independently (e.g., getting dressed, showering), cues and prompts used as accommodations need to be carefully considered. In this case, support should focus on providing cues in such a way that the person may be able to do the task independently in the future. When spoken instructions are used to assist a person, the immediate results are often positive as the person does what is said. However, the spoken words may inadvertently become part of the task and a person may continue to need a supporter to say, "Put on your sock," long after the sequence is learned. Speaking involves relationship. If the task is not one of relationship, speaking during the task about how to do it should be kept to a minimum. (For more information on the effective use of cues and prompts, see Donnellan, LaVigna, Negri-Shoultz, & Fassbender, 1988.)

Use of Scent   Accommodations using smell can also be very effective for some individuals. The scent of coffee can get many of us moving in the morning. Certain scents can relax some individuals and help them regulate their actions. Other scents, such as food cooking, can bring a person to the kitchen. Some people have reported success in using a form of classical conditioning, where a scent becomes associated with relaxation and self-control and is used to elicit those feelings during times of stress. As many people have negative reactions and profound sensitivity to scents, caution should be exercised in exploring scent as an accommodation.

Defining the Task   When an individual has difficulty maintaining an action or attending to a task, it often helps to choose tasks with clear beginnings and endings, such as stacking chairs, making popcorn, emptying waste baskets, and washing very dirty dishes. Even if the task does not have a clear beginning or end, you can create them by using time markers, such as a bell ring. It is also helpful to make the transformation or result of an activity more salient or obvious. Using color is an excellent way to achieve this. You can use opaque foams and colored cleansers for scrubbing. Colored paper to end a stack can work as well. Teaching a motor pattern "rule" can help some individuals with both initiating and maintaining an action. Examples of this would be cleaning from one corner to another, washing each plate in a specific motion, and taking everything from the counter top and putting it on the table.

Accommodations for Perceptual Differences

Each person has a unique and individual sensory system. An accommodation for one person may be a trigger for another. It is important to have knowledge of the individual and understand how their perceptual differences may challenge them. It may be helpful to work with sensory integration specialists, occupational therapists, physical therapists, or other professionals for specific guidance.

Environmental accommodations may help some people by fine-tuning the aspects of an environment that promote a person's optimum participation and reduce stress. The accommodations below are a sampling, useful for some people in some situations.

Materials   Many materials may assist in sensory integration and body comfort, thereby reducing stress levels for some individuals. The following materials have been successfully used as accommodations: tumble form chairs, bean bag chairs, chewy and crunchy things, tube necklaces, "feel good box," black light, weighted vest, foot or hand vibrators, light box, tinted glasses, earplugs or earphones, and heavy, padded clothing.

Reduce Sound   Some individuals are sensitive to a variety of sounds. Pay special attention to background noise and sudden noises. Notice how competing noise, white noise, and loud noises affect a person's ability to pay attention. Remember that sometimes the senses mix. For example, for some people a loud noise may affect their ability to see things clearly or to remain standing. A way to reduce auditory reverberation might be to use carpet, cork flooring, ceiling tiles, and/or large padded furniture. It is vitally important to have quiet spaces to get away from the stimulation of daily activity.

Reduce Clutter and Distractions   Visual perception can also be challenging for many individuals. Reduce visual clutter while keeping materials visible and accessible. Reduce glare and visual refraction by turning off unnecessary lighting, especially fluorescent lighting; using matte finishes on surfaces and walls; using lamps instead of overhead lights; choosing low wattage light bulbs; and using soft colored light that cuts down contrast and color contrast in a room. Choice of colors for walls, floors, and furniture are important. Solid colors for the walls sometimes help people with depth perception differences to judge distances. One plain wall in a room can provide a visually "quiet" space. Floors and walls should not be the same color. Some people report being able to move better when the floor pattern is compelling, such as floor tiles in a black and white pattern. An example of this is presented in the film *Awakenings*, where a patient is able to cross the room once the black and white pattern has been continued (Sacks, 1990). In the bathroom, a floor that contrasts in color to the toilet and other fixtures is helpful to some. Too much sameness among colors of walls, floors, furniture, and fixtures may make it difficult to see them as separate. The furniture might be positioned around the periphery of the room in order to move around the room more freely or "navigate" without barriers or obstacles.

Understanding Touch   Individuals have reported many accommodations concerning touch. Some people have difficulty with being touched and have learned to accommodate by avoiding the touch of others. Touch may be easier for some to tolerate if it is firm touch rather than light touch and is predictable or rhythmical. Grandin (Grandin, 1995; Grandin & Scariano, 1986) created a "squeeze machine" that provided firm pressure to her body that helped relieve intense anxiety and stress. Some individuals report that hugs and massage help provide comfort and kinesthetic feedback, while for others, such intense touch can be very uncomfortable or cause agitation.

Experimenting with Different Modalities   Combining input from different sensory channels may be difficult for some people. Try stressing one modality at a time. For example, use fewer gestures when speaking, use touch sparingly, and signal your intention to touch before doing so. It is also important to not expect eye contact while a person listens. Consider that movement of others in the area may compete for attention. Experiment to find the right combinations for accommodating to a person's perceptual differences.

Accommodations for Speaking and Interactions

When interactions and speaking are difficult for a person, interpersonal accommodations that explore ways to develop and sustain a relationship are important. Interpersonal accommodations are aspects of support that focus on accommodating a person's differences within the relationship. When people do not use words to communicate and have difficulty using their bodies to express meaning, others sometimes assume the person does not understand what is being said. People who do not have a full range of facial expressions or cannot use their bodies or voices to express emotions are sometimes thought to not have feelings. People have told us that this is one of the most devastating aspects of learning, sensory, and movement differences. Speak to people directly. Although a person's disability may affect various aspects of interaction, it is most helpful to speak to people in a way that acknowledges their competencies. If comprehension appears to be a problem, use augmentation to add meaning to your words; explain yourself in several different ways or illustrate your meaning in some other way, through pictures with words modeling the activity. People must feel that they are part of the communication world in order to find the motivation needed to participate. Provide people with information, friendship, humor, and intellectual stimulation. Do not be afraid to ask an individual about the best way to support him or her.

A partner in an interaction with a person who senses and moves differently may consider accommodating or adapting communication in ways that may not be obvious to most people. Small changes may have a large impact on a person's ability to participate. During an interaction, remember that the melody of your voice may add or distract from your meaning. Try speaking with more or less intonation in your voice, using a soft melody to your voice, whispering, or speaking in a rhythm. A slower pace is often helpful for anyone when the person, place, or activities are unfamiliar. Pause after speaking (sometimes up to 20 seconds) and allow extra time for a person to respond (Miranda & Donnellan, 1986). Creating or maintaining a rhythm during the conversation may be helpful for some. If the individual is swaying or moving in a certain way, it may be helpful to match that movement or rhythm.

An interpersonal accommodation with great significance for many people is a partner who does not demand eye contact in order to continue an interaction. The lack of direct eye-to-eye gaze simplifies listening for some and produces a comfort that allows an easier flow of speech and other forms of expression. Some individuals need more personal space or distance between them and their partner, while others need to be in physical contact with a partner in order to stay with an interaction. For some individuals, physical contact can allow the emergence of speech.

Many people and their families report a benefit from an accommodation that combines touch, rhythm, communication, and emotional support to type or point to produce written language. This is sometimes called facilitated communicating. Support to the person's hand, wrist, arm, shoulder, or back helps some individuals communicate. This accommodation has been the center of research and media attention, much of it negative. Nonetheless, since the mid-1990s when the controversy was at its peak, some people who type to talk have worked hard to establish the validity and reliability of their words (Biklen & Cardinal, 1997). Some who began typing with physical support are now able to type without touch, but may need the presence of a trusted facilitator who provides other supports important for communicating (Broderick & Kasa-Hendrickson, 2001; Mukhopadhyay, 2000; Rubin et al. 2001). There are many resources available for those interested in knowing more about facilitated communicating (Biklen, 1993; Biklen & Cardinal, 1997; Brandl, 1999; Crossley, 1997; Donnellan, Sabin, & Majure, 1992).

Accommodations for Emotional Regulation and Expression

Each of us has specific ways to modulate our emotions and to reduce emotional overload, although we often use these accommodations unconsciously. We use emotional accommodations to regulate both positive and negative emotions as may be seen on television game shows where winning and losing contestants struggle to "keep it together" with loud screaming, attempts to fight back tears, jumping up and down, wringing of hands, and repetitive speech, such as, "Oh my gosh, oh my gosh, oh my gosh!"

Some people with autism report that they work very hard to control emotions, both the initiation of the right emotion and the regulation of the intensity of the emotion. Many report "unfiltered emotions," or difficulty identifying which emotion one is feeling. They report that others often misunderstand their behaviors and their attempts to control emotions, partly because the context or source of an emotional stressor may not be evident or problematic to those around them. Imagine those game show contestants emoting strongly while standing in line at the grocery. Within the store context, the contestants would appear totally inappropriate.

The challenges with which people with autism struggle are often extreme. The most obvious emotional accommodation is to support and promote the confidence and self-esteem of people. Assuming and expressing confidence in a person can be a powerful support and should not be underestimated. Some individuals report that they can sense when a supporter is annoyed or frustrated. Humor can be used to distract a person from an anxious mood and make a situation seem less serious. The attitudes of supporters, whether or not these are specifically expressed, may affect an autistic person's performance, just as they affect the rest of us.

Some people report difficulty with knowing which emotion they are expressing. It may be helpful to let a person know when you see a fleeting sign of a positive emotion. Although a person may appear to be focused on other things and not show conventional signs and signals of relationship, they may be interested in and want relationships with other people. Let them (and others) know that you can see they are acting friendly, even if the signs and signals are unusual or fleeting.

It may be best to discuss difficulties of past behavior during calm and quiet times rather than bringing them up before or during an activity when there may be a problem. While briefing a person just before entering a challenging situation may serve as a reminder for some, for others, it may highlight the problems that they may encounter. In contrast, people report that when others express confidence in their abilities and highlight their competencies, they enter a situation with less anxiety. Some people report that when they are focused on self-control and a supporter brings up the topic of behavior to avoid, the person is more likely to have a problem. As with stuttering or other movement difficulties, naming a behavior to avoid sometimes causes that behavior to happen. Many people report that distraction from thinking about the behavior is more effective than direct reference to it. If one must talk about behavior in a situation, the focus should be on the positive behavior rather than the negative.

During difficult times, when a person needs assistance to maintain self-control, reduce the need to interpret the meaning of your words and use clear language with clear references. Keep conversational "banter" to a minimum, indicate topic switches clearly, and be clear in your intentions and message. Provide the person with more space, both physical space and spaces in the inter-action. Having a space to self-regulate helps some individuals with emotional regulation and expression. Consider teaching a person to leave or avoid sources of provocation.

When a person is vulnerable or is having difficulty with emotional expres-sion or regulation, try to monitor and limit the emotional load of the interaction. Individuals report a loss of sense of control at transition times or shifts from the expected. Some report feelings of performance anxiety with exposure of self and the experience of being the center of attention as too scary. Some report hyperexperienced sensations and emotions that can build when triggered by in-tense situations. The experience is too much feeling and may lead to destruction of one's own work, objects in the environment, attacking one's own body, or shutting down.

Emotions can build up, get mixed up, or become "stuck." "A little bit scared" can turn into terror, yet may be expressed by laughing. "A little bit upset" can turn into furious. "A little bit amused" can turn into manic, hysterical laughing. Direct confrontations may be raw, exposing, and emotionally provoking. When a person is vulnerable or losing control, a direct reference to the situation may be very unhelpful. Often, distraction and indirect references work better. Make a nonverbal offer, for example. Hold out your hand as an offer of support or gently push an object in the person's direction rather than ask if the person wants it. Try using the third person when describing what needs to be done: "When a person feels confused, it sometimes helps to . . . ," and then suggest a course of action. Direct your comments to "another" person or speak to the materials in front of you. Use objects to illustrate or explain interactions.

CONCLUSION

In this chapter, we suggest that the first-hand accounts of individuals with the problems associated with autism provide a rich source of evidence for the pres-ence of sensory and movement differences and disturbances in the lives of these individuals. We have an emerging awareness that behaviors may not be what they seem. We need to rethink many of our previous assumptions regarding people's behavior, paying attention to the insights of people labeled with autism, as well as published literature on sensory and movement differences. Some of the implications informing our thinking include (1) self-stimulatory behaviors may not be volitional or pleasurable; (2) automatic, habitual, impulsive, or over-learned responses may be difficult for a person to inhibit; (3) random bursts of activity, rapid fatigue, lethargy, or disturbances of a person's overall behavior may signal acute difficulties organizing and regulating sensation and movement;

and (4) overreacting or not responding may be related to sensory integration and movement difficulties. These difficulties often are not evident to us because we are constrained by our neurotypical experience and social judgments and by the communication difficulties inherent in autism. Additionally, we suggest that the difficulties these labeled people have regulating and organizing thought, sensory, perceptual, motor, and emotional experience may cause, and even be exacerbated by, stress. It is not our intention to develop yet another set of characteristics to add to the plethora of diagnostic checklists available in our field. Rather, we hope to connect the experience of individuals with autism to the wide range of information about sensory and movement differences found in the literature beyond the field of autism.

We offer the notion of accommodations which was introduced and brilliantly presented by Luria (1932/1976) and by Sacks (1990) as a model of support. Personalized accommodations can be added to the other positive supports recommended for individuals with the labels of autism and other developmental differences. Personalized accommodations are also consistent with the principles of Person-Centered Planning, as discussed and practiced by many of our colleagues (e.g., Cattermole & Blunden, 2002; Falvey, Forest, Pearpoint, & Rosenberg, 1997; O'Brien & O'Brien, 1998; Snow, 1994). Our experience and that of our many colleagues who espouse such a personal and practical approach has the added benefit of expanding our own sense of empathy for those who have an often stressful experience navigating the ordinary events of life. To borrow from the words of the great physician and philosopher, Maimonides, once we can begin to understand their experience, we can never again see in these people anything but ourselves.

Acknowledgment

Extracts from the unpublished dissertation, *Exploring Movement Differences in Autism through First-hand Accounts,* are reprinted with the permission of Karen Strandt-Conroy.

References

Ahuja, N. (2000). Organic catatonia: A review. *Indian Journal of Psychiatry, 42*(4), 327–346.

American Psychiatric Association. (1987). *Diagnostic and statistical manual of mental disorders: Revision* (3rd ed.). Washington, DC: Author.

Ayres, A. (1979). *Sensory integration and the child.* Los Angeles: Western Psychological Services.

Baltaxe, C., (1981). Acoustic characteristics of prosody in autism. In P. Mittler (Ed.), *Frontiers of knowledge in mental retardation, volume 1: Social, educational, and behavioral aspects* (pp. 223–233). New York: Pro Ed.

Baltaxe, C., & Simmons, J., (1977). Bedtime soliloquies and linguiatic competence in autism. *Journal of Speech and Hearing Disorders, 42,* 376–393.

Baron-Cohen, S., (1989). Do autistic children have obsessions and compulsions? *British Journal of Clinical Psychology, 28*, 193–200.

Barron, J., & Barron, S. (1992). *There's a boy in here.* New York: Simon & Schuster.

Bartak, L., Rutter, M., & Cox, A. (1975). A comparative study of infantile autism and specific developmental receptive language disorder: I. The children. *British Journal of Psychiaty, 126*, 127–145.

Bebko, J., & Lennox, C. (1988) Teaching the control of diurnal bruxism to two children with autism, using a simple cueing procedure. *Behavior Therapy, 19*, 249–255.

Bender, L. (1947). Childhood schizophrenia: Clinical study of one hundred schizophrenic children. *American Journal of Orthopsychiatry, 17*, 40–56.

Biklen, D. (1990). Communication unbound: Autism and praxis. *Harvard Educational Review, 60*, 291–314.

Biklen, D. (1993). *Communication unbound: How facilitated communication is challenging traditional views of autism and ability/disability.* New York: Teachers College Press.

Biklen, D., & Cardinal, D. (Eds.). (1997). *Contested words, contested science: Unraveling the facilitated communication controversy.* New York: Teachers College Press.

Blackman, L. (1999). *Lucy's story: Autism and other adventures.* Brisbane, Australia: Book in Hand.

Bond, S. (1986). *The gait of adolescent males with autistic behaviors: A pilot study.* Unpublished master's thesis, McMaster University School of Graduate Studies, Hamilton, Ontario.

Brandl, C. (1999). *Facilitated communication case studies: See us smart!* Ann Arbor, MI: Robbie Dean Press.

Brasic, J., Barnett, J., Will, M., Nadrich, R., Sheitman, B., Ahmad, R., Mendonca, M., Kaplan, D., & Brathwaite, C. (2000). Dyskinesias differentiate autistic disorder from catatonia. *CNS Spectrums, 5*(12), 19–22.

Brenner, S., Friedman, A., & Merrit, H. (1947). Psychiatric syndromes in patients with organic brain disease. 1. Diseases of the basal ganglia. *American Journal of Psychiatry, 135*, 1242–1243.

Broderick, A., & Kasa-Hendrickson, C. (2001). "Say just one word at first": The emergence of reliable speech in a student labeled with autism. *Journal of the Association for Persons with Severe Handicaps, 26*(1), 13–24.

Campbell, M., et al. (1972). Lithium and chlorpromazine: A controlled crossover study of Hyperactive severely disturbed young children. *Journal of Autism and Childhood Schizophrenia, 2*, 234–263.

Carr, E. (1979). Teaching autistic children to use sign language: Some research issues. *Journal of Autism and Developmental Disorders, 9*, 345–359.

Cattermole, M., & Blunden, R. (2002). *My life: A person-centered approach to checking outcomes for people with learning difficulties.* Worchester, England: BILD Publications.

Cesaroni, L. (1990). *Exploring the autistic experience through first-hand accounts from high-functioning individuals with autism.* Unpublished doctoral dissertation, University of Toronto, Ontario.

Cesaroni, L., & Garber, M. (1991). Exploring the autistic experience of autism through first hand account. *Journal of Autism and Developmental Disorders, 21*, 303–313.

Chaplin, R. (2000). Possible causes of catatonia in autistic spectrum disorders. *British Journal of Psychiatry, 177*, 180.

Chess, S. (1972). Neurological dysfunction and childhood behavioral pathology. *Journal of Autism and Childhood Schizophrenia, 2,* 299–311.

Churchill, D., & Bryson, C. (1972). Looking and approach behavior of psychotic and normal children as a function of adult attention or preoccupation. *Comprehensive Psychiatry, 13,* 171–177.

Clark, P., & Rutter, M. (1977). Compliance and resistance in autistic children. Journal of Autism and Childhood Schizophrenia, 7, 33–34.

Comings, D., & Comings, B. (1991). Clinical and genetic relationships between autistic-pervasive developmental disorder and Tourette syndrome: A study of 19 cases. *American Journal of Medical Genetics, 39,* 180–191.

Cowley, G. (2000, July 31). Understanding autism. *Newsweek,* 46–54.

Cowley, G. (2003, September 8). Boys, girls and autism. *Newsweek,* 42–50.

Crossley, R. (1997). *Speechless: Facilitating communication for people without voices.* New York: Penguin.

Curcio, F. (1978). Sensorimotor functioning and communication in mute autistic children. *Journal of Autism and Childhood Schizophrenia, 8,* 181–189.

Curcio, F., & Piserchia, E. (1978). Sensormotor functioning and communication in mute autistic children. *Journal of Autism and Childhood Schizophrenia, 8,* 181–189.

Damasio, A., & Maurer, R. (1978). A neurological model for childhood autism. *Archives of Neurology, 35,* 777–786.

Dawson, G., & Adams, A. (1984). Imitation and social responsiveness in autistic children. *Journal of Abdormal Child Psychology, 12,* 209–226.

DeMyer, M. (1975). Research in infantile autism: A strategy and its results. *Biological Psychiatry, 10,* 433–450.

DeMyer, M. (1976). Motor, perceptual-motor and intellectual disabilities of autistic children. In L. Wing (Ed.), *Early childhood autism* (2nd ed., pp. 169–196) Oxford: Pergamon Press.

DeMyer, M., Alpern, G., Barton, S., DeMyer, W., Churchill, D., Hingtgen, J., Bryson, C., et al. (1972). Imitation in autistic, early schizophrenic, and non-psychotic subnormal children. *Journal of Autism and Childhood Schizophrenia, 2,* 263–287.

DeMyer, M., Hingtgen, J., & Jackson, R. (1981). Infantile autism reviewed: A decade of research. *Schizophrenia Bulletin, 7,* 388–451.

Donnellan, A. (1999). Invented knowledge and autism: Highlighting our strengths and expanding the conversation. *The Journal of the Association for Persons with Severe Handicaps, 24*(3), 230–236.

Donnellan, A. (1999). Invented knowledge and autism: Highlighting our strengths and expanding the conversation. *The Journal of the Association for Persons with Severe Handicaps, 24*(3), 230–236.

Donnellan, A., LaVigna, G., Negri-Shoultz, N., & Fassbender, L. (1988). *Progress without punishment: Effective approaches for learners with behavior problems.* New York: Teacher's College Press.

Donnellan, A., & Leary, M. (1995). *Movement differences and diversity in Autism/ Mental Retardation.* Madison, WI: DRI Press.

Donnellan, A., Leary, M., Miller, J., Lapos, M., Doran, C., & Marquette, J. (2003). *Exploring accommodations: Some things to consider when supporting people with learning, sensory, and movement differences.* Madison, WI: DRI Press.

Donnellan, A., Sabin, L., & Majure, L. (1992). Facilitated communication: Beyond the quandary to the questions. *Topics in Language Disorders, 12*(4), 69–82.

Earl, C. (1934). The primitive catatonic psychosis of idiocy. *British Journal of Medical Psychology, 14,* 230–253.

Falvey, M., Forest, M., Pearpoint, J., & Rosenberg, R. (1997). *All my life's a circle: Circles, maps & paths.* Toronto: Inclusion Press.

Favell, J., McGimsey, J., & Jones, M., (1978) The use of physical restraint in the treatment of self-injury and as a positive reinforcement. *Journal of Applied Behavior Analysis, 11,* 225–241.

Feldenkrais, M. (1972). *Awareness through movement.* New York: HarperCollins.

Frith, U. (1970). Studies in pattern detection in normal and autistic children. *Journal of Abnormal Psychology, 76,* 413–420.

Frith, U. (1971). Spontaneous patterns produced by autistic, normal, and subnormal children. In M. Rutter (Ed.), *Infantile autism: Concepts, characteristics, and treatment* (pp. 113–131). London: Churchill-Livingstone.

Frith, U., & Hermelin, B. (1969). The role of visual and motor cues for normal, subnormal and autistic children. *Journal of Clinical Psychology and Psychiatry, 10,* 153–163.

Gabony, P. (1991). Research supplement: Self-injurious behavior: A unitary phenomenon or a set of diverse behaviors? *British Journal of Special Education, 18* (Research Suppl.) 59–63.

Gedye, A. (1989). Extreme self-injury attributed to frontal lobe seizures. *American Journal on Mental Retardation, 94,* 20–26.

Geller, B., Guttmacher, L. & Bleeg, M. (1981). Coexistence of childhood onset pervasive Development disorder and attention deficit disorder with hyperactivity. *American Journal of Psychiatry, 138,* 388–389.

Gillberg, C., Rosenhall, U., & Johansson, E., (1983), Auditory brainstem responses in childhood psychosis. *Journal of Autism and Developmental Disorders, 13,* 19–32.

Gittelman, M., & Birch, H. (1967). Childhood schizophrenia: Intellect, neurologic status, perinatal risk, prognosis, and family pathology. *Archives of General Psychiatry, 11,* 620–634.

Goldfarb, W. (1956). Receptor preferences in schizophrenic children. *Archives of Neurology and Psychiatry, 76,* 643–653.

Guess, D., & Carr, E. (1991) Emergence and maintenance of stereotypy and self-injury. *American Journal on Mental Retardation, 96,* 299–319.

Grandin, T. (1995). *Thinking in pictures: And other reports from my life with autism.* New York: Doubleday.

Grandin, T., & Scariano, M. (1986). *Emergence: Labeled autistic.* Novato, CA: Arena.

Gray, C. (1994). *Comic strip conversations.* Arlington, TX: Future Horizons.

Gray, C. (2000). *The new social story book: Illustrated edition.* Arlington, TX: Future Horizons.

Groden, J., Cautela, J., LeVasseur, P., Groden, G., & Bausman, M. (1991). *Imagery procedures for people with special needs: Breaking the barriers II.* Champaign, IL: Research Press.

Hale, M. & Hale, C. (1999). *I had no means to shout!* Bloomington, IN: First Books.

Hare, D., & Malone, C. (2004). Catatonia and autistic spectrum disorders. *Autism 8*(2), 183–195.

Hoffman, W., & Prior, M. (1982) Neuropsychological dimensions of autism in children: A test of the hemispheric dysfunction hypothesis. *Journal of Clinical Neuropsychology, 4,* 27–41.

Hutt, C., Hutt, S. J., Lee, D., & Ounsted, C. (1964). Arousal and childhood autism. *Nature, 204*, 909–919.

Hutt, C., & Ounsted, C. (1966). The biological significance of gaze aversion with particular reference to the syndrome of infantile autism. *Behavioral Science, 11*, 346–356.

Hutt, S. J., Hutt, C., Lee, D., & Ounsted, C. (1965). A behavioral and electroencephalographic study of autistic children. *Journal of Psychiatric Research, 3*, 181–197.

Jollife, T., Lansdown, R., & Robinson, C. (1992). Autism: A personal account. *Communication, 26*, 12–19.

Jones, V., & Prior, M. (1985). Motor imitation abilities and neurological signs in autistic children. *Journal of Autism and Developmental Disorders, 15*, 37–46.

Kahlbaum, K. (1973). *Catatonia*. (Y. Levij & T. Pridan, Trans.). Baltimore, MD: Johns Hopkins University Press. (Original work published in 1874)

Kanner, L. (1943). Autistic disturbances of affective contact. *Nervous Child, 2*, 217–250.

Kanner, L. (1944). Early infantile autism. *Journal of Pediatrics, 25*, 211–217.

Kern, L., Koegel, R., & Dunlap, G. (1984). The influence of vigorous versus mild exercise on autistic stereotyped behaviors, *Journal of Autism and Developmental Disorders, 14*, 57–67.

Konstantareas, M. (1985). Review of the evidence on the relevance of sign language in the early communication of autistic children. *Australian Journal of Human Communication Disorders, 13*, 77–97.

LaVigna, G. (1977). Communication training in mute, autistic adolescents using the written word. *Journal of Autism and Childhood Schizophrenia, 7*, 135–149.

Leary, M., & Hill, D. (1996). Moving on: Autism and movement disturbance. *Mental Retardation, 34*(1), 39–53.

Leary, M., Hill, D., & Donnellan, A. (1999, November). *Autism: Myths and misunderstandings*. Presented to the School of Psychology, University of Michigan, Ann Arbor.

Lovaas, O., et al, (1971). Selective responding by autistic children to multiple sensory input. *Journal of Abnormal Psychology, 77*, 211–222.

Lovett, H. (1996). *Learning to listen: Positive approaches and people with difficult behavior*. Baltimore, MD: Paul H. Brookes.

Loveland, K., & Landry, S. (1986). Joint attention and language in autism and developmental language delays. *Journal of Autism and Developmental Disorders, 16*, 335–349.

Lund, C., Mortimer, A., Rogers, D., & McKenna, P. (1991). Motor, volitional and behavioural disorders in schizophrenia 1: Assessment using the modified Rogers scale. *British Journal of Psychiatry, 158*, 323–336.

Luria, A. R. (1976). *The nature of human conflicts*. New York: Liveright. (Original work published in 1932)

Masterson, B., & Biederman, G. (1983). Propeioceptive versus visual control in autistic children. *Journal of Autism and Developmental Disorders, 13*, 141–152.

Maurer, R. (1992). *The neurology of facilitated communication* (audiotape from proceedings, Autism Society of America). Albuquerque, NM: Audio Archives.

Maurer, R. (1993). *What autism and facilitated communication have to teach us about the neurology of relationship* (audiotape from lecture). Toronto, Ontario: MacKenzie Group International.

Maurer, R., & Damasio, A. (1982). Childhood autism from the point of view of behavioral neurology. *Journal of Autism and Developmental Disorders, 12,* 195–205.

McKean, T. (1994). *Soon will come the light.* Arlington, TX: Future Horizons.

Meiselas, K. et al (1989). Differentiation of steriotypies from neuroleptic-related dyskinesias in autistic children. *Journal of Clinical Psychopharmacology, 9,* 207–209.

Menolascino, F. (1965). Psychoses of childhood: Experiences of a mental retardation pilot project. *American Journal of Mental Deficiency, 70,* 83–92.

Mirenda, P., & Donnellan, A. (1986). Effects of adult interaction style on conversational behavior in students with severe communication problems. *Language, Speech, and Hearing Services in Schools, 17,* 126–141.

Mirenda, P., Donnellan, A., & Yoder, D. (1983) Gaze behavior: A new look at an old problem. *Journal of Autism and Developmental Disorders, 13,* 397–409.

Morrison, D., Miller, D., & Meija, B. (1971). Effects of adult verbal requests on the Behavior of autistic children. *American Journal of Mental Deficiency, 75,* 510–518.

Mukhopadhyay, T. R. (2000). *Beyond the silence.* London: National Autistic Society.

Mundy, P., Sigman, M., & Kasari, C., (1990). A longitudinal study of joint attention and language development in autistic children. *Journal of Autism and Developmental Disorders, 20,* 115–128.

Nash, J. (2002, May 6). The secrets of autism. *Time, 159*(18), 46–56.

O'Brien, J., & O'Brien, C. L. (1998). *A little book about person-centered planning.* Toronto: Inclusion Press.

Ornitz, E. (1974). The modulation of sensory input and motor output in autistic children. *Journal of Autism and Childhood Schizophrenia, 4,* 197–215.

Ornitz, E., & Ritvo, E. (1968). Perceptual inconstancy in early infantile autism. *Archives of General Psychiatry, 18,* 78–98.

Ornitz, E., & Ritvo, E. (1976). The syndrome of autism: A critical review. *American Journal of Psychiatry, 133,* 609–621.

Paccia, J., & Curcio, F. (1982). Language processing and forms of immediate echolalia in autistic children. *Journal of Speech and Hearing Research, 25,* 42–47.

Patterson, J. (2002a). *Social behavior of individuals with autism found in first-hand accounts.* Unpublished master's thesis, University of San Diego, San Diego.

Patterson, J. (2002b). *Movement differences: Data collected from first-hand accounts of autism.* Unpublished manuscript.

Prior, M., & Hoffman, W. (1990). Brief report: Neuropsychological testing of autistic children through an exploration with frontal lobe tests. *Journal of Autism and Developmental Disorder, 20*(4), 581–590.

Prior, M., & Macmillan, M. (1973). Maintenance of sameness in children with Kanner's syndrome. *Journal of Autism and Developmental Disorders, 20,* 581–590.

Prizant, B., & Duchan, J. (1981). The functions of immediate echolalia in autistic children. *Journal of Speech and Hearing Disorders, 46,* 241–249.

Prizant, B., & Rydell, P. (1984). Analysis of functions of delayed echolalia in autistic children. *Journal of Speech and Hearing Disorders, 27,* 183–192.

Prizant, B., & Wetherby, A. (1985). Intentional communicative behaviour of children with autism: Theoretical and practical issues. *Australian Journal of Human Communication Disorders, 13,* 21–59.

Ramachandran, V., & Hubbard, E. (2003). Hearing colors, tasting shapes. *Scientific American,* May, 53–59.

Rapin, I. (1987). Searching for the cause of autism: A neurologic perspective. In

D. Cohen & A. Donnellen (Eds.), *Handbook of autism and pervasive developmental disorders* (pp. 710–717). New York: Wiley.

Realmuto, G., & August, G. (1991). Catatonia in autistic disorder: A sign of comorbidity or variable expression? *Journal of Autism and Developmental Disorders, 21,* 517–528.

Realmuto, G., & Main, B. (1982). Coincidence of Tourette's disorder and infantile autism. *Journal of Autism and Developmental Disorders, 12,* 367–372.

Richer, J., & Coss, R. (1976). Gaze aversion in autistic and normal children. *Acta Psychiatrica Scandinavica, 53,* 193–210.

Ritvo, E. et al. (1971). Effects of L-dopa in autism. *Journal of Autism and Childhood Schizophrenia, 1,* 190–205.

Rogers, D. (1992). *Motor disorder in psychiatry: Towards a neurological psychiatry.* Chichester, England: Wiley & Sons.

Rolider, A., & Van Houten, R. (1985). Movement suppession time-out for undesireable behavior in psychotic and severely developmentally delayed children. *Journal of Applied Behavior Analysis, 18,* 275–288.

Rubin, S., Biklen, D., Kasa-Hendrickson, C., Kluth, P., Cardinal, D., & Broderick, A. (2001). Independence, participation, and the meaning of intellectual ability. *Disability & Society, 16*(3), 415–429.

Rutter, M. (1966). Prognosis: Psychotic children in adolescence and early adult life. In J. K. Wing (Ed.), *Early childhood autism* (pp. 83–98). Oxford: Pergamon Press.

Rutter, M., (1974). The development of infantile autism. *Psychological Medicine, 4,* 147–163.

Rutter, M., Greenfield, D., & Lockyer, L. (1967). A five to fifteen year follow-up study of infantile psychosis. II. Social and behavioral outcome. *British Journal of Psychiatry, 113,* 1183–1199.

Sacks, O. (1990). *Awakenings.* New York: Harper Perennial.

Schopler, E., Reichler, R., & Renner, B. (1986). *The childhood autism rating scale (CARS).* Los Angeles: Western Psychological Services.

Simon, N., (1975). Echolalic speech in childhood autism. *Archives of General Psychiatry, 32,* 1439–1446.

Snow, J. (1994). *What's really worth doing and how to do it.* Toronto, Ontario: Inclusion Press.

Sorosky, A., et al. (1968). Systematic observations of autistic behavior. *Archives of General Psychiatry, 18,* 439–449.

Strandt-Conroy, K. (1999). *Exploring movement differences in autism through firsthand accounts.* Unpublished doctoral dissertation, University of Wisconsin-Madison.

Strandt-Conroy, K., & Donnellan, A. (in preparation). *Autism and movement differences: Evidence from self-reports.* Unpublished manuscript.

Sverd, J. (1991). Tourette syndrome and autistic disorder: A significant relationship. *American Journal of Medical Genetics, 39,* 173–179.

Thelen, E. (1995). Motor development: A new synthesis. *American Psychologist, 50*(2), 79–95.

Thelen, E., & Smith, L. B. (1994). *A dynamic systems approach to development and cognition.* Cambridge, MA: MIT Press.

Vilensky, J., Damasio, A., & Maurer, R. (1981). Gait disturbances in patients with autistic behavior. *Archives of Neurology, 38,* 646–649.

Volkmar, F. (1986). Compliance, noncompliance, and negativism. In E. Schopler &

G. Mesibov (Eds.). *Social behavior in autism* (pp. 171–188). New York: Plenum Press.

Volkmar, F., Hoder, E., & Cohen, D. (1985). Compliance, 'negativism', and the effects of treatment structure in autism: A naturalistic, behavioral study. *Journal of Child Psychology and Psychiatry, 26*, 865–877.

Walker, H., & Coleman, M. (1976). Characteristics of adventitious movements in autistic children. In M. Coleman (Ed.), *The autistic syndrome* (pp. 135–144). Amsterdam: North Holland.

Wallace, B. (1975). Negativism in verbal and nonverbal responses of autistic children. *Journal of Abnormal Psychology, 84*, 138–143.

Wetherby, A., & Prutting, C. (1984). Profiles of communicative and cognitive-social abilities in autistic children. *Journal of Speech and Hearing Research, 27*, 364–377.

Williams, D. (1992). *Nobody nowhere.* New York: Avon.

Williams, D. (1994). *Somebody somewhere.* New York: Times Books.

Williams, D. (1996a). *Like color to the blind.* New York: Times Books.

Williams, D. (1996b). *Autism: An inside-out approach.* London: Jessica Kingsley.

Williams, D. (2003). *Exposure anxiety—The invisible cage: An exploration of self-protection responses in the autism spectrum disorders.* London, Jessica Kingsley.

Winchel, R., & Stanley, M. (1991) Self-injurious behavior: A review of the behavior and biology of self-mutilization. *American Journal of Psychiatry, 148*, 306–317.

Wing, L., & Attwood, A. (1987). Syndromes of autism and atypical development. In D. Cohen & A. Donnellan (Eds.), *Handbook of autism and pervasive developmental disorders* (pp. 3–19). New York: Wiley & Sons.

Wortis, J. (1958). Schizophrenic symptomatology in mentally retarded children. *American Journal of Psychiatry, 115*, 429–431.

Young, S. (2000). *Tears fall you can't see: Autism, personhood and expression of self.* Unpublished doctoral dissertation, University of Wisconsin-Madison.

Young, S., & Donnellan, A. (1997). *Rethinking autism and mental retardation: A review of what we think we know.* Unpublished manuscript.

9 Therapist Insights in Working with Stress in People with Autism Spectrum Disorder

Lawrence Bartak, Verity Bottroff,
and Joanna Zeitz

This chapter provides a detailed way of understanding the behavior that people with autism may present. Analysis of the person's behavior in such detail makes it possible to understand the degree and kinds of stress being experienced. This analysis is intended to assist in the development of an effective means of stress reduction. Stress may be reduced in the individual, their family members, and also in other people associated with them, such as peers, teachers, or support staff. The chapter will then describe effective procedures for stress reduction. We represent a merging of theory and practice in the efficient management of stress in people with autism.

DEVELOPMENTS IN CONCEPTUALIZATION ABOUT AUTISM

Following the description of autistic disorder by Kanner (1943), many workers in the field viewed it as a pattern of severe emotional disturbance arising from maladaptive parental child rearing practices, possibly compounded by a personality disorder in parents (Bettelheim, 1976).

From about 1965, psychological studies of children with autism (Bartak, Rutter, & Cox, 1975; Churchill, 1978; Cox, Rutter, Bartak, & Newman, 1975; DeMyer et al. 1972; Frith & Hermelin, 1969; Hermelin & O'Connor, 1970) formed the basis for a new approach to autism. It was established that children with autism could be reliably psychologically assessed and that there were characteristic patterns of cognitive ability showing a clear pattern of relative deficits. It was shown that there was no evidence of deviant personality in parents or of deviant patterns of relationships in families. This body of data has resulted in a switch of emphasis away from psychodynamic and psychiatric approaches with procedures, such as play therapy, aimed at resolving areas of conflict in the child, and in psychotherapy of parents. Attention has been focused on intervention directed to the child's pattern of autistic behavior (Baron-Cohen & Howlin, 1993, 1998) and this pattern is now described in reasonably standardized terms in systems such as the *International Classification of Diseases* (ICD-10; World Health Organization, 1992) and the *Diagnostic and Statistical Manual of Mental Disorders*, fourth edition, text revision (*DSM-IV-TR*; American Psychiatric Association [APA], 2000). However, these systems present autistic disorder as an aggregated set of behaviors, and intervention tends to be based on behavioral and special educational approaches. Education has become the main focus in treatment, although other interventions including medication may be of supplementary use, but not as a basic "cure," for autism (Wing, 1996).

More recent experience with increasing numbers of adults, persons with high-functioning autism, those with Asperger's syndrome and those with partial degrees of autism, such as pervasive developmental disorder not otherwise specified, or "atypical autism," highlights the limitation of current diagnostic approaches. Many of the differences between individuals with autism can be viewed as individual differences in personality and temperamental traits unconnected with autism. There are three consequences of this shift of emphasis. First, there is a need to focus on the individual as a whole person with many normal aspects of behavior, and with autistic behavior as a subcomponent of the totality of their behavior. Many things that people with autism do may be understood as normal behaviors (whether acceptable or unacceptable) and interpreted developmentally. Second, there is a need to focus on the range of behaviors that are specific to autism, but to develop a dynamic model of them with an understanding of primary deficits which lead to secondary and tertiary behavioral consequences, depending on the demands of their environment. This is to say that there are probably basic deficits in people with autism, but these then interact with environmental factors to produce secondary behavioral consequences with further disturbance if the individual is not adequately understood. Third, there is a need to describe each of the deficit areas in more depth to allow for more detailed and individualized assessment and more effective program planning as a result. The major deficit areas as described in *DSM-IV-TR* and ICD-10 systems are far too general and do not provide scope for detailed descriptions of the dynamic functioning of individuals. This chapter addresses this situation by providing a dynamic model of autism that highlights deficits in social functioning and problems of arousal. It proposes the value of individual psychotherapy within a transdisciplinary approach and, finally, describes an intensive treatment program based on this model.

DYNAMIC MODEL OF AUTISM

Systems such as *DSM-IV-TR* (APA, 2000) describe basic criteria of autism as involving the development of delayed and deviant social behavior by 3 years of age, delayed and disordered communication, and the presence of ritualistic and stereotyped patterns of behavior. As noted above, such description is unsatisfactory because the terms used are too general and do not lead to any consideration of whether some components are more basic than others. An alternative scheme to be described here lists basic deficits and describes effects of these deficits at three consequent levels of analysis (fig. 9.1).

A wide range of research studies over many years (Bartak, Rutter, & Cox, 1975; Churchill, 1978; Cox, Rutter, Bartak, & Newman, 1975; DeMyer et al. 1972; Frith & Hermelin, 1969; Hermelin & O'Connor, 1970; Rutter, 1999), as well as developmental changes in children with autism growing to adulthood (Howlin, 1997; Howlin & Goode, 1998), suggest a pattern of primary deficits that show little relative change through development. Absolute levels of ability, of course, can and often do show considerable improvement as the child grows up. Most children with autism develop better social skills, language, and problem-solving skills as they get older. However, a basic pattern of relative deficits appears to endure well into adulthood. These deficits include (1) a delay and deficit in the processing of information to do with other people's feelings, motives, and behavior within the social context; (2) delay and deficit in receptive and expressive language processing; and (3) deficits in executive function skills involving weak central coherence (Pennington & Ozonoff, 1996). It is not clear whether these deficits are independent of each other or, for example, whether some aspects of the deficit in social functioning are a consequence of weak central coherence.

In any event, it would appear that given the postulated primary deficits, a number of secondary effects may flow from them. Ritualistic behaviors, such as insistence on sameness and collection of strange objects, seem to indicate an attempt to focus on detail and control one's environment in the face of the significant deficits in perception of pattern and capacity, and to remediate these through communication with others. In this view, the third cardinal diagnostic feature of autism is thus seen as a secondary consequence of basic deficits. Oddities of expressive social behavior, such as the aloof/passive/active—odd/stilted, overformal, quartet of Wing (1996) can similarly easily be understood as consequences of primary deficits, as can poor common sense, poor sensory integration, and poor consensual validation of ideas about other people's behavior. Poor sensory integration is commonly a major problem of children with autism spectrum disorders. However, it is placed among the secondary features in the current model, as a substantial range of clinical experience indicates that sensory integration seems dependent on the person's understanding of their environment. As their comprehension of language and social situations improves, their

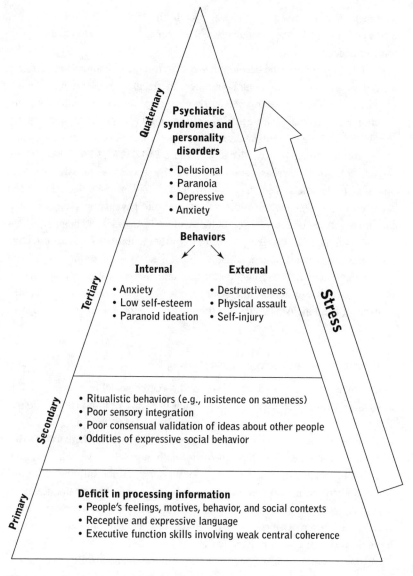

Figure 9.1. Dynamic model of autism.

sensory integration follows suit, both in general and on a moment-to-moment basis.

If radical and poorly thought-out attempts at intervention are made with a view to extinguishing secondary behaviors such as obsessive rituals, then tertiary behavioral effects may appear (as in any normal person whose strategies for control of their environment are systematically blocked). Tertiary effects that may be present following increased stress would include internalizing behaviors such as anxiety, low self-esteem, and paranoid ideation, or externalizing behaviors such as destructiveness, physical assault on other people, and self-injury. Many components of these behaviors will be seen at times in individual children with autism.

Failure to recognize the developmental features and dynamic and functional aspects of such behaviors, with consequent ineffectual intervention strategies, may lead to further or quaternary features emerging, especially in older or high-functioning individuals. These may be seen as a kind of crystallization of tertiary behavioral disturbance into patterns which represent psychiatric syndromes and personality disorders on axes 1 and 2 in the *DSM-IV-TR* (APA, 2000). These include delusional disorder, paranoid personality disorder, depressive disorder, and anxiety disorders. The stage is then set for diagnostic confusion between the occurrence of autistic disorder and a comorbid psychiatric syndrome, and quaternary effects of autism resembling psychiatric disorder and being misdiagnosed. Such confusion is likely to result in further inability to provide effective intervention strategies in general, and with respect to stress in the person with autism in particular. The dynamic model of autism places special emphasis on the consequences of autism for social functioning and invites a more detailed analysis of the deficits of social functioning that are inherent in the disorder.

Classification of Deficits of Social Interaction

In autism, a major area of deficit involves disordered social functioning. While this has generally been explained as a deficit in theory of mind (Baron-Cohen, 1991, 1993, Baron-Cohen, Leslie, & Frith, 1985, 1986), we propose a focus on disordered pragmatic functions. "Pragmatic" is interpreted here as referring to moment-to-moment interactive behavior with others, both verbally and non-verbally. In this context, the term pragmatic references not only the social and communicative aspects of verbal language, but also nonverbal analogues in behavior. Assessment of pragmatic functions by speech pathologists has generally been limited to verbal aspects, which are rated on checklists or rating scales with limited overlap in lists of pragmatic functions.

A more general model of pragmatic functions with applicability to the kinds of deficits seen in autism would involve a number of dimensions, including aspects of interactive function such as channel, direction, competencies, content, language level, and centro-peripheral processing.

Channel

A channel of communication is essentially verbal or nonverbal. Verbal components include semantic aspects, such as processing literal meaning and processing implied meaning. Nonverbal aspects include tone of voice, facial expression, body language, gesture, and signing systems.

Direction

Direction is receptive or expressive. Implied in direction is capacity for initiation, involving mostly expressive skill in the short-term with long-term receptive skill, and responding, involving a mixture of receptive and expressive skill with shorter-term central processing of received input. Many children with autism display marked distress on being required to respond, compared with their competency when able to initiate social interaction. This suggests that the differentiation of initiating and responding competency is important in intervention for these children.

Competencies

Competency is derived directly from the work of Perkins (2000) in applied linguistics. Perkins has noted that there are three areas of pragmatic competency that can be discriminated, including cognitive, socio-cognitive, and affective components. Cognitive areas of competency comprise knowledge of the domain of discussion or area of behavior. You have to know what you are talking about, or what you are engaged in, in order to interact with someone else in some verbal or nonverbal activity. Executive function skills are also necessary. These are concerned with planning and organization in problem solving, or dealing effectively with one's environment. There are probably five or so distinct components, any of which may be impaired:

- staying on task, including impulse control and knowing that tasks have a beginning, middle and end
- processing single items of information or whole arrays of information, switching between them, and sometimes attending to both simultaneously
- evaluating the relative importance of individual pieces of information
- suppressing unimportant or irrelevant pieces of information
- monitoring one's own performance and reevaluating the relative importance of individual pieces of information as necessary.

Other essential cognitive skills include long-term memory, shorter-term memory, and some degree of inferential ability if interpersonal interaction is to proceed in a progressive goal-directed manner.

Affective components involve the capacity to be reinforced by interaction with other people, that is, to find it rewarding to interact with others. Socio-cognitive components include cognitive skills focused on interaction with others. These would include theory of mind (Baron-Cohen, 1991, 1993; Baron-Cohen, Leslie, & Frith, 1985, 1986) and pragmatic rules concerned with effective conduct of discourse governing such features as topic change and maintenance, level of abstraction, and other stylistic matters. Effective conduct of conversation may involve competence in the executive function skills outlined above and their application to the moment-to-moment demands of the conversation. Knowing when to change the topic or stay with it, how to emphasize what is new information, and knowing what new information the listener wants are all competencies that are required on each turn of the conversation. Confusion resulting from the lack of some or all these skills is a major source of stress in high-functioning people with autism spectrum disorders. Theory of mind is likely to be more complex and to require more detailed assessment than is commonly described. Theory of mind includes:

1. Knowing that other people have feelings, thoughts, and motives
2. Receptive skills to decode facial expressions, body language, social contexts, and tone of voice
3. Knowing what others feel, think, and desire (based on competency in the first two items)
4. Knowing what one feels, thinks, or wants
5. Receptive skills to decode one's own facial expression, body language, or tone of voice
6. Knowing the effect of one's own behavior on others.

Wing's (1996) active—odd group may have competency in items 1 through 3, but be impaired in items 4 through 6; many people with Asperger's disorder may have competency in 1 through 5, but be impaired in 6. It is likely to be important to estimate skills in each of these areas for efficient program design.

Content

In general, over the short-term, interactive behavior may be seen as serving a limited number of broad objectives: (1) greeting or initiating (opening a conversation or nonverbal equivalent); (2) mutual goal-directed actions (in conversation, maintaining topic; in play, pursuing the main objective); (3)action that is not goal directed (talking about something else like the weather or engaging in some behavior not relevant to the mutual activity); (4) meta-linguistics or meta-behavioral action (commenting on the activity, statements about changing the activity or topic); and (5) concluding actions (terminating the conversation or the activity, taking leave). Competencies in each of these areas of content may vary.

Language Level

Quality of conversational interaction is dependent on level of language competence and nonverbal equivalents, if interactive behavior can be conceptualized. In language, competency will extend from single-word utterances, through phrase speech, to mature sentence structure. Nonverbal equivalents will extend from single discrete pieces of behavior, to coordinated sequences of nonverbal interactive behavior.

Centro-peripheral Processing

At the most central level, semantic competence will result in discrete words or representations of discrete pieces of behavior. More peripherally, syntactic systems and nonverbal equivalents will link words into utterances or representations of behaviors into more global representations of behavioral sequences. Phonological and other motor systems will realize utterances or other behavioral sequences as expressive behavior both verbal and nonverbal in the environment or the interpretation of such behavior on the part of others in the interaction. Any of these components may be specifically impaired and require focused intervention to reduce stress in the individual with autism.

A MODEL OF STRESS

The reaction of a person with autism to stress, as with anyone who is stressed, will be determined by a number of interacting factors, which are described below.

First, arousal intensity refers to the level of intensity of emotional arousal. This is one of the temperamental traits developed by Thomas, Chess, and Birch (1969). Arousal intensity is probably partly dependent on the sensitivity and reactivity of the individual's central nervous system. It is also likely to be a function of the accuracy and comprehensiveness of the person's perceptual skills and their understanding of the stressor—that is, their capacity to clearly understand the nature of the events, persons, or objects that are the source of stress.

Second, people differ in the speed with which they become aroused and in the speed with which high arousal dies away. This concept of activation and decay of arousal was originally formulated by Pavlov (Gray, 1964) as a dimension of central nervous system mobility. This is likely to affect the degree of stress experienced by people, depending on its interaction with the duration of the stressor in the environment. In persons with rapid arousal build-up, even very short-term stress is likely to trigger a significant stress response . However, longer-lasting stressors may cause more stress in people with slower build-up and decay because they are likely to remain highly aroused even after the stressor is removed.

People also vary in their capacity to sustain goal-directed, effective behavior while highly aroused. Pavlov (Gray, 1964; Nebylitsyn & Gray, 1972) described this capacity as central nervous system strength. Alternatives to effective behavior in high arousal include the development of inhibitory behavior, such as freezing, or less mature and regressive behavior, such as tantrums and destructive actions (Gray, 1987). Some factors can modulate stress arousal. We know that the presence of supports in the person's environment can reduce the arousing effect of stressors on the individual. Similarly, learned adaptive comprehension behaviors, in other words, having a greater understanding, or more accurate and detailed perception of the nature of the stressor, may also reduce the stress response.This may be similar to the learning that takes place through many systems of psychotherapy. Finally, individuals can learn to reduce their physiological arousal in the face of stressors through relaxation training. Such learning may be directed toward changing the level of arousal or may be directed toward speed of activation and decay of arousal.

Some combination of the six factors described above, along with the characteristics of the person's competencies, will determine the degree of stress on the individual. Some factors, such as learned adaptive behaviors, can be changed directly through intervention. Others, such as central nervous system response characteristics, cannot be easily changed but can be compensated through aspects of other factors, including positioning of environmental support factors or buffers. In general, a program for stress reduction consists of two major parts. First, the degree of stress on the individual needs to be assessed in terms of the model of stress, as well as in terms of the person's cognitive, problem-solving, affective, and interpersonal functioning (as described earlier in this chapter). Second, we then need to build up stress-reducing factors in the individual that involve the development of environmental buffers and learned, adaptive behaviors of both kinds. These include buffers, learned, adaptive comprehension behaviors, and learned, adaptive relaxation behaviors.

PSYCHOTHERAPY

Psychotherapy has been regarded as irrelevant to autism ever since autistic disorder was recognized as a brain-based developmental disorder of information processing (Rutter, 1983), rather than as a pattern of family-induced emotional disturbance. However, for those individuals with sufficient verbal fluency, such as people with very high-functioning autism and those who combine Asperger's syndrome with normal or above-normal intelligence, modified psychotherapy may be relevant for reducing stress. Traditional psychotherapies of various kinds involve a conversational interaction with a focus on problems that the client presents. These are then interpreted either covertly or overtly by the therapist in terms of some theory of causation in the person's life experience. Attempts are made to clarify the problem for the client by explicating areas of emotional conflict or by reducing confusion.

In autism, when people have enough verbal fluency for a conversational approach to therapy, an alternative psychotherapy may be relevant. In this case, after focusing on problems, the therapist can adopt a teaching approach that focuses on analysis of stress that result from a lack of understanding, perceiving, or effectively dealing with the stressor. Then, the therapist teaches the client how to apply new rules for understanding a given situation and helps the client develop effective behavioral strategies to deal with problems. Sometimes with high-functioning individuals, a traditional psychotherapy may be added. This approach recognizes that people with autism have emotional conflict and confusion, the same as people who are not affected by autism.

Transdisciplinary Approach

A transdisciplinary approach implies that some staff will be specialized in skills that others share to a lesser degree. It also acknowledges that some skills are exclusive to certain staff and others are equally shared across all groups. The models of autistic disorder and of stress reactions developed above are complex. It follows that it would be necessary for each component of a comprehensive intervention package to deal with stress in people with autism spectrum disorders to be designed by a specialist with expertise relevant to the specific component. Sometimes that component may also be carried out by that specialist. However, in other circumstances, the component could be carried out by other staff with a specialist supervising the staff member who devised the component.

Family Factors

The person with autism exists in a family social context, just as all other people do. A comprehensive approach to stress will also require some analysis of the familial context of the individual. A systems approach (Minuchin, 1985) may be useful in such analysis, looking for features such as enmeshment, role diffusion, and positive and negative feedback mechanisms. Analysis of stress in other family members may well be part of this. Teaching adaptive behaviors to other family members could be relevant, and these might include applied behavioral techniques and systematic assertiveness training to develop assertive skills in parents.

Theory to Practice: A Model of Intervention

An Intensive Intervention Program (IIP) for individuals with an autism spectrum disorder and challenging behaviors was the focus of a three-year research project (Bottroff, Bullitis, Murphy, & Zeitz, 2001; Bottroff & Zeitz, 2002). The model of support and intervention for working with individuals and their families reflects a dynamic model of autism as presented in figure 9.1. The remainder of this chapter details the quaternary, tertiary, secondary, and primary effects of the disorder on both the person as well as on the family. It also provides a framework for support and intervention with illustrative case applications.

Quaternary Effects

The target population of Bottroff and colleague's (Bottroff, Bullitis, Murphy, & Zeitz, 2001; Bottroff & Zeitz, 2002) project was a subgroup of high-functioning individuals with autism spectrum disorder, most of whom were diagnosed with

Asperger's syndrome, all demonstrating challenging behaviors causing risk to themselves and/or others in their environment (e.g., physical harm, mental distress). Profiles of the 15 individuals (14 males and 1 female, ranging in age from 10 to 17 years with a mean age of 12.8 years), reflect quaternary features of the model. For example, all the participants were receiving some degree of psychiatric consultation and medication for challenging behaviors. Multiple diagnosis was also evident with 75% of the participants having received at least one other diagnosis, including psychiatric syndromes ($n = 4$ with conduct disorder, $n = 6$ with depression), as well as comorbidity of attention-deficit hyperactivity disorder (ADHD $n = 9$), dyslexia ($n = 5$), and Tourette's syndrome ($n = 2$). It is not clear whether these were genuine dual diagnoses or diagnostic confusion. For example, one participant had received five diagnoses over time. This situation suggests additional stress factors for the individuals, as well as evidence of the inability of service systems to provide appropriate supports and interventions. The latter was one of the criteria for entry into the IIP. Other interventions had been tried, but without success. The most extreme example of a quaternary feature within this selected group was a suicide attempt by an 11-year-old boy.

Effect on Family

The major effect of quaternary features on the families was reported in a preentry questionnaire and family worker counseling sessions and observations. The situation can best be described as a crisis situation within the family. This group of families reported stress levels resulting in clinical depression, and antidepressant medication was prescribed for the majority of mothers (> 90%) and some fathers (20%). For example, one mother described being on suicide watch over her son when he realized that his long-awaited attempt to attend an alternative school had failed. She spent hours holding her son as he sobbed, "I do not belong in this world. It is too cruel for me, mummy. I need to end it all now. Please get me out of here. I just can't stand it any longer. I beg you." In response to such situations, she would break down crying on the laundry room floor, feeling so helpless and alone, thinking there was only one way out.

Tertiary Effects

A number of assessments were conducted to determine the student's skill level. One of the assessment tools used was the Social Skills Rating System (SSRS; Gresham & Elliott, 1990), which gives a rating of problem behaviors from the perspective of the individual's parents and teachers. All parents rated their child as exhibiting more problem behaviors than 98% of their peers, both in externalization and internalization of behaviors. These included physical and verbal aggression toward family, teachers, peers, and property. Wherever possible (i.e., school was accepting responsibility for a student), teachers (50%) completed the

SSRS and their ratings reflected those of the parents. The students' ratings on the Reynolds Adolescent Depression Scale (RADS; Reynolds, 1986) concurred with the clinical diagnoses reported (40%).

Effect on Family

The education system was struggling to support the students in mainstream classrooms. All participants except one home-schooled student had been suspended or excluded from several schools, and the majority attended only part-time schooling with a policy of telephoning the parents (at any time and at the teachers' discretion) to have the child removed from the class.

A major outcome for all mothers, and some fathers, was the physical anxiety reaction experienced when the telephone rang during school times. For example, parents reported a sick feeling, a panicked feeling, or a feeling of dread. Reactive interventions, such as a teacher requesting a parent remove the child from the school environment, which target behavior in the tertiary stage, created a significant increase in stress for families and individuals with autism spectrum disorder. This can exacerbate internalizing and externalizing behavior to further result in quaternary reactions such as anxiety disorder, depression, and other psychiatric syndromes in the child, as well as generating significant anxiety and depression in the parents.

Secondary Effects

Assessment results generally demonstrated an extreme discrepancy between students' overall patterns and levels of cognitive functioning and their social, emotional, and functional behavior. For example, one student at chronological age of 10 years, 0 months, scored a full scale IQ of 101, and a Vineland Adaptive Behavior Scale score of 5 years, 1 month, with interpersonal relationship skills of 3 years, 2 months. Poor sensory integration became so apparent in the participants that an occupational therapist with sensory integration training and experience in working with individuals with autism spectrum disorder was included on the professional team. For example, the sound of a sibling chewing cereal at breakfast time was registered by one participant as so abhorrent that his distress manifested in physical aggression toward the sibling and his belongings. Poor consensual validation of ideas about other people was also demonstrated in his insistence that his sibling was chewing loudly just to annoy him.

This poor consensual validation is particularly noticeable when developing peer relationships. For example, most of the participants demonstrated initiation skills toward peers, but the ability to develop the relationship beyond an initial stage was restricted by their difficulty in interpreting the intention of the peers' reciprocal behavior. This contributed to the victimization and bullying of participants. Self-reports and parental reports indicated that all participants experienced victimization and bullying. A study conducted in South Australia by Cole (1997) demonstrated that children with autism spectrum disorder are at greater risk of peer victimization and rejection compared with their peers.

Effect on Family

The significant discrepancy between overall intelligence and social-emotional understanding, with associated difficulties inhibiting behavior, presents as a major issue within families, particularly for siblings. Siblings and parents become the targets and victims of the frustration experienced by the individuals with autism spectrum disorder. Conversely, this discrepancy in development contributes to the individual with autism spectrum disorder becoming the target of victimization and bullying at school.

The participants in the IIP also demonstrated difficulties controlling their emotions with teachers. When interacting with teachers and other students, a "fight-or-flight" reaction was evident, with family members often left dealing with the outcomes.

Primary Effects

The qualitative differences and delays in social and emotional development, communication, and executive functioning may be independent of each other, associated with, or a result of a primary deficit, which may be one of these areas. A search for the primary deficit has been a research focus over many years, such as theory of mind (Baron-Cohen, 1989, 1991, 1993; Baron-Cohen, Leslie, & Frith, 1986; Leslie & Frith, 1990), and affect and emotion (Hobson, 1986, 1991, 1994). The importance of such knowledge lies in the ability of clinicians to develop strategies to alleviate the primary deficits, which will in turn prevent or reduce secondary effects. In the absence of this information, the intervention strategies developed for individuals within the IIP, in particular the cognitive-behavioral techniques, focused on the range of developmental areas associated with the primary features of the disability such as social-emotional and communication, as well as elements within the model of pragmatic functions outlined previously.

The affective component within the pragmatic dimension highlights the capacity of the individual to derive some pleasure from interacting with others. The desire for interaction, to be part of the peer group, and to develop friendships becomes apparent as individuals with an autism spectrum disorder approach adolescence (Bottroff, 1998). This phenomenon was evident for the participants within the IIP, as was their anxiety associated with attempts to gain entry and status within the peer group. An appreciation of the connection between the desire, level of social-emotional development to achieve the desire, and associated anxiety is expressed vividly through the following personal account from Donna Williams (2003): "The biggest problem was that my social desire had so over-taken the level of social-emotional development that I couldn't easily combine feelings with being social. I was being driven as strongly outward as I was in-ward, attacking myself and attacking others, diverting attention onto everything and being as confusing as I was confused" (p. 47). She uses the term "exposure anxiety" to convey the survival or self-protection mechanism which is activated when feeling loss of control and stress associated with "self-in-relation-to-other" interactions (p. 10).

Effect on Family

Knowledge of the primary characteristics associated with autism spectrum dis-order and their effects on the individuals are important in understanding percep-tions of the personal and physical environment. The development of a profile of each individual within the IIP is a preliminary step in devising intervention and support strategies. Both therapists and parents gain from sharing their percep-tions. For example, parents reported feeling less frustrated and annoyed by their child's behavior, sometimes perceived as "defiant and naughty," when they were provided with information about the primary characteristics of the disability in relation to their child's behavior. Afterward, parents are more receptive to the implementation of suggested strategies, perhaps because they now can put the behavior in context.

Support and Intervention

The intervention model trialed in the IIP research project was originally de-veloped because of requests for crisis support from family members of peo-ple with high-functioning autism and Asperger's disorder presenting with very challenging behavior. These adolescents and young adults presented with ter-tiary and quaternary characteristics, including suicide attempts, substance abuse, violence, and aggression, sometimes resulting in criminal proceedings or tem-porary institutionalization in a psychiatric hospital with subsequent family cri-sis and breakdown. In particular, a young adolescent with Asperger's disorder (pseudonym Andrew) had been in various types of accommodation supported by numerous service providers with minimal success. He exhibited violent out-bursts, illicit drug-taking, and "pseudo" suicidal attempts (as diagnosed by his psychiatrist) requiring many emergency admissions to a hospital. Professional service providers struggled to keep him stable, happy, and healthy. Although he was generally pleasant to staff, he did not respect the staff's life experiences or see them as understanding his experiences. His life was discussed and acted upon by third parties on a regular basis and he had little control of his life. Through his contacts, he met a homeless, older adolescent (pseudonym Sam), whom he invited to live with him without informing supporting agencies or family. Sam hid from staff and the two supported each other very well.

Andrew stopped taking illicit drugs because Sam had taken drugs and did not recommend it. He stopped taking overdoses and his violence decreased. The support of a person who was loyal to him and respected and understood his experiences was critical in motivating him to change some of his self-destructive behavior. Sam would support Andrew in coping with professionals challenging his behavior. On some occasions, Sam would agree with the professionals, but on others, he supported Andrew to disagree. Eventually, Sam attended Andrew's support meetings. Sam helped Andrew to say what he wanted and he argued for his needs. Andrew was no longer a solitary figure in a room of professionals.

A high level of reactionary crisis intervention from legal and medical services into an individual's life may cause a sense of loss of control over his or her life. This can increase stress and heighten arousal resulting in fight and flight reactions, primarily the former. These reactions, together with the loss of trust and respect for people and no motivation to change, presented a major challenge for proactive support and intervention.

Taking into consideration Andrew and Sam's experiences, Zeitz's (2000) model provided mentor support, intervention strategies, and counseling for individuals with autism spectrum disorder and their families. Motivation, trust, and choice were key components for engaging the cooperation of the student with autism spectrum disorder. The model was adopted for the research project that initially targeted adolescents with autism spectrum disorder and was subsequently adapted for the younger children. The support structure and some key individual intervention strategies will become the focus for the remainder of the chapter (fig. 9.2).

Case Management

Case management provided a consistent intervention focus and essential coordination of supports and services, including a point of contact for communication between supporting professionals. Principles for case management and individualization of program interventions include the following:

- assessment of function of behavior, intellectual ability, independent living skills, and social skills
- individual support from a mentor
- individual counseling, including cognitive-behavioral approach
- parent and sibling information and support sessions
- regular communication and liaison with school community
- regular communication and liaison with supporting medical practitioners
- mediation between family and student
- individual home plan for behavioral change
- maintenance plan, including community connections for on going support.

Intervention Model

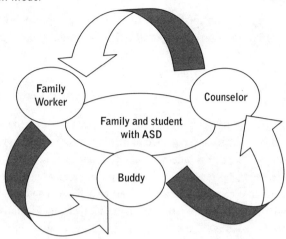

Intervention components and timetable

1 Case Management		
2 Assessment	3 Family Support 4 Individual Support	5 Maintenance

1	2	3	4	5	6	7	8	9	10	11	12

Months

Figure 9.2. Support roles.

Assessment

A broad baseline was obtained before intervention began. Depression scales, social skills scales, functional behavior, intellectual ability, and general behavior were assessed. For a majority of the participants, these assessments indicated depression and anxiety that required medical intervention. The assessments highlighted individual strengths and weaknesses that needed to be considered when developing individualized interventions strategies. The assessments also provided a comparison of views from key people in the life of the student with autism spectrum disorder and highlighted inconsistencies across the student's environment. Examples of these assessments were reported earlier in this chapter.

Family Support

Family support that was offered to the family members separately from the child with autism spectrum disorder provided an opportunity to talk about concerns, both related and unrelated to the child with autism spectrum disorder.

Maintenance

A maintenance plan is intended to assist with transitioning support for people with autism spectrum disorder to specialized services and generic community groups.

Individual Support

As a result of crisis interventions and the consequential lack of trust, support from a mentor was adopted as a method of helping restore positive and motivating relationships with professionals and family. The mentor was a nonauthoritarian role model who respected the student's experiences, thoughts, and feelings. Mentors had a sound knowledge of autism spectrum disorder and offered the student feedback (interpretation) on the communication and interactions of others. The mentor (referred to as a "buddy") attended therapy sessions with the student, spent time in the community involved in an activity motivating to the student, and talked with the student about the topics discussed in the therapy sessions. The role of the mentor can best be described as a "social" interpreter on the student's shoulder, that is, a "Jiminy Cricket" (Matthews & Williams, 1988). This relationship was time limited and was gradually withdrawn. It was part of the mentor's role to help the student connect with community support and activities. The student attended weekly sessions with the counselor and discussed critical issues for the student, including:

- interpreting other people's communication and expectations
- discussing strategies for working through conflicts and seeing situations from another person's perspective
- managing anxiety and stress levels
- dealing with anger and aggression
- gaining a greater understanding of autism spectrum disorder
- developing strategies for dealing with harassment
- understanding community living and community norms.

The sessions were not about forcing change by applied consequences, but rather about helping the student explore the likely social consequences of a particular sequence of behavior. Cognitive behavior therapy strategies were developed to assist in mapping the potential actions, thoughts, feelings, and beliefs of people involved in particular circumstances. This helped the students understand the process of decision making and consequent actions. The students were then provided with an explanation of the development of reputation. The purpose of this intervention was to provide the students with a greater understanding of how their reputation may limit their life choices, such as future education and career choice. A student may wish to stay in mainstream schooling rather than in a special small class, but due to his reputation for aggressive behavior, this decision may be made for him.

The following is an example of the application of the model with an adolescent with autism spectrum disorder and his mother:

> Tom, who was 15 years old, was referred to the program because of his physical and verbal aggression toward his mother. His school reported incidents of harassment and victimization, poor grades and poor attendance. At the first session of the intervention program Tom had been suspended from school for property destruction. Tom felt this was grossly unjustified. He presented at the program with a sullen defiant attitude. Tom received support from Julie, his buddy, twice a week for three hours each time. Julie attended a group session with Tom that included the other students and their buddies. She also supported him at a counseling session and met with him in the community for a recreational activity of his choice.
>
> The sessions explored conflicts he was experiencing at home and at school. Tom's family met with the family support worker each week. This occurred initially without Tom's involvement, allowing the family to express their frustration at Tom's behavior and attitude without feeling compromised or restrained by his feelings or reactions. Toward the end of the six months of intervention, Tom was invited to the family session with Julie. The family support worker supported the other family members and the counselor mediated the session. Issues that had been causing the greatest conflict in the house were raised for discussion and actions assigned to individuals to promote change.

Individual Intervention Strategies

The individual counseling sessions are activity-based to promote motivation and attention. The person with autism spectrum disorder is involved in the visual depiction of the sessions. This may be presented through drawing on a white board, the use of a video camera, or the use of a subject of interest, such as Pokemon or Digemon characters used to act out scenarios. Motivation to participate is essential. The immediate issues concerning the student must take priority. For example, if the student's greatest concern is how to respond to peer harassment, then this needs immediate attention. If the student anticipates a solution to issues troubling him or her, motivation to participate in the program may increase and stress may reduce because a stressor has been addressed. A sense of respect and worth is more likely to be gained if students feels their concerns are taken seriously. Trust and a sense of respect are vital to a good working relationship and essential when coping with challenges to one's behavior.

Concrete mapping of connections between concepts (e.g., thoughts, feelings) was a critical component of the methodology, such as Vermeulen's (2000) description of three activities of the brain—receiving, processing, and responding. This provides a starting point for discussing "processing," or the thinking and feeling aspects associated with behavior. Attention is given to the difference between thoughts and feelings. Initially a list of emotions is made using the descriptive words offered rather than typical terms. These may be color-coded to aid classification of important people, such as family members, at a later stage. To expand the list, the students are presented with hypothetical situations. Following is an example of one hypothetical situation used within the IIP:

> A boy is at his first day in a new school and it is lunchtime. (How does he feel?) He doesn't have any friends yet, so he borrows a basketball and goes to the school basketball court to play by himself. (How is he feeling?) Three other boys from his class are playing together at the other end of the court, and they ask if he would like to join in. (How does he feel?) He joins in, and, while they are playing, one of the other boys accidentally throws the ball, and it breaks a window on a school building. (How does he feel?) All the boys run. The boy is still standing there as a teacher walks around the corner. (How does he feel?) The teacher asks if he knows what happened. (How does he feel?)

A number of different activities were used to confirm students' understanding of feelings and maintain their motivation to participate. Drawing facial expressions on the white board or the computer to represent each emotion was one such activity. After drawing facial expressions, the student listed five of the emotions that best describe him, and then created a story about himself, including feelings.

Using the hypothetical situation again, after discussing feelings, the student is asked what he or she believes the boy may be thinking at each stage. Often the student will continue to state feelings, not thoughts, and at this point a discussion of the separation of thoughts and feelings begins. This is critical groundwork for the use of the Action, Thought, Feeling, Action, and Reputation (ATFAR) strategy (fig. 9.3).

The ATFAR strategy is a framework for breaking down the interactions between two or more people into separate parts (initially this involves actions, thoughts, and feelings) to assist analysis of a third person's intentions. The student can then gain an insight into the way that his actions are viewed by others. For students who are able to conceptualize the process, reputation is added to the framework. A therapist must consider the motivation of the student to participate. As noted earlier in relation to affective components of normal pragmatics, students must find it rewarding to interact with others. Students need to recognize there will be a benefit if they learn the framework. Therefore, it is essential that the therapist personalize the strategy to make it motivating enough for the student to want to learn. The use of a recent incident in which the student felt he had been treated in an unjust way by another person may assist in gaining the student's interest. This may be a useful starting point for learning about the ATFAR framework. The following is an example of a personal incident:

> John was very upset about being suspended from school. John's description of what happened was that "another boy pushed me and I was taken to the office and suspended—nothing happened to him!" While drawing the scenario, setting the scene (therapist and/or student), John was asked to describe what happened.

Figure 9.3. Action, thought, feeling, action, reputation.

Describing the Action and Thought

Plotting through the action is an essential step to deciphering the motives of other people involved in the incident. This process helps the student view the scenario through the third person's eyes. Using concrete steps helps the student form associations—that is, connections between other people's experiences and actions. It is important that, as the scenario is being described, it is drawn or acted out. The analogy of a film director and use of a video camera to make a short movie of the scene can be very motivating.

The scene can be set using available people, such as a buddy and a counselor, to play the different characters in the scenario. The student describes the scene and actions to the actors and a script is written. The scene is filmed. To develop an understanding of events, the actions have to be sequential and connected, highlighting obvious gaps in the story.

John's description of the incident involving school suspension was as follows. "He pushed me. I was taken to the office and suspended and nothing happened to him." John was asked, "Why did the boy push you?" and "What happened just before the boy pushed you?" Eventually the following story sequence was constructed.

> During lunch break John was playing with a ball, and three girls who often teased John started to do so. He tried to walk away, but they followed him around, continuing to tease him. He started to cry and the girls left. The boy who John hit was watching and laughing. John threw a stick at the boy and it hit him on the head. The boy started to cry. The boy pushed John and John hit him again with another stick.

John was asked to list all the people involved so that each character could be assigned an "actor." He was then asked to set the positions and describe what each person "looked like" (feeling), or, "How would you describe their faces?" That is, what feelings did they convey through facial expression at different stages throughout the scenario? In the above scenario, the student described the other child as crying and angry. This allows the therapist to refer back to the ATFAR and add the third person's feelings to the beginning of the example. The student is then asked why the child was crying and angry: "What had happened to upset him?" In this example, the student's response was, "I threw a stick at him because he was laughing at me."

This process helps the student plot through a scenario addressing all parties' roles, rather than just his or her own perspective. The aim is to help students understand that can change their thoughts about the incident if necessary and, most important, reduce their anger, resulting in alternative actions with a subsequent reduction in build-up of tension and stress.

The student is then asked how he or she felt: "What were your feelings at the time of the incident?" If a thought is given instead of a feeling, then this is labeled as such, and the student is asked again, with examples of feelings. When the student's thoughts and feelings have been explored and recorded in drawing and writing, his or her action (response) is discussed. At this point it can be useful to return to the original "unjust action" and, working backward, discuss with the student what the thoughts and feelings of the other person may have been. A common response is, "I have no idea." The counselor explains that information for deciphering the feelings of others is available to the student. A discussion of the depiction of feelings through facial expression and body language then helps the students surmise the third person's feelings.

Exploring Emotions

Students are asked which colors they would assign to their family members. A discussion takes place of the main color they assign to each person and how they can tell this person is best represented by the color suggested. This opens up communication on the physical and verbal cues of emotion, such as body language, intonation, and facial expression.

Below is a part of a list of feelings given by John, who was 12 years old. It is important that the list is fun to compile. The therapist and buddy join in listing as many feelings as possible, writing down the description of each exactly as the student says, including profanities (within reason) and invented words. The average number of emotions generated by students and buddies in the IIP was 65. The students are given a packet of felt pens with 20 colors and asked to draw a line next to each feeling using the color they think best represented the feeling.

John's list

BLUE: sad
GREY: depressed, bored, nervous, regretful
PURPLE: lonely
GREEN: sick, shameful weird, curious
PINK: puzzled, surprised
YELLOW: proud, fun, jolly, good, happy, excited
RED: embarrassed, powerful, furious
BLACK: not wanted
DARK GREEN: stupid
No color: uncomfortable, interested

Brother = blue (sad)
Mum = yellow + gray (happy and depressed)
Dad = red (furious)
Sister = pink (puzzled)
John = black (not wanted)

Other activities that explore emotions include:

- videotaping emotions
- acting out emotions playing a game of "emotions charades"
- creating a facial expression pictionary
- cutting out expressions from magazines and make up stores to fit the picture.

A focus on emotions associated with family members facilitates an exploration of the behavioral issues within the family. The ATFAR strategy is used to demonstrate the interactions that are taking place and how conflicts can be reduced.

Reputation

Apparently, all of the students in the project were very motivated by a desire to have friends. This desire appeared to be no less than that of the average person (Bottroff, 1998). Taking this into consideration, the therapist used this motivation to challenge the students on their belief about the effect their behavior had on other people's desire to be friends with them. To begin this work, each student was asked to guess how a classmate might describe him to a new student in the class. Working with components of the ATFAR strategy, a list of what other people see and their possible thoughts about their observations was compiled. To assist this process, the analogy of a video can be used again, returning if necessary to the method described above of scripting, acting out, and filming an incident. The students were asked what would be seen by a person watching the video.

When working with students who have challenging behavior, a discussion on the formation of reputation then takes place. Once again, using the ATFAR strategy, the students are told that if an action is seen once by another person, that person may have a thought or opinion about the student. If the same behavior is witnessed again, the person may recall the previous incident and confirm to himself that the previous thought about that person was indeed accurate. The behavior witnessed repetitively (e.g., kindness, aggression, excitability) becomes a label and forms the student's reputation with that person. Reputations are easily talked about: "That's John over there. He is a very kind person." The students are told that the more extreme a behavior is, the more it is noticed, and the quicker it becomes part of a reputation. People can know about a person's reputation before meeting him or her. For example, "I have heard John is a very kind person." Negative reputations can limit a person's choices. For example, "I have heard

John can be aggressive, and I don't think it would be a good idea to invite him to the train show." This concept is explored step-by-step with the students.

Below is an example of responses given by Brian, 14 years of age, with Asperger's syndrome, who was regularly suspended from school for violent behavior. He was asked, "How do you think the other students at school would describe you?" His answer included, "intelligent, absent from school, and someone who wants space to get away from it all (people)."

He was asked, "How do you think the teachers at school would describe you?" He listed the same characteristics as he did for the students' list, but his teachers' list also included, "clumsy, lazy, lacking concentration, and violent."

Changing a Reputation

Reputations can be changed, but they have to be changed in the same way they were made. This discussion leads to the question of how the student would like to be viewed by others. Brian was asked, "What would you like your reputation to be?" His answer was to list positive characteristics, including "intelligent, efficient worker, peaceful, good at English, and sense of humor."

Once the reputation has been explored and the motivation for changing behavior established, work on relaxation and management of anxiety can increase, with the aim of learning a new way other than explosive reactions to cope with stress.

Valuable Additions

A valuable addition to the IIP model has been the inclusion of biofeedback equipment to assist in motivation and understanding of the progressive muscle relaxation technique. This relaxation technique is supported by the pioneering work of Groden, Cautela and Groden (1989).

Another successful component of the IIP model was the addition of the Alert Program (Williams & Shellenberger, 1994) for the younger students. Dunn and Donaldson (2001) describe the benefits of the Alert Program as assisting children to self-regulate their arousal level using sensory input and the analogy of a car engine running high, just right, or low. In addition, it was determined that an occupational therapist was needed in the transdisciplinary team to carry out appropriate assessments and to make subsequent recommendations for practice. A study by Alexander (1998) demonstrated that the Alert Program can be adapted for children with autism spectrum disorder with positive outcomes.

Strategies were developed to help students adapt to stressful environments, such as maintaining on-task behavior in a classroom when the noise level escalates. Strategies "to keep their engines running just right," may include time-out in a quiet room engaging in a special interest activity, a physical activity such as running around a school track or playground, a weighted blanket over the student's lap, or wearing a weighted vest. Students were also provided with a toolbox in which they placed objects to help them adjust their level of arousal. For example, if feeling anxious, they could use a stress ball from their toolbox.

Use of the principles and strategies associated with the Alert Program illustrates some of the key features associated with the dynamic model of autism described in the beginning of this chapter. The Alert Program focuses on a primary effect of the condition of autism spectrum disorder, expressed as central nervous system response characteristics and the development of the student's awareness of his level of arousal, together with an understanding of how different environmental factors affect arousal levels. Environmental supports (buffers) are then introduced, providing the student with a method of self-control, which in turn should improve sensory integration (secondary effects), reduce anxiety (tertiary effects), and reduce subsequent quaternary effects. Similarly, the cognitive-behavioral methods adopted in the individual counseling sessions focused on developing awareness and understanding of people's feelings, motives, behavior, and social contexts (ATFAR), all recognized as primary effects associated with autism spectrum disorder. The intention of this approach was to reduce inappropriate validation of ideas about other people (secondary effects), with a consequential reduction of tertiary behaviors, both internal (e.g., anxiety, low self-esteem, paranoid ideation) and external (e.g., destructiveness, physical assault, self-injury). An overall result of this approach is a reduced probability of the development of psychiatric syndromes and personality disorders (e.g., anxiety, depression, paranoia).

Evaluation of the Intensive Intervention Program

The major aim of the IIP was to improve family quality of life. Interviews were conducted with the students, their mentors, and parents to evaluate the effectiveness of the program in relation to this outcome. An analysis of the results indicated support for the model of intervention. For example, the following comments were received from one mother when she discussed the value of the specific roles within the model: "The way everything linked in—the buddy, counselor and family worker . . . everyone working as a group . . . this helped us sort out her behavior. No one bit could be eliminated."

Positive changes in the students' behavior reported by their parents were improvements in social skills, including appreciation of other people's feelings and a reduction in aggression and depression. As expressed by one mother, "[The] depression [is] not as bad. There have been no pictures [the child would draw gruesome pictures], head banging, or hurting himself. Also no hurting other children (including siblings)." There were also improvements in behavior in school settings, with increased attendance, and one student had his best school report. Before the program he wanted to leave school. Parents reported a calmer, more relaxed family environment and that they were "now functioning as a family, [child] is more relaxed, positive in his perception of life including seeing his 'inappropriate' behavior from an understanding of the negative reactions of others."

Students perceived improvements in their behavior. The adolescent students reported improvements in anger management and interpersonal skills, including more awareness of other people's emotions, whereas the younger students focused on the anger management (teaching me not to hit; how to control temper). Younger students found talking about behavioral issues with the counselor a challenging experience; however, the older students were more able to appreciate the value of the counselor's role: "I could see where she was coming from and what she was doing" (this is a good example of theory of mind). Other comments included the following:

- helped me to understand things and talk about things that were difficult to talk about
- helped me through things, such as how to stop an argument before it starts
- clarified my thoughts and ideas about people and reputation
- helped me manage anger and emotions.

The students' responses suggested that they viewed the mentor as a confidant and support, someone "to hang out with" who helped them in group sessions, meetings, and interviews. Comments from the staff who adopted the "buddy role" indicated that this was initially challenging. The most difficult aspect was the ability to maintain a nonauthoritarian role while providing the student with information on the potential consequences of chosen actions on his reputation without appearing judgmental. This required a shift in their personal attitudes toward social conventions and a review of their method of influence over another person's choices.

The phasing out of the program was the major concern raised by all participants. Some parents feared that the positive behavioral changes in their children would not be maintained. Though counselors were available for both parents and students should they require any further support and in the event of any crises, minimal support was required for 90% of the families. One family whose son has multiple diagnoses, including psychiatric syndromes, and other family members with diagnosed disabilities, including Asperger's syndrome, has required more substantial support. This situation demonstrates the increased challenges for professionals when quaternary effects are evident.

The following quote is an example of the maintenance of positive behavioral outcomes in this unsolicited correspondence from a mother, 12 months after the completion of the IIP: "I opened a letter to find an invitation to a Challenging Behaviors Workshop. I put it aside and [her child] picked it up, read it, and asked, 'I don't have any challenging behaviors, do I mum? You can imagine how pleased I was to be able to tell him he hasn't got any challenging behaviors at all!"

Conclusion

We have presented dynamic views of autism and of the development and management of stress in people with autism spectrum disorder. We have attempted to show how consideration of a combination of these approaches leads to more effective and comprehensive stress reduction. Success here is likely to prevent primary and secondary features of autistic disorders from escalating into tertiary and quaternary features, with consequent escalation of costs. Some costs are personal, both for the person with autism and for their family members. Others are financial, both for families and for state and federal resources that maintain support services for people with disabilities and other special needs. Effective attention to reduction of unnecessary stress in people with autism is likely to result in significant emotional and financial cost benefits to everyone concerned. However, of primary importance is the achievement of an increase in quality of life for individuals with an autism spectrum disorder and their families.

References

Alexander, V. (1998). *A pilot study of the relationship between sensory processing and anxiety in boys with Asperger's syndrome*. Unpublished doctoral dissertation, Flinders University, Adelaide, Australia.

American Psychiatric Association (2000). *Diagnostic and statistical manual of mental disorders: Text revision* (4th ed.). Washington, DC: Author.

Baron-Cohen, S. (1989). The autistic child's theory of mind: A case of specific developmental delay. *Journal of Child Psychology and Psychiatry, 30*(2), 285–297.

Baron-Cohen, S. (1991). The theory of mind deficit in autism: How specific is it? *British Journal of Developmental Psychology, 9*, 301–314.

Baron-Cohen, S. (1993). From attention-goal psychology to belief-desire psychology: The development of a theory of mind, and its dysfunction. In S. Baron-Cohen, H. Tager-Flusberg, & D. Cohen (Eds.), *Understanding other minds: Perspectives from autism* (pp. 59–82). New York: Oxford University Press.

Baron-Cohen, S., Leslie, A. M., & Frith, U. (1986). Mechanical, behavioural and intentional understanding of picture stories in autistic children. *British Journal of Devleopmental Psychology, 4*, 113–125.

Baron-Cohen, S., & Howlin, P. (1993). The theory of mind deficit in autism: Some questions for teaching and diagnosis. In S. Baron-Cohen, H. Tager-Flusberg, & D. Cohen (Eds.), *Understanding other minds: Perspectives from autism* (pp. 466–480). New York: Oxford University Press.

Baron-Cohen, S., & Howlin, P. (1998). *Teaching children with autism to mind-read: A practical guide for teachers and parents*. New York: Wiley & Sons.

Baron-Cohen, S., Leslie, A. M., & Frith, U. (1985). Does the autistic child have a 'theory of mind'? *Cognition, 21*, 37–46.

Baron-Cohen, S., Leslie, A. M., & Frith, U. (1986). Mechanical, behavioural and intentional understanding of picture stories in autistic children. *British Journal of Developmental Psychology, 4*, 113–125.

Bartak, L., Rutter, M., & Cox, A. (1975). A comparative study of infantile autism and specific developmental receptive language disorder: vol. I. The children. *British Journal of Psychiatry, 126*, 127–145.

Bettelheim, B. (1976). *The empty fortress*. New York: Free Press.

Bottroff, V. (1998). The development of friendships and the puzzle of autism. In K. Rigby & P. Slee (Eds.), *Children's peer relations* (pp. 91–105). London: Routledge.

Bottroff, V., Bullitis, E., Murphy, C., & Zeitz, J. (2001). Individual needs and integrated practices for individuals with Asperger syndrome and their families. In *Proceedings of the National Autism Conference: Positive Steps Forward*, Adelaide, Australia.

Bottroff, V., & Zeitz, J. (2002). A model of support and intervention for individuals with Asperger syndrome and challenging behaviour and their families. In *Proceedings of the Inaugural World Autism Congress: Unity through diversity*, Melbourne, Australia.

Churchill, D. W. (1978). Language: The problem beyond conditioning. In M. Rutter & E. Schopler, *Autism: A Reappraisal of concepts and treatment* (pp. 71–84). London: Plenum Press.

Cole, C. (1977). *Victimisation of children with autism spectrum disorder in mainstream schools*. Unpublished honors thesis, Flinders University, Adelaide, Australia.

Cox, A., Rutter, M., Bartak, L., & Newman, S. (1975). A comparative study of infantile autism and specific developmental receptive language disorder: vol. II. Parental characteristics. *British Journal of Psychiatry, 126*, 146–159.

DeMyer, M. K., Alpern, G. D., Barton, S., DeMyer, W. E., Churchill, D. W., Hingtgen, J. N., Bryson, C. Q., Pontius, W., & Kimberlin, C. (1972). Imitation in autistic, early schizophrenic, and non-psychotic subnormal children. *Journal of Autism and Childhood Schizophrenia, 2* (3), 264–287.

Dunn, L. S., & Donaldson, C. (2001). Integration of the sensory-motor approach within the Classroom. In R. A. Huebner (Ed.), *Autism: A sensory-motor approach to management* (pp. 297–311). Austin, TX: Pro-ed.

Frith, U., & Hermelin, B. (1969). The role of visual and motor cues for normal, subnormal and autistic children. *Journal of Child Psychology and Psychiatry, 10*, 153–163.

Gray, J. A. (1964). *Pavlov's typology: Recent theoretical and experimental developments from the laboratory of B M Teplov*. Oxford: Pergamon Press.

Gray, J. A. (1987). *Psychology of fear and stress*. Cambridge, England: Cambridge University Press.

Gresham, F. M., & Elliott, S. N. (1990). *Social Skills Rating System: Manual*. Circle Pines, MN: American Guidance Services.

Groden, J., Cautela, J. R., & Groden, G. (1989). *Breaking the barriers: The use of relaxation for people with special needs* [Video]. Champaign, IL: Research Press.

Hermelin, B. A., & O'Connor, M. A. (1970). *Psychological experiments with autistic children*. Oxford: Pergamon Press.

Hobson, P. (1986). The autistic child's appraisal of expressions of emotion. *Journal of Child Psychology and Psychiatry, 27*(3), 321–342.

Hobson, P. (1991). Against the theory of 'Theory of Mind'. *British Journal of Developmental Psychology, 9*, 33–51.

Hobson, P. (1994). Understanding persons: The role of affect. In S. Baron-Cohen, H. Tager-Flushberg & D. Cohen (Eds.), *Understanding other minds: Perspectives from autism* (pp. 204–227). Oxford: Oxford University Press.

Howlin, P. (1997). *Autism: Preparing for adulthood*. London: Routledge.

Howlin, P., & Goode, S. (1998). Outcome in adult life for people with autism and Asperger's syndrome. In F. R. Volkmar (Ed.), *Autism and pervasive developmental disorders* (pp. 209–241). Cambridge, England: Cambridge University Press.

Kanner, L. (1943). Autistic disturbances of affective contact. *Nervous Child, 2,* 217–250.

Leslie, A. M., & Frith, U. (1990). Prospects for a cognitive neuropsychology of autism: Hobson's choice. *Psychological Review, 97*(1), 122–131.

Minuchin, P. (1985). Families and individual development: Provocations from the field of family therapy. *Child Development, 56,* 289–302.

Matthews, J., & Williams, J (1988). *The self–help guide for special kids and their parents.* London: Jessica Kingsley.

Nebylitsyn, V. D., & Gray, J. A. (1972). *Biological bases of individual behaviour.* New York: Academic Press.

Pennington, B. F., & Ozonoff, S. (1996). Executive functions and developmental psychopathologies. *Journal of Child Psychology and Psychiatry, 37,* 51–87.

Perkins, M. (2000). The scope of pragmatic disability: A cognitive approach. In N. Muller (Ed.), *Pragmatics in speech and language pathology: Studies in clinical applications.* (pp. 7–28) Amsterdam: John Benjamin.

Reynolds, W. M. (1986). *Reynolds adolescent depression scale (RADS).* Lutz, FL: Psychological Assessment Resources, Inc.

Rutter, M. (1983). Cognitive deficits in the pathogenesis of autism. *Journal of Child Psychology and Psychiatry, 24,* 513–531.

Rutter, M. (1999). Two-way interplay between research and clinical work. *Journal of Child Psychology and Psychiatry, 40*(2), 169–188.

Thomas, A., Chess, S., & Birch, H. G. (1969). *Temperament and behaviour disorders in children.* New York: New York University Press.

Vermeulen, P. (2000). *I am special: Introducing children and young people to their autistic spectrum disorder.* London: Jessica Kingsley.

Williams, D. (2003). *Exposure anxiety–The invisible cage: An exploration of self-protection responses in the autism spectrum and beyond.* London: Jessica Kingsley.

Williams, M. S., & Shellenberger, S. (1994). *How does your engine run? A leader's guide to the Alert Program for self-regulation.* Albuquerque, NM: Therapy Works.

Wing, L. (1996). *The autistic spectrum: A guide for parents and professionals.* London: Constable.

World Health Organization (1992). *International statistical classification of diseases and related health problems: Tenth revision.* Geneva, Switzerland: Author.

Zeitz, J. (2000). *Intensive intervention: Pilot project.* Unpublished report. Autism Association of South Australia, Adelaide, Australia.

IV

Strategies for Coping with Stress

10   *Stress and Coping among Family Members of Individuals with Autism*

Beth A. Glasberg, Megan Martins,
and Sandra L. Harris

Raising children in our contemporary culture is inherently stressful for many parents. The popular media is full of often contradictory advice about effective parenting, many nuclear families live far away from the support of their extended family, both parents are often employed and have little time for reflection in a life packed full of demands, and single-parent families face all of the tasks of day-to-day family life with only one adult to meet these multiple needs. Parents worry about the real and perceived hazards their children face each day, including the temptation of substance abuse, premature sexual activity, seduction of children by Internet predators, violence in the schools, and so forth. It is not surprising that many parents worry about how effectively they can raise their children and whether they are making the right decisions.

Given this general context of stressful demands, it is especially striking that parents of children with autism report more stress-related discomfort than do their peers who are raising typically developing children (e.g., Fong, 1991). The purpose of this chapter is to review the sources of stress in the lives of family members of children with autism and to consider some of the ways these families cope with the stressors they encounter. First, we briefly consider the question of what stress is and how one measures it. Then, we explore to what extent family members of people with autism differ from other families in their level of stress. In addition to examining stress in the nuclear family, we review the modest literature on how members of the extended family, especially grandparents, view their grandchild with autism. The latter part of the chapter focuses on the coping strategies that family members use to solve the problems of their family and their own discomfort. Well-functioning families of people with autism have something to teach all of us about dealing with life's demands.

DEFINING AND MEASURING STRESS

When we use the term "stress" in this chapter, we refer to the many large and small events occurring throughout our days that create discomfort. The stressors can range in severity from being stuck in a traffic jam to being the victim of an earthquake. The stressors can vary in duration from adjusting one's schedule to pick a child up at school early one day, to providing daily care for a family member with a serious physical illness. Many stressful events, such as natural disasters or illness, are beyond our control. Nonetheless, we can often acquire some control over how we cope with these events. People differ in the ways in which they think about and deal with stressors, and understanding how some people cope well may be useful in helping others address the consequences that follow from stressful events.

We experience the effects of stress in our bodies and in our minds. As described elsewhere in this book, a variety of explanatory models of stress have been created. These models examine the relationship among the mind—body factors that are involved in responses to stressors. For example, the physiological aspects of stress include such bodily sensations as headaches, fatigue, and other forms of physical discomfort that are often problematic for people in stressful situations. One can also consider the cognitive aspects of stress, such as anxious or dysphoric thoughts, or the emotional aspects, such as feelings of depression or anger. It is probably useful to think of these various manifestations of stress as different aspects of the same phenomenon. For individuals who are experiencing stress, all these factors may weigh heavily in their experience, as would the interpersonal issues that are created by the stressful event. Because there is no one way to measure stress, stress levels are often inferred based on measuring variables believed to be related to stress, such as behavior problems, feelings of depression, feelings of anxiety, or medical problems.

Stress may be short-term (acute) or ongoing (chronic) in nature. A family whose breadwinner is out of work for a few weeks might experience considerable stress for a short period, and then settle back to familiar routines. In contrast, a family that includes a child with autism is faced by a situation likely to result in a chronic increase in stress levels. The ongoing level of discomfort is greater than in other families, compounded by some episodes of even more intense stress when they face a crisis, such as searching for an educational placement for their child or seeking a group home for their young adult (Blacher & Hanneman, 1992; Harris, Glasberg, & Delmolino, 1998; Marsh, 1992).

A number of studies have looked at how stress levels change across the life span, both in families raising typically developing children (e.g., McCubbin &

Figley, 1983) and those that include a child with a disability (e.g., Harris, Gill, & Alessandri, 1990; Wikler, 1986). This research usually reflects the understanding that family life is inherently stressful because of the normative, life cycle events that every family encounters, such as the birth of a child, the death of a grandparent, or children leaving for college, as well as other less normative, but still common, events such as the death of a parent or a divorce (e.g., McCubbin & Figley, 1983). The investigator who studies the impact of chronic stress on the family of a child with autism must take into account the impact of these more normative stressors, as well as the influence of the child's autism.

A good example of an event that has very different implications if it is normative within the family's life cycle or occurs out of the cycle is provided by Baker and Blacher (2002), who note that, for most families, the decision to place a child in residential care results in good post-placement adaptation by the parents. However, the process appears to be more helpful for parents of adults. For parents of younger children, this same decision may be associated with more stress. They suggest that the placement decision for an adult more closely resembles the normative events of adulthood, while a placement decision for a child is a more jarring decision for a family. Thus, an effective coping strategy for a child of one age may be less effective at a different age.

From a research perspective, it is also important to explore whether there are unique or more intense stressors for families raising a child with autism as compared to other serious challenges in childhood, including mental retardation, physical disabilities, or chronic or life-threatening illnesses. When doing research on autism, it is common to use children with mental retardation as a comparison group because these families also face significant demands in their lives (e.g., Weiss, 2002).

STRESS AND THE NUCLEAR FAMILY

Although having a family member with any illness, handicap, or disability may be challenging, the unique combination of impairments associated with autism may place family members at an especially high risk for difficulties with psychological adjustment (e.g., Holmes & Carr, 1991; Morgan, 1988). Research on parenting a child with autism suggests that the experience is more stressful for mothers than parenting either a child who is developing normally or a child with Down's syndrome (e.g., Donovan, 1988). Although we found no data specific to stress in fathers of children with autism, research suggests that fathers of children with various disabilities experience more stress than fathers of children without disabilities. Furthermore, fathers are just as stressed as mothers of children with disabilities (Dyson, 1997). Taken together, the above findings suggest that, like mothers of children with autism, fathers of children with autism are likely to exhibit even more stress than fathers of children with other disabilities.

In a similar vein, mothers of children with autism are more likely to report symptoms of depression than mothers of children with other developmental disorders (Weiss, 2002). Although fathers of children with various developmental disorders show less depression than do mothers, the degree of depression experienced by fathers is related to the depression of their wives (Trute, 1995). Therefore, one might anticipate greater degrees of depression among fathers of children with autism than among fathers of children with other developmental disorders.

A child's lack of social responsiveness may be one factor that makes autism particularly stressful for a parent. The burden of care for a child with autism exceeds that associated with a typically developing child, but also the expressed affection that usually reinforces a parent for his or her sacrifices is either absent or significantly diminished in an autistic child. In severe cases, children with autism may not respond any differently to their parents than they do to other adults (Schreibman, 1988). Additionally, because children with autism may have difficulty learning even the most basic of social norms, such as the difference between what is acceptable in public versus private settings (Monat, 1982), or what is dangerous versus what is safe (Wing & Attwood, 1987), the parent may be subjected to many embarrassing or frightening situations.

Parents of individuals with autism have to adopt multiple new roles. For example, to ensure that a child receives the best possible education, parents may need to become knowledgeable about instruction, as well as about how to advocate for the provision of best practice in their child's school setting. Furthermore, to ensure that they maximize their child's learning opportunities in the home, many parents of children with autism become expert teachers. Finally, due to disagreements about what constitutes an appropriate education, parents may need to become knowledgeable about laws pertaining to education and other legal issues.

Although parents of children with other disabilities are also asked to adopt these roles, the unique challenge associated with autism is the lack of a unified or generally accepted best practice. Applied Behavior Analysis (ABA) is the only approach to working with students with autism that has significant empirical support (e.g., New York State Department of Health, 1999), but a standardized treatment protocol for autism does not exist. Many families and professionals have a strong belief in or commitment to alternative approaches. Even within ABA, there are a multitude of decisions to make in creating an appropriate program for an individual student. This leaves families in a position in which they may receive a number of conflicting outside recommendations as to what is best for their child, which in turn leaves more room for disagreement with school districts or other service providers and more room for doubt about approaches incorporated by families for use in the home.

The situation described above can heighten parental stress in a variety of ways. First, the multiple roles that parents assume lead to significant demands on their time, money, and energy without a concomitant increase in resources. This balance of demands versus resources is an important variable in determining whether an event will become a stressor (Lazarus, 1966). Second, these multiple demands may limit opportunities for families to develop friendships outside their family (Tunali & Power, 2002). Because friendships can buffer the effects of stressful experiences for mothers of children with autism (e.g., Weiss, 2002) and are associated with decreased levels of depression in fathers of children with disabilities (Trute, 1995), demands associated with autism may have a doubly stressful impact. In fact, Boyd (2002) found a lack of social support to be among the most powerful predictors of depression and anxiety in mothers of children with autism. Despite these findings, the impact of social support appears to be complex. Dyson (1997) found no differences in levels of social support reported by parents of children with disabilities and parents of children without disabilities. Nevertheless, the parents of individuals with disabilities were still experiencing greater degrees of stress. Perhaps social support acts to decrease the impact of stress by reducing the probability that it will lead to depressive symptoms.

Finally, the absence of a standardized treatment protocol for students with autism may also contribute to stress among parents, in that beliefs about the efficacy of the treatment being used are associated with lower levels of stress (Hastings & Johnson, 2001). If professionals disagree about recommendations for treatment, then a parent cannot be expected to have confidence about the efficacy of the approach. Additionally, questioning one's choices regarding a treatment approach may lead to a decreased overall sense of efficacy on the part of parents. Because increased self-efficacy has been shown to temper the effects of behavior problems in leading to anxiety and depression in mothers of children with autism and anxiety in fathers of children with autism (Hastings & Brown, 2002), the lack of clarity regarding best practice in autism may be particularly problematic for parents.

Other studies have examined the impact of behavior problems as distinct from self-efficacy. Because aggressive behaviors are commonly seen among individuals with autism (Paul, 1987), this line of research becomes vitally important. Preliminary research indicates that child behavior problems intensify the experience of stress among mothers of children with disabilities, but not among fathers (Hastings, 2003). Hastings (2003) found that maternal stress was also affected by the mental health status of the father, but the reverse did not hold true. These findings contrast with those of Trute (1995), who found that depression in each spouse was related to that of their partner. Again, it seems that the variables that affect stress level differ slightly than those that lead to depressive symptoms.

Aggressive behaviors may also increase stress more for parents raising more than one child. Because of the dangerous nature of aggression, parents of children with autism may be more likely to intervene in disputes among siblings than parents of children without handicaps. Although the directionality is not clear, Dunn (1988) points out that parental intervention in conflict is positively correlated with the frequency of conflict. High rates of conflicts among siblings can add another potential stressor to a parent's already full plate.

The increased risk for aggression and conflict may be stressful for the sibling as well as for the parents. Rodrigue, Geffken, and Morgan (1993) view sibling interactions as powerful components of socialization that help to develop instrumental and affective relationship skills. They explain that while positive and frequent interactions provide important sources of emotional support, negative and infrequent relations may disrupt the psychological adaptation process. Additionally, children with autism usually require more parental attention than children without autism (Cutler & Kozloff, 1987). Dunn's (1988) review also found a relationship between differential behavior on the part of parents and conflict frequency.

In their review of research examining siblings of children with chronic illnesses, Gallo and Knafl (1993) identify numerous characteristics of illnesses that affect sibling adjustment. Because many of these characteristics are variable dimensions for autism as well, they may help improve our understanding of the experiences of parents and siblings of affected individuals. First, Gallo and Knafl (1993) show disease course to be an important factor. Relapsing or episodic disorders lead to more stress for the sibling than those disorders with more stable or predictable courses. As a disorder with an unpredictable course, autism may be more stressful in this regard.

Next, Gallo and Knafl (1993) suggest that the functioning level of the child with an illness affects his or her relationship with a sibling. Although studies of illnesses have yielded discrepant results (e.g., Wilson, McGillivray, & Zeitlin, 1992), it is clear with regard to autism that its associated functional limitations restrict the range of activities that the siblings can share. One might reason that siblings of more severely affected individuals experience fewer shared activities than siblings of high-functioning individuals. In her exploration of sibling relationships involving a child with autism, Harris (1994) described the detrimental effects of language and motor deficits on a sibling relationship. She explains that while the birth of a younger child may initially lead to sibling rivalry, this typically changes at approximately 3 or 4 years of age. Because the younger child has gained the motor ability to play and the ability to communicate, he or she becomes more reinforcing to the older child. Harris points out that for a child with autism, these abilities may not emerge until much later, if at all. Alternatively, these skills may develop in a way that is qualitatively different from those of a typically developing child. Consequently, the formation of the sibling relationship may suffer.

Having a brother or sister with high-functioning autism may carry its own unique challenges. The disability in these individuals may be less visible. Therefore, a sibling might have higher expectations for a brother or sister and become more frustrated with perceived inequities in responses, interaction, or parental demands. In fact, Gallo and Knafl (1993) highlighted illness visibility as an important characteristic affecting sibling adjustment. Unfortunately, they were unable to draw clear conclusions from the literature. With regard to autism, the disability at all functioning levels is not physically visible, but rather is behaviorally visible. These behavioral deviations might lead to questions from outsiders. A layperson may not understand the unusual behavior they observe and may inquire about it. Demands to explain a child's behaviors to strangers can be tiresome to parents and overwhelming to siblings, many having neither the language to respond nor a clear understanding of the disability itself.

Finally, Gallo and Knafl (1993) suggest that the time of onset may contribute to the variability in outcomes among siblings of children with illnesses. They explain that in a disorder with a later onset, as opposed to a congenital disorder, a relationship has already begun to form between the siblings. A strong preexisting relationship may present more of a loss for a sibling or parent, but can provide the foundation for more positive interactions after the illness or disability has emerged. In the case of autism, these foundations may prove particularly important, as the social impairment associated with autism might make forging bonds more difficult later on.

Research comparing the experience of older and younger siblings of individuals with autism has not yielded consistent results about the impact of a preexisting relationship. This might be due to a variety of factors. First, it is not clear whether there is "a time before autism" in an affected individual's life. Some parents describe knowing something was wrong with their child almost from birth, whereas other parents say confidently that they saw very typical development followed by regression. Research based on review of videotapes of 1-year-old children suggests that there are subtle differences, early on, that only a trained eye might perceive (Osterling, Dawson, & Munson, 2002). Whether this "time before autism" exists, parents certainly experience a loss of their expectations for the child as the disability unfolds. Older siblings may experience this as well, depending on their age at the time of their brother's or sister's birth.

The impact of birth order might be overshadowed by the impact of the role that a sibling is assigned in relation to a brother or sister with autism. Farber (1960) suggested that younger siblings placed in caretaking roles for older siblings may experience "role tension," or anxiety, conflict, and resentment at having been placed in a position of role overload. Despite this widely accepted theory, more recent research does not support this idea. Brody, Stoneman, Davis, and Crapps (1991) studied same-sex, school-aged sibling dyads in which the older sibling had mental retardation while the younger was typically developing. Their results showed that, although role asymmetries involving the younger child taking on more managing, helping, and teaching roles did emerge, no differences in affective tone while interacting surfaced. In another study, Stoneman, Brody, Davis, Crapps, and Malone (1991) found that while younger school-aged, same-sex siblings of children with mental retardation often engaged in role reversals in that they acted as caregivers for the older child, increased involvement in caregiving was associated with less conflicted sibling relationships rather than with more.

In a similar vein, Celiberti and Harris (1993) taught school-aged siblings of children with autism to teach appropriate play responses using behavioral techniques. As a result, not only did the play skills of the children with autism improve, but also the siblings were rated as more confident, more interested in the child with autism, more enthusiastic, and more effective following the training. Their new skills generalized and were maintained over time. Furthermore, Harris (1994) reports that subjective evaluations of videotapes used for the study reveal that the affect of the siblings becomes more positive as their skill level with the play methods increases. Like siblings of children with mental retardation, it appears that siblings of children with autism benefit from assuming a teaching or managing role. While this may occur at the cost of interactions as a playmate, the functional competencies of the child with a disability would likely have limited their ability to engage in sustained play, regardless of the sibling's behavior (Stoneman et al., 1991). Assumption of a teaching role may provide the only opportunity for reinforcing interaction with the sibling. In turn, this may decrease any stressful or maladaptive adjustment that might have resulted in response to the challenges of growing up with an individual with autism.

Research suggests that the roles assigned by parents to siblings who are not disabled in relation to their disabled siblings tend to vary across gender and birth order (Boyce & Barnett, 1993). For example, Stoneman, Brody, Davis, and Crapps (1988) found that older sisters of children with mental retardation had more childcare responsibilities for their sibling than any other category of sibling of an individual, either with mental retardation or without handicaps. Lobato, Faust, and Spirito (1988) found that sisters of children with handicaps received significantly fewer privileges and more restrictions than brothers. Breslau (1982) hypothesized that younger siblings get less attention due to the care demands of the child with a disability. Because older sisters and younger brothers of children with illnesses or disabilities have repeatedly been shown to evidence the most difficulty with adjustment (Breslau, 1982; Lobato et al. 1988), it has been hypothesized that differing roles and responsibilities mediate outcome.

Given the evidence discussed above indicating the positive effects of assuming a caregiving role, the difficulties experienced by older sisters typically assigned a caregiving role are confusing. One possible explanation is that, in moderation, assumption of a caregiving role is adaptive. Nevertheless, either overburdening a child, as may be the case with some older sisters, or oversheltering a child, as may be the case with some younger brothers, may lead to increased stress and adjustment difficulties.

As a group, siblings of children with autism and other disabilities do not show evidence of increased stress or adjustment problems. Rodrigue et al. (1993) found no differences in self-concept between siblings of children with autism and siblings of children with either Down's syndrome or no handicap. Similarly, Boyce and Barnett's (1993) review concludes that most studies reveal no differences in self-concept between siblings of persons with mental retardation and siblings of children without handicaps. Out of nine studies assessing the self-concept of siblings of children with illnesses or disabilities (Howe, 1993), only three found that these children showed mild decrements, and these only achieved statistical significance due to their consistency across the group.

Although most empirical investigations have failed to document an increased rate of significant pathology among siblings of children with autism and other disabilities, reports of clinicians working with this population suggest that these children might harbor concerns that go undetected by the standardized instruments used in most of the research to date (e.g., Belchic & Glasberg, 1995; Glasberg & Belchic, 1996). Supporting this claim are the findings of Bagenholm and Gillberg (1991), who used a semi-structured interview composed of open-ended questions and found that siblings of children with autism expressed more negative views of their sibling relationship; reported more problems with their siblings disturbing or breaking things; were more concerned about the future of their sibling; played less with their sibling; felt lonelier; and had fewer friends than either siblings of children with mental retardation or siblings of children without any handicap. Standardized instruments, such as those used by Stoneman et al. (1988), may not pick up these types of daily hassles or dissatisfactions that are associated with an increased stress level.

Additionally, subtle differences have been noted among siblings of individuals with illnesses or disabilities. In his review of research on siblings of children with physical disabilities and chronic illnesses, Howe (1993) found that in 4 of 11 studies, the target siblings evidenced more internalizing symptoms than children with healthy siblings, but the symptoms were not clinically significant in degree. Similarly, Rodrigue et al. (1993) found that siblings of children with autism manifested both more internalizing and externalizing behavior problems than siblings of children with either Down's syndrome or no handicap, but the mean scores of the group fell within the normative range. The findings of Glasberg (1998) echo these results in that, as a group, the degree of adjustment and behavior problems among siblings of children with autism fell within the normal range. However, there were many more individuals who exhibited significant degrees of acting out behaviors, as well as internalizing problems such as anxiety or depression, than would be expected based on the incidence in the general population. Similarly, in their work with siblings of children with varied special needs, Lobato, Barbour, Hall, and Miller (1987) found an increased incidence of significant internalizing and externalizing behavior problems despite group averages in the normative range. In all the studies described above, sibling behavior problems were assessed through parent report. These findings suggest that some parents of siblings see an extremely low number of adjustment problems, whereas others see an extremely high number of adjustment problems.

Because stress is so closely tied to behavior problems and adjustment, it seems that there is great variability in the responses of different children to the same stressor.

STRESS AND THE EXTENDED FAMILY

Although parents and siblings most directly bear the brunt of the stress involved in having a family member with autism, other family members, including grandparents, aunts, uncles, and cousins, also react to the child's autism. There is little research on the experiences of these extended family members.

We know that grandparents often have a significant emotional investment in their grandchildren, both because grandchildren bring joy into their lives and because they are symbols of the continuity of the generations (Mueller & Elder, 2003). Any serious illness, including childhood cancer or chronic disabilities such as autism, is a source of substantial stress for grandparents and other members of the extended family, just as it is for parents (Scherman, Gardner, Brown, & Schutter, 1995). Grandparents are concerned both for the child and for the parents who must deal with the demands created by the child's autism; they also feel a sense of loss and concern for themselves as well. Their dreams of the joy of spending time with and relating to their grandchild can be seriously challenged by the behavior of the child with autism.

One study of the grandparents of children with autism compared how mothers, fathers, grandmothers, and grandfathers described their child or grandchild with autism, the parents' description of the impact of the child on their own lives, and the grandparents' perception of how their adult child's life was affected by the grandchild's autism (Harris, Handleman, & Palmer, 1985). In general, grandparents showed an understanding of the experience of their adult child and their grandchild. When we found a difference between the two adult generations, it was the grandparents who had a more positive view of the impact of the child on the life of the parents and of their own relationship with their adult child. For example, while both mothers and fathers said that things had gotten worse in the family since the birth of the child with autism, grandparents did not recognize the degree of this change. Similarly, although the mothers of children with autism reported that their child was demanding and that they felt discomfort when people asked about the child, the grandmothers did not recognize these feelings.

There were also interesting differences among grandparents. In general, grandmothers (as compared to grandfathers), showed greater understanding of the experience of their adult child, and the most empathic understanding came from the mother's mother, while the least empathy was that between fathers of an autistic child and their own fathers. Our research showed that although they had a more optimistic view than their daughters, the maternal grandmothers overall were quite attuned to their daughter's lives, even though they did not understand the full extent of the daughter's burden. We also found that maternal grandparents visited the family more often than did paternal grandparents. These findings are consistent with the observation that maternal grandparents of typically developing children tend to have a closer relationship with their grandchildren than do paternal grandparents (Chan & Elder, 2000). Not surprisingly, adults who have a good relationship with their parents draw more support from the older generation after the birth of a child with a disability than parents who have a less satisfactory relationship (Mirfin-Veitch, Bray, & Watson, 1997). When there is conflict between the generations, the grandparents may be a source of stress for parents (Hastings, Thomas, & Delwiche, 2002).

The observation of greater optimism on the part of grandparents is consistent with other work suggesting that grandparents may tend to idealize their grandchildren and attend less to problems (Bengtson & Robertson, 1985). This idealization suggests that they may, as a group, be less vulnerable to the stress of having a grandchild with autism than are the parents. Of course, grandparents also typically have much less responsibility for rearing grandchildren, and the child's autism does not impact on their lives in a daily way.

When we explored the extent to which grandparents and parents agreed in their view of the developmental status of the child with autism, we found significant differences between the generations (Glasberg & Harris, 1997). Parents and grandparents independently filled out the General Development Scale of the Minnesota Child Development Inventory (Ireton & Thwing, 1972). Although parents and grandparents agreed with one another about the child's developmental skills in many respects, the ratings made by paternal grandparents were significantly different from ratings by the father. The paternal grandparents underestimated the child's developmental achievements in comparison to the father, and the less contact they had with the family, the more they missed the mark. Consistent with our earlier observation about the empathic understanding and greater contact with the maternal grandmother (Harris et al., 1985), maternal grandmothers described their grandchild in terms that aligned closely with the mother's description.

UNDERSTANDING STRESS IN THE FAMILY OF AN INDIVIDUAL WITH AUTISM

As described above, there are a variety of ways to think about stress. When hearing the word stress, some people think of tension in their bodies, some think of anxious thoughts, and others think of challenging situations. This difficulty in definition has led to multiple theoretical and empirical approaches to understanding stress. One of the most widely accepted models involves a concept called "appraisal" (Lazarus, 1966). According to this approach, the stress response involves a relationship between the person and the environment. When one sees the demands of the environment as exceeding one's resources, stress results. This model outlines additional steps that an individual goes through as part of appraising a situation, including (1) defining an event, (2) determining the degree of self-relevance, and (3) assessing the implications of the event with regard to the individual's motives. Viewed from this perspective, it is easy to see how events themselves cannot be seen as inherently stressful. Instead, it is the appraisal process that determines an event's stressful impact.

In using Lazarus's (1966) model to examine the impact of living with a family member with autism, numerous variables emerge that impact stressful outcomes. First, understanding autism and its associated behavior problems or skill deficits can be challenging for adults and children alike. Understanding either a major event, such as obtaining a diagnosis, or the smaller everyday events associated with the disorder may be challenging for family members. For example, if a child with autism rejects the social overtures of a parent or sibling, will they define this as a part of the disability or as a lack of feeling? Their emotional responses to these two contrasting attributions would be very different.

To continue through the appraisal process, having a family member with autism will be highly relevant to one's own life and sense of self, particularly if the family members live together. Assigned roles may also play a large part because the greater an individual's responsibility for the family member with autism, the greater the degree of personal relevance will result. For a parent, assuming the roles of advocate and teacher described earlier in this chapter may require sacrificing employment or other personal pursuits, which would certainly imply a high degree of personal relevance.

Further, for parents who have imagined and planned for a typically developing child, autism is counter to their dreams. This stressor may be reexperienced as certain plans a parent has for a child fail to be realized. This reminder of thwarted goals may emerge during larger life events, such as the birthday that would have heralded a bat mitzvah or communion, or during simpler moments, like going to a hockey game that a father always imagined attending with his son.

Finally, appraisal involves the assessment of demands versus resources; the results of this assessment will vary by individual family members in terms of finances, available social support, supportiveness of a school system, support of siblings by parents, and other variables. Families with a wealth of resources prior to the disability may experience "loss stress" in response to the onset of autism as compared to those whose resources were stretched tighter in raising a typically developing child.

COPING STRATEGIES FOR PARENTS

The question of how parents cope effectively with the stress created by raising a child with autism or another disability has captured the continuing attention of investigators (e.g., Bristol, 1984; Factor, Perry & Freeman, 1990; Weiss, 2002).

It is important to remember that the changes are not always negative. A balanced look at the experiences of parents of children with autism and other forms of developmental disabilities suggests that many families experience positive life changes from raising their child with a disability. For example, Scorgie and Sobsey (2000) described "transformational outcomes" in the lives of many parents. Their participants described three domains of change, including personal growth, better relationships with other people, and a change in life view or spirituality. The potential for this kind of change in perspective is important to keep in mind when helping parents develop an adaptive and life-enhancing, rather than depressive or helpless, view of the meaning of their child's autism and how they, as parents, might respond.

In a study of the family system and methods of coping, Sivberg (2002) found higher levels of effective coping correlated with lower levels of family strain. He argues that parents should learn and use as many effective coping methods as they can. He points to such examples as being thoughtful about how one distributes attention to the child with autism and other children in the family, and not viewing the child with autism as the sole source of strain within the family.

The literature suggests there are two general categories of coping that can be helpful in dealing with stress. These include instrumental behaviors, such as learning to use the methods of applied behavior analysis to solve learning and behavior problems posed by a child with autism, and palliative methods, such as support groups or therapy to address one's feelings or cognitions about raising a child with autism. Both categories can be helpful, and they are not mutually exclusive; changes in one's feelings and cognitions by palliative means can result in more focus and energy for instrumental behaviors, and effective use of instrumental strategies can influence feelings and thoughts. For example, a father who is feeling depressed and helpless to deal with his daughter with autism might initially respond to an intervention such as cognitive behavior therapy (CBT) to address his depression and reframe some of his thoughts about his daughter's disability. The resulting shift might energize him to take a class in applied behavior analysis and develop effective home programs for his child, and that in turn might influence his feelings and thoughts about his daughter.

Altering one's thoughts plays a key role in how many parents cope with autism. Weiss (2002) studied mothers of children ages 2–7 years with autism and with mental retardation, as well as a group of women whose children were following a more typical developmental pattern. She found that mothers of children with autism who had a sense of control over events in their lives, who felt a commitment to a set of values or beliefs, and who looked upon challenges as opportunities were more effective at coping than those who did not embrace this approach. Having friendships that increased the mother's sense of self-esteem were also related to effective coping, as was feeling supported by her spouse. Dyson (1997) identified cognitive variables that lead to decreased stress for fathers, the most important of which was a perception that the family emphasizes the personal growth of individual members. In a study of Latino families of children with developmental delays, Skinner, Correa, Skinner, and Bailey (2001) found that religious faith, even more than practicing or identifying with a certain religion, was sustaining to many families. Parents often used their faith as way to understand what the child's disability meant to them. Gray (2003) also found faith to be important to the mothers of individuals with high-functioning autism and Asperger's disorder that he studied.

Adhering to positive views about the experience of having a child with a disability can be an important palliative coping strategy (Hastings & Taunt, 2002). Tunali and Power (2002) give an example of how mothers of children with autism may shift their thoughts to deal with the challenges of raising their child. These authors compared mothers of children with autism with other women who had typically developing children. They found that women who were raising children with autism put less emphasis on the importance of career success and were less likely to endorse the idea that mothers of young children should work outside of the home than did other mothers. Mothers of autistic children also tended to spend more of their leisure time with their extended family than did the comparison mothers. The mothers of children with autism also expressed less concern about what other people thought about their child. Another coping strategy used by many of the mothers of children with autism was to place a higher value on partner support and the importance of the parental role, as compared to the other women who more strongly endorsed intimacy and shared leisure as important in their marriage and family life. In summarizing their findings, Tunali and Power (2002) commented that, as a whole, mothers of children with autism cope with the demands of raising their child by redefining what is most important to them as mothers and wives.

Instrumental interventions can help parents change their thoughts and feelings about themselves or their child. For example, it is possible to increase the sense of self-efficacy of parents of children on the autism spectrum. Sofronoff and Farbotko (2002) provided Parent Management Training (Judge, 1997) to parents of children with Asperger's disorder. This training was aimed at helping parents deal more effectively with the behavior problems demonstrated by their child. After training, the parents reported fewer behavior problems by their child and a greater sense of personal self-efficacy. Similarly, Russell and Matson (1998) taught fathers basic behavioral intervention skills, such as how to provide clear instructions and apply correct consequences. All the fathers showed improved skills at the end of training, and all the children demonstrated increased compliance to their fathers' instructions. However, no clear impact on the stress level of fathers was demonstrated. When embarking on parent training, Moes and Frea (2002) note that taking the family context into account when teaching parents management skills can improve the impact of the behavioral support plans.

Whitaker (2002) also explored the benefits of parent education. Whitaker described a preschool program for children with autism in which parents were given considerable help in understanding how autism influences their child's behavior, applying specific teaching methods to their child's behavior, and thinking about their child's educational needs in the transition from preschool age to school age. Although there were no comparison families, the interview data from the participants suggested that these parents found the services very helpful in meeting their child's needs. The value of helping parents understand the implications of their child's autism on his or her behavior and learning were also illustrated in interviews with parents about the diagnostic process (Midence and O'Neill, 1999).

Although it has been widely suggested that men are more likely to use problem-focused (instrumental) coping strategies and women are more likely to use emotion-focused (palliative) coping strategies, the results of Gray's study (2003) challenge this assumption. In his qualitative analysis of interviews with mothers and fathers of children with high-functioning autism and Asperger's disorder, Gray found that both mothers and fathers used the two most popular coping strategies equally. The most popular strategy reported was anticipation and planning. This involves thinking through the demands of upcoming situations, anticipating possible problems, and preventing or preparing for them. The next most popular strategy is the opposite of the first. This strategy is described as "taking it one day at a time," which involves making few commitments and making decisions on a moment-to-moment basis. For example, a parent relying on this approach might cancel their plans for the day if they see their child has awakened in a difficult mood.

Other strategies reported by parents in the Gray (1993) study did differ by the parent's gender. Mothers were more likely to practice therapies with the child at home to change behaviors and more likely to separate the child from their siblings to prevent problems. In contrast, fathers reported that they preferred to keep their child busy with play and other activities when they are at home, and that they may go to work or spend more time at work as a coping strategy. The option of going to work was a critical difference between mothers and fathers who participated in this study. Wide discrepancies in caregiving responsibilities were identified in this study, with mothers doing most of the childcare, even when they were employed outside of the home. An overarching theme of the interviews was the notion that although both mothers and fathers were experiencing being a parent of a child with a disability, the actual contact with the realities of the situation was much more direct for mothers. As one father explained, "The father essentially has respite care five days a week." This finding clearly applies to traditionally structured families only.

COPING STRATEGIES FOR SIBLINGS

As described above, the outcomes associated with growing up with a sibling with a disability are varied. Some studies have indicated that siblings are more likely to experience adjustment problems, such as increased rates of aggression, social isolation, learning problems, or lower reported self-concept (Boyce & Barnett, 1993). Other studies have concluded that siblings are not at greater risk for problems such as these (Gamble & Woulbroun, 1993). In fact, some studies have indicated that there may be some positive effects of having a sibling with a disability, including increased tolerance of others and more compassion toward others (Boyce & Barnett, 1993). The impact of the stress associated with having a sibling with autism varies according to several factors, one of which is probably the coping strategies that siblings know and use.

Recall that coping strategies refer to attempts to reduce the effect of a stressor, either by changing one's perception of the stressor or by directly altering it. There are numerous coping strategies that siblings have reported using or that their parents have reported observing in their children. Researchers have also reported sibling use of particular coping strategies (Gamble & Woulbourn, 1993). Some of these include seeking support (talking to a friend or parent about a problem); physical or verbal aggression (hitting sister because I wanted her to stop); problem-solving skills (asking a parent to put locks on door to keep out sibling who breaks toys); avoidance (not thinking about it); physical exercise; cognitive restructuring (looking at the bright side of things); or self-soothing (telling oneself that things are bound to get better). Children tend to use a variety of coping strategies and different coping strategies over time. However, younger children use fewer coping strategies than do older children (Donaldson, Prinstein, Danovsky, & Spirito, 2000).

Rather than examining each coping strategy individually, researchers have developed a number of ways to categorize the coping strategies that children use. Gamble and McHale (1989) divided coping strategies by their function (alter the environment vs. regulate emotion) and their technique (direct action vs. cognition). Based on these divisions, the authors identified four categories of coping responses: cognitions about other people or the situation, such as, "My brother doesn't like to play with me because he has autism, and that makes it hard for him to play with anyone"; cognitions about self, such as, "I'm a very likeable sister"; behaviors directed toward the environment, such as, "I'll ask mom to teach my brother to play with me"; and behaviors directed toward self, such as, "I'll just play at my friend's house every day instead of coming home." They found that siblings of children with disabilities generally used the same coping strategies as siblings of typically developing children. However, they did find that children with siblings who had disabilities used more cognitive strategies in dealing with others.

This finding is consistent with other findings that siblings of children with disabilities may use cognitive techniques more often than active coping strategies (Gamble & McHale, 1989). This may be because their brothers and sisters with disabilities are less likely to respond to more typical active strategies aimed to change their behavior (e.g., asking them to play). Also, their parents may be more likely to prohibit such behavior by the sibling if it upsets the child with a disability. Further, children in general have less control over the events that occur in their lives and may have to use more cognitive strategies than adults. Gamble and McHale (1989) also found that children who used more cognitive strategies were likely to have higher depression and anxiety symptoms. This may indicate that the cognitive strategies used by the children are not as effective as desired. Interventions with children should focus on teaching them active coping strategies (i.e., sharing feelings with parents) and on manipulating the environment to reinforce those strategies (i.e., encouraging parents to respond to their child when they express their feelings).

Many siblings have misconceptions about autism that result in emotions they find difficult to express (Harris & Glasberg, 2003). Misinformation about the disorder may lead to a sibling's belief that they can "catch" autism and fear of spending time with their sibling. A lack of knowledge about the many people who are coming in and out of the house to visit their sibling may lead to resentment or the need to compete for attention from adults. Support and discussion groups provide a context for siblings to express these types of feelings about their sibling's disorder and to learn more about the disorder.

Research on support groups has primarily reported that siblings benefit from increased knowledge about their sibling's condition and has reported high participant satisfaction (Lobato & Kao, 2002). The activities of siblings groups have been based on meeting the needs of siblings that are described in the literature, including meeting other children who have siblings with disabilities, discussing joys and concerns with other siblings, learning from other siblings about how they handle common situations, discussing the implications of the disorder, and teaching parents and professionals about the needs of siblings (Meyer & Vadasy, 1994). Recently, Lobato and Kao (2002) expanded upon previous research and evaluated a sibling support group on these factors, as well as adjustment to the disorder, connectedness with other siblings, and global behavioral functioning. The authors found increased knowledge and connectedness, as well as decreased behavioral problems, following participation in the group. Further, these improvements were maintained at a 3-month follow-up.

Despite these encouraging findings, much is still unknown about support groups, including which components of the groups are necessary for changes observed in siblings. In their groups, Lobato and Kao (2002) held sessions about improving sibling knowledge, increasing family communication, labeling and managing emotions, and problem-solving skills. There was some focus on individual sibling needs, as well as on social or recreational activities where children were able to connect with siblings who were similar to them. Further, simultaneous groups were held in which the parents of the siblings participated in a number of activities that were integrated with the sibling groups' agendas. It is unknown which components of the groups were responsible for changes observed in siblings.

In addition, research on sibling groups has focused on the needs of children aged 8–13 years. There is less known about meeting the needs of younger siblings, older adolescent, and adult siblings who may have special concerns of their own (Harris & Glasberg, 2003). For example, groups for adult siblings might include discussions with parents about the family's plan for the future or sharing accurate information about what is known about the genetics of autism and the likelihood of the sibling having a child with the disorder. Further, many of the sibling group activities have been designed for siblings of children with various disorders and disabilities, including physical disabilities and chronic illnesses. Although many of the challenges for these children are similar, there may be particular challenges associated with being a sibling of an individual with a developmental disability or autism.

Some siblings may not know how to interact with their brother or sister with autism. Researchers have reported lower rates of sibling interaction in children with autism and their siblings than between children with autism and their parents (El-Ghoroury & Romanczyk, 1999). Clinicians have hypothesized that siblings are interested in interaction with their disabled brothers and sisters, but their attempts to interact have been punished by unsatisfying interactions (Harris & Glasberg, 2003). Negative sibling relationships have also been associated with sources of sibling stress, such as worries about the sibling with autism's future and perception of parental favoritism toward their sibling (McHale, Sloan, & Simeonsson, 1986).

Thus, improving relationships between siblings may decrease the stress associated with having a sibling with autism. Celiberti and Harris (1993) demonstrated that siblings can acquire behavioral skills that facilitate play between siblings, such as giving clear directions, using social praise to reward good behavior, and correctly prompting siblings to engage in play behaviors. The authors also found that all of the siblings who participated in the study were rated by independent raters as more confident, more interested in the child with autism, and more pleased by their interactions with their sibling. Additionally, it has been shown that parents can be effective instructors of the behavioral skills that may improve interactions between siblings and ultimately improve sibling relationships (Harris & Glasberg, 2003). Acquiring these skills is an excellent example of a coping action that changes the nature of the stressor and consequently impacts one's emotional response.

COPING STRATEGIES FOR THE EXTENDED FAMILY

There is little, if any, research on the specific coping strategies of members of the extended family of the child with autism. From our extensive clinical experience providing support groups for parents of children with autism and our conversations with grandparents, we are aware of the many things the extended family can do to support the nuclear family. These strategies may also allow the extended family members to feel that they have a significant and valued role in helping parents raise their child.

Offering instrumental help to the family is potentially a very valuable role for the members of the extended family. Research on a neonatal intensive care unit (Prudhoe & Peters, 1995) and with children with developmental disabilities (Sandler, Warren, & Raver, 1995) suggests that support from members of the extended family, including grandparents, is sometimes more helpful to parents than professional assistance. For example, learning how to care for the child with autism and taking him for an occasional weekend or evening, or taking all the children in the family for a special treat, are examples of ways to offer this meaningful support (Katz & Kessel, 2002). Another example is being certain that when the family is invited to holiday gatherings, provision is made to ensure that the large number of people present do not create an excessively stressful situation for the child with autism. This could be achieved by arranging for the child to play in one room and having a variety of attentive adults rotate through the room for brief periods so that the parents can enjoy the gathering and not be confined to coping with the needs of their child. Doing the weekly grocery shopping, taking a typically developing child to extracurricular activities each week, or providing other support for the routines of the family can also be quite helpful.

Emotional support is important as well. Expressing sincere admiration for the efforts of the parents of the child with autism, being a sounding board, and being a source of reassurance are all potentially helpful. In offering support, it is also vital to take one's cue from the parents. We have suggested elsewhere (Harris, 2002) that it is important for the senior generation to be supportive without being intrusive. This holds true for the wider extended family as well. The parents of a child with autism often have to make complex decisions about their child's treatment, and this process can be complicated if they feel that the rest of the family is "second-guessing" or disapproving of their decisions. Although it is fitting to offer one's opinion when asked, it is important to respect the right of parents to make their own decisions for their child.

Many of the coping strategies that are helpful for parents of children with autism may also be helpful for the rest of the family. For example, instrumental activities such as learning about autism and becoming skilled in ways to teach new behaviors to the child may give one a greater sense of effectiveness. The emotional needs of a loving grandparent, aunt, or cousin are also important to consider. Finding support among one's own support network can help members of the extended family deal with their feelings without burdening their adult children with the need for comfort.

FUTURE RESEARCH

Although a significant body of literature is developing regarding the impact of autism on the family, there are still numerous questions left unanswered. First, more information is needed on the relationship between self-reported stress and outcomes thought to be related to stress. In various studies discussed previously, we see that the group reporting the most stress is not necessarily the group demonstrating the greatest degree of anxiety or depression. Neither has the relationship between self-reported stress and health been studied in this population. Perhaps as more information about stress is gathered in the general population, we will be able to use these models to better understand the impact of stressors related to autism on family members.

Next, although we still need much more information on mothers of individuals with autism and other disabilities, the amount of research evaluating mothers dwarfs that studying fathers, siblings, grandparents, or other extended family members. In our many years of combined clinical experience, we have seen wide variability in the involvement of these other family members with the individual with autism. We have worked with grandmothers who conduct therapy sessions with their grandchild three days per week and adult siblings who pursue doctorates in the study of autism, spurred by their involvement with their own siblings. Varying levels of involvement make these individuals critical in the outcomes for individuals with autism and their parents. The impact of varying degrees of involvement on these different family members also remains unknown.

Furthermore, the impact of cultural factors, such as minority background or decreased access to services due to living in a rural area is virtually unknown. Similarly, families raising children with autism in inner cities or with few financial resources have very different experiences from those with more affluent backgrounds. Identifying and offering support needed by these populations is an area of critical importance. Furthermore, the family structures of some of these groups differ from that of the groups with whom research is being conducted. Perhaps grandmothers or neighbors who help with childcare should be the targets for training and intervention in some communities.

SUMMARY

Autism does not just affect individuals—it affects families, and its effects are profound. Autism requires families to redefine their expectations of what their day-to-day lives will be like and to redesign their long-term hopes, plans, and dreams. Features specific to autism may make this disorder even more challenging for families than are other developmental disorders. In response to this demand, many families experience a great deal of stress. However, for many other families, autism does not seem to have as stressful an impact. In fact, most family members of individuals with autism are not exhibiting significant difficulties with adjustment. There are numerous variables influencing the degree of stress that family members experience. First, the interaction between the demands of the situation and the individual's preexisting resources can have an effect on adjustment. Second, thoughts about having a family member with autism, as well as actions to improve upon challenging characteristics of this situation, can ease or increase a burden. Finally, support from others in many forms can be helpful. The impact of autism on any individual family member cannot be predicted without a full understanding of a number of complex variables.

References

Bagenholm, A., & Gillberg, C. (1991). Psychosocial effects on siblings of children with autism and mental retardation: A population based study. *Journal of Mental Deficiency Research, 35*, 291–307.

Baker, B., & Blacher, J. (2002). For better or worse? Impact of residential placement on families. *Mental Retardation, 40*, 1–13.

Belchic, J. K., & Glasberg, B. A. (1995, May). *Creating a discussion group for siblings of children with developmental disabilities.* Program presented at the Philadelphia Conference on Developmental Disabilities for Parents and Professionals, Philadelphia, PA.

Bengtson, V. L., & Robertson, J. F. (Eds.). (1985). *Grandparenthood.* Beverly Hills, CA: Sage.

Blacher, J. B., & Hanneman, R. A. (1992). Family life cycle issues and mental retardation. *American Journal on Mental Retardation, 96*, 607–616.

Boyce, G. C., & Barnett, W. S. (1993). Siblings of persons with mental retardation: A historical perspective and recent findings. In Z. Stoneman & P. W. Berman (Eds.), *The effects of mental retardation, disability and illness on sibling relationships* (pp. 145–184). Baltimore, MD: Paul H. Brookes.

Boyd, B. A. (2002). Examining the relationship between stress and lack of social support in mothers of children with autism. *Focus on Autism and Other Developmental Disabilities, 17*, 208–215.

Breslau, N. (1982). Siblings of disabled children: Birth order and age spacing effects. *Journal of Abnormal Child Psychology, 10*, 85–96.

Bristol, M. M. (1984). Family resources and successful adaptation to autistic children. In E. Schopler & G. B. Mesibov (Eds.), *The effects of autism on the family* (pp. 289–310). New York: Plenum Press.

Brody, G. H., Stoneman, Z., Davis, C. H., & Crapps, J. M. (1991). Observations of the role relations and behavior between older children with mental retardation and their younger siblings. *American Journal on Mental Retardation, 95*, 527–536.

Celiberti, D. A., & Harris, S. L. (1993). Behavioral intervention for siblings of children with autism: A focus on skills to enhance play. *Behavior Therapy, 24*, 573–599.

Chan, C. G., & Elder, G. H., Jr. (2000). Matrilineal advantage in grandparent-grandchild relations. *Gerontologist, 40*, 179–190.

Cutler, B. C., & Kozloff, M. A. (1987). Living with autism: Effects on families and family needs. In D. J. Cohen & A. M. Donnelan (Eds.), *Handbook of autism and pervasive developmental disorders* (pp. 513–527). New York: Wiley & Sons.

Donaldson, D., Prinstein, M. J., Danovsky, M., & Spirito, A. (2000). Patterns of children's coping with life stress: Implications for clinicians. *American Journal of Orthopsychiatry, 70*, 351–359.

Dunn, J. F. (1988). Annotation: Sibling influences on childhood development. *Journal of Child Psychology and Psychiatry and Allied Disciplines, 29*, 119–127.

Dyson, L. L. (1997). Fathers and mothers of school-age children with developmental disabilities: Parental stress, family functioning, and social support. *American Journal on Mental Retardation, 102(3),* 267–279.

El-Ghoroury, N. H., & Romanczyk, R. G. (1999). Play interactions of family members towards children with autism. *Journal of Autism and Developmental Disorders, 29,* 249–258.

Factor, D. C., Perry, A., & Freeman, N. (1990). Brief report: Stress, social support, and respite care use in families with autistic children. *Journal of Autism and Developmental Disorders, 20,* 139–146.

Farber, B. (1960). Family organization and crisis: Maintenance of integration in families with a severely mentally retarded child. *Monographs of the Society for Research in Child Development, 25.*

Fong, P.L. (1991). Cognitive appraisals in high-and low-stress mothers of adolescents with autism. *Journal of Consulting and Clinical Psychology, 59,* 471–474.

Gallo, A. M., & Knafl, K. A. (1993). Siblings of children with chronic illnesses: A categorical and noncategorical look at the selected literature. In Z. Stoneman & P. W. Berman (Eds.), *The effects of mental retardation, disability, and illness on sibling relationships* (pp. 215–234). Baltimore, MD: Paul H. Brookes.

Gamble, W. C., & McHale, S. M. (1989). Coping with stress in sibling relationships: A comparison of children with disabled and nondisabled siblings. *Journal of Applied Developmental Psychology, 10,* 353–373.

Gamble, W. C., & Woulbroun, E. J. (1993). Measurement considerations in the identification and assessment of stressors and coping strategies. In Z. Stoneman & P. W. Berman (Eds.), *The effects of mental retardation, disability, and illness on sibling relationships* (pp. 287–319). Baltimore, MD: Paul H. Brookes.

Glasberg, B. A. (1998). *The development of a child's appraisal of a sibling's autism.* Unpublished doctoral dissertation. Rutgers: The State University of New Jersey.

Glasberg, B. A., & Belchic, J. K. (1996, April). *Creating a discussion group for siblings of children with developmental disabilities.* Program presented at the meeting of the New Jersey Center for Outreach and Services for the Autism Community, East Brunswick, NJ.

Glasberg, B. A., & Harris, S. L. (1997). Grandparents and parents assess the development of their child with autism. *Child and Family Behavior Therapy, 19,* 17–27.

Gray, D. E. (2003). Gender and coping: The parents of children with high-functioning autism. *Social Science and Medicine, 56(3),* 631–642.

Harris, S. L. (1994). *Siblings of children with autism: A guide for families.* Bethesda, MD: Woodbine House.

Harris, S. L. (2002). Ask the editor. *Journal Autism and Developmental Disorders, 32,* 147.

Harris, S. L., Gill, M. J., & Alessandri, M. (1990). The family with an autistic child. In M. Seligman (Ed.), *The family with a handicapped child* (2nd ed., pp. 269–294). Boston: Allyn & Bacon.

Harris, S. L., & Glasberg, B. A. (2003). *Siblings of children with autism: A guide for families* (2nd ed.). Bethesda, MD: Woodbine House.

Harris, S. L., Glasberg, B., & Delmolino, L. (1998). Families and the developmentally disabled adolescent. In V. B. Van Hasselt & M. Hersen (Eds.), *Handbook of psychological treatment protocols for children and adolescents* (pp. 357–370). Mahwah, NJ: Erlbaum.

Harris, S. L., Handleman, J. S., & Palmer, C. (1985). Parents and grandparents view the autistic child. *Journal of Autism and Developmental Disorders 15*, 127–137.

Hastings, R. P. (2003). Child behavior problems and partner mental health as correlates of stress in mothers and fathers of children with autism. *Journal of Intellectual Disability Research, 47*, 231–237.

Hastings, R. P., & Brown, T. (2002). Behavior problems of children with autism, parental self-efficacy, and mental health. *American Journal on Mental Retardation, 107(3)*, 222–232.

Hastings, R. P., & Johnson, E. (2001). Stress in UK families conducting intensive home-based intervention for their young child with autism. *Journal of Autism and Developmental Disorders, 31* (3), 327–336.

Hastings, R.P., & Taunt, H. M. (2002). Positive perceptions in families of children with developmental disabilities. *American Journal on Mental Retardation, 107*, 116–127.

Hastings, R. P., Thomas, H., & Delwiche, N. (2002). Grandparent support for families of children with Down's syndrome. *Journal of Applied Research in Intellectual Disabilities, 15*, 97–104.

Holmes, N., & Carr, J. (1991). The pattern of care in families of adults with a mental handicap: A comparison between families of autistic adults and Down syndrome adults. *Journal of Autism and Developmental Disorders, 21*, 159–176.

Howe, G. W. (1993). Siblings of children with physical disabilities and chronic illnesses: Studies of risk and social ecology. In Z. Stoneman & P. W. Berman (Eds.), *The effects of mental retardation, disability, and illness on sibling relationships* (pp. 185–214). Baltimore, MD: Paul H. Brookes.

Ireton, H. R., & Thwing, E. J. (1972). *Minnesota Child Development Inventory Manual.* Minneapolis, MN: Behavioral Science Systems.

Judge, S. L. (1997) Parental perceptions of help-giving practices and control appraisals in early intervention programs. *Topics in Early Childhood Special Education, 17*, 457–476.

Katz, S., & Kessel, L. (2002). Grandparents of children with developmental disabilities: Perceptions, beliefs, and involvement in their care. *Issues in Comprehensive Pediatric Nursing, 25*, 113–128.

Lazarus, R. S. (1966). *Psychological stress and the coping process.* New York: McGraw-Hill.

Lobato, D., Barbour, L., Hall, L. J., & Miller, C. T. (1987). Psychosocial characteristics of preschool siblings of handicapped and nonhandicapped children. *Journal of Abnormal Child Psychology, 15(3)*, 329–338.

Lobato, D., Faust, D., & Spirito, A. (1988). Examining the effects of chronic disease and disability on children's sibling relationships. *Journal of Pediatric Psychology, 13*, 389–407.

Lobato, D. J., & Kao, B. T. (2002). Integrated sibling-parent group intervention to improve sibling knowledge and adjustment to chronic illness and disability. *Journal of Pediatric Psychology, 27*, 711–716.

Marsh, D. (1992). *Families and mental retardation: New directions in professional practice.* New York: Praeger.

McCubbin, H. I., & Figley, C. R. (Eds.). (1983). *Stress and the family: Vol. 1. Coping with normative transitions.* New York: Brunner/Mazel.

McHale, S. M., Sloan, J., & Simeonsson, R. J. (1986). Sibling relationships of children with autistic, mentally retarded, and nonhandicapped brothers and sisters. *Journal of Autism and Developmental Disorders, 16*, 399–413.

Meyer, D. J., & Vadasy, P. F. (1994). *Sibshops: Workshops for siblings of children with special needs*. Baltimore, MD: Paul H. Brookes.

Midence, K., & O'Neill, M. (1999). The experience of parents in the diagnosis of autism. *Autism, 3,* 273–285.

Mirfin-Veitch, B., Bray, A., & Watson, M. (1997). 'We're just that sort of family': Intergenerational relationships in families including children with disabilities. *Family Relations, 46,* 305–311.

Moes, D. R., & Frea, W. D. (2002). Contextualized behavioral support in early intervention for children with autism and their families. *Journal of Autism and Developmental Disorders, 32,* 519–533.

Monat, R. K. (1982). *Sexuality and the mentally retarded*. San Diego, CA: College Hill Press.

Morgan, S. B. (1988). The autistic child and family functioning: A developmental family-systems perspective. *Journal of Autism and Developmental Disorders, 18,* 263–280.

Mueller, M. M., & Elder, G. H., Jr. (2003). Family contingencies across the generations: Grandparent-grandchild relationships in holistic perspective. *Journal of Marriage and the Family, 65,* 404–418.

New York State Department of Health (1999). *Clinical practice guidelines: Report of the recommendations: Autism/pervasive developmental disorders, assessment and intervention for young children (Age 0–3 Years)*. Albany, NY: Author.

Osterling, J. A., Dawson, G., & Munson, J. A. (2002). Early recognition of one-year-old infants with autism spectrum disorder versus mental retardation. *Development and Psychopathology, 14*(2), 239–251.

Paul, R. (1987). Communication. In D. J. Cohen & A. M. Donnelan (Eds.), *Handbook of autism and pervasive developmental disorders* (pp. 61–84). New York: Wiley & Sons.

Prudhoe, C. M., & Peters, D. L. (1995). Social support of parents and grandparents in the neonatal intensive care unit. *Pediatric Nursing, 21,* 140–146.

Rodrigue, J. R., Geffken, G. R., & Morgan, S. B. (1993). Perceived competence and behavioral adjustment of siblings of children with autism. *Journal of Autism and Developmental Disorders, 23,* 665–674.

Russell, D., & Matson, J. (1998). Fathers as intervention agents for their children with developmental disabilities. *Child and Family Behavior Therapy, 20*(3), 29–49.

Sandler, A. G., Warren, S. H., & Raver, S. A. (1995). Grandparents as a source of support for parents of children with disabilities: A brief report. *Mental Retardation, 33,* 248–250.

Scherman, A., Gardner, J. E., Brown, P., & Schutter, M. (1995). Grandparents' adjustment to children with disabilities. *Educational Gerontology, 21,* 261–273.

Schreibman, L. (1988). *Autism*. Newbury Park, CA: Sage.

Scorgie, K., & Sobsey, D. (2000). Transformational outcomes associated with parenting children who have disabilities. *Mental Retardation, 38,* 195–206.

Sivberg, B. (2002). Family system and coping behaviors. *Autism, 6,* 397–409.

Skinner, D. G., Correa, V., Skinner, M., & Bailey, D. B. (2001). Role of religion in the lives of Latino families of young children with developmental delays. *American Journal on Mental Retardation, 106,* 297–313.

Sofronoff, K., & Farbotko, M. (2002). The effectiveness of parent management training to increase self-efficacy in parents of children with Asperger disorder. *Autism, 6,* 271–286.

Stoneman, Z., Brody, G. H., Davis, C. H., & Crapps, J. M. (1988). Childcare responsibilities, peer relations, and sibling conflict: Older siblings of mentally retarded children. *American Journal on Mental Retardation, 93*, 174–183.

Stoneman, Z., Brody, G. H., Davis, C. H., Crapps, J. M., & Malone, D. M. (1991). Ascribed role relations between children with mental retardation and their younger siblings. *American Journal on Mental Retardation, 95*, 537–550.

Tunali, B., & Power, T.G. (2002). Coping by redefinition: Cognitive appraisals in mothers of children with autism and children without autism. *Journal of Autism and Developmental Disorders, 32*, 25–34.

Trute, B. (1995). Gender differences in the psychological adjustment of parents of young, developmentally disabled children. *Journal of Child Psychology and Psychiatry, 36*(7), 1225–1242.

Weiss, M.J. (2002). Hardiness and social support as predictors of stress in mothers of typical children, children with autism, and children with mental retardation. *Autism, 6*, 115–130.

Whitaker, P. (2002). Supporting families of preschool children with autism. *Autism, 6*, 411–426.

Wikler, L. (1986). Periodic stresses of families of older mentally retarded children: An exploratory study. *American Journal on Mental Retardation, 90*, 703–706.

Wilson, C. J., McGillivray, J. A., & Zeitlin, A. G. (1992). The relationship between attitude to disabled sibling and ratings of behavioral competency. *Journal of Intellectual Disability Research, 36*, 325–336.

Wing, L., & Attwood, A. (1987). Syndromes of autism and atypical development. In D. J. Cohen & A. M. Donnellan (Eds.), *Handbook of autism and pervasive developmental disorders* (pp. 3–19). New York: Wiley & Sons.

11 Communication and Stress in Students with Autism Spectrum Disorders

Diane Twachtman-Cullen

> Man has a limited capacity for change. When this capacity is overwhelmed, the capacity is in future shock.
>
> —Alvin Toffler

It appears that we have arrived at that unenviable state known as "future shock." Modern life is a veritable treadmill of stressors. The changes that have occurred in society since Toffler's (1970) prescient warning more than 30 years ago about the effects of rapid change on the psyche have been monumental, outstripping our ability to keep up and deal with them. Before the Information Age caught society in its grip, the flow of information was deliberate enough to enable people to actually deal with it. Technology has changed all of that. Today, instant messaging, cellular telephones, and e-mail keep us constantly in touch. Ironically, these modern "conveniences" have been anything but convenient; that is, instead of simplifying life, they have added layers of complexity. They have also robbed us of downtime and leisure at a point in our evolution when these things are most urgently needed. In short, technological progress has not come without a price. To wit, it has created unreasonable demands on our time, given us far more information than we can handle, and stretched our internal coping mechanisms to the breaking point. Worse yet, there is no relief in sight.

The acceleration of new information is staggering. The United States is a world leader in the storage of new information, producing approximately 40% of all stored data (Lyman & Varian, 2003). Lyman and Varian further state that this figure pales by comparison to the information that flows through electronic media (e.g., telephone, radio, television, Internet), which is estimated at approximately 3.5 times that which is recorded in storage media.

Adding to this, the disintegration of the nuclear family, the cultural turbulence caused by worries about homeland security, the relatively recent spate of school violence, and corresponding concerns regarding the long-term effects of bullying are a near-perfect recipe for the uncontrollable type of stress that has become an inescapable part of modern life. Our children, in particular, have not escaped the ravages of stress.

Institutions of education, as a microcosm of the larger society, present their own unique stressors for children. For example, the kindergarten of the past has evolved into a no-nonsense environment where academics overshadow the lessons of fairness and sharing that children used to learn through play and that were once a mainstay of the preschool curriculum. Today, the demands of state-generated, standardized competency tests have created a pressure cooker atmosphere for both teachers and students alike, throughout the grades. Likewise, the inexorable push toward inclusive education has created a complex web of obligations and events that take teachers out of the classroom to attend meetings regularly and often, while at the same time requiring them to meet the needs of students who require widely disparate teaching content, methods, and techniques.

Within this atmosphere, consider the plight of the child with an autism spectrum disorder (ASD). Even in the best of times and under the most serene circumstances—neither of which accurately describes modern life—stress is an endemic part of life for individuals with ASD. Combine the spillover effects of stress from both the school environment and the larger society with the internal stress that is part and parcel of ASD, and you have all of the conditions necessary for a virtual "perfect storm" of stress-related consequences: frustration, confusion, overload, and in the worst of circumstances, shutdown. These states of being are all too familiar in the lives of students with ASD.

It should be obvious that the need for stress-reduction strategies for students on the spectrum has never been greater or more urgent. What may not be as obvious is the fact that stress reduction has become a mainstream concern and, as such, it needs to become a mainstream "event." Hence, anything that can be done to reduce stress or to enable children to manage it will go a long way toward improving the quality of school life for all children—those with ASD and their neurotypical peers. This chapter explores the complex, multidimensional relationship between communication and stress in children with ASD. It is based on the premise that because of the neurological and physiological challenges associated with conditions on the autism spectrum and the endemic communication challenges seen in this population, these children are uniquely vulnerable to stress. Cognitive and social-cognitive predisposing factors are considered, as well as the pragmatic and processing deficits that feed into the stress cycle. I also examine the nature of the environmental demands that serve as the context within which stress occurs. Finally, the use of strategies for stress reduction and management are discussed.

GOOD AND BAD STRESS

The word "stress" has taken on such negative connotations in society that it is hard to believe that stress is simply the body's response to the demands that are made upon it (Selye, 1974). Having said that, it is important to note that not all stresses are necessarily bad for the organism; or, more to the point, not all stressors are created equal. There is such a thing as good stress (Jensen, 1998; Selye, 1974). This type of stress is known as eustress. Happy events such as marriage or the birth of a child usually result in eustress. Bad stress is aptly known as distress. Unhappy events such as divorce or the death of a loved one typically cause distress.

Indeed, stress may be considered a double-edged sword. On the one hand, mild stress can prime the system and motivate the individual to operate at peak performance levels. On the other hand, severe stress can debilitate both the individual and his or her performance. Two questions come to mind. First, is there such a thing as an optimal level of stress? Second, is there such a thing as too little stress? The answer to both questions is yes, but what constitutes optimal or insufficient levels of stress vary from person to person. The following examples may help to illustrate these phenomena.

Many people have had the experience of being seated in a busy restaurant, expecting service to be less than optimal due to the number of patrons, and being pleasantly surprised when both the food and the check arrive in a timely manner. Conversely, those same people have probably also had the experience of walking into a restaurant that wasn't at all busy, expecting the service to be exemplary under the circumstances, and finding quite the opposite to be true. The mechanism at work is quite simple to understand. In the first situation, the number of people in the restaurant serves to motivate the wait staff to move quickly and "stay on top of their game." In other words, the level of stress may be considered optimal from the perspective of priming the system to operate at peak efficiency. In the second situation, there appears to be too little stress to prime the system and motivate the wait staff to operate efficiently. As a result, they appear to be operating in slow motion. Having said that, it is important to note that there is a fine line between optimal stress and distress, and this has significant ramifications for individuals with ASD. Consider again the moderately busy restaurant scenario. All that is needed to tip the balance in the optimal situation toward the distress side of the scale is to add one or more of the following stressors: an increased number of patrons, too few wait staff, or a kitchen staff unable to keep up with the demand.

Individuals with ASD have neurological compromises and unique challenges that make the line between optimal stress and distress even finer than it is for the general population. For example, compromises in the physiological arousal mechanism can result in chronic states of underarousal or overarousal. In the former state, the child actually requires a relatively high degree of stimulation in order to respond optimally; there is often a narrow band between optimal and overload. In other words, a child with ASD who is chronically underaroused may need a great deal of stimulation to provoke a desired response, but even minimal stimulation beyond that point may catapult the child into an overload situation. This experience is perhaps best understood in terms of the phenomenon known as recruitment in severe hearing loss, where although it may take as much as 80 dB of sound for the individual to hear a signal, a mere 20 dB more may bring him or her to the threshold of pain. Under such circumstances, the regulation of stimulation is more of an art form than a science.

In the case of overarousal, the system is already in a state of distress, making any amount of stimulation a stressful event. Since both of these arousal states are internally based, it is incumbent upon caregivers to exercise vigilance with regard to recognizing and monitoring the individual's external signs of distress so that they can "titrate" the amount and type of stimulation to fit the circumstances. Indeed, anything that caregivers can do to monitor and regulate the amount of stimulation to which individuals with ASD are exposed will go a long way toward minimizing the stress associated with overarousal. The importance of this cannot be overstated because impairment in the executive function system negatively impacts the ability of the individual with ASD to self-regulate.

COGNITIVE AND SOCIAL-COGNITIVE FACTORS IN STRESS

Executive Function

In addition to the internal physiological mechanisms (e.g., compromises in the arousal mechanism, sensory issues) that make children with ASD uniquely vulnerable to stress, neurologically based cognitive and social-cognitive deficits also predispose the child to stress. Though more subtle than the physiological factors discussed earlier, these neurological compromises not only interfere with the body's self-regulatory mechanism, but also create a web of stress that is particularly problematic in complex, high-demand environments.

The construct of executive function (EF) is the "high priestess" of the cognitive system, the executive "comptroller" of organized, goal-directed behavior (Twachtman-Cullen, 2000a). Welsh and Pennington (1988) describe the components of the EF system as, "a) an intention to inhibit a response or to defer it to a later more appropriate time; b) a strategic plan of action sequences; and c) a mental representation of the task, including the relevant stimulus information encoded in memory and the desired future goal-state" (pp. 201–202). These components make it possible for individuals with an adequate EF system to maintain attention to the task at hand, control their impulses, engage in mental planning activities, exercise flexibility in the use of strategies, transition from one activity to another, and self-monitor their behavior so that changes can be made as the situation or circumstances require. In short, all these activities acting in concert with one another underpin the important task of self-regulation. This is no small task, considering that Borkowski and Burke (1996) refer to the act of self-regulation, an area of acknowledged difficulty in ASD, as "the basis for adaptive learning and thinking" (p. 238).

Inherent in the concept of EF is that of working memory, defined by Barkley (1996) as "the means by which a stimulus or signal is kindled, sustained, and held or symbolically fixed in mind and prolonged 'on-line' while parallel processing of the content of the signal takes place" (pp. 315–316). The tasks subsumed under the rubric of EF enable neurotypical individuals to deal with the demands of a complex, rapidly moving social world by enabling them to analyze what is needed, select appropriate strategies for dealing with it, and monitor their behavior based on the demands of the situation so that appropriate adjustments can be made.

In contrast, consider the plight of those with ASD. These individuals have well-recognized difficulty in all of the areas of executive functioning noted above. They are known to be distractible, impulsive, and inflexible. Their problems with transitions are legion, as is their difficulty monitoring and adjusting their behavior to suit situational needs. Lacking an internal set of directions to guide behavior (i.e., self-regulatory control mechanisms), individuals with ASD are at the mercy of their immediate context and surroundings—a situation that leads to disorganization and lack of control, and one that is a near constant source of anxiety and stress.

Theory of Mind

Theory of mind is a social-cognitive construct that is intimately related to the pragmatics of communication and to social understanding and expression. In fact, many of the well-known problems in communication and language that individuals with ASD manifest are linked to their theory of mind deficits (Baron-Cohen, 1988; Frith, 1989). For example, one of the most recognized features of language use in individuals with ASD is their propensity for literal expression and interpretation. This is quite illuminating from the perspective of theory of mind, since the essence of the problem in literal communication is the inability to recognize the intentions of others. Consider, for example, the answer that a young man with autism gave when asked who was the author of *The Emperor's New Clothes*. He replied, "The person who wrote it." Had the young man been aware that the questioner wanted to know the name of the author, he would likely have answered the question differently.

Indirect requests are also instructive from a theory of mind perspective. For example, many years ago I asked the husband of a college professor with Asperger's syndrome if his wife was literal. He replied, "Is she literal? If I say, 'Can you pass the salt,' she says 'yes'!" As in the previous example, had the woman been aware that, despite the literal meaning of the words, her husband nonetheless intended for her to pass the salt, she would not have interpreted the question as one that was merely seeking information on her ability to carry out the act. Intentionality, as it turns out, is at the very heart of theory of mind. According to Baron-Cohen (1995), "In decoding speech we [must] go way beyond the words we hear or read, to hypothesize about the speaker's mental states" (p. 27). In fact, Baron-Cohen reduces the quest for meaning of an utterance or written narrative to its lowest common denominator: What does the speaker or writer intend for the listener or reader to understand?

Normal variations aside, neurotypical people have an adequate theory of mind—an instinctive sense that people have different ways of thinking and feeling about things, as well as an understanding that no two minds are alike. Some of our most common expressions underscore this point. For example, when we say, "different strokes for different folks," we are acknowledging that things that appeal to one person might not appeal to another. Likewise, implicit in the expression, "If I were you," is the recognition that I am not you—the inference being that thought processes and ways of looking at things differ from person to person.

To have a theory of mind is to be able to attribute mental states to others, a process Simon Baron-Cohen (1995) and Uta Frith (1989) refer to as "mentalizing." In other words, we use mental state terms to help us understand what people mean in order to make sense of their behavior, such as, "She's crying because she feels badly," or, "He's studying hard because he really wants a good grade on the test." Nonautistic individuals mentalize, or "form mental state hypotheses," quite naturally in response to the external behavior that people exhibit. The importance of attributing mental states to others cannot be overstated. This mental practice

- helps us to understand, or make sense of, a person's behavior
- enables us to use the information that is gleaned to predict what a person might, or might not do
- provides the basis upon which we may modify and/or adjust our own behavior to meet the needs of the situation.

In contrast, the compromises in theory of mind that are seen in individuals with autism interfere with their ability to make sense of behavior, predict what a person is or is not likely to do, and adjust their behavior to accommodate the situation and circumstances. Problems in these essential interactive processes create a great deal of stress and anxiety in children with ASD and leave them ill-equipped to deal with a world that they have difficulty understanding.

Consider the plight of a 10-year-old boy with high-functioning autism and a functional language system. Desiring a cookie, he walks into the kitchen and says to his mother, "Can I have a cookie?" His mother is humming happily as she works, having just received a phone call from a dear friend. She says to her son, "Sure. Take two cookies." The young boy, though elated at the prospect of receiving two cookies, is nevertheless perplexed regarding why he is able to get two cookies on this day, when on so many others his request has been denied. In an attempt to understand his mother's behavior—and consummately unmindful of her nonverbal cues signaling "good mood"—he might hypothesize that she gave him two cookies because it was four o'clock. (Lacking a theory of mind, it is easy to make the wrong connections! Note also that, unlike the mental state hypotheses of neurotypical people noted above, this child's hypothesis has nothing to do with internal mental state.) The next day—at exactly four o'clock—the boy goes into the kitchen and asks his mother for a cookie. Muttering under her breath and slamming the cabinet door shut, she whirls around and says, "Of course not. It's much too close to supper." Unmindful of the nonverbal cues that signal "bad mood," the little boy is at a loss to understand his mother's behavior, particularly since the family eats at exactly the same time every night—five o'clock. The point is that absent a well-defined theory of mind that would enable him to read his mother's nonverbal behavior, the boy would undoubtedly have difficulty determining why he was able to get two cookies the night before and none on this evening. While he's trying to figure things out, his 5-year-old, neurotypical brother rounds the corner, takes one look at his mother, and decides instantaneously to abandon his request for a cookie. Notwithstanding that he is 5 years younger than his brother, he reads his mother's behavior, recognizes that she is in a bad mood, predicts that she probably won't give him a cookie, and modifies his behavior accordingly by leaving the room. Moreover, he does all of this in a split second, without consciously engaging in the process of reasoning.

What this example illustrates is that it is not enough to have language, as this high-functioning 10-year-old boy did. It is also important to be attuned to the nonverbal communicative signals that infuse situations with meaning, for it is these types of mental-state activities that provide the information necessary to comprehend and use language effectively to make things happen and to guide behavior overall. Furthermore, when individuals with ASD can't use language to effect desired outcomes because they make the wrong connections, the result is clearly a stressful event that interferes significantly with their understanding of the world. Moreover, because theory of mind deficits interfere with the "causal-explanatory framework" (Tager-Flusberg, 1997), which is so critical for making inferences and interpreting behavior, these deficits also have an impact on executive functioning in general and on information processing in particular.

Information Processing

The deceptive simplicity with which information processing takes place in neurotypical people belies its complex and multidimensional nature. The ability to adequately process information requires competence in the higher-order processes involving executive function. It also requires an array of complex understandings related to theory of mind and pragmatics. As important as these processes are, however, they alone are insufficient to handle all that is involved in the multifaceted process of handling information in real time. Referring to information processing as "the final common pathway" for the exchange of meaning, Twachtman-Cullen (2000b) notes that "issues related to depth, manner, and speed of processing, as well as those related to many intangibles, such as cohesion, vigilance, and meta-cognitive/meta-linguistic awareness" (p. 241) all interact with aspects of theory of mind and pragmatics to make the processing of information possible.

Several studies have demonstrated that the matrix of understandings involved in information processing eludes even the most able individuals with ASD. This is largely a function of their grounding in procedural knowledge (i.e., knowledge for doing things), and their weaknesses in declarative knowledge (i.e., knowledge about things; Goldstein, Minshew, & Siegel, 1994; Minshew, Goldstein, & Siegel, 1995; Minshew, Goldstein, Taylor, & Siegel, 1994). According to Twachtman-Cullen (2000b), procedural knowledge is required for more concrete, straightforward operations such as reading decoding and rote memorization—areas of relative competence in individuals on the autism spectrum. Declarative knowledge, on the other hand, is required for more abstract operations such as concept formation, critical thinking, language and reading comprehension, and information processing. Hence, even when these children are able to understand the more straightforward, literal elements of language, they nonetheless have difficulty understanding and processing figurative language. For example, an individual with ASD may easily grasp what is meant by the sentence, "I have a dog," while at the same time find inexplicable its figurative counterpart, "That movie was a real dog!" Likewise, difficulty understanding that a word may have multiple meanings would undoubtedly interfere with comprehension. For example, if a child with autism knows only one meaning for the word "fair," as in operating according to the rules in a game, the child is not likely to understand the following: "Although she was fair of face, he was the fair-haired boy." It should be obvious that to understand this utterance one would need to understand not only the meaning of the word "fair" in the context in which it occurs, but also that of the figurative expression, "fair-haired." Needless to say, this would take into account an appreciation for context and the ability to read between the lines, neither of which is an area of strength in ASD. Finally, it should be obvious that the time involved in such ruminations would undoubtedly slow down and interfere with real-time information processing.

At this juncture, it is important to point out that while there is undoubtedly a specific physiological basis for delayed processing in some individuals on the spectrum, there may also be other individuals for whom delayed processing is merely an artifact, secondary to language comprehension difficulty involving, for example, multiple meanings of words or figurative language.

Notwithstanding whether comprehension difficulty stems from natural or artifactual causes, the effect on information processing will be the same. Specifically, these individuals will have difficulty taking in information, relating it to what is already known, assimilating it into the existing fund of knowledge, and transferring it to the appropriate storage area so that it may be retrieved when needed (Twachtman-Cullen, 2000a). Anything that interferes with this complex, labor-intensive process is likely to cause stress, the result of which is to further compromise the individual's ability to process information. Hence, a vicious cycle is created.

STRESS AND PRAGMATICS

Pragmatics refers to the use of language for social communication purposes. Of all of the aspects of language behavior that could go wrong in ASD, it is the pragmatic elements that are the most profoundly affected, given that they have deep roots that extend into the processes involving theory of mind, executive function, and information processing. There are three main aspects of pragmatics, each of which also relates directly to theory of mind, and each of which can serve as a breeding ground for stress: pragmatic functions of communication; presuppositional knowledge; and the four maxims of communication.

Pragmatic Functions of Communication

The pragmatic functions of communication refer to the reasons people speak. Specifically, people speak to perform certain communicative functions, such as making requests, commenting on things, asking questions, protesting, and negotiating. Individuals with autism who are at the less able end of the autism continuum often exercise the pragmatic functions of communication by engaging in aberrant behavior. This is particularly true in the case of the nonverbal or minimally verbal individuals. For example, in the absence of being able to appropriately request a desired food item, the less able child with autism may simply take the item from someone else's plate. Likewise, the child who is unable to say, "no," in the conventional way may act out to communicate his or her intent. Characteristically, caregivers do not generally treat these types of behaviors as attempts to communicate (i.e., as means to desired ends), but rather as behavior problems (i.e., as ends in themselves) that must be extinguished. This type of misjudgment creates layers of stress for children with ASD. First and foremost, there is the stress that issues from not being able to make needs known. Next, there is the stress involved in having honest attempts at communication—unconventional and aberrant though they are—erroneously viewed as purely negative and, in some cases, as willful behavior. Finally, there is the ultimate frustration that accrues from being punished for a behavior the child is at a loss to understand or control. As if this is not enough, add to it the lost opportunities for the child to learn more effective ways of communicating.

Deficits in the pragmatic functions of communication are not reserved solely for those individuals at the less able end of the autism continuum. Indeed, the inability to express one's needs and desires results in a great deal of frustration for those with high-functioning autism and Asperger's syndrome, as well. Twachtman-Cullen (2003) recounts the story of Michael, a preschool child with Asperger's syndrome whose abiding pleasure in life was words—saying them, but mostly writing them. Despite the fact that Michael had a good deal of language at his disposal, he didn't use it for anything beyond the repetitive act of saying and writing disjointed strings of unconnected words. When the teacher was asked about the way in which Michael requests things that he wants, she replied, "He just gets them himself." Such independence is often a red flag signaling pragmatic impairment, or a lack of knowledge regarding how to use language to make something happen.

One day Michael spied a desired toy on a high shelf. He brought a chair over to the cupboard so that he could climb on it and claim his prize. Discouraged from doing so by his teacher in order to motivate him to use his words to request, Michael was asked to tell the teacher what he wanted, and told that she would get it for him. There was silence while Michael alternately paced the floor anxiously and stared up at the toy longingly. During the several minutes that he engaged in this anxious pacing behavior, his teacher made numerous overt attempts to prompt a verbal request, all to no avail. After several minutes of mounting frustration, Michael walked away dejectedly. He approached an easel on the other side of the classroom, ostensibly to indulge in his favorite pastime, writing strings of unrelated words. Instead, he wrote a single word, help, and then he walked away, looking sad. It was clear to both his teacher and to me that, notwithstanding an enviable lexicon and the ability to speak, Michael lacked the critical pragmatic knowledge that he could use his language as an instrument of social causality, and as such, he could effect a change in the behavior of his caregivers simply by using his words to request help. On that day, Michael's stress and anxiety were palpable.

Presuppositions

A second aspect of pragmatics concerns presuppositional knowledge and consists of the judgments that speakers make about their listeners' needs with respect to informational content, communicative style, and other situational elements, such as context. For example, to know what information to convey, we have to be aware of what our communicative partner already knows, in addition to what new information the individual needs to make sense of the message. Neurotypical speakers easily adjust their communicative styles to suit the needs of their communicative partners and the circumstances. For example, we would use a more formal communicative style with a person in authority than we would use with a family member or dear friend. In addition, we would use a different style of communication (and vocabulary) in the context of a football game than we would use at a formal dinner party. All of these pragmatic decisions require an adequate theory of mind and a high degree of social understanding.

A lack of competence in presuppositional knowledge can cause individuals with ASD to say and do things that neurotypical people construe as inappropriate (or worse yet, dangerous), a situation that can cause them unimagined stress. Consider the following scenario that occurred coincidentally in the aftermath of the Columbine school shooting: Eleven-year old Matthew, frustrated by his paraprofessional support person's refusal to let him spend a few more minutes on the computer said, "If I had a gun I'd shoot you." When Matthew's mother arrived at the school to pick him up that afternoon she found her son in the principal's office with two police officers, a look of abject terror on his face. Unable to comprehend his plight, Matthew was nonetheless suspended from school for several days. His anxiety over the incident never did dissipate, and he was later diagnosed with post-traumatic stress disorder. The stress involved in making presuppositional judgment errors is all the more devastating in an atmosphere of zero tolerance.

Four Maxims of Conversation

The third aspect of pragmatics that shares an intimate association with theory of mind relates to the conversational maxims (Grice, 1975; Twachtman-Cullen, 2000b). These are the rules of discourse by which neurotypical speakers cooperate in their conversations with one another.

The first rule is that of quantity. This rule requires the speaker to convey only the amount of information necessary to convey his or her meaning. Saying too much or too little would violate this rule. For example, when a young man with Asperger's syndrome talks nonstop about Amtrak trains without regard to the social distress signals of his communicative partner, he is violating the rule of quantity.

The second maxim is that of quality. This rule concerns the truth-value of utterances. Lying and confabulation (i.e., saying something untrue that the speaker, nevertheless, believes to be true) would constitute a violation of this rule. If a little girl with high-functioning autism tells a fanciful story of how she encountered a house in which a family of bears lived, her confabulatory statements are likely to provoke ridicule by her classmates.

The third maxim has to do with the relevance of utterances. Off-topic comments and tangential remarks constitute a violation of this rule. More able individuals with ASD are often told such things as, "You're off topic," and "Stick to the topic." These types of directives can be a source of stress, particularly if the child has no idea what the word topic means, let alone how to stay on it.

The final maxim is that of clarity. This rule obligates the speaker to convey information in a manner that is clear and understandable to the listener. Beginning an utterance in the middle of a thought without providing adequate background information (a situation that happens often in ASD) constitutes a violation of this maxim. Because this usually results in a lack of understanding of the child's communicative intent, it is yet another source of stress for the child with ASD.

To summarize, the type of knowledge needed to follow the unwritten rules of discourse is not only social in nature, but also intimately connected to one's ability to make judgments about the contents of other people's minds. It should also be obvious that the compendium of pragmatic or, socially based knowledge needed to be a competent communicator is not only rich and multifaceted, but also largely implicit. In other words, even though competent communicators are constantly making pragmatic decisions to regulate both their comprehension and expression of information, they are largely unaware of those decisions because pragmatic decision-making is wired into our subconscious and takes place in milliseconds of time during the actual discourse event.

It is for all of these reasons that the entire area of pragmatic communication with its roots in executive function, theory of mind, and information processing is fraught with "land mines" for individuals with ASD. These land mines make it tricky at best and tremendously stressful at worst to negotiate the social world at all, let alone in the competent, flexible, and fluent manner that is the norm for neurotypical individuals.

COMMUNICATION–BEHAVIOR–STRESS CONNECTION

Rousseau (1963) said, "When children begin to talk they cry less. This progress is quite natural; one language is substituted for the other." In these few simple words, Rousseau captured the essence of the pragmatic axiom—that all behavior communicates, regardless of whether there is the intent to do so. Watzlawick, Beavin, and Jackson (1967) in their classic treatise on the pragmatics of communication go even farther by stating, "Behavior has no opposite. In other words, there is no such thing as nonbehavior or, to put it even more simply: one cannot *not* behave. Now, if it is accepted that all behavior in an interactional situation has message value, i.e., is communication, it follows that no matter how one may try, one cannot *not* communicate. Activity or inactivity, words or silence all have message value: they influence others and these others, in turn, cannot *not* respond to these communications and are thus themselves communicating" (pp. 48–49, emphasis in original).

People seem to understand and accept the pragmatics of communication, at least at some unconscious level, when applied to neurotypical infants and toddlers who lack a sophisticated language system. Hence, when a baby cries we interpret his or her behavior as having message value and answer by checking to see if the baby is hungry, needs a diaper change, or is in discomfort due to some other cause. Likewise, when a toddler has developed some verbal language with which to express simple pragmatic functions, such as requesting a cookie or juice, we don't automatically expect that the child will be able to use that language in situations that require an understanding beyond his or her ability level. The pragmatic communicative function of protesting offers an interesting example that also has implications for children on the autism spectrum.

Suppose that a neurotypical toddler requests an object that contains small parts that present a choking hazard. The caregiver's refusal to grant the request will likely be met with protest behavior, due to the toddler's lack of understanding of the adult's position. Because the child is too young to use more advanced forms of protesting that make use of reasoning or negotiation, he or she is likely to communicate frustration by crying and/or engaging in a full-blown tantrum. Responsible and knowledgeable caregivers would likely understand the child's difficulty comprehending the concept of danger and would probably try to soothe the child's feelings or use distraction to interrupt the protest behavior. Implicit in this type of reaction is the pragmatic knowledge—unconscious or otherwise—that the child is communicating his or her frustration but lacks the necessary language skills to do so in a more appropriate manner. Under such circumstances, one does not hold the child to standards that are inappropriate, such as insisting that the child use words to express complex thoughts and feelings. Neither does one punish the child for being unable to do so.

Now consider the situation involving an 8-year-old nonverbal boy with autism. At snack time, his teacher asks, "What do you want?" The boy, absent a conventional way of answering the question and requesting a cookie, reaches out and takes one off of a classmate's plate. The teacher admonishes him for "stealing" the cookie and takes it away from him. The boy engages in immediate protest behavior, crying and banging his hands on the table in frustration because the teacher's response is inexplicable to him. After all, viewed from his perspective, it is clear that he has answered the teacher's request in the only manner in which he is able—behaviorally (i.e., by taking the cookie off the plate). Unlike the situation involving the toddler in the first example, this situation provokes harsh judgment regarding the child's inappropriate behavior and perhaps even a trip to time-out.

For whatever reason (and indeed there are many), the pragmatic axiom is not regularly applied to the child with ASD. Specifically, there is rarely an assumption on the part of the adult that the behavior is an attempt to fulfill the pragmatic function of communication—that it is a means to a desired end. Instead, the behavior is viewed as an end in and of itself, and as such it is judged swiftly and harshly as inappropriate behavior. Herein lies a major disconnect: the lack of recognition of the relationship between communication and behavior, a situation that causes the individual with ASD needless stress and anxiety.

The previous example is a scenario that plays out on a daily basis in class-room after classroom serving students with autism who have significant pragmatic challenges. Specifically, individuals with autism who lack a conventional communication system often respond in idiosyncratic or aberrant ways, and caregivers regularly respond in a manner so as to discourage that behavior. So common is the practice of responding to the behavior instead of to its communicative intent that the implications of this practice receive little attention. Notwithstanding the commonness of the practice, it is nonetheless deeply disturbing and inimical to the child's interests, particularly when one considers its effect on the stress levels of students with autism.

The phenomenon of paradoxical communication can shed light on the underlying mechanisms that cause the child stress in this type of situation, as there are many parallels to it in the example of the boy at snack time. Watzlawick, Beavin, and Jackson (1967) define paradox within the context of pragmatic communication as "a contradiction that follows correct deduction from consistent premises" (p. 188). Returning to the example above, it is clear that the child understood the question when the teacher asked, "What do you want?" He responded to its intent pragmatically in the only way that he could given his low level of pragmatic knowledge, and then he was confronted with the contradictory response of having the cookie taken away from him by the very person who had asked him if he wanted it in the first place. According to Watzlawick, Beavin, and Jackson (1967), "a person caught in such a situation is in an untenable position" (p. 195), a predicament that is not only emblematic of stress, but also exacerbated by the lack of control inherent in conditions of untenability. The effect that a lack of control has on stress levels is discussed in the next section.

INVERSE RELATIONSHIP BETWEEN COMMUNICATION AND STRESS

As the level of stress increases beyond the point considered optimal, there is a corresponding decrease in one's ability to communicate effectively. This is as true for individuals who are neurotypical as well as for those on the autism spectrum. Consider how difficult it would be to effectively and efficiently communicate one's thoughts under conditions of severe stress, even if the person were to possess an intact language system. The opposite is also true: as the level of stress decreases, it generally becomes easier to express one's thoughts and ideas. Although these principles hold true for both neurotypical people as well as those with ASD, there are important differences between the two populations. Given that pragmatic impairment is considered to be pathognomonic of the disorders along the autism continuum, the ability to communicate is always problematic at some level in individuals with ASD (Twachtman-Cullen, 2000a, 2000b), a situation that is not generally the case for neurotypical people. Hence, individuals with ASD are starting out from a compromised position—a circumstance that leads to yet another communication–stress paradigm.

In this paradigm, decreased ability to communicate one's thoughts, needs, and desires, which is the case in ASD, leads to increased stress and anxiety. Carter (1999) relates the story of a young boy who learned through painstaking repetition and practice to point to the object of his desire and to wait for an adult to respond. Prior to learning this alternative communicative behavior, the child would simply grab whatever it was that he wanted, not unlike the boy in the example discussed earlier. Inexplicably, from time-to-time, the child would engage in a massive tantrum for no apparent reason. The mystery was solved when one day the father saw his child through a window standing alone in a room pointing to the cupboard where the biscuits were kept. According to Carter (1999), "The father decided to stay at the window and watch. After about five minutes of hopeless pointing, the boy started to get upset and after ten [minutes] he was distraught. Within fifteen minutes he was gripped by a full-scale tantrum. Evidently, the child had been waiting for a biscuit to be given to him" (p. 141). If actions speak louder than words, then surely this child's behavior speaks volumes with respect to the stress involved in not being able to communicate one's wishes or, as in this case, not even being able to understand the most basic idea of communication—that in order to send a message there needs to be someone available to receive it.

Although there is a great deal of commonality regarding stressors for neurotypical people, individuals with ASD can be "stressed out" by things that neurotypical people would neither characterize, nor even recognize, as stressful. Consequently, things that serve as potential stressors for individuals with ASD are likely to go unnoticed, given that they are often below the neurotypical individual's level of consciousness and hence difficult to relate to and understand. One way to guard against this is to understand the syndrome of autism and its intimate affiliation with anxiety and stress. Another is to exercise conscious vigilance regarding potential sources of stress because, when it comes to dealing with the ravages of stress, an ounce of prevention is worth a pound of cure. This can be accomplished by monitoring the environment for potential sources of stress, by taking proactive steps to reduce their impact, or by eliminating them wherever possible.

EFFECT OF EXTERNAL STRESSORS

Although the particulars regarding what constitutes a stressful event and what doesn't vary from person to person, the broad categories of stressors are generally the same. One universal set of stressors may be placed under the rubric of environmental demands. Unlike the inverse relationship between communication and stress, the relationship between environmental demands and stress varies proportionately. In other words, whereas low-level environmental demands place little external stress on individuals with ASD, high-level demands generally result in increased stress, concomitant with decreased ability to communicate. For example, minimally verbal children who are barely at a two-to-three word utterance level are likely to become highly frustrated and shut down completely when pressured to respond with complete sentences. Similarly, when students are called upon without warning in class and required to give specific information quickly, they may be too stressed to do so during such a cognitively demanding moment. Furthermore, when the idiosyncratic communicative attempts of individuals with ASD are ignored, misinterpreted, or held in disdain by uninformed caregivers, the net result is to heap stressor upon stressor on children who are already maximally stressed by the constraints of their disability. This situation is all the more dire when there is a real or perceived lack of control over one's circumstances.

One of the most potent factors influencing a person's response to stress is that of control. A classic series of animal experiments illustrates the detrimental effects of lack of control. Maier and Geer (1968) placed dogs in cages equipped with grids through which mild electric shocks were delivered. There was no way for the dogs to escape. In other words, there was no way for the dogs to control their unpleasant situation. After a while—and only when the dogs became chronically resigned to their circumstance—the experimenters eliminated the shocks on one side of the cage. They then physically dragged the dogs to the safe side of the cage so that they could experience the difference between the side with the electrified grid and the one that offered respite. The researchers found that it took scores of physical manipulations to the safe side of the cage to get the dogs to begin to reengage in more proactive behavior because they had learned to be helpless in a situation over which they lacked control. What is most telling about these findings is that the dogs' learned helplessness was highly resistant to change even after the possibility of control was restored to them.

According to Peterson, Maier, and Seligman (1993), the results of research regarding the effects of lack of control on human beings suggest an even stronger connection than that found in animal studies. Moreover, this is true regardless of the specific source of lack of control. For example, "social class is a key indicator of control, because the lower down you are in social standing, the less opportunity and training you are likely to have to influence events that impinge on your life" (Bartels, n.d.; see http://www.abc.net.au/science/slab/stress/control.htm).

Surely among autistic individuals, there is little opportunity and even less training in ways to exercise appropriate control over one's life. Moreover, if the yardstick of social standing were applied to individuals on the autism spectrum, they would be hard-pressed to measure up. Finally, although lack of control has a similar effect on both neurotypical people and those with ASD, it is the latter population for whom lack of control is most pervasive. This stems from the pragmatic communication deficits that are a defining feature of conditions on the autism spectrum, since pragmatic impairment robs individuals with ASD of the power to use language in a communicatively competent manner to exercise control over their lives. Lest one doubt the power inherent in the ability to communicate, consider the words of Daniel Webster: "If all my possessions were taken away from me with one exception, I would choose to keep the power of communication, for by it, I would regain all the rest."

COLLISION BETWEEN INTERNAL AND EXTERNAL STRESS FACTORS IN THE SCHOOL SETTING

In considering the effect of stress on student learning, two factors are important to consider. First, students with ASD are generally more vulnerable to stress than are their neurotypical peers (Groden, Diller, Bausman, Velicer, Norman, & Cautela, 2001; Groden & LeVasseur, 1995; Groden, LeVasseur, Diller, & Cautela, 2002), and perhaps even more than other special needs students, this stress negatively impacts their ability to communicate. Second, language is the means by which all academic subjects are pursued. Consequently, when stress debilitates the comprehension and use of language in students with ASD, it will not only have a detrimental effect on their overall comfort level, but it will also adversely affect their educational performance. It is not easy to escape this stress scenario because the educational environment itself can be a source of significant stress for students with ASD. This is particularly true today with the emphasis on inclusive education.

While it is well beyond the scope of this chapter to discuss the pros and cons of inclusion, one might argue that when it comes to determining the benefits of inclusion, we may be asking the wrong questions with respect to individuals with ASD. There is a dearth of studies looking specifically at the effect of environmental stressors on the well-being of students with ASD. Yet it is common to hear parents report that their children "hold it together throughout the day," only to have meltdowns when they arrive home. Likewise, teachers often report that their students with ASD regularly exhibit task-avoidance behavior such as aggression and bolting when academic or other pressures mount.

These behavioral reactions are not difficult to understand when one considers that students with ASD present unique challenges that impact their ability to benefit from the inclusive classroom setting. For one thing, students with ASD tend to remain calmer and more focused in simpler, low-demand environments, given their propensity to react negatively to high stimulation and their vulnerability to distractions—both of which abound in the inclusive classroom setting. These students also tend to have difficulty with the information processing demands and pace of mainstream environments, many of which contain too much auditory input and precious few visual supports.

According to Jensen (1998), the number of threats that neurotypical students are exposed to on a regular basis in the school environment is "endless." Hallways and playgrounds have become ideal environments for bullying, and sometimes humiliation and lack of discipline reign supreme in the classroom. To make matters worse, Jensen (1998) states, "At a typical school, nearly every decision, from length of time on learning to whom to work with, is dictated and managed outside student control" (p. 59). If these things are stressful for students who are neurotypical, how much more stressful are they for students with ASD who are regularly overwhelmed by environmental demands and constantly bombarded by information that they are unable to understand? Factor in the lack of control that comes with an inability to use language as a means of controlling the events and circumstances of their lives, and you have a recipe for disaster—fight, flight, or shutdown. Although these states of being are appropriate for survival, they are distinctly inappropriate for learning.

In discussing the effect of survival mode on learning, Jensen (1998) states, "Survival always overrides pattern-detection and complex problem-solving. Students are less able to understand connections or detect larger levels of organization. This fact has tremendous implications for learning. Learning narrows to the memorization of isolated facts" (p. 57). The deleterious effect on learning may be even more profound for students with ASD than it is for neurotypical students because the tasks that are most affected by stress are those that require an optimal learning stance. For example, pattern-detection and complex problem-solving are rooted in declarative knowledge, which is an area of known disability in students with ASD. Moreover, the memorization of isolated facts is a function of procedural knowledge, which is an area of known strength in ASD. The question that comes to mind is, Does excess stress in the school environment relegate students to a procedural level at the same time it prevents them from accessing the higher-order processes needed for more advanced learning tasks? More research is needed before this question can be answered.

STRATEGIES FOR STRESS REDUCTION AND MANAGEMENT

The first thing that needs to be said about stress reduction in ASD is that it requires caregivers to understand both the internal and external factors that predispose students to stress. The importance of this cannot be overstated, as such knowledge provides a roadmap for intervention. For example, if caregivers understand that students with autism find chaotic, unpredictable environments stressful, they will know to increase predictability and routine. Likewise, if they understand that because of their executive function deficits students with ASD are unable to hold things in working memory or to behave in an organized, goal-directed manner without external supports, they will know to provide the visual and organizational supports that these students need to be successful.

Furthermore, if caregivers understand that students with autism—particularly if they lack a conventional communication system—are likely to use idiosyncratic or aberrant behavior to express their wants and needs, they will be less apt to judge them as behaviorally disordered and more inclined to teach them alternative communicative behaviors. Correct responses can go a long way toward reducing the students' level of stress and anxiety.

There are also specific communication strategies that can help individuals with ASD cope with the stress that results from their pragmatic difficulties. For example, because these individuals are generally more adept at processing visual as opposed to auditory cues, manual signs can be used to aid verbal comprehension, thereby reducing the stress involved in having to rely solely on the auditory channel. The use of manual signs on a consistent basis can also enable individuals with ASD to use expressive language (Daniels, 2001), thereby reducing the stress of being unable to express simple needs and desires. Similarly, the use of pictures can facilitate comprehension and expression and thus minimize the stress associated with problems in these skill areas. Daniels (2001), recognizing the difficulty that children with autism have with the processing of verbal language, states, "Sign language, pictures, or pictographs illustrating the steps of a task are much easier for them to understand than words" (p. 97).

It is the primary responsibility of the caregiver to exercise constant vigilance regarding the potential sources and signs of stress so that they can take steps to mitigate the effects of stress or to provide appropriate coping strategies for dealing with them. For example, control factors can act as buffers to ameliorate the effects of environmental demands. In other words, giving an individual greater control over his or her life can go a long way toward mitigating the effects of stress. One simple way to do this is to offer the student more choices. Another is to provide more opportunities to refuse something when it is appropriate to do so.

It is unlikely that caregivers will be able to eliminate all of the sources of stress to which individuals with ASD are exposed. That being the case, attention should be given to stress management. There are many techniques for teaching children to cope with stress; however, the three techniques discussed below are uniquely appropriate to individuals with ASD.

The first of these techniques is physiological. According to Groden et al. (2001), "stress is the physiological reaction of the body to life situations" (p. 207), so anything geared toward helping the body regain a state of equilibrium would be an effective stress reduction or stress management strategy. The sensory diet is one such technique designed for this purpose (Wilbarger & Wilbarger, 1991). It consists of a program of planned sensory input and motor output individualized to the specific needs of the student. While the diet itself may be implemented by teachers, parents, and/or paraprofessionals, the actual selection of program components and the ongoing monitoring/adjusting of the program require the expertise of an occupational therapist. If these guidelines are met, the sensory diet can be an effective technique not only for stress management, but also for enabling the student with ASD to be more available for learning.

Social stories (Gray & White, 2002) provide an excellent technique for increasing social understanding in students with ASD. Using this technique can go a long way toward stress reduction and management, given that many stress reactions are the students' response to situations that they do not comprehend or that take them by surprise. Social stories can help prepare the individual with autism for what he or she can expect, thereby increasing both understanding and predictability. Anything that can be done to increase the individual's ability to understand and predict what the social world has in store will increase the comfort level of the student.

An even more powerful technique for stress reduction and management is that of cognitive picture rehearsal. This instructional strategy has its roots in learning theory, particularly that of "covert conditioning" (Groden et al., 2002). This type of conditioning holds that the same learning principles that apply to observable behaviors also apply to those that cannot be directly observed. According to Groden and LeVasseur (1995), "Cognitive picture rehearsal is an instructional strategy that uses repeated practice of sequence of behaviors by presenting the sequence to the child [or adult] in the form of pictures and an accompanying script. This procedure holds that pleasant events following a behavior increase the probability of that behavior occurring again" (p. 288).

Cognitive picture rehearsal is ideally suited to individuals with ASD, given their strengths in the visual domain. Picture rehearsal is also unique in its ability to help individuals learn new and more appropriate responses and, at the same time, reduce and manage stress.

SUMMARY

Stress and anxiety affect everyone. However, neurotypical people have more strategies at their disposal with which to deal with stress. In contrast, individuals with ASD are at a distinct disadvantage when it comes to dealing with stress and anxiety, given their physiologic makeup and the cognitive and social-cognitive factors that predispose them to stress and anxiety. In this chapter I have discussed how deficits in executive function, theory of mind, and information processing create a stressful internal environment that affects both the individual's understanding of and response to the world, and his or her ability to communicate in a manner that makes the control of one's life and circumstances possible. I have also considered the relationship between stress and such external factors as environmental demands, control issues, and educational setting. Finally, stress reduction and management strategies were presented that help make the world a more hospitable place for those with ASD.

References

Barkley, R. A. (1996). Linkages between attention and executive functions. In G. R. Lyon & N. A. Krasnegor (Eds.), *Attention, memory, and executive function* (pp. 307–325). Baltimore, MD: Paul H. Brookes.

Bartels, J. (n.d.). Stress control. From material first broadcast as a four-part series on *The Health Report* on ABC Radio National, November, 1998 Available: http://www.abc.net.au/science/slab/stress/control.htm [accessed March 8, 2004].

Baron-Cohen, S. (1988). Social and pragmatic deficits in autism: Cognitive or affective? *Journal of Autism and Developmental Disorders, 18,* 379–402.

Baron-Cohen, S. (1995). *Mindblindness: An essay on autism and theory of mind.* Cambridge, MA: MIT Press.

Borkowski, J. G., & Burke, J. E. (1996). Theories, models, and measurements of executive functioning: An information processing perspective. In G. R. Lyon & N. A. Krasnegor (Eds.), *Attention, memory, and executive function* (pp. 235–261). Baltimore, MD: Paul H. Brookes.

Carter, R. (1999). *Mapping the mind.* Berkeley, CA: University of California Press.

Daniels, M. (2001). *Dancing with words: Signing for hearing children's literacy.* Westport, CT: Bergin & Garvey.

Frith, U. (1989). *Autism: Explaining the enigma.* Oxford: Basil Blackwell.

Goldstein, G., Minshew, N. J., & Siegel, D. J. (1994). Age differences in academic achievement in high-functioning autistic individuals. *Journal of Clinical and Experimental Neuropsychology, 16,* 671–680.

Gray, C., & White, A. L. (2002). *My new social stories book.* New York: Jessica Kingsley.

Grice, H. P. (1975). Logic and conversation. In R. Cole & J. Morgan (Eds.), *Syntax and semantics: Speech acts.* New York: Academic Press.

Groden, J., & LeVasseur, P. (1995). Cognitive picture rehearsal: A system to teach self-control. In K.A. Quill (Ed.), *Teaching children with autism: Strategies to enhance communication and socialization* (pp. 287–306). Albany, NY: Delmar.

Groden, J., Diller, A., Bausman, M., Velicer, W., Norman, G., & Cautela, J. (2001). The development of a stress survey schedule for persons with autism and other developmental disabilities. *Journal of Autism and Developmental Disorders, 31,* 207–217.

Groden, J., LeVasseur, P., Diller, A., & Cautela, J. (2002). *Coping with stress through picture rehearsal: A how-to manual for working with individuals with autism and developmental disabilities.* Providence, RI: Groden Center.

Jensen, E. (1998). *Teaching with the brain in mind.* Alexandria, VA: Association for Supervision and Curriculum Development.

Maier, S., & Geer, J. (1968). Alleviation of learned helplessness in a dog. *Journal of Abnormal Psychology, 73,* 256–262.

Minshew, N. J., Goldstein, G., & Siegel, D. J. (1995). Speech and language in high-functioning autistic individuals. *Neuropsychology, 9,* 255–261.

Minshew, N. J., Goldstein, G., Taylor, H. G., & Siegel, D. J. (1994). Academic achievement in high-functioning autistic individuals. *Journal of Clinical and Experimental Neuropsychology, 16,* 261–270.

Peterson, C., Maier, S., & Seligman, M. (1993). *Learned helplessness.* New York: Oxford University Press.

Rousseau, J. J. (1963). *Emile.* London: J. M. Dent.

Selye, H. (1974). *Stress without distress.* Philadelphia: Lippincott.

Tager-Flusberg, H. (1997). Language acquisition and theory of mind: Contributions from the study of autism. In L. B. Adamson & M. A. Romski (Eds.), *Communication and language acquisition: Discoveries from atypical development* (pp. 135–160). Baltimore, MD: Paul H. Brookes.

Toffler, A. (1970). *Future shock.* New York: Random House.

Twachtman-Cullen, D. (2000a). *How to be a para pro: A comprehensive training manual for paraprofessionals.* Higganum, CT: Starfish Specialty Press.

Twachtman-Cullen, D. (2000b). More able children with autism spectrum disorders: Sociocommunicative challenges and guidelines for enhancing abilities. In A. M. Wetherby & B. M. Prizant (Eds.), *Autism spectrum disorders: A Transactional development perspective* (pp. 225–249). Baltimore, MD: Paul H. Brookes.

Twachtman-Cullen, D. (January-February, 2003). The effect of theory of mind deficits on communication and social behavior in individuals with ASD: An introduction. *Autism-Asperger Digest,* pp. 16–19.

Watzlawick, P., Beavin, J. H., & Jackson, D. D. (1967). *Pragmatics of human communication: A study of interactional patterns, pathologies, and paradoxes.* New York: W. W. Norton.

Welsh, M. C., & Pennington, B. F. (1988). Assessing frontal lobe functioning in children: Views from developmental psychology. *Developmental Neuropsychology, 4,* 199–230.

Wilbarger, P., & Wilbarger, J. (1991). *Sensory defensiveness in children aged 2–12: An intervention guide for parents and other caregivers.* Denver, CO: Avanti Educational Programs.

12 *Understanding the Role of Stress in Autism*
The Key to Teaching for Independence

Janice E. Janzen, M. Grace Baron,
and June Groden

> An autistic child can be helped only if a serious attempt is made to see the
> world from his point of view, so the adaptive function of much of his behavior
> can be understood in the context of his handicaps.
>
> —Lorna Wing

A person's perspective of the world depends on the way he or she processes information. This chapter affirms the wisdom of Lorna Wing's early call for taking the perspective of those whom we aim to teach. It also proposes that an understanding of the causes and the effects of stress can help teachers understand the perspective of those with autism spectrum disorders (ASD). And finally, it provides all those who teach and support persons with autism a foundation of practical strategies to decrease stress, maximize learning, and increase independence

When the perspective of those who have ASD is understood, it is possible to determine more accurately why they do the things they do and what is likely to help decrease their stress and allow them to focus and learn more effectively. Without that understanding, interventions will be based on misperceptions developed from experiences with typically developing peers. Interventions based on misperceptions are unproductive and will most likely increase stress and anxiety and decrease the ability to focus, learn, and function efficiently.

UNDERSTANDING PERSPECTIVE

Stress, anxiety, and panic are common for those with ASD (Attwood, 1998; Groden, Cautela, Prince, & Berryman, 1994; Groden et al., 2001; Hardy, 1985; Myles, Cook, Miller, Rinner, & Robbins, 2000), leading to an inability to focus on instruction, to learn, and to understand basic social interaction; problems with communication and problem-solving skills; and an increasing number and intensity of behavior problems. Klinger and Dawson (1992) frame these stressful responses as problems of arousal regulation. While novel stimuli provide rich stimulation and resulting learning opportunities for typical children, those with autism appear to have an unusually restricted range of optimal stimulation. They become easily overaroused and overwhelmed by novel and unpredictable stimuli, and, in turn, demonstrate a characteristic way of processing information, or cognitive learning style.

Individuals with ASD tend to process information in a wholistic or gestalt manner (Prizant, 1983). This contrasts with a more typical analytic style in which sensory information is taken in and sorted quickly to identify the critical information and block out or discard irrelevant, background details, or "noise." Then the bits and pieces of new information are integrated with bits and pieces of old information and filed away with a meaningful label. This analytic process provides the foundation for cause/effect learning. As one has more experiences with the same or similar situations, the earlier information can be recalled, reanalyzed, and modified. Analytic processors are automatically able to recall, analyze, integrate, modify, or expand their understanding of a situation to apply to other situations. In contrast, when wholistic or gestalt processors encounter something new, all the details of the situation are taken in as a chunk and stored quickly without analysis for meaning. This means that everything that occurs within the person's sensory range at the same time, or closely together in time, is likely to be firmly linked and recorded together like a snapshot or a videotape and stored in long-term memory—often without accurate meaning or a relevant label.

Bogdashina (2003) presents a fuller picture of this cognitive style in a recent integration of research and first-person reports of the sensory-perceptual experience of persons with autism: "Gestalt perception is often overwhelming and may lead to all sorts of distortions during the processing of information, such as fragmented perception, hypersensitivity, fluctuation between hypersensitivity and hyposensitivity, delayed processing, etc." (p. 48). For example, a snapshot of a situation in class could include the teacher, the notes on the board behind teacher, the clock over the teacher's head that reads 1:12, the flag beside the board, the teacher's red shirt, and the head of the person in the desk sitting in front. In addition, the chunk of information could include other sensory information that occurred at the same time—the sound of the car horn outside the window, the flickering lights overhead, the sound of the furnace fan, the smell of the bread baking in the cafeteria, the words of the teacher's lesson, the feel of their shirt's scratchy label, and every thing else that was happening at that time, all stored together without the ability to analyze it—with no distinction between relevant and irrelevant information.

Bogdashina (2003) further suggests that the "overflow of sensory information that cannot be filtered and/or processed simultaneously may cause distortions in perception" (p. 52). She outlines a number of compensatory behaviors such as shutting down all the sensory channels as self-protection, or closing down some channels, or "monoprocessing," to focus intently on the information being received by only one channel. Her analysis enriches our understanding of the difficulties those with ASD may have recalling and manipulating information flexibly, and learning the full meaning of the language, of concepts and rules, cause and effect, and problem-solving skills.

Table 12.1 details the learning and thinking difficulties associated with gestalt processing, as well as the positive effects associated with such a cognitive style. These attributes provide a broader base for understanding the perspective of individuals with autism and for selecting effective intervention strategies. Although these characteristics or effects are generally present in those with autism spectrum disorders, there will be considerable variation in the pattern and intensity of features displayed by any individual.

The Teacher's Role and Goal

To maximize learning, teachers, parents, and other mentors not only have to understand the individual's perspective; they must serve as interpreters. The interpreter's primary goal is to provide respectful and effective support that will enable those with ASD to achieve their highest potential and to live an independent and satisfying life as an adult. To accomplish this, a first task is to establish a comfortable and trusting relationship with the individual. The presence of a trusted friend and a social support network will help decrease the stress response and allow the individual to function more effectively (Sapolsky, 1994). A second task is to provide information and assistance to the learner in order to resolve problems that are triggered by stress. Only then will it be possible to teach new skills.

The interpreter's role is a collaborative one. Parents, teachers, and all other mentors involved with the individual who has ASD must share information and solve problems together. Collaboration brings together information from all settings to facilitate problem solving, to identify the functions of a problem behavior, and to develop effective support systems that will match the need in all settings, thus reducing stress and confusion.

Finally, the interpreter must distinguish between providing support to prevent or resolve problems and overprotection. Overprotection is unproductive even when based on kind and well-meaning motives. Those who are overprotected and shielded from the realities of the world are not likely to learn how to deal independently with stress, to solve problems, or to become more competent in the world. Those who are guided and supported to learn the skills to solve their own problems will become more independent and live a more satisfying life.

To form authentic relationships, provide supports and teach effectively, interpreters not only have to understand the unique processing style common to

Table 12.1. Characteristics of gestalt processing

Processing strengths or attributes can include the ability to:

- Process visual information quickly and meaningfully
- Take in chunks of information quickly (one-trial learning)
- Learn long routines quickly, exactly as taught
- Remember and recall concrete information for a long time
- Understand and use concrete, context-free information and rules
- Concentrate intently on topics of specific interest

Processing difficulties or deficits can include problems with:

- Scanning to select and focus on relevant information
- Modulating sensory input
- Screening out irrelevant background information
- Interpreting language and rules literally and inflexibly
- Retrieving information in the appropriate sequence in order to
  - Learn cause/effect relationships
  - Predict future events from past experiences
- Adapting to new and novel information
- Processing auditory information
- Attaching accurate meaning to sights and sounds
- Understanding the perspective of others
- Understanding the subtleties of social, cultural, and language rules
- Perceiving time and time concepts accurately

Predictable traits or characteristics can include:

- High anxiety and stress that can accelerate quickly
- Variable performance with an ability to do things one day but not another
- Naïve, guileless and, vulnerable to bullying
- Inability to understand social rules; awkward or inappropriate in social situations
- Honest and not adept at deceiving; generally do not try to impress others
- Inability to defend or explain themselves; rarely blame others
- Tendency to be perfectionists
- Tendency to be compliant and even overly compliant when they understand exactly what to do

---

those with autism. They must also build knowledge and skills in three key areas: (1) the relationship of stress to problem behaviors, (2) strategies to reduce stress, and (3) strategies to provide instruction to maximize independence.

RELATIONSHIP OF STRESS TO PROBLEM BEHAVIORS

Behavioral analysis has evolved over the years to include an appreciation of the function and meaning, or "communicative intent," of problem behavior (Groden et al., 2001; Groden, Stevenson, Groden, 1993; LaVigna & Donnellan, 1986; Meyer & Evans, 1989; O'Neill, Horner, Albin, Storey, & Sprague, 1990). Behavior can serve a number of different functions that must be identified in order to develop effective interventions. A comprehensive functional analysis provides the information needed to understand the meaning or purpose of challenging behaviors, including those that appear to be reflexive and unintentional. Four concepts can guide and expand the search for the function or meaning of the challenging behaviors of autism (Janzen, 2003).

1. *Behavior is communication.* A behavior can be a logical response to the current situation or an effort to regulate conditions that do not match the need. For example, one boy with autism worked diligently for some time. Once tired, he was not able to communicate conventionally his desire to quit. Instead, he yawned and stretched, then pushed the work material away. When his teacher failed to identify this behavior as a signal of fatigue and continued to make demands, the boy fell to the floor screaming.

2. *Behavior can be a logical response to the environment in which it was first learned.* If the history of the behavior is lost, it will be difficult to determine the exact meaning or need and to determine an effective intervention. For example, one young man without a system for communication would run from one side of the room to another and bang against the windows. After many behavior programs failed to stop this potentially dangerous behavior, a functional assessment of the problem revealed that this behavior occurred when he was bored. This had begun after he attended an ice hockey game when he was a boy and appeared to be an attempt to entertain himself. With this information, his interpreter added more physical activities to his daily calendar and taught him where and when it was safe to play hockey.

3. *Behavior can be an attempt of the brain to keep itself stimulated or in equilibrium.* For example, repetitive stereotypic behaviors can serve as a release of tension. Observations have shown that these behaviors are used most often when bored, tired, anxious, overwhelmed by sensory stimulation, excited, and frustrated. One young man who had been taught to keep his hands down said, "When I look the most relaxed, I am the most tense and upset" (Cesaroni & Garber, 1991).

4. *Behavior can be an outward expression of an inward state.* Worries, fears, fatigue, and anxiety also have a significant effect on tolerance and control. Many self-injurious behaviors may be first triggered by physical pain (Groden et al., 1994; Marsella & Marsella, 1991). For example, one girl began hitting her face and jamming her fist in her mouth. It was ultimately determined that she had an infected tooth. After treatment, she no longer hit her face.

Such challenging behavior can be seen as a response to stressors from one's external or internal environment. People with ASD are often overwhelmed by the abundance of sensory "noise" in the world, have difficulty making sense of the environment, have difficulty identifying and finding solutions to their problems, and they are often unable to ask for assistance when needed—a prime situation for increased stress. Other chapters in this volume elaborate a stress perspective for understanding and treating the problems of autism. The remainder of this chapter provides strategies to help those with ASD maintain that optimum level of stress needed to support learning and increase independence. Janzen (1999, 2003) elaborates the key concepts of this chapter and provides reproducible forms and detailed examples and applications of a number of assessment and teaching strategies outlined below.

Identifying Stressors

The process for identifying stressors begins with understanding the learner's unique sensory, spatial, and motor functioning; physical problems; information processing differences; and the ability to understand symbols and to communicate effectively.

Various instruments can help identify stressors for an individual with autism (Bramston & Bostock, 1994; Bramston & Fogarty, 1995; Groden et al., 2001; Janzen, 2003). The most valuable information is obtained when all the people involved with the individual can collaborate and share information from various situations and settings as they complete these assessments. Stressors that are typical for students with autism include sensory-perceptual, cognitive, or social events such as:

1. *Physical problems.* The pain and discomfort that accompany many illnesses increase stress, which is often expressed behaviorally. Self-injury, head-banging, or slapping various parts of the body are often the first signs of headaches, sinus infections, allergies, earaches, and other physical problems.
2. *Sensory overload.* This can include noise and confusion, flickering lights, texture of clothing, crowding and movement during transitions, odors, and other distractions, including sounds of a distant train, traffic in the street outside, and people talking in the hall.
3. *A missing bit of critical information.* A student may misunderstand or misinterpret something or be unable to ask for clarification in response to questions such as, who, what, where, when, how, and what then.
4. *People.* The normal behavior of other people lead to a level of stimulation that overwhelms those with ASD. Direct eye contact is extremely stressful, even painful for some. In typical social exchanges, people talk at the same time, use too many words, have shrill voices, laugh, get too close, make demands, have odors, and so on.
5. *Changes.* It is often stressful when something is new or changed, or when something familiar is missing. For example, one young student fell apart and did not know what to do when he arrived at school and the principal was not in his familiar place to greet him. When another young man arrives home each day, he circles the house to line everything up in its familiar place. Only then can he relax.
6. *Interruptions and transitions.* Unexpected interruptions in the middle of a familiar routine or activity can be stressful, as can the increasing noise, confusing movement, and unpredictable situations that occur during transitions.

7. *Boredom and waiting.* Problems often occur when those with ASD do not know what to do while waiting, do not know how long they will need to wait, do not know where to wait, or do not know what will happen next.

Identifying Behavioral Signals of Stress

Intense and severe behavior problems generally begin with small, subtle behavioral signals that indicate confusion, anxiety, or fatigue. For example, subtle signals might include a frown, a stretch, or a yawn. These precursors may lead to other signs of resistance including stereotypic behavior, disorganized behavior, general apathy or "freezing," self-injury, emotional outbursts, or leaving the situation. Students with autism have few adaptive alternatives for communicating about or resolving their stressful situations.

Individual students often exhibit a fairly consistent sequence of observable behavior in response to stress; some escalate slowly through several levels of intensity, but others can escalate quickly to a crisis level. For example, when one student begins to get tired during a one-on-one session, he places his hand lightly over the teacher's. If she does not recognize and interpret this subtle signal correctly and continues making demands, his hand drops down and he lightly pinches her hand. If that signal is ignored, his behavior escalates to screaming and falling to the floor. Another student misinterpreted his teacher's comment and thought he would not see his favorite movie as promised. He quickly stood up and placed his hands around his teacher's throat. Because the teacher knew him very well, she understood his confusion and quietly said, "Finish your math, and then you can see the movie." He quickly sat down and returned to work.

Identifying the Phases of the Stress Response

All people respond to life's inevitable stressors with a predictable ebb and flow of stressful and calmer periods throughout the day and over the years. The same holds true for people with autism. Although certain individuals, including persons with autism, may have an exaggerated, more immediate, or more intense response to stressors, it is likely that the phasic nature of the stress response is the same for all people. Figure 12.1 illustrates a proposed general four-level response to any stressful incident.

The subtle behavioral signals of the escalation level increase in intensity as stress increases. At the peak of intensity, or crisis level, we see reflexive, panic-like responses with potentially dangerous behavior. In the deescalation phase, the stress level drops below the line of equilibrium, and the person shows little energy, motivation, or ability to focus until after a certain period of rest or recovery. This is a period when the individual is vulnerable, when any seemingly minor demand can trigger a return to the crisis level. Finally, in a period of equilibrium, an optimum range of tolerable stress allows the individual to be at ease

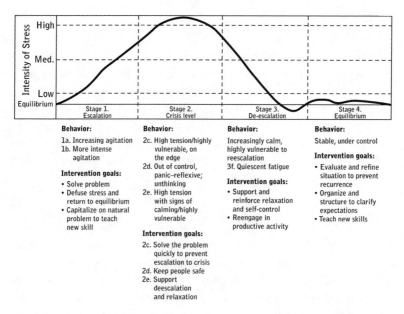

	Stage 1. Escalation	Stage 2. Crisis level	Stage 3. De-escalation	Stage 4. Equilibrium
Behavior:	1a. Increasing agitation 1b. More intense agitation	2c. High tension/highly vulnerable, on the edge 2d. Out of control, panic–reflexive; unthinking 2e. High tension with signs of calming/highly vulnerable	Increasingly calm, highly vulnerable to reescalation 3f. Quiescent fatigue	Stable, under control
Intervention goals:	• Solve problem • Defuse stress and return to equilibrium • Capitalize on natural problem to teach new skill	**Intervention goals:** 2c. Solve the problem quickly to prevent escalation to crisis 2d. Keep people safe 2e. Support deescalation and relaxation	**Intervention goals:** • Support and reinforce relaxation and self-control • Reengage in productive activity	**Intervention goals:** • Evaluate and refine situation to prevent recurrence • Organize and structure to clarify expectations • Teach new skills

Figure 12.1. Profile of stress: basis for matching interventions to needs.
(© 1996 by Marvin M. Janzen and Janice E. Janzen, Trustees of the Marvin M. and Janice E. Janzen Family Trust. Reproduced with permission of Harcourt Assessment, Inc. All rights reserved.)

and to focus on instruction. As noted earlier, the range of equilibrium may be generally very narrow for people with autism.

Interpreters who know the individual well and who are alert can identify the earliest behavioral signals of stress, identify the reason for the stress, and can then intervene and provide the appropriate support before the stress escalates to the crises point, thus facilitating a more rapid return to the stage of equilibrium—that optimum level of stress when the individual can focus on productive activity. However, this is not all that the interpreter needs to do. If nothing more is done, the situation will recur over and over again, and the individual with autism will never learn to become independent in managing stress. When the learner is at the equilibrium, the interpreter can reorganize and clarify the stressful situation and teach skills to maximize self-control (e.g., communication, relaxation response, problem-solving skills).

Lack of awareness of the impact of stress and the phases in responding to stress results in unnecessary and often dangerous delays in learning and a waste of critical teaching time. The remainder of this chapter details the interpreter's key strategies and tasks for optimal teaching and learning and provides intervention strategies that will reduce the impact of stress in the lives of students with autism.

STRATEGIES TO REDUCE STRESS

Once interpreters have developed a supportive relationship with an individual who has ASD and have learned to identify the his or her behavioral signals of stress, they must decide how to intervene. The intervention and instructional process is guided by an awareness of the four stages of a stress response and involves three dynamic and interrelated tasks: evaluate and refine (stage 1), organize and structure (stage 2), and teach new skills (stage 3). Both cognitive and behavioral strategies are integrated and used during each of these three tasks to maximize learning.

Task 1. Evaluate and Refine

At the first sign of a stress response, the interpreter's role is a reactive one, thinking and acting quickly to identify the situational trigger as well as the specific phase of the learner's stress response. The interpreter then selects the intervention priority, either priority 1 (to prevent a crisis), priority 2 (to maintain the flow of the activity), or priority 3 (to capitalize on a natural opportunity to strengthen skills).

Priority 1. Prevent a Crisis

If stress is escalating to the stage 2 level, the first priority is to prevent a behavioral crisis using the following sequence of strategies. First, reduce demands and pressures quickly. Do not get closer or make demands for eye contact, do not demand an explanation, an apology, or choice, and do not threaten (e.g., "If you don't stop screaming, you can't have recess!"). Do not grab, hold, or crowd the student. Do remain calm; model calm breathing; move slowly and use a quiet voice.

Second, ignore the behavior but acknowledge the message. Avoid labeling the behavior (by saying, "Don't. . . .") because even hearing about the behavior can increase stress. Identifying the behavior is not productive; it doesn't tell the student what to do, and the negative attention can serve to strengthen the behavior. Instead, use a reflective listening strategy to acknowledge the message in the learner's behavior; for example, "Are you tired and want to quit work?" or "I'll help you, then you can take a break." This valuable strategy informs the individual that his or her unspoken message was heard. This reflective listening strategy supports relaxation and helps focus attention on the interpreter's words. (See *Strategies for Giving Verbal Information* later in this chapter for more details on the use of the reflective listening strategy.)

Finally, tell the learner what to do right now to help reduce the stressfulness of the situation. Keep the instructions simple, using as few words as possible, such as, "Put your hands in your pockets," or "Go to your quiet place." Visual cues (e.g., cards, line drawings) can also clarify what the student should do. It is important to reinforce any small signs of self-control. For example, even if the individual only stops screaming to take a breath, say softly and without touching, "Good. You took a deep breath. You can relax."

Priority 2. Maintain the Flow of the Activity

If the student's stress response is at a low or moderate level and not approaching the crisis level, a teacher should aim to maintain the flow of the activity. For example, if a learner makes an incorrect response in an instructional routine and appears somewhat agitated but not at a crisis point, a teacher can repair the situation immediately by either refining the instructional sequence or delaying the instruction until a period of equilibrium returns. Or, when a problem occurs during the initial instruction of a new skill or routine (when errors should be avoided), a quick refinement of the instructional sequence can prevent further errors. Such refinements may include inserting a more effective prompt (e.g., a cue card, a point, touch to direct attention) or altering the arrangement of materials. However, if refinement of the task is impractical or may publicly embarrass the student, ignore the behavior, acknowledge the problem, and provide direction and/or assistance to solve the problem quickly. Later, clarify the directions and reteach the task before reengaging in the activity.

Priority 3. Capitalize on the Natural Problem to Strengthen New Skills

A low or moderate stress level and the right situation can provide a "teachable moment" for learning or strengthening a new skill. General strategies for this procedure includes acknowledging the problem, cueing the use of the new skill to resolve the problem, and quietly highlighting the solution, the effort, and the accomplishment. This strategy encourages the student's active involvement to solve the problem and gives access to natural reinforcement to maintain the learning. For example, one child screamed while pulling on the doorknob. Dad quickly held out the child's picture communication board and said, "Want to go outside?" as he helped the child point to the correct picture. While opening the door, he said, "Oh, you want to go outside, I'll open the door for you."

Task 2. Organize and Structure

An interpreter who is aware of the impact of stressors in a learning environment can, by careful organization, create an environment that maintains a state of equilibrium. An organized, distraction-free, and predictable environment contributes to effective teaching and learning (Dawson & Osterling, 1997) and can compensate for the information processing differences of students with autism.

A teacher can organize and structure space, time, events, as well as verbal directions and instruction to highlight relevant information to visually clarify exactly what to do, where to do it, when to start, how to do it, what to do next, what does it look like when it is finished, and so on. This process not only reduces stress, but it also leads to more efficient learning and to independence. A number of organizational strategies help the interpreter create a physical and social environment that facilitates learning, and accommodates the gestalt processing style of students with autism.

Organize Physical Space

An organized physical environment can reduce the perceptual and motor problems of students with autism. An organized environment can communicate expectations, reduce sensory overload, and provide a safe and secure learning environment. Table 12.2 summarizes strategies for organizing a student's physical space.

An interpreter can reduce environmental stressors by creating a setting that provides information to a learner about basic questions such as, "Where am I supposed to be? Where can I find the . . . ? Where do I start? Where do I finish?" For example, a student who regularly runs out of his classroom, can be taught to respond to a STOP sign at the exit of the area and return to his seat. Similarly, simple accommodations in a learning setting can make it possible to respond with self-control to a potentially disruptive stressor. For example, a student can learn to put in earplugs whenever she hears painful sounds (e.g., a train approaching). Also, for people with autism, strong interests and unexpected abilities paired with the inability to understand cause–effect relationships can lead to dangerous situations. It is critical to identify and address potential safety issues in the physical environment. Furthermore, special supervision may also be needed to manage emergencies in every setting. For example, if an individual hides to protect himself from the noise of fire alarms or the confusion of an unexpected change, it must be clear who is responsible for getting him to safety in an emergency.

Organize Events in Time

The ability to predict and prepare for events and to plan and anticipate pleasant future events helps people deal with unpleasant or frustrating situations. In fact, Sapolsky (1994) reports that unpredictability is a major cause of stress. Persons with autism often have difficulty predicting future events, so they may neither anticipate pleasurable events nor prepare themselves for changes. Also, those with autism generally have little control of their lives and are often taken into new or stressful settings and situations with little or no preparation. Should they resist or try to avoid the confusion and stress present in these unfamiliar situ-

Table 12.2. Organizing the physical environment to reduce stress and maximize learning

Objective	Strategies	Examples
Clarify the environment	Highlight the boundaries of specific areas to keep the walkways clear	• Arrange furniture and rugs to mark walkways • Use tape markers on floor •˙Use twine, yarn, a thin rope, crepe paper strips, or signs to highlight entry and exit
	Highlight the location of events and materials	• Label work or play areas • Place labels (or pictures) on shelves and containers to highlight where things belong • Use clear containers so the contents are in view
	Highlight and provide instruction to identify and use the signs and markers that are naturally available in the evironment:	• In the gym, banks, post office, checkout stands, stop lights, and other barriers, such as sidewalks and low fences
Reduce sensory overload	Assess the individual's sensitivities and the sensory demad of the environment	• Teach to wear ear plugs, hats with visors, pull down window shades, etc., to block irritating sounds, glaring or flickering lights.
	Provide organized and structured areas that are free of distractions.	• Provide separate areas for instruction in new skills, and personal area for work and/or "calming"
Increase safety and security	Do safety check	• Store dangerous chemicals securely
	Assign special supervision to manage emergencies	• Special safety covers for fans, windows, and locks.

ations, their freedom and options become even more limited. To protect themselves from these highly stressful situations, they may develop rigid, inflexible routines and become even more isolated. Without intervention, any unexpected change will trigger a stress response that can lead to severe behavioral outbursts. One solution is a carefully designed schedule and a simple but clearly organized calendar to clarify expectations and provide predictability.

An individualized calendar system is a critical element of any positive behavioral support aimed at decreasing stress-related behavior problems. When the individual with autism reviews this specialized calendar consistently each morning and references it throughout the day, and when the calendar is flexible to match changing situations, it provides a natural teaching structure for other central goals for an educational plan (Janzen, 2003). These include the practice of language (i.e., concepts related to time, space, events, settings) and skills for communicating preferences and decisions; increased opportunity for active and independent learning without artificial reinforcers; and opportunity to teach flexibility and tolerance for new and changing events. Organizing events in time requires that a teacher develop an individualized reinforcing schedule, develop a calendar system to support and communicate that schedule, and provide other supportive systems to clarify time and events.

Develop an Inherently Motivating Schedule   This scheduling process is based on two basic behavioral principles:

1. If a reinforcing event occurs immediately as a direct result of effort and action, it is more likely that the same effort and action will be repeated and strengthened (Skinner, 1953).
2. If a preferred activity immediately follows a less preferred activity, it is likely that the less preferred activity will increase its value and become a more preferred activity—a new reinforcing event (Premack & Collier, 1962).

However, the opposite is also true. If a less-preferred or disliked activity consistently follows a liked activity, the liked activity can become less-preferred and even disliked. Therefore, liked and disliked activities cannot simply be alternated; rather, familiar and tolerated activities are used as buffers, as illustrated in table 12.3.

The process for developing an effective schedule begins with an assessment to identify the individual's liked, tolerated, and disliked activities, people, and locations or settings. People with ASD often have very different preferences than their peers, and often they have very few liked activities. Teachers, parents and other interpreters can share information from all settings and together modify or make adaptations to ensure that naturally reinforcing activities are available at the critical times.

Once the assessment is complete, a schedule can be developed that will provide motivation with natural activities. Table 12.4 outlines some of the basic principles for organizing the events to match each individual's needs.

Develop the Calendar Systems   An effectively designed calendar is easily accessible and interests and motivates the student to use it independently. Individualized decisions must be made regarding which type of symbol best represents events and what type of calendar format is most understandable and easiest to manage.

On one hand, if the symbols are too simple, a student will not be motivated to attend to them. On the other hand, if the symbols are too abstract, the student

Table 12.3. Formula for sequencing events in time to capitalize on the reinforcing qualities of the activities

---

Activity 1: Moderately liked activity—a pleasant beginning

Activity 2: Familiar and tolerated activity

Activity 3: Most disliked activity (perhaps a new skill or a hard task)

Activity 4: Most liked activity

Activity 5: Familiar or tolerated activity

Activity 6: Another familiar or tolerated activity

Activity 7: Another disliked activity

Activity 8: A different highly liked activity

Activity 9: Familiar or tolerated activity

    (Continue to rotate as above)

Final Activity: Pleasant and liked activity—a positive ending

---

will not attach the correct meaning to the symbols. For example, a 3-year-old with ASD may be interested in the printed words and be able to read, yet a 10-year-old with some speech, who is quite competent in a number of areas, may still require pictures or object symbols.

A tendency to interpret information literally and concretely complicates the process of symbol selection, especially if the symbol already has a specific meaning. For example, if a ball is used to represent a PE class, the individual may believe that he will only play ball in the PE class and may become very upset if told to put the ball down to run a race. For another individual the use of a picture of a coat to symbolize recess time led to an expectation that she must always wear a coat before going to recess. On hot spring days when her coat was left at home, she refused to go outside because she felt she must always have a coat to go outside.

Similarly, individuals with autism may be unable to sort and select the relevant information from the irrelevant and focus on some insignificant detail of the symbol. For example, one student was given a photo of his backpack. When asked what was in the picture, he replied, "Telephone." Indeed, the background of the picture showed his sister talking on the phone. In another situation, when Greg's teacher held up a picture of the school bus and said, "What is this?" he quickly replied, "Number 56." He was correct, for the picture from a commercial set had a tiny #56 in the upper corner. Greg had a passion for numbers and was so focused on the numbers that he simply could not see the picture. Later when it was time to go home, he was shown a black and white line drawing of a bus with no distracting elements and was told, "This is a picture of the school bus.

Table 12.4. Principles for organizing events in time to achieve maximum benefit

Principles	Strategy	Examples
Schedules must be flexible.	Tailor the amount of time spent in each activity depending on the individual's age, tolerance, attention span, and whether the activity is liked or disliked (familiar or new).	• Time spent on a liked activity should be longer than the time spent on a difficult/disliked activity. • A disliked or hard activity should end at the peak of performance before stress escalates and inappropriate behaviors accelerate. Ending at the peak of performance rewards hard work rather than inappropriate behavior. • Decrease time demands when tolerance is low and the stress level begins to escalate, thus avoiding a crises. Use reflective listening strategies and contingencies (see table 12.6). • Provide a concrete way to clarify how much work must be done
Schedules need variety to increase motivation and flexibility.	Use variety to increase motivation and flexibility and to emphasize the importance of checking the schedules. If the schedule remains the same from day to day, the routine is memorized and the calendar is no longer important.	• Change one or more elements of the schedule each day, a different activity, time sequence, location, or a different interpreter.
Schedules must be balanced daily to include activities with differing requirements.	Increase motivation and ensure that reinforcing activities are scheduled appropriately.	• Balance the type of activities and the new/hard/disliked activities must be balanced with the liked and familiar activities as per the formula in table 12.3.
	Ensure that the student has opportunities to learn a broad range of skills in a broad range of settings.	• Include fine motor/gross motor, quiet/noisy, 1:1/independent/plus cooperative activities, as well as in small and large group sizes, and in various settings.

It means it's time to go home." He immediately attached the correct meaning to the picture. Because persons with autism can often take in, learn, and remember chunks of concrete information quickly (Prizant, 1983), the symbols used should be simple, clear, and free of extraneous details. Generic, black-and-white line drawings have many advantages for those with autism. If designed simply, black-and-white line drawings are free of irrelevant elements that interfere with accurate associations and generalizations (Groden & LeVasseur, 1995). Some learners can begin with real objects to represent an activity, then transition rather quickly through a sequence from generic black and white line drawings, to line drawings labeled with the printed word, and finally on to the printed word alone. Other students need not progress through the various levels of symbol types and are able to begin with written word symbols.

Considerations for overall calendar design are similar to those for determining the type of symbols to use. The calendar should be free of decorative or extraneous details. The calendar should also be simple and easy to adapt since, ideally, it will need frequent alterations to match the student's increasing skill and changing needs. If the student is to benefit from the calendar system, it must be used. It will only be used if it is understandable, if it is in an easily accessible location, or if it is easy to carry around.

Provide Other Visual Systems to Clarify Time and Events   The individually designed calendar clarifies the sequence of events that will occur during a day, but it does not specifically clarify the parts or steps of each event in a way to answer the students' unspoken questions, such as "Where? What supplies will I need? How much do I do? How will I know when I am finished? Where do I start?" These questions can be answered by incorporating mini-calendars, checklists, cue cards, transition cues, or semantic maps to provide the visual structure to support self-monitoring and greater independence. Any successful calendar system must be supported by some or all of these supplemental systems to accommodate the differing needs of each student.

In summary, this process of organizing and visually structuring the schedule of events in time is very efficient because it increases predictability, reduces stress, and provides a format for teaching many lessons and skills at the same time. This process also provides opportunities to make choices, solve problems, and move independently throughout the day, increasing teaching and learning time. However, the optimum affect can only be achieved when the schedule is flexible, has variety, is visually represented in a calendar that can be easily referred to throughout the day, is supported with other visuals, and is continuously evaluated and refined to meet the individual's changing needs.

The individually developed schedule that is visualized on a simple calendar is perhaps the most valuable positive behavior support tool. The long-term goal of this process is for those with ASD to independently manage their own time and to use standard calendars and appointment books as adults. Hodgdon (1995,

1999) and Janzen (2003) provide more in-depth information for teaching and solving problems related to the use of schedules, calendars, and other visual systems.

Organize and Structure Verbal Information

It is generally accepted that most students with autism who can hear have very good, perhaps even excellent, rote memory abilities—that is, the ability to receive or take in and store verbal information quickly. However, certain auditory processing deficits result in a number of learning and behavioral problems. Because people with ASD do not provide consistent and easily understood feedback, they receive less verbal input and have fewer opportunities to learn the language and to communicate. To reverse this cycle, students need access to verbal information in a form they can understand. Hearing the language in natural contexts is a prerequisite for understanding and using the language for speaking, reading, and writing. However, it is not enough for interpreters to simply spend more time talking to these individuals. The critical element is to know when to talk and how to talk. The following guidelines and strategies for organizing and structuring verbal information address three verbal procedures for clarifying information and to reduce stress: (1) parallel talking, (2) reflective listening, and (3) using contingencies. These procedures will increase the ability to understanding the language, reduce stress, and increase motivation.

Strategies for Giving Verbal Information   In essence, one talks to those with ASD at the same times and for the same reasons one talks with those who do not have ASD. However, because of their extreme sensory sensitivity, unique cognitive style, and extreme literalness, people with ASD require more concise information given in such a way as to avoid confusion and increasing stress. For example, requiring eye contact during interactions or instruction is painful, distracting, and stressful for some; therefore, eye contact should not be required simply for compliance. To guide their attention to the material or object under discussion, calmly and quietly say the individual's name, touch their shoulder, use pauses, small gestures, or tapping prompts to direct their attention. The student may demonstrate attention by a peripheral or a fleeting glance or by pausing or quieting down as if listening.

Verbal directions must be clear, specific, literal, and concise. For example, while handing a book to the individual, instead of saying, "Put it over there," point to the blue table and say, "Put this book on the blue table." Leave out extraneous words and phrases such as polite forms (i.e., "Are you ready to work now?" or, "Would you like to . . . ?") The individual must be specifically told what to do, rather than telling them what not to do. For example, a negative statement such as, "If you don't do . . . , you can't play outside," will confuse the literal student who is likely to only hear the end and believe he will never be able to go outside again. Contingency statements must be stated positively to clarify the work required in order to receive the reinforcer.

Students with ASD often need extra time to process verbal directions and commands in order to generate and produce an appropriate response. Repeating requests too fast or talking louder will add to the confusion-triggering stress responses. Therefore, give directions or state requests with a calm voice and pause for at least 30 seconds before repeating or rephrasing the direction. It is generally more helpful to clarify directions with visual cues such as pictures.

When teaching a skill or routine that will ultimately be an independent activity, pair a verbal description of the materials and the steps of the routine with the actions. For students with autism, verbal prompts, cues, and even simple conversations may not only distract the learner from the natural or adapted visual cues, but may also become firmly embedded into what should be an independent activity. To avoid this, the instructor should first highlight the visual prompts and then systematically fade from the routine. These strategies and suggestions are summarized in table 12.5.

Three verbal strategies, parallel talking, reflective listening, and contingencies, not only teach the meaning of the language, but they also clarify information to reduce stress. Parallel talking is a process for matching language to action; that is, it is a way to provide literal, clear, and descriptive language to clarify ongoing actions. This process provides a powerful opportunity for those with ASD to hear and relate the language to the natural context to facilitate language learning and use. Reflective listening matches language to emotions and is used when a person has a problem and anxiety begins to escalate. This strategy identifies and clarifies the problem, expresses concern, and establishes a mutually respectful relationship, thus defusing the stress and anxiety. A contingency is a contract that specifies and clarifies expectation; it defines the work to be performed and the payoff. When used appropriately, a contingency provides a structure for understanding the language, teaching sequencing, and cause—effect relationships. Contingencies increase motivation and provide a means to predict and prepare for coming events thus reducing stress and problem behaviors. The strategies for using these procedures are outlined in table 12.6.

Those with ASD are generally very compliant if they truly understand what it is they are to do. Therefore, if a direction is not followed, it is possible that some small detail of the direction is not clearly structured for understanding. Interpreters must be prepared to teach and highlight the meaning of the direction, both visually and verbally. Then they must be prepared to provide the assistance to carry it out quickly and ensure that the correct response is firmly associated with the direction.

In summary, an organized physical and social learning environment adds visual clarity to space, time, events, and verbal information to answer those critical

Table 12.5. When to talk, when to stop talking, and how to talk

When to talk	When stress is at a low to moderate level during stages 1 and 4
	• To provide information to solve problems and defuse stress.
	• During social interactions, to have fun and share experiences.
	• When introducing new objects, information or a skill.
	• At the beginning and the end of each day—to review the schedule of events for the day, to review the day and prepare for the next day.
	• When providing positive feedback.
When to stop talking	When stress is escalating near the stage 2 level and until stress decreases in stage 3.
	• After the introduction of a new skill or routine—nonverbal cues and prompts should be incorporated to support independence.
	• After asking a question or giving a direction that requires a verbal or motor response, pause to give processing time before repeating.
How to talk effectively	Speak calmly, softly, and clearly to accommodate auditory sensitivity.
	• Use accurate and precise language to prevent confusion.
	• Use normal tone, rate, and expression (i.e., no baby talk).
	• Express a complete thought.
	• Give directions clearly, literally, and concisely.
	• Leave out extraneous words (e.g., polite forms, sarcasm).
	• Ask questions only if there are real choices and options.
	• Clarify the words with visual supports and references (e.g., cue cards, lists, picture sequences).

questions, "What? When? Where? How? How long? What's next?" Those with ASD can learn to understand the verbal world if care is taken to match words to their immediate needs, level of stress, their feelings, and action, especially when clarifying the words with visual systems. These visual support systems may never be totally withdrawn; rather, they are modified and adapted to meet changing needs. The goal is to ensure that those with ASD, just like everyone else, will be able to use these visual systems (e.g., lists, charts, calendars, and appointment books) to navigate and adapt in confusing and busy world throughout their lifetime.

Task 3. Teach New Skills

The third major task for preventing stress-related problems is to teach new skills. In addition to functional academic skills, interpreters must also develop and expand competence and independence by teaching relaxation and self-monitoring skills, functional communication skills, problem-solving skills, choice-making

Table 12.6. Three valuable verbal strategies: parallel talking, reflective listening, and contingencies

Strategy	Directions for use
Parallel talking	
A receptive language strategy that provides clear, literal, and descriptive language to clarify natural, ongoing actions, events, and emotions to facilitate language learning and use.	• Used during the natural daily routines that directly involves the student, such as, eating, dressing, riding in the car, or playing with an object. • Label the people, objects, actions, events, and emotions as they occur, much as a sportscaster describes a game so clearly that a listener knows exactly what is happening. • Use gestures to direct attention and clarify the meaning. • Make no demands, ask for no responses—this is relaxed, receptive language process. • Pause or break the stream of talk before giving a direction or asking a question to give learner time to shift attention.
Reflective listening	In stage 1 when anxiety begins to escalate, recognize the earliest behavioral signals of stress.
Matches language to emotions and problems and to a solution.	• Quickly scan the environment for cues to identify the cause of the problem. • Tentatively verbalize the feeling and the problem (i.e., "You look worried, are you afraid that . . . ").
Expresses concern and recognizes that a problem exists.	• Pause for some kind of subtle acknowledgement, such as quick eye contact, relaxing shoulders, moving closer, or very quiet as if listening.
Defuses stress and sets the stage for solving the problem.	• Suggest a way to resolve the problem and provide assistance. • If the cause cannot be identified, or if it is a problem with no available solution, the following kinds of statements can help: "I understand that you want to see your mother right now, but she is away. She will be here on Sunday." Take the student to the calendar and circle the date. "Right now, you can jump on the trampoline until the timer goes off and it will be time for . . . " (Provide assistance to check off each passing day.) "I'm sorry, I cannot understand what you need. You can get a drink and sit in your rocking chair now. When the timer goes off we will try again (or, it will be time to . . .)"

Table 12.6. (continued)

Strategy	Directions for use
Contingency statements	Contingencies are useful at stages 1 and 4, and if used with caution, they may be used in stages 2 and 3.
Provide a structure for decreasing stress and problem behaviors while achieving a number of critical goals	• The daily schedule with reinforcing activities arranged throughout the day is the foundation for using contingencies.
Teaches cause/effect relationships	• State contingencies positively, the work first and then the payoff, for example: "As soon as you do . . . , you can . . . ," or, "Do 2 more . . . then it will be time to . . ." Negatively stated contingencies increase stress.
Increases motivation to work, to try and to persist	• State a contingency at the peak of performance to reward working and persistence. Otherwise, it becomes a bribe that rewards inappropriate behavior. • The payoff must be truely valued and must be delivered as stated.
Prepares for transitions and increases flexibility	• Contiongencies can be renegotiated to accommodate a student's changing tolerance levels (i.e., "You are working very hard, I will help you finish this now, and then you can . . .")
Develops natural activity reinforcers	• Contingency statements may need a visual component, such as, a line drawing of the work then the payoff, or a check off system to clarify the amount of work.

Note that all procedures must be modified to match the learner's age, level of ability, and level of stress.

skills, and social skills. When those with ASD learn to use these critical skills independently, they will gain more control over their lives.

Teaching is best carried out while the individual's stress is at the stage 4 level of equilibrium, as illustrated in the profile of stress (fig. 12.1). Even in this stage, however, interpreters' alertness to the early behavioral signals of stress will help refine the instructional process or the environment and maintain productive attention and learning. The field of applied behavior analysis provides the foundation for designing and delivering instruction precisely to ensure that students learn discrete skills and make systematic generalizations. These behavioral principles provide a broad range of techniques and strategies that can be specifically selected, adapted, and applied to match each individual's needs at any specific time (Dunlap, Kern, & Worcester, 2001). Interpreters must become so familiar with these behavioral principles and strategies that they can use and adapt them automatically and unobtrusively in any situation. Many texts are available to guide effective discrete trial instruction to those with ASD (e.g., Fovel, 2002; Maurice, Green, & Luce, 1996). The remainder of this chapter addresses the process for teaching critical skills in the context of natural routines (Brown, Evans, Weed, & Owens, 1987; Falco, Janzen, Arick, Wilgus, & DeBoer, 1990).

Teach Functional Skills and Independence in the Context of Routines

Although students with autism have the potential to learn the skills or lessons they are taught, teachers and parents often fail to teach all the small, but critical, steps or skills that lead to true independence. These individuals must be taught many more specific lessons to achieve independence than are needed by their peers without ASD who learn so many skills automatically. An individually designed calendar serves to reduce stress by clarifying the sequence of events to be carried out each day, but a calendar does not provide the details to clarify the various parts or steps of each activity or event.

The process of teaching in the context of functional routines capitalizes on the ability of those with ASD to learn total routines quickly and to be highly motivated to repeat and complete those familiar routines. Studies have shown that the opportunity to repeat a familiar routine serves as a natural reinforcer for those with autism (Goetz, Sailor, & Sailor, 1985). There are other advantages to teaching functional skills in the context of routines; this process increases the level of predictability and supports transitions from one event to another, thus reducing stress. But perhaps the most valuable aspect of this process is that many critical skills can be taught in the context of a single routine and rehearsed frequently with natural variations, thus promoting generalization and self-management.

Organize Events as Routines   An event is anything that occurs in a certain place or at a certain time throughout a day or week, such as getting ready for the school bus, a PE class, a medical appointment, going to a movie with a friend, a job at the local library, taking a shower, and going to bed. Each event can be conceptualized as a routine, and every day is filled with a sequence of such routines. Each routine includes common components that must be completed to achieve the goal of learning and using the routine independently.

Five essential components of any routine include skills required to initiate, to prepare, to perform essential steps, to terminate, and to transition to next event of the routine. Supplemental/enrichment components include (1) solving problems, (2) communicating and socializing, (3) making choices and decisions, and (4) self-monitoring. Adding and teaching these components help address unexpected situations and opportunities in a routine and thereby promote independent adjustment. Organizing events as routines ensures that all the steps required will be addressed to complete the event from beginning to end and to move fluently on to the next event. This process promotes generalization, self-management, and increases predictability (Brown, Evans, Weed, & Owens,1987; Falco et al., 1990).

Although it is not essential to organize every event of the day as a routine, it is important to organize those that have the potential for creating stress, such as when introducing a new event, when major changes will be made in a familiar routine or event, and when those routines that are causing an elevated level of stress.

Designing the Instruction of a Routine   Below are seven steps for designing the instruction of any routine:

1. Define the purpose or critical effect of the routine.
2. Assess to identify the sequence of steps or actions—from the signal to initiate through to termination and transition to the next routine.
3. Identify the natural cues (or signals) to initiate each step and any natural cues, prompts, and reinforcers that will be available in the setting.
4. Identify and develop needed visual support systems to clarify the purpose of the routine, and the sequence of steps leading to independence.
5. Identify and plan for introducing the variations to promote generalization—different settings, different problems, and different opportunities for socialization.
6. Plan the process for introducing the new routine—develop the visual systems to support the routine.
7. Prepare the monitoring plan to chart progress and problems.

Teaching any routine rests squarely on a traditional task analysis (step 2 above) to identify all the essential motor actions necessary for completing a task. However, if self-directed participation is the goal, then a broader, more functional assessment of the goal and context of the routine is needed. Such an analysis can determine which additional skills must be taught for self-initiation and completion of the routine and how to self-correct for potential stressful situations that may occur within the routine. For example, teaching a laundry routine would include self-initiation of the routine upon seeing the laundry basket full of dirty clothes and ending when the dry clothes are folded and returned to the appropriate place. A fuller assessment can determine the individual's current abilities, which steps are done independently, and which will need support systems (e.g., mini-calendars, checklists, cue cards). However, one must know what to do if the detergent bottle is empty, if the drier does not work, if the door bell rings, what to do while the clothes are washing and drying, and what to do after the clothes are folded and placed in a drawer. A teacher can anticipate such potentially stressful events by asking a series of questions related to the routine: "What is required? When do I do it? Where do I do it? How do I do it? How much? What do I do if . . . ? What then? How will I know that I'm finished?" A student's independence in any routine can be enhanced by teaching self-managed strategies to ask and respond to such questions and correct or elaborate the basic routine.

Teaching Functional Routines   Once the instructional plan and the visual support systems have been developed, introduce the routine in a familiar distraction-free setting prior to the initial instruction. Use the parallel talking strategy (see table 12.6) while reviewing each step of the routine illustrated on a visual checklist to ensure that the student understands the labels for the objects and actions and makes the correct associations. Some students benefit from viewing videotape of another person conducting the routine. Introduce the tape several days before the student participates in the routine to allow them time to review it several times (Biederman, Fairhall, Raven, & Davey, 1998; Buggey, Toombs, Gardener, & Cervetti, 1999).

Once the student is familiar with the routine and it is listed on their daily schedule, move with the student to the appropriate location. Then model and parallel talk through the routine while referring to the steps on the visual checklist. Depending on the situation, the student may or may not participate in some of the motor actions on the first day. It is sometimes helpful to repeat, "Today I will do . . . , and tomorrow you will do it and I will help you."

As the student begins to conduct the routine, use pointing, touch, or blocking prompts as needed to prevent errors and verbalize only to highlight specific labels or actions. If an error is made, direct the student back to the previous cue without verbalizing or highlighting the error. Simply refer to the visual system and say, "Let's try that again." Then provide subtle prompts to prevent a repeat of the error. After a few days, tell the student, "Today I won't talk while you work, but I will be here to help you."

Some individuals will require more time than others to become comfortable with a new routine. But with adequate preparation and appropriate visual supports, these students are often able to master a routine in a relatively short time. Therefore, before they have mastered the routine firmly, the variations must be added. For example, set up problems that require the student to ask for assistance. The interpreter should stand farther away and provide assistance nonverbally only if critically necessary.

There is a risk that prompts will become a part of the routine and decrease independence. This is especially true of verbal directions and prompts. If used they should be eliminated quickly. Continue to evaluate and refine the sequence as needed to prevent recurring errors and to add variations to increase the student's flexibility.

A well-planned functional routine ensures that all the critical elements of the routine are addressed so the student can be successful and as independent as possible now and in the future. A functional routine provides a way of thinking to prepare for new and changing events, and a well-planned routine provides a structure for increasing independence in many different situations and settings. While communication, social, relaxation/self-management, problem-solving skills, and choice making skills may be introduced and practiced in more structured settings, it is important to integrate them into functional routines as soon as possible. Parents, teachers, job coaches, and other interpreters should be aware of any new skills that are being taught, not only to reinforce them when the student uses them in the natural world, but also to prompt their use when needed in other settings.

SUMMARY

An intervention process based on the profile of stress (fig. 12.1) provides the foundation for understanding the perspective of those with ASD. When their perspective is understood, interpreters can be alert to the earliest signals of increasing stress. The interpreter can then evaluate and refine the setting or situation to help the student return to the state of equilibrium and maintain focus on learning. When a trained interpreter is present to organize and structure the environment and instruction for persons with autism, the learning rate increases, and stress-induced behavior problems are decreased. The potential benefits of doing this may also include an authentic engagement and enjoyment in learning, greater independence, and a rewarding life.

References

Attwood, T. (1998). *Asperger's syndrome: A guide for parents and professionals.* London: Jessica Kingsley.

Bogdashina. O. (2003). *Sensory perceptual issues in autism and Asperger syndrome: Different sensory experiences—different perceptual worlds.* New York: Jessica Kingsley.

Biederman, G. B., Fairhall, J. L., Raven, K. A., & Davey, V. A. (1998). Verbal prompting, hand-over-hand instruction, and passive observation in teaching children with developmental disabilities. *Exceptional Children, 64*(4), 503–511.

Bramston, P., & Bostock, J. (1994). Measuring perceived stress in people with intellectual disabilities: The development of a new scale. *Australia and New Zealand Journal of Developmental Disabilities, 19,* 149–157.

Bramston, P., & Fogarty, G. J. (1995). Measuring stress in the mildly intellectually handicapped: The factorial structure of the Subjective Stress Scale. *Research in Developmental Disabilities, 16,* 117–131.

Brown, F., Evans, I., Weed, K., & Owens, V. (1987) Delineating functional competencies: A component model. *Journal of the Association for Persons with Severe Handicaps, 12*(2), 117–124.

Buggey, T., Toombs, K., Gardener, P., & Cervetti, M. (1999). Training responding behaviors in students with autism: Using videotaped self-modeling. *Journal of Positive Behavior Interventions, 4,* 205–214.

Cesaroni, L., & Garber, M. (1991). Exploring the experience of autism through first hand accounts. *Journal of Autism and Developmental Disorders, 21*(3), 303–313.

Dawson, G., & Osterling, J. (1997). Early intervention in autism: Effectiveness and common elements of current approaches. In M. J. Guralnick (Ed.), *The effectiveness of early intervention: Second generation research* (pp. 307–326). Baltimore, MD: Paul H. Brookes.

Dunlap, G., Kern, L., & Worcester, J. (2001). ABA and academic instruction. *Focus on Autism and Other Developmental Disabilities, 16*(2), 129–136.

Falco, R., Janzen, J., Arick, J., Wilgus, K., & DeBoer, M. (1990). *Project QUEST inservice manual: Functional assessment of student needs and functional instruction for communication, social interactions, self-management, and choice.* Portland, OR: Department of Special and Counselor Education, Portland State University.

Fovel, J. T. (2002). *The ABA program companion.* New York: DRL Books.

Goetz, L., Sailor, G., & Sailor, W. (1985). Using a behavior chain interruption strategy to teach communication skills to students with severe disabilities. *Journal of the Association for Persons with Severe Handicaps, 10*(1), 21–30.

Groden, G., Stevenson, S., & Groden, J. (1993). *Understanding challenging behavior: A step-by-step behavior analysis guide.* Providence, RI: Manisses Communications Group.

Groden, J., Cautela, J. R., Prince., & Berryman, J. (1994). The impact of stress and anxiety on individuals with autism and other developmental disabilities. In E. Schopler & G. B. Mesibov (Eds.), *Behavioral issues in autism* (pp. 177–194). New York: Plenum Press.

Groden, J., Diller, A., Bausman, M., Velicer, W., Norman, G., & Cautella, J. (2001). The development of a stress survey schedule for persons with autism and other developmental disabilities. *Journal of Autism and Developmental Disorders, 31*(2), 20–217.

Groden, J., & LeVasseur, P. (1995). Cognitive picture rehearsal: A system to teach self-control. In K. Quill (Ed.), *Teaching children with autism* (pp. 287–306). Albany, NY: Delmar.

Hardy, P. M. (1985, July). *Anxiety and panic disorder in autism.* Paper presented at the annual Meeting and Conference of the National Society of Autistic Children, Los Angeles, CA.

Hodgdon, L. (1995). Solving social-behavioral problems through the use of visually supported communication. In K. Quill (Ed.), *Teaching children with autism* (pp. 265–285). Albany, NY: Delmar.

Hodgdon, L. (1999). *Solving behavior problems in autism: Improving communication with visual strategies.* Troy, MI: Quirk Roberts.

Janzen J. (1999). *Autism, facts and strategies for parents.* San Antonio, TX: Therapy Skill Builders.

Janzen, J. (2003). *Understanding the nature of autism: A guide to the autism spectrum disorders.* San Antonio, TX: Therapy Skill Builders.

Klinger, L .G., & Dawson, G. (1992). Facilitating early social and communicative development in children with autism. In S.F. Warren & J. Reichle (Eds.), *Communication and language intervention series, Volume 1: Causes and effects* (pp. 157–186). Baltimore, MD: Paul H. Brookes.

LaVigna, G. W., & Donnellan, A. M. (1986). *Alternatives to punishment: Solving behavior problems with non-aversive strategies.* New York: Irvington.

Marsella, A., & Marsella, B. (1991, Spring). The medical side of behavior. *The Advocate: Newsletter of the ASA, 15.*

Maurice, C., Green, G., & Luce, S. C. (1996). *Behavioral intervention for young children with autism: A manual for parents and professionals.* Austin, TX: Pro-Ed.

Meyer, L. M., & Evans, I. M. (1989). *Non-aversive intervention for behavior problems: A manual for community and residential settings.* Baltimore, MD: Paul H. Brookes.

Myles, B. S., Cook, K. T., Miller, N. E., Rinner, L., & Robbins, L. A. (2000). *Asperger syndrome and sensory issues: Practical solutions for making sense of the world.* Shawnee Mission, KS: Autism Asperger.

O'Neill, R. E., Horner, R. H., Albin, R. W., Storey, K., & Sprague, J. R. (1990). *Functional analysis of problem behavior: A practical assessment guide.* Sycamore, IL: Sycamore.

Premack, D., & Collier, G. (1962). Analysis of non-reinforcement variables affecting response probability. *Psychological Monographs: General and Applied, 76*(5). Washington, DC: American Psychological Association.

Prizant, B. M. (1983). Language acquisition and communicative behavior in autism: Toward an understanding of the "whole" of it. *Journal of Speech and Hearing Disorders, 48,* 296–307.

Sapolsky, R. M. (1994). *Why zebras don't get ulcers: A guide to stress, stress-related diseases, and coping.* New York: W. H. Freeman.

Skinner, B. F. (1953). *Science and human behavior.* New York: Macmillan.

Wing, L. (1980). Foreword. In C. Webster, M. Konstantareas, J. Oxman, & J. Mack (Eds.), *Autism: New directions in research and education.* New York: Pergamon Press.

13 Asperger's Syndrome and Problems Related to Stress

Tony Attwood

We all experience stress to some degree, but children with Asperger's syndrome experience far more stress in their day than their peers. The first section of this chapter examines the possible causes of stress for any child, with particular attention to why these potentially stressful situations are more severe and prolonged for children with Asperger's syndrome. The next section describes methods to measure the degree of stress. In the final section of the chapter, I present a program to reduce stress levels.

POSSIBLE CAUSES OF STRESS

Social Interaction

The *Diagnostic and Statistical Manual of Mental Disorders, Fourth Edition—Text Revision* (*DSM-IV-TR*; American Psychiatric Association, 2000) diagnostic criteria for Asperger's syndrome includes failure to develop peer relationships appropriate to developmental level. My clinical experience suggests that the maturity of the children in the concept of friendship is at least two years behind their peers. However, it is not simply a matter of developmental delay, as there are attributes, such as eye contact, that are unusual for any of the developmental stages in social development (Church, Alisanski, & Amanullah, 2000). Young children with Asperger's syndrome may not have the motivation to interact with their peers in the classroom, on the playground, or at home. Encouragement to play and work with other children can be met with resistance and precipitate stress. Later in their development, the same children may want to play with their peers, but become aware of their social immaturity and difficulty interpreting and responding appropriately to increasingly complex social cues and rules. These children can also have a strong sense of social justice and insist that their peers or adults do not break social rules. When those rules are changed or broken, children with Asperger's syndrome become distressed, confused, and angry. This also causes stress. Finally, the child may make and maintain friendships, but this is achieved by an existing intellectual effort rather than intuition, with a conspicuous sensitivity to making a social error.

Programs to reduce social isolation and encourage social inclusion may facilitate the development of friendships, but they can also lead these children to be vulnerable to tormenting and bullying by their peers. Not every child in the class or playground is a potential friend. Young children with Asperger's syndrome may not be aware of the malicious intentions of some of their peers. As their social reasoning matures, they can experience significant stress as a result of teasing and victimization. This can be of particular concern to parents and teachers during their adolescence.

Communication

Children with Asperger's syndrome may have a remarkable vocabulary and development of syntax, but they usually have significant problems with the pragmatic aspects of language. They are not naturally skilled in the art of conversation. Their problems can include a tendency to make a literal interpretation, such that metaphor, sarcasm, and idioms can be very confusing. There can also be a problem understanding the relevance of changes in prosody that convey emotion and indicate hidden meanings. Difficulties with communication can also include problems with auditory discrimination, which can lead to a difficulty focusing on the teacher's voice when other children are talking.

Children with Asperger's syndrome may also have difficulty explaining their thoughts using speech. An example of this characteristic was a teenager, Daniel, who had remarkable visual reasoning skills. I was explaining to his teacher that she could improve the students' understanding of the course work by remembering that "a picture is worth a thousand words." He overheard the conversation and replied that in his mind he has the picture, but not the thousand words to describe it. The impairments in translating mental images and thoughts into speech increase the children's level of stress.

Cognitive Abilities

The profile of cognitive abilities of children with Asperger's syndrome is quite unusual. Analysis of the profile on a standardized intelligence test can indicate whether the child is a "visualizer," with a natural ability, for example, in engineering, or a "verbalizer," with a natural ability for reading. Many children with Asperger's syndrome have achieved reading, mathematics, and spelling abilities with little tutoring at a precocious age, or they have been developmentally delayed in these abilities and required considerable assistance.

There is a tendency for children with Asperger's syndrome to be at the extremes of ability in academic subjects at school, with conspicuous talents and deficits, and an overall IQ in the normal range. The pattern can include an encyclopedic long-term memory and expertise in a special interest, such as specific forms of transport, electronics, nature, the arts, and science. The child appears to be a "little professor." This can lead others to have an anticipation of advanced cognitive maturity and hence stress from unmet expectations.

Research on attention-deficit disorder (ADD), executive function, and Asperger's syndrome have confirmed characteristics of being impulsive, having poor attention (especially when lacking motivation), reduced organizational and planning skills, and impaired working memory (Eisenmajer et al., 1996; Nyden, Gillberg, Hjelmquist, & Heiman, 1999; Ozonoff, South, & Miller, 2000; Pennington & Ozonoff, 1996). Attempts to overcome these characteristics will obviously result in stress, which is experienced by both the child and teacher.

I have identified differences in cognitive styles that can also contribute to greater stress. Many children with Asperger's syndrome are perfectionists with a pathological fear of making a mistake. They tend to look for and overly focus on their mistakes, as well as those of others. Whereas other children accept a certain proportion of errors in their work and abilities, children with Asperger's syndrome can perceive themselves more as adults and anticipate a level of their own performance far greater than one would expect for children of their age. They can have an extraordinary ability to identify mistakes that would be overlooked by others. They tend to focus on the details rather than the gestalt, failing to grasp the whole picture, a characteristic described as weak central coherence (Frith & Happe, 1994). When they publicly identify the errors of a teacher or parent, they may consider that the adult should be grateful to them for pointing out their mistake; however, the adult may not be so generous, and the child can be confused at the adult's resulting annoyance.

The theoretical model of weak central coherence may also explain another characteristic of Asperger's syndrome. Everyday life requires that we easily identify the pattern or sequence of events in our lives. Having a tendency to focus on the detail rather than on the gestalt or pattern can result in great distress if there are minor and, to others, irrelevant changes in expectations or routine. Children with Asperger's syndrome may see the world as consisting of unconnected fragments and are often desperate to create and maintain order to avoid what appears to be chaos. Changes in routine can result in conspicuous confusion and distress. The children may try to avoid situations that are unfamiliar, that lack clear structure, or that are new because they have no anticipated script of events. They may actively avoid situations that involve surprises, such as receiving a present. If equipment, routines, and schedules are changed or out of order, there is intense anxiety or fear of what may or may not happen due to impaired central coherence. They may respond by imposing their expectations and, if prevented from establishing and imposing control, the children can become very distressed and emotional.

Impaired Theory of Mind

The extensive research on social cognition and theory-of-mind skills confirms that children with Asperger's syndrome have considerable difficulty identifying and conceptualizing the thoughts and feelings of other people and themselves (Baron-Cohen & Jolliffe, 1997; Baron-Cohen, O'Riordan, Stone, Jones, & Plaisted, 1999; Heavey, Phillips, Baron-Cohen, & Rutter, 2000; Kleinman, Marciano, & Ault, 2001; Muris et al., 1999). To use a more colloquial phrase, they lack empathy.

The interpersonal and inner world of thoughts and feelings appears to be uncharted territory for children with Asperger's syndrome. This can result in confusion in social situations, especially where the intentions of others are not obvious. These children may have difficulty in the following areas:

- distinguishing between deliberate and accidental intentions
- reading the social/emotional messages in eye movements, facial expressions, tone of voice, and body language
- recognizing that they hurt someone's feelings, or knowing how to repair their feelings
- recognizing cues, such as when it is appropriate to interrupt or not, signs of boredom, or embarrassment.

Impaired theory-of-mind abilities can have other implications. If this characteristic is not recognized by others, children with Asperger's syndrome can be labeled as disrespectful, disobedient, and deliberately rude. They do break the social rules and fail to respond to the warning signs, but this is due to a neurological disorder that impairs the ability to recognize and respond to social signals. It is neither a character fault nor due to defective parenting skills or inadequate behavior management programs.

Research using new neuroimaging technology has identified structural and functional abnormalities of the amygdala of subjects with autism and Asperger's syndrome (Adolphs, Sears, & Piven, 2001; Baron-Cohen, Ring, Wheelwright, Ashwin, & Williams, 2000; Critchley et al., 2000; Fine, Lumsden, & Blair, 2001). The amygdala regulates a range of emotions including anger, fear, and sadness; thus, we also have neuroanatomical evidence that suggests there will be problems with the perception and regulation of emotions. The child will experience stress because they are "mind-blind" and because of the challenging intellectual effort needed for the comprehension, expression, and cognitive control of emotions in others and themselves.

Sensory Experiences

Children with Asperger's syndrome may have difficulty perceiving social cues, but they can have a remarkable acuity in their sensory perception. The most common sensory sensitivity is for auditory experiences. Unexpected or loud noises, such as a dog barking, can be frightening, or a particular high-pitched continuous noise, such as a small electric motor in a hand dryer or vacuum cleaner, can be perceived as unbearably intense. A cacophony of sounds as occurs in a shopping center, supermarket, or school playground can be overwhelming. Tactile sensitivity can be a source of irritation and distress. Young children may have an intense dislike of the texture of play materials, such as shaving foam, sand, or specific types of clothing fabrics. The various types and intensities of touch in social interactions that occur in greetings and demonstrations of affection can be perceived as unpleasant. There can be a tactile sensitivity associated with particular parts of the body. Hair-washing can be stressful, and sensitivity on the soles of the feet may lead to an avoidance of wearing shoes or walking on particular surfaces.

Such children can be sensitive to the aroma, taste, and texture of specific foods. Their diet may be restricted to the same bland food, and great distress occurs when they are expected to eat age-appropriate food that they perceive as intensely unpleasant. The sensitivity to aromas can cause the avoidance of perfumed soaps, deodorants, and cleaning products. There can also be a sensitivity to light intensity with an avoidance of bright or sunlit environments. In contrast, these children may not react to pain and extremes of temperature as expected. They may have a stoic tolerance of physical discomfort and not communicate their distress to others or seek comfort from a parent. Thus, the sensory world can be overwhelming and a source of considerable stress that may not be obvious to those who do not understand the nature of Asperger's syndrome.

Motor Clumsiness

We are only starting to recognize and explore the problems experienced in motor coordination and dexterity. When walking, and especially running, children with Asperger's syndrome can have a gait that is ungainly or immature. Ball-catching skills can be affected by problems with timing and coordination. Difficulties with manual dexterity can affect the use of utensils and self-care skills such as dressing, and when associated with problems of balance, cause delays in acquiring skills like riding a bicycle. These abilities can eventually be mastered before the children start school, but are then followed by difficulties with handwriting and the coordination required for physical education classes. The children can be especially distressed by their difficulty in handwriting and avoid some educational activities because they are expected to write. Some physical education classes can be a source of stress due to the expectation of the physical education teacher and the public criticisms or humiliation by their peers.

ASSESSMENT OF STRESS LEVELS

We are starting to become more aware of the long-term and short-term indicators of stress. The long-term indicators can be an increase in the severity of expression of some of the diagnostic characteristics of Asperger's syndrome. There can be an increase in time spent in solitude and being absorbed in their special interest. In the short-term, there can be an increase in the rigidity in thought processes, routines, and problem-solving methods, as well as actions and demands that enforce consistency, avoidance, and control in their daily experiences. The children can become oppositional, hyperactive, and critical of themselves and others. There can also be an increase in the intensity of emotional reactions to stress with episodes of panic, anger, or tears.

A mood or stress diary can be used to analyze any cyclical changes or times of day and specific triggers or circumstances that are more likely to increase stress levels. The child's individualized stress levels can be assessed on a daily or hourly basis using a numerical rating. The range may be from 0 to 20, with 0 to 4 being a relatively stress free period and 16 to 20 indicating high levels of stress. Over time, a pattern may emerge to suggest that the children have cyclical or tidal expressions of stress. They may become more prone to stress during particular seasons, or in response to changes, such as temporarily living in the home of a step-parent.

Children with Asperger's syndrome can temporally inhibit their overt signs of stress in situations where they want to maintain their abilities and composure. For example, the children can be "angels" at school, with the teacher commending them for their ability to cope with distress. However, when they arrive home, their parents describe them as "devils." They have suppressed their stress and agitation but release the energy at home. This is not necessarily because the parents are in some way causing the distressed behavior at home or because they are unable to manage their child. The children recognize the importance of remaining calm at school to avoid consequences and to create a persona of success, but the effort can only be endured if there is a chance to release their suppressed stress at home.

The formal assessment of stress can include the administration of a range of self-report scales and questionnaires, completed by the children, their parents, and teachers. The Stress Survey Schedule for Persons with Autism and Developmental Disabilities is an excellent instrument for measuring stress (Groden et al., 2001). Other instruments may need to be modified for this particular clinical group, as they may find open-ended questions difficult to complete due to characteristics of alexithymia, which is the inability to know the word that defines a particular level of emotion. They may be more able to accurately describe their response using a numerical representation of the gradation of experience by using numbers or metaphors, such as using a thermometer to illustrate the degrees of expression. To minimize word retrieval problems, multiple-choice questions can be used in preference to open-ended sentence completion tasks. A pictorial dictionary of feelings can be used as additional cues for a diary or logbook assessment measures. The concept of a measuring instrument for stress can also be used to assess or measure changes in stress levels from minute to minute. For example, a gauge with a rotating needle can be made, as in a speedometer, and the children can move the needle to indicate their stress levels. The gauge can be placed on their desk at school and as the teacher passes by the desk, they can see the position of the needle. Thus, stress levels can be expressed simply by moving the position of the needle rather than communicating their feelings in words and gestures.

Sometimes the children may not be able to perceive their inner perception of stress and early warning signals of increasing emotional arousal. Biofeedback training can be used to increase their awareness of the internal cues. For example, I have used machines that measure galvanic skin response to enable these children to see and hear their level of stress. Training can also include being more aware of the physiological, behavioral, and cognitive signs of stress. This can include being more aware of breathing, heart rate, and perspiration, as well as behaviors and actions associated with stress, such as clenched fists or teeth, and the cognitive signs of rigid thinking and feelings of frustration and intolerance.

Parents may report that the build up of stress is not represented on a graph of intensity and time as a gradual incline, but as an almost vertical escalation, or "explosion." The emotional response or energy levels appear almost as an on/off switch set at maximum volume. Thus, there is a very brief period to alert the child or others to an imminent rapid escalation of stress and a subsequent decreasing ability to control the emotion.

Finally, there needs to be an assessment of the stress levels and emotion management strategies of parents and teachers. Unfortunately, the stress and emotionality of those around them can only add fuel to the fire. When others become agitated or affectionate, the child with Asperger's syndrome can be more confused and stressed.

Triggers of Stress

There are specific events that can result in severe stress and rapid loss of control of feelings. The most common events that precipitate stress are change and surprises. When a child is referred to me with an autistic spectrum disorder (ASD) who has recently had a deterioration in behavior and emotions, my first questions are about any changes in routines, teaching staff, accommodation, or expectations. The child with Asperger's syndrome has a limited ability to cope with change. Insistence on sameness is one of the diagnostic characteristics that can increase when the child is stressed.

Another trigger is the number of people in a situation. I suggest that it is possible to eliminate all the diagnostic signs of Asperger's syndrome in a particular child. When children are alone, perhaps in their bedroom or playing on the computer, they have no need of social or communication skills and can do what they want to do in their own way. The classic diagnostic signs of Asperger's syndrome have disappeared. As soon as another person enters the bedroom, the signs of Asperger's syndrome become conspicuous. A child may be reasonably able to cope with the social reasoning and communication requirements if there is only one person to relate to, but the level of stress and characteristics of Asperger's syndrome can be proportional to the number of people present. A crowded playground or shopping mall can be a trigger for quite agitated behavior and increase the signs of Asperger's syndrome.

One of the most dramatic triggers of stress is the experience of confusion and failure. As already discussed, children with Asperger's syndrome can be perfectionists with high personal expectations, a tendency to focus on mistakes rather than what is correct, and be less likely to have the flexible thinking to consider alternative strategies, such as trying another way or asking for help. When frustrated they can quickly become overly emotional, inhibiting access to their strength—logic. I explain to older and more able children with Asperger's syndrome that when they become anxious, their IQ drops 30 points, and when they become angry it drops 60 points.

Experiencing public humiliation, social rejection, and teasing can also be significant triggers for stress and agitated behavior. Unfortunately, many children with Asperger's syndrome perceive advice from adults and their peers as criticism, which can also be a significant trigger. Another trigger is distress from being interrupted, which is rather ironic because the child may frequently interrupt others. Other potential triggers include confusion from sensory overload, someone breaking the social rules (as perceived by the child with Asperger's syndrome), and the emotionality of others. The child can be aware that others are expressing strong emotions to each other, which can range from affection to anger, but the child can only understand and tolerate a narrow waveband of emotion in other people, even if the feelings are not directed at themselves.

STRESS MANAGEMENT STRATEGIES

The remainder of this chapter details a number of strategies to reduce stress for children with an autistic spectrum disorder. Using the metaphor of a toolbox to "fix the feeling," clinicians and caregivers alike can help individuals build a personalized stress and emotion-management program.

Emotional Toolbox

When someone is stressed, there is a need to escape (flight), solve a problem, or end a threat (fight). The human body makes physical and mental changes to resolve the situation. One of the changes is an increase in physical and mental energy. Programs for emotion management can be conceptualized as programs to manage energy.

The emotional toolbox program begins with an explanation to the child of how an increase in emotions and energy can be adaptive characteristics for animals and humans in terms of the fight-or-flight response. When there is a genuine threat, for example, of being eaten by a predator or losing territory to a competitor, the brain and body react with an increase in energy and an adaptive change in thinking and behavior. This primitive but evolutionary successful response was essential for human survival. However, in our modern society, we can react with the same degree of energy in stressful situations that are not life threatening. Children with Asperger's syndrome often enjoy learning about animals and history. This model can be used to explain the child's changes in thinking, emotions, and behavior in particularly stressful situations.

From an early age, all children will know a toolbox contains a variety of different tools to repair a machine or fix a household problem. The strategy I have developed is to identify different types of tools to fix the problems associated with negative emotions, especially anxiety, anger, and sadness. The range of tools can be divided into those that constructively release or reduce energy and those that improve thinking. I work with the child and family or with the teacher to identify different tools that help "fix the feeling," as well as to identify tools that can make the emotions or consequences worse. Paper and pen are used by the participants during a brainstorming session of drawing a toolbox and pictures with descriptions of different types of tools and activities that can encourage constructive emotion management.

Physical Tools

A hammer can represent tools or actions that physically release energy. A picture of a hammer is drawn on a large sheet of paper and participants suggest safe physical activities (see box 13.1).

For young children, energy-releasing tools may include running, bouncing on the trampoline, or swinging on a swing set. For older children, sports practice and dancing can be used to let off steam. For example, a child chose playing a game of tennis as one of his physical tools because it "takes the fight out of me." Other activities may include cycling, swimming, and playing the drums. Some household activities, such as recycling, can provide a satisfying release of energy: crushing cans or packaging; or tearing old clothes to make rags can be an activity to repair the feelings of frustration. Kitchen activities can include squeezing oranges or pounding meat. Adults can consider some aspect of gardening or renovations.

Some children with Asperger's syndrome have already identified that a physical tool and destruction is a very effective "quick fix" to end the feeling but have not been careful in choosing the focus of their physical release. If they break something to release stress, it is preferable that the energy is channeled into a constructive activity.

Relaxation Tools

Relaxation tools help calm the person and lower their heart rate. A paintbrush could be used to illustrate this category of tools. Calming activities may include drawing, reading, and listening to music (see box 13.2).

Children with Asperger's syndrome often find that solitude is their most relaxing activity. They may need to retreat to a quiet, secluded sanctuary as an effective emotional repair mechanism. Young children may relax by gentle rocking actions, singing, or engaging in a repetitive action. This may include manipulating an object, such as a stress ball or worry beads. Other relaxing activities used by children with an ASD can be misinterpreted as self-stimulatory behaviors. Examples include completing a favorite jigsaw puzzle many times and frequently watching the same videotape. Children with ASD have a strong preference for routines and predictability. When you know the dialogue, scenes, and outcome of a television program or movie it can have a calming effect, as there will be no surprises.

Other relaxing activities can include massage, a brief doze, or good sleep as well as applying relaxation activities that have been practiced beforehand that focus on breathing and imagery. For adults, some routine chores, such as housecleaning, can be a repetitive action that results in satisfaction and relaxation when complete. Teachers can also use this strategy; when they notice the child is becoming distressed, they can suggest a high-status responsibility that will enable the child to leave a situation or to become distracted by an activity that restores order and consistency. For example, the teacher could suggest that the child leave the class to take an important message or document to the school office or tidy a bookshelf, placing all the books in alphabetical order.

Social Tools

Social tools use people as a means of managing feelings. The goal is to find and be with someone who can help change the mood. A two-handled saw can be used to represent social activities or individuals that can repair feelings (see box 13.3).

The social activity will need to be enjoyable and without the stress that can be associated with social interaction and play with peers. The social contact may be with adults, who have a natural ability to make the child feel good. This should be someone who genuinely admires or loves the child, gives compliments, and manages to say the right things to repair the feelings, such as a family member—perhaps a grandparent who has time to be patient with the child—or a friend.

Box 13.1 Physical Activity Tools

• Physical exercise: walk, run, trampoline
• Sports: basketball or dancing
• Creative destruction: recycling
• Bite an apple
• Break a pencil

People with Asperger's syndrome are more likely to have a successful social interaction with a one-on-one interaction. Communication using Internet chat lines can be a successful social activity that can be an emotional repair mechanism. The person with Asperger's syndrome may have greater eloquence and insight in disclosing their thoughts and feelings by typing rather than talking. You do not need skills with eye contact and reading a face, or changes in vocal tone or body language, when engaged in an online conversation. The chat line can include other people with Asperger's syndrome who have genuine empathy and may offer constructive suggestions to repair a mood or situation.

Sometimes the best friend may be a pet. Despite the negative mood or stressful events of the day, dogs are delighted to see their owner, show unconditional adoration, and enjoy the company of their owner. A positive action that may help repair negative emotions is to help someone or to be needed (i.e., an altruistic act). I have noted that some children, and especially adults, with Asperger's syndrome can change their mood when helping others. This can include activities such as helping someone who has difficulties in an area of the child's talents or expertise; for example, helping an adult fix a problem with a computer or helping a classmate with a subject such as mathematics. Adults with Asperger's syndrome often enjoy volunteer work, particularly with the elderly, very young children, and animals. Being needed and appreciated is a significant emotional repair mechanism for all of us.

Thinking Tools

Another type of tool can be used to change thinking or knowledge. Children can nominate the type of tool, such as a screwdriver or wrench, to represent this category of emotional repair. They are encouraged to use their intellectual strength to control their feelings using a variety of techniques. Self-talk can be used, such as "I can control my feelings," or "I can stay calm," when they are under stress. The words can be reassuring and encourage self-esteem. Liane Holliday-Willey (2001), who has Asperger's syndrome, has created a series of statements such as, "I will ask for help when I need it,"and "I will be patient with those who need time to understand me." Evan, a young man with Asperger's syndrome, was discussing thinking tools with me and created the strategy of making an "antidote" to poisonous thoughts. The procedure is to provide a comment that

Box 13.2 Relaxation Tools

- Music
- Solitude
- Massage
- Reading
- Repetitive action
- Sleep
- Art
- Stress ball
- Pleasures book

counteracts negative thoughts. For example, the poisonous thought, "I can't do it" can be neutralized by the antidote, "The smart thing to do is ask for help." It is necessary to determine the child's negative or poisonous thoughts in a particular situation and together create a personalized antidote that is remembered or written on a card so that the antidote is carried with the child, to be "administered" when needed.

Another thinking tool is to put the event in perspective. The approach is to use logic and facts with a series of questions such as, "Is there another shop where we could buy that particular computer game?" or "Will children teasing you about your interest in astronomy prevent you from being a successful astronomer?"

Children with Asperger's syndrome have a great interest in acquiring knowledge, and a special type of thinking tool is to create a project on the source of stress. For example, one source of extreme distress may be the sound of a restroom hand dryer. The project can include dismantling a hand dryer to see how it works and being reassured that it switches off after people have dried their hands. There can be a comparison of different dryer models and the exploration of which restrooms have a dryer. The project can be written as a science project or as a social story (Gray, 1998).

One thinking tool that can be used by children with Asperger's syndrome may not be the choice of other children. Children with Asperger's syndrome usually enjoy achieving academic success. When they are stressed, the teacher may instruct them to complete a school activity that they enjoy and for which they have a natural talent. Many children with Asperger's syndrome enjoy correctly completing classroom activities, such as solving math problems or spelling. If this is the preferred activity, then this tool can be suggested when they are stressed so that they can achieve success and self-confidence, which will prevent an increase in stress levels. Other children would probably try to avoid academic tasks when stressed.

Cue-controlled relaxation is also a useful thinking tool. The strategy is for children to have an object in their pocket that symbolizes or has been classically conditioned to elicit feelings of relaxation. For example, a teenage girl

Box 13.3 Social Tools

- Talk to a family member or friend
- Talk to a pet
- Share the problem
- Seek a second opinion
- Find someone to help change the mood
- Develop close friends

with Asperger's syndrome was an avid reader of fiction, and her favorite book was *The Secret Garden,* by Frances Hodgson Burnett. She kept a key in her pocket to metaphorically open the door to the secret garden, an imaginary place where she felt relaxed and happy. A few moments touching or looking at the key helped her contemplate a scene described in the book, relax, and achieve a more positive state of mind. Adults can have a special picture in their wallet, such as a photograph of a woodland scene that reminds them of solitude and tranquility.

Special Interest Tools

A survey of special interests examined the role the interest plays in the lives of the people with Asperger's syndrome (Bashe & Kirby, 2001). The major functions were an experience of intense enjoyment, security, comfort, and relaxation, as well as the facilitation or avoidance of social interaction. For children with Asperger's syndrome, finding a rare specimen of the interest can be experienced as an intensely pleasurable moment. This may be in contrast to a lack of success with social play, making friends, and some academic and daily living activities. Children with Asperger's syndrome may have relatively fewer pleasures in life, and the special interest can be the "silver lining" to a somewhat gloomy life, a natural antidepressant.

In the general population, rituals and repetition are commonly used to reduce anxiety. One of the characteristics of the special interests is their repetitive and ritualistic nature. An adolescent with Asperger's syndrome had a great interest in Japanese culture and performed the elaborate and ritualized Japanese tea ceremony whenever she felt anxious. Luke Jackson (2002), a teenager with Asperger's syndrome, describes the cataloging of the examples of his interests as a means of "personal defragmentation." If one is considering imagery as part of a stress reduction program, then children with Asperger's syndrome could be encouraged to think of their special interest.

In behavioral learning theory terms, the repetitive action, thought, or interest becomes a form of negative reinforcement; it is soothing and helps you feel calmer. It is interesting that the degree of motivation and duration of time spent on the interest is proportional to the degree of stress (Bashe & Kirby, 2001). The more the person experiences stressors such as change, failure, and low self-esteem, the more the interest becomes obtrusive, dominant, or bizarre. If the child has few means of enjoyment and relaxation, what may have started as a source of pleasure and tranquility under conditions of stress can become a compulsive act reminiscent of an obsessive-compulsive disorder (OCD). This problem can occur when children have very few tools in their emotional toolbox. If the special interest is their only source of relaxation or escape, then the interest can become irresistible. Being prevented from achieving uninterrupted access to their only emotional restorative creates even more stress. A program of controlled or timed access can be introduced to ensure the time spent on the interest is not excessive. Unfortunately, time goes quickly when you are enjoying yourself. There may need to be some negotiation and compromise regarding the duration of access. The special interest can be a useful tool in the toolbox but must be one of many tools.

Other Tools

There are other types, or categories, of tools that can be included in the toolbox, which may be typical of the general population or unique.

Medication is often prescribed to manage or repair emotions. If the child is showing clear signs of an anxiety disorder or depression, then medication such as a selective serotonin reuptake inhibitor (SSRI) can be recommended as a potential emotion management tool. Some children with Asperger's syndrome also have signs of attention-deficit hyperactivity disorder (ADHD). One of the characteristics of a combination of the two disorders is for the child to react impulsively when experiencing emotional arousal. These children have a tendency to react without cognitive reflection, such as retaliating to an act of another child that caused emotional discomfort without first determining if the act was accidental or considering the consequences of retaliation. A trial of stimulant medication may reduce emotionally impulsive actions.

Some children with Asperger's syndrome have a cyclical fluctuation of emotions. A mood diary can determine the amplitude and wavelength of any cyclical pattern. The administration of an anticonvulsant could achieve a reduction in amplitude so that the child does not experience the extremes of emotion.

When the concern is anger, as described in this chapter, emotion management can be conceptualized as energy management. An antipsychotic medication can reduce the child's energy levels. The medication is prescribed as a sedative, not to treat signs of schizophrenia.

Clinical experience has confirmed the value of medication, but there are some concerns, often voiced by parents and children themselves. One concern is that, at present, we do not have longitudinal studies of the long-term effect of using psychotropic medication on young children. Another concern is the effect on the child's clarity of thought. From my clinical experience, many children report that medication slows their thinking and cognitive skills. Children and adults with Asperger's syndrome often value their clarity of thought. As one adult with Asperger's syndrome described, "It was like I was locked out of my own home." The medication not only reduces the low moods; it can also reduce the exhilaration experienced during time spent on the special interest. There can, therefore, be a problem of patient compliance in taking the medication consistently. However, as a matter of practicality, expediency, and in the absence of psychological therapies, medication may be the primary tool offered by support services.

Other potential tools for the toolbox are enjoyable activities, such as watching a favorite comedy—laughter is often the best medicine. Children with Asperger's syndrome can enjoy jokes typical of their developmental level and be remarkably creative with puns and jokes (Werth, Perkins, & Boucher, 2001). Another tool is to read the autobiographies of adults with Asperger's syndrome for encouragement and advice. We now have several autobiographies written by children and adults with Asperger's syndrome, which can be remarkably inspirational.

Another tool category, which could be described as an environmental tool, involves the assessment of the child's sensory world identifying strategies to avoid specific sensory experiences, such as determining the position of the child's desk in class to reduce the general level of noise, distraction, and interruption. Sensory integration therapy or the use of tinted Irlen lenses in glasses or as overlays to reading materials can reduce the distress caused by aspects of the child's environment and sensory perception.

A tool that can encourage self-control is the offer of a prize or reward. The reward may be to earn access to preferred activities, the special interest, or even money. Some children with Asperger's syndrome are natural capitalists. If the child is having organizational problems or has impaired executive function, reward strategies need to be in place at school and home, particularly when the child is engaged in completing homework.

A tool that can be used for some children and that seems especially effective with girls with Asperger's syndrome, is to act as a person they know or admire who could cope with the situation. In high school, speech and drama classes can be used to role-play what to do and how to think in specific situations.

The concept of a toolbox can also be extended and used in group activities to compare the effectiveness of tools used by different participants in the group and the possibility of "borrowing" a tool. An interesting and extremely valuable by-product of this strategy is that it can teach children with Asperger's syndrome how to repair the emotions of themselves and their family members and friends.

Inappropriate Tools

There must be a discussion of inappropriate tools (one would not use a hammer to fix a computer) in order to explain how some actions, such as violence and thoughts of suicide, are not appropriate tools or emotional repair mechanisms. For example, one client would slap himself to stop negative thoughts and feelings. Another tool that could become inappropriate is the retreat into a fantasy world (perhaps imagining they are a superhero), or to engage in retaliation. The use of escape into fantasy literature and games can be a typical tool for ordinary adolescents, but it is of concern when it becomes the dominant or exclusive coping mechanism. The border between fantasy and reality may be unclear, and the thinking may become delusional. The program also needs to consider whether teenagers are using drugs and alcohol to manage their stress levels and mood, and whether legal prescription medication would be safer and more effective. Other inappropriate tools would be taking stress out on someone else (e.g., their younger siblings), self-injury, and the destruction of something valuable or precious.

It is also necessary to evaluate tools used by parents and teachers and to remove any tools from the toolbox that may be inappropriate or counterproductive. Children with Asperger's syndrome are often confused by certain emotions, and this can be the case with the expression of affection. They may fear what they do not easily understand, and affection from others may not be an effective mechanism to repair their feelings. A teenage boy with Asperger's syndrome said, "I get angry when someone tries to cheer me up," and a younger child, when asked if a hug would help when he was upset, replied with an emphatic, "No, I get madder." Children with ASD can perceive gestures of affection as uncomfortable and not comforting. The children are annoyed that they are being squeezed or confused as to why someone would want to kiss their cheek. Social stories, developed by Carol Gray (1998), can be used to explain to the children why other people respond to their distress by gestures and words of affection. This can reduce their confusion and increase their tolerance of affectionate behavior in others. Parents, friends, family members, and teachers will need to be aware that affection is a powerful emotional restoration tool for themselves, but not necessarily for children with Asperger's syndrome. Demonstrating affection could "add fuel to the fire." Sometimes affection can be used as an emotion repair mechanism or tool in the toolbox, but the level of expression may be much less demonstrative than would be used with a typical child.

Punishment can be another inappropriate tool. Stating the punishment for a particular behavior can be perceived as a threat, which could inflame the situation and may not be a wise approach. There may be a time and a place to discuss consequences, but when children are rapidly losing the cognitive control of their emotions, stating a punishment could make self-control less likely.

Unusual Tools

Unusual tools or responses are also considered. The child may laugh when expected to show remorse (Berthier, 1995). Crying and laughing are both tension-releasing mechanisms; unfortunately, the child with Asperger's syndrome may not know or be able to recognize which release mechanism is appropriate for the social context. An example of another unusual response was explained during a group session on sadness; a teenage girl with Asperger's syndrome explained that, "Crying doesn't work for me, so I get angry." Clinical experience suggests that tears may be rare as a response to feeling sad, with a more common response being anger. The program includes developing a range of conventional means of emotional expression, repair mechanisms, and explaining why some of their reactions are misinterpreted by others.

Another tool or mechanism that appears to be unusual is that of quickly resolving grief and anger. This characteristic can be of concern to the child's family who expect the classic signs of prolonged and intense grieving; they consider the person as uncaring. This can also occur with anger; the child may quickly express intense anger that ends as quickly as it began. However, this rapid recovery in both grief and anger is simply a feature of Asperger's syndrome.

Different Tools for Different Levels of Stress

When the level of stress is low, the preference may be for relaxation tools or for the distracting and enjoyable aspects of the special interest. As the level of stress becomes greater, the options may include greater use of thinking and social tools. When the stress and energy levels are very high, physical tools may be recommended as an emotional repair mechanism. At this point, the advice is not to expect the child to explain the causes of the stress using speech. When extremely agitated, children are at their least insightful or eloquent. The most effective tools can be solitude to enable them to calm down or vigorous physical activities from the collection of physical tools.

Clinical experience with the concept of an emotional toolbox has provided some interesting comparisons between children with Asperger's syndrome and typical children who naturally have a much wider range of tools, the most popular and effective being social tools. Children with Asperger's syndrome often need active encouragement to develop and use other people as a means of repairing their feelings. Physical acts are often the first tool used to quickly and effectively discharge the emotion. Emotion management is usually achieved by actions rather than by reflection and relaxation.

Practice

Once the children have a new toolbox, it is necessary to start practicing using the tools in a graduated sequence of assignments. The first stage is for the adult to model the appropriate thinking and actions in role-play with the children, who then practice with the adult or other group members, vocalizing their thoughts to monitor their cognitive processes. A form of graduated practice is used, starting with situations associated with a relatively mild level of distress or agitation. A list of situations, or triggers, is created from the assessment conducted at the start of the program, with each situation written on an adhesive note. The children use the emotion thermometer or a measuring instrument to determine the hierarchy or rank order of situations. The most distressing situations are posted at the upper level of the thermometer. As the program progresses, the children and adult work through the hierarchy. After practice during the training session, the children are asked to apply their new knowledge and abilities in real situations. After each practical experience, the children and adult consider the degree of success and debrief, using reinforcement for achievements such as a "boasting book," or certificate of achievement.

One of the issues during the practice stage is generalization. Children with Asperger's syndrome tend to be quite rigid in terms of recognizing when the new strategies are applicable in a situation that does not obviously resemble the practice sessions. It will be necessary to ensure that strategies are used in a wide range of circumstances and that once an appropriate stress management strategy has proved successful, no assumption will be made that the strategy will continue to be used in all settings.

The duration of the practice stage depends on the degree of success and list of situations. Gradually the adult provides less direct guidance and support, to encourage confidence in independently using the new strategies. The goal is to provide a template for current and future problems.

Does the program described in this chapter work in practice? I have developed the strategies over many years of clinical experience with personal stories of success. The program has now been evaluated using an independent team of psychologists based at the University of Queensland. Sofronoff, Attwood, and Hinton (2005) describe the design of the study, using randomly allocated experimental and control subjects. Subsequent publications will provide more information on the assessment measures used in the study and long-term results. At this stage in the research process, it does appear that, in practice, the program can make a significant improvement in children's ability to understand and manage their emotions and the stress in their lives.

References

Adolphs, R., Sears, L., & Piven, J. (2001). Abnormal processing of social information from faces in autism. *Journal of Cognitive Neuroscience, 13*, 232–240.

American Psychiatric Association. (2000). *Diagnostic and statistical manual of mental disorders: Text revision.* (4th ed.). Washington, DC: Author.

Baron-Cohen, S., & Jolliffe, T. (1997). Another advanced test of theory of mind: Evidence from very high functioning adults with autism or Asperger syndrome. *Journal of Child Psychology and Psychiatry, 38*, 813–822.

Baron-Cohen, S., O'Riordan, M., Stone, V., Jones, R., & Plaisted, K. (1999). Recognition of faux pas by normally developing children and children with Asperger disorder or high functioning autism. *Journal of Autism and Developmental Disorders, 29,* 407–418.

Baron-Cohen, S., Ring, H. A., Bullmore, E. T, Wheelwright, S., Ashwin, C., & Williams, S. C. R. (2000). The amygdala theory of autism. *Neuroscience and Biobehavioral Reviews, 24,* 355–364.

Baron-Cohen, S., Ring, H. A., Wheelwright, S., Bullmore, E. T., Brammer, M. J., Simmons, A., & Williams, S. C. R. (1999). Social intelligence in the normal autistic brain: An FMRI study. *European Journal of Neuroscience, 11,* 1891–1898.

Bashe, P., & Kirby, B. L. (2001). *The oasis guide to Asperger's syndrome.* New York: Crown.

Berthier, M. L. (1995). Hypomania following bereavement in Asperger's syndrome: A case study. *Neuropsychiatry, Neuropsychology and Behavioural Neurology, 8,* 222–228.

Church, C., Alisanski, S., & Amanullah, S. (2000). The social, behavioural and academic experiences of children with Asperger's syndrome. *Focus on Autism and other Developmental Disabilities, 15*(1), 12–20.

Critchley, H. D., Daly, E. M., Bullmore, E. T., Williams, S. C. R., Van Amelsvoort, T., Robertson, D. M., et al. (2000). The functional neuroanatomy of social behaviour. *Brain, 123,* 2203–2212.

Eisenmajer, R., Prior, M., Leekman, S., Wing, L., Gould, J., Welham, M., & Ong, N. (1996). Comparison of clinical symptoms in autism and Asperger's disorder. *Journal of the American Academy of Child and Adolescent Psychiatry, 35,* 1523–1531.

Fine, C., Lumsden, J., & Blair, R. J. R. (2001). dissociation between 'theory of mind and executive functions in a patient with early left amygdala damage. *Brain Journal of Neurology, 124,* 287–298.

Frith, U., & Happe, F. (1994). Autism: Beyond "Theory of Mind." *Cognition, 50,* 115–132.

Gray, C. A. (1998). Social and comic strip conversations with students with Asperger syndrome and high-functioning autism. In E. Schopler, G. Mesibov, & L. J. Kunce (Eds.), *Asperger's syndrome or high-functioning autism* (pp. 167–198). New York: Plenum Press.

Groden, J., Diller, A., Bausman, M., Velicer, W., Norman, G., & Cautella, J. (2001). The development of a stress survey schedule for persons with autism and other developmental disabilities. *Journal of Autism and Developmental Disorders, 31*(2), 207–217.

Heavey, L., Phillips, W., Baron-Cohen, S., & Rutter, M. (2000). The awkward moments test: a naturalistic measure of social understanding in autism. *Journal of Autism and Developmental Disorders, 30,* 225–236.

Holliday-Willey, L. (2001). *Asperger syndrome in the family: Redefining normal.* London: Jessica Kingsley.

Jackson, L., (2002). *Freaks, geeks and Asperger's syndrome.* London: Jessica Kingsley.

Kleinman, J., Marciano, P., & Ault, R. (2001). Advanced theory of mind in high functioning adults with autism. *Journal of Autism and Developmental Disorders, 31,* 29–36.

Muris, P., Steerneman, P., Meesters, C., Merckelbach, H., Horselenberg, R., van den Hogan, T., & van den Hogan, L. (1999). The TOM test: A new instrument for assessing theory of mind in normal children and children with pervasive developmental disorders. *Autism and Developmental Disorders, 29,* 67–80.

Nyden, A., Gillberg, C., Hjelmquist, & Heiman, M. (1999). Executive function/ attention deficits in boys with Asperger disorder, attention disorder and reading/ writing disorder. *Autism, 3*, 213–228.

Ozonoff, S., South, M., & Miller, J. (2000). DSM-IV defined Asperger disorder: Cognitive, behavioural and early history differentiation from high-functioning autism. *Autism, 4*, 29–46.

Pennington, B. F., & Ozonoff, S. (1996). Executive function and developmental psychopathology. *Journal of Child Psychology and Psychiatry Annual Research Review, 37*, 51–87.

Sofronoff, K., Attwood, T., & Hinton, S. (2005). A randomised controlled trial of a CBT intervention for anxiety in children with Asperger syndrome. *Journal of Child Psychology and Psychiatry. 46,* 1152–1160.

Werth, A., Perkins, M., & Boucher, J. (2001). Here's the weavery looming up. *Autism, 5*(2), 111–125.

14 The Experience of Bereavement for Those with Developmental Disabilities

Patricia A. Wisocki

> Yet belief in the inevitability of death does not diminish our anguish when it arrives.
>
> —Naguib Mahfouz

The capacity for grief is a universal experience among humans, and even among nonhuman primates, independent of learning processes (e.g., Mineka & Suomi, 1978). Grief is a normal response to loss. Only under certain circumstances may it become a form of pathology and require therapeutic intervention. Yet, a portion of the human population, specifically those with autism and other developmental disabilities, has been thought to be exempt from grieving because of two mistaken assumptions. The first assumption is that autistic individuals are unable to understand the finality, irreversibility, or the inevitability of death (Speece & Brent, 1984). The second assumption is that persons with autism are unable to form strong attachment bonds that could produce feelings of personal loss and mourning (Deutsch, 1985; McDaniel, 1989), perhaps due to shallow emotional reserves. When a loss occurs, persons with developmental disabilities are often shielded from experiencing mourning rituals (including attendance at wakes and funerals, visits to cemeteries, even passing time with or saying goodbye to a dying loved one) out of a fear of "upsetting" the person with developmental disabilities (Seltzer, 1989). If the individual displays an excessive, intense, or disruptive grief reaction, it is often misinterpreted as a part of the individual's overall symptom pattern and is discouraged (Carder, 1987; Lipe-Goodson & Goebel, 1983). These assumptions may lead caregivers to mislabel, ignore, or inappropriately treat grief reactions as "problem behaviors."

Another problem relates to the lack of education provided to individuals with autism and other developmental disabilities. Considerations about death education and grief counseling are rarely included in Individual Educational Plans (IEP) or treatment programs for persons with developmental disorders (Yanok & Beifus, 1993). Thus, people with developmental disorders may not be prepared to deal well with the loss of loved ones or to participate in mourning rituals. Likewise, it is rare that caregivers are trained to console or counsel those who are grieving. If grief is not recognized in individuals with developmental disabilities, those individuals may suffer additional stress and behavioral problems (Kloeppel & Hollins, 1989).

This chapter presents (1) case examples of bereavement among those with developmental disabilities; (2) a review of the typical stages of grief, contrasted with what is known about the bereavement experiences of those with developmental disabilities; (3) a psychological model of stress in which grief is an example; (4) an application of the stress model to the population of those with autism and other developmental disabilities; (5) the relationship between grief and depression for those with developmental disabilities; (6) the problem of pathological grief; (7) the influence of cognitive and developmental factors on the experience of bereavement; and (8) educational programs that have been developed to teach those with developmental disabilities about death and to assist with bereavement.

Although the general topic of bereavement has been extensively studied, the research and clinical evidence pertinent to bereavement and those with developmental disabilities is meager, necessitating extrapolation from the broader to the narrower field in some areas. Thus, let us look first at some case examples of bereaved persons with developmental disabilities to examine the range of difficulties that could occur. Personal information has been changed to protect client identity.

CASE EXAMPLES OF BEREAVEMENT

Robert, a 39-year-old man with signs of severe autism, experienced the loss of his father a year after his sister died. Although Robert had been extremely close to his father, he had not been permitted to participate in the funeral rituals. This was because the family did not want to upset him and because they were fearful that Robert's behavior would be embarrassing to them or difficult to handle as they went through the mourning rituals. Robert was told, however, that his father had died. In his day program, Robert asked continuously about his father: where was he, when was he coming to take him to a favorite restaurant, when could he visit him. He also expressed intense fear of being in the dark and of going into the ground. These repetitive questions were seen by the day care staff as part of his overall pattern of autism. They were uncomfortable with the content of the questions and were uncertain as to how to deal with Robert. Finally, they relied on using the same strategies to which they were accustomed when dealing with repetitive and persistent speech—either ignoring him or telling him that he needed to refer those questions and concerns to his residential caregivers. At one point, Robert said he wanted to be with his father, producing concerns among the staff that Robert would attempt suicide to achieve that goal. The staff did not understand that these behaviors were part of the normal grieving process. Robert was expressing his feelings about the loss of a valued person and was most likely demonstrating a need for comfort and reassurance. He was preoccupied with memories of his father and recalled the enjoyable associations he had with him.

Camille, a 26-year-old woman with moderate autism, was concerned about the pregnancy miscarriage experienced by her caregiver. Camille had been informed of the various developmental stages of the expected child and was looking forward to holding the baby, as had been promised by the staff person. She was devastated, as were many of the other clients, when told that there would be no baby. Camille demonstrated grief in terms of sadness, disruption of her work schedule, and constant questioning of the caregiver, who was herself grieving. Camille also expressed anger at the caregiver for denying her the opportunity to see and hold the baby. This example reminds us of how closely relationships may develop between clients and caregivers; and it is a good example of the impact anticipation has on behavior. Camille was not able to understand the concept of death in this case, perhaps because she had never seen or touched the baby from whom she was anticipating pleasure.

Billy, a 4-year-old nonverbal child with severe autism, whose young father had died suddenly of a heart attack, could not understand what had happened to his father and was unable to communicate his feelings about the loss. His behavior, already disruptive at home, became even more difficult to control. He demonstrated an increased frequency of enuresis, tantrum behavior, and inattentiveness to stimuli. The problems attributed to autism became exaggerated in the absence of his father. His mother was at a loss as to how to comfort Billy and explain to him what had happened. As we will see later, Billy's age most likely compounded the difficulties with communication. A child under the age of 5 is generally unable to understand what it means for someone to die.

Joe, a 28-year-old man with mild mental retardation, experienced the loss of a pet dog that had been part of his family for 14 years. He did not speak fondly of the pet, but was angry, saying he was glad the dog had died and, "good riddance." Joe said that his other pets were more important to him. Joe's behavior, however, changed in significant ways. He became more aggressive and more demanding in social relationships and often expressed his opinions in a belligerent way. He spoke frequently about the deceased pet to staff and other clients at his day care placement.

Judy, a 30-year-old woman with mild autism who was often violent and self-abusive, had lost her father several years earlier, but still talked about him as a person who had loved her and indulged her, in contrast to her mother who did none of those things. Whenever she was denied some activity or object or asked to shoulder some responsibility at home, she mentioned that her father would never have refused her or asked her to do any of the things requested. This refrain continued to upset her mother, who felt that she herself had "moved on with her life" and wanted her daughter to do so as well.

STAGES OF BEREAVEMENT

Bereavement is thought by many to occur in stages, although it is not certain that a person must grieve in an ordered sequence or that anything harmful happens if a person does not do so. With each stage, the time limits may vary, and the intensity experienced may differ markedly as a function of individual and environmental variables. Let us look briefly at what these stages are, keeping in mind that there is no set pattern to what any individual will experience when grieving.

Stage 1: Shock

During the first stage of bereavement, the bereaved person experiences a dazed sense of unreality or numbing that may last several hours or several days, and he or she often reports feeling isolated from the world.

Stage 2: Protest and Yearning

In the second stage, the bereaved person recognizes the loss but does not entirely accept it. He or she feels intense pain and longing for the deceased and protests the loss by means of a variety of "searching" behaviors, including dreams about the dead person, "finding" him or her in familiar places, hallucinations, and so forth. This is also a time of agitation, heightened physiological arousal, and restlessness, sometimes alternating with a feeling of deceleration.

The bereaved is preoccupied with memories of the lost person and focuses attention on those aspects of the environment that have pleasant associations with the deceased person. This stage typically lasts for several months.

Stage 3: Disorganization and Despair

In the third stage, the bereaved accepts the fact of the loss and abandons attempts to recover the lost person but continues to grieve for the deceased. The bereaved person commonly experiences apathy, withdrawal, loss of energy and despondency, loss of sexual interest, poor socialization, diminished appetite, sleep disturbances, and other behavioral and somatic problems. He or she may experience conflicting emotions and moods, such as despair, hostility, shame, guilt, anger, and irritability. This stage is the most enduring, complex, and difficult phase of the grief process, often lasting a year or more.

Stage 4: Detachment, Reorganization, and Recovery

The characteristics of the third stage are ultimately relieved when the bereaved develops new ways of perceiving and thinking about the world and his or her place in it. A person regains hope and confidence in him- or herself and is able to enjoy life again. Most often, this involves the establishment of new roles, relationships, and sense of purpose in life. It is not unusual for a person to grieve for several years before a relatively adequate readjustment occurs. Feelings of grief may be triggered continuously by holidays and dates that mark meaningful events for the bereaved.

EXPRESSION OF GRIEF BY PERSONS WITH DEVELOPMENTAL DISABILITIES

Persons with developmental disabilities demonstrate expressions of grief similar to persons without developmental disabilities. In a study in which 37 adults with mild to severe mental retardation were interviewed about their past experiences with loss through death, the effect of the loss on their lives, and how they dealt with the bereavement process, Harper and Wadsworth (1993) found that (1) a significant proportion of the population (29 people of 37) indicated an accurate cognitive understanding of death; (2) clients reported concerns about the deaths of relatives, roommates, and pets, and the loss of care providers who had changed jobs; (3) more than a quarter of the population interviewed indicated problems of loneliness, anxiety, sadness, and depression following the death of a relative or care provider; (4) almost half the population reported having dreams about the person who had died; and (5) the large majority said they did not talk with others about death. These clients had experienced their losses at various time intervals from the date of the interview, including 6 months, 1 year, 2 years, and from 2 to 3 years. When queried about "circumstances when bereavement (in their opinion) became dysfunctional" (p. 324), the typical response was 1 year, followed by 6 months, with a range from 1 or 2 days to more than 5 years. As reported in this same study, the authors surveyed 100 people who worked professionally with people with mental retardation about their personal experiences in assisting clients during times of personal loss. These professionals reported that they had observed the following frequent reactions to grief on the part of the bereaved clients: crying, sadness, irritability, sleep difficulties, fatigue, loss of appetite, hostility toward others, body aches, anxiety, and confusion. These professionals also reported a number of lifestyle changes in their clients, including a reduction in physical activity, social isolation, a preference for passive activities, a decrease in the number of activities, and poor hygiene. Loss and grief reactions were noted in some cases to precipitate a decrease in daily functional living skills as well.

The behavior described by both the clients and the professional caregivers in the study by Harper and Wadsworth (1993) are similar to the behaviors portrayed in bereavement stages 1, 2, and 3 presented earlier. Those with developmental disabilities who participated in these studies indicated shock over their losses; they felt intense pain and longing for the deceased and protested the loss by a variety of searching behaviors; and they experienced a host of psychological, social, and physical problems similar to those described in bereavement stages 2 and 3. The one area for which data are not provided in this study is the final one—detachment, reorganization, and recovery. The issue of coping with grief is addressed in the last part of this chapter.

GRIEF AS A STRESSOR

There is no question that the death of a loved one is a stressful experience. As a stressor, bereavement has been implicated in the development of disease and illness (e.g., Elliott & Eisdorfer, 1982; Lindemann, 1950; Osterweis, Solomon, & Green, 1984; Selye, 1976).

Bereavement expressed as "death of a spouse," or "death of a close family member," and "death of a close friend" ranks high on the list of Holmes and Rahe's (1967) Social Readjustment Rating Scale. These events were rated, respectively, as numbers 1, 5, and 17 as requiring the most intense readjustment for an individual. Bramston, Fogarty, and Cummings (1999) found that more than half of the people with an intellectual disability identified death as a significant stressor in their lives. The loss itself, the person's attempt to cope with the loss, and the environmental disruption resulting from the loss creates an internal imbalance for the bereaved person.

According to the cognitive stress theory of Lazarus and Folkman (1984), "Psychological stress is a particular relationship between the person and the environment that is appraised by the individual as taxing or exceeding his or her resources and endangering his or her well-being" (p. 19). There are three distinct elements of the definition that are important to consider. The first element is the emphasis on the relationship between demands and resources that affect the extent of the stress experienced in a particular situation. Thus, the emphasis is neither placed exclusively on the demands of the situation nor exclusively on the resources of the person.

The second element is the individual's cognitive appraisal of the situation, which determines why and to what extent a situation is viewed as stressful. A situation is considered irrelevant if it has no implications for the individual's well-being; it is benign if it will preserve or improve the individual's well-being; and it is stressful if it is appraised as harmful, threatening, or involving a loss. Once the stressful nature of a situation has been identified, the individual must evaluate his or her coping options to determine the most effective strategy for achieving success. The extent of the stress experienced depends on the relationship between what is perceived as the danger and what are the resources one has to deal with the danger. As new information becomes available to the person, the cognitive appraisal process may change.

The third element has to do with coping methods, which are defined as "constantly changing cognitive and behavioral efforts to manage specific external and/or internal demands that are appraised as taxing or exceeding the resources of the person" (Lazarus & Folkman, 1984, p. 141). The extent to which the individual will experience a situation as stressful depends on the coping resources he or she has. These resources may reside within the person and may include health and energy levels, social skills, positive beliefs, self-concept, self-control ability, and problem-solving capability. The resources may also be derived from the environment, such as money, housing, and social support. Because people do not always use the resources available to them, Lazarus and Folkman introduced the notion of constraints to indicate factors that restrict the way people employ the resources available to them.

Let us now try to apply this cognitive model of stress to bereavement among those with autism and other developmental disabilities. First, we consider the demands of the situation. An individual with developmental disabilities and those involved in his or her care may be regarded as a small social organization with a differentiated system of roles regulating behavior. All members of the social group spend a great deal of time with each other, often forming strong attachment bonds. In addition, the maintenance of routine is extremely important. Changes in routine, or even transitions from one place or event to another, may result in displays of anxiety. The loss of any person in this social group marks the end of a close relationship and imposes change on the other members of the group. Tasks performed by the person will have to be assumed by another member of the group or assigned to a person new to the social group, making for an additional change for all.

For the person with developmental disabilities, the loss of a loved one may bring about a change of residence, a change in employment, the loss of visitors, or other sources of social support, which in turn may result in a decrease in attention, activities, and physical care, poor hygiene, and loss of financial status. He or she may also face other environmental upheavals, like moving in with a new roommate or learning to work with a new care provider. Even the loss of a beloved pet with a long history of attachment to an individual may have a significant impact on that individual's life. Another source of stress for grieving individuals stems from the failure of others to recognize their expressions of grief and from their inability to "work through" the grieving process. Wadsworth and Harper (1991) have gone so far as to say that profound stress from these changes may precipitate a psychiatric illness in individuals with mental retardation.

Second, we consider the person's coping resources. There is a great deal of individual variability in this area. To a large extent, the person's ability to cope with loss will depend on his or her personality traits, personal skills and strengths, financial resources, and social supports. The availability of social support and the ability to access and maintain it is of prime importance (Hansson, 1986). Thus, one might argue that a person who has been taught self-control procedures, including ways to appraise a situation cognitively in a positive way, one who has a positive self-image, and one who has been provided with social skills, will most likely be better able to cope with loss than a person with deficits in any of those areas. Further, a person who has acquired knowledge and experience about death, mourning rituals, and ways of interacting with others over the death of a loved one will have an advantage in his or her ability to cope with the loss.

The availability of a social network is extremely important to the grief process. The bereaved person must be able to talk about the loss, express his or her feelings, and explore the effect of the loss on one's life. To know that others have had similar experiences and feelings is also a big help to the bereaved. And the knowledge that a person is able to rely on others for support should reduce anxiety and feelings of loneliness.

There is virtually no empirical evidence on the coping resources or coping processes displayed by those with developmental disabilities in the experience of bereavement. Several educational programs have been developed, however, to assist those with developmental disabilities handle losses in their lives. These programs will be examined later in this chapter.

DEPRESSION AND BEREAVEMENT

When stress is added to grief, especially if the stress is prolonged, depression and other pathological grief reactions are likely to develop (Stroebe & Stroebe, 1987). Grief and depression are closely related phenomena (Averill, 1979). According to Harper and Wadsworth (1993), such depression-linked behaviors as fatigue, sadness, loss of energy, irritability, lowered self-esteem, poor hygiene, loss of appetite, increased isolation from others, and a reduction in "acting out" behaviors are among the major manifestations of a grief reaction for those with developmental disabilities; these occur with high frequency.

For caregivers, it is difficult to know if the client is experiencing grief-related depression, a psychiatric case of clinical depression, or a physical problem. Often caregivers decide on the second diagnosis and resort to behavioral treatment interventions or psychotropic medications for the behaviors exhibited (Moise, 1985) instead of simply providing support and the opportunity to express one's emotions. Further, the use of these methods does not typically encourage the development of coping strategies to deal with the bereavement experienced. Grief-related depression is generally time-limited and may be less debilitating to the individual than a serious case of clinical depression.

It appears from the research of Stoddart, Burke, and Temple (2002) that depression is more likely than is anxiety to be alleviated for the bereaved after a group intervention, again underscoring the transient nature of grief-related depression. These authors tested 21 bereaved, middle-aged persons with intellectual disabilities before and after a group therapy experience focused on bereavement and found that depression scores were significantly changed after the group intervention, but anxiety and understanding about death were not changed.

PATHOLOGICAL GRIEF

If grief has continued for an extensive time (usually more than a year) and the bereaved person shows no sign of recovering from the loss, or if the grieving behaviors put a person at serious physical or psychological risk (e.g., from self-injury, threat of suicide, extreme aggressiveness, refusal to eat, extreme passivity or withdrawal, or hallucinatory reactions), the grief may be considered pathological (Wahl, 1970). When the bereaved denies that the death occurred or becomes morbidly preoccupied with the death of a person, the grief may also be regarded as pathological and require clinical interventions.

The bereaved may manifest widely varying responses and, to a large extent, it will be the family and other caregivers of the client who determine the inappropriateness or appropriateness of the grief reactions. One must make a judgment about pathological grief in light of the full range of normal grief against which the behavior in question is being compared. One must also recognize the physiological, social, and psychological variables that might influence an individual's grief reaction (Rando, 1984).

In considering situations in which bereavement becomes pathological among those with developmental disabilities, the survey conducted by Harper and Wadsworth (1993) revealed that approximately 10–15% of grieving clients suffered intense grief reactions, which could be considered dysfunctional. These reactions were headaches, difficulty breathing, loss of orientation to surroundings, loss of body function, hyperactivity, suicidal statements, pretending to be dead, increase in sexual behavior, "bizarre actions," hearing voices, or seeing things not present. These responses are similar to those experienced by people who do not display developmental disabilities.

INFLUENCE OF AGE AND COGNITIVE FACTORS ON BEREAVEMENT

Two factors, among others, that affect grief reactions are chronological age and cognitive abilities. According to Raphael (1983), bereaved children up to the age of 5 years manifest anxiety or aggressive behavior, fears about separation, temper tantrums, periodic loss of bowel and bladder control, and sleep disturbances.

Indeed, several clinical researchers (Bowlby, 1980; Rutter, 1966) have found that bereaved children under the age of 5 are more susceptible to the pathological effects of grieving than are older children.

Raphael (1983) has pointed out that children between 6 and 10 years old may appear to be unaffected by the loss of a loved one and demonstrate emotional control. They may be trying to appear mature, or they may be afraid of feeling vulnerable or appearing "different" to their peers. Children in this age group often assume the role of caretaker to a younger sibling, or even a parent. They often demonstrate excessive guilt and think about things they might have done differently to prevent the person from dying. Phobic and hypochondriacal behaviors also become prominent in this age group, with children becoming preoccupied with personal failings and making mistakes.

Bereaved preadolescents and adolescents manifest many of these same behaviors, but include new patterns of response (Corr & Corr, 1996). They generally keep their emotional reactions private and are cautious about every thing they say and do. They rarely confide in others or accept condolences, being especially anxious to fit in with their peers at all costs. Adolescents may go to one or both extremes of behavior. They may become depressed and withdrawn after a death, avoiding regular activities and even close friends, or they may run away from home or indulge in excessive risk taking through drugs, alcohol, promiscuity, or reckless driving. Some bereaved adolescents become preoccupied with the "unfairness" of death or make judgments about how others react to death, presumably as a way to exert intellectual control over a highly emotional event. They may also feel guilty about their possible previous insensitive behavior to the deceased person and other perceived personal flaws and errors in the past. Finally, it is not unusual for adolescents to try to assume the role of caretaker in the family.

Baker and Sedney (1996) have outlined seven ways in which the grief reactions of children differ from those of adults. First, the reactions of children are often less intense just after a death has occurred, but they last longer, thereby extending the bereavement process for them. Second, children need adult parenting figures who are consistently available and able to help them work through painful feelings brought on by the loss (Furman, 1974). Third, children under the age of 11 are not as cognitively able to understand the nature and implications of death. Fourth, children use different ways to cope with loss, such as distraction, clinging to familiar routines for comfort, denying the loss, and using fantasy (Sekaer, 1987). Fifth, when the child experiences the loss of a parent, his or her grief reactions are affected by a strong need to identify with the attributes of the person who has died instead of trying to distance oneself, which is a more common reaction for adults. Sixth, because a child's development of self is still in process, a child is affected more deeply by a loss in childhood. Seventh, it is difficult to ascertain when grieving has terminated and normal development resumes because the process of grieving is closely interwoven with the developmental processes in children.

In studying early elementary school children without developmental disabilities, Jenkins and Cavanaugh (1985) found a positive correlation between a child's understanding of human mortality and chronological age and the acquisition of verbal skills. The older the child, the better able he or she was to have a realistic concept of death. The same has been found true for older adults with mental retardation. Seltzer (1989) found that elderly adults with mental retardation acquired a more accurate conceptualization about death than younger adults with comparable cognitive abilities. Seltzer attributed this difference to the life experiences acquired through the aging process.

Intellectual impairments and communication deficits are other factors that may complicate the grieving process. Koocher (1973) demonstrated that a child's individual level of cognitive development is a more important influence on his or her death concepts than chronological age alone. As Piaget (1951) has outlined, cognitive and language development for a child under the age of 3 is too poorly developed to convey an accurate concept of death. Between the ages of 3 and 5 years, death is seen as reversible; the dead are often presumed to be asleep. Between the ages of 5 and 9 years, children begin to understand that death is final, but they see it only in reference to other people. After age 10, death is seen as permanent, inevitable, and associated with the termination of bodily activities. Wolfenstein (1966, 1969) wrote that children do not have the ability to tolerate the pain of bereavement necessary to achieve satisfactory separation from a loved one until adolescence. Wolfenstein (1966) also felt that a period of "trial mourning" is a normal part of adolescent development and is necessary for mourning a loss.

Kennedy (2000) attempted to determine if Piagetian level (Piaget, 1951) of cognitive development, verbal comprehension knowledge, social inference skill, and experience with death affected the understanding of death in 108 adults with a mean IQ of 53. Kennedy found that IQ was a significant factor in understanding what death means, along with previous experience with death in the form of having lost a loved one, having participated in death-related events, and having talked to someone about death and dying. Piagetian level of cognitive development was not related to how people understood death, but it did moderate the relationship between one's skill at forming verbal concepts and understanding death.

Perhaps most significantly, the results from this study indicated that the adults with mental retardation were similar to children without mental retardation in how they conceptualized death (Kennedy, 2000). Thus, it appears that cognitive age is an important factor in understanding death, along with life experiences which involved death and dying. It is not necessary, however, that a person's cognitive age be high in order to understand death. Chronological age is also an important factor. Children under the age of 10 generally do not have much experience with death and the dying process, so they do not have a firm grasp on the finality of death. One suspects that the effects of experience would wipe out the protections of age. The lower limits of cognitive age in understanding death and how intellectual development interfaces with chronological age and experience and the advantages brought by each factor are still unclear.

INTERVENTIONS

The way one adjusts to a loss is influenced by a multiplicity of interwoven factors, including the quality of the relationship between the people involved, the quality and availability of a social network, the manner in which the death occurred, the degree to which the loss was anticipated, the developmental and cognitive level of the bereaved person, the spiritual and religious training of the bereaved, age and gender, previous experiences with loss, and the bereaved person's general anxiety about death and illness.

It is important to remember that grieving is a natural, human process. It is not pathological to feel sadness at the loss of a familiar and loved person, pet, or object. When a loss occurs, we should not immediately try to change the grieving behaviors we see in clients. Persons with developmental disabilities need to be consoled in their grief like anyone else. They need to explore their feelings about the loss and verbalize those feelings. They need room to express their sadness in whatever way is feasible. They should not, upon displaying signs of grief, necessarily be medicated or placed in a more restrictive environment to come to terms with their grief.

The individual with developmental disabilities may experience problems in expressing emotions and adapting to changes in relationships (Day, 1985; Harper, Wadsworth, & Fowler, 1991; Oswin, 1985). Some of these problems may be avoided if the person with developmental disabilities receives instruction about death and the grieving process and if they are taught ways to cope with the feelings of loss. One such program of "death education" has been developed by Yanok and Beifus (1993). They developed a curriculum, called Communi-cating About Loss and Mourning (CALM), which was field tested on verbally expressive adults with mental retardation. Twenty-five clients from sheltered workshops served as the experimental group, while 25 others were the controls. The mean ages of the participants in the groups were 35 and 45 years old, respec-tively. Each group had a mean IQ of 49. Using animate and inanimate objects and pictures of people at different stages in life, in eight 50-min sessions, the investigators successfully taught participants to (1) distinguish between living organisms and inanimate objects within the natural environment; (2) understand that all living things ultimately die; (3) realize that death is a permanent condi-tion; (4) demonstrate an awareness of the meaning of fatal accidents, terminal illnesses, and natural causes of death; and (5) define pertinent spoken vocabulary words (e.g., burial, cemetery, deceased, funeral, mourning, perish). Sessions consisted primarily of guided group discussions of individual and shared death experiences, with encouragement to share personal thoughts and worries.

The methods used to bring about positive results were varied and creative. One method involved providing experience with death-related accoutrements by means of field trips to area funeral homes, cemeteries, and churches and participating in discussions about death with funeral directors, physicians, and the clergy. Yanok and Beifus (1993) taught clients socially appropriate behavior at funeral homes and cemeteries by using media presentations of actual or enacted burial rites. They taught that it was acceptable to demonstrate sorrow in public and that, in some cases, indifference or relief might also be a reasonable human reaction to the death of a stranger or long-suffering loved one. With modeling, rehearsal, feedback, reinforcement, and practice in the natural environment, they instructed clients how and when to display grief, behave appropriately at funeral services, and convey condolences to others who are bereaved.

Yanouk and Beifus (1993) recommend that the CALM program be implemented on a weekly basis over a period of several months, rather than on successive days over a brief period. They maintain that it is best to provide a review and guided discussion of material from previous classes before teaching a new lesson and that clients be encouraged to speak freely about their own mortality, as well as that of others.

Another model of helping bereaved persons address specific personal loss has been developed for children by Baker, Sedney, and Gross (1992). Although there is no evidence in the literature that this model has been used with children or adults with developmental disabilities, it deserves some attention here. This model focuses on presenting tasks for the bereaved at different stages (early, middle, and late) after the loss has been experienced. It is useful for people with developmental disabilities who have little experience with death and/or loss and it is fairly concrete in explaining ways to intervene at different times in the grief process. It promotes the idea that grief-related behavior is directed to certain goals.

Early-phase tasks of grieving focus on explaining that someone has died, what death means, and that the client is personally safe. The client may worry that he or she will die as well or that the other people that they know may die too. As a result, the client may engage in a variety of self-protective mechanisms, such as denial, distortion, and emotional, or even physical, isolation from others. They may avoid overstimulation and try to protect others in the setting, requiring the caregiver to provide extra emotional support during this time.

Baker et al. (1992) recommends that the client be included in the mourning ritual, especially if it is a family member who has died. If it is a staff member who has died, or another client, and it is unlikely that the grieving person would ordinarily be included in the mourning practices, although some memorial service marking the loss is probably useful. Efforts should be made to elicit questions from the client, answer them thoroughly, and tolerate his or her attempts to cope with the loss. Depending on the client, it may be necessary to make sure that daily routines are maintained in order to provide environmental consistency.

Middle-phase tasks include accepting and emotionally acknowledging the reality of the loss, exploring and reevaluating the relationship to the person who died, and facing the psychological pain that accompanies the realization of the loss. The relationship to the deceased is explored as fully as possible through stories about him or her, focusing on both good and bad memories. In this phase the client needs to realize that the deceased will not return. Painful feelings of loss and despair must be weathered with the support from the staff and family members.

It is possible that the client will have ambivalent feelings about the deceased, such as angry feelings at being abandoned, or guilt over something that was done and has been associated with the person who has died. It is helpful to discuss these feelings in a supportive context and encourage positive memories of the deceased.

Late-phase tasks relate to the reorganization of an individual's sense of identity and of significant relationships. First, the client needs to develop a new sense of how he or she fits into the social group in the absence of the deceased, while still understanding that someone has been lost and that connections to that person remain. Second, the client needs to develop new relationships without an excessive fear of loss and without having to compare the new person with the one who has died. Sometimes the need to make new attachments is so urgent that problems may develop when new people are introduced into the social group of the client. Third, the client must be able to consolidate and maintain his or her relationship to the deceased. Fourth, the client must be able to return to his or her typical schedule and resume the pattern of living that was interrupted by the loss. Finally, the client must be able to cope with the periodic resurgence of painful affect, usually at special anniversaries where there is a reminder of the loss.

CONCLUSIONS

Grief is a normal and universal experience among human beings. The sorrow of loss is shared by all, including those with developmental disabilities. As we have seen, people with developmental disabilities are able to understand the meaning, finality, and irreversibility of death, despite cognitive and developmental limitations. They are able to feel grief and its effects, in terms of both anxiety and depression.

Although some educational programs have been developed to help persons with developmental disabilities address personal losses and participate in the mourning rituals attendant on a death, more are needed. It is hoped that death education will become a part of individual education plans and that caregivers will themselves be educated to deal sensitively with the bereavement issues of their clients.

Acknowledgment

Portions of this chapter have been presented in depth elsewhere by Averill and Wisocki (1981) and Wisocki and Averill (1987).

References

Averill, J. (1979). The functions of grief. In C. Izard (Ed.), *Emotions in personality and psychopathology*. New York: Plenum Press.

Averill, J., & Wisocki, P. (1981). Some observations on behavioral approaches to the treatment of grief among the elderly. In H. J. Sobel (Ed.), *Behavior therapy in terminal care: A humanistic approach* (pp. 125–150). Cambridge, MA: Ballinger.

Baker, J., & Sedney, M. A. (1996). How bereaved children cope with loss: An overview. In C. A. Corr & D. M. Corr (Eds.), *Handbook of childhood death and bereavement*. New York: Springer.

Baker, J., Sedney, M. A., & Gross, E. (1992). Psychological tasks for bereaved children. *American Journal of Orthopsychiatry, 62*, 105–116.

Bowlby, J. (1980). *Attachment and loss: Vol. 3. Loss, sadness, and depression*. New York: Basic Books.

Bramston, P., Fogarty, G., & Cummings, R. (1999). The nature of stressors reported by people with an intellectual disability. *Journal of Applied Research in Intellectual Disabilities, 12*, 1–10.

Carder, M. M. (1987). Journey into understanding: Mentally retarded people's experience around death. *Journal of Pastoral Care, 4*, 18–31.

Corr, C., & Corr, D. (Eds.). (1996). *Handbook of childhood death and bereavement*. New York: Springer.

Day, K. (1985). Psychiatric disorder in middle-aged, elderly mentally handicapped. *British Journal of Psychiatry, 147*, 665–668.

Deutsch, H. (1985). Grief counseling with the mentally retarded clients. *Psychiatric Aspects of Mental Retardation Reviews, 4*, 17–20.

Elliott, G., & Eisdorfer, C. (Eds.). (1982). *Stress and human health: A study by the Institute of Medicine, National Academy of Sciences*. New York: Springer.

Furman, E. (1974). *A child's parent dies: Studies in childhood bereavement*. New Haven, CT: Yale University Press.

Hansson, R. (1986). Relational competence, relationships, and adjustment in old age. *Journal of Personality and Social Psychology, 50*, 1050–1058.

Harper, D., & Wadsworth, J. (1993). Grief in adults with mental retardation: Preliminary findings. *Research in Developmental Disabilities, 14*(4), 313–330.

Harper, D., Wadsworth, J., & Fowler, C. (1991, October). Grief and loss with older adults with mental retardation: A pilot study of current status and needs. Paper presented at the SIG/Aging Conference, Lexington, KY.

Holmes, R., & Rahe, R. (1967). The social readjustment rating scale. *Journal of Psychosomatic Research, 11*, 213–218.

Jenkins, R., & Cavanaugh, J. (1985). Examining the relationship between the development of the concept of death and overall cognitive development. *Omega: Journal of Death and Dying, 16*, 193–199.

Kennedy, E. J. (2000). The impact of cognitive development and socialization factors on the concept of death among adults with mental retardation. *Dissertation Abstracts International: Section B. The Sciences and Engineering* (p. 1111). University Microfilms International.

Kloeppel, D., & Hollins, S. (1989). Double handicap: Mental retardation and death in the family. *Death Studies 13*, 31–38.

Koocher, G. (1973). Childhood, death, and cognitive development. *Developmental Psychology, 9*, 369–375.

Lazarus, R., & Folkman, S. (1984). *Stress, appraisal, and coping.* New York: Springer.

Lindemann, E. (1950). Modifications in the course of ulcerative colitis in relationship to changes in life situations and reaction patterns. *Research Publications of the Association for Research in Nervous and Mental Disorders, 29*, 706–723.

Lipe-Goodson, P. S., & Goebel, B. L. (1983). Perceptions of age and death in mentally retarded adults. *Mental Retardation, 21*, 68–75.

McDaniel, B. A. (1989). A group work experience with mentally retarded adults on the issues of death and dying. *Journal of Gerontological Social Work, 13*, 187–192.

Mineka, S., & Suomi, S. (1978). Social separation in monkeys. *Psychological Bulletin, 85*, 376–400.

Moise, L. (1985). In sickness and death. *Mental Retardation, 16*, 397–398.

Osterweis, M., Solomon, F., & Green, M. (Eds.). (1984). *Bereavement reactions, consequences, and care.* Washington, DC: National Academy Press.

Oswin, M. (1985). Bereavement. In M. Kraft, J. Bicknell, & S. Hollins (Eds.), *Mental handicap: A multidisciplinary approach* (pp. 197–205). Ballierre, England: Tindall.

Piaget, J. (1951). *The child's conception of the world.* London: Routledge & Kegan Paul.

Rando, T. (1984). *Grief, dying, and death: Clinical interventions for caregivers.* Champaign, IL: Research Press.

Raphael, B. (1983). *The anatomy of bereavement.* New York: Basic Books.

Rutter, M. (1966). *Children of sick parents.* London: Oxford University Press.

Sekaer, C. (1987). Toward a definition of "childhood mourning." *American Journal of Psychotherapy, 41*, 201–219.

Seltzer, G. B. (1989). A developmental approach to cognitive understanding of death and dying. In M. Howell (Ed.), *Serving the underserved: Caring for people who are both old and mentally retarded* (pp. 331–338). Boston: Exceptional Parent Press.

Selye, H. (1976). *The stress of life* (2nd ed). New York: McGraw-Hill.

Speece, M. W., & Brent, S. B. (1984). Children's understanding of death: A review of three components of a death concept. *Child Development, 55*, 1671–1686.

Stoddart, K., Burke, L., & Temple, V. (2002). Outcome evaluation of bereavement groups for adults with intellectual disabilities. *Journal of Applied Research in Intellectual Disabilities, 15*, 28–35.

Stroebe, W., & Stroebe, M. (1987). *Bereavement and health.* Cambridge, MA: Cambridge University Press.

Wadsworth, J., & Harper, D. (1991). Grief and bereavement in mental retardation: A need for a new understanding. *Death Studies, 15*, 281–292.

Wahl, C. (1970). The differential diagnosis of normal and neurotic grief following bereavement. *Psychosomatics, 11*, 104–106.

Wisocki, P., & Averill, J. (1987). The challenge of bereavement. In L. Carstensen and B. Edelstein (Eds.), *Handbook of clinical gerontology* (pp. 312–321). New York: Pergamon Press.

Wolfenstein, M. (1966). How is mourning possible? *Psychoanalytic Study of the Child, 21*, 93–123.

Wolfenstein, M. (1969). Loss, rage, and repetition. *Psychoanalytic Study of the Child, 24*, 432–460.

Yanok, J., & Beifus, J. A. (1993). Communicating about loss and mourning: Death education for individuals with mental retardation. *Mental Retardation, 31*, 144–147.

15 Diagnosis and Treatment of Anxiety Disorders in Individuals with Autism Spectrum Disorder

Luke Y. Tsai

It is appropriate to address the assessment and treatment of anxiety disorders in a volume on stress and coping in autism spectrum disorder (ASD) for several reasons. Anxiety and stress are related conditions in that they both involve physiological arousal. As such, anxiety is always accompanied by stress. In addition, the presence of anxiety disorders can create great difficulties and stress in an individual's life because anxiety disorders can be debilitating; they are often associated with isolation, depression, substance abuse, and other forms of psychopathology. People with anxiety disorders are three to five times more likely to go to a doctor and six times more likely to be hospitalized for psychiatric disorders than people without anxiety disorders (Anxiety Disorders Association of America, 2004). Furthermore, an anxiety disorder may quite frequently be a comorbid psychiatric disorder that has been misdiagnosed or unrecognized in individuals with ASD. Finally, the caregivers of individuals with ASD usually have additional stress when their children develop comorbid anxiety disorders. Therefore, it is crucial that caregivers learn about early recognition of anxiety disorders in their children with ASD to ensure early and effective treatment.

This chapter reviews anxiety disorders in individuals with either an autistic disorder or Asperger's disorder and uses the term ASD to indicate that the information being presented can be applied to both. Building on an overview of the comorbid psychiatric disorders of both autistic disorder and Asperger's disorder, I outline a process of medical assessment and general psychosocial treatment of anxiety disorders. I conclude with guidelines for psychopharmacological assessment and treatment of anxiety disorders in ASD. The recommendations herein are developed mainly from my experience with persons with ASD. I hope that these recommendations will be helpful as strategic decision guides rather than as prescriptive formulae to physicians, caregivers, and families alike.

COMORBID PSYCHIATRIC DISORDERS OF AUTISTIC DISORDER

Several medical conditions that have been recognized with a relatively high frequency in individuals with autistic disorder. About 30% of people with autistic disorder also have seizure disorders, 2–5% have fragile X syndrome, and 1–3% have tuberous sclerosis. Many individuals with autistic disorder also develop other behavioral or psychiatric symptoms in addition to the core autistic symptomatologies (e.g., impairment in social interaction, impairment in communication, and restricted, repetitive and stereotyped patterns of behavior, interests, and activities) that may be considered clinical manifestations of comorbid psychiatric disorders. In fact, there is an accumulation of case reports describing specific types of psychiatric disorders in individuals with autistic disorders. These include reports of unipolar and bipolar affective disorders, obsessive-compulsive disorder (OCD), schizophrenia, and Tourette's syndrome (reviewed by Tsai, 2003a). There are consistent reports of a comorbidity for autism and anxiety disorders. Estimates of cormorbid disorders include 17% (Ando & Yoshimura, 1979), 23% (Chung, Luk, & Lee, 1990), 25% (Szatmari, Bartolucci, Bremner, Bond, & Rich, 1989) and 46% (Gillott, Furniss, & Walter, 2001). Other studies report rates ranging from about 60% (Rutter, Greenfeld, & Lockyer, 1967), 73% (Le Couteur et al., 1989), and 74% (Fombonne, 1992).

COMORBID PSYCHIATRIC DISORDERS OF ASPERGER'S DISORDER

Information about the incidence of comorbid psychiatric disorders in Asperger's disorder has been quite limited due to its relatively short history of acceptance as a distinct clinical entity by professionals in the United States. Nonetheless, there are reported cases of psychiatric disorders such as Tourette's disorder, attention-deficit hyperactivity disorder (ADHD), affective illness or depression, OCD, and schizophrenia in individuals with Asperger's disorder (reviewed by Tsai, 2003b).

Tantam (2000) stated that anxiety was an almost universally comorbid condition with Asperger's disorder. Green, Gilchrist, Burton, and Cox (2000) examined psychiatric and social functioning in 20 individuals with Asperger's disorder, ages 11–19 years, with full-scale IQ scores above 70. The researchers found that 35% of the adolescents with Asperger's disorder met the ICD-10 (*International Classification of Diseases, 10th revision*; World Health Organization, 1992) criteria for generalized anxiety disorder (GAD), and 10% met the criteria for a specific phobia. The Asperger's disorder group had significantly

more symptoms of worry, hypochondria, panic, specific fears, and obsessive ruminations and rituals than the control group with a diagnosis of conduct disorder.
Mental status exams also revealed more physical signs of anxiety, nonfacial tics,
and abnormal emotional responsiveness in the Asperger's disorder.

COMORBID ANXIETY DISORDERS OF AUTISM SPECTRUM DISORDER

When autistic disorder and Asperger's disorder are viewed as a spectrum disorder, some clinicians have cited anxiety as a common feature of ASD (Attwood,
1998; Tantam, 2000). Although still lacking in breadth, a small body of research
on anxiety in individuals with autism spectrum disorder has been emerging in
recent years. Kim, Szatmari, Bryson, Streiner, and Wilson (2000) examined the
prevalence of anxiety and mood problems in a sample of 59 children with autism
and Asperger's disorder with IQ scores above the cut-off for mental retardation.
The researchers found that 13.6% of the children in the study scored at least
two standard deviations above the mean on a parent report measure of generalized anxiety and on the internalizing factor, which includes generalized anxiety,
separation anxiety, and depression.

DIAGNOSING ANXIETY DISORDERS IN INDIVIDUALS WITH ASD

Individuals with ASD represent a diverse clinical picture, which often makes diagnosis and treatment difficult. One factor that leads to confusion for clinicians
making diagnostic and programming decisions is the wide variability of characteristics within the spectrum of autism. It has been observed that when anxiety
symptoms do exist in individuals with ASD, only those individuals with high-
functioning autistic disorder or Asperger's disorder are more likely to receive
an additional diagnosis of anxiety disorders (*Diagnostic and Statistical Manual of Mental Disorders, Fourth Edition—Text Revision* [*DSM-IV-TR*]; American Psychiatric Association [APA], 2000). Clinicians are usually reluctant to
make additional psychiatric diagnosis in the lower functioning or nonverbal individuals with autistic disorder who are incapable of providing diagnostic information via diagnostic interviewing or patient self-report scales (Tsai, 1996).
The lack of reliable and valid alternative diagnostic methods applicable to the
lower functioning or nonverbal autistic population is another contributory factor
to the lower rate of anxiety disorders reported by general practitioners. Moreover, many symptoms of anxiety disorder (e.g., panic attacks, avoiding noisy and
crowded places) tend to be interpreted as aberrant behaviors by many clinicians
who lack knowledge of and experience in anxiety disorders in individuals with
ASD. Nevertheless, even individuals with high-functioning autistic disorder or

Asperger's disorder usually do not know that they are suffering from anxiety disorders. Hence, they usually do not report or complain of their anxiety symptoms.

To render more effective treatment of people with ASD, the current assessment technology must be advanced and refined. To accomplish this goal, some modifications of the contemporary diagnostic criteria of certain psychiatric disorders, including anxiety disorders, may be required when dealing with the autistic population. For example, a diagnosis of GAD should be considered in lower functioning individuals with ASD even in the absence of clear verbal report of symptoms by the individuals.

Furthermore, the reported high rate of anxiety disorders in this group make it critical to distinguish not only the types of anxiety disorders but also commonly comorbid psychiatric disorders such as depression, ADHD, and substance abuse (Clark et al., 1995; Curry & Murphy, 1995) so that an effective treatment or intervention plan can be developed and implemented to improve these individuals' overall well-being.

DEFINITION AND SUBTYPES OF ANXIETY DISORDERS

Currently, the *DSM-IV-TR* (APA, 2000), considers the following disorders as subtypes of anxiety disorders: GAD (includes overanxious disorder of childhood); separation anxiety disorder; social phobia, or social anxiety disorder; specific phobia (formerly simple phobia); panic disorder without agoraphobia; panic disorder with agoraphobia; agoraphobia without history of panic disorder; obsessive-compulsive disorder; selective mutism (formerly elective mutism); post-traumatic stress disorder; acute stress disorder; anxiety disorder due to medical condition or substance use; and anxiety disorder not otherwise specified.

This chapter explores the connection of autism with seven types of anxiety disorders listed above and excludes six types for which little information is currently available, or which may have low comorbidity with autism.

Generalized Anxiety Disorder

The essential features of GAD are excessive, persistent, uncontrollable anxiety, and worry about everyday things. The focus of GAD worry can shift. Adults usually focus on issues like job, finances, health of both self and family, and marriage, but their focus can shift to more mundane issues, such as chores and car repairs. Children and adolescents with GAD worry a great deal about future events, peer relationships, social acceptability, competency, and pleasing others. Unlike children with social phobia or specific phobia, children with GAD have numerous and diffuse worries that are not limited to a specific stimulus or environment. They are often described by their parents as "worry warts" and as overly conscientious. Children and adolescents with GAD tend to overestimate the likelihood of negative consequences, predict catastrophic outcomes for future events, and underestimate their ability to cope with unfavorable situations (Albano, Chorpita, & Barlow, 1996). The intensity, duration, and frequency of the worry are disproportionate to the issue, and the worry can cause clinically significant distress or impairment in social, occupational, or other important areas of functioning.

To qualify for a *DSM-IV-TR* diagnosis of GAD (APA, 2000), the following symptoms must occur more days than not for at least 6 months or longer. Three of the following six symptom groups are required for adults, but only one is needed in children: (1) motor tension, shakiness, jitteriness, jumpiness, trembling, tension, muscle aches, inability to relax, eyelid twitch, furrowed brow, strained face; (2) fidgeting, restlessness, easy startle, feeling on edge; (3) fatigability; (4) vigilance and scanning, hyperattentiveness, distractibility, difficulty in concentrating or mind going blank; (5) irritability, impatience; and (6) sleep disturbances, including difficulty falling or staying asleep, or restless, unsatisfying sleep.

In addition, GAD tends to be associated with autonomic hyperactivities including sweating, heart pounding or racing, rapid or irregular heartbeat, cold, clammy hands, dry mouth, dizziness, lightheadedness, paresthesia (tingling in hands or feet), upset stomach, hot or cold spells, frequent urination, diarrhea, nausea, discomfort in the pit of the stomach, lump in the throat, flushing, pallor, high resting pulse, high respiration rate, or breathing problems.

Separation Anxiety Disorder

Separation anxiety is a normative part of development, typically beginning around 6 or 7 months old, peaking around 18 months, and decreasing after 30 months. However, subclinical features of separation anxiety may persist into childhood and early adolescence. When separation anxiety develops outside these normative parameters, is persistent and excessive, and is associated with significant distress or impairment of daily functioning, a diagnosis of separation anxiety disorder should be considered.

Separation anxiety disorder is characterized by developmentally inappropriate and excessive anxiety about being apart from the individuals to whom a child is most attached. When separated from a parent or attachment figure, the child frequently worries excessively that harm may come to himself or to a loved one. The following are the symptom groups usually associated with separation anxiety disorder: (1) recurrent excessive distress when separation from home or major attachment figures occurs or is anticipated; (2) persistent and excessive worry about losing, or about possible harm befalling the major attachment figures (e.g., serious accident, death); (3) persistent and excessive worry that an untoward event will lead to separation from a major attachment figure (e.g., getting lost, being kidnapped); (4) persistent reluctance (e.g., displaying procrastination during the morning routine before school) or refusal to go to school or elsewhere because of fear of separation; (5) persistently and excessively fearful or reluctant to be alone or without major attachment figures at home or without significant adults in other settings; (6) persistent reluctance or refusal to go to sleep without being near a major attachment figure or reluctant to sleep away from home; (7) repeated nightmares involving the theme of separation; and (8) repeated complaints of physical symptoms (such as headaches, stomachaches, nausea, or vomiting) when separation from major attachment figures occurs or is anticipated. To qualify for a *DSM-IV-TR* diagnosis of separation anxiety disorder (APA, 2000), a child must have three of the above eight symptoms, and the child must have the symptoms for at least 4 weeks and an onset before age 18.

Social Phobia (Social Anxiety Disorder)

Social phobia is characterized by an intense fear of one or more situations, usually social or performance situations in which a person is exposed to unfamiliar persons or to scrutiny by others. The most commonly feared situations are public speaking or performing, attending social gatherings, dealing with authority figures, and social interactions such as speaking to strangers or asking directions. Although some individuals with social phobia have very circumscribed fears, such as eating or writing in public or using public restrooms, most of them fear or avoid many different types of social situations.

Individuals with social phobia fear being evaluated and criticized, fear being the center of attention, or fear that they might be embarrassed in some way. They commonly fear that others will find some fault with them; that others will notice their physical signs of anxiety; that others will consider them weird, unattractive, or stupid; or that they will do or say something foolish or embarrassing. Adults with social phobia usually recognize that their fears are unfounded or excessive, but suffer them nonetheless. However, this feature of cognizance may be absent in children with social phobia.

Onset of social phobia is usually in mid- to late adolescence, but an increasing number of studies are documenting the characteristics of social phobia in children and younger adolescents (Beidel, Turner, & Morris, 1999; Black, 1996; Francis, Last, & Strauss, 1992; Spence, Donovan, & Brechman-Toussaint, 1999). These studies have found that the disorder is valid, is not uncommon in clinical populations, and is associated with significant impairment. Children with social phobia are prone to excessive shyness, tend to cry or to have tantrums, and tend to cling to or hide behind their mothers when confronted with a feared social situation. They may be reluctant to attend school. Adolescents with social phobia may have great difficulty with dating or establishing any relationships with members of the opposite sex. Children and adolescents with social phobia may avoid participation in classroom activities, avoid class presentations, do poorly on tests or in presentations, avoid physical education class, and avoid taking part in age-appropriate social activities. Their fears are centered in peer settings rather than social activities involving adults, with whom they may feel more comfortable.

Somatic symptoms are common in social phobia including racing heart or palpitations, sweating, blushing, tremulousness, light headedness, and diarrhea. These symptoms may be indistinguishable from a full-blown panic attack. Individuals with social phobia may fear that others will notice the somatic manifestations of their anxiety (e.g., tremulousness, sweating, blushing) and that this will cause further embarrassment or ridicule.

Specific Phobia

Specific phobia is characterized by a marked and persistent fear that is excessive or unreasonable, cued by the presence or anticipation of a specific object or situation (e.g., flying, heights, animals, receiving an injection, seeing blood) that provokes immediate anxiety (*DSM-IV-TR*; APA, 2000). The anxiety response may be accompanied by a variety of somatic symptoms. In children, it may be expressed by crying, tantrums, freezing, or clinging. The avoidance, anxious anticipation, or distress in the feared situation interferes with a person's normal routine, social relationships, or academic (or occupational) functioning, or there is marked distress about having the fear. The stimulus is either avoided or endured with intense anxiety. By definition, adults recognize that the fear is excessive or unreasonable, although children may not.

According to the *DSM-IV-TR* (APA, 2000), there are five subtypes of specific phobia: (1) animal type, (2) natural-environment type (e.g., fears of storms, heights, water), (3) blood—injection—injury type, (4) situational type, including fear cued by specific situations, such as tunnels, bridges, flying, or driving, and (5) "other." Animal type, natural-environment type, and blood—injection—injury type all usually begin in childhood. Situational type has a bimodal onset, with one peak in childhood and another in early adulthood. Situational type appears to be closely related to panic disorder with agoraphobia (Verburg, Griez, & Meijer, 1994).

School phobia is sometimes used broadly with reference to children who refuse or resist going to school for any reason. A more precise use of the term "school phobia" would be restricted to describing a child's fear of something specific about the school situation, such as a specific teacher or peer, taking a shower after physical education class, or something encountered on the way to school (Black, 1995).

In assessing the fears of children and adolescents, it is important to maintain a developmental perspective because some fears are common and appropriate at young ages. Determining at what point the anxiety becomes "clinical" can be a fine distinction. Infants' fears diminish during the preschool years. Preschool children are typically afraid of strangers, the dark, animals, or imaginary creatures. Children of elementary school age are more likely to be afraid of animals, darkness, threats to their own safety, or thunder and lightning. Older children are more concerned with health, social, and school fears. Adolescent fears may focus more on failure, sex, or agoraphobia (Marks, 1987). If the fears persist into older ages, or if there is significant and persistent distress or functional impairment, then clinical evaluation is indicated.

Agoraphobia

In the *DSM-IV-TR* (APA, 2000), agoraphobia is not a codable disorder. However, agoraphobia often, but not always, coincides with panic disorder. Agoraphobia is characterized by a fear of having a panic attack in a place from which escape is difficult or embarrassing, or in which help may not be available in the event of having an unexpected or situationally predisposed panic attack or paniclike symptoms. Agoraphobic fears typically involve characteristic clusters of situations that include being outside the home alone; being in a crowd or standing in a line; being on a bridge; and traveling in a bus, train, or automobile.

Individuals with agoraphobia tend to refuse to leave their home for years at a time. Others develop a fixed route, or territory, from which they cannot deviate, for example the route between home and work, and it becomes impossible for these people to travel beyond what they consider to be their safety zones without suffering severe anxiety.

Panic Disorder

According to the *DSM-IV-TR* (APA, 2000), panic disorder is characterized by recurrent, unexpected panic attacks, and with at least a month of persistent concern about having additional attacks, worry about the implications of the attacks (e.g., somatic preoccupations), or other behavioral changes related to the attacks.

A panic attack is defined as the abrupt onset of an episode of intense feeling or discomfort, which peaks in approximately 10 min, and includes at least four of the following groups of symptoms: a feeling of imminent danger or doom; the need to escape; palpitations, pounding heart, or accelerated heart rate; sweating; trembling or shaking; shortness of breath or a smothering feeling; a feeling of choking; chest pain or discomfort; nausea or abdominal discomfort; feeling dizzy, unsteady, lightheaded, or faint; derealization (feelings of unreality) or depersonalization (being detached from oneself); a fear of "going crazy" or losing control; a fear of dying; paresthesia (numbness or tingling sensations); and chills or hot flushes.

There are three types of panic attacks:

1. Unexpected or uncued—the attack "comes out of the blue," without warning and with no discernable reason.
2. Situational or cued—situations in which an individual always has an attack, for example, upon entering a tunnel.
3. Situationally predisposed—situations in which an individual is likely to have a panic attack, but does not always have one.

An example of the third type would be an individual who sometimes has attacks while driving. Unexpected panic attacks are required for the diagnosis of panic disorder. Situationally bound panic attacks are more characteristic of specific phobia and social phobia. Situationally predisposed panic attacks are common in panic disorder, but they also occur in individuals with specific phobia and social phobia.

Panic attacks are the hallmark of panic disorder, but they are also associated with other anxiety disorders, including specific phobia, social phobia, OCD, and post-traumatic stress disorder. Panic disorder may occur either with or without agoraphobia. Individuals with panic disorder may avoid situations where panic attacks are feared (e.g., elevators, subway trains, grocery stores). These individuals have panic disorder with agoraphobia.

The frequency and severity of panic attacks varies from person to person. An individual may have repeated attacks for weeks, while another may have short bursts of very severe attacks. Individuals with panic disorder often worry about the physical and emotional consequences of the panic attacks. Many become convinced that the attacks indicate an undiagnosed illness and will submit to frequent medical tests. Even after tests reveal negative findings, they may remain worried that they a have physical illness. Some individuals will change their behavioral patterns in the hopes of preventing having another attack. For example, individuals with panic disorder may stop exercising because they experience the physiological arousal as too frightening due to its resemblance to a panic attack.

The age of onset of panic disorder varies from late adolescence to the mid-thirties. Relatively few suffer from the disorder in childhood (Abelson & Alessi, 1992). However, there are cases of both prepubertal and adolescent-onset panic disorder described in the literature (Biederman et al., 1997; King, Ollendick, & Mattis, 1997). Several studies of adults with panic disorder have reported that many patients recalled the onset to be in childhood or adolescence (Thyer, Parrish, Curtis, Nesse, & Cameron, 1985; von Korff, Eaton, & Keyl, 1985). The symptoms, course, and associated complications and comorbid psychiatric conditions in children and adolescents with panic disorder appear to be similar to that observed in adults with panic disorder. Cognitive symptoms are reported less frequently than somatic ones (King et al., 1997).

A common feature in children and adolescents with panic disorder is comorbid separation anxiety disorder (Black, 1995). Children with early development of separation anxiety disorder are at an increased risk for later development of panic disorder (Biederman et al., 1993). Many children and adolescents with prepubertal onset of panic disorder also manifest symptoms of separation anxiety disorder (Black, 1995). An association between adult-onset panic disorder and childhood anxiety, specifically separation anxiety disorder, has also been reported (Gittelman & Klein, 1984).

Obsessive-Compulsive Disorder

Obsessive-compulsive disorder is characterized by uncontrollable obsessions and/or compulsions (*DSM-IV-TR*; APA, 2000). Obsessions are recurring unwanted ideas, thoughts, images, or impulses that are intrusive (i.e., ego-dystonic), inappropriate, or unpleasant, and that cause the individual to experience a high degree of anxiety. Some common obsessions are unwanted ideas or thoughts, including persistent fears that harm may come to oneself or to a loved one; a belief that one has a terrible illness; religious scrupulousness; thoughts about contamination (e.g., when an individual fears coming into contact with dirt, germs or "unclean" objects); persistent doubts, such as whether one has turned off the iron or stove, locked the door, or turned on the answering machine; extreme need for symmetry or exactness or an excessive need to do things perfectly or in a particular order; aggressive impulses or thoughts, such as being overcome with the urge to yell "fire" in a crowded theater, or aggressive images that usually include sexual imagery.

Compulsions are repetitive behaviors or rituals performed by the person with OCD to neutralize the anxiety caused by obsessive thoughts. Compulsions are incorporated into the person's daily routine and are not always directly related to the obsessive thought. For example, a person who has aggressive thoughts counts floor tiles in an effort to control the thought. Some of the most common compulsions are cleaning constantly, with frequent and lengthy washing of hands, taking many showers a day, constantly cleaning one's home because of worry of contamination by germs; checking several or even hundreds of times to make sure that the stove is turned off and the doors are locked; counting steps from one spot to the other or counting book/magazine pages; silently repeating a name, word, phrase, or action over and over; taking an excessively slow and methodical approach to daily activities; endlessly rearranging objects in an effort to keep them in precise alignment with each other; hoarding useless items, such as old newspapers, junk mail, and even broken appliances—sometimes reaching the point that entire rooms are filled with saved items. Some people affected by OCD have regimented rituals, while others have rituals that are complex and changing. For OCD to be diagnosed, the obsessions and/or compulsions must take up a considerable amount of the individual's time, at least 1 hour every day, and interfere with normal routines, occupational functioning, social activities, or relationships.

Generally, people with OCD know that their obsessive thoughts are sense-less and that their compulsions are not really necessary. Most struggle to banish their unwanted, obsessive thoughts and to prevent themselves from engaging in compulsive behaviors. In contrast, some individuals with OCD attempt to hide their disorder rather than seek help and often are successful in concealing their obsessive-compulsive symptoms from friends and co-workers. Onset of OCD is usually gradual and most often begins in adolescence to early adulthood. Un-like adults, children with OCD do not realize that the obsessions and compul-sions, which are most often of the washing, checking, and ordering variety, are excessive.

The symptoms of OCD may become less severe from time to time, but the symptoms are usually chronic. OCD tends to last for years, even decades. This disorder can interfere with one's ability to concentrate, and it is not uncom-mon for an individual to avoid certain situations. For example, someone who is obsessed with cleanliness may be unable to use public restrooms. People with OCD who struggle against their compulsions often develop a dysphoric mood and become irritable, tense, and depressed.

ANXIETY DISORDERS AND COMORBIDITY IN NON-ASD POPULATIONS

Kendall, Brady, and Verduin (2001) investigated comorbidity in childhood anx-iety disorders. In their sample, 79% of children with a primary diagnosis of an anxiety disorder had at least one comorbid diagnosis. The most frequent comor-bid diagnoses were simple phobia, social phobia, and GAD. The study found that participants with comorbid diagnoses displayed more severe internalizing symptoms than participants with only a single anxiety disorder.

Anxiety disorders often present with other comorbid psychiatric disorders such as depressive disorder, OCD, and ADHD (Biederman, Newcorn, & Sprich, 1991; Masi, Mucci, Favilla, Romano, & Poli, 1999). Woodward and Fergusson (2001) conducted a 21-year longitudinal study of 1265 New Zealand children. They found that among those with anxiety disorders there was a significant asso-ciation between adolescent-onset anxiety disorders and later risks of additional anxiety disorders, major depression, dependence on illicit drugs, and failure to attend college.

A poorer prognosis has been found in children with anxiety disorders and comorbid disorders (Last, Hanson, & Franco, 1997; Masi et al. 1999; Manassis & Hood, 1998). Studies have reported that children and adolescents with co-morbid anxiety and depressive disorders present with greater symptom severity (Bernstein, 1991; Last, Perrin, Hersen, & Kazdin, 1996) and have a poorer re-sponse to treatment (Berman, Weems, & Silverman, 2000; Brent et al., 1998). In addition, children with anxiety disorders are at risk for developing alcohol abuse in adolescence (Manassis & Monga, 2001).

The following section illustrates and discusses the behavioral and medical assessment process used to determine whether medication treatment is appropriate for individuals with ASD and anxiety disorders. It is important that the parents and other caregivers of these individuals are aware of the purpose and the process of such assessments because they will, and should be, directly involved in the process. Their full cooperation will influence the choice of evaluation methods and the reliability of evaluation results.

Behavioral and Medical Assessment

Both behavioral and medical assessments have three primary functions:

- to identify and classify a case on the basis of distinguishing characteristics
- to determine the nature and causes of the problematic behaviors or symptoms
- to provide guidelines for effective intervention.

Both types of assessments focus on the specifics of the behaviors or symptoms of concern and take into account other factors, such as the characteristics of the individual, family, and environment that influence the behaviors or symptoms. The assessment should also pay attention to the strengths of the individual being evaluated. Thus, the combined behavior and medical interventions not only aim to decrease inappropriate and undesirable behaviors, but also to increase appropriate and desirable behaviors and maximize growth and development. Many unsuccessful attempts at changing an individual's behaviors or symptoms are due to an incomplete assessment, an inaccurate assessment, or no assessment at all. Although a good assessment does not guarantee a successful outcome, it certainly can lead to a more effective intervention.

Clarifying the Concerned Symptom/Behavior among Nonmedical Caregivers

Although clarifying the problem behaviors or symptoms seems an obvious first step in the assessment process, its importance cannot be overemphasized. If a caregiver of an individual has a concern or question concerning the anxiety disorder in the individual, it is essential that all the caregivers of the individual agree on the concern to be addressed. It is possible that one caregiver's opinion of the individual's behaviors or symptoms is quite different from those of the other caregivers. Some individuals with Asperger's disorder or high-functioning autism may be able to report their symptoms or may have questions about the feelings or symptoms that have been bothering them. Thus, the first step in the assessment process is for the involved caregivers or team members and the individual with ASD to meet, clarify, and understand the behaviors or symptoms of concern. The team members usually include parents or legal guardians, teachers, a speech therapist, an occupational therapist or a job coach, a school administrator or employer, and a psychologist or behavioral therapist. It is very important that all caregivers involved with the individual's care have the same concept and understanding of the behaviors/symptoms of concern. The target behaviors/symptoms must be observable and measurable. The team then should carry out a functional behavioral analysis to help clarify the function, or motivation, including whether the behaviors or symptoms are environmentally maintained reactions to specific events, or individuals, or result from internal neurophysiological or neurochemical source.

Functional Behavioral Analysis

Often behaviors of concern are not exhibited in the physician's office and a physician must rely on the report of families and professionals for a full assessment. An experienced and qualified professional (usually a psychologist or a behavioral therapist) should carry out a complete functional behavioral analysis (see chapter 1 in this volume). The results from the functional behavioral analysis should be presented at a follow-up team meeting. Deciding to refer for further medical assessment is appropriate when the team members agree that data indicate the behaviors or symptoms of concern may not be solely the result of environmental cues or consequences.

Physicians generally do not include functional behavioral analysis information in the diagnoses of their patients, often due to economic reasons, time pressures, or lack of knowledge of the utility of such an analysis. All caregivers are strongly encouraged to learn more about functional behavioral analysis through reading or workshop attendance.

Medical Assessment and Diagnosis

Medical assessment is a complex process that involves directly observing and recording the individual's behaviors, symptoms, complaints, and concerns. It also takes into account social, cultural, biological, and developmental influences on the individual. Hence, assessment of an individual's "behavioral problems" necessitates a multimethod and interdisciplinary approach. Representatives of many disciplines must work together to make a full assessment of an individual's weaknesses or disabilities, as well as strengths and abilities. The physician should select methods that would include the involvement of all caregivers to provide information appropriate to the nature of the presenting problems useful for the final diagnosis of the individual.

Traditionally, the term "diagnosis," as it has been used by the medical profession, emphasizes understanding a patient's presenting complaints, using a diagnostic system to classify the behaviors or symptoms of concern, finding the cause or causes of medical disorders, and prescribing potentially effective treatment to eliminate symptoms or cure the underlying illness. The medical assessment and diagnosis in individuals with ASD involves the same basic techniques as in the nonautistic population, although greater reliance on gathering clinical information from family and caregivers may be necessary.

Physician Qualifications

A physician needs four kinds of knowledge to provide high-quality medication assessment and treatment of individuals with ASD: (1) normal child and family development; (2) assessment and diagnosis of ASD and comorbid neuropsychiatric disorders; (3) general theories and principles of behavioral, psychological, educational, occupational, sensory, and speech/language assessments, and knowledge of how to select these assessment methods and to communicate findings to the individual of concern and his parents and/or caregivers; and (4) experience in providing intervention services to individuals with ASD and related neuropsychiatric disorders.

A GUIDE TO MEDICAL ASSESSMENT AND DIAGNOSIS

The following section summarizes a model for medical assessment to guide both medical practitioners and parent and nonmedical advocates (Tsai, 2001).

Step 1: Initial Contact

At initial contact, the parent or caregiver is asked to specify the type of diagnostic evaluation desired and the reasons for making the request.

Step 2: First Assessment Session

At the time of the first session, the physician should review the report of functional behavioral analysis, completed questionnaires, videotapes, and other available information. Information can be gathered through interviews, direct observations, speech and language assessment, mental status assessment, physical and neurological assessment, and laboratory tests.

Interviews

Commonly used interview formats include unstructured interviews, structured interviews, semi-structured interviews, symptom checklists, and computer-based interviews. Important information can include past medical history, such as hospitalizations, allergies, use of substances, current medications, trauma, disorders of central nervous system, disorder of eyes, ears, nose, and throat, disorder of respiratory system, cardiovascular diseases, gastrointestinal disorders,

disorders of urinary tract, and disorders of endocrine system. Also, a review of family neuropsychiatric history may provide information on inherited thyroid disease, Huntington's disease, anxiety disorders, OCD, and Tourette's syndrome.

Some individuals with high-functioning autistic disorder or Asperger's disorder are capable of relating fairly well verbally as long as the communications are not overly complex. Establishing rapport is vital with these individuals. Hence, knowledge of the cognitive developmental characteristics of individuals at different ages and appropriate interview skills are essential to conducting a successful interview with a verbal individual with ASD.

Observations

Direct observation includes the contemporaneous recording of spontaneously occurring, externally observable, behavioral events. Typically this can be done while the child is at play or in interaction with a caregiver. Observation of a child's selection of play materials and how the child plays with them can be a valuable source of information about his intellectual and language development, special interests, leisure time skills, social relationships and interaction skills, feelings, thoughts, worries, and anxieties. Such a method is particularly important and useful in gathering information from nonverbal, lower functioning, and uncooperative individuals. Direct observation can also provide objective record of behaviors such as crying or whimpering, inactivity, withdrawal, agitation, stuttering, tremors, and nervousness. These behaviors may relate to depressive and/or anxiety disorders. From observational data, areas requiring more formalized testing can be identified.

Speech and Language Assessment

Given the potential of psychotherapeutic medications to alter speech and language skills, some baseline assessment is desirable. If there is any doubt, a full-scale evaluation of speech and language should be conducted through a referral to a qualified speech and language pathologist.

Mental Status Assessment

The mental status examination focuses on the individual's appearance; mood or affect; orientation to time, place and person; thought processes and verbalization; neuromuscular integration; awareness of problems; and cognitive function.

Physical and Neurological Assessment

Because different behavior problems, symptoms, or side effects of medications may mimic other medical or psychiatric disorders, the physical and neurological assessment may reveal medical problems or disorders previously missed;

new, unrelated medical problems or disorders; incorrect earlier diagnosis; or adverse effects associated with various treatments. It is important to make an accurate differential diagnosis that will directly impact on the nature and course of medication to be prescribed. The other major reason for a careful and complete physical and neurological assessment is to establish the baseline physical and neurological status prior to medication therapy for monitoring and preventing the development of side effects.

Laboratory Tests

Although laboratory tests can never replace clinical acumen in any medical specialty, they can play a significant role in explaining and quantifying biological factors associated with various medical and psychiatric disorders. Also, few diagnoses of mental or psychiatric disorders can be confirmed by current laboratory tests. Hence, laboratory studies should be ordered only for specific diagnostic considerations, such as thyroid studies to evaluate depression or anxiety and for baseline assessment where the proposed medication(s) could alter organ systems (e.g., assessments of thyroid function before lithium is instituted). The following are the commonly considered laboratory measures in evaluating anxiety disorders: electrocardiogram (ECG), catecholamine and enzyme assays, metabolic screening, thyroid function tests, liver and kidney function tests, serum measures, and illicit drug screening.

Caregivers of individuals with ASD should know that not all the laboratory measures and tests promoted by nonmedical professionals or the media need to be done as routine screens or tests. Particularly, many tests recommended by advocacy groups and/or media tend to be new tests that may not be supported by scientific evidence demonstrating that they meet minimum criteria of effectiveness. Inaccurate, false-positive results can cause profound anxiety and require additional testing that can be increasingly invasive and costly. They can also deplete society's limited medical resources. Physicians can and should refuse to order tests that would violate their medical and ethical judgment.

Step 3: Further Assessment

To confirm or clarify a physician's working first impressions, other assessments may be warranted and can include additional home and school observation, problem- or disorder-specific questionnaires/rating scales sent to the individual's teacher or job supervisor, or the client and family may be referred to allied health professionals for further assessment.

Step 4: Diagnosis

Diagnosis is best made through a process of analysis and synthesis that brings together the results of all the data analyses by each of the interdisciplinary team members. Having obtained the necessary information from subjective and objective sources, the next step is the development of a preliminary diagnostic impression based on ICD-10 (WHO, 1992) or *DSM-IV-TR* (APA, 2000).

Step 5: Developing an Intervention Plan

The interdisciplinary team of specialists jointly prescribe a comprehensive intervention plan specifically for anxiety disorders that may include psychotherapy, behavior therapy, cognitive behavior therapy, and pharmacotherapy for the individual and his caregivers. Often there is also the need to consider and treat other co-existing psychiatric symptoms (e.g., depression, obsessions, compulsions). The intervention plan should prioritize the identified behaviors or symptoms of concern and decide which behavior or symptom should be dealt with first.

Step 6: Communicating Findings and Treatment Recommendations

When the physician communicates the findings of the assessment to the caregivers, he or she provides the critical link between the assessment and intervention processes and sets the stage for intervention. Information should be communicated to the individual and his or her caregivers through feedback conferences, reports, and letters.

TREATMENT OF ANXIETY DISORDERS

Experts believe that anxiety disorders are caused by a combination of biological and environmental factors and the disorder is treatable. Success of treatment, however, varies with the individual. Treatments that have demonstrated effectiveness include the psychosocial therapies known as behavior therapy, cognitive therapy, cognitive-behavior therapy; medications; or combined therapy of psychosocial treatments and medications. The effectiveness of psychosocial and medication treatments can be enhanced by involvement of the family in treatment and careful consideration in the choice of a therapist.

Involvement of Other Family Members

The effectiveness of psychosocial and medication treatments can be enhanced by involvement of the family in treatment. Individuals with ASD often need help from their family members to achieve the goals of effective treatment. Individuals with both ASD and anxiety disorders and their family members may spend months, even years, without knowing what is wrong. This can be frustrating and put a strain on their relationships. This strain is not necessarily alleviated once there is a diagnosis. Recovery can be a long process. Household routines tend to be disrupted. Sometimes special plans need to be made. The person with the disorder may be reluctant to participate in typical social activities. These factors can have a negative impact on family dynamics. It is critical for family members to keep in mind that the recovery process is stressful for them, too. They should build a support network of relatives and friends for themselves.

Family members often want to help the individual with both ASD and anxiety disorder, but do not know how. Family members should learn as much as they can about anxiety disorders, which will help them know what to expect from the illness and from the recovery process. They should also learn when to be patient with the individual with the disorder and when to push. They should learn how to modify expectations during stressful periods, and learn to be flexible and try to maintain a normal routine.

Choosing a Therapist

As described earlier, the physician who performs the diagnostic assessment should discuss the treatment plan or options with the individuals with ASD and their caregivers. Such a discussion should also include choosing a therapist. The physician may offer to provide the treatment or might refer the family to other mental health professionals for further treatment. It is important to feel comfortable with the potential therapist. The individual and the caregivers should speak to the therapist in his or her office. If the individual and the caregivers feel uncomfortable with the potential therapist and would rather see someone else, they should not be embarrassed to indicate their desire.

Questions to Ask the Therapist

During the initial consultation, the individual and the caregivers may have many questions about the therapist's treatment method, training background, and fees. A therapist should be willing to answer any questions. If a therapist is reluctant to answer questions, find someone else who will. The following are some questions suggested by the Anxiety Disorders Association of America (2004) to ask a therapist during the initial consultation:

- What training and experience do you have in treating anxiety disorders?
- What is your basic approach to treatment?
- Can you prescribe medication or refer me to someone who can, if it proves necessary?
- How long is the course of treatment?
- How frequent are treatment sessions and how long do they last?
- Do you include family members in therapy?
- Will you or a staff member go to the home of a phobic person, if necessary?
- What is your fee schedule, and do you have a sliding scale for various financial circumstances?
- What kinds of health insurance do you accept?

Psychosocial therapies include behavior therapy, cognitive therapy, and cognitive-behavioral therapy. The following sections describe the components of cognitive-behavior therapy (CBT), which includes both behavior therapy and cognitive therapy, and summarize the literature on efficacy of CBT with anxiety disorders in non-ASD populations. Psychosocial therapies, however, require a certain level of cognitive functioning; they may not be appropriate for individuals with middle to low functioning ASD. Nonetheless, caregivers, including physicians, should conduct a careful assessment of the individual's suitability for the psychosocial therapies.

In cognitive-behavior therapy (CBT), the therapist and patient work together as a collaborative team. The therapist acts as an observer, a teacher, and a coach. The therapist teaches coping skills and, in some types of CBT, points out logical contradictions in the patient's patterns of thinking and behavior. Meanwhile, patients learn to move toward and engage their anxiety and employ skills used in therapy to cope with it on a daily basis between sessions.

Components of CBT that have been most commonly used include psychoeducation, self-monitoring, exposure, relaxation training, cognitive restructuring or therapy, social skill training, the rehearsal of newly learned relaxation, and cognitive coping responses. Not all components would be used in individuals with just one subtype of anxiety disorders. However, it is common that most components, if not all, would be used because individuals with anxiety disorders tend to have comorbid subtypes of anxiety disorders.

Psychoeducation

At the beginning of treatment, therapists provide patients/caregivers with information about the nature of the disorder from a cognitive-behavioral perspective. Interventions commonly include a discussion of the role of thoughts and avoidance patterns in helping cue and maintain anxiety episodes and a review of the physiologic source of anxiety related symptoms. Home reading assignments that further explain the CBT conceptualization and treatment components are usually used to enhance independent learning in CBT. The purposes of these interventions are to (1) help patients become a more active collaborator in treatment because all interventions are to be applied, ultimately, in the absence of' the therapist and (2) help break the experience of anxiety attacks into identifiable elements and provide a rationale for the interventions to follow (Rayburn & Otto, 2003).

Self-monitoring

Teaching patients to objectively observe their anxious responses and trigger environmental cues is essential to most CBT. The earlier a patient learns to identify incipient anxiety or worry, the more effective the deployment of coping responses to reduce the anxiety will be. Therapists and patients work together in sessions to determine characteristic cognitive, somatic, affective, and behavioral reactions involved in their anxious responding; to determine how these internal reactions causatively relate to each other, such as what individuals think affects how they feel and how they feel affects what they think; and to determine the external environment and perceptions of threat. They do so through devices, such as discussions of recent anxious or worrisome periods during the past week and imaginary reliving of stressful events. Patients are then encouraged to observe themselves and their inner and outer worlds between sessions in order to identify other cues involved in their anxious process (Borkovec, Newman, & Castonguay, 2003).

Cognitive Therapy/Restructuring

Anxiety disorders centrally involve inaccurate perceptions or beliefs of potential threats and worrisome reactions predicting negative future events. Patients with anxiety disorders tend to overestimate the probability of negative outcomes, such as, "I will fail my science test tomorrow," as well as the degree of catastrophe of these outcomes: "My parents and my teacher will be very upset with me." The goal of cognitive therapy is to help patients evaluate their thoughts and beliefs about the meaning and consequences of the somatic symptoms of anxiety attacks.

A variety of strategies are used to help patients recognize the content of their thinking, evaluate its accuracy, and guide themselves more effectively. Basic cognitive therapy involves four sequential steps: (1) identifying the patient's negative thoughts (i.e., how he or she is thinking) and the beliefs about self, world, and future that underlie those thoughts; (2) helping patients evaluate the accuracy of those thoughts through examination of their logic, probability, and past evidence; (3) helping patients generate alternative, more objective and accurate interpretations, predictions, and ways of believing; and (4) helping patients use these new perspectives whenever anxiety and worry are detected, and engage in deliberate behavioral experiments to provide further evidence to support them (Borkovec et al., 2003).

Regular thought monitoring in response to situational, emotional, and physiologic cues is used to help patients become better observers of their current thoughts and to evaluate systematically the objective evidence for and against the veracity of these thoughts. For example, patients are asked to note the situation (e.g., being in a crowded supermarket), the emotional and physiologic sensations (e.g., nervousness, increased heart rate, sweating, dizziness), and the cognition (e.g., "I am going to have a heart attack"). Patients are encouraged to write down the worry and what they are afraid might happen any time they notice themselves worrying. At the end of each day, they review prior entries and identify whether an outcome relevant to a particular worry has actually occurred. If so, they rate whether the outcome turned out poorly or well and whether they coped with the outcome poorly or well. Using this monitoring method, patients direct their attention to what actually transpires. The Socratic dialogue/method is used to help patients come to their own conclusions about the way things actually are or are likely to be in the future, in contrast to their customary negative interpretations. Patients then are taught to challenge these catastrophic thoughts and to adopt alternative and more accurate cognitive responses, such as, "I have never had a heart attack in these situations in the past and chances are that I am not going to have a heart attack now" (Rayburn & Otto, 2003).

Patients are encouraged to try out various ways of seeing things more accurately and to constantly modify those perspectives in response to new information that they are learning through observations of the way things actually are. Patients are also encouraged to bring additional positive values to the engagement of the present moment. By using these rational thoughts in lieu of their customary negative interpretations in exposures to anxiety-provoking situations, patients are provided with a cognitive-coping strategy, which, over time and repetition, will allow them to modify their habitual negative beliefs about anxiety-provoking situations. They learn to spend increasing time in the present rather than in their minds and the future. In this way, a positive approach to life and to stressful or anxiety-provoking situations is cultivated (Hambrick, Weeks, Harb, & Heimberg, 2003).

Another strategy is to help patients learn to establish a brief worry period each day and to postpone any detected worries during the day to that period. Such an approach can help them temporarily let go of their worrying, focus their attention back on the task at hand or on present moment reality, and achieve some greater degree of environmental control over this internal process. The worry period is then used to apply cognitive therapy skills to generate alternative perspectives for the postponed worry for use the next time that worry occurs.

Rehearsal of Coping Responses

Cognitive-behavior therapy emphasizes gradual change through frequent practice of new, more adaptive actions. For patients with anxiety disorders, learning to relax and see things more accurately represents new ways of acting with which they have little familiarity. However, most cognitive approaches to the treatment of anxiety disorders are closely tied to exposure and are rarely purely cognitive. Consequently, rehearsing their new coping skills has always been incorporated into CBT treatments for anxiety disorder.

Patients are taught to detect anxious or worrisome feelings in daily living and/or to generate those feelings in the therapy session. Then, patients practice deploying their cognitive and/or relaxation coping skills in response to those cues. This is sometimes accomplished with the use of graduated exposures to commonly confronted stressful situations. In a therapy-session of rehearsals, patients repeatedly engage in imagery rehearsals with one set of anxiety and worry cues until they are experiencing success at rapidly reducing the anxiety before moving on to another representative set of external and internal cues. These rehearsals presumably increase the habit strength of new coping responses and help establish daily anxiety cues as reminders to rapidly deploy those new responses upon incipient anxiety detection.

During the therapy session, in addition to above imagery rehearsals, patients may also be taught to imagine the most likely outcomes relevant to a particular worry (based on preceding cognitive-therapy analyses) and encourage them to immediately replace any catastrophic thoughts or images concerning worrisome outcomes with images of these more realistic outcomes during their daily living (Borkovec et al., 2003).

Exposure Treatment/Interventions

Patients with anxiety disorder often hold beliefs that engaging in safety behaviors would help them to deal with their anxiety and that the implementation of safety behaviors will prevent feared catastrophes. For example, individuals with social anxiety disorder may choose not to contribute to conversations (safety behavior) for fear of saying the wrong thing and being criticized by others. However, they may have denied themselves the opportunity to learn that they could have managed the situation adequately without doing so.

Exposure treatment involves exposing patients to anxiety-provoking situations without allowing them to use safety behaviors. The aims of exposure treatment are to help patients access their negative thoughts and to obtain evidence to evaluate these thoughts. When an individual is exposed to the anxiety-provoking situation, such as making a speech in front of classmates, but does not encounter the feared outcome (e.g., "everyone will laugh at me"), natural conditioning processes involved in fear reduction take place. The individual is also confronted with information that contradicts their negative and distorted beliefs.

The first stage of exposure treatment is the collaborative development of a rank-ordered list of situations that provoke anxiety for the patient. Then the patient is encouraged to put himself or herself into these feared situations, starting with situations low on this rank-ordered list.

Exposure treatment is most effective when patients pay full attention to the anxiety-provoking situation and allow the inevitable rush of anxiety and arousal to occur. However, some patients may try to distract themselves from the situation as it unfolds, or they may focus attention on the threatening aspects of the situation that may prevent them from attending to what is actually happening. Therefore, it is important to instruct the patients to maintain focus on the anxiety-provoking situation.

The patients are also asked to remain in the situation until their anxiety naturally begins to subside. As a sense of mastery in the lesser situation is obtained and it no longer elicits distressing levels of fear or anxiety, the patients are encouraged to approach the higher ranked and more anxiety-provoking situations, and gradually work towards the situations they find most difficult. Exposure to anxiety-provoking situations may be administered by means of imagery; role-play with the therapist or therapy assistants; confronting anxiety-provoking situations in everyday life outside of session; or by a combination of these methods. Furthermore, exposure treatment is often combined with other treatment components, such as applied relaxation or cognitive techniques (Hambrick et al., 2003).

Exposure treatment protocols may differ in the degree of therapist involvement, as well as the length, number, and interval between exposure sessions. Exposure treatment can be carried out as an individual therapy—one patient with one therapist—or as a group therapy with four to eight patients, balanced with regard to age and sex, and led by male and female co-therapists. The patient(s) and the therapist(s) typically meet for 12 weekly 2- to 2.5-hr sessions. The first two sessions are devoted to providing patients with a cognitive-behavioral model of anxiety disorders and to introducing the concepts of exposure, homework, and cognitive therapy. Structured exercises are used to teach patients the concepts and procedures involved in the identification, logical analysis, and disputation of negative automatic thoughts. During the remaining 10 sessions, therapists plan graduated individualized exposure role-plays for each patient to examine and to modify their negative thoughts before, during, and after exposure to anxiety-provoking situations. Therapist-directed, cognitive-restructuring exercises and coaching are integrated with exposure to the situations to provide opportunities for testing the veracity of patients' negative thoughts. Furthermore, homework assignments are developed for each patient at the end of each session; these usually consist of exposures to real-life situations. When approaching anxiety-provoking situations outside of group sessions, patients are encouraged to use cognitive-restructuring skills before, during, and after the homework event (Hambrick et al., 2003).

In the case of panic disorder, interceptive exposure techniques are used to target the patients' fears of their own physiologic anxiety sensations. With the help of specific procedures (e.g., hyperventilation or head-rolling to induce dizziness, lightheadedness, tingling), patients systematically confront feared somatic sensations. For example, patients who are afraid of throat-tightening because they believe they will not be able to breath are asked to do tongue-pushing to deliberately induce throat-tightening. This exposure allows them to test catastrophic fears about these sensations, as well as to learn that they will not lose control of their breathing. The exposure also provides them with an opportunity to rehearse alternative responses, such as simply noting the sensations while doing nothing to control or avoid them. With repeated exposure, patients find that they no longer fear the symptoms. Consequently, the symptoms lose their ability to elicit panic episodes (Rayburn & Otto, 2003).

Exposure treatment may also involve patients engaging in situational (in vivo) exposure exercises. For example, in patients with agoraphobia in the early stages of the treatment, the patient and therapist together establish a hierarchy of situations the patient avoids due to the situation's ability to elicit panic. Throughout the treatment, patients confront these situations in a stepwise manner, starting with moderately anxiety-provoking situations. Common examples of in vivo exposures are riding in an elevator, going to the grocery store, standing in a crowd of people, or riding on a subway train. The majority of the in vivo exposures are typically performed as homework assignments. However, it is also possible to engage in some of them in the context of therapy sessions in which a therapist accompanies the patients to these situations. The patients are encouraged to resist the urge to leave when they start feeling anxious. Instead, they are instructed to stay in the feared situation until the fear subsides. Through these experiences, the patients gradually overcome their agoraphobic avoidance and relearn that the once-feared places and circumstances are safe (Rayburn & Otto, 2003).

Relaxation Training

Individuals with anxiety disorders often experience excessive physiologic arousal when confronted with or in anticipation of feared situations. Effective relaxation strategies provide patients with a means of coping with these physiologic manifestations of anxiety, as well as a method of cultivating relaxation as a way of living moment to moment. Relaxation techniques are also used for creating effectively pleasant present moments upon which to focus, instead of the illusions about the future that their minds are constantly creating in their worrisome thinking (Hambrick et al., 2003).

Effectively applying relaxation involves three skills to be acquired in treatment, including:

- recognition of the early sensations of anxiety and physiologic arousal
- proficiency in achieving a relaxed state quickly while engaging in daily activities
- use of relaxation strategies in anxiety-provoking situations.

Patients are trained in relaxation during treatment sessions. The relaxation training involves exercises aimed at the progressive relaxation of different muscle groups. The relaxation practices focus on particular muscle groups, tensing for 5 to 10 sec, releasing the tension, and noticing the difference between sensations accompanying tension and relaxation. Progressive muscle relaxation begins with larger muscle groups in order to achieve relaxation rapidly. Patients may be taught cue-controlled relaxation, which involves the repeated pairing of a word (e.g., "relax") with a relaxed bodily state, and then using the word as a cue to achieve a relaxed state during everyday activities (Hambrick et al., 2003). Patients may also receive additional relaxation techniques, such as slowed diaphragmatic breathing, meditation, and pleasant imagery. As patients with anxiety disorders tend to have rigid and habitual cognitive, affective, somatic, and behavioral ways of responding to life situations, using multiple relaxation methods provides patients with flexibility and choice among several coping responses (Borkovec et al., 2003).

The patients are asked to practice their techniques once or twice a day to strengthen their ability to rapidly produce relaxation. They are also encouraged to use this response whenever they notice incipient anxiety or worry during their self-monitoring, and to cultivate relaxation as a manner of being throughout the day (Borkovec et al., 2003).

Social Skills Training

Social skills training is primarily used for social anxiety disorder. It is based on the premise that socially anxious individuals exhibit behavioral deficiencies (e.g., poor eye contact or body posture, poor conversation skills) that elicit negative reactions from others, thereby causing social interactions to be anxiety inducing for the individuals. Social skills training comprises several techniques designed to reduce these deficiencies. These techniques include therapist modeling, behavioral rehearsal, corrective feedback, social reinforcement, and homework assignments (Hambrick et al., 2003).

However, any therapeutic efficacy of social skills training is not necessarily attributable to the remediation of deficiencies in the patient's repertoire of social skills. It may be due to the training aspects (e.g., repeated practice of feared social behaviors), the exposure aspects (e.g., confrontation of feared situations), or the cognitive elements (e.g., corrective feedback about the adequacy of one's social behavior) inherent in the instruction of such skills. Thus, social skills training is usually combined with other techniques, such as cognitive therapy or exposure in a mixture of group and individual formats (Hambrick et al., 2003).

Prevention of Relapse

Cognitive-behavior therapy for panic disorder also includes a relapse prevention component. The last two or three therapy sessions are devoted to the prevention of relapse. The therapist encourages the patient to identify potential problem areas that he or she may encounter and think of possible solutions based on knowledge gained from therapy. During these final sessions, therapist and patient may also establish a written relapse prevention contract. This contract includes an outline of specific skills learned in therapy and concrete plans for using these skills under certain circumstances. A formal contract may be helpful in terms of motivating patients to apply cognitive-behavioral tools in the future (Rayburn & Otto, 2003).

Importance of Family/Parental Involvement

Studies have been conducted to evaluate the role of parental involvement in the treatment of child anxiety disorders (Barrett, Dadds, & Rapee, 1996; Cobham, Dadds, & Scence, 1998; Mendlowitz et al., 1999). Barrett and colleagues (1996) found that significantly more children who participated in a CBT intervention that included a family therapy component were free of their anxiety diagnosis, at post-treatment and at 12-month follow-up, than children who participated in CBT without parental involvement. However, at 6-year follow-up, the superiority of the CBT plus family therapy was no longer present (Barrett, Duffy, Dadds, & Rapee, 2001). Cobham and colleagues (1998) compared the efficacy of child-focused CBT and child-focused CBT plus parental anxiety management for children with anxiety disorders. Results indicated that the parental anxiety management component increased the efficacy of the CBT component only for children with at least one anxious parent.

Importance of Early Intervention

Dadds et al. (1999) evaluated the potential benefits of prevention and early intervention with children demonstrating symptoms of anxiety. Almost 2000 Australian children ages 7–14 years were screened for anxiety symptoms in their classrooms. After screening and diagnostic interviewing, 128 children were selected for inclusion. Children selected for inclusion either had subclinical features of an anxiety disorder or met criteria but had low severity ratings. Participants in the 10-week evaluation were assigned to either a child and parent intervention or a monitoring group. After 10 weeks, both groups showed improvement. At the 6-month follow-up assessment, the benefit was maintained in the treatment group only, with a decrease in number of baseline anxiety diagnoses and a lower rate of new anxiety disorders. Only 16% of children who received the preventive intervention developed a new anxiety disorder compared with 54% in the monitoring condition. At the 2-year follow-up assessment, only the treatment group showed gains with a durable reduction in anxiety symptoms and decreased likelihood of developing new anxiety disorders (Dadds et al., 1999).

EFFICACY OF CBT FOR ANXIETY DISORDERS IN NON-ASD POPULATIONS

Cognitive Behavior Therapy for Generalized Anxiety Disorder

Prior reviews and meta-analyses concur that the evidence consistently supports the efficacy of traditional CBT for GAD. Indeed, CBT for GAD is listed as an empirically supported treatment by the Task Force for the Dissemination and Promotion of Empirically Supported Treatments (Chambless et al., 1998).

The effects of CBT have routinely maintained or increased their degree of improvement at the 6-month or 12-month follow-up assessments. It appears that targeting one process of anxious functioning (e.g., conditions using cognitive therapy, somatic anxiety using relaxation techniques) for a long enough period ultimately results in therapeutic changes in the other processes, whereas providing the multiple cognitive and behavioral coping skills inherent in CBT appears to be clinically most useful when treatment duration is relatively brief.

Although the results are very encouraging, some methods of assessing the degree of clinically significant change suggest that only about half of GAD patients receiving CBT return to normal levels of anxiety. Some investigators have argued that GAD may be the most difficult anxiety disorder to treat (Borkovec et al., 2003).

Although a number of psychosocial approaches exist for treating anxiety disorders in children (e.g., CBT, psychodynamic psychotherapy, play therapy, supportive therapy), CBT is the only one whose efficacy is supported by data from randomized controlled studies (Labellarte, Ginsburg, & Walkup, 1999). Barrios and O'Dell (1998) list major groupings of treatment components common to CBT interventions for anxious children: desensitization, prolonged exposure, modeling, contingency management, and self-management or cognitive strategies. Results indicated that after treatment, 73% of children who received individual CBT and 50% of children who received group CBT no longer met diagnostic criteria for their primary anxiety disorder, whereas only 8% of children in the waiting-list control group no longer met criteria. Results indicate that the treatment gains associated with individual CBT versus group CBT were not significantly different. Treatment gains were maintained at the 3-month follow-up assessment. Berman and colleagues also reported no significant difference between treatment outcome for anxious children treated with individual versus group CBT (Berman et al., 2000).

Cognitive-Behavior Therapy for Panic Disorder

All CBT treatments for panic disorder include exposure and cognitive elements. Some programs emphasize exposure exercises, whereas others focus on formal cognitive therapy techniques that involve exposure in the form of behavioral experiments. Since the 1980s, a great deal of research has emerged in support of the efficacy of CBT for panic disorder in adults (Barlow & Cerney, 1988), and in children and adolescents (Drobes & Strauss, 1993; Hoffman & Mattis, 2000).

Research suggests that in terms of long-term outcome, CBT applied as a monotherapy appears to result in more stable gains than treatment combining CBT and medication. CBT offers beneficial outcome when applied during any of a number of phases of the disorder. It should be considered as an effective first-line treatment for the disorder and for patients who have not responded to, or who have exhibited only partial improvement, with pharmacotherapy. CBT can also be of particular benefit during the medication discontinuation phase. Finally, brief CBT interventions have shown promise in stemming the tide of new cases of panic disorder in vulnerable individuals (Rayburn & Otto, 2003).

Cognitive-Behavior Therapy for Social Anxiety Disorder

A large number of outcome studies have been conducted in the last two decades. To evaluate the efficacy of CBT for social phobia, meta-analytic strategies have been increasingly used to examine this large and growing literature. Patients receiving CBT demonstrate substantial improvement in social anxiety symptoms after treatment. CBT has been found to be effective not only in the short-term studies, but also in follow-up investigations. Treatment gains are maintained after CBT ends. Most patients either maintained their gains or made additional improvements.

Many CBT treatments for social anxiety disorder comprise heterogeneous procedures, often including behavioral techniques (e.g., exposure, relaxation, social skills training), and/or cognitive strategies. Studies have been carried out to assess the efficacy of the various CBT procedures. Research indicates that treatments using both cognitive strategies and exposure are the most efficacious. Social skills training or relaxation training do not appear to be indicated for every patient and may have less impact on the patient who is socially facile or who reports little physiologic arousal, respectively. It also appears that individuals who demonstrate more cognitive change (as assessed with measures of rational thinking, positive and negative self-statements, or thought listing procedures after behavior tests) show greater improvements in social anxiety after receiving CBT (Hambrick et al., 2003).

To date, there are only a few studies that demonstrate the efficacy of CBT for children or adolescents with social phobia (Albano, Marten, Holt, Heimberg, & Barlow, 1995; Beidel, Turner, & Morris, 2000; Hayward et al., 2000; Spence, Donovan, & Brechman-Toussaint, 2000).

Cognitive-Behavior Therapy for Specific Phobia

The most successful treatment approach for children with specific phobia appears to be graduated in vivo exposure in combination with contingency management and self-control strategies (Morris & Kratochwill, 1998; Silverman et al., 1999). In vivo exposure involves gradually bringing the child into contact with progressively more stressful variations on phobic stimuli. Habituation and teaching the child to cope with the anxious feelings are the two primary principles that underlie this approach. Contingency management techniques entail using differential reinforcement to shape the phobic child's behavior. Desired behaviors (e.g., approaching phobic stimuli) are rewarded, and maladaptive behaviors (e.g., avoidance behaviors) are not. Self-control strategies use the cognitive tools of self-evaluation and self-reward to accomplish the same ends.

PSYCHOPHARMACOTHERAPY

The art and science of psychopharmacotherapy, or "medication therapy," have expanded rapidly since the 1980s. In particular, the contributions made by neuroscience have facilitated the development of new psychotropics. It is critical that physicians continually assimilate new information about recent advances. It is equally important that consumers (individuals with ASD and their caregivers) continually obtain the necessary drug information and become familiar with the use of various drugs.

The decision to implement drug treatment must be based on a sound diagnosis. If medication is likely to be both effective and safe, the physician should consider it. However, the immediate and long-term side-effects, or evaluation of the risk–benefit ratio for an individual, must be considered before prescribing a specific medication. Pharmacotherapy, should be only a part of a comprehensive intervention program that includes psychosocial interventions that include family counseling and individual and group therapies, cognitive therapy, behavior therapy, CBT, special education intervention, occupational therapy, and speech and communication therapy. Without these additional therapies, the therapeutic advantages of medication treatment usually disappears after prolonged use of medications, or after medications are discontinued.

Drug treatment should be reserved for those individuals whose symptoms are sufficiently severe as to impede normal emotional and social development or the ability to learn. Medication can be very useful in the treatment of anxiety disorders. It is often used in conjunction with one or more of the therapies mentioned above. Anti-anxiety medication can be either a short-term or long-term treatment option. Depending on the specific indication, if medication therapy is effective, it should proceed at an optimal dosage for a period of 4 to 6 months. After this time, the drug should be discontinued for about 4 weeks to permit evaluation of the need for continued treatment.

Individuals with ASD or their parents are understandably hesitant about taking any medication without knowing which ones are appropriate and safe to use. Many individuals with ASD do not like to take psychotropic medications for fear that they may be stigmatized. Many parents also do not like to give their children medications because they worry that taking medications will stigmatize their children.

Individuals with ASD should not be forced to take medications, nor should the medications be disguised or inaccurately described. It is important to find out why the individual does not want to take the medicine. It is important to educate and to involve the individuals, particularly those with high-functioning autistic disorder or Asperger's disorder, in the discussion of his or her anxiety disorders and of the goal of treatment. Discussion should be at a developmentally appropriate level.

The individual with ASD is the center of pharmacotherapy, and the patient should be involved in the entire process as much as possible. The caregivers should make every effort to help the patient understand the reason and purpose of taking the medications. Even very young children can have the medication explained in ways they can understand. The caregivers should encourage the individuals to ask questions and express feelings. If necessary, appropriate and sensitive counseling can help overcome any fear or worry about taking medication, such as fear that the medication may diminish self-control or cause them to be stigmatized by others who know they must take medication. Understanding the reason for taking the medicine and the long-term treatment goals helps individuals feel better about themselves and function better at school or at work.

The educational process should continue throughout the entire treatment relationship. It often involves clarifying issues as they arise. If this is done properly, the individual becomes a helpful ally throughout the treatment. This approach prevents the development of a negative attitude or a misperception toward the use of the medication. Individuals with ASD should be given the responsibility of taking their own medications so that they are taking the important role in the treatment process.

Some Helpful Questions and Answers

To help individuals with ASD and their caregivers develop better understanding of how medications are used in anxiety disorders, the most frequently asked questions and answers about treating anxiety disorders with medications are presented below. Individuals with ASD and their legal guardians should have a right and a choice to not receive medication therapy. The diagnosing physician should also provide information concerning alternatives to medication, such as CBT and other psychosocial treatments.

What Medications Are Typically Used to Treat Anxiety Disorders?

The preferred medication for most anxiety disorders is buspirone (Buspar) or the selective serotonin reuptake inhibitors (SSRI). The SSRI group of medications includes fluoxetine (Prozac), sertralin (Zoloft), paroxetine (Paxil), fluvoxamine (Luvox), citalopram (Celexa), escitalopram (Lexapro), venlafaxine (Effexor), and nefazodone (Serzone). However, the Food and Drug Administration (FDA) has limited the use of SSRIs in youth with anxiety disorders to Prozac, Zoloft, and Luvox. Furthermore, in March 2004, the FDA issued a Public Health Advisory on Cautions for Use of Antidepressants, particularly the SSRIs. Although there is no clear link between the use of SSRIs and suicide, the FDA recommended that physicians, patients, families, and caregivers closely monitor both adults and children who take SSRIs, particularly for depression, a frequent co-existing condition of anxiety disorders.

Tricyclic antidepressants (TCA; medications with a three-ring chemical structure) are less commonly used in the treatment of anxiety disorders. They are the second line of drugs of choice because there is a potential for development of tolerance and dependence, as well as the possibility of abuse and withdrawal reactions. The tricyclic group of medications include imipramine (Tofranil), amitripryline (Elavil), desipramine (Norpramin), doxepin (Sinequan), nortriptyline (Pamelor or Aventyl), and protriptyline (Vivactil)] and benzodiazepines [BZDs; e.g., alprazolam (Xanax), diazepam (Valium), chlordiazepoxide (Librium or Librax) and lorazepam (Ativan)]. Treatments using BZDs can be considered on a short-term basis, alone, or in combination with buspirone, an SSRI, or a TCA while waiting for the SSRI or TCA to reach therapeutic level.

How Do Anti-Anxiety Medications Work?

The exact pharmacological mechanism of all the anti-anxiety medication is unclear. Nonetheless, it is known that the primary cellular actions of the anti-depressants are on the monoamine neurotransmitter system. The monoamine neurotransmitters include acetylcholine, norepinephrine, serotonin, and dopamine. Generally, the antidepressants act by influencing the metabolism and/or reuptake of these neurotransmitters, which results in functionally increased levels of available neurotransmitters. They can block the symptoms of panic, including rapid heartbeat, terror, dizziness, chest pains, nausea, and breathing problems.

The properties of the above BZDs are similar to those of the sedative-hypnotics. The various sedative effects differ mainly in milligram potency, dose—response curves, and onset and duration of action. All are general depressants of brain function and decrease anxiety. To varying degrees, all have the potential for dependency with tolerance and severe withdrawal symptoms. They are addictive and have cross-tolerance and cross-dependence. On the whole, low-potency and/or long-acting medications like Valium are preferable because their adverse effects have been far better researched. Also, the high-potency and/or short-acting medications tend to cause more problems of dependence, rebound, and withdrawals.

A relatively newer category of nonsedating, nonaddictive anxiolytic drugs is now available (e.g., buspirone). The molecular structure of buspirone is uniquely different from other anti-anxiety medications. Buspirone lacks hypnotic, anti-convulsant, and muscle-relaxant properties. Thus, it differs from the BZDs in that it does not impair motor skills. The newer drugs do not appear to act synergistically with alcohol, and they are likely to possess a much lower potential for abuse, dependence, and withdrawal syndrome than the BZDs. Despite having no FDA approved indications for use with persons younger than 18 years of age, the use of buspirone with children and adolescents is of great interest to child psychiatrists because of its minimal sedation and low potential for abuse.

How Should Anti-Anxiety Medications Be Taken?

Dosage of anti-anxiety medications varies, depending on the type of drug, the person's body chemistry, age, and, sometimes, body weight. Physicians usually start with low dosages and gradually raise them until reaching the desired effect without the appearance of troublesome side effects (i.e., titrating dosages). The lag in clinical response may be as much as several days to weeks. The lag time is apparently related to delays in achieving therapeutic blood levels and the interval required to affect neurotransmitter systems. The patient should take the drug for several weeks at maximum doses before the doctor considers the treatment a failure.

Except for some early adjustments, the patient usually does not have to use divided doses of anti-anxiety medications. A single dose taken in the morning usually is adequate, though in some individuals divided doses may be needed. Some medications may cause drowsiness and sleepiness if taken during daytime. The drugs should be taken at bedtime (particularly when the clinician takes advantage of the sedative side-effects to help treat associated insomnia).

Adequate compliance with treatment is a major issue affecting the potential for a successful outcome. Most patients and their parents do not routinely follow instructions for the use of medications or other aspects of treatment. About 50% of the prescriptions filled each year are not taken correctly. Although physicians usually emphasize that the use of medications as prescribed is important to treat specific problems or disorders, individuals with ASD and their parents may be ambivalent or forgetful about taking or giving medications as prescribed. Previous studies have shown that people tend to forget to take their medications when doctors prescribe a multiple, daily-dose regimen. When physicians ask patients to take their medications four times a day, the patients tended to miss more doses than those being asked to take the medications three times daily. Similarly, those on a three-dose daily regimen missed more doses than those on a two-dose daily regimen, and those on a two-dose daily regimen missed more doses than those on a once-a-day regimen. Many psychotherapeutic medications can be given once a day, either administered in the evening or upon waking. Whenever possible, the individual and the caregivers should ask the prescribing physician about taking medications in a single, daily dose. Taking medication once daily facilitates compliance and spares the individual the embarrassment of taking medication in front of schoolmates or co-workers. The individual or the caregivers should ask the prescribing physician for a printed treatment plan that includes instructions for taking the medication. Caregivers should help the individual learn how to use the treatment plan to enhance the compliance of taking medications according to the instructions.

If an individual with ASD has difficulty with taking medication orally due to the taste or size of the medication, ask the pharmacist to use flavorings to sweeten a bitter taste, mask strong medicine with a pleasant flavor, or create a liquid-form medication. The pharmacist can also dye medications with a favorite color. This will add just a miniscule cost, but it may make life easier for both the individual and their caregivers, as well as reduce the risk of noncompliance.

Some medical experts are concerned about a lack of federal oversight. They worry that flavorings can dilute a medication or dangerously alter its chemical structure. Pharmacists, however, consider the flavorings harmless and perhaps even beneficial because the individuals are more likely to take the full dose. I am not aware of the Food and Drug Administration receiving any reports that flavored drugs have caused harm.

One particularly risky and potentially dangerous practice is that of taking tablets or capsules without water or other liquid. Liquids assist the pills' progress to the stomach where they will dissolve and yield their contents. If possible, always use liquid medicine rather than pills for very young children. If the medicines are tablets or capsules, at least 100 ml (half a cupful) of liquid (water or a favorite soft drink) should be provided. Otherwise, pills could lodge in the esophagus and cause physical damage to its lining.

Once the effective dosage is established, the dosage is maintained for several weeks or months, and thereafter the prescription is evaluated for the lowest effective dose for as long as the anxiety disorder continues. This involves a gradual downward adjustment of the dosage until the individual requires no medication. This process usually takes 6 months or more from the start of the medication treatment.

How Can One Tell If the Medication Is Working?

An individual with ASD, the caregivers, and the prescribing physician should together obtain baseline measures before starting any medication. Document any symptoms or signs that resemble psychotherapeutic medication-induced side-effects, such as hyperactivity and tics. The individual and his or her caregivers should regularly measure frequency and severity of the behaviors or symptoms being treated over an entire course of treatment to document the clinical effects of the medications. In addition to direct observational procedures, use behavioral checklists. Several instruments developed for the general population have been modified for use among those with developmental disorders, including ASD. It is important that all the behavioral measures follow the rule of reliability including inter-rater reliability to avoid placebo effect being misinterpreted as true treatment effect. This approach also provides an opportunity for physician and all other caregivers to collaborate and to ensure the best quality of care.

When certain medications (e.g., TCAs) are used, the physician should regularly monitor the blood level of these medications. Such laboratory drug monitoring can provide the necessary information on how rapidly an individual eliminates the drug so the dose can be adjusted to maximize safety and efficacy. Although psychotherapeutic medications have important benefits, there is no effective medication that does not have side effects. Everyone involved in caring for an individual with ASD must pay attention to the development of adverse effects throughout the entire course of treatment, and all efforts must be made to minimize side effects. The effects of psychotherapeutic medications on a child's brain are not fully understood, and it is not known whether medications produce long-lasting and irreversible effects. Caregivers should regularly and systematically question the individual, if he or she is verbally capable, about the development of any possible side effects. In addition, direct observational procedures, side-effects checklists, and blood level monitoring of certain medications should be done to monitor the side effects.

What If the Individual Develops Side Effects?

Side effects caused by buspirone and SSRIs are often mild and transient and frequently do not require discontinuing the medication. Individuals on a medication or their caregivers should call the prescribing doctor with any questions or concerns regarding possible side effects during the course of treatment. The dose of the medication may need to be adjusted and/or the medication treatment may need to be discontinued. Some individuals may have side effects to one SSRI, but not to others, so a trial of a different SSRI may be needed if side effects develop to the initial medication.

How Long Will It Take for the Medication to Work?

Initiation of medication treatment usually does not produce an immediate decrease in symptoms of anxiety. Improvement in the individual's symptoms may begin to occur after a week or more of treatment, although an initial treatment trial of 4–6 weeks may be needed to assess clinical response, particularly with a SSRI.

Can Anti-Anxiety Medication Be Used with Other Medications?

Anti-anxiety medications may interact with some over-the-counter medications. Call and check with the prescribing doctor or check with the pharmacist who dispenses the prescribed medication before adding any over-the-counter medications to avoid potential medication interactions.

How Frequently Should the Physician See the
Individual, and How Long Will the Individual
Need to Take Medicine?

The phase (e.g., acute, relapse, recurrence) of a disorder or a problem of concern is of critical importance in terms of the initial intervention and the duration of treatment. During the initial acute phase of psychopharmacotherapy, the physician should see the individual at least once a week. Once the acute episode has been adequately alleviated, usually after several weeks of treatment, an ongoing medication maintenance program can begin to prevent a relapse back into the acute phase. The individual can be seen less frequently, such as monthly or bimonthly, to review therapeutic response and development of side-effects.

Medication adjustment is usually a trial-and-error technique. With the possible exception of stimulants in ADHD, medication response in ASD tends to occur in slow motion. Avoid changing medications or dosages before the necessary interval of time for a response. In general, if an individual has not responded to a medication within 4 weeks while the dosage is in the therapeutic range, it is unlikely he or she will respond at a later date. The medication should be discontinued gradually (over about 2 weeks) while a second medication is instituted and its dosage is slowly increased.

There are no firm guidelines regarding when to discontinue medication. Nonetheless, the nature of a disorder or problems of concern may determine how long someone must take a psychotherapeutic medication. In cases with positive therapeutic response, medication treatment should proceed at optimal dosage for periods of 4–6 months. The medication should be gradually tapered and then discontinued for at least 1–2 months to permit evaluation of the need for continued treatment, as well as assessment of the development of side effects, such as growth changes or neuromuscular abnormalities.

This reassessment should not take place at the beginning of a school year to ensure that the individual has acclimated to a new classroom. This approach is to prevent erroneous decisions being made on the basis of a "honeymoon" effect with a new teacher that may occur during the initial stages of the academic year. A better time to do the reassessment is 2–3 weeks after summer break starts. If there is no significant difference in the child's behavior when medicated, then treatment may be discontinued for a longer period.

The individual with ASD, his or her parents or legal guardians, or the prescribing physician may terminate medication treatment. At this juncture, the potential for recurrence should be clearly discussed in the context of the risk—benefit ratio.

If an individual with ASD has been on a medication for several months or years, withdrawal must be done very slowly. Sudden withdrawal from a medication can cause severe reactions. Sometimes it takes several weeks to withdraw a person from a medication they have taken for many years. If a new medication is tried for just a few weeks, and it is not effective or has bad side effects, it can usually be withdrawn immediately.

Choosing Effective Medications

The following recommendations for choosing effective medications for anxiety disorder are not a substitute for an informed discussion between individuals with ASD or their caregivers and the prescribing physicians. This section provides a decision-making method that incorporates a growing database for the optimal use of drug therapies in clinical practice. When sufficient research data are lacking, suggestions are offered based on my own cumulative clinical and research experience. The goal is to provide a logical treatment strategy that can be readily comprehended and for parents to discuss with their child's physician who is not familiar with ASD. The following sections describe some principles usually implied in medication therapy. Appropriate selection of psychotherapeutic medication is based on multiple considerations, including medical, patient and family, physician, social, and economic factors.

Medical Factors

Symptoms can be seen as the behavioral manifestations of underlying brain pathology, and treatment plans are formulated on this assumption. Most medication treatments are currently dictated by a specific diagnosis. Hence, the selection of medication depends on the known effectiveness of a certain class of medications for a certain clinical diagnosis. For example, a physician will usually select one of the serotonin reuptake inhibitors (SRI) as the first-line medication for OCD. However, the individual may have to try several different medications in the class before finding a suitable one or ruling out that class.

Usually, there are a number of medication options, so it is important to choose the medication that has the best risk—benefit ratio. For example, studies have shown that SRIs, antidepressants, and BZDs all can improve anxiety disorders. However, the SRIs have the best result qualitatively and the fewest side effects, so there is little reason to use the others as the first-line medication of choice except when SRIs fail or produce unacceptable side effects such as severe irritability or insomnia.

Physicians usually avoid prescribing those psychotherapeutic medications that have a high rate of drug–drug interactions or that have adverse effects in certain populations. A physician's call for therapeutic medications usually can be satisfied by a thorough knowledge of one or two medications in each therapeutic category. The individual will benefit if the physician avoids the temptation to choose from many different newer medications for the individual's treatment. The individual's parents and caregivers should also refrain from demanding that the physician prescribe a particular medication that they have heard about from other parents or caregivers, especially if the individual's physician uses it infrequently or has never used it. When certain medications require preliminary and follow-up laboratory tests (e.g., TCAs), physicians tend not to select them as first-line medications because individuals with ASD tend to cooperate poorly with the laboratory procedures.

Some medications are clearly indicated during an acute phase of treatment, but not for maintenance or prophylactic purposes. For example, BZDs are effective for controlling acute anxiety disorder, but they are ineffective in preventing a relapse or in maintenance due to the tendency of developing physical dependence. Conversely, certain medications may not be useful for acute management but are exceptionally beneficial for maintenance. For example, lithium is not effective in controlling agitation during the acute phase of manic-depressive disorder or episodic temper outbursts with physical aggression, but it is quite effective in preventing a relapse of manic-depressive disorder.

Patient and Family Factors

Selecting appropriate medication requires comprehensive information about the patient, including current functioning and diagnosis, past medical and psychiatric history, and family medical and psychiatric history. It is crucial that the caregivers maintain an up-to-date medical record. For example, many medications may lower the threshold for seizure or interact with anticonvulsants to either enhance or diminish their treatment effectiveness. Therefore, it is critical for the physician to know about a patient's history of seizure disorder, previous use of and response to any medication, and current medications.

Prior personal (and possibly family) history of a good or poor response to a specific medication usually is an important factor in making the first-line choice for a subsequent episode. Physicians usually avoid prescribing a medication that had side effects in an individual or family members.

Physician Factors

Physicians vary immensely in their general approach to use of medications. Most doctors grow comfortable with a set of basic strategies at the beginning of their careers and then use them over and over again. While medical researchers may continuously validate new medications, tests, and operations, practicing physicians may lag behind, favoring known options instead. Some physicians practice evidence-based medicine, search the medical literature for specific research studies, and choose the medication that has shown the strongest treatment effect for a particular disorder or syndrome. Unfortunately, sometimes personal needs or biases, such as being the first and only physician in the community who knows something about the new medication, may influence a physician's choice of medication. If the individual or caregiver has any concern about a physician's motive or knowledge, they should get a second opinion.

Social Factors

Some parents may be under pressure from the school or workplace to do something about their child's problem behaviors or emotional disturbances. If certain nonmedical professionals involved in caring of individuals with ASD strongly believe in psychopharmacotherapy, they may advocate for certain medications, sometimes based on media reports. This factor may impinge on both physician and parents in selecting medication.

Economic Factors

Pharmaceuticals are a big business, and drug companies have a limited patent period in which to recoup very expensive investments in the development and marketing of new products. Drug companies use every legitimate marketing technique to sell their products, with an increasing emphasis on projecting an image of being interested in helping physicians help their patients. This factor may influence the physician's choice of medications. In contrast, third-party payers (insurance companies, HMOs) tend to encourage their participating physicians to use generic brands or less expensive brand-name medications.

Determining the Treatment Priority

When there are multiple behaviors and/or emotional concerns, the treatment team should determine the treatment priority. If at all possible, treatment should begin with one medication for the most urgent problem.

If an individual has multiple behavioral problems or emotional disturbances, and if there is no acute crisis that requires the simultaneous use of several medications to control all problems or symptoms of concern, the treatment team should choose the one problem or symptom that is of the greatest concern and that is the most likely to respond quickly to a selected medication.

Use the following criteria to prioritize the behavior or emotional concerns:

1. The first-priority category consists of any behavior that leads to a direct hazard to the health or safety of the individual or other people.
2. The second most serious category includes disruptive and/or destructive behaviors such as running or screaming in the classroom, house, or job place; throwing tantrums; and kicking, throwing or breaking objects.
3. The third category includes behaviors that pose a severe threat to the self-esteem of the individual, such as poor social skills and extreme shyness at group times.
4. The fourth category includes any other behavior, such as baby talk and stereotyped movements (e.g., hand-flapping, clapping).

If one medication is effective, it is simpler than juggling two or three. The physician should begin with the one medication believed to be the most effective with the fewest side effects. Such monotherapy (i.e., using only one medication) is still the best practice in terms of enhancing compliance, avoiding drug–drug interaction, minimizing side effects, and measuring the treatment effect and side effects. When treatment effects are not satisfactory, adding other medications may be warranted. (See Tsai (2001) for guidelines for co-pharmacy and poly-pharmacy.)

Determining the Optimal Dosage

Some people may respond better to one medication than another, some may need larger dosages than others, and children differ significantly from adults in their pharmacokinetic capacities. Because there is no certain way of determining beforehand which medication will be effective, the doctor may have to prescribe first one, and then another, until one is effective. The treatment is usually continued for a minimum of several months.

Before starting a medication, the doctor, the individual with ASD, and his or her caregivers should discuss a plan for reaching the optimal dosage. All involved in the medication treatment should agree on how quickly the dose will be increased and what the maximum level will be. Like any other medication, psychotherapeutic medications do not produce the same effect in everyone. Age, sex, body size, body chemistry, habits, and diet are some of the factors that can influence a medication's effect. For some medications, however, the optimal dose is unrelated to weight, age, or illness severity. The optimal therapeutic dose for many psychotherapeutic medications is subject to wide inter-individual variation.

To determine the optimal dosage, many clinicians prefer to titrate dosage (i.e., gradually increase or decrease the dosage). This approach relies on closely monitoring the changes of behaviors or symptoms. In addition to the behavioral observations and ratings by the caregivers, it is important to find out the individual's subjective feelings and reactions to the medication. Many individuals with ASD can verbalize their feelings when asked to do so. They may report a sensation of being slowed down, being irritable, or feeling calmer or more attentive at school or at the workplace once a therapeutic dosage has been attained. If the individual is a young child and/or less verbal, the physician has to rely heavily on the caregivers' reports to determine the optimal dose of medications.

Some physicians may prefer to use standardized doses based on the individual's body weight when reliable body weight based dosage information is available. Physicians can measure certain medications in the blood to guide clinical use. This approach may be more helpful in cases where reliable informants are not available to report whether the individual is taking the medication, as well as in cases where the prescribed medications have known therapeutic range of blood levels. Generally, once the doctor has determined a medication's therapeutic effect, the lowest possible maintenance dose that is within the therapeutic range should be prescribed.

A physician commits a major error by prescribing ineffectively low doses of a medication that exposes individuals with ASD to many risks without the benefits of medication therapy. On the other hand, there is an insidious tendency in medicine to operate on the principle that more is likely to be better. Some physicians give persons with ASD an excessively high maintenance dose of medications that can interfere with intellectual function and, in the case of antipsychotic medications, may hasten the development of tardive dyskinesia, a neurological problem caused by the long-term use of neuroleptic drugs. There is often a lag of 2–6 weeks before a psychotherapeutic medication begins to act. The apparent lack of effect in this phase may lead to unwarranted increases in dosage or discontinuation of the medication.

Due to relatively large liver size in proportion to body weight in children, on the one hand, they tend to need higher doses relative to body weight when compared to adults. On the other hand, children tend to have less adipose tissue and less protein binding when compared to adults and may have more medication available for bioactivity and, potentially, more side effects. Children are vulnerable because their bodies are developing at a very rapid pace and may therefore be physically more susceptible to the actions of medications. Caregivers need to be vigilant about the risk–benefit ratio if medication therapy is being considered for a child younger than 4 years old.

EVIDENCE-BASED MEDICATION TREATMENT OF ANXIETY DISORDERS IN NON-ASD POPULATION

Investigators in the field of autistic disorder have carried out some psychopharmacological studies based on the knowledge and experiences learned from other psychiatric disorders (Tsai, 2003a). However, medication treatment specific to anxiety disorders in ASD has rarely been carried out (Tsai, 2003a). At the present, in terms of doing medication treatment of anxiety disorders in individuals with ASD, one has to rely on the information learned from non-ASD populations.

Medication Treatment of Anxiety Disorders in Non-ASD Adults

Drug treatments in adults with GAD have been reviewed (Gorman, 2003; Rickels & Rynn, 2002). The reviews suggest that current effective medications for patients with GAD include anxiolytic BZDs, including alprazolam (Xanax), chlordiazepoxide (Librium or Librax), diazepam (Valium), lorazepam (Ativan), clonazepam (Klonopin); buspirone, and SSRIs including venlafaxine (Effexor), paroxetine (Paxil), sertraline (Zoloft) citalopram (Celexa), and escitalopram (Lexapro). Benzodiazepines have long been used to treat anxiety and are appropriate in short-term treatment situations, however, their adverse side-effect profile (i.e., potential to produce dependency and withdrawal symptoms) and their inability to treat depression, commonly comorbid with GAD, render them less than ideal in many situations (Gorman, 2003). Buspirone has demonstrated efficacy in treatment of GAD, but it shows very little effect in treatment of comorbid depression and it has a slow onset of action. Antidepressants like paroxetine and venlafaxine are effective in treatment of both anxiety and concurrent depression (Gorman, 2003). Tricyclic antidepressants such as imipramine (Tofranil) may substantially reduce symptoms of anxiety but are not considered as first-line therapy because of their side effect profile (Rickels & Rynn, 2002).

Few people with social phobia seek professional help despite the existence of beneficial treatment approaches. There is limited systematic data assessing pharmacotherapy of social anxiety disorder. The efficacy, tolerability, and safety of the SSRIs, evidenced in randomized clinical trials, support these agents as first-line treatment. The benzodiazepine clonazepam and certain monoamine oxidase inhibitors may also be of benefit (Van Ameringen et al., 2003). Buspirone has been studied for the treatment of social phobia (Apter & Allen, 1999). A recent study appears to show that citalopram (Celexa) may be a safe and effective treatment for generalized social anxiety disorder, including patients who have failed to tolerate or respond to a prior treatment trial (Simon, Korbly, Worthington, Kinrys, & Pollack, 2002).

Treatment of social phobia may need to be continued for several months to consolidate response and achieve full remission. The SSRIs have shown benefit in long-term treatment trials, while long-term treatment data from clinical studies of clonazepam are limited, but these trials support the drug's efficacy. In light of the chronicity and disability associated with social phobia, as well as the high relapse rate after short-term therapy, it is recommended that effective treatment be continued for at least 12 months (Van Ameringen et al., 2003)

Research on the optimal treatment of panic disorder has been undertaken, and numerous randomized, controlled trials have been published. Selective serotonin reuptake inhibitors have emerged as the most favorable treatment, as they have a beneficial side-effect profile, are relatively safe, and do not produce physical dependency. High-potency benzodiazepines, reversible monoamine oxidase inhibitors, and TCAs have also shown efficacy (Pollack, Allgulander, Bandelow, Cassano, Greist et al., 2003).

Medication Treatment of Anxiety Disorders in Non-ASD Children and Adolescents

This section presents some of the medications that have been studied systematically in the treatment of childhood anxiety disorders in non-ASD populations (Allen, Leonard, & Swedo, 1995; Kutcher, Reiter, & Gardner, 1995; Velosa & Riddle, 2000). Although the data are limited, they do provide some directions for physicians who would use medications in individuals with both ASD and anxiety disorders.

Open-label (Birmaher et al., 1994; Fairbanks et al., 1997) and controlled studies (Research Unit on Pediatric Psychopharmacology, 2001; Rynn, Segueland, & Rickels, 2001) have demonstrated the efficacy and short-term safety of SSRIs for children and adolescents with separation anxiety disorders, social phobia, and GAD. In a review of studies using SSRIs in the short-term treatment of children and adolescents with anxiety disorders or major depression, it was suggested that after remission of target symptoms, a drug-free trial should be considered. It was further recommended that the medication-free trial should occur during the first period of low stress, after a year of SSRI treatment. If a youth relapses during the period without medication, the SSRI should be restarted (Pine, 2002).

Five studies of TCA trials for separation anxiety disorder or school refusal have reported contrasting findings. One of these studies supports the use of TCAs to treat separation anxiety disorder with or without school refusal (Gittelman-Klein & Klein, 1973), and another of the studies supports combining a TCA with CBT for anxious-depressed teenagers with severe, refractory symptoms (Bernstein et al., 2000). The other three studies had problems with either small sample sizes (Bernstein, Garfinkel, & Borchardt, 1990; Klein, Koplewicz, & Kanner, 1992) or low medication dosage (Berney et al., 1981). Nonetheless, these studies suggest that a TCA may be considered for targeting anxiety symptoms in children and adolescents.

There are limited data on the efficacy of benzodiazepines in the treatment of GAD or separation anxiety disorder in children and adolescents. The existing studies are limited by small sample sizes and short duration of treatment (Graae, Milner, Rizzotto, & Klein, 1994; Simeon et al., 1992). Side effects of benzodiazepines may include sedation, incoordination, slurred speech, and tremor (Kutcher, Reiter, Gardner, & Klein, 1992). Behavioral disinhibition has been reported in children and adolescents taking clonazepam (Graae et al., 1994; Reiter & Kutcher, 1991). Physical and psychological dependence after long-term use in adults is of substantial concern (Salzman, 1989). The risk of tolerance and dependence in children has not been adequately studied (Velosa & Riddle, 2000). One consideration may be using a benzodiazepine in a highly anxious child on a short-term basis, alone or in combination with an SSRI or a TCA while waiting for the antidepressant to reach therapeutic dosage. Although no controlled studies of the psychopharmacological treatment of panic disorder have been done in children, case reports suggest that childhood-onset panic disorder may be similar in its pharmacological response to that seen in adults (Black & Robbins, 1990; Kutcher & MacKenzie, 1988). Although no systematic treatment trials of SSRIs in children have been conducted, SSRIs are emerging in clinical practice as the first-line medication treatment of choice. Preliminary evidence in support of the use of paroxetine is provided by the 83% response rate reported in a recent open-label study of 18 children and adolescents with panic disorder (Masi et al., 2001). Although pharmacological treatments have not been shown to be effective for specific phobias, many children with specific phobias also have generalized anxiety or other anxiety disorders and may benefit from pharmacotherapy (Fyer, 1987).

Strategic Use of Medication to Treat Anxiety Disorders and Comorbid Psychiatric Disorders in ASD

Table 15.1 summarizes general recommendations for medication treatment of anxiety disorders in ASD for consideration by treating physicians. All cases are, of course, unique, and no prescriptive authority is intended in this presentation. Some special considerations are warranted and discussed here in the treatment of acute anxiety, OCD, and two disorders (depression and ADHD) that often co-occur with anxiety disorders in this population.

Generalized Anxiety Disorder

Ideally, in treatment of acute anxiety, the medication chosen should be administered with the lowest possible dose for the shortest possible time. Dosages should be flexible rather than arbitrary and should be taken intermittently at a time of increased symptoms rather than on a fixed daily schedule. In general, 1–7 days of medication treatment is recommended for a reaction to an acute situational stress, although 1–6 weeks of treatment may be needed for short-term anxiety due to specific life events. Clinical judgment plays a major role in the decision to continue anxiolytic treatment beyond 4–6 weeks. Although long-term administration may maintain initial improvement, it is unlikely to result in further gains. The chronic nature of anxiety disorders and the frequency of eventual relapse after treatment discontinuation suggest that in some individuals long-term treatment may be indicated. Periodic reassessment of the efficacy, safety, and necessity of long-term anxiolytic therapy is necessary because the high rate of comorbidity for GAD with other psychiatric disorders suggests that an alternative approach (such as adding an antidepressant while tapering of an anxiolytic drug) may be more appropriate in certain individuals.

Obsessive-Compulsive Disorder

The use of SSRIs to treat OCD bears a special caution. Clinical evidence clearly indicates that most individuals relapse if SSRIs are discontinued suddenly. To prevent this, after effective medication has been used for 6 months, physicians should taper the dose gradually until symptoms reemerge and then increase to the dose level administered right before the symptoms reemerged. Follow up should be performed every 2–3 months.

Depression

When depression is present, an SRI may be added while anxiety disorder is being treated with a BZD. If there is no response or insufficient response, sequential

Table 15.1. Strategic medication for anxiety disorders

Disorder	Recommendation	Alternatives (in strategic order)
Generalized anxiety disorder		
Acute anxiety episode		
Mild	CBT	BZD
Moderate/Severe	BZD + CBT	Add Buspar
Chronic anxiety		
With prior BZD	Add Buspar; taper BZD	
Without prior BZD	Buspar	Add BZD; taper Buspar or BZD; add Antidepressant (TCA or SSRI)
Panic disorder		
Panic attacks		
Mild	CBT	Add SSRI or a TCA; add Alprazolam or Clonazepam
Moderate	TCA or SSRI and CBT	Add Alprazolam or Clonazepam
Severe	TCA or SSRI and Alprazolam or Clonazepam & CBT	Add Depakote with or without BZD
Agoraphobia		
Mild	CBT	Add SSRI or a TCA; add Alprazolam or Clonazepam
Moderate	TCA or SSRI	Add Alprazolam or Clonazepam
Severe	TCA or SSRI or Alprazolam and CBT	Add Depakote with or without BZD
Social phobia	CBT	Add SRI; add Alprazolam or Clonazepam
Specific phobia	CBT (systematic desensitization)	Add Propranolol
Obsessive-compulsive disorder or symptoms		
Mild	CBT	Add SSRI or Anafranil (as the last choice if history of seizures)
Moderate/Severe	SSRI and CBT	Sequential trials of SSRI or Anafranil (as the last choice if history of seizures)
Maintenance	Continue effective medication for 6 months; taper dose gradually	

BZD, benzodiazepine; CBT, Cognitive-Behavioral Therapy; SSRI, selective serotonin reuptake inhibitors; TCA, tricyclic antidepressants.

431

trials with other SRIs are warranted. If SRIs are unsuccessful, alternative and sequential strategies include using a TCA, sequential trials with other TCAs and buspirone (Welbutrin), and the addition of a mood stabilizer (e.g., Depakote) and ECT.

ADHD

In low- to middle-functioning individuals or in high-functioning individuals with other neurological disorders, treatment for anxiety disorders comorbid with ADHD can begin with a TCA. If there is no or insufficient response, sequential trials with other TCAs are warranted. Welbutrin or Natrexon can be prescribed for inattention, impulsiveness, and hyperactivity. Sequential trials with Catapres, Tenex, and Haldol can address hyperactivity and impulsiveness.

In high-functioning individuals without other neurological disorders, treatment can begin with Ritalin, or Dexedrine, or Adderall. If there is no or insufficient response, sequential trials with Ritalin, Dexedrine, Adderall, or Cylert can follow. If there is still no or insufficient response with all of the above stimulants, sequential trials with TCAs, Wellbutrin, Natrexon, Catapres, Tenex may be used.

Efficacy and Applications of Combined Therapy

Examining how medication therapy, CBT, or a combination of these therapies contribute to improvement can help determine which patients benefit from which intervention in the treatment of anxiety disorders.

Few studies have directly compared the relative efficacy of CBT and pharmacotherapy for social anxiety disorder. Preliminary results support the efficacy of both pharmacotherapy and CBT for social anxiety disorder. Pharmacotherapy may show somewhat greater acute efficacy and may be associated with quicker response. CBT may confer greater protection against relapse. However, information is extremely limited for how CBT and pharmacotherapeutic interventions might work together in the treatment of social anxiety disorder (Hambrick et al., 2003).

Meta-analytic review of the panic treatment-outcome literature indicates approximately equal outcome is achieved by both pharmacotherapy and CBT during the acute treatment phase (Rayburn & Otto, 2003). Cognitive behavior therapy has demonstrated efficacy in the acute and long-term treatment of panic disorder. An integrated treatment approach that combines pharmacotherapy with CBT may provide the best treatment (Pollack et al., 2003).

As most people will enjoy acute improvement with either CBT or pharmacotherapy, it is tempting to consider combination treatment as a strategy to boost efficacy. However, one should not automatically assume that a combination of two effective treatments is better than one intervention alone. Although there is some evidence for synergistic effects, this relationship appears to be especially complex. There is good evidence that CBT can extend the gains from pharmacotherapy when added sequentially or as an initial strategy, and there is limited evidence that pharmacotherapy holds promise for CBT nonresponders. However, for the addition of pharmacotherapy to CBT, there are some indications that any additive effects achieved during the acute treatment period may come at a cost to longer-term outcome because some of the benefits of CBT provided during medication treatment may be lost when medication is discontinued (Rayburn & Otto, 2003). Furthermore, the combination of interventions may result in decreased treatment efficacy if individuals receiving both medication and CBT believe that the medication is the primary agent of change and they consequently invest less in the CBT.

One also needs to keep in mind that not all cognitive-behavioral techniques may combine equally well with medications. For instance, medications that inhibit the experience of anxiety, such as benzodiazepines, may be relatively poorer candidates for combination with exposure techniques (Hambrick et al., 2003). Little is known about the ways in which specific CBT techniques are best combined with specific pharmacotherapies. In fact, there remains much to learn about the best methods of combining the different techniques of CBT and various medications.

Nonetheless, it would be of great interest to know the relative efficacy of different methods of starting and sequencing of these treatments. For example, one might start an individual on medication first to take the edge off his or her anxiety or fears. The medication can then be phased out as the individual learns cognitive-behavioral skills for coping with anxious arousal. CBT can also be used to help individuals discontinue medications on which they have become psychologically or physically dependent. A similar strategy might be used with individuals who have used medications successfully but who may be likely to relapse on medication discontinuation. CBT is offered during the process of medication tapering, allowing the individuals to learn how to respond to cues present during and after the withdrawal of medication effects. CBT might also be used to augment gains in partial responders to pharmacotherapy (Hambrick et al., 2003).

Which Treatment Modality Should Be Considered?

Given that CBT, pharmacotherapy, and combined therapy can offer promising treatment outcome, on what basis should one modality of treatment be selected over the other? So far, there are no data indicating how individuals should be matched to one of the treatment modalities based on characteristics of their symptom profile (Rayburn & Otto, 2003). Factors such as cost, user friendliness, availability, treatment response, and maintenance therapy may be helpful when considering a treatment modality.

Cost

Examination of the costs of the treatments may help the decision making. Current data indicate that individual CBT is somewhat more costly than pharmacotherapy during the acute 4-month treatment phase, but then it quickly makes up its initial costs over follow-up, so that after one year it was found to be roughly half as costly as medication therapy. Group CBT provides cost savings relative to pharmacotherapy starting in the acute treatment phase and extending forward, so that it was less than 25% of the costs of pharmacotherapy by the end of the 1-year study (Rayburn & Otto, 2003).

User Friendliness

CBT appears to be an especially tolerable treatment, as estimated by dropout rates in clinical trials. Part of the acceptability of CBT may come from its relatively quick onset of action, well within the time frame of antidepressant treatments for panic disorder. For example, studies of CBT indicate improvements as early as the second session, with evidence of incremental improvement thereafter (Rayburn & Otto, 2003).

Availability

The greatest limitation of CBT is the availability of CBT providers. That is, many communities and clinics may not have access to CBT providers. Pharmacotherapy is much easier to obtain in most communities. Hence, medication therapy alone, or in conjunction with dynamic treatment, tends to be a common form of treatment. For clinicians considering referral to a CBT specialist, professional associations, such as the Association for the Advancement of Behavior Therapy (www.aabt.org) or the Anxiety Disorders Association of American (www.adaa.org) can help identify CBT specialists in a given area.

Treatment Response

CBT appears to be an effective strategy when patients do not respond to pharmacotherapy. Examination of outcome for patients who are either partial responders or nonresponders to an adequate dose and duration of pharmacotherapy indicates that brief CBT offers an efficacious alternative (Rayburn & Otto, 2003).

Maintenance Therapy

Long-term efficacy is an important consideration in treatment selection, as maintenance treatment is recommended for at least 12–24 months, and in some cases, indefinitely (Pollack et al., 2003). It is generally accepted that to maintain treatment gains from pharmacotherapy, medications need to be continued over the long term. Indeed, when medications are discontinued after acute treatment, relapse rates in the range of 54–70% are common. Even with continuation treatment, there is some evidence that ongoing slippage in treatment gains may occur regardless of the use of single agent or combined pharmacologic strategies. In contrast, there is good evidence that individuals can use CBT as a strategy to discontinue their pharmacotherapy while maintaining or extending treatment gains (Rayburn & Otto, 2003).

References

Abelson, J. L., & Alessi, N. E. (1992). Discussion of child panic revisited. *Journal of American Academy of Child and Adolescent Psychiatry, 31*, 114–116.

Albano, A. M., Chorpita, B. E., & Barlow, D. H. (1996). Childhood anxiety disorders. In E. J. Mash & R. A. Barkley (Eds.), *Child psychopathology* (pp. 196–241). New York: Guilford Press.

Albano, A. M., Marten, P. A, Holt, C. S., Heimberg, R. G., & Barlow, D. H. (1995). Cognitive-behavioral group treatment for social phobia in adolescents: A preliminary study. *Journal of Nervous & Mental Disease, 183*, 649–656.

Allen, A. J., Leonard, H., & Swedo, S. E. (1995). Current knowledge of medications for the treatment of childhood anxiety disorders. *Journal of American Academy of Child and Adolescent Psychiatry, 34*, 976–986.

American Psychiatric Association. (2000). *Diagnostic and Statistical Manual of Mental Disorders: Text revision* (4th ed.). Washington, DC: Author.

Ando, H., & Yoshimura, I. (1979). Effects of age on communication skill levels and prevalence of maladaptive behaviors in autistic and mentally retarded children. *Journal of Autism and Developmental Disorders, 9*, 83–93.

Anxiety Disorders Association. (2004). *Statistics and facts about anxiety disorders.* Silver Spring, MD: Anxiety Disorders Association. Available: http://www.adaa.org/mediaroom/index.cfm.

Apter, J. T., & Allen, L. A. (1999). Buspirone: Future direction. *Journal of Clinical Psychopharmacology, 19*(1), 86–93.

Attwood, T. (1998). *Asperger's syndrome: A guide for parents and professionals.* Philadelphia: Jessica Kingsley.

Barlow, D. H., & Cerney, J. A. (1988). *Psychological treatment of panic.* New York: Guilford Press.

Barrett, P. M., Dadds, M. R., & Rapee, R. M. (1996). Family treatment of childhood anxiety: A controlled trial. *Journal of Consulting & Clinical Psychology, 64*, 333–342.

Barrett, P. M., Duffy, A. L., Dadds, M. R., & Rapee, R. M. (2001). Cognitive-behavioral treatment of anxiety disorders in children: Long-term (6-year) follow-up. *Journal of Consulting & Clinical Psychology, 169*, 135–141.

Barrios, B. A., & O'Dell, S. L. (1998). Fears and anxieties. In E. J. Mash & R. A. Barkley (Eds.), *Treatment of childhood disorders* (2nd ed., pp. 249–337). New York: Guilford Press.

Beidel, D. C., Turner, S. M., & Morris, T. L. (1999). Psychopathology of childhood social phobia. *Journal of American Academy of Child and Adolescent Psychiatry, 38*, 643–650.

Beidel, D. C., Turner, S. M., & Morris, T. L. (2000). Behavioral treatment of childhood social phobia. *Journal of Consulting & Clinical Psychology, 68,* 1072–1080.

Berman, S. L., Weems, C. F., & Silverman, W. K. (2000). Predictors of outcome in exposure-based cognitive and behavioral treatments for phobic and anxiety disorders in children. *Behavior Therapy, 31,* 713–731.

Berney, T., Kolvin, I., Bhate, S. R., Garside, R. F., Jeans, J, Kay, B., & Scarth, L. (1981). School phobia: A therapeutic trial with Clomipramine and short-term outcome. *British Journal of Psychiatry, 138,* 110–118.

Bernstein, G. A. (1991). Comorbidity and severity of anxiety and depressive disorders in a clinic sample. *Journal of American Academy of Child and Adolescent Psychiatry, 30,* 43–50.

Bernstein, G. A., Borchardt, C. M., Perwien, A. R., Crosby, R. D., Kushner, M. G., Thuras, P. D., & Last, C. G. (2000). Imipramine plus cognitive-behavioral therapy in the treatment of school refusal. *Journal of American Academy of Child and Adolescent Psychiatry, 39,* 276–283.

Bernstein, G. A., Garfinkel, B. D., & Borchardt, C. M. (1990). Comparative studies of pharmacotherapy for school refusal. *Journal of American Academy of Child and Adolescent Psychiatry, 29,* 773–781.

Biederman, J., Faraone, S. V., Marrs, A., Moore, P., Garcia, J., Ablon, S., Mick, E., Gershon, J., & Kearns, M. E. (1997). Panic disorder and agoraphobia in consecutively referred children and adolescents. *Journal of American Academy of Child and Adolescent Psychiatry, 36,* 214–223.

Biederman, J., Newcorn, J., & Sprich, S. (1991). Comorbidity of attention deficit hyperactivity disorder with conduct, depressive, anxiety, and other disorders. *American Journal of Psychiatry, 148,* 564–577.

Biederman, J., Rosenbaum, J. F., Bolduc-Murphy, E. A., Faraone, S. V., Chaloff, J., Hirshfeld, D. R., & Kagan, J. (1993). A three-year follow-up of children with and without behavioral inhibition. *Journal of American Academy of Child and Adolescent Psychiatry, 32,* 814–821.

Birmaher, B., Waterman, G. S., Ryan, N., Cully, M., Balach, L., Ingram, J., & Brodsky, M. (1994). Fluoxetine for childhood anxiety disorders. *Journal of American Academy of Child and Adolescent Psychiatry, 33,* 993–999.

Black, B. (1995) Separation anxiety disorder and panic disorder. In J. S. March (Ed.), *Anxiety disorder in children and adolescents* (pp. 212–234). New York: Guildford Press.

Black, B. (1996). Social anxiety and selective mutism. In L. J. Dickstein, M. B. Riba, & J. M. Oldham (Eds.), *American Psychiatric Press Review of Psychiatry* (Vol. 15, pp. 469–495). Washington, DC: American Psychiatric Press.

Black, B., & Robbins, D. R. (1990). Panic disorder in children and adolescents. *Journal of American Academy of Child and Adolescent Psychiatry, 29,* 36–44.

Black, B., & Uhde, T. W. (1995). Psychiatric characteristics of children with selective mutism: A pilot study. *Journal of American Academy of Child and Adolescent Psychiatry, 34,* 847–856.

Borkovec, T. D., Newman, M. G., & Castonguay, L. G. (2003). Cognitive-behavioral therapy for generalized anxiety disorder with integrations from interpersonal and experiential therapies. *CNS Spectrum, 8,* 382–389.

Brent, D. A., Kolko, D. J., Birmaher, B., Baugher, M., Bridge, J., Roth, C., & Holder, D. (1998). Predictors of treatment efficacy in a clinical trial of three psychosocial treatments for adolescent depression. *Journal of American Academy of Child and Adolescent Psychiatry, 37,* 906–914.

Chambless, D. L., Baker, M. J., Baucom, D. H., Beutler, L. E., Calhoun, K. S., Crits-Christopf, P., et al. (1998). Update on empirically validated therapies, II. *The Clinical Psychologist, 51*, 3–16.

Chung, S. Y., Luk, S. L, & Lee, P. W. (1990). A follow-up study of infantile autism in Hong Kong. *Journal of Autism and Developmental Disorders, 20*, 221–232.

Clark, D. B., Bukstein, O. G., Smith, M. G., Kaczynski, N. A., Mezzich, A. C., & Donovan, J. E. (1995). Identifying anxiety disorders in adolescents hospitalized for alcohol abuse or dependence. *Psychiatric Service, 46*, 618–620.

Cobham, V. E., Dadds, M. R., & Scence, S. H. (1998). The role of parental anxiety in the treatment of childhood anxiety. *Journal of Consulting & Clinical Psychology, 66*, 893–905.

Curry, J. F., & Murphy, L. B. (1995). Comorbidity of anxiety disorders. In J. S. March (Ed.), *Anxiety Disorders in Children and Adolescents* (pp. 301–320). New York: Guilford Press.

Dadds, M. R., Holland, D. E., Laurens, K. R., Mullins, M., Barrette, P. M., & Spence, S. H. (1999). Early intervention and prevention of anxiety disorders in children: Results at 2-year follow-up. *Journal of Consulting & Clinical Psychology, 67*, 145–150.

Drobes, D. J., & Strauss, C. C. (1993). Behavioral treatment of childhood anxiety disorders. *Child and Adolescent Psychiatric Clinic of North America, 2*, 779–794.

Fairbanks, J. M., Pine, D. S., Tancer, N. K., Dummit, E. S. III, Kentgen, L. M., Martin, J., Asche, B. K., & Klein, R. G. (1997). Open Fluoxetine treatment of mixed anxiety disorders in children and adolescents. *Journal of Child and Adolescent Psychopharmacology, 7*, 17–29.

Fombonne, E. (1992). Diagnostic assessment in a sample of autistic and developmentally impaired adolescents. *Journal of Autism and Developmental Disorders, 22*, 563–581.

Francis, G., Last, C. G., & Strauss, C. C. (1992). Avoidant disorder and social phobia in children and adolescents. *Journal of American Academy of Child and Adolescent Psychiatry, 31*, 1086–1089.

Fyer, A. J. (1987). Simple phobia. *Modern Problems of Pharmacopsychiatry, 22*, 174–192.

Gillott, A., Furniss, F., & Walter, A. (2001). Anxiety in high-functioning children with autism. *Autism, 5*, 277–286.

Gittelman-Klein, R., & Klein, D. F. (1973). School phobia: Diagnostic considerations in the light of Imipramine effects. *Journal of Nervous and Mental Disease, 156*, 199–215.

Gittelman, R., & Klein, D. F. (1984). Relationship between separation anxiety and panic and agoraphobic disorders. *Psychopatheology, 17*(Suppl. 1), 56–65.

Gorman, J. M. (2003). Treating generalized anxiety disorder. *Journal of Clinical Psychiatry, 64* (Suppl. 2), 24–29.

Graae, F., Milner, J., Rizzotto, L., & Klein, R. G. (1994). Clonazepam in childhood anxiety disorders. *Journal of American Academy of Child and Adolescent Psychiatry, 33*, 372–376.

Green, J., Gilchrist, A., Burton, D., & Cox, A. (2000). Social and psychiatric functioning in adolescents with Asperger syndrome compared with conduct disorder. *Journal of Autism and Developmental Disorders, 30*, 279–293.

Hambrick, J. P., Weeks, J. W., Harb, G. C., & Heimberg, R. G. (2003). Cognitive-behavioral therapy for social anxiety disorder: Supporting evidence and future directions. *CNS Spectrum, 8*(5), 373–381.

Hayward, C., Varady, S., Albano, A. M., Thienemann, M., Henderson, L., & Schatz-berg, A. F. (2000). Cognitive-behavioral group therapy for social phobia in female adolescents: Results of a pilot study. *Journal of American Academy of Child and Adolescent Psychiatry, 39*, 721–726.

Hoffman, E. C., & Mattis, S. G. (2000). A developmental adaptation of panic control treatment for panic disorder in adolescence. *Cognitive and Behavioral Practice, 7*, 253–261.

Kendall, P. C., Brady, E. U., & Verduin, T. L. (2001). Comorbidity in childhood anxiety disorders and treatment outcome. *Journal of American Academy of Child and Adolescent Psychiatry, 40*, 787–794.

Kim, J. A., Szatmari, P., Bryson, S. E., Streiner, D. L., & Wilson, F. J. (2000). The prevalence of anxiety and mood problems among children with autism and As-perger syndrome. *Autism, 4*, 117–132.

King, N. J., Ollendick, T. H., & Mattis, S. G. (1997). New clinical panic attacks in adolescents: Prevalence, symptomatology, and associated features. *Behavioral Change, 13*, 171–183.

Klein, R. G., Koplewicz, H. S., & Kanner, A. (1992) Imipramine treatment of chil-dren with separation anxiety disorder. *Journal of American Academy of Child and Adolescent Psychiatry, 31*, 21–28.

Kutcher, S. P., & MacKenzie, S. (1988). Successful Clonazepam treatment of adoles-cents with panic disorder. *Journal of Clinical Psychopharmacology, 8*, 299–300.

Kutcher, S., Reiter, S., & Gardner, D. (1995). Pharmacotherapy: Approaches and applications. In J. S. March (Ed.), *Anxiety disorders in children and adolescents* (pp. 341–385). New York: Guilford Press.

Kutcher, S. P., Reiter, S., Gardner, D. M., & Klein, R. G. (1992). The pharmacother-apy of anxiety disorders in children and adolescents. *Psychiatric Clinics of North America, 15*, 41–67.

Labellarte, M. J., Ginsburg, G. S., & Walkup, J. T. (1999). The treatment of anxiety disorders in children and adolescents. *Biological Psychiatry, 46*, 1567–1578.

Last, C. G., Hansen, C., & Franco, N. (1997). Anxious children in adulthood: A prospective study of adjustment. *Journal of American Academy of Child and Adolescent Psychiatry, 36*, 645–652.

Last, C. G., Perrin, S., Hersen, M., & Kazdin, A. E. (1996). A prospective study of childhood anxiety disorders. *Journal of American Academy of Child and Adoles-cent Psychiatry, 35*, 1502–1510.

Le Couteur, A., Rutter, M., Lord, C., Rios, P., Robertson, S., Holdgrafer, M., & McLennan, J. (1989). Autism Diagnostic Interview: A standardized investigator-based instrument. *Journal of Autism and Developmental Disorders, 19*, 363–387.

Manassis, K., & Hood, J. (1998). Individual and familial predictors of impairment in childhood anxiety disorders. *Journal of American Academy of Child and Ado-lescent Psychiatry, 37*, 428–434.

Manassis, K., & Monga, S. (2001). A therapeutic approach to children and ado-lescents with anxiety disorders and associated comorbid conditions. *Journal of American Academy of Child and Adolescent Psychiatry, 40*, 115–117.

Marks, I. M. (1987). *Fears, phobias, and rituals*. New York: Oxford University Press.

Masi, G., Mucci M., Favilla L., Romano, R., & Poli, P. (1999). Symptomatology and comorbidity of generalized anxiety disorder in children and adolescents. *Compre-hensive Psychiatry, 40*, 210–215.

Masi, G., Toni, C., Mucci, M., Millepiedi, S., Mata, B., & Perugi, G. (2001). Paroxetine in child and adolescent outpatients with panic disorder. *Journal of Child and Adolescent Psychopharmacology, 11*, 151–157.

Mendlowitz, S. L., Manassis, K., Bradley, S., Scapillato, D., Miezitis, S., & Shaw, B. F. (1999). Cognitive-behavioral group treatments in childhood anxiety disorders: The role of parental involvement. *Journal of American Academy of Child and Adolescent Psychiatry, 38*, 1223–1229.

Morris, R. J., & Kratochwill, T. R. (1998). Childhood fears and phobias. In T. R. Kratochwill & R. J. Morris (Eds.), *The practice of child therapy* (3rd ed., pp. 91–131). Needham Heights, MA: Allyn & Bacon.

Pine, D. S. (2002). Treating children and adolescents with selective Serotonin Reuptake Inhibitors: How long is appropriate? *Journal of Child and Adolescent Psychopharmacology, 12*, 189–203.

Pollack, M. H., Allgulander, C., Bandelow, B., Cassano, G. B., Greist, J. H., Hollander, E., David, J., Nutt, D. J., Okasha, A., & Swinson, R. P. (2003). WCA Recommendations for the long-term treatment of panic disorder. *CNS Spectrum, 8*(Suppl. 1), 17–30.

Rayburn, N. R., & Otto, M. W. (2003) Cognitive-behavioral therapy for panic disorder: A review of treatment elements, strategies, and outcomes. *CNS Spectrum, 8*(5), 356–362.

Reiter, S., & Kutcher, S. (1991). Disinhibition and anger outbursts in adolescents treated with Clonazepam (letter). *Journal of Clinical Psychopharmacology, 11*, 268.

Research Unit on Pediatric Psychopharmacology Anxiety Study Group. (2001). Fluvoxamine for the treatment of anxiety disorders in children and adolescents. *New England Journal of Medicine, 344*, 1279–1285.

Rickels, K., & Rynn, M. (2002). Pharmacotherapy of generalized anxiety disorder. *Journal of Clinical Psychiatry, 63*(Suppl. 14), 9–16.

Rutter, M., Greenfeld, D., & Lockyer, L. (1967). A five to fifteen year follow-up study of infantile psychosis: II. Social and behavioural outcome. *British Journal of Psychiatry, 113*, 1183–1199.

Rynn, M. A., Sequeland, L., & Rickels, K. (2001). Placebo-controlled trial of Sertraline in the treatment of children with generalized anxiety disorder. *American Journal of Psychiatry, 158*, 2008–2014.

Salzman, C. (1989). Treatment with antianxiety agents. In *Treatments of psychiatric disorders: A task force report of the American Psychiatric Association* (Vol. 3, pp. 2036–2052). Washington, DC: American Psychiatric Association.

Silverman, W. K., Kurtines, W. M., Ginsburg, G. S., Weems, C. F., Rabian, B., & Serafini, L. T. (1999). Contingency management, self-control, and education support in the treatment of childhood phobic disorders: A randomized clinical trial. *Journal of Consulting & Clinical Psychology, 67*, 675–687.

Simeon, J. G., Ferguson, H. B., Knott, V., Roberts, N., Gauthier, B., Dubois, C., & Wiggins, D. (1992). Clinical, cognitive, and neurophysiological effects of Alprazolam in children and adolescents with overanxious and avoidant disorders. *Journal of American Academy of Child and Adolescent Psychiatry, 31*, 29–33.

Simon, N. M., Korbly, N. B., Worthington, J. J., Kinrys, G., & Pollack, M. H. (2002). Citalopram for social anxiety disorder: An open-label pilot study in refractory and nonrefractory patients. *CNS Spectrums, 7*(9), 655–657.

Spence, S. H., Donovan, C., & Brechman-Toussaint, M. (1999). Social skills, social outcomes, and cognitive features of childhood social phobia. *Journal of Abnormal Psychology, 108*, 211–221.

Spence, S. H., Donovan, C., & Brechman-Toussaint, M. (2000). The treatment of childhood social phobia: The effectiveness of a social skills training-based, cognitive-behavioural intervention, with and without parental involvement. *Journal of Child Psychology and Psychiatry, 41*, 713–726.

Szatmari, P., Bartolucci, G., Bremner, R., Bond, S., & Rich, S. (1989). A follow-up study of high functioning autistic children. *Journal of Autism and Developmental Disorders, 19*, 213–225.

Tantam, D. (2000). Psychological disorder in adolescents and adults with Asperger Syndrome. *Autism, 4*, 47–62.

Thyer, B. A., Parrish, R. T., Curtis, G. C., Nesse, R. M., & Cameron, O. G. (1985). Ages of onset of DSMIII anxiety disorders. *Comprehensive Psychiatry, 26*, 113–122.

Tsai, L. Y. (1996). Brief Report: Comorbid psychiatric disorders of autistic disorder. *Journal of Autism and Developmental Disorders, 26*, 159–163.

Tsai, L. Y. (2001). *Taking the mystery out of medication in autism/Asperger syndromes*. Arlington, TX: Future Horizons Inc.

Tsai, L. Y. (2003a). Autistic Disorder. In J. W. Wiener & M. K. Dulcan (Eds.), *Textbook of child and adolescent psychiatry* (3rd ed., pp. 261–315). Washington, DC: American Psychiatric Press.

Tsai, L. Y. (2003b). Other Pervasive Developmental Disorders. In J. W. Wiener & M. K. Dulcan (Eds.), *Textbook of child and adolescent psychiatry* (3rd ed., pp. 317–349). Washington, DC: American Psychiatric Press.

Van Ameringen, M., Allgulander, C., Bandelow, B., Greist, J. H., Hollander, E., Montgomery, S. A., Nutt, D. J., Okasha, A., Pollack, M. H., Stein, D. J., & Swinson, R. P. (2003). WCA Recommendations for the longer-term treatment of social phobia. *CNS Spectrum, 8* (Suppl. 1), 40–52.

Velosa, J. F., & Riddle, M. A. (2000). Pharmacologic treatment of anxiety disorders in children and adolescents. *Child and Adolescent Psychiatric Clinics of North America, 9*, 119–133.

Verburg, C., Griez, E., & Meijer, J. (1994). A 35% carbon dioxide challenge in simple phobias. *Acta Psychiatrica Scandinavia, 90*, 420–423.

von Korff, M. R., Eaton, W. W., & Keyl, P. M. (1985). The epidemiology of panic attacks and panic disorder. *American Journal of Epidemiology, 122*, 970–981.

Woodward, L. J., & Fergusson, D. M. (2001). Life course outcomes of young people with anxiety disorders in adolescence. *Journal of American Academy of Child and Adolescent Psychiatry, 40*, 1086–1093.

World Health Organization. (1992). *The ICD-10 classification of mental and behavioral disorders: Clinical descriptions and diagnostic guidelines*. Geneva: Author.

Index